Collective Bargaining and Labor Relations

9/1/90

Read Chapter 13

— notes on employment
practices

Collective Bargaining and Labor Relations

Cases, Practice, and Law

University of Louisville

Attorney at Law

Merrill Publishing Company
A Bell & Howell Information Company
Columbus Toronto London Melbourne

Cover illustration: Merrill Publishing/Jim Browning

Published by Merrill Publishing Company
A Bell & Howell Information Company
Columbus, Ohio 43216

This book was set in Garamond and Helvetica

Administrative Editor: Tim McEwen
Production Coordinator: Carol Sykes
Art Coordinator: Lorraine Woost
Cover Designer: Cathy Watterson

Library of Congress Catalog Card Number: 87-62692
International Standard Book Number: 0-675-20876-9
Printed in the United States of America
1   2   3   4   5   6   7   8   9—92   91   90   89   88

Dedicated to

My wife, Colleen, for her support and understanding; my pride and joy, Shari; and my cute little baby, Amber

My husband, Michael D. Ward, for his support; my children, Jasper and Kevin, for their patience; my mother, Eunice A. Heavrin, for her example; my father, William T. Heavrin, in loving memory for his unending confidence in my abilities

Preface

Collective bargaining and labor relations is a dynamic and rapidly changing field. The techniques developed in the 1930s and 1940s no longer suit the new demands and problems of today. Technology, foreign competition, and the general public's less sympathetic attitude have forced dramatic changes in how labor relations must be conducted. At the same time, management is aware that union members are better educated, more sophisticated, and less tolerant of unfair policies and "take it or leave it" attitudes.

We have combined our negotiating, labor law, and teaching experiences to develop a text for readers who need a practical working knowledge of labor relations terms, practices, and law. This text introduces collective bargaining and labor relations with an emphasis on the "real world" applications students will face on the job. Sections of actual labor agreements, as well as cases from arbitrator decisions, the National Labor Relations Board (NLRB), and the courts, illustrate and emphasize contemporary issues of collective bargaining and labor relations.

Many changes in this second edition are the direct result of ideas and suggestions of faculty and students who used the first edition. In addition, our nation's labor laws and practices have significantly changed in some areas due to court decisions, NLRB rulings, and the rapidly changing environment of union and management relations. These recent changes have also been incorporated.

Each chapter presents the material according to the following student-oriented format:

☐ Labor News, a summary of a news event in labor relations, opens each chapter.
☐ Introductory statements detail the concepts, techniques, and examples to be covered in the chapter.

☐ Key terms appear in boldface and are defined in context.

☐ New case studies at the end of each chapter show students theory and applications in the light of actual labor negotiations involving companies and organizations they know.

☐ Summaries, key terms, review questions, and endnotes reinforce key concepts, help students monitor and assess their progress, and suggest resources for further study and research.

With this pedagogical approach, theory is integrated with the "bread and butter" issues at the core of most actual negotiations. Included in the text are traditional methods of estimating wage and benefit items and computerized costing methods, which are part of today's most sophisticated bargaining techniques. Negotiation techniques are clearly described and wage and benefit issues covered in depth, giving students a hands-on feel for how theory is used in actual situations. Labor relations history and labor laws are highlighted throughout to help students see how the flow of events fosters particular legislation—and vice versa.

In addition to the Labor News chapter opening sections and the new case studies of actual NLRB or court decisions, some of the interesting new features of this edition include

☐ Discussions of recent labor events, such as the 1986–87 steel industry record strike, and significant court decisions, such as the U.S. Supreme Court's 1986 affirmative action trilogy decisions, NLRB rulings, and the 1986 OSHA "right-to-know" law.

☐ Examination of emerging significant labor issues, such as the legal battle over employer drug screening, retraining rights, termination-at-will, and "pay-back" agreements.

☐ Trends in negotiation, such as the increase in profit-sharing plans, two-tier wage systems, and health care cost containment programs, as well as the rapid decline in negotiated cost-of-living adjustment clauses (COLAs).

☐ Sections of labor agreements, to illustrate how issues such as seniority, vacation pay, and subcontracting are negotiated. Many examples of actual labor agreements are provided.

This text is comprehensive in its treatment of the environment of labor relations, the activity of collective bargaining, and the need for administering an agreement after it has been signed.

☐ Part I traces the development of collective bargaining. Chapter 1 presents the historical context for modern labor relations and statutes. Chapter 2 discusses labor unions and member loyalty, and how the National Labor Relations Act defines union responsibilities and individual rights.

☐ Part II examines the collective bargaining process. Chapter 3 details provisions of the National Labor Relations Act, how bargaining units are formed and chosen, and the types of units in the work force. Chapter 4 discusses what employer conduct is construed as unfair labor practice. Chapter 5 deals with labor agreements, negotiating techniques, and overcoming an impasse.

☐ Part III covers costing of labor contracts. Primary issues include direct wages and salaries (Chapter 6) and benefits (Chapter 7).

☐ Part IV looks at operational processes. Issues of job security and employee seniority are presented in Chapter 8. In Chapter 9, the basic principles of collective bargaining agreements, methods of enforcement, the NLRB and court intervention, grievance and arbitration procedures, and pressure tactics are explored. Chapter 10 defines individual rights under collective bargaining agreements, and Chapters 10 and 11 present widely used procedures involving grievance and arbitration awards and strikes.

☐ Part V covers additional issues related to collective bargaining. Chapter 12 compares public employee and private unions and procedures for resolving disagreements, settling impasses, and administering contracts in the public sector. Chapter 13 explains civil rights and equal pay legislation and their impact upon labor agreements. In Chapter 14 present and future trends are examined: mechanization of the workplace, growth of service industries, flextime, the four-day week, job sharing, and the relationship of the union to the "new" labor force of women and minorities.

☐ Appendixes A and B provide ready reference to the text of the National Labor Relations Act and the Labor-Management Relations Act.

A comprehensive instructor's manual to this text contains a student-tested test bank of 600 multiple choice and true/false questions written by the authors. Answers to review questions, discussions of cases, and additional cases for study are provided. Adopting professors will also receive *The Collective Bargaining Newsletter,* a semiannual update of NLRB actions, court decisions, union activities, and other labor events. Sample student handouts will be included.

A supplement to this text, *Collective Bargaining Simulated: Computerized and Noncomputerized Formats,* 2nd edition, by Michael R. Carrell and Jerald R. Smith, presents a classroom-tested simulation of a contract negotiation in two parts:

☐ A costing program shows students how to cost out various wage and benefit proposals.

☐ A complete negotiation simulation involves students directly in an actual labor contract negotiation.

Students (management) can negotiate directly with the computer (labor) on a wide range of economic and noneconomic items. Students can also negotiate with each other individually or in teams using a computerized costing program as a tool.

Acknowledgments

We wish to thank sincerely those individuals whose help made this book possible. During our individual careers, several people have been particularly helpful: Dean Robert Taylor of the University of Louisville; Dean William H. Peters of American University; John Vahaly, Richard Herden, Frank Kuzmits, Bruce Kemelgor, John Paul

Nelson, Joe Grant, Robert Myers, David Liebson, and Leonard Jaffee of the University of Louisville; Andrew Hailey of the University of Southern Mississippi; Dean Stuart Van Auken of California State University, Chico; Dean John Dittrich, of Bloomsburg University; Dean Lynn Spruill of Oregon State University; Marc Wallace, Jim Gibson, and Joe Massie of the University of Kentucky; William Sharbrough of The Citadel; Robert Cosenza of Pepperdine University; Frank X. Quickert, Jr., Diane LeRoy, Sally Haynes, Robert P. Benson, Jr., and Kay Wolf of the City of Louisville; and the following friends: Joe Corradino, Don Ridings, Bill Heavrin, Nancy Holland, and Barbara Burns.

For their editorial suggestions on style and content we wish to thank David L. Leightty, labor attorney; Lucretia B. Ward, writer; Marilyn Byrne, writer; Chris Heavrin and Barbara Elliott, attorneys. Also for their special contribution, John G. Bischof and William M. Lutes of ARCO Metals Company; Del Melcher and Jim Cain of the Mechanical Contractors Association of Kentucky, Inc.; Dale Detlefs of Mercer-Meidinger, Inc.; John Bruce of the Iron Workers Local No. 70, A.F.L.-C.I.O.; Lynn Hampton, C.P.A.; and Ralph Orms, President, Kentucky Fraternal Order of Police.

Our warmest regards to our staff: Karen Barnett, Laura Ahrens, Colleen Wilson, Sharon Mills, Karen Richardson, Brenda Lahue, Kathy Ostermiller, Gwen Price, Brenda Mathis, and Janet Dossett.

Special recognition to the University of Louisville School of Business Summer Research Committee, John Vahaly, Chairman, for the summer release time for this project.

A personal thank you to a friend and supporter for many years, Harvey I. Sloane, County Judge/Executive. We are grateful to those who reviewed the text for their help and suggestions: David R. Bloodsworth, University of Massachusetts; Larry Donnelly, Xavier University: Robert C. Miljus; Roger Wolters, Auburn University; Louis White, University of Houston at Clear Lake; and Steven Willborn, University of Nebraska at Lincoln.

Finally, we would like to thank the schools that adopted the first edition of this text for providing invaluable feedback:

Auburn University at Montgomery	Hofstra University
Bunker Hill Community College	Howard University
California State University, Los Angeles	Jackson Business Institute
Cañada College	Kennesaw College
Central Michigan University	Lafayette College
Central Washington University	Longview Community College
City University of New York	Longwood College
Clearwater Christian College	Lummi Community College
Corpus Christi State University	Merrimack College
Creighton University	Miami University
De Paul University	Middlesex County College
Eastern Illinois University	Morehead State University
Edison State Community College	Muskegon Community College
Elizabeth City State University	New York University
Georgia College	Niagara University
Grand Valley State College	Norfolk State University
Gwynedd-Mercy College	North Adams State College

Northern Arizona University
North Texas State College
Ohio Dominican College
Ohio University, Athens
Pennsylvania State University, University Park
Philadelphia College of Textiles and Science
Pima Community College
Purdue University, Calumet
Ramapo College of New Jersey
Robert Morris College
Rollins College
Saint Louis Community College at Meramec
Saint Martin's College
Seton Hall University
Shawnee State Community College
Southeastern Massachusetts University
SUNY College of Technology at Utica/Rome
Texas Southern University
Texas Southmost College

University of Arkansas at Little Rock
University of California, Los Angeles
University of Central Florida
University of Cincinnati
University of Colorado, Colorado Springs
University of Iowa
University of Louisville
University of Minnesota at Duluth
University of Missouri, Columbia
University of Oregon
University of Rhode Island
University of Southern Mississippi
University of Virginia
University of Wisconsin—Oshkosh
Victoria College
Washington State University
Webster College
Western Carolina University
West Georgia College
West Virginia University
Williamsport Area Community College
Wright State University

Contents

Chapter 7
Employee Benefits Issues   *193*

PART IV
OPERATIONAL PROCESSES   *235*

Chapter 8
Security and Seniority   *237*

Chapter 9
Implementing the Collective Bargaining Agreement   *263*

Chapter 10
Grievance and Disciplinary Procedures   *291*

Development of Collective Bargaining

Collective Bargaining— A Legal and Historical Overview

LABOR NEWS

A & P Competes with Worker Participation, Bonuses

Only a few years earlier the Great Atlantic & Pacific Tea Company was near ruin. The union was forced to accept wage givebacks in an effort to survive. In exchange, the United Food and Commercial Worker's Philadelphia level negotiated bonuses if sales increased, in addition to worker participation in running the stores. By 1986 the "new" management announced a doubling of its market share in Pennsylvania under the New Super Fresh Food Markets. In Philadelphia, since the program began in 1982, A & P has paid out about $10 million in worker bonuses and considers the program a success. In fact, A & P has converted stores to the new Super Fresh line in Minnesota, Maryland, Virginia, and Washington, D.C.

Robert Wolper, a Philadelphia union official, started the worker participation concept. However, he warns the program has not been a panacea. As a critical part of the program, managers must adjust to workers' involvement in decision making at every level, and, says Wolper, "it's not a smooth process."

Source of data: "Worker Participation at Some A & P Stores Gives the Chain a Boost," The Wall Street Journal (Jan. 6, 1987); p. 1.

Collective bargaining is the process by which union leaders representing groups of employees negotiate specific terms of employment with designated representatives of management. This process has existed in the United States for almost two hundred years and began in 1792 when the Philadelphia Cordwainers (shoemakers) formed a local trade union to bargain for higher wages. While their action is historically viewed as the beginning of collective bargaining in the United States, current practices were largely formed by federal statutes enacted in the 1930s and 1940s and court decisions interpreting those statutes. Thus the modern era of collective bargaining is only about fifty years old.

What Is Collective Bargaining?

The term *collective bargaining* originated in the British labor movement. But it was Samuel Gompers, an American labor leader, who developed its common use in this country. The following is a modern-day definition:

> Collective bargaining is defined as the continuous relationship between an employer and a designated labor organization representing a specific unit of employees for the purpose of negotiating written terms of employment.[1]

According to the definition, collective bargaining must be recognized as a *continuous* process, beginning with the negotiation of a contract through the life of the contract with almost daily interpretation and administration of its provisions. In recent years the process has also come to include the handling of employee grievances in most labor agreements and, if necessary, arbitration of such grievances in a final and binding decision.

The *employer* referred to in the definition may be one or more related organizations joined together for purposes of collective bargaining. The labor organization bargains on behalf of a specific group of employees recognized by the National Labor Relations Board (NLRB) or by agreement between the employer and employees. Under United States law, the labor organization is given the right to represent all employees of the bargaining unit. This gives the union leadership leverage in negotiation since management cannot seek competing unions to negotiate other agreements.

The **terms of employment** generally negotiated include the price of labor, e.g., wages and benefits; work rules, including hours of work, job classifications, effort required, and work practices; individual job rights, e.g., seniority, discipline procedures, and promotion and layoff procedures; management and union rights; and the methods of enforcement and administration of the contract including grievance resolution.[2]

The American system of collective bargaining and labor relations has often been characterized by confrontation—the "screw the boss" and "keep the union in its place" syndromes.[3] However, most union and management officials view collective bargaining as a rational, democratic, and peaceful way of resolving conflict between labor and management. Of approximately 150,000 collective bargaining agreements, only 2 percent have resulted in strikes. Ninety-eight percent of all cases involving collective bargaining have ended in successful, peaceful negotiations. This record is the result of years of "fine tuning" the collective bargaining process in the United States.[4] The news media usually report only those cases involving picketing, strike activities, or other work disruptions. Seldom do we see reports on cases such as the Bagdad Copper Mine in Arizona, where the company offered guaranteed lifetime employment since 1929 and has never experienced significant labor unrest. In fact, the U.S. Department of Labor reported that in 1985, unions struck less often and the strikes involved fewer workers than in any year since 1946.[5]

People sometimes falsely assume since they are not union members, the activities of labor-management relations do not affect them. In recent years, however, the general public has felt the impact of collective bargaining processes. Millions of travelers missed their scheduled flights due to the 1981 Air Traffic Controllers strike. Sports fans saw the 1982 professional baseball and football seasons substantially shortened, while cities lost a great deal of money due to canceled games. And telephone customers had their service disrupted due to the 1983 Telecommunications Workers strike. People have suddenly realized that collective bargaining affects everyone in ways never considered before. Indirect effects of collective bargaining might include higher costs for products produced by union labor, and higher costs for products produced by nonunion labor whose management wishes to remain nonunion.

Collective bargaining can be found in countless meeting rooms all across the country. Representatives of management and labor sit across a bargaining table negotiating a labor contract. Teams of negotiators haggle over appropriate wage levels, hours of work, and other conditions of employment. If the industry is large enough, the public may be aware of the progress of the negotiations. People may be afraid of a breakdown that could result in a strike. The parties could then expect federal mediators to join into the process, hopefully bringing the labor dispute to a successful and peaceful conclusion.

The process of collective bargaining is an accepted part of labor-management relations in this country. Such was not always the case. Employers viewed decisions on wages, hours, and conditions of employment as the inviolate prerogative of management. They did not choose to share decision making with their employees. But the employees would not accept unilateral decisions. They realized that the employers' profit depended upon their labor and that they should not be denied their share of the rewards.

The struggle between labor and management and its resolution has resulted in today's collective bargaining process. To understand that process is to know the forces that shaped it.

Early Judicial Regulation

Prerevolutionary America saw little division between the employers and employees. The economy of the Colonies was primarily agricultural with some handicraft trade.

Basic goods were supplied by skilled laborers: shoemakers, tailors, carpenters, printers, smiths, and mechanics. The growth of the economy benefited these laborers who, because their skills were scarce, could enjoy relatively high wages and job security. They were largely self-employed and dealt with consumers on an equal footing.

Following the American Revolution, some of these skilled workers became shop owners employing others to fill orders that became more frequent as the economy began to build. Their need to produce goods in an increasingly competitive market demanded cheaper production cost and lower wages. Thus a clearer distinction between employer and employee began. Skilled workers of a single craft formed associations and societies to protect their handiwork and their livelihood. Their method of action was to agree on a wage scale and then pledge to work only for an employer who would pay those wages. The response from the employer to this erosion of management rights was swift and decisive. Using a very supportive court system, those workers were charged with criminal conspiracy in a series of cases known as the **Cordwainers conspiracy cases.**[6]

The Cordwainers Conspiracy Cases

In the Cordwainers conspiracy cases the court stated that the common law of criminal conspiracy was the law of America. In other words, if two or more people conspired to commit an illegal act, they were then guilty of conspiracy whether they ever completed the particular illegal act. Early American labor law was interpreted by judges and based on English Common Law. Whereas English judges had largely relied upon statutes to find criminal conspiracy in labor cases, U.S. judges, who often shared a common background with employers, chose to find legal precedents in the common law for protecting the employer's property rights over the employee's job rights.[7]

In the 1806 Philadelphia Cordwainers case, the court considered the mere "combination" of workmen to raise wages an illegal act. The court felt such combinations were formed to benefit the workers and to injure nonparticipants. Public outcry over judicial interpretation of combinations led later courts to find other grounds for declaring them illegal.

In a New York Cordwainers case three years later (*People* v. *Melvin*), the court dismissed the idea that it was illegal merely to combine. But it denounced using a combination of workers to strike because it deprived others, primarily the employers, of their rights and property. And in an 1815 Pittsburgh case, the court clearly characterized the offense involved in organizing workers as conspiracy to impoverish a third person, be it the employer or another worker willing to work against the combination's rules.

The threat of criminal conspiracy charges and the depression following the War of 1812 practically destroyed the fledgling labor movement. When prosperity returned, the demand for skilled labor put the employees in a better bargaining position, and combinations of skilled laborers began again.

Employers responded to this attempt by labor to again enter the decision-making process by taking employee combinations to court. "Conspiracy" cases against the New York Hatters (1823), Philadelphia Tailors (1827), and Philadelphia Spinners

(1829) questioned the legality of the means used to force the employer to meet labor's demands—picketing, circulation of scab lists, and the sympathetic strike. Before labor could rally from such attacks by the courts, another depression weakened the demand for labor, and the combinations lost their bargaining power.

Industrialization

During the 1830s, the American factory system was coming into being, and the struggle between employer and employee intensified. Factories substituted mechanical power and machinery for muscle power and skills. Industrialization necessitated large capital outlays and a concentration of labor. Mass production for national and even international markets began to develop. By the Civil War the textile, the boot and shoe, and the iron industries were ready to take the final step to a modern mechanized operation.

The monopolistic practices of the employer during the 1860s encouraged the employees to unionize.[8] The need for the joint action of laborers in this newly mechanized environment was expressed by Jonathan C. Fincher, an organizer of a union for machinists and blacksmiths.

> . . . In the early days of mechanism in this country but few shops employed many men. Generally the employer was head man; he knew his men personally; . . . if aught went astray, there was no circumlocution office to go through to have an understanding about it. But as the business came to be more fully developed, it was found that more capital must be employed and the authority and supervision of the owner or owners must be delegated to superintendents and under foremen. In this manner men and masters became estranged and the gulf could only be bridged by a strike, when, perhaps, the representatives of the working men might be admitted to the office and allowed to state their case. It was to resist this combination of capital, which had so changed the character of the employers, that led to the formation of the union. . . .[9]

Because of this need for workers to meet the employer as an equal, the courts began to move away from finding workers guilty of criminal conspiracy.

The conspiracy doctrine was further narrowed during *Commonwealth* v. *Hunt,* which involved a stubborn journeyman who worked for less than union scale and repeatedly broke other union rules.[10] Union members caused his dismissal by refusing to work with him, and his complaint led to the criminal conspiracy charge. The court found that criminal conspiracy required either an illegal *purpose* or resort to illegal *means.* In this instance, the purpose was to induce workers to become union members and abide by union rules and hence, was not illegal. And the means, refusing to work with a worker who did not comply, was not unlawful because no contract was breached. The court upheld the workers' right to organize and to compel all workmen to comply with the union scale.

Use of Labor Injunctions

Abandonment of the criminal conspiracy doctrine by the courts did not signal judicial acceptance of unions. Nor did it enhance the employer's relationships with unions.

Indeed, judicial and business attitudes toward union activities became even more hostile as viable union organizations sought to use economic measures to regulate the terms and conditions of their employment.

The labor incidents cited in the following paragraphs coincide with the growth and development of national labor organizations. The employers' acts, supported by court reaction to these incidents, took on national importance and to a large extent created the need for a national labor policy.

The Railway Strike of 1877

The Depression of 1873 had again placed labor at the mercy of the employers. The treatment of workers by railroad companies was typical of this period. Railroad companies had, through various capitalization schemes, produced large dividends for wealthy stockholders while consistently losing money. To compensate, railway rates increased and wages were reduced. The workers' discontent reached desperation after a 35 percent wage cut in three years, irregular employment, increases in railway hotel and transportation costs (use of which was necessitated by work schedules), and a suppression of union activities.

In 1877, numerous eastern lines announced a new 10 percent cut in wages, and the workers in Maryland began a strike. The **railway strike** spread quickly and violently to West Virginia, Kentucky, Ohio, Pennsylvania, New York, and Missouri. State militia dispersed one gathering in Pittsburgh, killing twenty-six people. Militia were called out in Kentucky, and federal troops fought with workers in Maryland, Ohio, Illinois, and Missouri. The strike lasted less than twenty days, but more than 100 workers were killed and several hundred badly wounded.[11] For the first time in the history of the U.S. labor movement, a general strike swept the country, and federal troops were called out to suppress it.

The embryonic labor movement realized the failure of this largely spontaneous strike stemmed from lack of organization. Propertied classes, terrified by the events of 1877, strengthened support of state militia. The construction of armories in major East Coast cities coincides with this period.[12]

Growth of National Unions

Prior to the Railway Strike there had been various unsuccessful attempts to develop a national trade union. In 1866 the National Labor Union (NLU) was formed. It advocated an eight-hour day, consumer cooperatives, restriction on immigration, a Department of Labor, and legal tender greenbacks. It did not consider collective bargaining one of its aims, nor were workers advised to strike to achieve their goals. The NLU floundered and disbanded six years after its creation, due to a preoccupation with currency reform and a lack of commitment to union goals.

The attempt to organize labor during the late 1800s fell into three camps. The **Noble Order of the Knights of Labor** (KOL), founded in 1869, was open to skilled and unskilled laborers and sought economic and social reform by political action rather than strikes. The members also sought to secure higher wages, fewer working hours, and better conditions through legislation. The KOL lacked a unified goal and philosophy. Often the needs of individuals conflicted, weakening the total effort. Another organization, the Socialist Labor Movement, sought total replacement of the capitalist system by socialism. Again, the lack of a concrete focus caused this movement to have limited popular appeal. A third group, the American Federation of Labor (AFL), was formed in 1886 under the leadership of Samuel Gompers, and had the sole policy of improving the position of skilled labor. Its program included standard hours and wages, fair working conditions, collective bargaining, and the accumulation of funds for union emergencies. More important, the AFL introduced the concept of business unionism to union management and leadership. A decentralization of authority allowed national unions trade autonomy, enabling them to make decisions for themselves. A particular craft or trade union had exclusive jurisdiction to insure protection from competition. The AFL rejected formation of a political labor party, preferring to work as a voting block within existing parties. At one of its initial meetings, the AFL prepared the following declaration of principles that embodied the spirit of the national labor movement:

> Whereas, a Struggle is going on in the nations of the civilized world, between the oppressors and the oppressed of all countries, a struggle between capital and labor which must grow in intensity from year to year and work disastrous results to the toiling millions of all nations, if not combined for mutual protection and benefits. The history of the wage workers of all countries is but the history of constant struggle and misery, engendered by ignorance and disunion, whereas the history of the non-producers of all countries proves that a minority thoroughly organized may work wonders for good or evil. It behooves the representatives of the workers of North America in congress assembled, to adopt such measures and disseminate such principles among the people of our country as will unite them for all time to come, to secure the recognition of the rights to which they are justly entitled. Conforming to the old adage, "In union there is strength," a formation embracing every trade and labor organization in North America, a union founded upon the basis as broad as the land we live in, is our only hope. The past history of trade unions proves that small organizations, well conducted, have accomplished great good, but their efforts have not been of that lasting character which a thorough unification of all the different branches of industrial workers is bound to secure.[13]

It was perhaps ironic that the unification of workers during the **Haymarket Square Riot** caused the AFL to monopolize the labor scene, overshadowing its predecessors.

The Haymarket Square Riot

The Haymarket Square incident took place in Chicago in 1886. Laborers called a general strike to demand an eight-hour day. A peaceful meeting, held to protest a police shooting of four strikers during a fight the previous day, ended with a bomb thrown into a group of police, killing one policeman and injuring others. The police opened fire and more strikers were killed or injured. Eight so-called anarchists, some of whom had not even been at the meeting, were tried and found guilty, not because of complicity in throwing the bomb, but because they held political beliefs that threatened accepted ideas.[14] One account describes the trial as follows:

Proceedings began before Judge Joseph E. Gary on June 21. The jury, consisting largely of businessmen and their clerks, was a packed one and the trial judge prejudiced.

. . . . these witnesses, all of them terrified and some of them paid, testified that the defendants were part of a conspiracy to overthrow the government of the United States by force and violence and that the Haymarket bomb and Degan's murder were the first blow in what was to have been a general assault on all established order. But their testimony was so filled with contradictions that the State was compelled to shift its ground in the midst of a trial. The core of the State's charge then became the allegation that the unknown person who had thrown the bomb was inspired to do so by the words and ideas of the defendants.

Thus the trial was transformed into a trial of books and the written word, a procedure which was later to be repeated in the United States. Endless editorials by Parsons and Spies were read. Interminable speeches by the defendants were recited to the jury. Excerpts were torn from the context of involved works on the nature and philosophy of politics and described as damning evidence against the conspirators. The political platform of the Working People's Association, its resolutions and statements were regarded as evidence involving the defendants in the murder of Degan. . . .

The press was there, of course, in all its glory, from every great city of the country. Thousands of words were printed daily in all parts of the country. From these dispatches we learn of the graceful, laughing society people beside Judge Gary on the bench, learn of the wives of the defendants, pale and haggard, their restless, bewildered children clinging to them, as they crowded together in the front row. We are informed that the courtroom was hot and suffocating, that the people packed together had scarcely room enough to wave the fans with which they had supplied themselves, and that the length of the trial, dragging on week after week, reflected the justice of American jurisprudence wherein even the guilty get all the impressive forms of the law before hanging. . . .

The verdict was almost a formality and the trial's big day arrived when the condemned men arose in court to accuse the accuser, to say why death sentence should not be passed upon them by Gary, and why it was not they but society that was guilty. They dominated the courtroom and they dominated the country that day. No newspaper was so conservative that it did not admit that the defendants in defying death and in defending the working class were both dignified and impressive.

Source: Richard O. Bayer and Herbert M. Morris, *Labor's Untold Story* (New York: United Electrical Radio and Machine Workers of America, 1955), pp. 98–99, by permission of United Electrical and Radio Machine Workers.

Four of the eight defendants were executed, one committed suicide, and the remaining three were sent to prison.[15]

Although the Knights of Labor had participated in neither the general strike nor the Haymarket Square incident, their public notoriety for more successful strikes led to the assumption that they had engineered the Haymarket upheaval. The public began to associate the Knights of Labor with violence and anarchy. Such criticism caused the Knights to lose support. The AFL began to dominate the labor movement.[16]

With the AFL in a dominant position, labor movement goals jelled. Leaders kept labor's ultimate goal—participation in the decision-making process—in sight. This meant collective bargaining and an arbitration system to resolve disputes with individual employers. On a national level, labor sought legislative actions to gain an eight-hour work day, to prohibit child labor, and to provide for worker's compensation in case of injury on the job.

The Pullman Strike of 1894

Interest was again focused on the railroads when workers in Illinois went on strike in 1894. These workers lived in Pullman's town, where wages were low and rents were high. A group of employees who made the Pullman cars demanded wages be restored to previous levels and rents be lowered. Since the demands were refused, these workers struck. In sympathy, another group of workers refused to switch Pullman cars. When switchers were fired, even more classifications of railway workers went on strike.

The reason behind this new solidarity was the American Railway Union established in 1843 by Eugene V. Debs. His was a new kind of industrial union that placed all workers into one organization, instead of dividing them into hostile craft unions.

When Debs started out as a labor organizer, he decried strikes and violence. But years of strike breaking by Pinkerton agents and rival unions, and the futility of intra-union struggles led to a change of heart. He is quoted as saying, "The strike is the weapon of the oppressed, of men capable of appreciating justice and having the courage to resist wrong and contend for principle."[17]

The **Pullman strike** was peaceful and well organized under his leadership. It shut down Illinois Central along with the Southern Pacific and Northern Pacific railroads. The boycott spread from Illinois to Colorado.

With the help of the federal government, railroad owners added mail cars to all trains. Strikers were then charged with interfering with mail delivery. Federal troops were brought in to break the strike. Although violence ensued, the strike continued.

The court enjoined the strikers—ordered them to stop—by applying the Sherman Antitrust Act.[18] This 1890 act declared that contracts, combinations, and conspiracies formed in restraint of trade and commerce were illegal. Theoretically directed at business, the court's injunction caused much controversy when applied to labor unions. Yet along with contempt of court sentences and fines, the injunction finally broke the Pullman Strike.

Debs was sentenced to six months in prison for contempt of court as a result of his participation. There he read Marx's *Das Kapital* and came to believe the labor struggle in America represented a struggle between the classes. He said, "The issue is Socialism versus Capitalism. I am for Socialism because I am for humanity."[19]

The lower court's application of the Sherman Antitrust Act to the Pullman Strike was later confirmed by the U.S. Supreme Court during another strike, known as the Danbury Hatter's case.[20] The Supreme Court stated that the act was designed to prevent conspiracies in restraint of interstate commerce and that a boycott was a form of this interference and therefore prohibited.

The Erdman Act

A key by-product of the Pullman Strike was the passage of the Erdman Act of 1898.[21] The United States Strike Commission formed by President Grover Cleveland investigated its cause and results, recommending a permanent federal commission to conciliate and, if necessary, decide railway labor disputes. Congress used this recommendation as its basis for passage of the Erdman Act. This act gave certain employment protections to union members and offered facilities for mediation and conciliation of railway labor disputes. While the legislation was limited to employees operating interstate trains, its mere passage suggested that federal regulation of the employer-employee relationship might be necessary to ensure peace in interstate industries.

Unions Gain a Foothold

The courts continued to use the injunction as a way to regulate union activity. In Case 1.1, an attempt to unionize mine workers resulted in a court-ordered injunction.

But not all court actions against organized labor were successful in discouraging their actions. In 1902, the United Mine Workers organized a strike of anthracite coal miners, demanding an increase in wages and union recognition. With the widespread support of boycotts and money for the workers, the United Mine Workers withstood federal troops and antitrust lawsuits. President Theodore Roosevelt stepped in and offered to establish a President's Commission to arbitrate. The offer was accepted by the workers almost immediately but the mine owners balked. Threatening to seize the mines unless the coal operators accepted a plan of arbitration, the President gained acceptance of his offer.[22] The Commission's recommendation included wage increases but fell short of union recognition.

Another successful strike during this period was conducted by textile workers in Lawrence, Massachusetts, in 1912. Again the strikers were supported by contributions from around the country. After nine and one-half weeks mill owners capitulated and met most of the workers' demands.

A 1913 strike by mine workers in Ludlow, Colorado, spurred the start of **company unions**. The mine owner, John D. Rockefeller, Jr., realized the inevitability of such workers' organizations. By instituting his own recognized employee organization and initiating reforms such as health funds and better living conditions, Rockefeller sought to eliminate the need for union recognition. Such company unions created the illusion of participation but lacked the essential element of labor and the employer meeting as equals at a bargaining table.

These successes increased the resolve of organized labor to establish viable collective bargaining relationships with employers. But the employers were not ready to yield control to their employees. When faced with an employee strike, employers resisted, seeking and often receiving support from the courts in the form of labor injunctions.

Prolabor Legislation

The Clayton Act

Public criticism of the use of the injunction against labor unions caused Congress to pass the **Clayton Act** in 1914.[23] This act sought to limit the court's injunctive powers against labor organizations. The Clayton Act stated that labor was not a commodity; that the existence and operation of labor organizations were not prohibited by antitrust; and that individual members of unions were not restrained from lawful activities. The act provided that neither the labor organization nor its members were considered illegal combinations or conspiracies in restraint of trade.

Still, courts continued to apply the Sherman Antitrust Act after passage of the Clayton Act by narrowly interpreting its provisions. The court felt that secondary strikes, boycotts, or picketing were not covered by the Clayton Act because of the employee-employer language and because legitimate objects of labor would not include strikes and activities if their purpose or effect was the unreasonable restraint of trade.

Though practically ineffective, passage of the Clayton Act signaled a hopeful period for labor organizations. With other political victories behind them, such as child labor laws, worker's compensation, and some limitations on working hours, members of the labor movement believed a new era was upon them.

The National War Labor Board

During World War I, President Woodrow Wilson formed the **National War Labor Board** to prevent labor disputes from disrupting the war effort. Formed to provide a means of settlement by mediation or conciliation of labor controversies in necessary war industries, it adopted self-organization and collective bargaining as its basic policy.[24] Federal recognition of labor rights continued and expanded when the federal government began to operate the railroads. After the war the National War Labor Board was abolished and railroads were returned to their owners. Despite the economic sense of avoiding labor disputes through cooperation, collective bargaining was no longer protected by the federal government.

The labor movement sustained losses in the early 1920s. Another postwar depression and labor's alleged association with Bolsheviks and Reds eroded public support. Even though the Clayton Act supposedly exempted labor unions from injunctions, the courts interpreted the Clayton Act as granting immunity only if an injunction was not necessary to prevent irreparable injury to property or its rights. In the broadest sense any labor action could injure property or property rights.[25] Case 1.2 is typical of the Court's interpretation of the Clayton Act.

Trade-union leadership and the rank and file turned to political action and industrial unionism to counteract their losses. They allied with the progressive movement, a loose coalition of farmers, socialists, and reformers who represented a populist view. Many people, fearing that the use of militia, federal troops, and court injunctions against unions represented a threat to the democratic process, adopted the progressive doctrine. That doctrine espoused the control of the political activities of corporations, graduated income and inheritance taxes, stringent conservation measures, federal regulations of the labor of women and children, and worker's compensation laws. The movement, while not widely embraced, successfully supported the passage of the Railway Labor Act.

The Railway Labor Act

This act passed in 1926 with the support of both labor and management.[26] It required railroad employers to negotiate with their employees' duly elected representatives. It provided for amicable adjustment of labor disputes and for voluntary submissions to arbitration.

As a result of the Railway Labor Act, Congress again fostered peaceful settlement of labor disputes through negotiation and mediation. The Supreme Court case upholding that act removed major judicial obstacles by supporting a national labor policy based on the affirmative legal protection of labor organizations.[27] Under the umbrella of the Commerce Clause of the United States, the Court said Congress could facilitate settlements of disputes and that

> The legality of collective action on the part of employees in order to safeguard their proper interests is not to be disputed . . . Congress . . . could safeguard it and seek to make their appropriate collective action an instrument of peace rather than of strife.[28]

Creation of a National Labor Policy

In 1929 the stock market crashed and the United States plunged into a major depression. The impact of the Great Depression on the workers was devastating. One-third of the country's work force was unemployed. Hoover's programs to combat unemployment served mainly to highlight the deprivation. The labor movement made more emphatic efforts to organize and demand recognition and became more politically active. The severity of conditions led to public sympathy for its problems.

For years this nation struggled over the right of workers to organize and to negotiate collectively with employers. Judicial solutions to the struggle were ineffective. Court decisions, by their nature, were confined to particular parties, to narrow situations, and to fixed time frames. Such decisions could not give national guidance. The judicial process was also time-consuming; neither labor nor management wanted disputes to drag on while the wheels of justice ground to a decision.

State legislation was also ineffectual, because organized labor transcended state boundaries. With few exceptions, the disruption of an industry in any one state affected industries throughout the country.

The Norris-La Guardia Act

Congress recognized the need for a national labor policy. The Erdman Act and the Clayton Act were the first steps in ensuring industrial peace based upon the balanced bargaining relationship of worker to owner.

The **Norris-La Guardia Act** (1932) was the next step in formulating a comprehensive national labor policy.[29] This act, like the Clayton Act, sought to restrict federal judicial intervention in labor disputes, thereby giving the unions an opportunity to grow. Courts could not enjoin strikes without actual violence, nor could they restrict the formation of a union or associated activities. The act also made illegal "yellow dog" contracts, in which employees pledged to refrain from union membership.

These protections were extended to secondary boycotts and strikes by expanding the employer-employee language of the Clayton Act.

The National Labor Relations Act (The Wagner Act)

The Great Depression and the selection of Franklin D. Roosevelt with strong labor support set the stage for passage of national legislation. Roosevelt quickly proved his interest in the plight of the worker. The National Industrial Recovery Act (1933) recognized workers' rights in selecting their own representatives.[30] Well intentioned but poorly constructed, the National Recovery Administration had no power to enforce the act, and industry largely ignored it. Within two years the National Industrial Recovery Act was declared unconstitutional.[31]

Relief of the unemployment problem continued by creation of such New Deal programs as the Civilian Conservation Corps (CCC), unemployment insurance, the Social Security program, and the Works Progress Administration (WPA). But these measures alone were not enough.

By 1935, the judiciary policy toward labor was

> one of selective suppression of organized labor's activities whenever they trenched too heavily upon the interests of any other segment of society. Commercial interests must not be injured by disruption of the interstate flow of goods; consumers and unorganized laborers must not be injured by wage standardization; employees and the public at large must not be injured by expansion of labor disputes through secondary boycotts.[32]

Senator Robert Wagner, a champion for labor, proposed an act that recognized employee rights to organize and bargain collectively. A quasi-judicial tribunal with the power and authority to enforce its own orders would be created. While the act was purported to protect the public from the disruption of interstate commerce resulting from labor disputes, Senator Wagner stated the act would also give the employee freedom and dignity.[33]

The **National Labor Relations Act** (also known as the **Wagner Act**) gave most private sector employees right to organize.[34] It required employers to meet with accredited representatives of a majority of their employees and to make an honest effort to reach agreement on issues raised. Employees now had the right to strike while the employer's retaliatory powers were limited under the act's unfair labor practice provisions. The **National Labor Relations Board (NLRB)** was created to enforce provisions of the act. Case 1.3, decided only three years after passage of the act, gives an interesting interpretation of the NLRB's powers.

By legislating the recognition of employee representatives and protecting the right to strike, Congress forced the employer to share the decision-making power with employees. Labor no longer depended upon work stoppages to get to the bargaining table, nor upon economic factors to determine its equality.

The entire thrust of the Wagner Act was to protect employees against employers and to establish a balance of bargaining power between the two. Later it was criticized for its one-sided nature but, at the time it was passed, organized labor had no leverage to pose a threat to management, thus equal protection for management seemed unnecessary.

Critics claimed the act was unconstitutional because, although it was based on the Commerce Clause, the latter did not specifically allow Congress to dictate the relationship between employers and employees. The National Labor Relations Board was careful in its activities, delaying adjudication on the constitutionality question until the Supreme Court upheld the act in a 1937 case, *Jones and Laughlin Steel Corporation*.[35] Labor-management relations improved somewhat under the Wagner Act but still remained uneasy. Exhibit 1.1 outlines the major provisions of the Wagner Act.

While the creation of a national labor policy dominated the labor scene in 1935, the character of the national labor union was also undergoing changes. The American Federation of Labor (AFL), a confederation of craft unions, had been the principal union model for a half century. However, in 1935 the Committee of Industrial Organizations, later called the Congress of Industrial Organizations (CIO), challenged the leadership of AFL by successfully supporting industrial unions. Membership in industrial unions was based upon employment in a particular industry, such as automobile, steel, or clothing, rather than a particular skill.

The CIO grew to five million members in less than twenty years under the leadership of John L. Lewis. This growth was attributed to the passage of the Wagner Act, the increased shift of the American economy from agriculture to manufacturing, and the heightened economic activity of World War II and the Korean War.

The Fair Labor Standards Act

The National Labor Relations Act was followed by the passage of the Fair Labor Standards Act in 1938.[36] This act applied primarily to employees engaged in interstate commerce and provided a federal minimum wage and a forty-four-hour week to be reduced to forty hours in three years. Passage of the act secured three main objectives of the labor movement: wages adequate to maintain a decent standard of living, shorter hours, and the abolition of labor by children under the age of sixteen.

World War II and the war effort brought a shortage of labor and more labor demands. Strikes brought charges that labor unions were unpatriotic. Congress, reacting to pressure, passed the Smith-Connally Act to control strikes injurious to the war effort.[37] Passage of this act showed a shift in political forces against strong federal support of union activities.

But the Wagner Act was still in place at the end of the war, and labor entered the postwar economic slump with considerable legal protection. The collective bargaining rights mandated by the act forced business to deal with labor on an equal footing. Supported by two Supreme Court decisions in the early 1940s, labor unions were allowed the use of peaceful picketing to inform the public of their alleged grievances and to elicit support for their cause.[38]

Widespread strikes during 1945–46 and wage drives in 1946–47 caused critics of the Wagner Act to increase the political pressure for amendment. The amendment's stated goal was to equalize its impact on employers. The relentless campaigning of the Chamber of Commerce and the National Association of Manufacturers, resentment over wartime strikes, and internal union irregularities began to turn the tide against organized labor.

Exhibit 1.1   Major provisions of the Wagner Act

Findings and Policy

☐ Denial by employers of employee collective bargaining leads to strikes, industrial unrest, and obstruction of commerce

☐ Inequality of bargaining power between employees and employers affects the flow of commerce and aggravates recurrent business depressions

☐ Protection of the right of employees to organize and bargain collectively safeguards commerce

☐ Policy of the United States to encourage practice and procedure of collective bargaining and the exercise of employees of their right to organize and negotiate

Rights of Employees

☐ To organize into unions of their own choosing

☐ To assist such labor unions

☐ To bargain collectively with their employer through representatives of their own choosing

☐ To strike or take other similar concerted action

Employer Unfair Labor Practices (illegal)

☐ Interfering with employee rights guaranteed by the act

☐ Refusal to bargain in good faith with employee representatives

☐ Discrimination against union members or employees pursuing their rights under the act

☐ Any attempt to dominate or interfere with employee unions

Representatives and Elections

☐ Employee representatives shall be exclusive representatives of the appropriate unit

☐ NLRB decides appropriateness of unit for bargaining purposes

☐ NLRB shall conduct secret ballot elections to determine employee representatives

National Labor Relations Board

☐ Members appointed by President of the United States

☐ Conducts elections to determine employee representatives of appropriate unit

☐ Exclusive power to prevent employer unfair labor practice

Numerous bills were introduced to change the Wagner Act—to weaken the powers of the National Labor Relations Board, to redefine appropriate bargaining units, to outlaw a closed union shop, to subject unions to unfair labor practices charges, and to limit strikes and other concerted activities. While these bills did not pass, they laid a foundation for the passage of the Taft-Hartley Amendments in 1947.

The Labor-Management Relations Act (Taft-Hartley Amendments)

For twelve years the Wagner Act gave unions the time and ability to grow strong. From 1935 to 1947 union membership went from 3 million to 15 million with some industries having 80 percent of their employees under collective bargaining agreements.[39] The image of organized labor in Congress was one of power—power to stop coal production during World War II and to shut down steel mills, seaports, and automobile assembly plants after the war.

A Republican Congress in 1946 introduced 200 bills on labor relations during its first week, and President Harry Truman proposed some revision of the nation's labor laws in his State of the Union Address. After extensive hearings by both the House and Senate, the 1947 Labor-Management Relations Act (known as the **Taft-Hartley Amendments**) was passed.[40] Although President Truman vetoed it, Congress overrode his veto and the bill became law on August 22, 1947.

Management saw the Taft-Hartley Amendments as a shift to a more balanced approach to labor relations. Labor unions were subjected to many of the same duties as employers. While the Wagner Act gave employees the right to organize, the Taft-Hartley Amendments recognized their right *not* to organize. Under the Wagner Act employers were required to bargain in good faith; under Taft-Hartley, that duty was extended to unions. The unfair labor practices section protecting employees from employer retaliation was expanded to protect employees and employers from labor unions' unfair labor practices. The Wagner Act had protected employees from being fired for joining a union; the Taft-Hartley Amendments protected employees from losing their jobs for not joining a union. The 1947 amendments recognized and gave preference to state right-to-work laws over bargained-for provisions in collective bargaining agreements that required union membership as a condition of employment. Exhibit 1.2 outlines the major provisions of the Taft Hartley Amendments.

Organized labor immediately began to work for the repeal of Taft-Hartley. Labor had, by opposing any change to the Wagner Act, shut itself out of congressional decision making, and demanded that Taft-Hartley be repealed before even discussing possible changes in the Wagner Act. This all-or-nothing approach backfired and Taft-Hartley was left unchanged. Labor legislation did not receive national attention again until 1957.

Certainly one response of the labor community to the passage of the Taft-Hartley Amendment was a reemergence of the "in union there is strength" approach to organized labor. The AFL-CIO merger in 1955 ended a twenty-year separation of the two dominant national labor organizations and enabled the united group to claim a total membership of 16.1 million workers, 10.9 million members from 108 AFL unions, and 5.2 million members from 30 CIO unions.

Besides fear of anti-union sentiment represented by the Taft-Hartley Amend-

Exhibit 1.2 Major provisions of the Taft-Hartley Amendments

Findings and Policy

☐ Certain practices of labor organizations, such as secondary strikes, burden and obstruct the free flow of commerce

☐ Elimination of such practices is necessary to guarantee rights of act

Rights of Employees

☐ To refrain from any and all union activities except union shop provision in valid collective bargaining agreements

Union Unfair Labor Practices

☐ Restraint or coercion of employees in exercise of their rights

☐ Discrimination against employee for not engaging in union activities

☐ Refusal to bargain in good faith with employer

Restrictions on Strike Activities

☐ No secondary strikes and boycotts

☐ Prohibits strikes conducted by one labor union to dislodge another labor union

☐ Outlaws strikes to force employers to make-work for union members

☐ Prohibits strikes during the term of a valid collective bargaining agreement unless employees give sixty days notice to employer and thirty days notice to the Federal Mediation and Conciliation Service (FMCS)

Right-to-Work Laws

☐ Gives states the right to outlaw union shop requirements in collective bargaining agreements so employees

can refrain from joining the union representing them at the bargaining table

ments, the merger was prompted by a desire to end union raiding where one union pirated members from the other. A change in leadership in both, as well as internal housecleaning by the CIO to rid itself of eleven communist front unions and by the AFL to expel the racket-ridden International Longshoremen's Union, created the mutual respect necessary to overcome past differences.

The Labor-Management Reporting and Disclosure Act of 1959

The famed McClellan hearings in 1957 set the stage for the second major change to the national labor policy since the Wagner Act. Initiated to investigate wrongdoings in the labor-management field, the Senate Committee soon unearthed corruption in some major unions. Charges of racketeering centered on threats that strikes would be called against employers and on incidents where union officials sold out the interests of union members for cash.[41] The public outcry for labor legislation to protect the internal operations of unions was noticed by political leaders, and congressional bills offering sweeping reforms were introduced. Labor supported reforms as long as amendments to the Taft-Hartley were included. Management also supported them as long as *their* amendments to Taft-Hartley were included. The mood created by the McClellan hearings was in management's favor, and the **Labor-Management Reporting and Disclosure Act of 1959** (known as the **Landrum-Griffin Act**) was passed.[42]

The Landrum-Griffin Act provisions amending the Wagner and Taft-Hartley acts further eroded the power of labor unions by limiting such economic activities as boycotts and picketing.

In regulating the internal operation of labor unions, the Landrum-Griffin Act introduced controls on internal handling of union funds. It established safeguards for union elections and in certain cases gave members the right to bring suit against the union. It also established due process rules for disciplining members. Unions were required, under the act, to have a constitution and bylaws and to file these and other disclosure documents with the Secretary of Labor.

Passage of the Landrum-Griffin Act signaled the end of significant changes to a national labor policy characterized by strong support of collective bargaining as a means of ending industrial strife. Successive chapters will discuss how that bargaining process is to be carried out under the provisions of the act.

Public Sector Collective Bargaining, 1962

The Wagner Act gave most private employees the right to collective bargaining. In January, 1962, President John F. Kennedy signed **Executive Order (E.O.) 10988** extending that right to most federal government employees. That executive order was subsequently amended by President Richard Nixon in E.O. 11491, and attempted to parallel private employee rights with one major exception. Public employees were denied the right to strike.

In 1978, Title VII of the Civil Service Reform Act replaced the executive orders as the legal protection for federal employee collective bargaining rights. While similar in most respects to the Wagner Act, the Civil Service Reform Act also prohibits employee strikes and mandates that all contracts contain a grievance procedure with binding arbitration as the final step.

Recent Labor Relations Issues

Very little labor-management legislation has been enacted in recent years. However, on the fiftieth anniversary of the passage of the Wagner Act, court and NLRB interpretations of existing legislation have continued to refine the nation's labor policy.[43]

The Health Care Amendments of 1974

In the early 1970s, it was recognized that 56 percent of all hospital employees had been excluded from the Wagner Act. As a result, Congress brought employees of privately owned nonprofit hospitals under its protection and restrictions by instituting the Health Care Amendments of 1974.[44] These amendments required that notice be given on contract negotiations and strikes to minimize the effects of labor disputes on the delivery of health care services.

The Labor Law Reform Act

In 1975, Congress amended the Wagner Act with passage of the common situs picketing bill, allowing construction unions to picket an entire worksite even though the labor dispute involved only one union. However, President Gerald Ford vetoed the bill and labor fell short of the support necessary to override the veto.

After President Jimmy Carter's election, the labor-backed labor reform act of 1977 represented yet another attempt to modify the nation's labor policy. The reform act required union representation elections to be held within thirty days of an election request. The purpose of this change was to enable labor to mitigate against employer anti-union activities during such an election. The law required employers to compensate their employees when the employer was found guilty of engaging in unfair labor practices; federal contracts were also withheld from such employers.

Despite Carter administration support for the labor reform act, passage was blocked by a Senate filibuster.

The 1981 Professional Air Traffic Controllers' Strike

The August, 1981, walkout of the air traffic controllers was the first declared national strike against the federal government. It presented President Ronald Reagan with perhaps the most difficult labor relations problem in modern times. Not only had a union broken the federal no-strike law and left hundreds of thousands of travelers stranded, but the **Professional Air Traffic Controllers' union (PATCO)** seemed to almost dare the President to try and replace its highly trained members.

President Reagan fired the striking workers after several weeks of negotiations. The Federal Labor Relations Authority (FLRA) revoked PATCO's right to represent its federal workers. The FLRA ruled that PATCO willfully violated federal laws by striking and thus violating the no-strike oath in the employment contracts. Transportation Secretary Drew Lewis is quoted as saying that the FLRA ruling ". . . . reaffirms a basic principle of our democracy, that no person or organization is above the law."[45] Probably more important to all government workers was the reality that these skilled, presumably irreplaceable workers were replaced. Equally hard for PATCO workers to accept was President Reagan's firm decision that no former PATCO striking member may ever work again as an air traffic controller.

The **PATCO strike** had no precedent. Union leaders, thinking the country could not survive without its members, risked massive fines, contempt-of-court orders, and jail sentences. The President decided that allowing any one government union to openly strike and win would open the door to the possible disruption of all public services, perhaps even that of the military.

Both sides may have miscalculated their positions. PATCO assumed that support from members of other unions and public demands for air service would force the government back to the bargaining table. President Reagan may have gambled that his stiff ultimatum—get back to work or be fired—would force most striking workers to reconsider. Instead, 13,000 of 15,000 continued to strike past the President's deadline. Union leaders were fined; some were even sent to jail. President Reagan's determination to uphold the law and still keep America flying eventually won out.[46]

The 1982 National Football League Strike

The elements of this labor-management clash in the fall of 1982 differed little from typical labor negotiation impasses. However, the nature of this highly popular professional sport assured coverage on the front page of most newspapers. Such publicity caused a national surfacing of interest in the status of collective bargaining.

Negotiations focused on how money from football revenues should be paid. The unions began by demanding a 55 percent share of the National Football League's gross revenues but compromised with a request of $1.6 billion over four years. The union proposal included a demand for distribution of the dollars by an established wage scale with incentives and performance bonuses. Management's position was that any percentage of the gross was unacceptable, but that it could offer $1.6 billion over five years. The parties also differed on wage scales with management preferring that each team decide its own salaries.

Negotiations dragged on for several weeks. They were marked by name-calling, extensive analysis of which side was losing the most, and hostile feelings by loyal football fans, who saw their season delayed and cut in half. When settlement was finally reached, neither side could boast of major concessions.

The 1983 AT&T Walkout

Nearly 700,000 unionized telephone workers broke a twelve-year labor peace on August 7, 1983. This strike was partially the result of an order by federal judge Harold Greene to divest AT&T into twenty-two local operating companies. The federal order, combined with the company's need to increase its use of high technology to remain competitive, gave union members ample reasons to fear future loss of jobs. Thus, their demands centered on employment security, although higher wages and benefits were also issues. Union negotiators asked that management and the unions jointly finance broad training and retraining programs to give members the necessary skills for the high technology jobs of the future. Management felt such a request went far beyond normal provisions for job security to a requirement of career security.[47]

The effects of modern technology at AT&T were even felt as a result of the strike. After the first two weeks, the company reported almost no interruption in service except for new installations. Ninety-seven percent of the calls were handled by automated computer systems, which had also enabled management to reduce the ratio of supervisors-to-workers from 5-to-1 to 2-to-1 in less than twenty years. By scheduling supervision on twelve-hour shifts and by postponing some work, AT&T was able to keep the strike from affecting most of its customers.

Management's ability to endure the strike due to automated equipment and longer shifts of supervision was something new. MIT professor Harley Saiken defined it as **telescabbing,** the use of modern technology as a substitute for labor during a strike instead of hiring scab labor.[48] Saiken further stated that many industries, including oil, steel, and utilities, will be able to maintain high production levels during strikes due to automation, thus taking away the unions' ability to disrupt production due to a strike.[49] Unions had lost one of their most important collective bargaining tools as a result of high technology. Although repair work, new installations, and some long-distance calls were affected by the strike, union leaders underestimated the ability of the company to continue its normal operations.

Shortly after AT&T announced its lack of interrupted services, the major union involved, the Communication Workers of America, went back to work. Other unions followed suit, generally settling for lower wage increases than demanded. However, AT&T gave up its demand that workers pay a part of their health insurance and agreed to a company-financed training and retraining program.

The 1985 Major League Baseball Strike

A strike in professional sports occurred again when major league baseball players left the playing fields in August of 1985—within two months of the end of the season. The dispute centered on the owners' contribution to the players' benefit plan and the system for salary arbitration. Players wanted the owners to continue to put one-third of their national television revenues into the players' benefit plans. Revenues from 1985 would have put such contributions into the $60 million range, an increase of $45 million a year. Owners felt such contributions excessive. Also, the owners felt the previous awards from arbitrators had resulted in inflated salaries, which they could no longer afford to pay. They proposed salary caps, which the players rejected.

The strike was settled within twenty-seven hours of its beginning. The agreement was praised for its reasonableness. Rather than paying one-third of the television revenues, the owners' contribution to the players' benefit plans increased from $17.2 million to $32.7 million a year. The owners gave up on the proposed salary cap, but the players agreed to increase the time of employment from two to three years before salary arbitration. The parties credited the quick settlement to both the memory of the fifty-day strike in 1981 and the owners' decision to allow the players access to their financial records. With information to support the owners' position that some teams were in serious trouble, the players were better able to sell compromise to their members.

The 1986 AT&T Contracts

When contract negotiations began again in the telephone industry in 1986, the realities of the Bell System breakup had set in. Over 30,000 employees had lost their jobs and 40,000 positions had been eliminated nationwide. The president of the Communication Workers of America, Morton Bahr, was called upon to offer innovative approaches to achieve the dual goal of employment competitiveness and employment security. Modest pay increases over the three years of the negotiated agreement with AT&T took second place to the job security offered by innovative job training provisions. Funded by corporate dollars, AT&T and the CWA jointly created a nonprofit organization to train workers seeking to upgrade their skills for emerging jobs at AT&T and those seeking careers outside AT&T. The CWA contracts with Bell South and Pacific Telephone followed similar patterns offering workers job retraining opportunities as a way to keep layoffs to a minimum.[50]

The 1986–87 Steel Industry Negotiations

For the first time in thirty years, the major U.S. steelmakers decided in the spring of 1986 not to bargain jointly. The prior use of **coordinated bargaining** enabled all the major steel producers to negotiate common wage rates and benefits with the United Steelworkers of America. All parties (including 450,000 workers) had also enjoyed relative harmony with an industry-wide no-strike agreement. However, foreign competition and weakening demand due to newer and cheaper steel substitutes had caused the industry to lose over $1 billion in the previous two years. Thus each steelmaker decided to negotiate separately a contract that could mean survival or bankruptcy.[51]

The steelworkers' union tried to negotiate concessions of wages and benefits with each steel producer based on its financial situation. Since USX Corporation (formerly U.S. Steel) was the only one of the major producers to have made a profit the previous two years, the union refused to grant similar economic concessions. The result was a bitter six-month strike—the longest steel strike in U.S. history. Neither side could really claim victory when it ended in January of 1987. The pressure to meet the needs of General Motors, the largest customer of USX, brought a settlement that gave USX concessions of $2.35 per hour. The union won early retirement for some workers, the reduction of subcontracting to nonunion labor, and a profit-sharing plan.[52]

Summary

In 1935, Congress articulated a national labor policy with the passage of the Wagner Act. That act was the culmination of over 100 years of organized labor's efforts to recognize the employee's right to bargain collectively. During that struggle, the labor movement faced hostile court decisions, economic depressions, and internal power struggles. The disruptive nature of work stoppages caused political leaders to seek a national solution to labor's problems. Under the Wagner Act, employees were free to organize and given the right to strike, and employers were required to bargain with employee representatives.

The Great Depression and the New Deal set the stage for Congress to pass legislation that not only protected organized labor but promoted its growth. Although the Taft-Hartley Amendments and the Landrum-Griffin Act modified the Wagner Act, its support of collective bargaining was not changed. Exhibit 1.3 summarizes the chronology of events in the U.S. labor movement.

Exhibit 1.3 Chronology of historical events in the U.S. labor movement

ERA OF UNION OPPOSITION

1790 **New York Printers Strike**   First strike by employees

1790s **First Unions**   Craft workers formed first known unions, including printers, shoemakers, tailors, carpenters, and bakers

1806 **Philadelphia Cordwainers Case**   Court found combination of employees illegal

1837 **Severe Depression**   Mass unemployment reduced union membership

1842 ***Commonwealth* v. *Hunt***   The conspiracy doctrine greatly narrowed

1860s **Civil War**   Buildup of coal, steel, and other war-related industries

1866 **National Labor Union**   Advocated consumer cooperatives, immigration restrictions; disbanded in 1872

1869 **Knights of Labor**   National social union formed to organize farmers, skilled and unskilled workers

1877 **Railway Strike**   More than 100 workers killed and several hundred wounded in first national strike

1886 **American Federation of Labor (AFL)**   Samuel Gompers led the first national trade union to advocate collective bargaining, trade autonomy, exclusive jurisdiction, standard hours, and better wages and working conditions

1886 **Haymarket Square Riot**   Several workers killed; others found guilty of anarchism. The Knights of Labor suffered the blame for the riot, shifting much of their support to the AFL

1890 **Sherman Antitrust Act**   Designed to break up corporate monopolies

1894 **Pullman Strike**   Rail workers demanded higher wages, lower rents. Strike ended by court orders under the Sherman Act. Strike led to passage of 1898 Erdman Act giving railroad employees employment protection

1913 **Colorado Mine Workers Strike**   Spurred the start of company unions by John D. Rockefeller, Jr.

1914 **Clayton Act**   Congress attempted to limit use of court injunction. First national pro-union legislation

1914 to 1918 **World War I**   President Wilson created the National War Labor Board to mediate labor disputes. The board also recognized employee collective bargaining rights during the war

1926 **Railway Labor Act**   Railroad employees were given collective bargaining rights and the right to use voluntary arbitration

---

ERA OF UNION SUPPORT

1929 **Stock Market Crash**   Beginning of Great Depression and 33 percent national unemployment

1932 **Norris-La Guardia Act**   Limited use of court injunction, made yellow dog contracts unenforceable

1935 **Wagner Act**   The Magna Charta of U.S. labor history. Within twelve years, union membership tripled in the U.S. Upheld by the Supreme Court in 1934. Created the NRLB

Exhibit 1.3   (continued)

1935	**Committee for Industrial Organization** John L. Lewis led industrial unions to split with AFL
1938	**Fair Labor Standards Act** Provided minimum wage, forty-hour week, overtime pay, and the abolition of child labor
1941 to 1945	**World War II** Widespread labor strikes during and after the war harmed the war effort and caused strong antilabor public sympathy

ERA OF STABILIZATION

1947	**Taft-Hartley Amendments** Amended Wagner Act to equalize the balance between labor and management. Also created the FMCS and right-to-work states
1952	**No-Raiding Pact** After seventeen years of bitter fighting, new labor chiefs in the AFL and CIO signed a no-raiding pact
1955	**AFL-CIO Merge** New unity spurred labor hopes for membership gains which failed to materialize (25 percent of labor force in 1955, 18 percent in 1988)
1959	**Landrum-Griffin Act** U.S. Senate hearing on labor corruption led Congress to establish stricter controls on union operations
1962	**Kennedy's Executive Order** Gave federal employees the right to organize but not to strike
1974	**Health Care Amendments** The Wagner Act was extended to include private, nonprofit hospital employees
1977	**Labor Law Reform Bill** Supported by President Carter and organized labor, a major revision of the NLRA passed the House but failed in the Senate
1983	**Labor-Management Racketeering Act** Proposed revision to NLRA passed the U.S. Senate. Labor leaders supported the act, which improves their public image
1987	**Longest Steel Strike in U.S. History** Ended after six months, signaling the demise of the once-proud industry (over 200,000 jobs lost in 10 years)

CASE 1.1   *Injunction*

Adapted from *Hitchman Coal & Coke Co.* v. *Mitchell,* 62 L.Ed. 260 (1917)

The Hitchman Coal and Coke Company had reluctantly accepted unionization in 1903. For the next three years it was plagued with strikes over mine workers' pay scales, causing considerable losses to the company. A two-month strike in 1906 resulted in a self-appointed committee of employees informing the company they could not afford to stay off the job and asking the company upon what terms they could return to work. The company said they could come back—but without the union. The employees agreed and returned to work.

Prospective employees were told that while the company paid the same wages demanded by the union, the mine was nonunion and would remain so; that the company would not recognize the United Mine Workers of America and would fire any man that joined. Each man employed assented to those conditions.

The United Mine Workers of America wanted to expand union mines in the area because nonunion mines tended to keep the cost of production low. Union mines could not compete and still grant workers the pay increases they demanded.

Union organizers repeatedly declared the need to organize the nonunion mines by means of strikes. They were determined to protect themselves from the unorganized mines. A plan was devised whereby the unionized mines would stay open while the nonunion mines would strike. The working miners would provide strike benefits for the strikers to insure their cooperation.

When the Hitchman Company was approached by union officials requesting recognition, the company refused and informed the union of the employment agreements not to unionize.

Representatives of the union began organizing the miners with the express intent of shutting down the mine until the company recognized the union. Their organizational means were limited to orderly and peaceful talks with individual workers and a few unobtrusive public meetings. The company sought and received an injunction against the union's activities.

Decision

The injunction was upheld on appeal. The U.S. Supreme Court reasoned that the company was within its rights in excluding union men from its employ and that, while the union was within its right in asking men to join, it could not injure the company when exercising that right. The Court found that the express intent of the union—to organize the workers to strike for recognition—would injure the company in two ways. It would interfere with the employer-employee relationships, and would cause a loss of profits.

Because the union's goals were illegal, the union's activities could be enjoined.

CASE 1.2   The Clayton Act

Adapted from *American Steel Foundries* v. *Tri-City Central Trades Council,* 66 L.Ed. 189 (1921)

The Tri-City Central Trades Council declared a strike on the American Steel Foundries to secure reinstatement of previous wage levels. Only two employees of the plant took part. The council arranged various groups of pickets near the entrance of the plant along the route employees took to the foundry. There was considerable evidence that the picketers warned the employees on their

way to and from work that they would be hurt if they did not quit. Violent methods were also pursued from time to time. An employee was physically assaulted by three of the pickets, and five employees were attacked by more than seven pickets. Other assaults were alleged.

The company sought and received an injunction against the council. The union claimed it was protected from injunction by the Clayton Act. The Clayton Act forbade the court from issuing an injunction to prevent peaceful persuasion by employees or those seeking employment in promotion of their side of a dispute. If, however, the methods used by the employees led to intimidation and obstruction, then the act would not prevent an injunction. The U.S. Supreme Court had to decide if the Clayton Act applied.

Decision

In this case the Court found that the activity was not peaceful. It stated that the location of the pickets along the entrance to the plant, the number of pickets at each location (4–12 in a group), and the alleged violent behavior of the pickets caused the activity to be unlawful. Therefore, the Clayton Act did not apply and an injunction was proper.

CASE 1.3   *The National Labor Relations Act*

Adapted from *National Labor Relations Board* v. *Fanstead Metallurgical Corporation*, 83 L.Ed. 627 (1938)

The corporation manufactures and sells products made from rare metals and is clearly subject to the commerce definition of the National Labor Relations Act.

A group of employees organized a union that the corporation refused to recognize. The union organized a sit-down strike in which about ninety-five employees occupied two key buildings of the corporation's facility. All work stopped.

The corporation asked the employees to leave and, when they refused, fired them. It obtained an injunction, which the employees ignored; law enforcement officials forcibly ousted and arrested them.

Production resumed and some of the strikers were hired back. However, others refused to return unless their union was recognized. The corporation had supported the organization of another independent union the National Labor Relations Board found to be a company union in violation of the act.

In light of that finding, the NLRB ordered the corporation to stop interfering with the rights of employees to organize and select their own bargaining representatives; to not dominate their labor organization; and to stop refusing to bargain with the employees' union.

The NLRB went one step further to effectuate its policies by ordering the corporation to reinstate all the striking employees with back pay, even if it involved discharging people hired since the strike. The corporation appealed the NLRB order.

Decision

The U.S. Supreme Court upheld the finding of an employer unfair labor practice for refusing to bargain with the union. It also pointed out that the employer's discharge of the employees was *proper* because the employees' actions while engaging in the strike were illegally to take and hold possession of the employer's property.

The Court was left to examine the authority of the NLRB to order the reinstatement of the strikers. The NLRB's reasoning was that since the strike was in response to an unfair labor practice, the act provided that the employees retained their status despite discharge for illegal conduct or, that as an alternative, the NLRB's authority was broad enough to order reinstatement to effectuate the purposes of the act.

The Court found the National Labor Relations Act's protection of employee activity is limited to lawful conduct. A lawful strike, the exercise of the right to quit work, is protected and the employees retain their employment status. But an illegal strike, one that includes the seizure of buildings to prevent their use by the employer, is outside the scope of the act.

The Court found that the NLRB's authority under the act was broad but not unlimited. The NLRB's authority to order affirmative action is limited to orders that will in fact restrain unfair labor practices, not punish an employer for past practices. Therefore, an affirmative order requiring the employer to recognize and bargain with the union was within its authority because of the impact upon the employer's future actions. But reinstatement of certain strikers who participated in an illegal act would not effectuate the purposes of the National Labor Relations Act to encourage peaceful resolution of labor disputes.

CASE STUDY *Secondary Boycotts*

Adapted from *Baldovin v. International Longshoreman's Association*, 626 F. 2d 445 (CA 5, 1980)

Facts

To protest the invasion of Afghanistan by the Soviet Union and to avoid giving the Soviet Union any economic benefit, the union refused to load cargo ships bound for the U.S.S.R. The refusal to work occurred in the United States and affected the farmers who produced the grain not loaded, as well as the companies and union members who loaded and transported the grain to the docks. The farmers and two shippers filed unfair labor practice charges against the union for an illegal secondary boycott. The NLRB sought to enjoin the union pending a ruling on the unfair labor practice charge. The union appealed the injunction.

Appeal

The NLRA prohibits secondary boycotts, that is, putting pressure on employer "B"

in order to affect employer "A," the real object of the dispute. The NLRB contended, in this case, that the union illegally boycotted the goods of the farmers and the shippers in order to harm the Soviet Union. The union's position was that its protest of the U.S.S.R. was not an activity affecting commerce under the NLRA and therefore not subject to its provisions. The power of the Congress to regulate labor is derived from its power over interstate commerce. The party that was the object of the dispute—the U.S.S.R.—was *not* subject to the provisions of the act, and its dispute with the U.S.S.R. was therefore incapable of affecting interstate commerce.

Questions

1. In this case, would you decide the union's boycott of U.S.S.R. cargo

ships to be an activity affecting interstate commerce or not? Give your reasons.

2. Even if there was an effect on interstate commerce, should the NLRA have been used to prohibit the union from its admittedly political activity? Why or why not?

3. Should U.S. unions protest U.S.S.R. actions and harm trade?

Key Terms and Concepts

Clayton Act

Company unions

Coordinated bargaining

Cordwainers conspiracy cases

Executive Order (E.0.) 10988

Haymarket Square Riot

Knights of Labor

Labor injunctions

Labor-Management Reporting and Disclosure Act (Landrum-Griffin Act)

National Labor Relations Act (Wagner Act)

National Labor Relations Board (NLRB)

National War Labor Board

Norris-La Guardia Act

PATCO (Professional Air Traffic Controllers) strike

Pullman strike

Railway strike

Taft-Hartley Amendments

Telescabbing

Terms of employment

Review Questions

1. Why is collective bargaining viewed as a continuous process?
2. What are the "terms of employment" that are generally negotiated in labor agreements?
3. What factors in the 1800s contributed to the growth of the American labor movement?
4. Describe the federal and court actions against union workers in the 1800s.
5. Did the Great Depression have any impact on the U.S. labor movement? If so, what?
6. Why did the Wagner Act have a major impact on employees' rights?
7. What is generally included in the "duty to bargain in good faith" as imposed by the National Labor Relations (Wagner) Act?
8. What is the general role of the NLRB? How and when was the NLRB created?
9. What circumstances prompted Congress to pass the Taft-Hartley Amendments? The Landrum-Griffin Act? What are the key provisions of these acts?
10. Why did President Reagan believe he had to fire the striking PATCO employees? What mistakes, if any, did PATCO make in calling a strike?

Endnotes

1. Gerald G. Somers, ed., *Collective Bargaining: Contemporary American Experience* (Madison, Wis.: Industrial Relations Research Assoc., 1980), pp. 553–56.
2. Ibid.
3. Scott A. Kruse, "Giveback Bargaining: One Answer to Current Labor Problems?" *Personnel Journal* 62, no. 4 (April 1983), p. 286.
4. *Why Unions?* American Federation of Labor and Congress of Industrial Organizations, pamphlet (Washington, D.C.: AFL-CIO, 1980).
5. "Major Union Strikes Reach a Low Point," *Courier-Journal,* Feb. 27, 1986.
6. Joseph Rayback, *A History of American Labor* (New York: Macmillan, 1959), pp. 54–57.
7. David P. Twomey, *Labor Law and Legislation* (Cincinnati: South-Western, 1980), pp. 7–8.
8. Maurice F. Neufeld, "The Persistence of Ideas in the American Labor Movement: The Heritage of the 1830s," *Industrial and Labor Relations Review* 35, no. 2 (Jan. 1982), p. 212.
9. John R. Commons, *History of Labor in the United States,* vol. 2 (New York: Macmillan, 1946), pp. 7–8.
10. Commonwealth v. Hunt, 45 Mass. (4 Met.) III (1842).
11. Samuel Yellen, *American Labor Struggles* (New York: Harcourt, Brace, 1936), pp. 3–38.
12. Rayback, *History of American Labor,* p. 135.
13. Stuart Bruce Kaufman, "Birth of a Federation: Mr. Gompers Endeavors Not to Build a Bubble," *Monthly Labor Review* 104, no. 11 (Nov. 1981), p. 24.
14. Yellen, *American Labor Struggles,* pp. 39–71.
15. Richard O. Bayer and Herbert M. Morris, *Labor's Untold Story* (New York: United Electrical, Radio, and Machine Workers of America, 1955), p. 99.
16. Rayback, *History of American Labor,* pp. 142–68.
17. Bayer, *Labor's Untold Story,* p. 119.
18. Sherman Anti-Trust Act, 15 U.S.C. sec. 1 (1982).
19. Lowe v. Lawler, 208 U.S. 274, 28 S.Ct. 301, 52 L.Ed. 488 (1908).
20. Bayer, *Labor's Untold Story,* p. 131.
21. Erdman Act, 30 Stat. 424 (1898), amended by Pub.L. 6, 38 Stat. 103 (1913); referenced in 45 U.S.C. sec. 101 (1976).
22. Rayback, *History of American Labor,* p. 212.
23. Clayton Act, ch. 323, sec. 1, 6, and 7, 38 Stat. 730 (1914); referenced in 15 U.S.C. sec. 12, 17, and 18 (1982).
24. Theodore Kheel, *Labor Law* (New York: Matthew Bender, 1982), pp. 5–24.
25. See Duple Printing Press Co. v. Deering, 254 U.S. 443, 41 S.Ct. 172, 65 L.Ed. 349 (1921); and Redford Cut Stone Co. v. Journeymen Stone Cutter's Association, 274 U.S. 37, 47 S.Ct. 522, 71 L.Ed. 916 (1927).
26. Railway Labor Act, 45 U.S.C. sec. 151 (1976).
27. Texas and New Orleans Railroad Co. v. Brotherhood of Railway & Steamship Clerks, 281 U.S. 548 (1930).
28. Ibid., 570.
29. Norris-La Guardia Act, 29 U.S.C. sec. 101 (1982).
30. National Industrial Recovery Act, Pub.L. 67, 48 Stat. 195 (1933); referenced in 7 U.S.C. sec. 601 (1982).
31. Schechter Poultry Corp. v. United States, 295 U.S. 495, 55 S.Ct. 837, 79 L.Ed. 893 (1937).
32. Charles J. Morris, ed., *The Developing Labor Law,* 2nd ed. (Washington, D.C.: Bureau of National Affairs, 1983), p. 12.
33. Morris, *Labor Law,* p. 28.

34. National Labor Relations Act, 29 U.S.C. sec. 151 et. seq. (1982).

35. Associated Press v. N.L.R.B., 301 U.S. 103 (1937); and N.L.R.B. v. Jones & Laughlin Steel Co., 301 U.S. 1, 57 S.Ct. 615, 81 L.Ed. 893 (1937).

36. Fair Labor Standards Act, 29 U.S.C. sec. 201 (1982).

37. War Labor Disputes Act, Pub.L. 89, 57 Stat. 163 (1943).

38. Thornhill v. Alabama, 310 U.S. 88 (1940); and Milk Drivers Local 753 v. Meadowmoore Dairies, Inc., 312 U.S. 287 (1941).

39. Morris, *Labor Law,* p. 35.

40. Labor-Management Relations (Taft-Hartley) Act, 29 U.S.C. sec. 141 et. seq. (1982).

41. Neil W. Chamberlain, *Sourcebook on Labor* (New York: McGraw-Hill, 1964), pp.26–29.

42. Labor-Management Reporting and Disclosure (Landrum-Griffin) Act, 29 U.S.C. sec. 401 et. seq. (1982).

43. Howard Lesnic, "The Supreme Court and Labor Law in the Fiftieth Year of the NLRA," *The Labor Lawyer* 1, no. 4 (Fall, 1985), pp. 703–719.

44. 29 U.S.C. sec. 152 (14) (1982).

45. Gisela Bolte, "Flying the Emptier Skies," *Time* 118 (Nov. 1981), p. 29.

46. Melinda Beck, "Who Controls the Air?" *Newsweek* 98 (Aug. 17, 1981), pp. 18–24.

47. Joann S. Lublin, "AT&T Walkout Could End by Weekend: Optimism Buoyed by Job-Security Talks," *The Wall Street Journal,* Aug. 18, 1983, p. 3.

48. John Breeher and Alexander Still, "Telescabbing: The New Union Buster," *Newsweek* 102 (Aug. 29, 1983), pp. 53–54.

49. Ibid.

50. "Greater Job Security through Training Program," *Resource* (Alexandria, Va.: American Society for Personnel Administration, Nov. 1986), p. 13.

51. Peter Perl, "Steel Firms Start Crucial Labor Talks," *The Washington Post,* March 9, 1986, p. K1.

52. J. Ernest Beazley, "USX, Union Tentatively Set Leaner Accord," *The Wall Street Journal,* Jan. 19, 1987, p. 3.

Unions

LABOR NEWS

Technology Changes in the Printing Industry

In the United States it has been common for as many as ten unions to exist at each major newspaper. From the very beginning the printing industry was organized by traditional craft unions, including compositors, stereotypers, platemakers, press operators, and so on. A major change began around the early 70s and has continued, until by 1987 the industry was composed of only three major unions: the Newspaper Guild (reporters, editors, white-collar workers), the International Typographical Union (compositors and mailroom workers), and the Graphic Communications International Union (pressroom and ancillary workers). The cause of this rapid trend toward fewer, more industrial unions in the printing industry was not management negotiators, government regulations, or even foreign competitors—it was unprecedented technological change.

New technology radically altered the traditional craft jobs in the printing industry. The clear distinction among the craft jurisdictions faded as technology blended jobs together, eliminating many. In the composing room new technology threatens to eliminate all jobs soon, forcing the International Typographical Union to call for "one big union" for the entire industry, which some union leaders are reluctant to encourage. Longstanding rivalries among printing unions have slowed merger attempts. The industry no longer has true craft unions; instead there are three "quasi-craft" unions, and in the future perhaps only one or two industrial unions will remain.

Source of data: Michael Wallace, "Technological Changes in Printing: Union Response in Three Countries," Monthly Labor Review *108, no. 7 (July 1985): pp. 41–43. Used by permission.*

In August of 1983, 675,000 employees of AT&T staged the first nationwide telephone company walkout in twelve years. Because of the technological systems, 97 percent of the company's business continued without noticeable problem. Despite this, the three unions involved were able to marshal their members for the strike. To understand the collective bargaining process it is necessary to understand the union and its relationship to its members.

The *labor union* is an organization of employees united in securing favorable conditions for wages, hours, and terms of employment from the employer. To qualify as a labor organization, the union must have the ability to meet with management and to bargain collectively for its members. The struggle for recognition of workers' rights to bargain collectively has created a national labor organization with a utilitarian structure. This chapter outlines part of that structure, details the union's responsibilities to its members, and explores the nature of unionism in this country.

Why Unionize?

The labor union developed as a means by which individuals could unite and have the collective power to accomplish goals that could not be accomplished alone. Whether that power is used to increase take-home wages, to ensure job protection, to improve working conditions, or simply to sit across the bargaining table as an equal with the employer, members believe that *in union there is strength!*[1]

Unions have been seen as very pragmatic organizations seeking to improve the economic and social conditions of their members. The success of their activities can be measured by the improvements in members' work conditions, and the perception members have of the union's effectiveness.

Although economists may debate to what degree unions cause workers' wages to increase, negotiated agreements do contain significant employment benefits.[2] Some nonwage elements include grievance procedures, seniority rights, and provisions to improve job satisfaction and security. Certainly companies that seek to prevent unionization are advised to approach their employees with similar employment benefits. Nonunion employers may also encourage employees' participation to determine the content of their work to increase employee job satisfaction and to decrease the need for a union.[3]

The following describes one employee's view of a union's effectiveness.

I am a forty-year-old male who has been in the work force for twenty-four years. I've worked for A&P (Meat Cutters Union), the Louisville Metropolitan Sewer District (nonunion), Wilder Flooring Company (Building Trades Union), Canada Dry Bottling Company (nonunion), Coca-Cola Bottling Company (Teamsters Union), American Synthetic Rubber Company, Olin Matheson (both Chemical and Rubber Workers Union), Murray Asphalt Company (nonunion), J.V. Reed Manufacturing Company (nonunion), General Electric (International Union of Electrical Workers), and for the last seventeen years I've worked for the Ford Motor Campany (United Automobile, Aerospace, and Agriculture Implement Workers of America [U.A.W.]).

The gut feeling that I and most of my rank-and-file coworkers have is that the leadership of the union on the international level has abrogated its responsibilities towards its members in favor of good public relations activities. The unions have paralleled the degeneration of leadership in the government (federal, state, and municipal); the American churches; the public schools; and the American manufacturing companies.

International Unions are today a big business in themselves. As such, they must also become, and have become, establishment companies.

This puts the rank-and-file in the nearly powerless position of working for, not in, the union, and also for the company. There have been classic examples in recent years of union leadership (president and executive boards) bringing contracts before the rank-and-file, recommending unanimous acceptance, and being overwhelmingly rejected. This, when the leadership should know exactly what the rank-and-file want and will approve, and should therefore bargain for with management.

But, for all the faults that union leadership has today, the unions are still needed (as is, for example, the government), for they are the only protection rank-and-file workers have. Companies, as always, are run by people whose main objective is making as large a profit as possible. Management (no matter what anyone says) is still in the adversary role towards workers. The companies' profits have to be split among stockholders, management bonuses and salaries, building programs, researching, marketing, advertising, and so forth. The only way the rank-and-file have of getting a fair share of this money is to have a strong, solid union that will affect the running of the companies.

I'm a union member and proud of it!

Source: Russell Heavrin, "Thoughts on Labor Unions by a Rank-and-File Member, circa 1983," Unpublished paper, by permission of Russell Heavrin.

This testimonial reflects the findings of a survey conducted by the U.S. Department of Labor.[4] The survey results showed that workers viewed unions as large and powerful institutions.

A final question . . . asked the extent to which the respondents saw union leaders as out to do what is best for themselves rather than what is best for their members . . . Approximately two-thirds of the respondents agreed that unions are more powerful than employers and that leaders are more interested in what benefits themselves than in what benefits union members.[5]

Despite this view, 80 percent of the respondents agreed that unions improved wages and job security for their members and protected them from the unfair labor practices of employers. The survey went on to examine the expectations of union members and how well the unions live up to those expectations. Three of the four main concerns expressed by the respondents reflected strong interest in the governance of the union: improving the handling of grievances, increasing feedback to members, and increasing the influence members have in running the union. The desire for improvements in the traditional bread-and-butter issues of wages, fringe benefits, job security, and safety and health came next in the listing of concerns. Finally, issues covering the quality of work were at the bottom of the respondents' priorities, although they seemed to be looking for an expansion of union activity into these areas.

Not surprisingly, the expectation of the union members exceeded the perception of union performance. However, 73 percent of the respondents indicated a general degree of satisfaction with their union, primarily with performance in traditional, economic bread-and-butter aspects of jobs.

A recent survey of union officials indicated that 63 percent of the officials surveyed thought their members did not know what the union did for them. For these union officials the causes of union membership decline could be attributed to labor's public image, the antilabor attitude of government, and the policies and structure of unions. Some officials felt that the union's past successes had raised members' standard of living and made them complacent. Similar improvements for nonunionized workers have eliminated their need to unionize.[6]

Why Workers Unionize

A key element to organizing workers is understanding why workers unionize. Although a union's collective bargaining success is usually measured by the wage increase it has negotiated, salary levels are not the primary reason workers organize.

Management's attitude toward employees, cited as the major factor in employee dissatisfaction, is manifested in the following areas:

1. Disregard for employees when making decisions that affect their jobs
2. No acknowledgment of the seniority of employees in wages, benefits, and layoffs
3. Unfair and inconsistent discipline
4. Beneficial treatment to employees who support management
5. No grievance procedure
6. An unsafe work environment
7. No attempt to regulate production to create job security
8. Inadequate training
9. No consideration of seniority for promotion purposes
10. Lack of communication; failure even to listen to employee complaints[7]

Overall, management's failure to include employees as part of the "team," involve them in decision making, or even inform them of the business's status, motivates employees to organize.

The recent increase of Japanese owned and operated businesses in the United States, primarily in the highly unionized automotive industry, has shown a marked contrast in management styles. To increase productivity, Japanese managers cultivate workers' loyalty by shortening or eliminating the distance between them, by giving employees a voice in management, and by minimizing layoffs. Allowing workers to participate in job-related decisions has increased efficiency. Training workers for more than one job cultivates flexibility, job pride, and ultimately more productivity. The relationship at these plants is good between management and employees represented by unions. And at unorganized plants, unions are having difficulties convincing workers they need a union.[8]

How Management Resists Unions

While unions decry loss of membership and search for new ways to organize and tap nontraditional areas of unionization, managers pursue specific maneuvers to keep unions out of their plants. To discourage organization, management must be willing to address workers' concerns and revamp existing employee relations systems to reflect changes not unlike those sought by unions.[9]

Ways to discourage unionization include the following:

1. Instituting valid performance reviews to ensure employees of nonpartial merit raises and promotions and to counter the seniority provisions usually contained in union contracts
2. Improving employee communication so managers sense discontent before it becomes major dissension
3. Establishing fair grievance procedures
4. Creating a pleasant office environment
5. Promoting potential union leaders to management
6. Pursuing a more people-oriented approach to dealing with employees overall[10]

Union Membership

The decline in union membership since the 1940s (Exhibit 2.1) can be traced to several factors. The number of new workers included in organizational elections per year has declined significantly, as has the success rate of unions trying to win those new workers in organizational elections. Unions have also lost existing members by losing decertification elections. The 1970s were particularly difficult for unions, as membership declined in highly unionized manufacturing industries hard hit by recession and foreign competition. Even if these industries had not lost employment, union membership would have declined due to unions' poor performance in certification and decertification elections.[11]

Exhibit 2.1   Union membership, 1935–1985

Year	Total Membership (thousands)	Percentage of Labor Force	
		Total	*Nonagricultural*
1935	3,728	6.7	13.2
1940	8,944	15.5	26.9
1945	14,796	21.9	35.5
1950	15,000	22.3	31.5
1955	17,749	24.7	33.2
1960	18,177	23.6	31.4
1965	18,519	22.4	28.4
1970	20,751	22.6	27.3
1975	21,090	20.7	25.5
1980	20,100	18.8	23.0
1985	17,400	17.8	19.1

Sources: U.S. Department of Labor, Bureau of Labor Statistics, Bulletin 2070, *Handbook of Labor Statistics,* (Washington, D.C.: Government Printing Office, 1980), p. 412.

Larry T. Adams, "Changing Employment Patterns of Organized Workers," *Monthly Labor Review* 108, no. 2 (Feb. 1985), pp. 25–31.

In the traditional union stronghold, production jobs in metropolitan areas, the proportion of union to nonunion employees declined from 73 to 51 percent from 1961 to 1984. This substantial drop in the nation's large cities was not limited to production workers; nonsupervisory office clerical workers in unions declined from 17 to 12 percent in the same period. Only part of the decline can be attributed to the employment shift toward service industries, because these shifts occurred *within* the union core of manufacturing and related clerical areas. The geographic area of greatest decline was the West, which dropped from 80 percent in 1961 to 48 percent in 1984. All other areas also showed declines: Northeast, 77 to 57 percent; South, 48 to 32 percent; and Midwest, 80 to 69 percent. Explanations of the production industry's decline of union membership include the move to less unionized Sunbelt states, the increased number of smaller and harder to organize plants, the trend toward building new facilities in rural, less unionized areas, and the dramatic increase in nonunion electronics production facilities as found in Silicon Valley near San Jose, California.[12]

Another response to dwindling union membership is the increased merger of labor organizations. In 1984, five mergers involved over 3.7 million members; in 1983, five mergers involved over 3 million members; and in 1983, six mergers involved over 2 million members. Although mergers of labor organizations have always been a part of the labor movement, the five years between 1979 and 1984 saw thirty mergers—35 percent of all mergers since 1955.[13]

Some people credit an enlightened management for its help in discouraging unionization. Younger workers, women, and minorities have never been courted by labor and now find traditional labor unions unresponsive to their needs, although the U.S. Department of Labor survey confirmed that these workers were as willing as white males to join unions if their job conditions warranted unionization.[14]

Avoiding unionization has become a major task of human resource managers in such traditional nonunion areas as health care, financial planning, and insurance companies. But these white-collar workers are obvious targets for organizational campaigns. Their responsibilities and education cause their expectations of respect and participation at their workplace to be higher even than assembly-line workers.[15] Clerical employees, the majority of which are women, are increasingly attracted to organizing, especially when the union organization is a young one geared toward their demographics.[16]

Unions have attempted with limited success to organize in these less traditional areas. The affirmative legislative environment of 1935–47 in the private sector and after the 1962 Presidential Executive Order in the public sector, does not exist today. Certainly the growth of union membership of the 1930s and 1940s cannot be repeated. And even though workers are facing bleak economic prospects, the large number of single people and two-wage families in the work force lessen the threat of the economic consequences of unemployment.

Many of the laws resulting from labor unions successfully satisfied the workers' needs and eliminated the need for a union. Certainly minimum wage, occupational health and safety, and workers' compensation laws protect workers in areas that unions have traditionally sought to improve. How long such laws would remain unchanged and enforced without continued union support is unknown. The advanced age of most labor leaders and the absence of young, aggressive, and imaginative replacements leave many workers believing unions could not answer today's challenges. The emergence of Richard Trumka, President of the United Mine Workers, and Vicki Saporta, organizer for the Teamsters, as union leaders may have dispelled some of those fears. However, the less than respectable image of labor unions has discouraged many workers from joining.

> Less than one hundred years ago, unions in the country were commonly considered criminal conspiracies. . . . The image of the union as a "low-class," disreputable organization still persists.[17]

Potential Growth

Organized labor in the 1980s has been unable to reverse its decline in membership, which began in the late 1950s (Exhibit 2.1). In fact, the decline from 1980 to 1985 was 2.7 million members, the sharpest four-year drop in U.S. history. The change from 20.1 million union workers in 1980 to 17.4 million in 1985 occurred when the total number of U.S. workers increased from 87.5 million to 91.3 million; thus the percentage of union membership fell from 18.8 percent in 1980 to 17.8 percent in 1985 (including agriculture, forestry, and fisheries). At its peak in 1945 union membership was 35.5 percent of all nonagricultural workers. However, the total number of union members had steadily *grown* during that period, underlying the seriousness of the 2.7 million drop from 1980 to 1985.[18]

Recent research in employee elections indicates union success can be increased by a greater emphasis on grass-roots organization. In addition, research indicates that increasing the number of certification elections held and the size of the units where possible, so long as the choice of organizational units is targeted to insure a steady victory rate, will increase union membership.[19] Narrowing the time for the conduct of the election will also improve the results for the unions.[20] Management, in its resistance to unionization, has been very successful in lengthening the time for an election and undermining union organization efforts. Another resistance tactic is giving workers more benefits so the gains of union representation are minimized. Decertification elections have become more frequent over the past decade, especially those involving a no-union choice.[21] Union leaders seeking to increase union membership must also keep current members in the fold by discouraging the "current union or no union" employee elections.

The AFL-CIO voted to put more emphasis on union organizational drives and added a new unit to assist member unions in planning and executing local organized campaigns. Their growth strategy is summarized as follows.

☐ Make new use of the concept of collective bargaining. Unions should tailor "models to the needs and concerns of different groups that provide greater flexibility in the workplace and greater reliance on mediation and arbitration . . . and address new issues of concern to workers," such as comparable worth and increased worker participation in decision making.

- ☐ Set up new membership categories. While many former union members are now in nonunion positions, they might still be interested in affiliating if costs were not prohibitive and services besides bargaining representation were offered.
- ☐ Provide direct services and benefits. The union suggested looking at providing services such as job referrals and supplemental insurance.
- ☐ Use corporate campaigns to deflect employer interference with attempts to form unions. Increase non-workplace pressure—called *corporate* or *coordinated* campaigns—on employers to allow for union development.
- ☐ Improve labor communications. This includes training members to act as representatives to the media to publicize union activity.
- ☐ Encourage union mergers.
- ☐ Establish organizing committees that would focus attention on a particular industry or region.[22]

The potential growth of unionism among professional workers is one of the brighter aspects of the total membership picture. Professional workers have been turning in increasing numbers to unionism as a remedy for their problems. Much of the growth in recent years has resulted from the expansion of collective bargaining in the public sector. In the private sector the growth of unionism among professionals may be more likely than is generally assumed. The resistance of professional workers to unionism may be weakening as evidenced by higher union success rates in professional unit elections than in all other units.[23]

What are the implications if this decline in membership continues into the 1990s? If the private sector nonconstruction union membership remains roughly constant and total U.S. employment continues to expand at the rate of 2.5 percent per year, the unionized share of the work force will not fall below 15 percent before 1995—plenty of time for events to change the current trend. However, an expansion of the unionized share of the work force probably would require *both* an increased rate of success in new elections and economic improvement in heavily unionized industries.[24]

Union Security

The preservation of existing strength and influence is a major issue facing unions in the 1980s. Security and the structure of the present organizations affect union preservation.

Union security refers to a union's ability to grow and to perform its exclusive collective bargaining role without interference from management, other unions, or other sources. A key element to a union's security is a provision in the collective bargaining agreement requiring employees to join the union and pay union dues as a condition of continued employment. Such a provision ensures the union and its members that all the employees who share the benefits of collective bargaining agreements pay for the union's cost. Required union membership increases the financial base of the union and may increase its ability to represent its members at the bargaining table.

Unions are concerned about their security for many reasons. For instance, a union is certified as the **exclusive bargaining agent** for only one year following a representation election. Rival unions can seek to organize its members during that short time. Although a union security provision cannot prevent such raiding, loyalties are developed and strengthened by participation in the union.

Laws

The passage of the National Labor Relations Act in 1935 reflected a congressional decision that collective bargaining should be encouraged to minimize industrial strife. The act guaranteed employees the freedom to choose their bargaining representative, and companies were prohibited from forming company unions, or from discriminating against union members. Yellow dog contracts, whereby employees agreed not to join unions in order to get hired, and blacklisting of union sympathizers were made illegal. The act allowed an employer to make an agreement with the union requiring union membership as a precondition to employment. As a result, the *closed shop* clause became common.

Union security increased union membership. Automatic **check-off provisions** in the contract authorizing the employer to withhold dues from a member's wages ensured that the union would receive payment.

Public reaction to the growth of union membership and numerous labor-management conflicts following World War II led to the 1947 passage of the Taft-Hartley Amendments to the National Labor Relations Act. Added to Section 7, which guaranteed freedom of organization, was a guarantee of the employee's right *not* to organize and engage in union activity. The closed shop was outlawed, although the amendments allowed union shops to be negotiated in future contracts. A union shop required union membership on or after thirty days of employment. The hiring power was, therefore, restored to the employer. However, while the act allowed union shops, it also permitted states to outlaw union shops. The so-called **right-to-work laws** permitted states to prohibit agreements requiring membership in a labor organization as a condition of employment. The Taft-Hartley Amendments even limited the dues check-off practice by requiring a written authorization from each union member.

Forms of Union Security

Union security clauses may take several basic forms:

1. *Closed shop*   Outlawed by the Taft-Hartley Amendments, the **closed shop** provision allowed the employer to hire only union members. In order to get a job, a person first had to join the union.

2. *Open shop*   No employee is required to join or to contribute money to a labor organization as a condition for employment under the **open shop**.

3. *Union shop*   A **union shop** provides that within a specific period of time, usually 30–90 days, an employee must join the union to continue the job with the company. Union membership under such a provision must be available on a fair and

nondiscriminatory basis and fees and dues must be reasonable. The National Labor Relations Act allows a majority of employees to vote to rescind the union shop authorization. This form of union security clause along with the check-off provision are most commonly found in collective bargaining agreements.[25]

4. *Union hiring hall*   A union hiring hall provision is typical of the construction, trucking, and longshoring trades. This form requires an employer to hire employees referred by the union, provided the union can supply a sufficient number of applicants. As long as the union refers union and nonunion members alike and does not require membership before the seventh day of employment, such provisions are legal.

5. *Agency shop*   **Agency shop** provisions require employees to contribute a sum equal to membership dues to the union, but they are not required to join the union. This provides the union the financial support of employees who benefit from their collective bargaining but retains the employee's right not to join the union.

6. *Maintenance of membership*   The **maintenance of membership** provision requires those who are union members at the time a union contract is entered into to remain union members but only for the duration of the agreement. Nonunion members are not required to join.

7. *Miscellaneous forms of union security*   A *preferential shop* requires the employer to give hiring preference to union members. The *check-off* of union dues from an employee's paycheck operates as a union security form because it protects the source of union funding and automatically keeps the employees in good standing with the union. This form of union security is often the only legal device available in right-to-work states. *Superseniority* gives union leaders top seniority for layoff purposes and indirectly increases union security by insuring the continuity of its leadership.

Recent board and court decisions threaten some of these traditional areas of union security. Superseniority rights are now limited to those union officials who are necessary to the actual administration of a collective bargaining agreement; being an office holder is not enough.[26] And increased restriction on the expenditure of union funds raised through agency shop agreements to those items directly related to collective bargaining has created financial difficulties for unions already suffering membership losses.[27]

Right-to-Work

Section 14(b) of the National Labor Relations Act states:

> Nothing in this act shall be construed as authorizing the execution and application of agreements requiring membership in a labor organization as a condition of employment in any state or territory in which such execution or application is prohibited by state or territorial law.

This provision allows states to enact laws prohibiting the union and/or agency shop forms of union security as seen in Case 2.1. Only twenty states, mostly in the West and the South, have done so.[28] Right-to-work legislation understandably evokes great emotions from both proponents and opponents.

Exhibit 2.2　(continued)

	ALL UNIONS			UNION AFFILIATION					
				AFL–CIO			Unaffiliated		
	Members[2]				Members[2]			Members[2]	
Year and industry group	Number[1]	Number (thousands)	Percent	Number[1]	Number (thousands)	Percent	Number[1]	Number (thousands)	Percent
Nonmanufacturing	96	9,998	46.0	70	7,811	46.0	26	2,186	45.9
Mining and quarrying (including crude petroleum and natural gas production)	14	428	2.0	10	149	.9	4	279	5.9
Construction	29	2,884	13.3	23	2,711	16.0	6	173	3.6
Transportation[4]	31	1,748	8.0	26	1,254	7.4	5	494	10.4
Telephone and telegraph	7	547	2.5	6	547	3.2	1	(3)	(3)
Electric, gas, and sanitary services (including water)	15	356	1.6	14	353	2.1	1	3	.1
Wholesale and retail trade	21	1,713	7.9	13	1,059	6.2	8	654	13.7
Finance, insurance, and real estate	7	51	.2	7	51	.3	—	—	—
Service industries[5]	50	1,990	9.2	29	1,548	9.1	18	276	5.8
Agriculture and fishing	7	44	.2	5	32	.2	2	12	.3
Nonmanufacturing (classification not available)	19	402	1.8	15	108	.6	4	294	6.2
Government	62	3,626	16.7	39	3,052	18.0	23	574	12.1
Federal	51	1,596	7.3	30	1,179	6.9	21	417	8.8
State.	19	473	2.2	17	412	2.4	2	61	1.3
Local	24	1,557	7.2	22	1,461	8.6	2	96	2.0

[1]These columns are nonadditive; many unions have membership in more than one industrial classification.
[2]Number of members computed by applying reported percentage figures to total membership, including membership outside continental United States. AFL–CIO data exclude directly affiliated locals. Total membership, moreover, may include retired and unemployed workers.
[3]Less than 0.05 percent or 500 members.
[4]Includes railroads, air, bus, truck, and water transportation; and allied services.
[5]Includes hotels, laundries, and other personal services; repair services, motion pictures, amusement, and related services; hospitals, educational institutions, and nonprofit membership organizations.
Note: Because of rounding, sums of individual items may not equal totals.

Source: U.S. Department of Labor, Bureau of Labor Statistics, *Handbook of Labor Statistics,* Bulletin 2070 (Washington, D.C.: Government Printing Office, December 1980), p. 408.

Types of Unions

Craft unions　The labor movement in this country began with associations and combinations of skilled workers who joined together for short periods of time to confront an employer on a specific job action. These associations were the bases of the craft unions.

Craft unions are made up of workers who have been organized in accordance with their craft or skill. "One craft, one union" is their slogan. For example, in the building construction industry, skilled workers include electricians, carpenters, bricklayers, and iron workers; in the printing industry, there are printers, typesetters, and engravers; in the service industry, barbers, cooks, and telephone workers; and in the manufacturing industry, millwrights, machinists, and tool-and-die makers.

The craft union, as an organization of skilled workers, is able to approach an employer on a much different footing than the industrial union. A craft union local typically seeks to organize all practitioners of its trade employed by a certain employer or within a specific geographic area. By doing so successfully, the craft union creates a union shop. Employers who need the services of a skilled laborer must employ a union member. Craft unions also seek to restrict the supply of skilled laborers so they can demand higher wages. Stringent apprenticeship programs consisting of several years of classroom instruction and on-the-job training limit craft union membership. And state or local licensing boards composed of members of the trade union can often restrict the number of licenses issued.

Union members enter the craft union after an apprenticeship of several years. Craft unionists remain members for their working lifetimes, moving from job to job as required but always remaining a part of their craft union. Even after retirement, their contact with the union remains as a tribute to their craft.

Labor agreements entered into by craft unions usually cover a geographic region rather than one employer. Union members may work for more than one employer within a year and still be covered by that same agreement. This is common when the building trades unions have negotiated a labor agreement with all the major construction companies in the area. Electricians, plumbers, drywallers, and other trades can go from job to job under the same agreement.

The **business agent** of the craft union is usually a full-time administrator paid by the union to handle negotiation and administration of the union contract as well as the day-to-day operation of the union hiring hall. On the job, one union member performs the role of **steward**; she may be the first person hired for that construction project, the most senior member of the construction crew, or a person chosen by the business agent. Stewards are the eyes and ears of the business agent. The steward's job is to make sure the contractor lives up to the agreement and to report to the business agent if he does not. This assures the business agent an active contact at each job site where the craft union is supplying laborers. There is, however, no continuing role for any *particular* steward in the craft union local. The steward's authority is limited to the job site and when that job is finished, the steward returns to regular union membership.

Industrial unions   While craft unions can be traced to the earliest days of this country, **industrial unions** have a wider and stronger base of mostly unskilled laborers. The slogan "One shop, one union" typifies the industrial union seeking to organize workers at one workplace with the same employer regardless of their jobs. The industrial union seeks to increase membership to ensure its influence.

Typical industrial unions include organizations of auto workers, rubber workers, textile workers, commercial workers, steelworkers, miners, and truck drivers. Increasingly, government employees such as firefighters, police, and hospital workers are organizing industrial-type unions.

The local industrial union most often is affiliated with a national or international union. Some national unions will negotiate **master agreements**, regional or national labor agreements covering wages, transfers, pensions, layoffs, and other benefits. The *local agreement* must be negotiated separately to cover matters of specific concern to the local union and the plant. An example of such a two-tiered agreement is the labor agreement between the United Auto Workers and Ford Motor Company. The table of contents in this particular master agreement includes the following:

Article I	Recognition
Article II	Union Shop
Article III	Dues and Assessments
Article IV	Company Responsibilities
Article V	Strikes, Stoppages, and Lockouts
Article VI	Representation
Article VII	Grievance Procedure
Article VIII	Seniority and Related Matters
Article IX	Wages and other Economic Matters
Article X	Miscellaneous
Article XI	Duration of Agreement[33]

The local agreement negotiated by Local 862, UAW Unit No. 2, includes the following:

Day off program
Employees information
Job posting agreement
Letters of understanding
Line spacing
Manning of medical facility
Miscellaneous agreement
Other miscellaneous agreements
Overtime agreement
Paid holidays
Seniority agreement
Shift preference agreement
Shift starting time[34]

Members of an industrial union often join the union *after* being hired simply because of a union shop provision in the contract. Members regard their union as their voice with the employer, and when employment ends, their membership usually ends as well.

The work of local industrial unions is typically administered by elected officials who are also full-time employees at the workplace. Their duties include negotiation and administration of the local union contract, normally with the assistance of a representative of the national or international union. This work is aided by elected *shop stewards* who form a permanent tier in the local industrial union hierarchy. At the departmental, shift, or line level, the shop stewards are the eyes and ears, voice, and strong right arm of the union. Their position enables them to communicate members' desires and complaints to union officials and to relay information back to the membership. Stewards participate in grievance adjustment and, through steward councils, assist in contract negotiations.

Levels of Unions

The four levels of unions are local unions, national (or international) unions, intermediate unions, and the federation of unions.

Local unions Unionized workers are members of a **local union** which is the organizational component of the labor union. It handles the day-to-day operations of the collective bargaining agreement, disposes of most grievances, manages strikes, and disciplines members. A local union may fill a social role in lives of its members, sponsoring dances, festivals, and other functions. It may be the focal point of the political organization and activity of its members.

A local union usually meets once a month to conduct business. At such meetings, annual elections are held, union issues discussed, and activities organized. Although this level is the most important to its members, attendance at the union meetings varies and is highest at times of crisis. Unlike paid business agents for craft unions, elected officials of local industrial unions are compensated by being given time off the job when conducting union business.

National (international) unions Typically, the local union is affiliated with a **national or international union**. Craft and industrial unions organize on a national basis and designate local unions by region. The national union serves as the local's parent, having created it. But a local union is considered a separate and distinct voluntary association owing its existence to the will of its members.

The relationship between a national union and its subordinate local unions is determined by the constitution, by-laws, and charter. The *charter* is a contract between the national and local organization and the members. The *constitution* and *by-laws* authorize the national union to function but also protect individual rights.

Constitutions are adopted or changed at conventions of representatives of member locals. Officers and executive boards are elected to take actions consistent with policies established by the convention. Most national unions allow their elected officials to hire and organize the union's administrative staff. Most unions have the following operational departments: executive and administrative, made up of president, vice-president, secretary-treasurer, and assistant; financial and auditing; organizational and service (to serve local unions); and the technical staff, which gives expert assistance in arbitration, labor laws, and data research.

The national union provides services to the locals, and the fundamental relationship is based on the services rendered. Services include organizing the unorganized workers within the jurisdiction of the local union. In appropriate circumstances, the national negotiates master agreements with nationwide employers and assists the local union in its local agreement. Even if no national contract is entered into, the national union assists the local unions in their contract negotiations through its research and educational services and may provide an expert negotiator. A national helps with grievance and arbitration administration, and provides support in strike activities. National unions play an important political and representative role on behalf of their locals in national and statewide political action. Local unions support the national unions with dues and fees.

Intermediate organizational units   Intermediate organizational units consisting of regional or district officers, trade councils, conference boards, and joint councils lie between national and local unions. For industrial unions, the intermediate office serves to bring the national office closer to the local unions to provide better services. For craft unions, joint councils often bring the various crafts together to give them better negotiating power with local construction employers, to coordinate their activities, and to assist in resolving jurisdictional disputes between craft unions.

Federation of unions   Perhaps the most familiar level of unions is the **federation of unions**, specifically the only U.S. federation of unions, the American Federation of Labor and Congress of Industrial Organization (AFL-CIO). Composed of approximately 95 national and international unions, the AFL-CIO has 55,000 local unions and 13.8 million members. Exhibit 2.3 illustrates its structure.

Federations were formed to increase union power. The federation acts as a national spokesperson for the labor movement. While the AFL-CIO is itself not a union, it represents U.S. labor in world affairs and coordinates union activities such as lobbying, voter registration, and political education. The federation also helps to coordinate activities aimed at organizing nonmember workers. The AFL-CIO assists in mediation and resolution of disputes between national unions that might otherwise result in work stoppages.

As with national unions, the officers, policies, activities, and business of the AFL-CIO are voted upon at periodic conventions, to which each national union sends delegates. Between conventions, the Executive Council, consisting of the president, secretary-treasurer, and thirty-three vice-presidents, convenes to handle such items as union corruption, charters of new internationals, and judicial appeals from member unions. The General Board is composed of the Executive Council plus the Chief Executive Officer of each affiliated union. The General Board rules on questions referred by the Executive Council, and includes items deemed to be politically sensitive and those requiring Council action by the AFL-CIO Constitution (see Exhibit 2.4).

Individual Rights within Unions

Duty of Fair Representation

The certified union for a bargaining unit is granted an exclusive right under the National Labor Relations Act to represent *all* of the employees in that unit, members and nonmembers alike. Individuals within that bargaining unit may not contract

Exhibit 2.3 Organization chart of the AFL-CIO

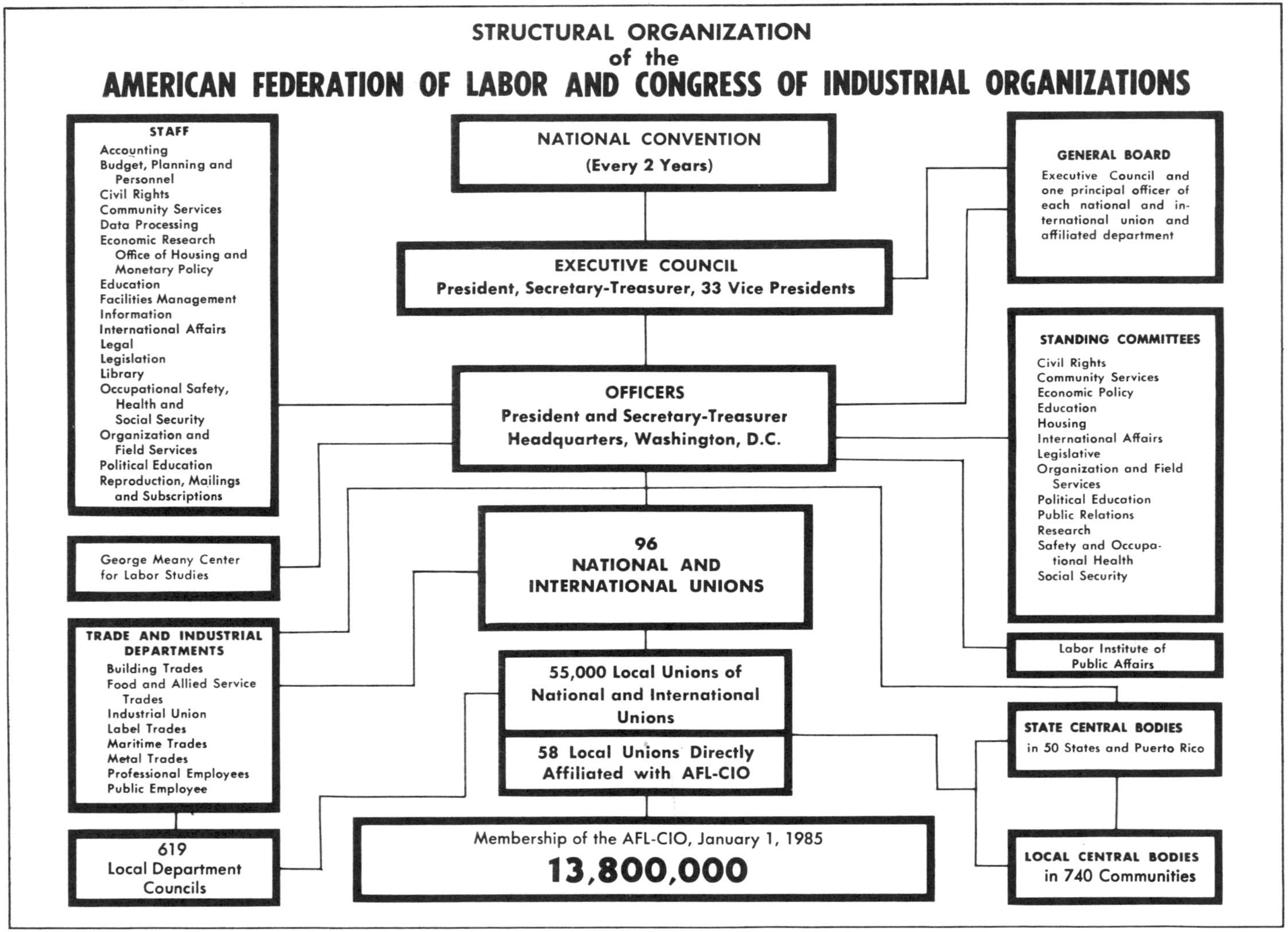

STRUCTURAL ORGANIZATION
of the
AMERICAN FEDERATION OF LABOR AND CONGRESS OF INDUSTRIAL ORGANIZATIONS

GENERAL BOARD
Executive Council and one principal officer of each national and international union and affiliated department

STANDING COMMITTEES
Civil Rights
Community Services
Economic Policy
Education
Housing
International Affairs
Legislative
Organization and Field Services
Political Education
Public Relations
Research
Safety and Occupational Health
Social Security

Labor Institute of Public Affairs

STATE CENTRAL BODIES
in 50 States and Puerto Rico

LOCAL CENTRAL BODIES
in 740 Communities

NATIONAL CONVENTION
(Every 2 Years)

EXECUTIVE COUNCIL
President, Secretary-Treasurer, 33 Vice Presidents

OFFICERS
President and Secretary-Treasurer
Headquarters, Washington, D.C.

96 NATIONAL AND INTERNATIONAL UNIONS

55,000 Local Unions of National and International Unions

58 Local Unions Directly Affiliated with AFL-CIO

Membership of the AFL-CIO, January 1, 1985
13,800,000

STAFF
Accounting
Budget, Planning and Personnel
Civil Rights
Community Services
Data Processing
Economic Research
Office of Housing and Monetary Policy
Education
Facilities Management
Information
International Affairs
Legal
Legislation
Library
Occupational Safety, Health and Social Security
Organization and Field Services
Political Education
Reproduction, Mailings and Subscriptions

George Meany Center for Labor Studies

TRADE AND INDUSTRIAL DEPARTMENTS
Building Trades
Food and Allied Service Trades
Industrial Union
Label Trades
Maritime Trades
Metal Trades
Professional Employees
Public Employee

619 Local Department Councils

Source: *This Is the AFL-CIO*, Publication no. 20 (Washington, D.C.: AFL-CIO, 1985), by permission of the AFL-CIO.

Exhibit 2.4 AFL-CIO structure

Structure of the AFL-CIO

Membership

The American Federation of Labor and Congress of Industrial Organizations (AFL-CIO) is made up of 95 national and international unions which in turn have more than 55,000 local unions.

The combined membership of all the unions affiliated with the AFL-CIO, as of January 1, 1984, was 13,800,000 workers.

Affiliated Organizations

In addition to the national and international unions, the AFL-CIO has state and city central bodies and trade and industrial departments.

There are *state central bodies* in each of the 50 states and Puerto Rico. The state bodies, composed of and supported by the different local unions in the particular state, function to advance the state-wide interests of labor and represent labor on state legislative matters.

Similarly, in each of 740 communities, the local unions of different national and international unions have formed *local central bodies*, through which they deal with civic and community problems and other local matters of mutual concern.

The *Trade and Industrial Departments* are separate organizations within the AFL-CIO which seek to promote the interests of specific groups of workers which are in different unions but have certain strong common interests.

Many of the national and international unions are affiliated with one or more of the eight such departments: Building and Construction Trades, Food and Allied Service Trades, Industrial Union, Maritime Trades, Metal Trades, Professional Employees and Public Employee. The eighth, the Union Label and Service Trades Department, seeks to promote consumer interest in union-made products and union services by urging the purchase of those products which bear the union label.

Policy Determination and Application

The basic policies of the AFL-CIO are set by its *convention*, which is its highest governing body. The convention meets every two years, although a special convention may be called at any time to consider a particular problem.

Each national and international union is entitled to send delegates to the convention, the number of delegates determined by the size of the union. Other affiliated organizations are entitled to be represented by one delegate each.

The governing body between conventions is the *Executive Council*, which is made up of the federation's President, Secretary-Treasurer, and 33 Vice-Presidents, all of whom are elected by majority vote of the convention.

The Executive Council carries out policies laid down by vote of the convention and deals with whatever issues and needs may arise between conventions. It meets at least three times a year.

The *executive officers* of the AFL-CIO are its *President, Lane Kirkland*, and *Secretary-Treasurer*, Thomas R. Donahue. They are responsible for supervising the affairs of the federation.

The President appoints a number of *standing committees* on particular subjects and directs the committees and staff departments in providing services to labor through organizing, legislative, international, public relations, educational, economic research and other activities.

A *General Board*, made up of the Executive Council members and a principal officer of each national and international union and each trade and industrial department, meets at the call of the President or the Executive Council to consider policy questions referred to it by the officers or the Executive Council.

American Federation of Labor and
Congress of Industrial Organizations
Lane Kirkland, *President*
Thomas R. Donahue, *Secretary-Treasurer*
Washington, D.C. 20006

Source: *This Is the AFL-CIO*, Publication no. 20 (Washington, D.C.: AFL-CIO, 1974), by permission of the AFL-CIO.

privately with the employer but must be represented by the recognized bargaining agent. In the traditional factory setting this **exclusivity rule** posed no particular problem for the individuals as long as the bargaining unit was appropriately formed. But today, nontraditional union members such as pro-football players, lawyers, and architects may find representation by the bargaining agent disadvantageous if the member is considered a superstar. Under this rule, a famous quarterback may have to accept the same salary as a member of the forward line, if that was the negotiated agreement.

The exclusivity rule giving the union the right to represent all members, however, is essential to the union's ability for proper representation at the bargaining table. Along with this right goes the **duty to fairly represent** *all* of the employees of the unit. Fair representation must be found both in the negotiation of the collective bargaining agreement and in its enforcement.

In a leading Supreme Court case, *Steele* v. *Louisville and N.R.R.,* a black railroad fireman asked the Court to set aside a seniority agreement negotiated by his union because it discriminated against minorities who were a part of the bargaining unit.[35] Although the Railway Labor Act under which the union had exclusive rights to bargain for the employees did not explicitly do so, the Court held that the act implicitly imposed a duty on the union to exercise its powers fairly on behalf of all those it acted for. Later court decisions found that the National Labor Relations Act imposed that same duty on its unions.

However, court decisions have acknowledged that contracts may have unfavorable effects on some members of the unit. The law does provide that such unfavorable effects cannot be the result of discriminatory treatment based on irrelevant or insidious considerations such as union membership or race, as suggested by Case 2.2. Guidelines on the resolution of such thorny issues as seniority, access to training programs, or promotion without a breach of the fair representation duty basically come from court decisions. A union must consider all employees and make an honest effort to serve their interests in good faith and without hostility and arbitrary discrimination.

Usually discrimination problems during contract negotiations can be easily detected and corrected. What may be more difficult to detect is whether the union has breached its duty of fair representation in contract enforcement; that is, whether the union chooses to follow the contract grievance procedure on behalf of the employee and whether it pursues such grievances fairly.[36] Under most collective bargaining agreements, the right to assert a violation of the agreement against the employer lies not with the individual employee, but with the union. Court action against the employer usually cannot be taken unless and until the employee exhausts that grievance procedure or alleges and proves that he or she was prevented from doing so by the wrongful action of the union. Thus, fair treatment of the employee by the union in administering a grievance is very important.

An employee must use the grievance procedure controlled by the union, but the employee does not have an absolute right to have a grievance pursued. In *Vaca* v. *Sipes,* the Supreme Court noted that a procedure giving the union discretion to supervise the grievance machinery and to invoke arbitration establishes an atmosphere for both parties to settle grievances short of arbitration.[37] The parties are assured that similar grievances receive similar treatment; thus, problem areas under the collective bargaining agreement can be isolated and perhaps resolved. Therefore, a breach of the duty to fairly represent an employee occurs only if the union's conduct toward the member is arbitrary, discriminatory, or in bad faith.

Some examples of the breach of that duty are obvious. Discrimination because of race, sex, religion, or nationality is clearly prohibited; age discrimination may not have the same protection. Some courts, prior to changes in federal law, sustained union decisions and actions that actually eliminated job rights of older employees. Such decisions were made in good faith and without malice.[38]

The merit of a grievance sought to be enforced by the employee is not paramount in a court's review of a union's actions. It is the actions of the union itself that the Court will review. If the union, in good faith and without discrimination, determines that a grievance should not be pursued, or if it indeed properly processed the grievance albeit unsuccessfully, it has not breached its duty to the employee.

An employee, however, who has been unfairly treated by the union has a cause of action against the union for the breach and against the employer for the underlying grievance.[39] This occurs when the union has acted in bad faith and with discrimination in not pursuing the grievance.

In a recent Supreme Court case, *Bowen* v. *The U.S. Postal Service,* the court apportioned the damages due the wrongfully discharged employee between the union and the employer by using the date of a hypothetical arbitration decision.[40] All back pay prior to that hypothetical date was due from the employer; all back pay from that date to the time of settlement was due from the union.

The Court reasoned that if the employee had been properly represented the employer's liability would have ended at the arbitration decision. All back pay benefits from that point forward were caused and should be paid by the union.

The effect of this decision on the union's ability to assess which grievances should be properly pursued has yet to be felt. Certainly unions have noticed the adverse financial possibilities of such open-ended liability. It is feared that the impact of the *Bowen* case on union leadership's decision-making process will erode its relationship with the rank and file.[41]

Union Democracy

Insuring the democratic operation of unions increases the individual's protection and rights. The justification for democratic unions is outlined in this abstract from the American Civil Liberties Union:

> First, a union in collective bargaining acts as the representative of every worker within the bargaining unit. It speaks for him, makes choices of policies which vitally affect him, and negotiates a contract which binds him. His wages, his seniority, his holidays, and even his retirement are all governed by this contract which becomes the basic law of his working life. The union in bargaining helps make laws; in processing grievances acts to enforce those laws; and in settling grievances helps interpret and apply those laws. It is the worker's economic legislature, policeman, and judge. The union, in short, is the worker's industrial government. The union's power is the power to govern the working lives of those for whom it bargains, and like all governing power should be exercised democratically.

Second, unions should be democratic because the power which they hold over the individual worker is largely derived from government. Labor relations acts such as the Wagner Act affirmatively protect the right to organize and place the government's stamp of approval on unionization. Even more, these statutes provide that government shall certify unions as the officially designated representatives and compel employers to recognize these unions as the exclusive representatives of all workers within the bargaining units. Unions, in the exercise of these powers derived from government, should maintain the same democratic standards required of government itself.

Third, unions should be democratic because their principal moral justification is that they introduce an element of democracy into the government of industry. They permit workers to have a voice in determining the conditions under which they shall work. This high objective of industrial democracy can be fulfilled only if unions which sit at the bargaining table are themselves democratic. Only to the extent that workers are allowed to participate in determining union policies do they become self-governing.

Source: Clyde W. Summers, Harry H. Wellington, and Allen Hyde, *Cases and Materials on Labor Law,* 2nd ed. (New York: Foundation Press, 1982), pp. 108–109, by permission of The Foundation Press, Inc.

The Labor-Management Reporting and Disclosure (Landrum-Griffin) Act of 1959 protects the democratic nature of unions. The act assures full and active participation by the rank and file in the affairs of the union. It accords protection of union members' right to participate in the election process. It requires high standards of responsibility and ethical conduct by union officials and protects members from the arbitrary and capricious whims of union leaders.

The Bill of Rights of Members of Labor Organizations established the machinery necessary to enforce this act. The rights under this Title I section include the right to nominate candidates and vote in union elections, and to attend membership meetings and participate in the deliberation of these meetings. Freedom to speak about union affairs and to assemble with union members was also reaffirmed. Title I protects union members from excessive charges because dues, fees, and assessments are decided by a majority vote of the membership as in Case 2.3. Members are given the right to sue the union and are assured due process protections in the union's disciplinary actions.

Under subsequent titles of the Landrum-Griffin Act, union members gained access to union financial reports; local unions received protection from their national organization in the assertion of trustee rights; the fair and democratic conduct of union elections was assured; and the fiduciary duty of union officials to their members was clearly outlined.

Summary

Unions seek to improve their members' living standard through better wages, job security, and social legislation. To do this, unions must seek their own security as the exclusive representative of the worker. Different types of unions emphasize the differences between skilled and unskilled workers. The craft union controls the availability of skilled laborers and can therefore exert great pressure. Industrial unions, in turn, include many unskilled employees to ensure their collective power.

The structure and relationship of the local union to its national or international organization differs between craft and industrial unions, although there are similarities. Most national affiliates assist the local unions in contract negotiations, administration of collective bargaining agreements, and strike activities.

A union seeks union security clauses in collective bargaining agreements ranging from union shops to dues check-off provisions to ensure the exclusive nature of its representation as well as its financial security. State right-to-work laws undermine that security and pose a great threat to unionization.

Individual employees have certain protections as members of labor unions, including guidelines on how they are to be represented in negotiation with the employer and in grievance procedures. In addition, the Landrum-Griffin Act assured the rank-and-file union members the right to participate in union politics and policies.

Labor organizations face the future with decreased membership, a changing national economy, and workers who have not yet participated in unionization.

CASE 2.1   *Right-to-Work Laws*

Adapted from *Retail Clerks International Association* v. *Schermerhorn,* 375 U.S. 96, 11 L.Ed. 179, 84 S.Ct. 219 (1963)

A class action suit was instituted in a Florida state court by four nonunion employees who sought injunctive relief against an employer and a union who had agreed to an agency shop arrangement in a collective bargaining agreement. The agreement did not require the employees to join the contracting union, but did require them to pay an initial service fee and monthly service fees to the union as a condition of employment. On the basis of the Florida Right-to-Work Law, the Florida Supreme Court held that the agency shop clause involved was illegal. The union appealed on the grounds that the National Labor Relations Act specifically allows agency shop provisions in collective bargaining agreements, only prohibiting agreements requiring membership. Because this agency shop agreement did not require membership in the union, the state's law should not be allowed to forbid it.

Decision

The Supreme Court upheld the Florida court's decision in finding that the agency shop clause was prohibited by Florida's Right-to-Work Law. The Court found that Section 14b of the National Labor Relations Act, which allows states to prohibit agreements requiring membership in a labor organization as a condition of employment, could not be so narrowly construed as the union had requested in this case or else the section would have no meaning. The state's Right-to-Work Law had to be interpreted to preclude any type of union security agreement allowed under federal law if the purpose of the act and the Taft-Hartley Amendments were to be effective.

CASE 2.2   *Duty of Fair Representation*

Adapted from *NAACP, Detroit Branch, The Guardians, Inc. et al,* v. *Detroit Police Officers Association et al.,* 28 EPD sec. 32, 498 (1981)

In October 1979 and in September 1980, the city of Detroit laid off approximately 1,100 police officers pursuant to the terms of the last hired, first fired seniority provisions contained in a collective bargaining agreement between the city and the defendants. Of the 1,100 officers laid off, approximately 800 were black. Individual black police officers and two organizations, the NAACP and The Guardians, Inc., brought suit against the union claiming that it had breached its duty of fair representation with regard to the layoffs. At the time, Detroit was under a court order upholding the city's voluntary affirmative action plan to offset the effects of past discrimination in the Detroit Police Department. The plaintiffs' claim against the union was that it breached its duty of fair representation under state law by discriminating against its black members. By enforcing the seniority-based layoff system, and by refusing to consider alternatives to layoffs in its contract negotiations, the plaintiffs argued that the union was aware that such action would perpetuate the effects of past hiring discrimination. In support of this assertion, the plaintiffs pointed out that when black officers requested by letter that the union accept the mayor's offer to discuss other options to avoid layoffs, the union never responded. Plaintiffs also asserted that the union was moti-

vated to accept the layoffs to reduce black voting strength within the union. They further contended that the union agreed to a wage freeze to avert a subsequent layoff situation in 1981 affecting more white officers.

The union claimed it had a bona fide seniority system under Title VII of the 1964 Civil Rights Act. The union stated that if it did act differently, it would be sacrificing contract rights of the majority in favor of the minority of its membership, thus violating its duty of fair representation to the majority. The union claimed that the plaintiffs showed no intentional discrimination and that it had always acted in good faith.

Decision

The U.S. District Court refused to grant the union a summary judgment because it felt issues presented by the plaintiffs in this case raised questions of fact concerning the union's behavior, and that sufficient proof needed to be shown before a decision could be made. The court did not decide whether Title VII of the 1964 Civil Rights Act, which insulates bona fide seniority provisions from attack, has an impact on the union's duty of fair representation. It simply found that a court needed to look at the facts.

CASE 2.3   *Union Democracy*

Adapted from *Bunz* v. *Moving Picture Machine Operators Protective Union Local 224,* 567 F.2d 1117 (1977)

The plaintiff is a member of the union that is the defendant in this case. During a strike the union officials imposed an assessment of $50 per month for any member who did not walk the picket line. The assessment was authorized by a referendum of the membership by a standing vote rather than by secret ballot. Plaintiff objected and a secret ballot was held with 59 percent of the members present voting for the assessment. The union's by-laws required that an assessment be approved by two-thirds vote of the members present. The union's attorney nonetheless ruled that the assessment had passed because the Landrum-Griffin Act provides that no special assessment can be levied except by a majority vote. Plaintiff sued the union, alleging improper implementation of the picket assessment, and the court granted the plaintiff's motion for summary judgment based on the fact that the Landrum-Griffin majority vote provision was a minimum requirement and that the union was free to enact and be governed by more stringent rules. The union appealed based on the fact that the court actually did not have jurisdiction to hear the case.

Decision

The Landrum-Griffin Act gives the court jurisdiction if any of the rights under the act have been infringed. Violation of the union's by-laws is not per se a violation of the Landrum-Griffin Act. However, the court found that the act provides that each member of a union be given an equal right to vote. In this case the court found a violation of the union's own by-laws in allowing a vote to pass by a majority vote rather than the stated two-thirds vote. Thus, the union violated members' rights to an equal vote.

CASE STUDY   *Duty of Fair Representation*

Adapted from *Teamsters* v. *National Labor Relations Board,* 587 F. 2d 1176 (CA D.C., 1978)

Facts

Unions representing employees in the nonferrous mining industry engage in nationwide coordinated bargaining. In this case negotiations for employees of the corporation were conducted by a negotiating committee representing four unions: Steelworkers, Laborers, Operating Engineers (collectively, AFL-CIO), and the Teamsters. The four unions were jointly certified to function as "the Union" in negotiating and signing an agreement. For years the relationship between the AFL-CIO and the teamsters had been adversarial, forming the basis for incidents to come.

At the start of negotiations, the company made clear its understanding that the negotiations would be conducted on a joint basis. And if and when it was informed by the spokesperson for the

"Union" (a member of the Steelworkers Union) that an agreement had been accepted, that in fact a new agreement existed.

Joint negotiations continued for about a month, but the company's offer fell short of the expected wage offer. The old contract expired and on October 1 the teamsters met and voted not to agree to any contract extensions and voted to go on strike. The teamsters informed the AFL-CIO of their vote and set up picket lines.

Later that evening, the company and the AFL-CIO negotiators met and agreed to a contract that included the expected wage increases. On October 2 the AFL-CIO unions met and ratified the agreements at meetings the teamsters were not allowed to attend. After the AFL-CIO vote the spokesperson called the teamsters to inform them of the vote, and called the company and notified them there was an agreement.

On October 3, both the AFL-CIO and company representatives told teamster officials and pickets that their strike was illegal because a contract was in effect. The teamsters told those officials that their ratification meeting would be held as soon as possible, but until the teamsters ratified the agreement the pickets would stay. The ratification meeting was held October 3 in the evening. The contract was ratified and the pickets removed.

Earlier on October 3, the AFL-CIO and company representatives had met to negotiate a strike settlement (back-to-work) agreement. The teamsters were not notified of nor invited to the meeting. The AFL-CIO proposed and the company accepted an agreement not to commence legal action against the AFL-CIO unions, but the company reserved the right to act against any "individual union" and to discharge or discipline any employee who continued to strike after ". . . 9:30 P.M. on October 2."

The company discharged two teamsters and suspended a third for picketing on October 2 and October 3 in violation of the no-strike clause. The teamsters filed charges against the company and the AFL-CIO. The case revolved around the AFL-CIO's breach of its duty of fair representation.

Lawsuit

The parties agreed on the principle of law that a union has the duty to represent all of the employees of a unit as part of its right to represent those employees exclusively. In this case the AFL-CIO unions were jointly certified with the teamsters to represent the company's employees. Therefore the AFL-CIO owed a duty to fairly represent the members of the teamsters union as well as its own unions. The parties disagreed on whether that duty was breached, however, in the following two causes of action.

1. Ratification Procedures

AFL-CIO position: The NLRA does not require a union to give its members the right to ratify an agreement it has negotiated. In effect, the teamsters had the opportunity to vote on the agreement when they voted October 1 not to continue the old contract. Their negative vote added to the AFL-CIO position would still have resulted in a passed contract. The teamsters had the same chance to vote on the contract on October 2 as the other unions but gave up on the chance by staying out on strike. Not allowing the teamsters to ratify the contract would be an internal union affair *not* governed by the duty to fairly represent under the act's exclusive representation section.

Teamsters position: Once the decision is made to seek a ratification vote of members before entering into an agreement, the union must allow all unit members an equal chance to vote.

The teamsters' October 1 vote cannot be counted as a ratification. In fact, the agreement had not even been reached at the time of that vote. No assumptions can be made as to how that vote would have come out if the agreement had been presented. Regardless of the legal reason ratification by union members is sought, it cannot be denied that the contract to be voted on would affect the members' employment for three years and therefore was subject to the fair representation section of the act.

2. Strike Settlement Agreement

AFL-CIO position: The teamsters were not disciplined because of the strike settlement but because they were on strike on October 2 and 3 in violation of a no-strike clause in a valid agreement. The teamsters were given notice that a contract existed and that they were in violation of it.

Teamsters position: When the

AFL-CIO representatives met on October 3 to negotiate a strike settlement, they proposed that strikers could be disciplined for being on strike after 9:30 P.M., on October 2. While the company representative contended the contract went into effect at that time, the notification was given to the company at 11 P.M., October 2. So the AFL-CIO actually provided that teamsters could be disciplined for violating a no-strike clause that was not even in effect for an hour and one-half.

Questions

1. Did the AFL-CIO representatives violate their duty to fairly represent the teamster members when they did not allow them to vote on the contract before telling the company it was approved? Why or why not?
2. Did the AFL-CIO representatives violate their duty to fairly represent the teamster members when agreeing to a strike settlement that would automatically penalize them?
3. Could the teamster representatives also be charged with violating their duty to fairly represent the members of the AFL-CIO unions by calling the strike?

Key Terms and Concepts

Agency shop

Business agent

Closed shop

Craft union

Dues check-off

Duty of fair representation

Exclusive bargaining agent/representative

Federation of unions

Industrial union

Intermediate organizational units

Local union

Maintenance of membership

Master agreement

National (or international) union

Open shop   Steward

Right-to-work   Union shop

Review Questions

1. How are craft and industrial unions different in their origins and basic concepts?
2. What are the different levels of unions? What are the basic objectives of each level and how do they work together?
3. Define union security and explain its importance to labor leaders.
4. Discuss why labor leaders have tried to repeal Section 14(b) (the right-to-work section) of the Taft-Hartley Amendments since its passage in 1947.
5. Why do many people believe that unions must be democratic?
6. What social and economic trends present major hurdles to union organizing during the remainder of this century?

Endnotes

1. Albert Rees, *The Economics of Trade Unions* (Chicago: University of Chicago Press, 1977), p. 30.
2. Daniel J. B. Mitchell, *Unions, Wage and Inflation* (Washington, D.C.: The Brookings Institution, 1980), pp. 1–22, 77–112.
3. James F. Rand, "Preventive-Maintenance Techniques for Staying Union-Free," *Personnel Journal* 59 (June 1980), pp. 497–99.
4. Thomas A. Kochan, "How American Workers View Labor Unions," Monthly Labor Review 102 (April 1979), pp. 23–31. See also George W. Bohlander, "How the Rank and File Views Local Union Administration—A Survey," *Employee Relations Law Journal* 8 (Autumn 1982), pp. 217–35.
5. Kochan, "American Workers," pp. 23–24.
6. Brian Heshizer and Harry Graham, "Are Unions Facing a Crisis? Labor Officials Are Divided," *Monthly Labor Review* 107, no. 8 (Aug. 1984), pp.23–35.
7. John P. Bucalo, Jr., "Successful Employee Relations," *Personnel Administrator* 31, no. 4 (April 1986), pp. 63–84.
8. Aaron Bernstein, "The Difference Japanese Management Makes," *Business Week*, July 14, 1986, pp. 47–50.
9. John P. Bucalo, Jr., "Successful Employee Relations," pp. 63–84.
10. Amos N. Okafor, "White Collar Unionization: Why and What to Do," *Personnel* 62, no. 8 (Aug. 1985), pp. 17–21.
11. William T. Dickens and Jonathan S. Leonard, "Accounting for the Decline in Union Membership, 1950–1980," *Industrial and Labor Relations Review* 38, no. 3 (April 1985), 323–34.
12. Philip M. Doyle, "Area Wage Surveys Shed Light on Declines in Unionization," *Monthly Labor Review* 108, no. 9 (Sept. 1985), pp. 13–20.
13. Larry T. Adams, "Labor Organization Mergers 1979–84: Adapting to Change," *Monthly Labor Review* 107, no. 9 (Sept. 1984), pp. 21–27.

14. Joseph R. Antos, Mark Chandler, and Wesley Mellow, "Sex Differences in Union Membership," *Industrial and Labor Relations Review* 33, no. 2 (Jan. 1980), pp. 162–69.

15. Daniel C. Stove, Jr., "Can Unions Pick Up the Pieces?" *Personnel Journal* 65, no. 2 (Feb. 1986), pp. 37–40.

16. Amos N. Okafor, "White-Collar Unionization," pp. 17–21.

17. Ross Stagner and Hjalmar Rosen, *Psychology of Union-Management Relations* (Monterey, Calif.: Brooks/Cole, 1965), p. 2.

18. Larry T. Adams, "Changing Employment Patterns of Organized Workers," *Monthly Labor Review* 108, no. 2 (Feb. 1985), pp. 25–31.

19. Marcus H. Sandner and Herbert G. Heneman III, "Union Growth Through the Election Process," *Industrial Relations* 20, no. 1 (Winter 1981), pp. 109–16.

20. Ronald L. Seeber and William N. Cooke, "The Decline in Union Success in NLRB Representation Elections," *Industrial Relations* 22, no. 1 (Winter 1983), pp. 34–44.

21. John C. Anderson, Charles A. O'Reilly III, and Gloria Busman, "Union Decertification in the U.S.: 1947–1977," *Industrial Relations* 19, no. 1 (Winter 1980), pp. 100–107; and "The Decertification Process: Evidence from California," *Industrial Relations* 21, no. 2 (Spring 1982), pp. 178–95.

22. "Huge 4-year Losses Renews Union Campaign to Spur Membership," *Resource* (American Society for Personnel Administration) April 1985, p. 5.

23. Robert L. Aronson, "Unionism Among Professional Employees in the Private Sector," *Industrial and Labor Relations Review* 38, no. 3 (April 1985), pp. 352–64.

24. Dickens and Leonard, pp. 323–34. See also Howard M. Leftwich, "Organizing in the Eighties: A Human Resources Perspective," *Labor Law Journal* 32, no. 8 (Aug. 1981), pp. 484–91. See also Paula B. Voos, "Union Organizing: Costs and Benefits," *Industrial and Labor Relations Review* 36, no. 4 (July 1983), pp. 576–91.

25. *Collective Bargaining: Negotiations and Contracts* (Washington, D.C.: Bureau of National Affairs, 1981), pp. 87.1, 87.3.

26. NLRB v. Niagara Madine & Tool Works, 117 LRRM 2689 (CA2, 1984); Local 900, International Union of Electrical Radio and Machine Workers v. NLRB, 727 F. 2d 1184 (D.D.C. 1984).

27. Ellis v. Railway Clerk, 466 U.S. 435, 104 S.Ct. 1883, 80 L.Ed. 2d 428 (1984).

28. States with right-to-work laws include

Alabama	Nevada
Arizona	North Carolina
Arkansas	North Dakota
Florida	South Carolina
Georgia	South Dakota
Iowa	Tennessee
Kansas	Texas
Louisiana	Utah
Mississippi	Virginia
Nebraska	Wyoming

29. Norman Hill, "The Double-Speak of Right-to-Work," *AFL-CIO American Federationist* 87 (Oct. 1980), pp. 13–16.

30. Barry T. Hirsch, "The Determinants of Unionization: An Analysis of Interarea Differences," *Industrial and Labor Relations Review* 33, no. 2 (Jan. 1980), pp. 147–61.

31. Kenneth A. Kovach, "National Right-to-Work Law: An Affirmative Position," *Labor Law Journal* 28 (May 1977), pp. 305–14.

32. Robert Swidinsky, "Bargaining Power Under Compulsory Unionism," *Industrial Relations* 21, no. 1 (Winter 1982), pp. 62–72.

33. *Agreement* between U.A.W. and Ford Motor Company, vol. 1, Feb. 13, 1982, effective Mar. 1, 1982, p. 4.

34. *Agreements* between Local 862, U.A.W., Unit no. 2, and Ford Motor Company, October 14, 1979, p. ii.

35. Steele v. Louisville and N.R.R., 323 U.S. 192, 15 LRRM 708 (1944).

36. Hines v. Anchor Motor Freight, Inc., 424 U.S. 554, 91 LRRM 2481 (1976).

37. Vaca v. Sipes, 386 U.S. 171, 64 LRRM 2369 (1967).

38. Goodlin v. Chinchfield R.R., 229 F. 2d 578, 37 LRRM 2515 (CA 6, 1956) cert. denied, 351 U.S. 953, 38 LRRM 2160 (1956).

39. George W. Bohlander, "Fair Representation: Not Just a Union Problem," *Personnel Administrator* 25, no. 3 (Mar. 1980), pp. 36–40, 82.

40. Bowen v. United States Postal Service, 112 LRRM 2281 (1983).

41. Thomas S. Francis, "The New Apportionment Rule Under *Bowen* v. *United States Postal Service,*" *Labor Law Journal* 35, no. 2 (Feb. 1984), pp. 71–91.

The Bargaining Process

Bargaining Unit Determination

LABOR NEWS

Milwaukee Spring II Case

In a major reversal of its own policy, the National Labor Relations Board has reconsidered its findings in Milwaukee Spring *and has decided that the company could relocate work done under a union contract to a non-union facility to avoid higher labor costs.*

The board ruled that such a move would indeed be legal, provided the company had fulfilled its bargaining obligation to the union concerning the move, and as long as the move was not barred by any type of work preservation provision in the contract. This most recent ruling supersedes the NLRB's earlier ruling in the same case; the earlier ruling had said that such moves during the term of an agreement violated employees' rights.

"An employer need not obtain a union's consent on a matter not contained in the body of the collective bargaining agreement," the board announced. "It is not for the board to create an implied work-preservation clause in every American labor agreement based on wages and benefits or recognition provisions," the NLRB concluded.

Source: "National Labor Relations Board Reverses Self on Legality of Moving Union Work," Resource pamphlet (Alexandria, Va: American Society for Personnel Administration, Feb. 1984), p. 7, by permission of American Society for Personnel Administration. 268 NLRB No. 87 (January 23, 1984)

The collective bargaining process is at the heart of the employer/employee relationship. That process, however, is not a simple one. The National Labor Relations Act as subsequently amended defines the process and limits the parties to it.[1] A group of employees cannot simply present their requests to the employer. Procedures must be followed to determine if those particular employees are protected by the act. A union purporting to represent the employees must prove that it does indeed represent them. And any particular group of employees who feel they have the same interests and desires and therefore should negotiate together may not satisfy the requirements of the act as an "appropriate" unit of employees for collective bargaining purposes. This chapter will explore the particulars of the act to learn when and how it can be used to determine parties subject to its provisions.

The National Labor Relations Board (NLRB)

The stated purpose of the National Labor Relations Act was to minimize industrial strife interfering with the normal flow of commerce. Using the authority of the Commerce Clause of the U.S. Constitution, Congress legislated a federally protected interest in the internal operations of certain industries.[2] That interest was in setting the legal process by which labor and management would bargain.

The act created a five-member National Labor Relations Board (NLRB) to administer its provisions. These board members are appointed for five-year-terms by the President and with the advice and consent of the U.S. Senate. The members' authority under the act enables them, through a wide range of remedies, to effectuate the purposes of the act and ". . . to protect the rights of the public in connection with labor disputes affecting commerce."[3]

Four basic principles of the act guide the NLRB's administration:

1. Encouragement of labor organizations and collective bargaining
2. Recognition of majority representation
3. Establishment of a prompt administrative machinery for enforcement instead of criminal sanctions
4. Imposition of sanctions or punishments even if other sanctions or punishments are found in other jurisdictions[4]

Jurisdiction of the National Labor Relations Board

Congress established certain jurisdictional tests to satisfy expected practical/legal criticisms of the act. The NLRB has jurisdiction over persons when there is a labor dispute affecting commerce; or when there is a controversy involving an employer, employee, or a labor organization. This jurisdiction has been found broad enough to include all representation and unfair labor practice proceedings. The tests must be met before the board is empowered to act.

Persons   The definition of a *person* under the National Labor Relations Act is all-inclusive, and involves "one or more individuals, labor organizations, partnerships, associations, corporations, legal representatives, trustees, trustees in bankruptcy, or receivers."[5]

Because the definition is so broad, few problems arise with finding a person in most disputes. However, entities otherwise exempt from the act because they are not considered as "employers" (namely, political subdivisions and railroads) have been able to invoke protections of the act against union-sponsored activities.[6]

Labor dispute   A labor dispute must exist for the board to exercise jurisdiction. The act defines *labor dispute* as ". . . any controversy concerning terms, tenure, or conditions of employment. . . ."[7] Labor disputes have been held to include employee-concerted activities such as strikes, walkouts, and picketing; unfair labor practices such as employers' refusal to bargain; and interference in employee rights. The term has also been interpreted to include investigation of the health and safety facilities of a work environment.

Included in the definition are controversies ". . . concerning the association or representation of persons in negotiating, fixing, maintaining, changing, or seeking to arrange terms or conditions of employment. . . ."[8] These controversies are usually addressed by the NLRB in its representation cases.

The definition also allows the board to take jurisdiction in proceedings involving secondary boycotts by stipulating that the controversy need not be between employers and employees only.[9] Although the act does not cover internal or interunion disputes, Case 3.1 provides an example of when a dispute between rival unions can result in NLRB action.

Affecting commerce   A broad definition of *commerce* under the statute gives the board authority in all but purely local disputes.[10] The board has jurisdiction if the labor dispute directly affects commerce. And, if the employer's operation affects commerce, any labor dispute involving that employer falls within the board's jurisdiction. The NLRB, under this theory, has taken jurisdiction over a manufacturer whose goods were to be transported interstate even though he was not engaged in out-of-state commerce.

To protect itself from the resulting multitude of backlogged cases, the NLRB is authorized to use its discretion and ". . . decline to assert jurisdiction over any labor dispute involving any class or category of employers, where . . . the effect of such labor dispute on commerce is not sufficiently substantial to warrant the exercise of its jurisdiction."[11]

To judge the substance of a dispute, the board has established jurisdictional standards using annual specific dollar amounts for different types of businesses. For example, for nonretail enterprises, a gross outflow or inflow of at least $50,000 in revenue is required for the NLRB to take jurisdiction, while retail establishments need gross business volumes of at least $500,000 per year and substantial interstate purchases or sales. This limitation is not absolute, however, and the board may enter cases of significant impact regardless of the dollar volume involved. An example of this is the NLRB's decision to examine handicapped workshop operations on a case-by-case basis. If it determines the operation is essentially rehabilitative it will not take jurisdiction. But it will if the workshop is primarily industrial with an economic purpose.[12]

The board has also judged the substance of a case and has removed itself from some controversies because of the type of employer involved. Such classes of employers include the employer who lacks sufficient control over employment conditions to bargain effectively and employers whose employees are subject to laws of a foreign country.[13]

Employees Employees, as included in the statutory definition, are entitled to the rights guaranteed by the act. Those include the right to self-organization; to form labor organizations; to bargain collectively; to engage in concerted activities for purposes of collective bargaining; and to refrain from such activities, unless there is a contract requirement to pay labor organization dues as a condition of employment.

The definition of *employee* is liberally construed, so stated exclusions in the definition become more important in determining who is *not* an employee. The types of workers not covered are agricultural workers; domestic servants; persons employed by a spouse or a parent; independent contractors; supervisors; individuals who work for employers subject to the Railway Labor Act; and employees of the United States government, the Federal Reserve Banks, the states or their political subdivisions.

Employers Employers under the act are subject to the unfair labor practices section, which emphasizes the duty to bargain collectively with employee representatives. The definition of *employer* also takes on broad connotations by listing those persons who are *not* employers: the United States government or a wholly owned government corporation (with the exception of the U.S. Postal Service by virtue of another federal law), the Federal Reserve Bank, a state or political subdivision, anyone subject to the Railway Labor Act, or any labor organization.[14]

Labor organizations *Labor organizations* are most commonly labor unions, but the NLRB recognizes other kinds of employee committees that represent their employees to employers.[15] Labor organizations are also subject under the act to the unfair labor practices section that places some limitations on strikes supported by the organization.

Preemption

A question of preemption arises when a field of activity, such as collective bargaining or labor relations, is subject to regulation by both the federal and state governments, and a decision must be made as to whether concurrent jurisdiction exists or if the federal government enjoys exclusive jurisdiction. Since the Constitution is clear that federal law is the supreme law of the land, a factual determination must be made as to whether Congress has entered and completely covered a field or activity.

The Supreme Court decided the preemption issue in a series of cases.[16] If an activity is the subject of state action and is clearly protected under Section 7 of the National Labor Relations Act, the state is totally preempted from the field and federal law controls. Section 7 provides employees the rights to self-organization; to form, join, or assist labor organizations; to bargain collectively; to engage in other concerted activities; or to refrain from doing all of these. If the activity sought to be regulated by the state clearly is prohibited by Section 8, the unfair labor practices section, the state is also totally preempted from the field. The Court went even further when it decided that the state would be preempted if the activity was arguably protected or prohibited by the act. However, the arguably protected or prohibited test was not to be applied in what the court described as a rigid manner.[17]

The preemption rule has two alternative bases. The first was the establishment of a uniform law of labor relations that serves federal interests. This law was to be centrally administered by an expert agency to promote predictability and ease in the nationwide judicial application of labor laws.[18] The second alternative was a congressional intention to leave certain peaceful, economic, self-help weapons to the free play of economic forces unregulated by any governmental authority. The National Labor Relations Act created a balance of power between labor and management, and the state should not be allowed to destroy that balance by outlawing or regulating particular actions.[19] An example of such a protected activity which the act left as an economic weapon is peaceful strikes. No state regulation of peaceful strikes is allowed.

Prior to the Landrum-Griffin Act, if an otherwise preempted activity fell within the NLRB's jurisdiction and the board did not exercise such jurisdiction because of its own limitation, the state still could not enter the field. However, Landrum-Griffin allows the board to cede jurisdiction, thereby allowing the state to regulate.

In determining an area arguably covered by the National Labor Relations Act, the Supreme Court recognized two exceptions. The first occurs when an activity is of mere peripheral concern to the purposes of the act; for example, a purely internal conflict between a union and a member. Or when the activity touches interest so deeply rooted in local feeling it compels state interest, the second exception can be used, and the state may intervene. Examples are enforcement of state laws prohibiting violence and obstruction of access to property or state laws concerning defamation. In some cases, the court has pushed the arguably test even further so preemption occurs only when the issues presented to the court are identical to those presented to the National Labor Relations Board. Parties then have a reasonable opportunity to invoke the protection of the National Labor Relations Act.

NLRB Authority in Representation Cases

The National Labor Relations Board (NLRB), in carrying out its lawful responsibilities, decides **representation cases**. Section 9(b) of the Labor-Management Relations Act authorizes the board to decide on a case-by-case basis the **appropriate unit** of employees for collective bargaining. The board exercises this power to guarantee employees the fullest freedom under the act, mainly, the right of self-organization.

The NLRB does not have rigid or constrictive regulations for dealing with recognition cases. It has wide discretion in its decisions, which courts will uphold absent a finding that the board acted arbitrarily.[20] Both the board and the courts recognize that more than one unit sometimes may be appropriate for collective bargaining. The board is not required to choose *the* most appropriate unit, only *an* appropriate unit.

Under Section 3(b) of the Labor-Management Relations Act, the board may delegate its authority to determine an appropriate unit to its regional directors, allowing itself discretionary review of such decisions. The board will review a decision if: a substantial question of law or policy is raised because of the absence of, or departure from, an officially reported board precedent; a regional director's decision on a substantial factual issue is clearly erroneous on the record and it affects the party's rights; the conduct of the hearing resulted in a legally prejudicial error; or there are compelling reasons for the board to reconsider a previously stated rule of policy.[21]

While there are no hard and fast rules in the act to determine appropriateness, there are certain limitations on the types of units and on workers to be included and excluded from units. Certain fundamental and logical policies should be followed in determining a unit.

Appropriateness

The basic underlying principle for the NLRB's determination of an appropriate unit is that only employees having a substantial mutuality of interest in wages, hours, and working conditions can be appropriately grouped in that unit. The logic is that the greater the similarity of working conditions, the greater the likelihood its members can agree on priorities and thus make the collective bargaining process successful.[22]

The following criteria are most often used in deciding what constitutes a rational unit:

1. Community of interest
2. History of bargaining
3. Desire of employees
4. Prior union organization
5. Relationship of the unit to the organizational structure of the company
6. Public interest
7. Accretion
8. Stipulated units
9. Statutory considerations

Community of interest   The **community of interest doctrine** attempts to quantify, by means of descriptive criteria, when workers should feel their individual interests are so similar it makes collective bargaining fruitful. The board has at various times enumerated these criteria: similarity of job functions and earnings, in benefits received or hours worked, and/or in job training or skills required; a high degree of contact and interchange among the employees; and/or geographical proximity and common supervision.[23] All of these can indicate a common interest or interests which, coupled with the other listed criteria, establish an appropriate unit. However, not all of the community of interest criteria have to apply: in a 1948 NLRB decision, common laborers who did not have common supervision were held to be an appropriate group because of their wage rates and *lack* of special skills.[24]

History of bargaining   If a bargaining unit and a particular employer have a history of bargaining, the board will recognize the appropriateness of the unit, in the absence of compelling reasons to the contrary, to ensure the employees' right of self-organization and to provide the stable labor relations sought by the board.

History of bargaining usually becomes a question when the board receives a request for decertification to allow for smaller or different bargaining units, or when a new class of employer has come under the board's jurisdiction, such as when the National Labor Relations Act was extended to the health care industry in 1974.

Although prior bargaining relationships are favorably considered by the board, such histories are not absolute. The board has disregarded history of bargaining in several cases when it contravened its policy of mixing clerical and production and maintenance personnel; when it was based on oral contracts; and when it reflected racial or sexual discrimination.[25]

Employee wishes   The **Globe doctrine** established the National Labor Relations Board policy to give weight to employee wishes when determining an appropriate bargaining unit.[26] Although the board cannot delegate the selection of a bargaining unit to employees, it may use the election process as a way to consult employees. In one such case,

> The Board provided for special balloting to determine the representation wishes of the employees. The situation involved a bargaining unit determination by the Board where a smaller craft unit and a larger industry unit were equally plausible. By permitting the employees in the smaller unit to indicate their preference, the Board was able to decide whether to leave the craft group in the smaller bargaining unit or to combine it with the larger group.[27]

Such consultation is especially helpful if two or more bargaining units are considered appropriate by the board's otherwise objective standards.

Employee unionization   The NLRB will consider the extent of unionization by a bargaining unit as one factor in unit determination, but not as a controlling factor. The question is still one of appropriateness and not of whether the wishes of a union can be honored. If the bargaining unit is otherwise appropriate, prior unionization can again indicate employee wishes. There is no prohibition to recognition as long as the unit is not otherwise prohibited.

The unit and company organizational structure   As discussed earlier, the considerations used to determine appropriateness are not legally binding formulas but an exercise in rational examination of the facts of an individual case. The NLRB recognized this from its earliest decision. In *Bendix Products Corporation,* 3 NLRB 682 (1937), the board stated, "The designation of a unit appropriate for the purposes of collective bargaining must be confined to evidence and circumstances peculiar to the individual case."[28] Under such a philosophy, a particular company may, because of its relationship to branch offices or its particular reporting policies, make an otherwise inappropriate unit appropriate for their employees.

The board must examine, in some cases, the internal operations of a company to ascertain those peculiarities. However, the board's decision may not be final, as can be seen in Case 3.2.

Public interest   One consideration added by the courts for review by the board is the public interest. Without much guidance provided by the courts, the board is to ascertain when its decision will serve the public interest. In making this determination, the NLRB must not be affected by the desires of the parties involved.[29]

Accretion   The **doctrine of accretion** allows the NLRB to add new classes of employees to existing units if their work satisfies the same criteria as the original unit; that is, community of interests, bargaining history, interchange of employees, geographic proximity, common supervision, and union wishes. However, such a determination is not automatic. If the new class of employees retains a separate identity, perhaps by virtue of its newness, it can be determined an appropriate unit.

Accretion offers the board a conflicting choice. Adding new employees to an established union preserves the stability so important under the act, but squeezing in new employees, under perhaps narrow similarities, constricts the employees' freedom of choice.

Stipulated units   The board's authority to determine an appropriate unit is not without limitations. A company and a union may **stipulate** to the board what they consider an appropriate **unit**. The courts have said the board may not alter the unit in such cases.[30] However, a stipulated unit may not violate principles in the National Labor Relations Act or established board policy, for example, by including supervisors.[31]

Statutory considerations   The NLRB is limited by specific sections of the act in determining appropriate bargaining units. Workers not included under the act's definition of employee may not be included in a unit. Moreover, the board may not determine a unit appropriate with both professional and nonprofessional personnel unless a majority of the professional employees has approved such a designation. A craft unit can seek recognition even if it previously had been part of a larger unit unless a majority of the employees in the craft votes against separate representation. And finally, guards cannot be included in a unit with any other employees.[32]

Other types of workers are excluded from appropriate units because of various board and court interpretations. Excluded are managerial employees, defined in board rulings as ". . . those who formulate and effectuate management policies by expressing and making operative the decisions of their employer."[33] Confidential employees are excluded if the nature of their work has a labor nexus; that is, if it involves the formation, determination, or execution of labor relations management policies, and if it involves access to confidential information concerning anticipated changes resulting from collective bargaining.[34] Temporary employees and in some instances part-time employees may also be excluded from appropriate units.

The lines drawn by court rulings and board interpretations are never totally clear. In *NLRB* v. *Yeshiva University,* it was determined that the faculty members were managerial employees because of their input into the academic product of the university.[35] As managerial instead of professional employees, they did not come under the protection of the National Labor Relations Act and could therefore not be recognized. Such a determination has a negative effect upon unionization in the academic sector.[36]

Types of Units

Certain types of units have evolved within the established principles of appropriateness. The act itself lists employer units, craft units, plant units, or their subdivisions.

Craft units   A **craft unit** is composed exclusively of workers having a recognized skill, such as electricians, machinists, and plumbers. Recognition questions for craft units usually come before the board when a group of craft employees wants to break away from an existing industrial union for **craft severance**. Congress has established the policy that the board cannot determine a craft unit inappropriate on the grounds that a different unit has been established by prior board determination, unless the majority of the employees in the craft unit vote against separate representation.

Despite this legislative policy, the NLRB has severely limited craft severance elections through a number of decisions. Under the *National Tube* doctrine,[37] the board identified certain industries whose operations were so integrated that craft workers could not be taken from the unit without affecting the stability of labor relations. And in the *Mallinckrodt Chemical Works*[38] decision, the board outlined the criteria it would use to allow craft severance; the application of these standards has greatly reduced incidents of craft severance.

The NLRB requires that the craft group be distinct from others in the unit by virtue of the skilled, nonrepetitive nature of its work. The board will examine the extent to which the group has retained its identity or, as the alternative, actually participated in the affairs of the larger unit. The impact of separating the craft unit from the whole is also a factor in the board's determination. Consideration of the particular bargaining history of the larger unit, as well as the history of collective bargaining in the industry as a whole, must be part of the board's deliberations. In some instances, the NLRB decision will be influenced by the degree to which the craft work is integrated with the unskilled work and is therefore essential to the production process. Finally, the board may examine the qualifications of the union seeking to represent the craft union for its experience as an agent for similar groups.[39]

Departmental units   Similar to a craft unit, a departmental unit is composed of all the members of one department in a larger organization. The board uses standards similar to those used for craft severance in determining one department an appropriate unit separate from the entire plant or company. An examination of the difference in skills and in training, the degree of common supervision, the degree of interchange with employees outside the department, and different job performance ratings have been used to allow a departmental unit to exist.[40]

Multiplant unit   Multiplant bargaining occurs between a company and a union, or unions that represent workers in one or more of its plants. A master agreement usually results. If all of the plants in a particular company are involved, it is also designated as a company-wide unit. Factors in determining whether a company-wide or **multiplant unit** is appropriate include the degree to which the plants are interrelated, whether the plants are subject to a common control from a strong central administration, or whether there is autonomy within a single plant. The NLRB will also consider the degree of exchange of employees among plants in the geographic area, whether the industry has an existing pattern of representation, or whether multiplant units always existed in the industry.

Multiemployer units   Collective bargaining can be conducted between a group of related employers and representatives of their employees. Factors to be considered in such a designation are whether there is an express or implied approval of all parties to enter into such bargaining relationship, or if the history of the bargaining in the industry implies an intent to consent to **multiemployer units**. The employer can withdraw from a multiemployer collective bargaining relationship before the date for modification or negotiation of a new contract. After bargaining has begun, an employer may withdraw only with the union's consent or upon showing unusual circumstances. The union consent ensures the stability necessary under the National Labor Relations Act, and unusual circumstances have been found by the board when there is a genuine bargaining impasse.[41]

Residual units   Workers do not always fit into neat packages, and the board has sometimes given recognition to odd collections of employees because of their common working situations or the close proximity of their working sites. The NLRB policy is that employees are entitled to separate representation if they are left unrepresented after the bulk of employees are organized. Employees such as sales and service personnel, and porters, janitors, and maids, who do not fit anywhere else, are **residual units**.

Remaining units   Because of exclusions contained in the act itself, professional employees and guards often have professional and guard units. Technical units contain employees with a high degree of skill and training who exercise independent judgment but fall short of professional status. The factors to be considered in determining a technical unit are the desires of the party, the bargaining history, the existence of a unit seeking self-representation, the separate supervision of the technical employees, the location of the workplace, similarity of work hours, and employee benefit packages. It often becomes a question of who should be included based on the level of skill and training, employee contact and interchange, and similarity of the working conditions. Departmental units are treated the same as craft units in severance cases. Office clerical units are commonly separated from production and maintenance units in a large plant because the board recognizes the common interest of office clerical employees regardless of previous bargaining history.

Employee Elections

The National Labor Relations Board's duties include the regulation of representation elections and campaigns. The board's objective is to preserve the right of employees to self-organization without outside and unwanted influences. Under the act, the bargaining agent is selected by a majority vote of unit members to be the exclusive representative for negotiation and administration of the agreement.

The procedures for conducting employee elections are codified. Cases decided by the NLRB have provided rules to supplement those procedures. The board is empowered to conduct elections by secret ballot and to certify the results. The main purpose and benefit of board certification is to resolve any question of representation.

Election Procedures

The steps in seeking the board's review of representation cases are described in the following paragraphs.

Step 1: Representation petition   The first step in the election process is to file a representation petition (Exhibit 3.1) at the office of the appropriate regional director. A union must present evidence of employee support before a representation election will be held. The NLRB requires designation by at least 30 percent of the bargaining unit employees, usually in the form of signed and dated authorization cards. The NLRB also accepts designations in the form of signed petitions and union application cards.[42]

National Labor Relations Board actions have several kinds of petitions. An **RC petition** can be filed by an employee, a group of employees, or a union representing employees seeking certification of an appropriate unit. An *RM petition* can be filed by an employer if one or more labor organizations claim representation status in an appropriate unit and the employer questions the representative's status. Also, when an employer has objective proof that the union no longer represents the majority of the employees, he or she may file an RM petition. An employer, employee, other individual, or a union may also use an *RD petition* to determine whether a recognized union still has the support of employees.[43]

Other types of petitions available are the *UD petition* that 30 percent or more of the employees file to rescind a union shop agreement; a *UC petition* requesting clarification of the composition of a bargaining unit currently certified; and an *AC petition* requesting that a change of circumstances be recognized, such as a change of union name or affiliation on a previous NLRB certification.

Petitions demonstrate sufficient employee interest or the actual type of representation case so the board may decide if it has jurisdiction. The board will assume the requisite employee interest and will accept an expedited election petition if it is filed within thirty days of the beginning of a recognitional or organizational picket.

Petitions requesting certification or decertification will normally only be accepted by the board if 30 percent of the employees in a unit favor such an election. This 30 percent is usually demonstrated by presenting cards authorizing the union to act as the employees' agent for collective bargaining. It can also be shown by a certification listing at least 30 percent of the employees of the represented unit as members in good standing of a union.

Another union may enter an election with a **showing of interest** that represents 10 percent of those in the unit in question. A cross-petition from another union may also be filed claiming representation of an appropriate unit different from the original unit but including some of the same people.[44]

Step 2: Investigation   The second step occurs when the regional director conducts investigations and a hearing, if necessary, to determine whether to proceed with an election. The employer's business must sufficiently affect commerce so as to rest jurisdiction in the NLRB. An actual representation question must exist and sufficient employee interest demonstrated. The requested unit is deemed appropriate and the bargaining agent qualified. Certain statutory time periods must be honored.

Step 3: Secret ballot election   The third step is the secret ballot election (see Exhibit 3.2). The NLRB has the responsibility to ensure a representative election is

Exhibit 3.1   Representation petition

Form NLRB-502
(11-64)

UNITED STATES OF AMERICA
NATIONAL LABOR RELATIONS BOARD

PETITION

Form Approved.
Budget Bureau No. 64-R002.14

DO NOT WRITE IN THIS SPACE

CASE NO.

INSTRUCTIONS.—Submit an original and four (4) copies of this Petition to the NLRB Regional Office in the Region in which the employer concerned is located.
If more space is required for any one item, attach additional sheets, numbering item accordingly.

DATE FILED

The Petitioner alleges that the following circumstances exist and requests that the National Labor Relations Board proceed under its proper authority pursuant to Section 9 of the National Labor Relations Act.

1. Purpose of this Petition (If box RC, RM, or RD is checked and a charge under Section 8(b)(7) of the Act has been filed involving the Employer named herein, the statement following the description of the type of petition shall not be deemed made.)

(Check one)

☐ RC-CERTIFICATION OF REPRESENTATIVE —A substantial number of employees wish to be represented for purposes of collective bargaining by Petitioner and Petitioner desires to be certified as representative of the employees.

☐ RM-REPRESENTATION (EMPLOYER PETITION)—One or more individuals or labor organizations have presented a claim to Petitioner to be recognized as the representative of employees of Petitioner.

☐ RD-DECERTIFICATION — A substantial number of employees assert that the certified or currently recognized bargaining representative is no longer their representative.

☐ UD-WITHDRAWAL OF UNION SHOP AUTHORITY—Thirty percent (30%) or more of employees in a bargaining unit covered by an agreement between their employer and a labor organization desire that such authority be rescinded.

☐ UC-UNIT CLARIFICATION—A labor organization is currently recognized by employer, but petitioner seeks clarification of placement of certain employees: (Check one) ☐ In unit not previously certified
☐ In unit previously certified in Case No. _____.

☐ AC-AMENDMENT OF CERTIFICATION—Petitioner seeks amendment of certification issued in Case No._____.

Attach statement describing the specific amendment sought.

2. NAME OF EMPLOYER	EMPLOYER REPRESENTATIVE TO CONTACT	PHONE NO.

3. ADDRESS(ES) OF ESTABLISHMENT(S) INVOLVED (Street and number, city, State, and ZIP Code)

4a. TYPE OF ESTABLISHMENT (Factory, mine, wholesaler, etc.)	4b. IDENTIFY PRINCIPAL PRODUCT OR SERVICE

5. Unit Involved (In UC petition, describe PRESENT bargaining unit and attach description of proposed clarification.)

Included

Excluded

6a. NUMBER OF EMPLOYEES IN UNIT:

PRESENT _____

PROPOSED (BY UC/AC)

_____

6b. IS THIS PETITION SUPPORTED BY 30% OR MORE OF THE EMPLOYEES IN THE UNIT?*

☐ YES   ☐ NO

*Not applicable in RM, UC, and AC

(If you have checked box RC in 1 above, check and complete EITHER item 7a or 7b, whichever is applicable)

Exhibit 3.1 (continued)

7a. ☐ Request for recognition as Bargaining Representative was made on .... and Employer
(Month, day, year)
declined recognition on or about .... *(If no reply received, so state)*
(Month, day, year)

7b. ☐ Petitioner is currently recognized as Bargaining Representative and desires certification under the act.

8. Recognized or Certified Bargaining Agent *(If there is none, so state)*

NAME	AFFILIATION
ADDRESS	DATE OF RECOGNITION OR CERTIFICATION

9. DATE OF EXPIRATION OF CURRENT CONTRACT, IF ANY *(Show month, day, and year)*	10. IF YOU HAVE CHECKED BOX UD IN 1 ABOVE, SHOW HERE THE DATE OF EXECUTION OF AGREEMENT GRANTING UNION SHOP *(Month, day, and year)*

11a. IS THERE NOW A STRIKE OR PICKETING AT THE EMPLOYER'S ESTABLISH-MENT(S) INVOLVED? YES .... NO	11b. IF SO, APPROXIMATELY HOW MANY EMPLOYEES ARE PARTICIPATING?

11c. THE EMPLOYER HAS BEEN PICKETED BY OR ON BEHALF OF ...., A LABOR
(Insert name)

ORGANIZATION, OF .... SINCE ....
(Insert address)   *(Month, day, year)*

12. ORGANIZATIONS OR INDIVIDUALS OTHER THAN PETITIONER (AND OTHER THAN THOSE NAMED IN ITEMS 8 AND 11c), WHICH HAVE CLAIMED RECOGNITION AS REPRESENTATIVES AND OTHER ORGANIZATIONS AND INDIVIDUALS KNOWN TO HAVE A REPRESENTATIVE INTEREST IN ANY EMPLOYEES IN THE UNIT DESCRIBED IN ITEM 5 ABOVE.   (IF NONE, SO STATE.)

NAME	AFFILIATION	ADDRESS	DATE OF CLAIM *(Required only if Petition is filed by Employer)*

I declare that I have read the above petition and that the statements therein are true to the best of my knowledge and belief.

....
(Petitioner and affiliation, if any)

By ....
(Signature of representative or person filing petition)   *(Title, if any)*

Address ....
(Street and number, city, State, and ZIP Code)   *(Telephone number)*

WILLFULLY FALSE STATEMENT ON THIS PETITION CAN BE PUNISHED BY FINE AND IMPRISONMENT (U.S. CODE, TITLE 18, SECTION 1001)

GPO 896-179

fairly and honestly conducted. In a 1948 case, the board stated that its function in representation proceedings was ". . . to provide a laboratory in which an experiment may be conducted, under conditions as nearly ideal as possible, to determine the uninhibited desires of the employees."[45] But the board recognized that the standards for election cases had to be judged against realistic standards of human conduct. When improprieties occur, certain factors should be weighed, such as the size of the unit, the circumstances of any alleged misconduct, and the real or apparent influence of the interfering party. Generally, the NLRB will only consider objectionable conduct in determining the validity of an election if it occurs during the critical period, that is, between the filing of an election petition and the election itself.

An employer may cause an election to be invalidated by threatening reprisals, offering promises of benefits during an election, indicating that the election itself is futile, or stating that a successful election will result in strikes and layoffs.

Employee actions may also influence the election certification. A union's agreement to waive union fees before an election has been considered an unfair labor practice. However, the facts presented in Case 3.3 reveal that such a union waiver was held not to have interfered with a valid election.

While elections may be voided because of misrepresentation or trickery, they will not be set aside solely because of misleading campaign statements or misrepresentation of fact. If parties, however, use forged documents so that the propaganda nature of the publication cannot be discerned or if NLRB documents are altered to indicate its endorsement, the election can be voided.[46]

Actions of third parties also may influence and invalidate an election. Employees who are not union agents will not influence an election if the union neither authorizes nor condones the conduct. Supervisors may exhibit pro-union sentiment unless it leads employees to believe the employer favors the particular union and they are expected to support it. Outside groups, newspapers, and public interest organizations may be considered in board hearings on elections if their activities have exacerbated employee fears of employer retaliations or reprisals. Even the NLRB agent may cause an election to be set aside if his or her action tends to destroy confidence in the election process or can be reasonably interpreted as impinging on the board's impartial election standards.

The board's rules prohibit either unions or employers from making speeches to mass groups of employees on company time within twenty-four hours of an election.

Exhibit 3.2 Request to proceed with election

FORM NLRB-4551
(10-62)

UNITED STATES OF AMERICA
NATIONAL LABOR RELATIONS BOARD

REQUEST TO PROCEED

In the matter of _____   _____
                          (Name of Case)   (Number of Case)

The undersigned hereby requests the Regional Director to proceed with the above-captioned representation case, notwithstanding the charges of unfair labor practices filed in Case No. _____.
It is understood that the Board will not entertain objections to any election in this matter based upon conduct occurring prior to the filing of the petition.

Date _____   _____

                                    By _____

                                          _____
                                                      (Title)

GPO 911-506

However, such meetings within twenty-four hours of an election do not violate these rules if voluntarily attended on the employee's own time.

Employers may assemble their employees and speak to them on company time if it is prior to twenty-four hours to the election and if the employer does not prevent, by rigid no-solicitation rules, access to the employees by the union representatives. On election day, prolonged conversations between either party and the voters are prohibited as are traditional campaign activities at the polling place. In recent studies of employee participation in representative elections, some questions have been raised as to what degree even a legal campaign discourages such participation.[47] If an employee perceives an election will be won or lost regardless of his vote, that employee may choose not to vote at all.[48]

In cases where an election involves three choices, for example, Union A, Union B, or no union, a **runoff election** may be required if none of the choices receives a majority of the votes cast. The two top vote getters are placed before the members of the bargaining unit again and the one receiving a majority vote can be certified.

> Under NLRB rules and regulations, "A runoff election is conducted only where: (a) the ballot in the original election contained three or more choices [i.e., two labor organizations and a 'neither' choice]; and (b) no single choice received a majority of the valid votes cast. Thus there can be no runoff where the original ballot provided for: (1) a 'yes' and 'no' choice in a one-union election; or (2) a 'severance' election." The ballot in the run-off election provides for a selection between the two choices receiving the largest and second largest number of votes in the original election.[49]

Step 4: Certification of election results   If the board is satisfied that the election represents the employees' free choice, the election is certified, the fourth step. Either no union is victorious or, if a union has gained a majority of those voting, that union is certified as the bargaining agent for the unit.

Certification benefits a union in a number of ways. It closes any challenges to the union's status as the exclusive bargaining agent for the particular unit. Its status is binding on the employer for at least one year during which time the employer must bargain with it. After the first year the employer must continue to bargain unless there is reasonable doubt the union continues to enjoy a majority vote of the unit. The board will not entertain petitions regarding rival certification for that unit within the one-year certification, nor within three years, if a valid contract is in effect. The certified union may strike against the employer under certain circumstances without fear of an unfair labor practice charge.

A union may seek recognition by the board to obtain the benefit of certification even if its status as an exclusive bargaining agent has not been challenged and the employer has agreed to bargain. The NLRB considers such a request as raising a question of representation.

Recognition without Elections

Election, while the most accepted way by which employees select their representatives, is not the exclusive method condoned by the NLRB. In a Supreme Court decision upholding a board bargaining order, the Court recognized two other valid means by which a union may establish majority status and thereby place a bargaining obligation upon the employer: a show of support through a union-called strike or strike vote; and the possession of cards, signed by a majority of employees, authorizing the union to represent them in collective bargaining.[50] In the **Gissel doctrine** the Court gave a stamp of approval for authorization cards as a substitute for an election *when* an employer's actions amounted to an unfair labor practice. The Court recognized that, if traditional remedies could not eradicate the lingering effects of the employer's conduct and permit the holding of a fair election, the union's authorization cards were a more reliable indicator of the employees' desires than an election, and a bargaining order should be issued. Limited use of authorization cards in lieu of elections seems well advised in light of research results indicating less than a one-to-one relationship between votes in an election and signatures on the authorization cards.[51] The board has also issued bargaining orders when the employer has gained independent knowledge of the union's majority status or has acknowledged the union's right to represent employees.

A question of representation may arise after a valid certification because of events outside of the control of the union or the board.

Voting Patterns

Significant time and money have been spent by unions and management researching why employees vote as they do in certification and decertification elections. In general employees will vote in what is perceived to be their best interest. Those who abstain from voting either do not desire a change in the status quo or plan to leave the organization. Aspects of their work life that influence their vote include compensation issues, work rules, and sources of grievances. Election campaigns by employers and unions appear to have little influence on the outcome of representation elections except among those employees who are initially undecided or indifferent. Generally, if employees are satisfied with their work environment, they vote against change— whether it is to keep an existing union or bring one in to represent them. If dissatisfied, they tend to vote for a change.[52]

Can employees exhibit loyalty to both the union and their employer? Research indicates that such dual commitment is strongest when a positive relationship exists between the employer and the union. However, when labor-management relations are poor, employees may be forced to choose, often resulting in employees giving their loyalty to the union. When they perceive that labor is too adversarial and they tire of divided loyalties, employees may choose union **decertification** (voting out the union) to end their strife.[53]

Decertification Elections

Also allowed under the act and supervised by the NLRB are decertification elections whereby the members of the unit vote to terminate an existing union's right to represent them in collective bargaining. Decertification elections most commonly occur when the initial year of union representation ends with no collective bargaining agreement, an existing contract will expire between sixty and ninety days, or a contract has expired and no new agreement is being negotiated.

The rules for a decertification election are similar to those for certification, with some exceptions. Only employees can file a decertification petition, which must include 30 percent of the eligible members of the unit. Again, the NLRB investigates the validity of the petition. If the union feels there is a problem with the petition or that an employer has unlawfully helped in the petition, it may file a blocking charge and delay the election until the unfair labor charge is resolved.

While an employer can in no way aid the filing of a petition, afterward, the employer, the employees who filed the petition, and the union may all engage in an election campaign. The rules for conducting a decertification election are the same as those for a representative election.

After the votes are counted, if a majority of the employees vote against the union, it is decertified. A tie vote counts against the union because it no longer enjoys a majority status. If the union wins, it continues to represent the unit, and another election is barred for at least a year.

Successorship

If there is a change in either a collective bargaining representative or an employer, parties to an unexpired collective bargaining agreement may not be certain of their status. This situation may exist when the union becomes decertified; because of a schism, merger, or change in union affiliation; or if the union simply becomes defunct and is replaced. Questions may arise by management when the sale of all or part of a business occurs, because of a merger or corporation consolidation, or if the corporation is reorganized. The courts refer to these situations as **successorship**.

The law on successorship provides that, if there is a genuine change in the collective bargaining representative, the existing collective bargaining contract, even if unexpired, is *not* binding on the successor representative. If a genuine change of employer exists but the employing industry remains substantially the same, the successor employer is required to recognize the existing collective bargaining unit and its representative, but is not bound by the agreement.

The National Labor Relations Act is essentially mute on the issue of successorship. The board generally has decided controversies through reliance on theories of representation and, if appropriate, on unfair labor practices. The law on successorship has come from Supreme Court rulings in a number of cases, the leading case being *National Labor Relations Board* v. *Burns International Security Services* in which the Court found a successor did not have to honor a predecessor's labor agreement.[54] However, the court held that, if certain criteria were met, a successor must recognize and bargain with the predecessor's union.

The following criteria have been established to determine if change in ownership or organization has affected the bargaining obligation:

1. There has been a substantial continuity of the same business operations
2. The new employer uses the same plant
3. The new employer has the same, or substantially the same, work force
4. The same jobs exist under the same working conditions
5. The same supervisors are employed

6. The new employer uses the same machinery, equipment, and methods of production
7. The new employer manufactures the same products or offers the same services[55]

If most of the criteria are met, the employing industry has remained substantially the same and the bargaining duty falls on the successor.

Summary

The National Labor Relations Act regulated the industrial relations of employers whose activities affect interstate commerce. The act guaranteed employees the right to self-organization and required the employer to bargain collectively with employee representatives. The National Labor Relations Board was established to enforce the act.

The board, in order to protect the employee rights guaranteed by the act, passes on the appropriateness of the selected bargaining units. The board also regulates and conducts union elections to ensure that employees exercise their freedom of choice.

Labor relations, as regulated by the National Labor Relations Act, is considered the exclusive domain of federal law. With a few exceptions, the National Labor Relations Board has primary jurisdiction in any labor dispute affecting commerce. State laws and regulations are not controlling.

CASE 3.1   *Jurisdiction*

Adapted from *National Maritime Union of America, AFL-CIO v. National Labor Relations Board,* 342 F.2d 538 (1965)

The previous owner of the vessel in question had a contract with the Marine Engineers Beneficial Association (MEBA), while the new owner had a contract with the National Maritime Union (NMU). When the ship docked, the MEBA picketed the pier in protest over the use of the other union. In retaliation NMU established pickets at various piers where ships with MEBA members were docked.

The picketing by NMU resulted in work stoppages because longshore personnel would not cross the picket lines and the picket lines prevented access to the docks by any other entrance.

The National Labor Relations Board found the NMU guilty of an unfair labor practice. While its attempt to protect itself from a rival union was lawful, the means it used was not. The NMU, instead of directing peaceful picketing at the rival union, put economic pressure on the employers involved. The NMU appealed the National Labor Relations Board's decisions on the grounds that the controversy was not a labor dispute under the act.

Decision

The court found that a labor dispute did exist. Normally the activities of two rival unions would not involve the National Labor Relations Act, but in this case, the activity of the NMU directly affected employers and employees. And the character of the underlying dispute—which union should be recognized—put it under the board's jurisdiction.

CASE 3.2 *Appropriate Unit*

Adapted from *Szabo Food Services, Inc.* v. *National Labor Relations Board,* 550 F.2d 705 (1976)

Employer is an industrial food service contractor supplying food service to nineteen cafeterias at ten United Aircraft Corporation locations. The employer considers these nineteen cafeterias to be a single operating unit. The unit has a district headquarters where its administration is centralized. All facets of the food service to these nineteen cafeterias are identical.

The union sought to organize a collective bargaining unit composed of three of these nineteen cafeterias. These three cafeterias are located five miles apart, have a combined work force of about fifty employees, and share a manager. The National Labor Relations Board found the unit appropriate based on the following:

1. The employees were under the common immediate supervision of a single manager
2. The three cafeterias were grouped together as a cost center for accountability
3. The unit manager retained control over day-to-day operations, especially in matters of hiring and firing
4. The cafeterias were five miles apart

while the other sixteen cafeterias were fourteen miles away
5. There was little employee interchange
6. There was no bargain history and no union seeking recognition for all nineteen cafeterias

The employer appealed the board's ruling.

Decision

The court recognized that the National Labor Relations Board has primary responsibility in determining a unit appropriate and such determination should be overturned only if arbitrary, unreasonable, or not supported by substantial evidence. It reviewed the board's reasons for determining the unit appropriate, and found that the board relied too heavily on the geographical proximity and the extent of union organization over the complete integration of the employer's managerial structure and labor relations policy. The cost center referred to by the board was merely an informational subdivision not indicative of financial independence; the responsibilities attributed to the local manager were overrated. In fact, the labor relations policy for all the cafeterias emanated from the district office. Based on these considerations, the court overruled the board's decision.

CASE 3.3 *Elections*

Adapted from *Vicksburg Hospital, Inc.* v. *National Labor Relations Board,* 653 F.2d 1070 (1981)

The union petitioned the National Labor Relations Board for certification as the bargaining agent for a unit composed of the hospital's nonprofessional service, maintenance, and technical employees. The hospital objected to the unit as overly broad, but the National Labor Relations Board found the unit appropriate and ordered the election to be held.

The union won the election and the hospital filed objections to the election charging that the union: offered economic inducements to employees who supported it by waiving initiation fees; misrepresented to employees various conditions of employment and their rights in the event of strikes; and misrepresented the government's role in the election by leading employees to believe the board supported the union.

The board found no grounds for the hospital's objections to the election and ordered it to bargain with the union. The hospital appealed.

Decision

The court noted that the board has wide discretion in determining whether an election was conducted fairly. The hospital must offer evidence of events from or about specific people and show that those events tended to or did influence the outcome of the election. In this case the union won by a wide majority so the influence would be very difficult to prove.

Offering to waive initiation fees for employees who sign authorization cards prior to an election can invalidate an election unless the offer extends to those who join after the election as well. In this case the hospital said the offer was ambiguous and therefore employees could have thought it was limited to before the election. The court found some ambiguity but not enough to show an undue influence on the outcome of the election.

The hospital's charge that the union misrepresented the employees' conditions during a strike was also dismissed by the court because the hospital had had an opportunity to, and did, rebut those union statements in a speech and in letters sent to employees.

In the matter of government support of the union, the hospital submitted a union pamphlet depicting Uncle Sam standing behind a union member with the caption, "Remember Uncle Sam Stands Behind You." While union conduct creating the impression that the government *encourages* employees to form unions may constitute grounds for setting aside an election, this leaflet did not exceed the bounds of permissible campaign propaganda. The pamphlet merely conveyed the message that the government protects the right to join a union.

The court upheld the election.

CASE STUDY   *Gissel Bargaining Order*

Adapted from *Medline Industries Inc.* v. *National Labor Relations Board* 593 F.2d 788 (CA 7, 1979)

Facts

The union lost a representation election by a vote of sixteen to five, with seven challenged ballots. The union charged the company with unfair labor practices and, based on the Gissel Bargaining Order, asked the NLRB to order the company to bargain with the union anyway. The NLRB found unfair labor practices and did so order. Although the company denied unfair labor practices, its appeal involved primarily the Gissel Bargaining Order.

Appeal

When an election is set aside because of unfair labor practices of the employer, the NLRB can order the company to bargain with the union if the union has obtained authorization cards from a majority of the employees in an appropriate unit.

The company contended that the union did not have enough cards; the union contended it did. There were four employees in dispute. The company contended the unit consisted of thirty-one employees; the union, twenty-nine. And the company contended that one of the sixteen authorization cards was invalid.

1. The union sought to exclude two members of the unit—one who was on sick leave and one who performed clerical duties. It was the union's position that although a member on leave would normally be considered part of the unit, the company had instituted a new personnel policy automatically terminating anyone on leave for more than twenty-one days. The employee in question had been on sick leave for over four months at the time of the unit count. The company pointed out that obviously the new personnel policy was not applied to this employee because he worked for one day during his extended leave, and was paid for it; and throughout his leave he enjoyed all the fringe benefits of an employee. As to the clerical worker, the union pointed out that clerical workers were excluded from the unit, and the employee was off the line doing clerical work 30 percent of the time. The company contended that her clerical time in the office was minimal and performed between 8:00 A.M. and 8:45 A.M., and at lunchtime. Her other clerical duties were done in the line area and were associated with the production line.

2. The company challenged the authorization card of one employee. In a Gissel case—because cards substitute for a secret ballot election—the signatures on the card must be obtained only by proper means. The company contended, based on the employee's testimony, that he was harassed for two or three days before signing the card, that he repeatedly stated that he did not want to sign the card, and that he was told signing the card was just for an election. The union claimed its admittedly repeated requests to the employee were not harassment but permissible pre-election campaigning and that, while he was told on one instance the card was only for an election, at a

general meeting he was told the cards would be presented to the company for recognition which the company could accept or reject.

Questions

1. If you were deciding this case, would you include the two employees in the unit total? Why or why not?
2. If you were deciding this case,

would you have accepted the disputed authorization card?

3. In this instance, the union had fifteen unchallenged authorization cards requesting an election but lost by only obtaining five unchallenged votes. Discuss some of the factors during an election campaign that could bring about this result.

Key Terms and Concepts

Accretion doctrine

Appropriate unit

Certification/Decertification

Community of interest doctrine

Craft severance

Craft units

Gissel doctrine

Globe doctrine

Multiplant, multiemployer units

RC petition

Remaining units

Representation cases

Residual units

Runoff election

Showing of interest

Stipulated units

Successorship

Review Questions

1. What is the purpose and jurisdiction of the NLRB?
2. Summarize the rights of employees and employers as provided by the National Labor Relations Act.
3. When are states totally restrained from the labor field, according to Supreme Court decisions?
4. What criteria do the NLRB consider when determining whether an appropriate unit of employees has substantial mutuality of interests?
5. How does the National Labor Relations Act limit the board's determination of the appropriate bargaining unit?
6. What are the steps the NLRB follows in a representation election?
7. How does certification benefit a union? Under what circumstances might the NLRB invalidate a certification election?

Endnotes

1. 29 U.S.C. sec. 151 et. seq. (1982); and 29 U.S.C. sec. 141 et. seq. (1982).
2. U.S., *Constitution,* sec. 8.
3. 29 U.S.C. sec. 151 (1982).
4. Ludwig Teller, *Labor Disputes and Collective Bargaining,* vol. 2 (New York: Baker, Voorhis & Co., 1940), p. 688.
5. 29 U.S.C. sec. 152 (1) (1982).
6. Plumbers & Steamfitters Local 298 v. County of Door, 359 U.S. 354, 79 S.Ct. 844, 3 L.Ed. 2d 872 (1959).
7. 29 U.S.C. sec. 152 (9) (1982).
8. Ibid.
9. Ibid.
10. Ibid. (6).
11. 29 U.S.C. sec. 164 (c) (1) (1982).
12. Cincinnati Association for the Blind v. N.L.R.B., 672 F.2d 567 (1982), discussed in *University of Detroit Urban Law Journal* 60 (Winter 1983), pp. 324–37.
13. Theodore Kheel, *Labor Law* (New York: Matthew Bender, 1982), chap. 8, p. 8–92.
14. U.S. Congress, 39 U.S.C. sec. 1209 (1982).
15. N.L.R.B. v. Cabot Carbon Co., 360 U.S. 203, 79 S.Ct. 1015, 3 L.Ed. 2d 1175 (1959).
16. San Diego Building Trades Council v. Garmon, 359 U.S. 236, 76 S.Ct. 773, 3 L.Ed. 2d 775 (1959); Amalgamated Association of Street, Electric Railway & Motor Coach Employees v. Lockridge, 403 U.S. 224, 91 S.Ct. 1909, 29 L.Ed. 2d 473 (1971); and Sears, Roebuck & Co. v. San Diego District Council of Carpenters, 98 S.Ct. 1745, 56 L.Ed. 2d 209 (1978).
17. Smith v. Evening News Association, 371 U.S. 195, 51 LRRM 2646 (1962); and Local 174, Teamsters v. Lucas Flour Co., 369 U.S. 95, 49 LRRM 2717 (1962).
18. Amalgamated Association, 403 U.S. 291.
19. Lodge 72, Machinists v. Wisconsin Employment Relations Comm., 427 U.S. 132, 96 S.Ct. 2548, 49 L.Ed. 2d 396 (1976).
20. May Dept. Stores Co. v. N.L.R.B., 326 U.S. 376, 66 S.Ct. 203, 90 L.Ed. 145 (1945).
21. *Labor Relations Reporter* (Washington, D.C.: Bureau of National Affairs, 1976), p. 4106.
22. James L. Perry and Harold L. Angle, "Bargaining Unit Structure and Organizational Outcomes," *Industrial Relations* 20, no. 1 (Winter 1981), pp. 47–59.
23. Short Stop Inc., 192 N.L.R.B. 184, 78 LRRM 1087 (1971); Mock Road Super Duper Inc., 156 N.L.R.B. 82, 61 LRRM 1173 (1966); Wil-Kil Pest Control, 440 F.2d 371 (7th Cir. 1971); and N.L.R.B. v. Saint Francis College, 562 F.2d 246 (3rd Cir. 1977).
24. Waterman S.S. Corp., N.L.R.B., 22 LRRM 1170 (1948).
25. Cases cited, in order of listing are: General Electric, 107 N.L.R.B. 21, 33 LRRM 1058 (1953); T.C. Wheaton Co., N.L.R.B. 14 LRRM 142 (1944); Safety Cabs, Inc., 173 N.L.R.B. 4, 69 LRRM 1199 (1968); and Land Title Guarantee & Trust Co., 194 N.L.R.B. 29, 78 LRRM 1500 (1971).
26. Globe Machinery & Stamping Co., 3 N.L.R.B. 294, 1-A LRRM 1122 (1937); and Short Stores, Inc., 192 N.L.R.B. 184, 78 LRRM 1087 (1971).
27. Harold S. Roberts, *Roberts Dictionary of Industrial Relations,* 3rd ed. (Washington, D.C.: Bureau of National Affairs, 1986), p. 243.
28. Teller, *Labor Disputes,* p. 918.
29. N.L.R.B. v. Delaware-New Jersey, Ferry Co., 128 F.2d 130 (3rd Cir. 1941).
30. Tidewater Oil Co. v. N.L.R.B., 358 F.2d 363 (2d Cir. 1966).
31. Ibid.
32. Labor-Management Relations Act, Sec. 9(b)(1)(2)(3); 29 U.S.C. sec. 159 b(1)(2)(3).

33. See National Labor Relations Board v. Textion, Inc., 85 LRRM 2945, (1975); and Palace Laundry Dry Clean Corp., N.L.R.B., 21 LRRM 1039 (1947).

34. N.L.R.B. v. Hendricks City Rural Electric Mem. Cor., 108 LRRM 3105 (1981).

35. 444 U.S. 672 (1980).

36. Clarence R. Dietsch and David A. Dilts, *NLRB* v. *Yeshiva University:* A Positive Perspective," *Monthly Labor Review* 106, no. 7 (July 1983), pp. 34–37; and Marsha Huie Ashlock, "The Bargaining Status of College and University Professors Under the National Labor Relations Laws," *Labor Law Journal* 35, no. 2 (Feb. 1984), pp. 103–11.

37. Charles J. Morris, ed., *The Developing Labor Law,* 2nd ed. (Washington, D.C.: Bureau of National Affairs, 1983), pp. 427–28.

38. 162 N.L.R.B. 387, 64 LRRM 1011 (1967).

39. Kheel, *Labor Law,* chap. 14, p. 53.

40. Stephens Produce, 515 F.2d 1373, 89 LRRM 2311 (CA 8, 1975).

41. Ibid., p. 80; and N.L.R.B. v. Beck Engraving Co., 522 F.2d 475 (3rd Cir. 1975).

42. Roberts, *Dictionary of Industrial Relations,* p. 668.

43. James P. Swann Jr., "The Decertification of a Union," *Personnel Administrator* 28, no. 1 (Jan. 1983) pp. 47–51.

44. Kheel, *Labor Law,* chap. 7A, p. 18.

45. Ibid., chap. 13, pp. 3–4.

46. Midland National Life Ins. Co. v. N.L.R.B., 263 N.L.R.B. 24, 110 LRRM 1489 (1982).

47. Herbert G. Heneman III and Marcus H. Sandver, "Predicting the Outcome of Union Certification Elections: A Review of the Literature," Industrial and Labor Relations Review 36, no. 4 (July 1983), p. 555.

48. Richard N. Block and Myron Roomkin, "Determinants of Voter Participation in Union Certification Elections," *Monthly Labor Review* 105, no. 4 (April 1982), pp. 45–47.

49. Roberts, *Dictionary of Industrial Relations,* p. 101.

50. N.L.R.B. v. Gissel Packing Co., 395 U.S. 575, 71 LRRM 2481 (1969).

51. Heneman, "Predicting the Outcome," p. 555.

52. Timothy P. Summers, John H. Betton, and Thomas A. Decatus, "Voting for and Against Unions: A Decision Model," *Academy of Management Review* 11, no. 3 (July 1986), pp. 643–55.

53. Harold L. Angle and James L. Perry, "Dual Commitment and Labor-Management Relationship Climates," *Academy of Management Journal* 29, no. 1 (March 1986), pp. 31–50.

54. 406 U.S. 272, 92 S.Ct. 1571, 32 L.Ed. 2d 61 (1972).

55. Morris, *Developing Labor Law,* p. 705.

Unfair Labor Practices

LABOR NEWS

Are Knitters Getting Fleeced in Vermont?

For 16 years Virginia Gray has made a second income knitting hats and sweaters at her snug Greensboro, Vt. home. But late last year a federal appeals court declared her livelihood illegal when it upheld an often overlooked "no homeworking" provision in the 1938 Fair Labor Standards Act. Since then Gray, 63, and the rest of Vermont's home knitters, mostly retired women or housewives with children, have been fighting for the right to work on their own terms. . . .

Because of subzero winter temperatures, icy roads, and a dearth of factories, Vermonters have always preferred working at hearthside. So in 1981 Secretary of Labor Raymond Donovan rescinded the decades-old ban on knitting outerwear at home. But when garment unions protested that Donovan's ruling could not prevent sweatshop conditions, the appeals court slapped on the ban again.

That came as a shock to the women, who had expected Donovan's decision to be the final word. "They hit us at a good time," says a bitter Audrey Pudvah, 27. "It was just before Christmas, and we were so blasted busy we really didn't have the time (to fight back)."

The Vermont knitters claim they make $5 to $10 an hour, well above the minimum wage of $3.35 an hour. . . . But lawyer Max Zimny, who appealed Donovan's ruling for the International Ladies' Garment Workers' Union, argues that on-site inspections are impractical and only a ban can prevent abuses. "This is not a union versus nonunion issue but one of labor standards," he says. "Nor is it an effort to unionize people in the home." . . .

"The union is always ready to consider exceptions which wouldn't collide with historic evils," he says. "We are never close-minded." For the time being, the Labor Department and the knitters have asked for a stay to allow the knitters to keep working while the Supreme Court decides on hearing their case. Donovan is trying to lift the ban on homework in knitted outerwear without riling the unions, and Sen. Orrin Hatch (R.-Utah) has proposed a bill to end such restrictions. Anyone who believes the knitters will quit, the women warn, is woolgathering.

Source: Condensed from Toby Kahn, "Vermont Home Knitters," People Weekly 21 (March 19, 1984), p. 64, by permission of Time, Inc.

The collective bargaining process requires the employer and the employee to meet and negotiate terms and conditions of employment. It is an uneasy relationship that requires give and take. Often one side does not choose to participate or to participate fully. The National Labor Relations Act recognizes that reluctance and by its terms seeks to legislate the behavior of the parties. Certain actions are deemed to be unfair if they run counter to the purposes of the act, and bad faith might be evidenced in the negotiation process by other actions. This chapter will explore aspects of unfair labor practices and breaches of the duty to bargain in good faith to see how such behavior frustrates successful collective bargaining.

Unfair Labor Practices by Employers

One of the primary objectives of the National Labor Relations Act was to encourage collective bargaining to minimize the industrial strife adversely affecting the free flow of commerce. To that end, the NLRB gave employees certain protected rights. Section 7 of the act, as amended by Taft-Hartley, enumerates these rights:

1. To self-organization
2. To form, join, or assist labor organizations
3. To bargain collectively through representatives of their own choosing
4. To engage in other concerted activities for the purpose of collective bargaining or other mutual aid or protection
5. To refrain from any or all of the above[1]

The act also lists **employer** activities considered **unfair labor practices** in violation of these rights:

1. Interference with, restraint, or coercion of employees in rights guaranteed under Section 7
2. Domination or interference with the formation or administration of a labor union
3. Discrimination against union members for their union membership
4. Discrimination against an employee for pursuing the rights under the act
5. Refusal to bargain collectively with representatives of its employees[2]

The basic right of employees to join together has always been protected under the freedom of association provision of the First Amendment to the United States Constitution. Prior to the National Labor Relations Act, however, no federal law protected the employee in the exercise of that right. The passage of the National Labor Relations Act balances the employer's property rights and the employees' organization and recognition rights according to the dictates of law and fact.

The Authority of the NLRB

An unfair labor practice charge comes to the National Labor Relations Board through procedures similar to election petitions. The party claiming injury files an appropriate form with a regional office of the NLRB (Exhibit 4.1). An initial investigation is held and if merit is found to the charge and the regional director cannot convince the parties to settle, a hearing is held before an administrative law judge. The decision of the administrative law judge may be appealed to the NLRB, which will decide the case through a subpanel of three members randomly selected by its executive secretary.[3]

As presidential appointees, board members are part of the political process, and their decision making should not be viewed as a pure exercise in administrative law. Recent studies indicate a high probability that board decisions in unfair labor practices reflect the appointing president's political philosophy toward labor-management relations. Frequent board turnover can influence the stability of decisions, having a negative impact upon the national labor-management relations policy.[4] Critics and supporters alike have seen a dramatic shift in board decisions since the beginning of the Reagan administration. Union attorneys cite a number of 1984 decisions as undermining employees' basic rights under the NLRA,[5] whereas management attorneys see the shift as the proper return to a middle ground with the board recovering from a pro-union bias.[6]

Union Organizational Campaigns

Employer interference with employee rights   The violation of Section 8(a)(1) of the National Labor Relations Act, dealing with interfering, restraining, or coercing employees in the exercise of their rights guaranteed by Section 7, can be direct through numerous types of interfering activities or indirect through violations of enumerated unfair labor practices actions.

To determine an unfair labor practice by an employer, the NLRB must find that the act interfered with, restrained, or coerced an action protected under the law. It must also be determined, under a reasonable probability test, that the employer's conduct could have an interfering, restraining, or coercive effect on employees. Within some constraints, the employer's motivation also must be weighed. Protected activities will be illustrated in specific examples.

The NLRB's reasonable probability test eliminates the need to prove *actual* interference, restraint, or coercion by the employer if it can be shown that the activity *tends* to interfere with the free exercise of protected rights.[7] The courts, however, distinguish between inherently discriminatory or destructive violations of employee rights when an employer could foresee the unlawful consequences, and those not so blatantly in violation. A hostile motive may be necessary to establish proof of an unfair labor practice if the activity itself can be objectively viewed as nondestructive. The kind of practice that most often evokes the need to prove intent is one motivated by a legitimate and substantial business justification.[8] In such cases, an actual intent to frustrate the purposes of the act must be found to warrant an unfair labor practice charge.

Protected activities   The right of self-organization and participation in a labor union includes the right to engage in organizational campaigns. In many cases, the exercise of that right directly opposes the employer's right to maintain a work environment. The courts have devised rules, based on the NLRB's opinion that

Exhibit 4.1 NLRB charge against employer form

FORM NLRB-501
(2-67)

FORM EXEMPT UNDER
44 U.S.C. 3512

UNITED STATES OF AMERICA
NATIONAL LABOR RELATIONS BOARD

CHARGE AGAINST EMPLOYER

INSTRUCTIONS: File an original and 4 copies of this charge with NLRB regional director for the region in which the alleged unfair labor practice occurred or is occurring.	DO NOT WRITE IN THIS SPACE
	Case No.
	Date Filed

1. EMPLOYER AGAINST WHOM CHARGE IS BROUGHT

a. Name of Employer	b. Number of Workers Employed

c. Address of Establishment (Street and number, city, State, and ZIP code)	d. Employer Representative to Contact	e. Phone No.

f. Type of Establishment (Factory, mine, wholesaler, etc.)	g. Identify Principal Product or Service

h. The above-named employer has engaged in and is engaging in unfair labor practices within the meaning of section 8(a), subsections (1) and _____ of the National Labor Relations Act,
(List subsections)

and these unfair labor practices are unfair labor practices affecting commerce within the meaning of the Act.

2. Basis of the Charge (Be specific as to facts, names, addresses, plants involved, dates, places, etc.)

By the above and other acts, the above-named employer has interfered with, restrained, and coerced employees in the exercise of the rights guaranteed in Section 7 of the Act.

3. Full Name of Party Filing Charge (If labor organization, give full name, including local name and number)

4a. Address (Street and number, city, State, and ZIP code)	4b. Telephone No.

5. Full Name of National or International Labor Organization of Which It Is an Affiliate or Constituent Unit (To be filled in when charge is filed by a labor organization)

6. DECLARATION

I declare that I have read the above charge and that the statements therein are true to the best of my knowledge and belief.

By _____   _____
      (Signature of representative or person filing charge)   (Title, if any)

Address _____   _____   _____
                                                                    (Telephone number)   (Date)

WILLFULLY FALSE STATEMENTS ON THIS CHARGE CAN BE PUNISHED BY FINE AND IMPRISONMENT (U.S. CODE, TITLE 18, SECTION 1001)

GPO 315-881

working time is for work, to balance the two interests. However, time outside working time is personal and may be used without unreasonable restraint, even on the employer's property. This includes lunchtime, break time, rest periods, and before and after the regular workday. The Supreme Court upheld this opinion in **Republic Aviation,** stating that rules prohibiting union solicitation by employees outside working time, even on employer's property, was an unreasonable impediment to self-organization.[9]

The courts, however, view organization by employees and organization by nonemployees as distinct when deciding upon the right of access to employer premises. A rule prohibiting nonemployee union organizers from solicitation on the employer's property will not be considered an unfair labor practice if there are other reasonable means to reach employees, and if solicitations by other nonemployee groups are also prohibited. However, if the union cannot find a reasonable means of reaching employees, perhaps because of the location or the nature of a business—for example, a business located in a company town or a lumber camp—a no-access rule would be an unfair labor practice.

Activities protected under the National Labor Relations Act include the following:

1. *Solicitation and distribution*   Oral solicitation by employees is allowed on the work premises during nonworking times. But distribution of union literature is restricted to nonworking times and areas. The board based this decision on employers' representations that such literature could clutter the workplace. No rule, however, is without exceptions. If justified by the nature of the business, a no-solicitation rule restricting employees even on nonworking time can be defended. Examples include department stores, restaurants, and patient care areas of hospitals where the public nature of the working area would prohibit normal interaction between employees. Conversely, an otherwise valid rule aimed only at nonemployees or employees during work time might be found an unfair labor practice by the employer if the institution of such a rule coincides with intensive union activity, the first violator of the rule is a union employee, other solicitations during work time are allowed, or a pattern of conduct hostile to union organization has been found. Exhibit 4.2 demonstrates the application of no-solicitation and no-distribution rules for both employees and nonemployees under current board decisions. Work "time" refers to that time when an employee is actually working and no solicitation may occur. Work "hours," on the other hand, are those hours when the company is open, including personal times such as lunch and breaks, during which the employee may be solicited.

2. *Union buttons or insignias*   Another protected activity is the wearing of union buttons or insignias. This right is balanced against the employer's right to conduct business. If a button or insignia should in particular circumstances cause a disturbance, present a health hazard, distract workers, cause damage to a product, or offend or distract customers, it may be prohibited. The NLRB in 1985, however, refused to allow an employer to discharge a construction employee who had a union insignia sticker on his helmet because no special circumstance existed to make the removal necessary to maintain production or discipline, or to ensure safety.[10]

Exhibit 4.2 Current no-solicitation and no-distribution rules

Rule	Employee Status	Time	Place	Legal Presumption
No Solicitation[1]	Employee and Nonemployee	Work "Time"	Work or Nonwork	Valid
No Solicitation[1]	Employee and Nonemployee	Work "Hours"	Work or Nonwork	Invalid
No Solicitation[1]	Employee and Nonemployee	Nonwork	Work or Nonwork	Invalid
No Distribution[2]	Employee	Work	Work	Valid
No Distribution[2]	Employee	Nonwork	Work	Invalid
No Distribution[2]	Employee	Work	Nonwork	Invalid
No Distribution[2]	Employee	Nonwork	Nonwork	Invalid
No Distribution[3]	Nonemployee	Work	Work	Valid
No Distribution[3]	Nonemployee	Nonwork	Work	Valid
No Distribution[3]	Nonemployee	Work	Nonwork	Valid
No Distribution[3]	Nonemployee	Nonwork	Nonwork	Valid

[1]For no-solicitation rules governing employees and nonemployees, "work" versus "nonwork" time was the key factor under *Essex*, and the *place* was irrelevant. Under DRW all such rules without clarification are presumptively invalid. Now, under *Our Way* the rule returns to *Essex*.

[2]For no-distribution rules governing employees, "workplace" is still a factor.

[3]In the case of no-distribution rules governing nonemployees, neither the time nor the place is a factor and all are presumptively valid where other means are available to reach the employees.

Source: Adapted from Thomas F. Phalen, Jr., "The Destabilization of Federal Labor Policy under the Reagan Board," *The Labor Lawyer* 2, no. 1 (Winter 1986), p. 31.

3. *Bulletin boards and meeting halls* Employees have no statutory right to use an employer's bulletin board. However, if the employees are allowed access to the bulletin board, the employer cannot censor the material to exclude union solicitation. Meeting halls fall under the same rule. If access has been allowed to employees on an unrestricted basis, use by employees for union organization cannot be the *only* exception. And if the physical location of the business makes other meeting places inaccessible, and the employer does not normally give employees access to the hall, her subsequent refusal might result in an unfair labor practice charge. In one 1986 case, the NLRB found an unfair labor practice when the company denied the union access to employee mailboxes it had been using to distribute literature for forty years. Although the company claimed the union could reach employees by other means, their denial was found discriminatory because other groups were allowed access to the mailboxes.[11]

Prohibited conduct Several activities constitute violations of the act because of their attempt to frustrate or to further union organizational efforts. Some common examples of **prohibited conduct** follow:

1. *Campaign propaganda and misrepresentation* When conducting representation elections, the board routinely ignores rhetoric, realizing that it is part of any

election campaign and usually will be disregarded by employees in making decisions. But such an attitude is flexible if the rights of the parties to an untrammeled choice are in jeopardy. In the *Midland National Life Insurance Company* case, the NLRB stated it would intervene in cases where forgery would render the voters unable to discern the propaganda nature of a publication.[12]

Misleading information on wage and fringe benefit data, usually proffered by the union to encourage unionization, is often seen by the board as exaggeration, but, if viewed by the courts as more serious, can cause the election to be invalidated.[13]

2.   *Threats and loss of benefits*   Unlike mere campaign rhetoric, the actual reduction or withholding of benefits as a method of combatting an organizational drive constitutes interference. Direct threats of economic reprisals issued to thwart a representation election will result in an unfair labor practice finding. These include discharge; loss of pay or benefits; more onerous working conditions; and threats of plant closure, physical violence, or permanent replacement of strikers.

It is more difficult to ascertain an unfair labor practice when threats of reprisals or promises of benefits are merely implied.

Under the *Gissel* case, an employer is not prohibited from communicating general views about unionism or predictions of the effect of unionization on the company, as long as such predictions involve consequences outside of the employer's control.[14] The Court added a subjective test of what the speaker intended and the listener understood to insure veiled threats would not coerce employee actions. To determine the coercive nature of a statement, a court should examine the total context in which the statement is made. Elements to be reviewed include the presence or absence of other unfair labor practice incidents, the actual content of the communication, the exact language used, the employer's history of dealing with unions, and the identity of the speaker.[15]

Statements as to the futility of selecting a bargaining agent and the inevitable coming of strikes, violence, and lay-offs if a union organizational drive is successful have also been found in violation of the act, as seen in Case 4.1.

3.   *Promise or grant of benefit*   The promise of economic benefits by the employer if employees reject unionization will violate the National Labor Relations Act, as will the promise or grant of economic benefits during an organizational campaign to influence the outcome of an election or to discourage organizational activities. The fact that there is no direct link between receipt of the benefit and a vote against the union is unimportant; the courts look to the implication of such largess. The employee may be impressed with the power of the employer's discretion to give and presumably take away benefits. However, the granting of benefits during a union campaign has not always been held a violation of the act. The board does not favor a per se approach but will examine each case within context. Clearly, offering money while urging a vote in a particular way will be considered coercive. In other cases, the board has found interference when salary increases were made in the context of repeated references to unionization, made effective just before an election, or announced before an election when there was no particular reason to do so.[16] On the other hand, a salary increase has been found not to interfere with the employee's right to organize when the timing, amount, and application of the increase was consistent with past practice.[17]

Unions can also be charged with unfair labor practices pertaining to promises. If the promise is within the bounds of what union representation can do for employees in relationship to their employer, it is probably not legally objectionable. However, promising economic benefits from the union itself, such as life insurance coverage or a waiver of union dues, has been found to be coercive.

    4. *Interrogation and polling of employees*   The NLRB originally viewed all employer interrogation of employees as to union sympathy as unlawful per se for two reasons: such interrogation instills a fear of discrimination in the mind of the employee, thereby restraining freedom of choice; and no purpose could be served by such inquiry except to identify employees with union sympathies.

    The courts, however, chose not to view it as a per se violation and instead examined it within the context of the inquiry. As a result, the board set its standard for polling of employees in the *Struksnes Construction, Inc.* case.

> Absent unusual circumstances, the polling of employees by an employer will be violative of Section 8(a)(1) of the act unless the following safeguards are observed: the purpose of the poll is to determine the truth of a union's claim of majority, this purpose is communicated to the employees, assurances against reprisals are given, the employees are polled by secret ballot, and the employer has not engaged in unfair labor practices or otherwise created a coercive atmosphere.[18]

    Individual or isolated questioning of employees is not a per se violation of the act. Tests of noncoercive questioning are whether an employer has a legitimate interest in the information sought, the employee is assured no reprisals will result from the answer, and there is no evidence of coercion in the interrogation itself. Such interrogation can arise when an employer attempts to prepare a defense for a National Labor Relations Board unfair labor practice proceeding. However, if under all the circumstances the interrogation reasonably tends to restrain or interfere with employees in the exercise of their rights, it will be held unlawful.

    The board has developed the following detailed criteria to protect the interests of both parties:

    a.   The purpose of the questioning must be communicated to the employee.
    b.   An assurance of no reprisal must be given.
    c.   The employee's participation must be obtained on a voluntary basis.
    d.   The questioning must take place in an atmosphere free from union animus.
    e.   The questioning itself must not be coercive in nature.
    f.   The questions must be relevant to the issues involved in the complaint.
    g.   The employee's subjective state of mind must not be probed.
    h.   The questions must not otherwise interfere with the statutory rights of employees.[19]

    5. *Surveillance*   Surveillance in almost any form has been held a violation of the unfair labor practices section of the National Labor Relations Act. The board has such an aversion to surveillance it will uphold findings even if the employees know nothing about it or the surveillance was only an employer's attempt to foster an impression of scrutiny. Encouraging surveillance and eavesdropping by union members has also been condemned by the NLRB.

Employer Domination of and Assistance to Labor Organizations

Under the National Labor Relations Act, employers' domination of and assistance to labor organizations are unfair labor practices. This provision obviously reflects the historic aversion to company unions of the 1930s used to discourage outside union organization. The National Labor Relations Act views employer interference in the internal workings of a union as a threat to the employee's free exercise of guaranteed rights.

The unlawful domination and assistance pertains only to labor organizations. Employee recreation committees, credit unions, social clubs, and the like may be initiated and supported by the employer without violation.

Labor organization To determine an unfair labor practice, it first must be established that a labor organization exists and that it is the focal point of the domination, interference, or assistance.

Obviously, a recognized bargaining unit certified by the NLRB presents no problem. But employee suggestion and improvement committees and similar active employee groups can be difficult to classify. The key elements of a unit looked for in most NLRB or court hearings are the organization's purpose and position to bargain with the employer regarding favorable conditions concerning wages, hours, and terms of employment. Adjustments of grievances concerning any of these issues would also qualify a group as a labor organization.

Employer domination and interference Once a labor organization is identified, the board will look for prohibited domination or support. *Support* is mere assistance to a favored union while *domination* means actual control of the union. An employer-created organization falls within the prohibited controls section of the act. Domination of a union may also be found when a union is not created by the employer. The employer's behavior toward an existing union may result in the employees' freedom of choice being unlawfully infringed. Courts have found domination when supervisors solicited union membership, the employer's attorney acted for the union in drafting its constitution and by-laws, and the employer allowed union officials on company time and property to pursue a union organization drive. Tests for domination are subjective from the standpoint of the employees.[20]

Another violation of this section is employer interference by friendly cooperation with the creation or operation of a labor organization. A suggestion in and of itself by an employer that a union be formed is not an unfair labor practice, but interference may be found if the suggestion is timed to counter an organizational drive by an outside union. After a union has been recognized, a violation may occur if supervisors and company executives who gained membership status prior to their promotions remain in the union.

Employer support and assistance While domination and control of a labor organization clearly violate the act, support and assistance of a labor organization by the employer presents a different problem. Often the suspect activities may be a manifestation of the employer's legal cooperation with the union. If the support does not have any effect on the employees' exercise of their rights guaranteed by the act and is trivial, no violation will be found.

Assistance or support that does violate the act is employer aid to one of two competing unions. The employer can unlawfully favor one union by giving direct assistance to its campaign drive, by allowing it exclusive use of company facilities, by supplying the union with employee names to aid in a raid of the other union's membership, by assessing and collecting union dues without signed authorization cards, and by recognizing the union when an election challenge is still pending or when majority status is in question. Financial support of a union, either directly by donating money or indirectly by, say, allowing the union to receive the profits from company-owned vending machines, are other violations of the support and assistance provisions.

In Case 4.2, employer/employee cooperation came under NLRB scrutiny for a determination as to whether the support involved employer domination.

Remedies   If employer control or interference in a labor organization is so extensive it results in employer domination, the board will disestablish the union. To ensure the removal of the employer from union activities, the board requires a public announcement that the company will cease bargaining with and will withdraw its support from the union. The employer must take no part in any reorganization by employees.[21]

If only support and not domination is found, the NLRB applies a less stringent remedy. Union recognition is withdrawn until the employer's support is eliminated and a new certification election is held.

Discrimination in Employment

Discrimination against employees, based upon their union activities, is an unfair labor practice and an obvious deterrent to successful collective bargaining. A violation of the act occurs when an employer encourages or discourages membership in any labor organization by hiring or tenure practices, or by using membership as a term or condition of employment.

Discrimination occurs when a union member is treated differently from a non-union worker, or because he is involved in union activity. Generally, the fact that a particular incident took place is not an issue. It is easy to ascertain that a refusal to hire, a discharge, or a change in an employment condition has occurred. The question for the board to resolve is whether the action was motivated by a desire to encourage or discourage union membership, and thereby discriminate against the member.

An employer has a right to select employees and take disciplinary action to maintain good business conditions. The NLRB must weigh claims of discrimination by the employee against claims by the employer that certain actions were taken for cause.

Discrimination cases fall into two categories. In *dual motive cases,* the employer puts forth two explanations for the action complained of. One constitutes a legitimate business reason and the other is a reason prohibited under the act. In a *pretext case,* the employer puts forth only the legitimate business reason, but the complainant asserts the prohibited reason is the true cause for the action. Approximately 60 percent of the unfair labor practice cases presented to the board involve a charge of discrimination for union activity. Prior to 1980, the board's test in these cases was to decide if the anti-union animus of the employer played a part in the complaint. If so, the employer was found to have violated the act. Since then, however, the board has required the employee to present a prima facie case that the anti-union animus of the employer played a substantial or motivating role in the complaint before requiring the employer to justify the action taken.[22]

Discriminatory acts by the employer in compliance with a *union shop* provision in a collective bargaining agreement do not violate the act. The act specifically allows a collective bargaining agreement to require that new employees join the union within thirty days of employment.

Applicants for jobs are protected by the act as well as those already employed. The language, "discrimination in regard to hire," could stand no other interpretation. Therefore, it is an unfair labor practice for an employer to refuse to hire an applicant because of union activities. It is also a violation to offer employment on the condition the applicant will not join or participate in a union.

Obvious acts of discrimination against employees regarding wages, hours, and working conditions will lead to charges of unfair labor practices. As discussed earlier, withholding benefits pending union recognition elections is an unfair labor practice if the purpose is to influence the election.

Discrimination can arise when an employer treats striking employees differently from nonstriking employees. For example, discrimination may be found if an employer announces that she will pay vacation benefits under an expired agreement to returning strikers, nonstriking workers, and strike replacements, but not to strikers.

Decisions on work assignments cannot be made if the goal is to decrease a union adherent's pay or benefits.

Except for the cited exception as to union shops, union acquiescence or cooperation in discriminatory activity will not relieve the employer from an unfair labor charge.

Although supervisors are not specifically protected, employers have been found guilty of unfair labor practices when discharging or disciplining a supervisor who has refused to engage in unfair labor practices, failed to engage in surveillance of employees' union activity, failed to coerce employees to renounce the union, failed to discharge union adherents, or testified before the National Labor Relations Board. The discharge or discipline of a supervisor in these instances is considered a violation of the act because of the coercive effect on employees.

Concerted activities Discrimination against employees for engaging in concerted activities violating the interference, restraint, or coercion provisions of the unfair labor practices section of the act also violates the discrimination for purposes of discouraging union membership provision. Although evidence of group action, not merely group concern, is required under current decisions of the board, recent circuit court decisions are expected to cause a reassessment of that standard.[23] It is expected that concerted activity will not be found in "personal gripe" cases but will be found when an individual employee seeks to protect his own statutory rights (and thereby his fellow workers') or improve the conditions of his employment.[24]

Concerted activity is any action by employees to legitimately further their common interests pursued on behalf of or with other employees and not solely by and on behalf of an individual.[25] The most common form of concerted activity is the strike. Concerted activity need not involve union leadership or membership to be protected. To establish concerted activity, certain elements must exist: the issue involved must be work related; the goal is to further a group interest; a specific remedy or result is sought; and the act itself must not be unlawful or improper.

The work-relatedness requirement is not stringently applied. The board has found many activities protected under the act:

1. Employees assisting another employer's personnel to unionize
2. Union resolution condemning employer's opposition to another union's strike
3. Union support of worker's compensation law changes
4. Union lobbying against the National Immigration Policy
5. Union lobbying against right-to-work laws[26]

Unprotected concerted activities occur when the employees are violent, act in breach of a contract, or engage in activities otherwise prohibited by the act, such as jurisdictional strikes or secondary boycotts. Employees can lose the protection of Section 7's concerted activities if they take actions disproportionate to the grievance involved. Disparaging an employer's product without clarification of the context of the dispute is such an action.

A **primary strike** is a type of concerted activity protected under the act if it is called for economic reasons or to protest unfair labor practices. Any retaliation against employees participating in a primary strike is therefore an unfair labor practice. However, if the employer has replaced strikers participating in an economic strike, he need only reinstate those for whom he has vacant positions. In contrast, employees participating in a strike to protest an unfair labor practice are entitled to reinstatement and back pay, even if they have been replaced. Unlawful activity during a strike may be grounds for discharging an employee and would not subject an employer to an unfair labor practice charge. Also, an employer who discharges employees for breaching a collective bargaining agreement will not be guilty of an unfair labor practice. However, discharging or otherwise discriminating against an employee for filing charges or giving testimony is, under the National Labor Relations Act, specifically designated as an unfair labor practice.

Other employee concerted activities protected under Section 8 (a)(3) or Section 8 (a)(4) are bringing a civil action against the employer unless done with malice or in bad faith; circulating a petition among coworkers calling for a union meeting to discuss current contract negotiations; complaining to local government authorities; and under some circumstances, refusing to cross a picket line.[27] Concerted activities not considered protected are serious trespass, destruction of property, violence, and participating in an unlawful strike in violation of a no-strike clause in an applicable collective bargaining agreement.[28]

Unfair Labor Practices by Labor Organizations

The Taft-Hartley Amendments to the National Labor Relations Act were a response to the perceived power of organized labor during the 1940s to dictate to the employer instead of meeting at the bargaining table as an equal. One aspect not previously covered by the National Labor Relations Act was the imposition against **labor organizations** of **unfair labor practice standards**. Exhibit 4.3 is a form used in filing charges against unions.

Restraint or Coercion of Employees

Unfair labor practice standards were applied to labor organizations to enforce an employee's right to refrain from union activities, which was granted by the Taft-Hartley Amendments. This includes protection to work without restraint from strikes, to refuse to sign union dues check-offs, and not to be coerced into accepting a particular union or any union at all.

The amendments did not impair the right of a labor organization to prescribe its own rules on members in good standing. And, if a union shop provision is part of a current collective bargaining agreement, an employee can be compelled to join the union after being hired and to pay dues or fees to retain employment.

The section of the amendments prohibiting unfair labor practices by unions can be violated only by a labor organization or its agent. Actions by individual employees not sanctioned by a union cannot subject the employee to an unfair labor practice charge.

The unfair labor practices provision prohibiting a union from restraining or coercing employees in the exercise of their guaranteed rights is not as broadly stated nor as strictly enforced as the mirror provision affecting employers. Violent or otherwise threatening behavior, or clearly coercive or intimidating union activities are necessary before the NLRB will find an unfair labor practice. Union propaganda and peer pressure present in a situation where employees belong to a union will not cause an unfair labor practice charge. Examine Case 4.3 for its facts in light of this criterion.

Specific activities are deemed to be in violation of the amendments:

1. Physical assaults or threats of violence directed at employees or their relatives
2. Threats of economic reprisals
3. Mass picketing that restrains the lawful entry or leaving of a work site
4. Causing or attempting to cause an employer to discriminate against employees
5. Discriminating provisions in collective bargaining agreements (union shop being an exception), for example, superseniority clauses for union members that do not exist for a legitimate purpose[29]

Duty of Fair Representation

A union is guilty of an unfair labor practice when it breaches its **duty of fair representation**. This duty requires that the union serve the interests of all members of

Exhibit 4.3 Charge against labor organization form

FORM NLRB-508 (4-73)	UNITED STATES OF AMERICA NATIONAL LABOR RELATIONS BOARD	FORM EXEMPT UNDER 44 U.S.C. 3512

CHARGE AGAINST LABOR ORGANIZATION OR ITS AGENTS

INSTRUCTIONS: File an original and 3 copies of this charge and an additional copy for each organization, each local and each individual named in item 1 with the NLRB regional director for the region in which the alleged unfair labor practice occurred or is occurring.	DO NOT WRITE IN THIS SPACE
	Case No.
	Date Filed

1. LABOR ORGANIZATION OR ITS AGENTS AGAINST WHICH CHARGE IS BROUGHT

a. Name	b. Union Representative to Contact	c. Phone No.

d. Address (Street, city, State and ZIP code)

e. The above-named organization(s) or its agents has (have) engaged in and is (are) engaging in unfair labor practices within the meaning of section 8(b), subsection(s) _____ (List Subsections) _____ of the National Labor Relations Act, and these unfair labor practices are unfair labor practices affecting commerce within the meaning of the Act.

2. Basis of the Charge (Be specific as to facts, names, addresses, plants involved, dates, places, etc.)

3. Name of Employer	4. Phone No.

5. Location of Plant Involved (Street, city, State and ZIP code)	6. Employer Representative to Contact

7. Type of Establishment (Factory, mine, wholesaler, etc.)	8. Identify Principal Product or Service	9. No. of Workers Employed

10. Full Name of Party Filing Charge

11. Address of Party Filing Charge (Street, city, State and ZIP code)	12. Telephone No.

13. DECLARATION

I declare that I have read the above charge and that the statements therein are true to the best of my knowledge and belief.

By _____
(Signature of representative or person making charge)   (Title or office, if any)

Address _____
(Telephone number)   (Date)

WILLFULLY FALSE STATEMENTS ON THIS CHARGE CAN BE PUNISHED BY FINE AND IMPRISONMENT (U.S. CODE, TITLE 18, SECTION 1001)

GPO 899-373

the bargaining unit without hostility or discrimination and in good faith and honesty. A breach occurs when the union acts in an arbitrary or discriminatory manner or in bad faith toward a bargaining unit member.

Areas in which a breach may occur include the following situations:

1. Discrimination against members of another union in a merger with that union by placing their names at the end of a seniority list
2. Refusal to pursue an employee's grievance because of the employee's race
3. Any actions motivated by discrimination on racial or sexual grounds
4. Failure to pursue a grievance on the basis of union politics[30]

Membership rules   A union may prescribe its own membership rules and can fine members to enforce them. Union rules must be properly adopted, must reflect a legitimate union interest, must not frustrate the national labor policy, and must be reasonably enforced against members, who can leave the union to escape the rule. Union rules also must pertain to internal matters and may not extend to the employer-employee relationship. For example, the union may assess fines for nonparticipation in a union-called strike, but failure to pay such fines cannot be invoked by the union to influence the employer to fire the employee. A union rule forbidding union membership to individuals who worked during a strike would not be upheld and would be opposed to the labor policy contained in the National Labor Relations Act.

Union restraint of employers   The National Labor Relations Act specifically protects the right of employers to select their own representatives for the purpose of collective bargaining and the adjustment of grievances. Any union attempt to restrain or coerce the employer in this selection is considered an unfair labor practice. Frequently, this charge arises when the union refuses to bargain with the negotiator or negotiating team sent by the employer, or when pressure is exerted by the union to remove a certain supervisor.

Duty to Bargain in Good Faith

The National Labor Relations Act established a national policy to encourage collective bargaining as a way to eliminate or to mitigate industrial strife obstructing commerce. Employees seek strength in numbers by joining employee organizations to insure equal bargaining powers. Under the National Labor Relations Act, employee organization is a *right,* protected and preserved.

However, once that right is exercised, a duty is placed upon both the employee organization and the employer to proceed to **bargain in good faith.**

Nature of the Duty

The Wagner (National Labor Relations) Act itself made it an unfair labor practice for an employer to refuse to bargain with representatives of his employees.[31] The NLRB, in enforcing that provision, imposed a good faith efforts test as a condition for compliance with this duty. The criteria established by the board included

1. Active participation in deliberations with an intention to find a basis for agreement
2. A sincere effort to reach a common ground
3. Binding agreements on mutually acceptable terms[32]

The board found indications of less than good faith when employers met directly with employees outside the bargaining process to reach an agreement not sanctioned by their representatives, when an employer refused to put the agreement in writing even after all issues were agreed to, or when an employer refused to make counterproposals.[33]

The comprehensive inclusion of unions in the unfair labor practices section of the National Labor Relations Act by the Taft-Hartley Amendments placed an equal obligation to bargain in good faith on employees. In addition, the board-imposed test of good faith to determine whether either party had refused to bargain was included in the amendments.[34]

The amendments also clarified what was meant by bargaining: to meet at reasonable times; to confer in good faith with respect to rates of pay, wages, hours of employment or other conditions of employment; and to execute a written contract if the parties reach an agreement. However, the obligation to bargain does not compel either party to agree to a proposal or to make a concession.

In addition, the amendments imposed the duty to bargain in good faith on the employer when the collective bargaining representative requests that the employer meet for purposes of collective bargaining. The completion of a representative election alone does not trigger the bargaining process. Until the employer has been asked, there can be no breach of the duty to bargain.

When the duty to bargain has arisen, the amendments require that negotiations be conducted in good faith with the view of reaching an agreement. Merely going through the motions without actually seeking to adjust differences does not meet this stipulation.

Totality of Conduct Doctrine

A **totality of conduct** test is applied to determine the fulfillment of the good faith bargaining obligation. If, in total conduct, a party has negotiated with an open mind in a sincere attempt to reach an agreement, isolated acts will not prove bad faith. On the other hand, actions that are not per se unfair labor practices may indicate bad faith bargaining when viewed in the totality of the bargaining process.

Boulwarism   Boulwarism is a "take it or leave it" bargaining technique. It derives its name from Lemuel R. Boulware, a vice-president for the General Electric Company, who negotiated for that company in the late 1940s. Using this technique, a company presents a comprehensive contract proposal which, in its opinion, has included all that is necessary or warranted. This form of negotiation eliminates any need to compromise in the employer's mind. Such a proposal is presented at the outset with the understanding that nothing is being held back for later trading, and employees are notified it is a final offer. This places the employer in the untenable position of not being able to negotiate. The NLRB declared an attitude of boulwarism a violation of the duty to bargain. It noted that while the formality of bargaining is followed, no illegal or nonmandatory subjects are insisted upon, and a clear intent to enter into an agreement is exhibited, there exists no serious intent to adjust differences and to reach a common ground.

A 1964 decision (confirmed in 1969) involving this procedure as practiced by the General Electric Company gave the NLRB a chance to examine the technique in detail. The company had examined all relevant facts and had anticipated union demands. It actively communicated its position to employees prior to the negotiation session. It presented what it considered a fair and firm offer although representations were made that new information could alter its position. The company was found to have failed in its duty to bargain in good faith because it failed to furnish information requested by the union; it had attempted to bypass the international union and to bargain directly with local unions; it had presented a "take-it-or-leave-it" insurance proposal; and it had, in its overall attitude and approach as evidenced by the totality of its conduct, failed in the good faith test.[35]

By the examination of the totality of conduct, the court expanded the understanding of the duty to bargain collectively by emphasizing the *collective* nature of the duty as contained in the National Labor Relations Act. Involvement is a bilateral procedure, allowing both parties a voice in the agreements reached. It is in direct opposition to the intent and purpose of the act for a party to assume the role of decision maker; an exchange of options must be presented and received with an open mind.

The technique of boulwarism, while generally used by an employer, has also been used by unions. In *Utility Workers (Ohio Power Company)*, the board found a union violating the duty to bargain in good faith when the union insisted that identical offers be made to several bargaining units and conditioned acceptance in any single unit upon submission of identical offers to all units.[36]

Surface bargaining   Another violation of the good faith duty can be evidenced by **surface bargaining**; that is, simply going through the motions without any real intention of arriving at an agreement. A totality test is used to determine surface bargaining. Surface bargaining can occur when a party has rejected a proposal, offered its own, and does not attempt to reconcile the differences; or when a party's only proposal is the continuation of existing practices.[37]

Extensive negotiation in and of itself will not justify a finding of surface bargaining since the National Labor Relations Act does not compel parties to agree to proposals or to make concessions. Hard bargaining on a major issue does not exhibit bad faith since a party is not required to yield on a position fairly maintained. Even if open hostility is exhibited by the parties, surface bargaining may not be charged if the totality of the bargaining process complies with the dictates of the act.

The National Labor Relations Board uses these factors when considering an unfair labor charge for surface bargaining:

1. Prior bargaining history of the parties
2. Parties' willingness to make concessions
3. The character of exchanged proposals and demands
4. Any dilatory tactics employed during negotiations
5. Conditions imposed by either party as necessary to reaching an agreement
6. Unilateral changes made during the bargaining process in conditions subject to bargaining
7. Communications by employer to individual employees
8. Any unfair labor practices committed during bargaining[38]

While the National Labor Relations Act does not require a party to make concessions, courts have consistently viewed a *willingness to make concessions* as evidence of good faith. Parties are encouraged to engage in **auction bargaining** in which parties state their positions, make proposals, and then trade off on those proposals to arrive at agreeable terms. Refusal to make any concessions evidenced by inflexibility on major issues can be held as bad faith. An intransigent attitude on some issues may be acceptable if bargaining continues on other issues.[39]

Agreement on many major bargaining subjects may be used as evidence of good faith even though one issue remains unresolved. For example, the company's refusal to agree to a change in a health and welfare plan in *John S. Swift & Co.* was not tantamount to an unfair labor practice because of its totality of conduct in negotiating and reaching agreement on virtually every other major bargaining issue.[40]

The National Labor Relations Board examines the *character of proposals and demands* to determine the good faith effort of the parties. While the mere presentation of a predictably unacceptable proposal will not justify a finding of bad faith if such proposal does not frustrate or unnecessarily prolong negotiations, presenting numerous new proposals after several months of negotiations or after some issues have been resolved can effect a finding of bad faith.[41] To insist upon the inclusion of a proposal with the purpose of thwarting the negotiating process violates good faith. But if such insistence, even on a nonmandatory subject, is based on a desire to resolve an issue of substance to a party and is not pushed to the point of impasse, bad faith may not be evidenced.

Proposals concerning the duration of a negotiated agreement can often evidence bad faith. When the proposed termination date is within a year and coincides with the end of the certification year of the bargaining unit, the board will find bad faith. The employer's refusal to discuss union dues check-off provisions is a breach of the good faith bargaining duty. This type of proposal frequently causes employers to adopt an adamant stand generally based on their objection to assisting in union organization. The National Labor Relations Board and subsequent court rulings have held such an intransigent position to be in bad faith.

In a landmark decision, the Supreme Court overruled an NLRB finding of bad faith by an employer insisting on a management functions clause.[42] The Court found that the union's proposal on that issue—an unlimited arbitration provision—contributed to the deadlock. Neither party refused to bargain and did indeed agree on other issues, thus the Court found that the board's determination that the employer had violated the National Labor Relations Act per se was not based on the totality of conduct but on the board's opinion of the substance of the proposal.

The degree to which either party stalls or uses **delaying tactics** to avoid collective bargaining is considered by the NLRB in its totality review. Obviously, a complete refusal to meet and to bargain violates the act. Scheduling meetings infrequently or canceling scheduled meetings can also evidence bad faith. Prolonged discussions on formalities designed to thwart the collective bargaining process will be considered bad faith. The number or length of time of negotiation sessions alone cannot determine good or bad faith, but the NLRB frequently reviews meeting history to determine an employer's charge of bad faith. And while there is no hard-and-fast rule as to how many or how long, a review of case decisions shows the *board's* preference for frequent meetings—79 in 11 months, 11 in 5 months, 11 in 4 months, 37 in 10 months.[43]

Because the duty to bargain includes bargaining on proper subjects, *imposing conditions* on the scope of bargaining will be scrutinized closely. If either party seeks to place restrictions on the bargaining process that make the process meaningless, a violation of the duty to bargain in good faith is found. Demanding concessions before bargaining begins will be viewed as evidence of bad faith.

An employer may show bad faith by requiring that an unfair labor practice charge be dropped before negotiations will begin, that a strike be terminated, or that the composition of the union's negotiation committee meet the employer's specifications.

Employers may be guilty of bad faith if they **unilaterally change conditions**, such as employees' wages, rates of pay, or hours of employment during contract negotiations. If such changes in benefits are considered better than those being offered at the table, bad faith is clearly evidenced.[44] The act seeks to avoid this attempt to bypass the union and to deal directly with employees. However, there are exceptions to this rule. If an impasse is reached, and is not the result of the employer's bad faith, a unilateral increase of benefits is not evidence of bad faith.

Bypassing the bargaining representation by attempting to *negotiate with employees* will often be held as a violation of the duty to bargain in good faith. The courts, in reviewing the National Labor Relations Act, found it was the employer's duty to recognize the union and conduct negotiations through the union rather than deal directly with employees. This is an obligation even if the employer traditionally had contracts with individual workers. The collective bargaining contract will supersede such contracts.[45] One exception to this rule is that if a union refuses a final offer, the employer may communicate that offer directly to employees.

The good faith test includes the duty to send negotiators to the table with sufficient *authority* to carry on meaningful negotiations. All attempts to delay commitment by the recourse of management representatives to check with some final authority are scrutinized closely for evidence of bad faith. However, the obligation of the union representative to take a contract back for a vote of union members before acceptance is not a violation of the duty to bargain in good faith.

Unfair labor practices during contract negotiations evidence bad faith. Threats to close a plant or to engage in discriminating layoffs during bargaining have been held in bad faith. To encourage the decertification of a union or to assist employees in the decertification process have also been found to obstruct the bargaining process.

Duty to Furnish Information

The employer has a duty to furnish information to the union enabling it to carry on the negotiation process. Often employees are unable to collect relevant data about an employer's business without the employer's cooperation. If the National Labor Relations Act did not support this duty to furnish information, much of the collective bargaining process would be futile. As with the duty to bargain, the duty to furnish information arises only after a request for information is made in good faith. A union may be subject to a charge of an unfair labor practice if it requests information only to harass or humiliate the employer.

    1. *Relevancy*   Within liberal interpretations, the NLRB has said that information requested must be relevant to the union's right to represent their members. The union need not prove that the particular information requested relates to a currently discussed item if the subject matter is part of the overall negotiations.

    2. *Financial information of company*   When an employer claims financial inability to meet a union wage demand, the financial information of the employer's company becomes relevant. The Supreme Court held that if such a claim by the employer is important enough to be made at the table, it requires some proof of its accuracy.[46] The board has extended this rule to actual claims of financial inability. Refusal to grant wage increases because the employer claims she could not stay competitive or would lose the profit margin was held by the board to invoke financial inability. Therefore, financial data becomes relevant. In the absence of such a claim, an employer's financial records can be denied the union's bargaining team. Nondisclosure of financial information may be seen by the employer as a reaffirmation of management prerogative and by the employees as an obstacle to effective bargaining.[47]

    3. *Prompt delivery of information in workable form*   Bad faith may be evidenced if requested information is not delivered in a timely manner or is delivered in an unreasonable, useless form. An employer may claim that compiling requested data is unduly burdensome, but he must be flexible and should suggest alternatives. If the information is given in a form generally accepted in business, a union's request for a different form will not be binding on the employer. And when the employer allows union access to all his records, he need not furnish information in a more organized form.

    4. *Information that must be furnished*   Almost all areas touching upon mandatory bargaining have been open to union requests for information. However, employers frequently refuse requests by the union to furnish wage information. The board, supported by lower courts and the Supreme Court, has found little if any justification for such refusals. The statutory requirement that wages be subject to collective bargaining extends to wages paid to particular employees, to groups of employees, and to methods of computing compensation. The union's right to information may include employees even outside of the bargaining unit or in other plants operated by employers.

Refusal to Bargain

The labor organization, like the employer, is charged with a duty under the Taft-Hartley Amendments to bargain in good faith. Failure to do so can result in an unfair labor practice charge. Basically, the good faith requirement is the same as for employers, and involves having an open mind in meeting and conferring with employers to reach an ultimate agreement. Refusal to sign an agreement the union and employer have come to terms on is an unfair labor practice. Insistence on being recognized as the exclusive bargaining agent for an inappropriate unit or when majority status is not held, is also an unfair labor practice.

Other unfair labor practices charged against a union will be explored in the contract negotiations discussed in the next chapter.

Summary

Employer unfair labor practices impede the collective bargaining process. Unfair labor practices, as contained in the act, include the interference with employees in the exercise of their rights; the domination of an employee union; the discrimination against union members; and the refusal to bargain.

The National Labor Relations Act imposed a duty to bargain in good faith on the employer and the labor organization, subject to its provisions. That good faith is evidenced by the total conduct of the parties toward the collective bargaining process.

Labor organizations also can be guilty of unfair labor practices. Because the National Labor Relations Act guarantees employees the right to refrain from union activities, attempts by labor unions to coerce employees to join is a violation. A union must fairly represent all of its members, and a breach of that duty is an unfair labor practice. The same is true of a union's duty to bargain in good faith with the employer.

CASE 4.1   *Unfair Labor Practice by an Employer*

Adapted from *National Labor Relations Board* v. *Sinclair Company,* 397 F.2d 157 (1968)

For twenty years the experienced and apprentice wire weavers of the company were represented by a union. But after a thirteen-week strike, the relationship ended. For almost thirteen years the employees were not represented by any union.

A new union began organizing employees and, having reached majority status, requested that it meet with the company. The company refused to recognize the union. An election was held and the union lost by a vote of 7–6. The union petitioned the NLRB to set aside the election because the pre-election conduct of the company's president was an unfair labor practice. The board agreed, set aside the election, and entered an unfair labor practice charge. The company appealed.

Decision

The court examined the pre-election conduct of the president. He had on numerous occasions, orally and in writing, urged the fourteen employees to reject the union. He claimed that the union's only weapon was a strike, and that the last strike had nearly ruined the company. He also warned that the company was still not financially secure and that a strike could close the plant. He denounced the particular union and its top officials as corrupt and strike happy. He added that the wire weavers' age and lack of education would make it difficult to find other jobs.

The company defended the pre-election remarks on the grounds that the remarks were true.

The court pointed out that an employer's predictions of economic consequences must be demonstrable, and not just based on the feelings of the employer. It also stated that the test of the coercive effect of such statements includes the total circumstances surrounding them.

The court affirmed the board's finding that the president's conduct interfered with the employees' exercise of a free and untrammeled choice in the election.

CASE 4.2   Domination

Adapted from *Hertzka & Knowles* v. *National Labor Relations Board,* 46 L.Ed., 2d 106 (1975)

The professional employees of a medium-sized architectural firm voted to be represented by a union. Over a year later, after months of unsuccessful negotiations, an employee petitioned for a decertification election.

The union lost the election. Immediately after the election, a partner in the firm called a meeting of partners and professional personnel to ask for suggestions on insuring management-employee dialogue.

An employee suggested a committee system whereby five in-house committees, composed of five employees and one management representative, would examine a different area of employee concern, such as wages. Two employees seconded his idea, and the plan was overwhelmingly approved. An employee suggested that the partners vote on the proposal, too. They did, and it passed unanimously. The committees met on company time without loss of pay. On some committees the managers voted, on some they did not.

The union filed an unfair labor practice charge against the employer for supporting and dominating a labor organization. The National Labor Relations Board agreed and ordered the employer to withdraw recognition and support of and to disestablish the employees' committees. The employer appealed.

Decision

The Supreme Court pointed out that there is a line between employer cooperation which the act encourages and employer domination which the act condemns. That line is crossed when, from the standpoint of the employee, freedom of choice has been stifled.

The Court found that the totality of circumstances in this case did not show such domination. Allowing the committees to meet on company time alone is not unlawful support. The Court noted that the idea for the committee system came from an employee and was supported and approved by other employees. Placing a management representative on the committees was also an employee's idea. The Court noted that the manager's vote, when he has a vote at all, is just one of six.

Under these facts, the Court reversed the board's finding.

CASE 4.3   *Unfair Labor Practice by a Union*

Adapted from *National Labor Relations Board* v. *District 65, Retail, Wholesale & Department Store Union, AFL-CIO* F.2d 745 (1967)

A union decided to try to organize employees of four direct mail companies. A plan was devised whereby a union organizer, accompanied by a group of persons acting on behalf of the union, would descend upon the four companies without permission and distribute union literature during working hours.

The nature of the union's conduct is illustrated by the following:

1. In the first incident, twenty-five men and women swarmed into the plant, moved to where employees were working, and began talking to employees about the union. All production stopped as a result of the commotion. When asked to leave, a union member suggested they call the police.
2. Two days later at another plant, twenty-five men and women entered by the front entrance and began talking to employees in the same manner as just described. At the same time, twelve men entered the plant from the rear and pushed by a manager who attempted to stop them. Again, work was at a standstill.
3. One company, fearing they would be next, hired a uniformed guard. Twenty-five union members found the door unlocked, pushed by the armed guard, threatened to kill him with his own gun, and created a commotion.

The board found the union violated the National Labor Relations Act section prohibiting unfair labor practices by labor organizations. The union appealed.

Decision

The court upheld the board.

The act forbids a union from restraining or coercing employees in the exercise of their rights. The court noted that one right is to refrain from collective bargaining activities. The union's conduct, which included threats and physical violence, constituted illegal coercion.

CASE STUDY   *Unionization*

Adapted from *National Labor Relations Board* v. *Exchange Parts Company,* 375 U.S. 405, 84 S.Ct. 457, 11 L.Ed. 2d 435 (1964)

Facts

The company was notified by the union that it was conducting an organizational campaign and requesting that an election be held to determine the employees' exclusive bargaining representative. Prior to that election but after it had notice of the election, the company informed employees it would be granting a floating holiday and that the employees could decide whether to take that holiday as an extra vacation day or on their birthdays. Immediately prior to the election the company sent employees a letter detailing its benefits granted to employees since 1949, with an estimate of the monetary value of the benefits and mentioning the birthday holiday. The letter further stated that the union could not grant these benefits but that only the company could do so. The letter also announced two new provisions that increased wages by recomputing overtime during holiday weeks and extended vacations by allowing employees to schedule them between two weekends. In the ensuing election the union lost.

Lawsuit

The union filed suit claiming that the company had violated the National La-bor Relations Act and that granting benefits to employees under these circumstances was an unfair labor practice. The lower court found that conferring employee benefits while a representation election is pending even for the purpose of inducing employees to vote against the union does not interfere with the protected right of the employees to organize.

Questions

1. The company in this case did not make its favors a condition of rejecting unionization. Although employees appeared to choose employer generosity over the union's ability to achieve results, were they actually denied the freedom of choice?

2. If the benefits granted are available to the employee without unionization, why should the employees unionize?

3. The union in this case brought suit after it had lost the representation election. Would it have been better if the employees had claimed an unfair labor practice instead of the union?

Key Terms and Concepts

Auction bargaining

Boulwarism

Concerted activities

Delaying tactics

Duty of fair representation

Employer unfair labor practices

Good faith bargaining

Labor organization unfair labor practices

Primary strike

Prohibited conduct

Republic Aviation case

Surface bargaining

Totality of conduct doctrine

Unilaterally changing conditions

Review Questions

1. What might the NLRB consider to be a breach of the good faith bargaining principle?
2. How does the NLRB review an unfair labor practice charge of surface bargaining?
3. Is an employer always required to furnish any data requested by a union during negotiations?
4. What are the rules employers and union organizers must follow during an organizational campaign?
5. Under what circumstances can an employer poll employees to determine their desire to join a union?
6. What is the difference between an employer's support and domination of a union?
7. When is an employer illegally discriminating against employees based upon their union activities?
8. What union activities are prohibited under the Taft-Hartley unfair labor practices provision?

Endnotes

1. 29 U.S.C. sec. 157 (1982).
2. 29 U.S.C. sec. 158(a) (1982).
3. Donald L. Dotson, "Processing Cases at the NLRB," *Labor Law Journal* 35, no. 1 (Jan. 1984), pp. 3–9.
4. William N. Cooke and Frederick H. Gautschi III, "Political Bias in NLRB Unfair Labor Practice Decisions," *Industrial and Labor Relations Review* 35, no. 4 (July 1982), pp. 539–49. See also Myron Roomkin, "A Quantitative Study of Unfair Labor Practice Cases," *Industrial and Labor Relations Review* 34, no. 2 (Jan. 1981), p. 256.
5. Thomas F. Phalen, Jr., "The Destabilization of Federal Labor Policy Under the Reagan Board," *The Labor Lawyer* 2, no. 1 (Winter 1986), pp. 1–31.
6. Fred W. Batten, "Recent Decisions of the Reagan Board: A Management Perspective," *The Labor Lawyer* 2, no. 1 (Winter 1986), pp. 33–46.
7. Cooper Thermometer Co., 154 N.L.R.B. 502, 59 LRRM 1767 (1965); and American Freightways Co., 124 N.L.R.B. 646, 44 LRRM 1202 (1959).
8. National Labor Relations Board v. Preston Feed Corp., 309 F.2d 346, (CA 4, 1962).
9. Republic Aviation, 324 U.S. 793, 16 LRRM 620 (1945).
10. Malta Co., 276 N.L.R.B. 171 (1985).
11. The Cincinnati Enquirer, 279 N.L.R.B. 149 (1986).
12. Midland National Life Ins. Co. v. N.L.R.B., 263 N.L.R.B. 24, 110 LRRM 1489 (1982).
13. James P. Swann, Jr., "Misrepresentation in Labor Union Elections," *Personnel Journal* 59, no. 11 (Nov. 1980), pp. 925–26.

14. National Labor Relations Board v. Gissel Packing Co., 395 U.S. 575, 71 LRRM 2481 (1969).

15. Gary L. Tidwell, "The Supervisor's Role in a Union Election," *Personnel Journal* 62, no. 8 (Aug. 1983), pp. 640–45.

16. James H. Hopkins and Robert D. Binderup, "Employee Relations and Union Organizing Campaigns," *The Personnel Administrator* 25, no. 3 (Mar. 1980), pp. 57–61.

17. Automated Prods., Inc., 242 N.L.R.B. 424, 101 LRRM 1208 (1979).

18. Struksnes Construction Co., 165 N.L.R.B. 1062,1063, 65 LRRM 1385 (1967).

19. Charles J. Morris, ed., *The Developing Labor Law,* 2nd ed. (Washington, D.C.: Bureau of National Affairs, 1983), pp. 125–26.

20. Federal-Magul Corp., Coldwater Distributors Center Division v. National Labor Relations Board, 394 F.2d 915 (CA Mich. 1968).

21. Morris, *Developing Labor Law,* p. 148.

22. David Vaughn, "Mixed Motives in Unfair Labor Practices," *New York University, 35th Annual National Conference on Labor* (New York: Matthew Bender & Co., 1983), pp. 169–94.

23. Prill v. National Labor Relations Board 755 F.2d 941 (D.C. Cir., 1985), and Ewing v. National Labor Relations Board, 119 LRRM 3273 (2nd Cir. 1985).

24. Anthony T. Oliver, Jr. and Bruce D. May, "Labor Relations: Are Lone Employees Protected Under Concerted Activity Laws?" *Personnel Journal* 64, no. 11 (Nov. 1985), pp. 123–26.

25. Meyers Industries v. Prill, 268 N.L.R.B. 73 (1984).

26. Morris, *Developing Labor Law,* pp. 136–47.

27. Ibid., pp. 147–58.

28. Ibid., pp. 159–64.

29. Ibid., pp. 174–81.

30. Ibid., pp. 1328–343.

31. 29 U.S.C. sec. 158(a)(5) (1982).

32. National Labor Relations Board v. Montgomery Ward & Co., 133 F.2d 676, 686 (CA 9, 1943), 12 LRRM 508.

33. Ludwig Teller, *Labor Disputes and Collective Bargaining,* vol. 2 (New York: Baker, Voorhis, 1940), p. 884.

34. 29 U.S.C. sec. 158(d) (1982).

35. National Labor Relations Board v. General Electric Co., 418 F.2d 736, 72 LRRM 2530 (CA 2, 1969) cert. denied, 397 U.S. 965, 73 LRRM 2600 (1970).

36. Utility Workers (Ohio Power Co.), 203 N.L.R.B. 230, 83 LRRM 1099 (1973).

37. U.S. Gypsum Co., 200 N.L.R.B. 132, 82 LRRM 1064 (1972).

38. Theodore Kheel, *Labor Law* (New York: Matthew Bender, 1982), pp. 16–31.

39. National Labor Relations Board v. Gellan Iron Works, Inc., 377 F.2d 894 (2d Cir. 1967).

40. John S. Smith and Co., 124 N.L.R.B. 394, 44 LRRM 1388 (1959).

41. National Labor Relations Board v. Fitzgerald Mills, 313 F.2d 260, 52 LRRM 2174 (CA 2, 1963).

42. National Labor Relations Board v. American National Insurance Co., 343 U.S. 395, 30 LRRM 2147 (1952).

43. Morris, *Developing Labor Law,* p. 595, note 275.

44. National Labor Relations Board v. Katz, 369 U.S. 736, 82 S. Ct. 1107, 8 L.Ed. 762 (1962).

45. JI Case v. National Labor Relations Board, 321 U.S. 332, 64 S. Ct. 576, 88 L.Ed. 762 (1944).

46. National Labor Relations Board v. Truitt Manufacturing Co., 351 U.S. 149, 38 LRRM 2024 (1955).

47. Robert E. Block, "The Disclosure of Profits in the Normal Course of Collective Bargaining: All Relevant Information Should be on the Table," *The Labor Lawyer* 2, no. 1 (Winter 1986), pp. 47–74.

Negotiating an Agreement

LABOR NEWS

Steel Ends Thirty-Year Peace Pact

No-strike clauses are usually highly sought by industry, but severe circumstances may alter their value. Since 1956 the U.S. steel industry enjoyed an industrywide no-strike agreement. In 1986 the six major U.S. steelmakers, after losing over $1 billion in two years, decided to bargain separately with the United Steelworkers of America. The firms' fierce competition for survival forced them to give up the safety of joint negotiations and the continuance of the no-strike pact. Each company tried to negotiate givebacks in wages and work rules, in addition to the $2 billion worth of givebacks negotiated in the previous five years. The union had already lost nearly 700,000 jobs in ten years despite the givebacks. Faced with crisis, the union shifted negotiating strategy and proposed tailored giveback proposals based on each firm's ability to pay as determined by sophisticated financial analysis. Each firm, hoping to avoid a strike, prepared a package that would give it a competitive edge with the other.

Adapted from: Peter Perl, "Steel Firms Start Crucial Labor Talks," The Washington Post, March 19, 1986, pp. K1, 7.

Central to the collective bargaining process are the actual negotiations carried out by the parties to reach an agreement. Artful use of this process can improve the relationship between an employer and the employees and result in a profitable agreement for both parties. Unsuccessful negotiations can lead to work stoppages and a loss of profits and benefits. This chapter examines different techniques of bargaining, details of the bargaining process, and solutions to the bargaining impasse.

The bargaining process usually begins when one party desires to terminate or amend an existing contract. Most agreements provide for the automatic extension of an existing contract past the expiration date, usually for one year. Either party may initiate new negotiations by providing written, explicit notice to the other party. A clause specifying automatic renewal and the process to begin new negotiations is included in most U.S. labor agreements.[1]

The Bargaining Process

The collective bargaining process begins long before the parties meet across the bargaining table. As discussed in previous chapters, the organization of units and the selection of the agent is a lengthy process necessary in determining the parties to a collective bargaining relationship.

People Who Bargain

Union representatives   Although there are as many types of negotiators as there are negotiations, some generalizations can be made. Generally, a local union's negotiating team is made up of certain ex-officio members, such as the president or one or more elected officers of the local union, and a chief steward or grievance committee member. In most negotiations involving craft unions, the business agent is part of the negotiating team and often the chief negotiator. For industrial unions a representative of the international union, who is a professional negotiator, is often available to guide and counsel local union officials.

Although international representatives have no official status during local negotiations, their experience often puts them in a leadership role. They give guidance on the grievance process and set the tone for negotiations and, in the case of impasse, for pressure tactics. They play the role of mediator or assume a militant stand to allow the local representatives to appear reasonable.

Whatever the makeup of the union's negotiating team, its authority is probably limited by the membership. The union members usually delegate only provisional and temporary authority to the negotiating team to make a settlement. Often, any final settlement must be presented to the total membership for a vote.

Management representative   The authority of the management negotiating team comes from top management and is generally a more complete delegation. Policy makers are often a part of the team. In negotiations involving a single employer, the representative may be the company's labor relations director or a production person and line executive; or there may be staff advisers such as the personnel director, financial officer, and a company lawyer. When a multiemployer association is involved, the companies often employ a labor relations advisor and negotiator, who is equivalent to the international representative. This professional serves a role similar to that of the union counterpart by promoting the multiemployer organization, by preparing management counterproposals, and by conducting negotiations.

Negotiating skills   Successful negotiations depend upon the knowledge and skill of the negotiators. They must, through careful preparations, become knowledgeable about their own and the other side's positions on the bargaining issues. They prepare and propose workable, attainable, and realistic issues within the framework of the negotiations. For example, negotiators may develop strong economic positions to give the parties bargaining room during the negotiation process.

To use the acquired knowledge wisely, a negotiator develops an understanding of the opposition. Listening skills and the ability to communicate clearly are two techniques he cultivates. A thick skin may be helpful as the other side may engage in personal attacks at some point in the negotiations. A negotiator realizes that such attacks are often necessary in satisfying a constituency.

The successful negotiator possesses personal integrity and courage.[2] At some point in the negotiations, agreements must be made. A negotiator's word and/or handshake is the basis for the agreement until and after it is committed to paper. The untrustworthy or faint of heart cannot bring collective bargaining negotiations to a successful conclusion.

Suggested attributes of the successful negotiator include the following:

1. Sets clear objectives
2. Doesn't hurry
3. When in doubt, calls for a caucus
4. Is prepared
5. Remains flexible
6. Continually examines why the other party acts as it does
7. Respects face-saving tactics employed by the opposition
8. Attempts to ascertain the real interest of the other party by the priority proposed
9. Actively listens
10. Builds a reputation for being fair but firm
11. Controls emotions
12. Remembers to evaluate each bargaining move in relation to all others
13. Measures bargaining moves against ultimate objectives
14. Pays close attention to the wording of proposals
15. Remembers that compromise is the key to successful negotiations; understands that no party can afford to win or lose all
16. Tries to understand people
17. Considers the impact of present negotiations on the future relationship of the parties[3]

Other parties to negotiations   The negotiator on the union's side represents the members of the appropriate bargaining unit and that unit retains most, if not all, of the decision-making authority. Realistically, the unit is usually influenced by a smaller group of active union members. They form the visible core of the larger bargaining unit. For example, they may be the members who participate in a union baseball team or work on the night shift. They attend the necessary meetings and make the policy that negotiators follow at the bargaining table.

The bargaining process may also be influenced by outsiders. Another bargaining unit may have established an industry precedent in a recently negotiated contract settlement. For example, when one of the three big auto companies settles a contract, the other two companies usually follow with similar wage increases.

Preparation and Choice of Bargaining Items

Many unions affiliate with larger international unions. If a master agreement is negotiated by the international, it controls all but local concerns. Preparation for negotiations on a master agreement is virtually nonstop, and the next year's preparations begin as soon as a contract is signed. Preparation for contract negotiation on a local level, while not that extensive, is still necessary.

The two stages involving preparation and choice of bargaining items are analysis and planning. In the *analysis stage,* information is gathered and **bargaining items** are decided upon, narrowing the issues to a manageable size. The *planning stage* forces the parties to evaluate and set priorities, along with making realistic decisions about its demands. The parties' attention is focused on achievable goals. The parties are then ready for the third stage of the collective bargaining process, *negotiations,* to be discussed later in this chapter.

Analysis stage   It is a function of law and common practice to decide what items to include in the collective bargaining session. The National Labor Relations Act provides that bargaining shall include rates of pay, wages, hours of employment, or conditions of employment.[4] Under enforcement of the unfair labor practice charge of refusal to bargain, the National Labor Relations Board determines which subjects fall under the law. The board and later the courts recognized three categories of bargaining subjects: those to be discussed, those that may be discussed, and those that cannot be discussed.

In the early years of the act, the board based its decisions on what constituted bargaining subjects by evaluating the history of the agreements. However, to protect unions and the collective bargaining process in its formative stage, the board found the discussion of union recognition clauses compulsory. Hence, union shops, dues check-offs, and the treatment of employees after a strike became part of the collective bargaining discussion.

In a case-by-case method, the board began to establish the list of subjects to be covered. The Supreme Court, in 1958, decided the **Borg-Warner case**, which distinguished between the treatment accorded subjects determined by the board to be mandatory and those determined to be permissive. The Court noted that while the attitude of the parties is important in determining the good faith required by the

Exhibit 5.1 Bargaining items

Mandatory	Permissive	Illegal
Rates of pay	Indemnity bonds	Closed shop
Wages	Management rights as	Hot cargo clause
Hours of employment	to union affairs	Separation of em-
Overtime pay	Pension benefits of	ployees based
Shift differentials	retired employees	on race
Holidays	Scope of the bargain-	Discriminatory
Vacations	ing unit	treatment
Severance pay	Including supervisors	
Pensions	in the contract	
Insurance benefits	Additional parties to	
Profit sharing plans	the contract such as	
Christmas bonuses	the international	
Company housing,	union	
meals, and discounts	Use of union label	
Employee security	Settlement of unfair	
Job performance	labor changes	
Union security	Prices in cafeteria	
Management-union	Continuance of past	
relationship	contract	
	Membership of bar-	
	gaining team	
	Employment of strike	
	seekers	

act, the issues being discussed are also important.[5] It became a legal question as to whether a proposal was one the parties were obliged to discuss. Exhibit 5.1 delineates mandatory, permissive, and illegal subjects.

If the subject is *mandatory,* a party may insist on its inclusion and the other party cannot refuse to discuss it. However, while compelled to bargain in good faith, neither party is legally obligated to compromise its stated position on a mandatory subject, and may even push the bargaining situation to an impasse.

Subjects deemed mandatory by the National Labor Relations Board include those issues actually listed in the act: rates of pay, wages, hours of employment, and other conditions of employment. Also included are issues the NLRB considers related to the subjects listed in the act.

In recent years several issues critical to unions, such as liquidation of a business, sale of assets, major operation changes, discontinuation of a product line, partial plant closings, and plant relocations, have been ruled permissive rather than mandatory. Since neither party may pursue a permissive issue to impasse, seldom can concessions be gained over a permissive subject.[6] The U.S. Supreme Court in its *Fibreboard Paper Products Corporation* v. *NLRB*[7] decision held certain management issues to be permissive, including subcontracting work, commitment of capital to labor-saving machinery, liquidation of assets, or terminating a business. The Supreme Court has also held that such issues should be permissive because they focus on economic profitability, which is wholly apart from the employment relationship.[8] These decisions have had a profound impact on unions' ability to win concessions on such issues at the negotiating table or alter major decisions affecting union security.

The board has defined wages as "direct and immediate economic benefits, flowing from the employment relationship."[9] Included in the discussion of wages are hourly pay rates, overtime pay, piece rates, incentive plans, shift differentials, paid holidays and vacations, and severance pay. Other forms of compensation are also included by the NLRB under the wage category and are therefore considered mandatory; they include the following:

1. *Pensions and insurance benefits*   While employers considered pensions and insurance benefits as separate from wages, the NLRB considered them as payment for services rendered and found an inseparable nexus between employees' current compensation and future benefits. However, retirement and pension plans are mandatory subjects for *active* employees only, and not retired members.

2. *Profit-sharing plans*   Profit-sharing plans are also considered as payment and enhancement of economic benefit. Such plans are usually structured to increase benefits to employees when company profits go up.

3. *Christmas and other bonuses*   A one-time or performance bonus may be a mandatory subject. The board has devised a test to determine whether such a bonus is a gift or part of the employees' compensation. The decision is based on

    a.   The consistency or regularity of the payment
    b.   The uniformity of the amount of payment from bonus to bonus
    c.   The relationship between the amount of the bonus and the pay scale of the employee
    d.   The taxability of the payment as income
    e.   The financial condition and ability of the employer to give the bonus

The board will determine it is a gift if

    a.   The bonus has been awarded intermittently over a very few years
    b.   The amount of the bonus is not uniform from year to year
    c.   The amount is not tied to the employees' salary
    d.   The awarding of a bonus depends upon the present financial condition of the employer

4. *Stock purchase plans*   Employers contend that stock purchase plans are not employee benefits but are simply an incentive for the employee to invest in the company. The National Labor Relations Board rejects that argument and deems such plans are a form of bargainable compensation.

5. *Merit wage incentives*   While a company may consider merit increases management's prerogative, the NLRB has said that because merit raises involve the

formation and application of standards affecting all wages, they must be considered a mandatory bargaining subject.

6. *Company housing, meals, and discounts*   The inclusion of these in the list of mandatory subjects depends upon the situation. Such items would be mandatory if the job required living or eating on company-owned premises.

Provisions detailing daily and weekly work schedules and requirements for overtime premiums are found in virtually all contracts.[10] Specific start and stop times, lunch and rest periods, and other scheduling rules are included. While scheduling work is normally a management prerogative, any change from the hours specified in the contract, no matter how minimal, is considered an unfair labor practice, even if it does not affect the employee's pay.

The board has stated that the phrase "conditions of employment" refers to terms under which employment status is given or withdrawn rather than physical working conditions. Conditions must have a material and significant impact directly affecting the employment relationship. Four major areas include the following:

1. *Employment security*   This covers all aspects of hiring and firing and granting tenure. Hiring and probationary periods, seniority, job-bidding procedures, promotions, and transfers must all be bargained, except for the nondiscriminatory promotion of employees to supervisory positions. The order and manner of layoffs and recalls, issues surrounding the discharge and retirement of employees, and contracting out work normally performed by members of the bargaining unit are also mandatory. In some instances, plant closings and relocations must be bargained. While courts have said a company is not required to negotiate an economically motivated decision to close or relocate a plant, the effects of such an action must be bargained.

2. *Job performance*   The day-to-day relationship between employer and employee is a mandatory subject of bargaining, and includes absenteeism, work breaks, lunch periods, discipline, and dress codes. Although safety practices must be discussed, management may still have the final say. Decisions concerning workloads and the number of employees necessary for a task are considered mandatory.

3. *Union security*   The protection of the union's representation status is a mandatory subject for bargaining. Such protection requires a thirty-day grace period before an employee must join the union, discontinuance of a union shop according to majority vote, and a prohibition against discharge of an employee for nonmembership in a union for any reason other than failure to pay dues.

4. *Management-union relationships*   All principles governing the discharge of collective bargaining duties and enforcement of collective bargaining agreements, including grievance and arbitration procedures, are considered mandatory.

If the subject is ***permissive,*** a party must withdraw it from bargaining if the other party does not voluntarily agree to its inclusion in the discussion. Both parties must agree for permissive subjects to be bargained. Under this scheme, it is a per se violation of the act to insist upon such a discussion to impasse, as in Case 5.1. Examples of permissive subjects include performance or indemnity bonds which protect the employer from liabilities in the quality of the union's work, and management's right to have an impact upon the internal affairs of the union.

Subjects deemed *illegal* by the act or the NLRB may not be proposed for discussion, and even if agreed to by both parties, would not be enforced by any court. These include violations of public policy, otherwise unlawful issues, and items inconsistent with the principles of the National Labor Relations Act. A closed shop requiring union membership before an employee is hired, racial separation of employees, and discrimination against nonunion members are illegal bargaining subjects.

If in the future a portion of the contract becomes illegal under a state or federal law, the **separability clause** in the contract becomes effective. The separability clause usually states that any portion of a contract conflicting with state or federal law is declared null and void without affecting other provisions. The clause may provide for the renegotiation of the issue if desired by either party.

Sources of bargaining items   Unions generally introduce most new items to be discussed at a collective bargaining session. While management generally reacts to such proposals, management can also initiate new items for discussion.

Union negotiation teams solicit member input in formulating demands. This can be done at general union meetings, at meetings with union stewards, through questionnaires, or by a suggestion box. Often bargaining items are formulated through analysis of the types of grievances filed and from recent arbitration awards. Problems detected at a lower level are passed on to be included in the collective bargaining talks. Management will often add line supervisors' suggestions on working conditions to its economic positions during negotiations.

Both union and management can also look to external sources for bargaining items. Recent contracts within the same industry can give both parties ideas on realistic, attainable proposals. Often the overall economic condition of the nation and the particular industry limits or expands bargaining demands.

Information necessary to support proposals and counterproposals can be obtained from such sources as the U.S. Department of Labor (Bureau of Labor Statistics) and Federal Reserve System, which publish economic data. National organizations such as the National Labor Relations Board, the Federal Mediation and Conciliation Service, and the Federal Labor Relations Council are directly involved in collective bargaining and can contribute primary information. Publications of the Bureau of National Affairs, Commerce Clearing House, and Prentice-Hall show national trends in contract settlement for comparison with local proposals. Special interest groups representing both labor and management collect a wide variety of information to help in contract negotiations, and include the National Association of Manufacturers (NAM) and the AFL-CIO.

In addition to general sources, each party is entitled to certain types of information from the opposition. Under the duty to bargain in good faith, a union may demand relevant information from the employer in preparing wage demands.

Planning stage   Planning and preparation may be the most critical elements in successful negotiations. In general negotiators plan effectively by

1. *Anticipation*   Each side, through research and members' input, must correctly assess those issues critical to both sides. The general mood greatly affects the early stages of negotiations. The key issues for each side and the possibility of a strike or other actions should be anticipated and a response prepared. A response such as a detailed counterproposal or a package of several items can center the conflict on the issues rather than personal emotions.

2. *Realistic objectives*   Prior preparation on all items of interest can help avoid costly mistakes during heated and lengthy negotiations. Negotiators should prioritize all objectives and develop a settlement range. Logical trade-offs among items of interest can be analyzed and prepared.

3. *Strategy*   Each party must evaluate the opponent's current needs as well as its own, review the bargaining history between the two parties, and prepare an overall strategy for negotiations. Important aspects to consider include personalities of negotiators, current financial and political position of each party, and outside influences such as the economy, product sales, and public support of unions. Strategy formulation helps both sides develop realistic expectations of how negotiations will proceed and what the final agreement will be. For example, senior union employees may be most unhappy with the current pension program, but a significant increase in the pension formula would require costly increases for all future retirees. Thus, in developing its strategy, management could develop an economic package including alternative combinations of one-time lucrative early retirement options with pay increases loaded toward younger employees.

4. *Agenda*   Both parties should develop an agenda for discussing all items in a logical manner and incorporate this in the written ground rules. For example, after settling problems with the current contract's wording (which may have arisen through grievance), negotiators can exchange noneconomic proposals and settle as many as possible. They should follow this with exchange of economic proposals dealing with smaller cost items first, keeping on the table the highest priority economic and noneconomic items.

Expectations must be established at the same time priorities are set. Successful collective bargaining may be impossible if the highest priority of one party is an item the other party is unlikely to negotiate.

To establish realistic objectives, the party considers patterns and trends in contract settlements of other employers in the industry and the local community. In an economy where a 4 percent cost-of-living raise is almost universal, a request for 12 percent may be unrealistic. The parties also examine their current and past bargaining relationship, along with their relative strength. For example, if contract negotiations have already been concluded with other employers in the same industry and this employer always follows their lead, it may be unrealistic to expect major deviations.

However, it is just as important to create optimistic bargaining objectives. Perceived as "frosting on the cake," such goals are within the realm of possibility but may be more indicative of the skill of the negotiator and the success of the negotiation process.

The parties should also prepare to accept certain pessimistic objectives. While these objectives are resisted during negotiations, they provide the negotiators room to maneuver without feeling stifled, and should be recognized when setting priorities.

Negotiation Sessions

The rules of the collective bargaining session are set usually by the parties at the opening session. If the parties have a long-standing relationship, establishing procedures can be very routine. But when the collective bargaining process is relatively new or when the parties have had bad labor relations, setting procedures can be as difficult, and as important, as bargaining on the issues.

Ground rules   The parties decide where, when, how often, and how long to meet. These and other procedures are often agreed to in writing as **ground rules** for negotiations. Exactly what is included in the ground rules varies greatly according to the desires of the negotiators and the bargaining history of the two parties. The following are examples of ground rules:

1.   All negotiation sessions will commence on the time, date, and location heretofore agreed upon by the parties.

2.   The chief negotiator for the company and the chief negotiator for the union shall be the chief spokespersons for the respective parties' interests. However, others present may speak as required or called upon by the negotiators.

3.   Insofar as practical and reasonable, the data introduced by either party at negotiations shall be made available to the other party.

4.   If either the company or the union intends to add a new member to its respective bargaining committee, the party adding the new member will notify the other party.

5.   Proposals and counterproposals will be made on typed copies as reasonable, and will be signed and dated by the appropriate party. The parties shall simultaneously exchange initial noneconomic and economic proposals at the appropriate times.

6.   Individual items agreed to by both parties shall be signed and dated and removed from the table. Any attempt to reintroduce or discuss those items shall be viewed as a breach of good faith.

7.   The company's chief negotiator and the union's chief negotiator shall have the authority to agree in substance on contract language and provisions. However, any agreement is preliminary and contingent upon a final contract. All preliminary agreements made regarding individual contract provisions shall be initialed and dated by both chief negotiators.

8.   If mediation is agreed to by both parties, the mediator picked by the parties shall be agreeable to both.

Negotiating teams are established. Neither side may dictate the membership of the other's negotiating team, but rules may be established as to how many members are allowed on each side and as to their official roles, such as spokesperson, recording secretary, or doorkeeper, who makes sure only authorized persons attend the negotiations. Negotiating teams are often kept as small as possible to allow for productive discussion. Each side must have a designated leader who makes commitments for the respective parties. Traditionally, union negotiating teams can only agree to propose the contract to the membership for acceptance.

A bargaining agenda is set to establish exchange of initial proposals, the order of discussion of bargaining items, and, if possible, how long to continue with one item if agreement is not forthcoming. A stalemate in the early stages of bargaining can sour the process, making agreement impossible. The number and length of bargaining sessions may indicate a party's reluctance to bargain in good faith, as in Case 5.2. If feasible, the agenda lists less controversial issues first so an atmosphere of agreement is fostered.

Economic and noneconomic proposals are usually separated. If economic data can be agreed upon, economic issues are easier to resolve. Generally, economic issues are negotiated as a package to insure a balanced settlement. Agreement is more easily reached on individual noneconomic issues than on a package.

Usually a decision is made on how to keep records of the negotiations. An accurate record keeps both parties honest during negotiations and when the final contract is proposed. A single outline of items discussed, proposals made on these items, what was agreed to or where disagreement arose, is prepared by one party and initialed by the other.

The negotiation site has private space to allow for a caucus by either party. It is decided in the initial session what the caucus and adjournment rights of both parties are to be. Misunderstanding in this area can lead one or the other party to stage a needless walkout while a strategic retreat could have served as a positive catalyst to settlement. Finally, parties should decide early on the role of a mediator, if they intend to resort to one in case of an impasse.

Posturing   The atmosphere of a collective bargaining session depends upon the attitudes of the parties involved. Their attitudes are influenced by their prior relationships, the economic circumstances of the employer, the basic employer's attitude toward unionization, and the leadership of the union. The relationship of the employer to the local union's international may also be a factor.

Whatever the particular atmosphere, labor negotiations follow a common pattern. The initial working sessions are no more than monologues wherein both parties present their list of demands. Often these sessions are open to the public, or at least well publicized to satisfy the negotiators' constituencies that proceedings are on the right course. The laundry list proposed by the parties purposefully includes bargaining items that can, and will, be bargained away during the negotiations with varying degrees of reluctance. This **posturing** stage is very important. It allows a certain amount of face-saving to the party who comes to the bargaining table with the least amount of bargaining power.

Within the posturing of negotiations, several common aspects of bargaining will likely rise and should be anticipated by the participants:

1. *Interdependence*   The conflict aspect of negotiations causes tempers to rise as parties become emotionally involved. However, both sides need to re-

member their goals are interdependent. Neither side can achieve success without the other.[11]

2. *Concealment*   During negotiations parties often conceal their real goals and objectives from the other side to enhance their opportunity for the best possible settlement. This is a characteristic of the negotiation process and should be expected. Every negotiator must decide how open and honest to be in communicating her needs and preferences. If a negotiator is completely open and honest, she often will settle for less than if she conceals her goals and fights harder for a better settlement. However, if a negotiator is completely deceptive about her goals, the talks may never move in the direction of a settlement. This dilemma of trust poses a key problem for negotiators: first discussions may reveal little of their true needs, only opening up in an effort to move discussions forward. As both sides begin to trust each other, this process becomes easier.[12]

3. *Packaging items*   It is difficult to achieve an agreement on all issues at one time. As many as fifty economic and noneconomic issues may be involved during negotiations; if all are left on the table at the same time, the process may become unwieldy. Instead, a few items may be packaged together, agreed to, and removed from further discussion, allowing both sides to achieve their goal on one or more items and thus establish trust in the process. The number of unresolved issues decreases as more packages are agreed to, moving negotiations toward completion. Packaging may at least narrow the list of disputed items to the high-priority issues for each side. The ground rules may require each chief negotiator to "sign off" on a package, signing and dating a written counterproposal detailing the items agreed to, thus removing them from further discussions.

4. *Throw-away items*   Negotiators, in their list of initial demands, may include items of no real value to their side, thus providing items to trade in exchange for others of high priority to their side. Throw-aways can be the basis of a successful bluff if the other side believes it has won a concession on an important item. While the throw-away items may have real value, they simply are not of high priority in comparison to other issues. A throw-away item for one side may, in fact, be a high-priority item for the other side.

When one side presents several demands during the initial session, only a few of which are of high priority, the tactic may be a "snow job." The strategy is to present many items that the other side must successfully research and on which they must develop proposals. In the process, the few items of real importance are "lost in the snow" or disguised.[13]

5. *Caucusing*   Much of the negotiating time is spent in the two parties meeting separately. After a proposal or counterproposal is received, a team usually asks for a caucus. There they can openly discuss the merits of the proposal and their willingness to accept it, or formulate a counterproposal. A major part of the strategy may be *not* to reveal at the table how the party feels about a proposal received from the other side. Even an obviously desirable proposal may lead to a caucus where the team accepts the proposal without emotion. An expression of happiness over one item may lead the other side to believe they need not give on further items. Caucusing is also used for resolving disagreement among members of the same team and gathering additional information about unanticipated or costly proposals.

6. *Flexibility*   The successful negotiation process requires the exchange of many proposals and counterproposals. Every proposal received should be studied and responded to by acceptance or a counter offer. Immediate rejection of a proposal infers inflexibility and a response of "we will only accept our position." This angers the other side and may in fact be bad faith bargaining. Also, most proposals must be carefully evaluated before their merits can be accurately estimated.

7. *Compromise*   The key to successful negotiations is compromise by both parties. If either side believes they will achieve every goal, then most likely no settlement will be reached. Instead, both parties must realize their goals are in direct conflict—if one side gains on an issue then the other side loses. If one side loses on too many issues, they may not sign the agreement, or if forced to sign then they certainly will be looking to "even the score" during the next round of negotiations.

At the end of most negotiations, spokespersons for each side are likely to say to the public, "We achieved the best contract we could—we wish we could have done better." Both sides will list issues they believe they won, and those where they desired something different. Since both sides achieved some of their goals, their negotiators "save face" with those they represent. Neither side declares themselves or the other side winners or losers but rather "tough negotiators."

Agreement   After the posturing, the real working sessions begin. Agreements are often made almost immediately on less important items. Usually these are non-economic items that both parties wish to resolve. When the bargaining on economic issues begins, the parties tend to back away from item agreement and look to total packaging. During negotiations, changing proposals must be analyzed for their cost. Until the total economic agreement is seen, neither party can be sure of its position. Negotiators can use different approaches to reach an actual agreement. Some examples follow.

1.   The parties can separate economic and noneconomic issues and agree on the noneconomic issues first. Changes improving grievance procedures, work rules, job evaluations, and similar items are often sought by both parties and can be more readily agreed to than issues involving costs and benefits.

2.   The parties can separate and discuss economic and noneconomic issues. Items can then be traded, with each side winning one item and giving up another until all the issues have been resolved.

3.   The parties can discuss each economic and noneconomic issue separately but may not agree to anything until all items are agreed upon. This total packaging approach, while perhaps more difficult, allows both parties the opportunity to evaluate the entire collective bargaining agreement before making a commitment.

Point of crisis   Finally, negotiators reach a decision. Once all of the proposals and counterproposals are on the table, the parties either agree or stop talking. If agreement cannot be reached, this may be the point of crisis. Various techniques such as mediation and arbitration are available to bring the parties back to agreement. Job actions such as strikes and lockouts, while receiving a great deal of publicity, are seldom used to resolve contract disputes. Ninety-five percent of all contracts are resolved without a job action.[14]

Contract   Once agreement has been reached, the contract is written. The contract language is very important, and should accurately state the parties' agreement, since they are expected to abide by it through its duration. Many grievance and arbitration actions stem from ambiguous contract language; the parties may even disagree on whether the language reflects what they negotiated.

The four areas most contracts cover are union security and management rights, the wage and effort bargain, individual security, and contract administration.

Bargaining Techniques

Labor and management meet across a negotiating table because of the National Labor Relations Act. The act requires that the parties bargain in good faith but provides that neither party has to agree to any particular proposal as long as it continues to bargain in good faith. Thus the act establishes the boundaries of the negotiation process but leaves the internal workings to the parties involved.

Over the years, the bargaining process has changed from an adversarial confrontation between the forces of capitalist and worker into a stylized ritual between the representatives of management and labor. Collective bargaining may be nothing but a process by which the negotiators seek to make the main terms of the agreement, which are already decided, acceptable to the parties.

Whether or not that observation is correct, collective bargaining has certainly changed from mere confrontation to a process by which labor and management sincerely attempt to resolve conflicting interests. Respect for the process, however, does not eliminate the conflict. The resolution of this conflict has been analyzed in numerous ways.

Labor negotiation has often been inaccurately compared to playing games. Games have a definite set of values and rules so parties know when they are winning and, more importantly, losing. There are no rules in negotiation except for those set by the parties, and the rules are often a part of the negotiation itself. The most important difference, however, is that negotiation is the art of compromise, assuring that neither party wins or loses everything.

Studies of the collective bargaining process seem to separate styles of bargaining into three categories. Styles focus on the parties involved (psychological or behavioral), on the issues to be decided (economic or analytical), and on the relative bargaining power of the parties (game theory or pressure bargaining).[15] Each approach has its strengths and weaknesses.

To focus on the parties making the decisions is perhaps the most realistic approach since the bargaining process is only as successful as the people who carry it out. However, analysis of the collective bargaining process through the relationship of the parties assumes a rational negotiator who compares benefits with the costs of a particular course of action and undertakes that course only when benefits exceed cost. It also assumes the negotiator is in total control, the parties have good information available, and all their assumptions are correct.

A study of collective bargaining assessing only the issues discussed can be comforting because of its simplicity. For example, comparing the cost of a strike for the employer and employee to arrive at each party's breaking point would seem an exact science. Still, this approach lacks an understanding of the emotions and knowledge of the parties involved.

A study of collective bargaining focusing exclusively on the relative bargaining power of the parties can overlook the personalities and the strengths or weaknesses of their positions on the issues. The focus is on muscle and how it is used to control the process.

The collective bargaining process is in reality a combination of the three styles. The parties interact on the issues using whatever advantage they have to achieve their goals. The key to successful bargaining lies in flexibility and in understanding and controlling the process. The following approaches are written in a "how-to" style, designed as a starting point for understanding the collective bargaining process.

Distributive Bargaining

Two parties are involved in distributive bargaining when they view the negotiations as a "win-lose" situation—the goals of one party are in direct conflict with those of the other party. Thus, any positive change in the current status of the issue causes a loss for the other side. Each party strives to bargain for a maximum share of the limited resources.[16]

In collective bargaining both sides may view the process as distributive bargaining. The limited resources include the monetary assets of the firm, which can be used for a variety of purposes—new equipment or machinery, dividend payments, higher wages, and so on. Another limited resource would be unfilled positions, so deciding who is promoted or transferred can be the subject of distributive bargaining. Other noneconomic issues, such as union security, employee grievances, and plant rules, can also be included. Both labor and management view any positive change from the current contract as something to be gained at the negotiation table and as a loss to the other party.

The distributive bargaining process can best be explained by five key elements:

1. *Target point*   The optimal goal or objective a negotiator sets for the issue, the target point, is the point at which the negotiator would most prefer to conclude negotiations.

2. *Resistance point*   The resistance point is maximum or minimum beyond which the negotiator will not accept a proposal. This is the negotiator's bottom line.

3. *Initial offer*   This is the first number or offer the negotiator presents as a written formal proposal.

4. *Settlement range*   The difference between the resistance points of labor and management is the range in which actual bargaining occurs, because anything outside the range will be quickly rejected by one party.

5. *Settlement point*   The heart of negotiations is the process of reaching agreement on one point within the settlement range, the settlement point. The

Exhibit 5.2   Distributive bargaining negotiation: First-year base wage increase (percentage)

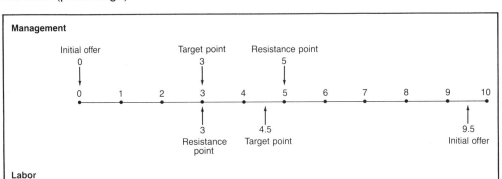

objective of both parties is to achieve a settlement point as close as possible to their target point.[17]

An example of the distributive bargaining process is illustrated in Exhibit 5.2. First both sides develop and keep confidential their target and resistance points. Labor has surveyed its members, reviewed similar contracts recently negotiated, and estimated the company's financial situation. Within a generally favorable economic package the negotiators set 4.5 percent as their target point but are willing to consider any offer above 3 percent, the resistance point, if the total package contains other economic benefits. They honestly believe the members would vote against any contract with less than a 3 percent increase, because inflation since the last negotiation has averaged 4 percent and recent contracts in the industry have included raises between 3 and 5 percent. Management negotiators set their target point at 3 percent, the lowest increase negotiated by any of their competitors. The company president has authorized them to accept an offer of up to 5 percent, the resistance point, if the total economic package is within a certain dollar amount.

Next, both sides choose their initial offers. Management decides a proposed wage giveback (decrease in base wage) might be considered bad faith bargaining since the company is in a reasonably good financial condition, so they initially offer a 0 percent increase, the lowest possible given the circumstances. Labor knows that no similar union has received more than 6 percent and therefore feels 9.5 percent (just under double digits) is as high an initial offer as can be made within the context of good faith bargaining. Both sides realize their initial offers must be less (greater) than their target point to allow room for negotiation "give and take" while also staying within what the other side would consider a reasonable and good faith offer. At the same time, both sides realize the other side's initial offer has left them room to negotiate and is not their last, best, or final offer.

Negotiations between the two sides now center on the 0–9.5 percent range. Both sides begin trying to convince the other to move from this initial offer. Neither side knows the target or resistance points of the other side. However, both sides will, through bargaining table discussion, begin to estimate the target and resistance points of the other side to determine if a settlement range exists and therefore a settlement point can be found. At the same time, each side strives to convince the other of the validity of their position. By presenting factual information, such as company records, copies of recent contracts, industry data, as well as persuasive information, such as employee survey data, negotiators hope to influence the perceptions of the party. Management may try to convince labor that to remain competitive and avoid layoffs, the company cannot afford an expensive settlement and is willing to take a strike if necessary. Labor may try to convince management of the members' determination to negotiate a high increase and their willingness to put on a successful strike.

Eventually, both sides believe they know, indirectly or directly, the other side's resistance point. For example, management might state, "We will seriously consider an offer under 5 percent if the total package is right," or labor might indicate, "Our members know no other local has settled for less than 3 percent." Now the negotiations center on the settlement range, both sides realizing there are many possible settlement points within the range.

Now the "hard" bargaining begins. Within the two-percent settlement range, each side carefully proposes a settlement point that, especially when wages are considered, may include other economic items in a package. And, most important, each negotiator is careful to propose only a settlement that he is prepared to accept. Within this range any offer might be accepted if both sides have a settlement point. Once proposed and accepted, it is too late to "hold out for a little more."

The settlement point is finally reached when one side achieves its target point, or both are willing to accept something less than their target points but within the settlement range. Factors such as the arguments of the other side, the total package, fatigue, or belief that "this is the best we can do," may influence negotiators to accept a settlement less than their target point.

Principled Negotiations

A process called **principled negotiations** was developed by the Harvard Negotiations Project and published in a book titled *Getting To Yes.* The essential element of the process is to be "hard on the merits, soft on the people."[18] The goal is to decide the issues presented at the negotiating table on their merits rather than through the traditional haggling process that focuses on what each side says it will or will not do. Substituting principled negotiations for the traditional pressure bargaining will theoretically result in a wiser agreement through a more efficient process improving the relationship of the parties.

The key element in principled negotiations is to separate the people from the problem. This insures a focus on interests, not positions; it generates a variety of possible options before a decision on a given position is made; and it insists that the result of the bargaining is based on some objective standard.

People Under the principled negotiation model, the first objective is to *separate the people from the problem.* This is accomplished by accepting the human element involved in negotiations. An understanding of the attitudes and perceptions of the parties is vital, along with the realization that not *what* is true but what the parties *believe* to be true is important. Neither party can convince the other of the legitimacy of its position without understanding the other party's perception of that position. Therefore, the first task of a negotiator is to understand the other party's perception. It is best to discuss these perceptions openly and to understand their importance to both of the parties. For example, during hard economic times, a union's noneconomic demands for job security may be more important to the union than management perceives. And yet if management can understand that importance, it should be easier to reach a mutually satisfactory agreement.

Perceptions can be changed. Consistent with the old adage, "actions speak louder than words," behavior inconsistent with the other party's perception can help change that perception. Unions expect management to approach the bargaining table determined to maintain the status quo. Thus, if management were to present original proposals to improve employee performance and so give an employee more job satisfaction, the union's perception of management might change.

Once a party's attitude is understood but cannot be changed, a proposal couched in terms consistent with that attitude may lead to agreement. The compromises involved in negotiation often mean a loss to one party or the other. To enable the party not to perceive such a compromise as a loss may successfully separate the person from the problem.

Emotion strongly affects the collective bargaining process. Both parties come to the negotiating process with personal feelings: there may be strong negative feeling generated by a historically bad labor climate, or a strong positive feeling of power may prevail. Recognize the emotions; allow their expression and let the parties express their pent-up frustrations. Releasing steam may defuse an otherwise explosive situation.

Finally, negotiating parties must learn to communicate.[19] Too often they are not really trying to converse, but are simply going through the motions. To communicate effectively a party must first actively listen and acknowledge what is being said. If necessary, a party should repeat in its own words what the other party has said to insure understanding. When speaking, a party should remember the goal is to persuade. Dialogue should be simple, with each side expressing its own position, then silence so the parties can digest what was said.

People can also be prevented from becoming a problem by building a working relationship before negotiations begin. A not-so-subtle tactic is mixing the seating of the two teams at a negotiating session. This increases the possibility that the parties will attack the problem rather than each other.

Interests   *Attacking the problem* is the second objective of principled bargaining. The parties are to focus on interests, not positions. Generally, parties come to the negotiating table with a laundry list of demands. Since a party has invested time, energy, and thought in that list, there is a strong tendency to defend it no matter how absurd it may be.

In principled negotiations, the parties are to develop an understanding of their real desires, concerns, and interests, rather than to simply list demands. The achievement of those interests is left for future resolution. Both sides have multiple interests and if those interests can be identified without the parties hardening into a particular position, conflict is eliminated.

Options   Once interests are identified, the third objective is for both parties to *seek as many options as possible in solving their conflicting interests.* More often than not, the interests of both parties can be satisfied in numerous ways. If creative thinking is applied, interests can overlap, allowing both parties to reach a successful compromise.

In order to seek numerous options, both parties must be willing to accept that there *is* more than one right answer. In seeking new solutions, a party must separate the acts of inventing and judging options. A proposal does not make a hard-and-fast position.

Options must be broadened. The belief that one party's gain will always result in the other party's loss often prevents successful bargaining. Therefore, options must be presented so both parties are allowed some advantage. When possible, identify interests that the parties share. For example, underlying every relationship between employer and employee is a shared interest in the health of the employer's industry; this fundamental interest must be present at the negotiating table. A creative negotiator will find ways to identify and explore shared interests, even as conflicting interests are negotiated.

Objective criteria   The fourth objective in principled negotiating is to have the *validity of each party's proposals judged by objective criteria.* For example, the parties could agree to ask for expert advice when discussing technological changes that might affect workers' jobs. Working together to understand the expert's advice can more easily lead to agreement. This enables either party to criticize the other party's proposal or to defend its own without destroying the relationship. It puts the parties in side-by-side negotiations against an objective third party, the criteria, instead of in a head-to-head confrontation. Agreement becomes easier when the basis of the agreement is recognized criteria.

Obviously, principled negotiation has its negative aspects. Realistically, parties in a negotiation do not often have equal bargaining power and so the temptation to engage in pressure bargaining may be strong. A party can try to keep the negotiations in a principled negotiations model by refusing to participate in pressure bargaining. Real communication is possible if the parties focus on the issues and resist reacting to attacks. Attacks on a position can be treated as an attack on the problem; the counterattack can then be limited to reasoned questions or criticisms on the issue involved.

Collective Bargaining by Objectives

Another method proposed as an alternative to pressure bargaining is **collective bargaining by objectives** (CBO). CBO is an adaptation of management by objectives (MBO) techniques to the collective bargaining process. In his book, *Collective Bargaining by Objectives,* Reed C. Richardson proposes a framework for negotiators in accomplishing the common, ordinary tasks involved in collective bargaining.[20]

Exhibit 5.3 contains the suggested outline to prepare for the collective bargaining process. Under this model, the subjects to be discussed at the bargaining table

Exhibit 5.3 Collective bargaining by objectives

Bargaining Items[a]	Priorities[b]	Range of Bargaining Objectives			Initial Bargaining Position[c]	Evaluation Results		
		Pessimistic	Realistic	Optimistic		P	R	O
Financial:								
Holidays	8	8 days	7 days	6 days	6 days	X		
Wages	1	10¢ first year; 10¢ second year	5¢ first year; 10¢ second year	5¢ first year; 10¢ second year	12¢ over three years		X	
Nonfinancial:								
Union security	12	Union shop	Modified union shop	Agency shop	Agency shop			X
Probationary period	20	30 days	60 days	90 days	120 days		X	

[a]Classify items in two groups: Financial and nonfinancial.
[b]Relative priority of each bargaining item to all bargaining items.
[c]Actual visible position taken at opening of negotiation (union initial proposal or company response or counteroffer)

Source: Reed C. Richardson, *Collective Bargaining by Objectives: A Positive Approach* (Englewood Cliffs, N.J.: Prentice-Hall, 1977), p. 151. Copyright © 1977, reprinted by permission of Prentice-Hall, Inc.

are listed in the first column. In the second column, the party rates the items, establishing priorities. The next three columns, entitled Range of Bargaining Objectives, enable the party to objectively evaluate the strength of a particular demand. The range of bargaining objectives include what the party would like to get (optimistic); what the party believes it will get (realistic); and what the party will accept (pessimistic). The initial bargaining position is stated in the sixth column, leaving the last three columns to record the results of the collective bargaining process.[21]

This exercise introduces discipline and provides a system for the negotiator's actions. Richardson lists the advantages of CBO as follows:

1. While structuring the approach to collective bargaining negotiations, the objectives approach is not at the expense of the flexibility so necessary to the give-and-take of negotiations.
2. It gives the negotiating team a real sense of direction and tangible goals (objectives) by which team members may measure their progress during negotiations.
3. It provides a more meaningful basis for data preparation, because positions and goals are specifically identified.
4. The range of bargaining objectives is in reality a settlement area toward which the negotiating team works, rather than the range so often described by writers of the field, whose minimum and maximum represent conflict or breakdown. The latter introduces negativism into the approach of the bargaining team, whereas the objectives approach effects a positive tone and thrust.
5. The team has a ready-reference, easy-to-scan blueprint that provides a confidential guide to strategy and tactics for all cost and noncost bargaining items, individually and/or collectively.

6. The identification of not just one goal but a range of possible settlement goals on each bargaining item requires by its very nature a more detailed and careful analysis.
7. Limiting the objectives approach to methodology makes it equally applicable and useful to private-sector bargaining, public-sector bargaining, or, for that matter, any type of bargaining situation.
8. Nothing is introduced into the methodology that is foreign to the normal bargaining situation.
9. It provides a better means of evaluating past negotiations as a useful experience base from which to launch a more effective plan for the next round of negotiations.
10. It may be used equally well as an effective tool for actual negotiations or as a stimulation device to train negotiators.
11. It provides (a) the parties individually with a safe and effective mechanism (agreed-upon settlement range) for delegating authority to their bargaining teams, and (b) a built-in means of establishing a rewards system for successful negotiations.

Source: Reed C. Richardson, *Collective Bargaining by Objectives: A Positive Approach* (Englewood Cliffs, N.J.: Prentice-Hall, 1977) pp. 109–10. Copyright © 1977, reprinted by permission of Prentice-Hall, Inc.

Collective bargaining by objectives demands that the parties make certain assumptions, and based on those assumptions, set priorities and establish an acceptable range of agreement prior to the beginning of the negotiation process. While stressing a rational and positive approach, this method recognizes the essentially adversarial nature of collective bargaining.

By establishing priorities, a party identifies those items it can bargain away and those having little or no room for compromise. Understanding priorities, therefore, allows the party to plan its strategy before the heat of negotiations so actions are based on real goals and values and not on emotions. Clearly delineating the objectives also puts the party in a position of confidence and certainty aimed at eliminating irrational actions during the negotiating process. The structural approach to priorities and the range of objectives allows for more complete delegation of authority to the bargaining team.

Certain guidelines must be followed in using CBO. The confidentiality of the information concerning priorities and the range of objectives must be preserved. As the basis for strategy and compromise, it becomes useless if the other party becomes aware of it. Also, this model does not include strike or lockout considerations. According to Richardson, "The objectives approach, while not ignoring pressure tactics, is based primarily on the achievement of goals through sound preparation and a careful, systematic approach to negotiation."[22]

Pressure Bargaining

"Power is the main thing unions and collective bargaining are all about."[23] An understanding of the use of pressure during labor negotiations is necessary in any study of collective bargaining.

The bargaining power model assumes that settlement in the collective bargaining process is determined by the relative bargaining power of each party. Simply stated, if it costs more to disagree than to agree, the party *will* agree. It is therefore an objective during collective bargaining to determine the costs associated with negotiations. Subsequent chapters discuss how to estimate costs for various contract proposals and provisions. However, the cost of agreeing or disagreeing *during* the collective bargaining process can be quite different.

The ultimate test of strength in the negotiating process is the union's ability to strike and the company's ability to take a strike. Before such action is undertaken, both sides either formally or by instinct, decide on a range within which settlement can be achieved. If either party refuses to enter that range, pressure must be applied.

In the pressure bargaining model, as with any model for collective bargaining, the parties must make sound assumptions. Miscalculations of the target point can lead to costly and futile actions.

Even under the pressure bargaining model, certain techniques lessen the chance of confrontation.

1. Use a bargaining book to record an accurate log of discussion, making areas of agreement and disagreement readily apparent.
2. Establish a habit of agreeing by beginning in the areas of common agreement and proceeding to the more controversial issues.
3. Present the other party with multiple choices, giving the other party an opportunity to select the least objectionable.
4. Try to keep bargaining sessions issue centered rather than people centered.
5. Judiciously use subcommittees and caucus times to defuse heated situations.[24]

Impasse

No matter what method of negotiations is followed, the parties at some point must agree or face an **impasse**. There are many reasons why negotiations could result in an impasse. The most obvious is that the interests of the two parties have not been reconciled. Another reason is that one party has no real intention of settling. Their overall strategy might include going to an impasse to show how inflexible the other party is. Also, during **pressure bargaining**, a strategic impasse may appear necessary to move the two parties closer together, and a genuine impasse results by simply miscalculating how close the parties really are.

Both parties have numerous options when an impasse occurs. One option is third-party intervention such as mediation or fact finding that could keep union negotiations open and workers on the job. Both sides may agree to continue the old contract on a day-to-day basis, maintaining wage and benefit levels, and preventing a strike or lockout. Or, union members can continue to work without a contract, taking whatever benefits the employer hands them. The employer can continue benefits at the previous contract level, increase them, or theoretically decrease benefits. The last usually indicates negotiating in bad faith. Another option is a lockout staged by an employer: he or she withholds employment to resist worker demands or gain concessions. Still another option is a strike called by a union.

Usually economic pressures during negotiations are initiated by the employees, because the union's goal in contract negotiations is to increase benefits while management's goal is to maintain the status quo or gain concessions.

A strike, however, may be called and/or endured for reasons other than a genuine inability to agree. One party may have merely miscalculated the breaking point of the opposition and increased a demand or refused a request once too often. Errors in strategy or in the interpersonal relations of the negotiator could preclude an opportunity for compromise. Management may want to liquidate surplus inventory while production is stopped by a strike. Union leaders may want to consolidate workers' support for their leadership, proving that a future strike threat has to be respected. Union leaders may feel the need for union solidarity that can be fostered only by a picket line. And often a strike is needed to vent member frustration over an inevitable but unsatisfactory contract settlement.[25]

An impasse may result after the negotiation teams have reached a tentative settlement and union membership rejects the contract. Such rejection may stem from a misjudgment of membership wishes by union officials or an inability to sell the agreement. One author contends, however, that rejection by the membership of a contract proposal is a strategy sometimes used by union leaders to increase the final settlement. This belief is supported by the fact that a small percentage of contracts are rejected if recommended by all or a majority of the negotiating team.[26]

Calling a Strike

Whatever the reason for an impasse, a decision to strike is not made lightly. In many instances the union negotiating team has called for a strike vote early in the negotiating process to prove its bargaining power when it becomes necessary to apply pressure. While such a vote strengthens the negotiator's hand, it needs to be carefully worked so that a strike deadline is not imposed, thereby tying the negotiator's hands. Slow-moving negotiations could become deadlocked; the deadline could destroy the negotiating atmosphere.

A union must weigh the cost of a strike against the probable benefit. A strike means loss of wages when wages may be quite high after years of successful union negotiations. Strike benefits also can be a drain on union funds. Workers risk losing their jobs, and even if they return to work, a strike can damage or destroy a good relationship with the employer. In addition, a union risks the loss of public sympathy with a strike. The success or failure of previous strikes and the availability of other jobs must also be considered.

Management's ability to withstand a strike depends upon the length of the strike, the type of business, and the preparation made.[27] Diminished profits must be anticipated even as operating costs continue; shutdown and reopening could increase those costs. A permanent loss of regular customers, as well as debasement of its public image, must also be considered.

Outside support may be found for both sides of a labor dispute. Striking workers may be eligible for such public assistance as food stamps and Aid to Families with Dependent Children (AFDC), as well as union strike benefits. Mutual Aid Pacts (MAP) or strike insurance may enable a company to recoup lost profits. However, such aid may only prolong a strike by eliminating the dollar incentive for settlement.

Empirical research about the possible causes of strikes has produced conflicting conclusions. To date, a model of the collective bargaining process accurately predicting or explaining strikes in the United States has not been produced.[28] Perhaps the causes are too numerous and unpredictable to be easily explained. Some research has shown that the state of the economy and political forces in labor relations are significant predictors of strike activity. Thus when negotiators believe that these factors are in their favor they are more likely to call a strike. These predictors are limited in their usefulness because they do not account for the specific factors involved in each individual strike decision.[29] Other studies have shown that strikes are more likely to occur when either management or labor fails to correctly estimate the level of interest in critical factors of the other party.[30] Management, for example, may underestimate the union members' concern over job security and the need for retraining rights or their perceived erosion of real wages due to inflation. Labor may not correctly estimate management's perceived need to adhere to a certain product-pricing policy or pressures from non-union or foreign market competition.

The cost of a strike has also been shown to affect the likelihood and the length of a strike. The employer considers costs such as loss of output, overtime costs to fill back orders, and the possible short-term and long-term effect on consumers and therefore marketshare. Some consumers may temporarily change to other products or supplies due to a strike. Then, due to their satisfaction with the new product or service or as an expression of dissatisfaction with the striking company, never return as customers. Profits and losses, increased legal and associated fees, and public image are also of concern to employers. The workers are primarily concerned with their loss of income during a strike. Union strike funds and government assistance seldom provide income equal to their previous take-home pay. Also to be carefully considered is the possible permanent loss of their jobs due to the eventual shutdown of the company or replacement by strikebreakers. Both sides consider their own strike costs in comparison to possible negotiation gains resulting from a strike. If the strike costs for the two parties are obviously unequal, that inequality translates into bargaining power for the side facing lower costs.[31]

A study of 1,050 negotiations in the United States between 1971 and 1980 revealed other possible strike determinants. Several factors were found to significantly affect the likelihood of a strike: (1) the proportion of males in the workforce, (2) product demand in the marketplace, (3) size of bargaining unit, (4) union density in the industry, and (5) the extent to which wages kept pace with inflation over the prior contract. Unions were more likely to strike when they contained more male members, product demand was high, the bargaining unit was large and located in a union-dominated industry, and wages had not kept pace with inflation.[32]

Types of Strikes

Economic weapons such as a strike are necessary to the collective bargaining process. Many such actions are protected under the National Labor Relations Act. The *primary strike,* one between an employer and employee, is analyzed later in this chapter. Chapter 9 will discuss the use of secondary economic pressure activities. To be protected under the act, a labor dispute must exist between the striking employees and their employer.

The act recognizes and handles two types of strikes differently. An **economic strike** is called to effect the economic settlement of a contract under negotiation. An **unfair labor practice strike** is called to protest an employer's violation of the National Labor Relations Act. For example, if a union member is fired for union activities, workers could stage a strike until the discriminatory practice is remedied.

Under either strike action the worker retains her status as an employee and thereby remains under the protection of the National Labor Relations Act. The worker's right to reinstatement after a strike will depend upon the type of strike. After an economic strike the employee is not entitled to reinstatement if the employer filled the job during the strike with a permanent employee. However, as demonstrated in Case 5.3, if the job has not been filled or becomes vacant when a replacement leaves, it can be reclaimed by the worker. Employees are entitled to reinstatement after an unfair labor practice strike even if the employer has filled their positions. Strike misconduct by the employee in either case can disqualify the worker from reinstatement.

A strike beginning as an economic strike may become an unfair labor practice strike if the union can prove that an employer is refusing to bargain in good faith. It is obviously to the union's advantage to do so, as it is to management's advantage to keep the strike an economic strike by continuing to negotiate in good faith. Management then has the option to hire replacement workers during the strike and keep the plant open, thereby lessening any adverse input caused by the strike. At the end of the strike the replacement workers can be retained, and the employer may have upgraded the work force with minimal disruption.[33]

All strikes, however, such as those undertaken by unlawful means or purposes, are not legal, and employees can be fired. Unlawful means of conducting a strike include

1. *Sit-down strike,* a takeover of the employer's property. This action is seen as a violation of the owner's property rights.
2. *Wildcat strike,* an economic strike conducted by a minority of the workers without the approval of the union, and in violation of a no-strike clause in an existing contract. While courts try to discourage such actions to insure the continued credibility of the union, these strikes may be sanctioned if actually called to protect one of the union's aims.[34]
3. *Violent activity,* removing any party who participates in the violence from the protection of the act.
4. *Partial strike,* including various types of job actions such as a work slowdown, refusal to work overtime, or an organized effort to have all workers call in sick. This action is seen as a violation of the owner's property rights. In the absence of an absolute strike, the employer cannot replace the workers to keep the operation going although the employer continues to be responsible for the worker's wages.

The National Labor Relations Act requires that a union desiring to terminate or modify an existing contract may not strike for sixty days after giving written notice to the employer or before the termination date of the contract, whichever occurs later. Also, the appropriate federal and state mediation agencies must be notified within thirty days. Any strike held during the sixty-day period is unlawful.

The National Labor Relations Act outlaws some consequences that workers might strike for. The following are unlawful ends that make a strike illegal:

1. *Jurisdictional strike,* called because two unions are in dispute as to whose workers deserve the work. For example, an electrical union could strike a construction site in protest of laborers being used to unload electrical supplies.

2. *Featherbedding strike,* when a union tries to pressure the employer to make work for union members through the limitation of production, the amount of work to be performed, or other make-work arrangements.

3. *Recognitional strike,* when a strike is called to gain recognition for another union if a certified union already represents employees.[35]

Picketing

The use of picket lines during a strike varies according to the type of union involved. A craft union strike generally uses only two or three pickets. The purpose of the picket is simply to inform other craft union members that a strike is in progress. Because craft union workers are skilled laborers, they cannot easily be replaced by workers who will not honor a picket line. Craft unions may employ larger picketing groups when protesting the use of a nonunion contractor.

An industrial union strike, however, often requires an active and large picket line to discourage unskilled laborers from keeping the production lines in operation. Mass picketing generally takes place at least at the start of a strike to persuade union members to join the strike and to keep strikebreakers away.

An employer may respond to mass picketing by obtaining a court injunction against the union to refrain from certain activities. An injunction, usually in the form of a temporary restraining order, is possible if the strike activities have included incidents of violence, personal injury, or damage to property. In such cases, the court can order specific restraints on the union's use of pickets—limiting, for instance, their number and location.[36]

Lockout

Although more infrequent, labor disputes may arise from an employer **lockout**. The employer may withhold employment to resist union demands or actually to force concessions from the union. The lockout can be accomplished by layoffs, shutting down, or bringing in nonunion workers. The employer again must measure the same factors involved in withstanding a strike when deciding to lock out the employees: loss of profits, cost of continued operations, possible loss of customers, and the effect on future labor negotiations.

Employer lockouts can be in violation of the National Labor Relations Act as an unfair labor practice if they are invoked to prevent unionization or to preclude collective bargaining before it begins.

Courts have supported both defensive and offensive employer lockouts under the Taft-Hartley Amendments. In *defensive* actions, employers are justified in a lockout if a threatened strike caused unusual economic loss or operational difficulties. When engaging in multiemployer bargaining, a strike against one employer can justify a lockout by the others to preserve the integrity of the multiemployer bargaining unit. *Offensive* economic lockouts have been justified after an impasse has developed during collective bargaining negotiation, or if the lockout was used to pressure employees to end the labor dispute on grounds favorable to the employer. The courts reasoned that an economic strike by employees seeks the same end and therefore the lockout is protected.[37]

No-Strike, No-Lockout Provisions

Most agreements contain provisions restricting the union's ability to call a strike and management's ability to stage a lockout. Usually either both or neither type of provision is negotiated since they are reciprocal in nature. No-strike and no-lockout clauses often contain similar, if not identical, language, falling into two general categories: (1) unconditional bans on interference with production during the life of the contract, and (2) conditional bans that permit strike or lockout under certain circumstances, usually one or more of the following:[38]

> Exhaustion of grievance procedure
> Violation of arbitration award
> Refusal to arbitrate dispute
> Noncompliance with portion of agreement
> Deadlocked contract reopener

The discipline or discharge of employees participating in illegal strikes under a no-strike provision may be permitted in the agreement. Most such clauses provide for appeal by the employee.[39]

Resolution of Impasse

When possible, an impasse should be avoided. Parties to negotiations can decide early on to seek a mediator to encourage joint problem solving. Using bargaining techniques, principled negotiations, and collective bargaining by objectives, pressure tactics can be avoided. By entering into negotiations long before the contract expiration date, some of the deadline pressure can be relieved. The use of joint labor-management study committees before and during the contract negotiations also can alleviate much of the conflict present in traditional bargaining sessions.

Still, an impasse often cannot be avoided, and resolution becomes one of the stages of negotiations. Sometimes a pressure tactic works and one of the parties reactivates negotiations more favorable to the opposing party. Often informal communication through a neutral third party enables the parties to resume talks to a successful conclusion. But traditionally an impasse is resolved by resorting to **mediation** and **arbitration** services.

1. *Mediation*   These services are available through the Federal Mediation and Conciliation Service (FMCS) and similar state agencies. A mediator assists in rescheduling negotiation sessions, reopening discussions, and making suggestions on possible areas of agreement. If an impasse has been caused by a mere misunderstanding of the parties' positions, an unbiased third party can often show them how close they actually are to agreement. If the impasse is caused by the substantive distance between the parties, a mediator must try to bring the respective proposals closer together.[40]

The mediator can only bring the parties together and keep them talking. He has no independent authority and will be successful only if trusted by both sides. Studies have confirmed that the qualities likely to aid a mediator in reaching a settlement are knowledge, expertise, impartiality, and sincerity.[41]

2. *Interest arbitration*   Although infrequently used in the private sector, this method involves the selection of a three-member panel to listen to both sides of a dispute and to make a final and binding decision on the details of the final agreement. Unlike contract arbitration, this process substitutes a panel for the negotiating parties in formulating a written contract.

3. *Final-offer arbitration*   This method requires both parties to submit their final offer to the three-member panel that has the authority to select one of the proposals. Final-offer arbitration gives the parties the motivation to make their final offers reasonable. Both parties realize that an unreasonable offer will have a lower chance of selection. Therefore, they strive to make their offer appear as fair and reasonable as possible.

In 1987 Detroit Tiger Jack Morris won a $1.85 million contract dispute through final-offer arbitration. The baseball players' union and major league owners had agreed to begin using the impasse resolution technique in 1974 to settle salary disputes. When the Tigers and their star pitcher could not reach a salary agreement they each presented their final offer to an arbitrator who could only choose one of the two offers and could not choose a compromise. The Tigers' last offer was $1.35 million—$500,000 larger than the previous largest final-offer arbitration award. Morris proposed $1.85 million based on his 123–81 record (most wins in the majors in the 1980s) and performance in the 1984 World Series.

4. *Mediation-arbitration*   A combination of items 1 and 2, in this method parties agree to bring in a mediator with authority to arbitrate *any* unresolved issues. Since the parties must agree to abide by the mediator-arbitrator's decision, they will likely agree on the substantive issues as well.

5. *Fact finding*   This method lies between mediation and arbitration. A hearing, similar to the one used in the arbitration process, is used to assemble and make the facts public through the media. But the fact-finding panel, like a mediator, can only recommend how an impasse may be resolved. Fact finding can be used to delay a strike, bring an unreasonable demand to the public's attention, create an atmosphere for new ideas, and, if reasonable recommendations are made, pressure a party into acceptance. This technique is used mostly in the public sector where such pressure is useful in forcing the parties to reach an agreement, especially if the facts show one side as unreasonable.

Summary

Individuals representing labor and management are involved in the collective bargaining process. Negotiators prepare for the negotiations, set priorities, and proceed in an honest and thorough manner. The National Labor Relations Act delineates areas of mandatory, permissive, and illegal negotiations. A good negotiator must also understand and value the human element, which is an integral part of the negotiating process. For some parties the give and take is as important as the end result. Knowing that while every demand was not met, the position and point of view was at least heard by the other party, can be part of a successful negotiation.[42]

Bargaining styles used in the collective bargaining process can focus on the relationship of the parties, on the issues to be decided, and on the relative bargaining power of the two sides. Principled negotiations emphasize getting the people involved in the negotiations to communicate on the issues. Collective bargaining by objectives borrows management-by-objectives techniques and proposes a framework for the negotiators by setting priorities and reasonable goals before the collective bargaining process is begun. Parties often use pressure bargaining techniques to further their bargaining objectives.

When the collective bargaining process breaks down, an impasse is reached. The parties can react to that impasse in various ways, with strikes being the most widely publicized reaction. Most often, however, mediation, arbitration, and fact finding are used to resolve impasses.

CASE 5.1 *Scope of Negotiation*

Adapted from *Houchins Market of Elizabethtown, Inc.* v. *National Labor Relations Board,* 375 F.2d 208 (1967)

During the course of collective bargaining, the union negotiator made statements to the effect that any contract proposal or recommendation would be subject to approval by employees. Toward the end of negotiations the company presented a written contract containing its counterproposals. After discussion, the union agreed to all the terms contained in the company's proposed agreement, but requested that additional items be included in the contract.

The company agreed to two of the proposals outright and suggested that the remaining three be discussed at the next bargaining session. Before the next scheduled bargaining session, the union informed the company that it was abandoning the three remaining proposals.

The company negotiator at this point reminded the union negotiator that the contract had to be approved by the employees. The union negotiator objected to the company's position, stating that membership approval was an internal matter and not something in which the company should get involved.

The company negotiator demanded that the issue of membership approval be added to the negotiations so a clause requiring such approval would be placed in the contract. The company refused to enter into the contract without such a vote.

The union filed an unfair labor practice charge for refusing to bargain in good faith, specifically for insisting on employee ratification as a condition precedent to execution of the contract upon which the parties had agreed.

Decision

The National Labor Relations Board found the company's insistence upon ratification by the bargaining unit did constitute an unfair labor practice. There was substantial evidence to support its finding that all terms of the contract had been agreed to at the time the company insisted on ratification by the employees.

On appeal, the court upheld the board's decision. Noting that the issue was not a mandatory bargaining item, the company had no right to refuse to enter into the agreement because the issue could not be resolved. The court also noted that the issue of ratification by the membership was exclusively within the internal domain of the union. The extent of authority delegated to the bargaining agent is for the union members to determine.

CASE 5.2   *Negotiating Procedures*

Adapted from *General Motors Acceptance Corp.* 79 LRRM 1663 (1972)

The company operated a wholesale and retail financing of motor vehicles in San Juan, Puerto Rico. The union organized eighteen field representatives in the San Juan branch in the fall and in November was certified as the employees' bargaining representative. Collective bargaining began on December 12. The negotiations lasted for eighteen months but were characterized by long delays between sessions when the company attempted to eliminate the union by withholding merit increases and soliciting letters from employees to repudiate the union. At the beginning of the negotiating sessions in December a year later, the company scheduled only three half days for bargaining and advised the union that if it wanted to continue to negotiate, it could go to the home office in New York.

In February, the union filed an unfair labor practice for refusal to bargain. The company refused to meet with the union again until the charge was withdrawn. The union withdrew the charge and the company agreed to meet in March for two more half days. In April, two half-day sessions were held; in May, three half days; in June, one day; and then negotiations broke down. The union again filed charges against the company for refusal to bargain in good faith.

Decision

The National Labor Relations Board found the company had refused to bargain in good faith. The board's rationale included the following: allowing only ten half days for bargaining during a six-month period, attempting to continue negotiations hundreds of miles from the plant, attempting to circumvent the collective bargaining unit and deal directly with employees.

CASE 5.3   *Economic Strikes*

Adapted from *National Labor Relations Board* v. *Fleetwood Trailer Company, Inc.*, 389 U.S. 375 (1967)

The company is a manufacturer of mobile homes employing about 110 persons. As a result of the breakdown in collective bargaining negotiations between the company and the union, about half of the employees struck. The company cut back its production and curtailed its orders for raw materials. The strike ended and a contract was signed. The union requested reinstatement of its strikers. The company explained that it could not reinstate the strikers because of the curtailment of production caused by the strike but that it intended to increase production to the full prestrike volume as soon as possible. Six strikers who applied for reinstatement were not hired. However, within six months of the strike six new employees who had not previously worked for the company were hired to fill jobs the striker applicants were qualified to fill. At a later date the six strikers were reinstated. The employees filed charges against the company, claiming it was an unfair labor practice to hire the new employees instead of the six strikers.

The NLRB trial examiner agreed with the employees and recommended that the company make the six employees whole for loss of earnings. The NLRB upheld the trial examiner's findings. The company appealed to the Court of Appeals. The court reversed the board's finding based on the fact the company did not have jobs for the six strikers on the date they applied for reinstatement; thus, not hiring them on that date was not a violation. The employees appealed the court's decision.

Decision

The Supreme Court found that the company did commit an unfair labor practice by not hiring the six striking employees when jobs became available. The Court found no merit to the fact that there were no jobs on the first date the employees applied. The Court stated that the basic right to jobs cannot depend upon job availability at the moment when applications are filed because the status of the striker as an employee continues until he has obtained regular and substantially equivalent employment. The Court recognized that frequently a strike affects the level of production and the number of jobs and that it is normal for striking employees to apply for reinstatement immediately after the strike and before full production is resumed. Then, if and when a job becomes available for which the striker is qualified, he is entitled to an offer of reinstatement. This right can only be defeated if the employer can show legitimate and substantial business justification for not re-employing. The company obviously had the applications of the striking employees on file and could show no legitimate business reasons for not hiring them when the jobs became available.

CASE STUDY   *Negotiating*

Adapted from *National Labor Relations Board* v. *Alterman Transport Lines, Inc.* 587 F.2d 212 (CA 5, 1979)

Facts

The company is an interstate trucking company with 98 percent of the stock owned by its president or his blood relatives. The president makes almost all of the company's decisions. The union received a bargaining order from the NLRB in October, 1972, and bargaining began in November, 1972. Between November, 1972, and December 30, 1974, when negotiations ceased, the parties met twenty-five times. The principal union negotiator was its president, who attended all the negotiating sessions but the last. The principal management negotiator was a vice president of operations who attended all the meetings accompanied by two lawyers. The company president attended the initial meeting and the last three.

At the first meeting when the union negotiator advised the company that any negotiated agreement was subject to the approval of the employees, the company president stated that the company's executive committee would have to ratify any agreement also. There was, however, no executive committee and the president alone intended to exercise the right of ratification.

The union's initial proposal was its master agreement covering over-the-road drivers. The company responded that the master agreement was written for dry-freight haulers and this company hauled wet freight. The union agreed to keep that fact in the negotiations. The negotiations bogged down for nine months on whether owner-operators were part of the unit. A decision by the NLRB that they were not was finally reached. Though slowed by this dispute, negotiations continued and some issues were agreed upon.

After the fifteenth and the twentieth session, in January and March of 1974, status sheets prepared by the company negotiator were given to the union negotiator. One such sheet appears in Exhibit 5.4.

Although the president was not directly involved in the negotiations, in late April he reviewed the negotiations file kept in his office and began to rewrite portions of the draft agreement. He arrived at a negotiation session and proposed his draft, which caused the union negotiator to object and accuse him of bad faith bargaining. The president asserted he was acting pursuant to his right of ratification. Two more sessions were held with more changes from the president. The negotiations stopped at the December 30, 1974, meeting when the president received a petition from 80 to 90 percent of the unit employees stating they no longer wanted representation by the union.

Exhibit 5.4   Negotiations status sheet

Name of Section	Status	Date
Preamble and existing operating practices	OK	3-8-73, 2-21-74
Contracting practices	OK	12-11-73
Bargaining unit	OK	1-11-74
Scope of agreement	Hold but OK	Discussed 1-11-74
Separability and savings	OK	12-11-73
Work week and work day	Hold	Set 5-10-73
Meals	OK	1-10-74
Unassigned employees	Withdrawn	1-11-74
Pay period	OK	1-10-74
Wages	Hold	Discussed 12-11-73
Holidays	Hold	Discussed 12-11-73
Vacation	Hold	Discussed 12-11-73
Seniority	OK	1-10-74
Federal and state regulations	OK	12-11-73
Nondiscrimination	OK	4-25-73
Stewards	OK	12-11-73
Management rights	OK	12-11-73
Work rules	OK	2-21-74
Grievance/arbitration	OK	12-11-73
Work stoppage/lockout	OK	2-14-74
Sick leave	Hold	Set 3-9-73, 4-4-73
Jury duty	OK	3-9-73
Discipline	OK	2-14-74
Interchangeability	Hold	Discussed 2-14-74
Employee examinations	OK	2-17-74
Maintenance of standards	OK	1-11-74
Existing operating practices	? See Preamble	2-14-74
Hiring of personnel	OK	1-10-74

Note: As of 2-21-74 the following articles or topics are either being held for economic reasons or have not been specifically discussed during negotiations.

1. Wage
2. Holidays
3. Vacation
4. Sick leave
5. Health and welfare
6. Pension
7. Work day/work week
8. Overtime
9. Length of contract
10. Check-off

The union charged the company with a violation of the duty to bargain in good faith.

Lawsuit

The company's position was as follows:

1. The president lawfully reserved the right of ratification at the first meeting.
2. A great deal of "spade work" was necessary because of the unique nature of the company's business.
3. That spade work was not done until the summer of 1974.
4. The president's entering into negotiations at that time was reasonable.
5. The president was merely exercising his right of ratification.

The union's position was as follows:

1. The negotiations prior to the president's involvement had resulted in tentative agreements in numerous noneconomic issues. These agreements had been reached through a give-and-take process involving mutual compromises. The president's alternative proposals, late in the game, were either a return to the company's original position or to an even more management-oriented position. His proposals bore no resemblance to any of the spade work that had been done over two years of negotiating.
2. While the individual proposals had only been tentatively agreed to, *major* changes to previously agreed-to provisions evidence bad faith. In this instance the president's proposals were harsher than the company's original proposals.
3. The uniqueness of the company's product would not necessitate two years of spade work on an issue such as a grievance procedure and then a totally different proposal by the president.
4. Negotiators must have some authority to speak for the company. In this case, the company's chief negotiator had not even seen the president's proposals prior to the negotiating session in which they were presented.
5. If the company's negotiating position was to be totally in the president's hands, he should have communicated his positions to his negotiators *before* the two years of meetings.
6. Using a negotiating session after two years of bargaining to present the company's position and then claiming it as his right of ratification was clearly bad faith bargaining.

Questions

1. Would you rule for the union or the company? Why?
2. Could the union have used either principled negotiations or collective bargaining by objectives techniques to resolve this agreement? Why or why not? And how?
3. Could establishing more specific ground rules have helped negotiations in this case? Why or why not?
4. If the company president intended to stall the negotiations, what, if anything, could the union negotiator have done to prevent it?

Key Terms

Arbitration	Mandatory bargaining subjects
Bargaining items	Mediation
Borg-Warner doctrine	Options in negotiations
Collective bargaining by objectives	Permissive bargaining subjects
Economic strike	Posturing
Fact finding	Pressure bargaining
Ground rules	Principled negotiations
Illegal bargaining subjects	Separability clause
Impasse	Unfair labor practice strike
Jurisdictional strike	Wildcat strike
Lockout	

Review Questions

1. What are the different styles used by negotiators?
2. Why are perceptions so important during the negotiation process? Why is listening critical to negotiators?
3. Can management by objectives be effectively used in labor negotiations? How?
4. Who are the principal parties involved in the collective bargaining process? What are their roles?
5. List some guidelines negotiators can use in aiding the negotiation process.
6. Why do negotiators use posturing during labor negotiation sessions?
7. Distinguish between mandatory, permissive, and illegal bargaining subjects.
8. What types of strikes could result in employees being legally fired?
9. Describe commonly used methods for resolving a negotiation impasse.

Endnotes

1. *Basic Patterns in Union Contracts,* 11th ed. (Washington, D.C.: The Bureau of National Affairs, 1986), p. 4.
2. Irving Paster, "Collective Bargaining: Warnings for the Novice Negotiator," *Personnel Journal* 60, no. 3 (Mar. 1981), pp. 203–7.
3. Reed C. Richardson, *Collective Bargaining by Objectives,* (Englewood Cliffs, N.J.: Prentice-Hall, 1977), p. 150, and Johanna S. Hunsaker, Philip L. Hunsaker, and Nancy Chase, "Guidelines for Productive Negotiating Relationships," *Personnel Administrator* 26 (Mar. 1981), pp. 37–40.

4. 29 U.S.C. sec. 159 (a) (1982).

5. National Labor Relations Board v. Wooster Division of the Borg-Warner Corp. 356 U.S. 342, 78 S.Ct. 718, 1 L.Ed. 2d 823 (1958).

6. Donna Sockell, "The Scope of Mandatory Bargaining: A Critique and a Proposal," *Industrial and Labor Relation Review* 40, no. 1 (Oct. 1986) pp. 19–34.

7. Fibreboard Paper Products Corp. v. National Labor Relations Board, 379 U.S. 203 (1964), pp. 210–23.

8. First National Maintenance Corp. v. National Labor Relations Board, 452 U.S. 666 (1981), pp. 677–89. Also Otis Elevator Company, 269 NLRB 891 (1984).

9. W.W. Cross & Co. v. National Labor Relations Board, 174 F. 2d 875 (1st Cir. 1949).

10. *Basic Patterns in Union Contracts,* 1986, pp. 7–8.

11. Roy J. Lewicki and Joseph A. Litterer, *Negotiation* (Homewood, Illinois: Richard D. Irwin, Inc., 1985) pp. 7–9.

12. Ibid.

13. C. Karrass, *Give and Take* (New York: Thomas Y. Crowell, 1974).

14. E. Edward Herman and Alfred Kuhn, *Collective Bargaining and Labor Relations* (Englewood Cliffs, N.J.: Prentice-Hall, 1981), p. 309.

15. David A. Dilts and Clarence R. Deitsch, *Labor Relations* (New York: Macmillan, 1983), p. 131.

16. Lewicki, *Negotiation,* pp. 75–82.

17. Ibid.

18. Roger Fisher and William Ury, *Getting to Yes* (Boston: Houghton-Mifflin, 1981), p. xii.

19. David A. Bender and William P. Curington, "Interaction Analysis: A Tool for Understanding Negotiations," *Industrial and Labor Relations Review* 36, no. 3 (April 1983), pp. 389–401.

20. Richardson, *Collective Bargaining,* p. xi.

21. Ibid., p. 151.

22. Ibid., p. 137.

23. Herman, *Collective Bargaining and Labor Relations,* p. 295.

24. Dilts, *Labor Relations,* p. 147.

25. Bruce E. Kaufman, "Bargaining Theory, Inflation, and Cyclical Strike Activity in Manufacturing," *Industrial and Labor Relations Review* 34, no. 3 (April 1981), pp. 333–55; and Bruce E. Kaufman, "Inter-industry Trends in Strike Activity," *Industrial Relations* 22, no. 1 (Winter 1983), pp. 45–57.

26. William H. Holley and Kenneth M. Jennings, *The Labor Relations Process* (Hinsdale, Ill.: Dryden, 1980), p. 204.

27. Stephen J. Cabot and Jerald R. Cureton, "Labor Disputes and Strikes: Be Prepared," *Personnel Journal* 60, no. 2 (Feb. 1981), pp. 121–24.

28. B. E. Kaufman, J. W. Skeels, M. Paldam, and P. J. Pedersen, "Replies," *Industrial and Labor Relations Review* 39, no. 2 (Jan. 1986), pp. 269–78.

29. Hoyt N. Wheeler, "Comment: Determinants of Strikes," *Industrial and Labor Relations Review* 37, no. 2 (Jan. 1984), pp. 263–69.

30. Martin J. Mauro, "Strikes as a Result of Imperfect Information," *Industrial and Labor Relations Review* 35, no. 4 (July 1982), pp. 522–38.

31. Dennis R. Make, "The Effect of the Cost of Strikes on the Volume of Strike Activity," *Industrial and Labor Relations Review* 39, no. 4 (July 1986), pp. 552–53.

32. Cynthia L. Gramm, "The Determinants of Strike Incidence and Severity: A Micro-level Study," *Industrial and Labor Relations Review* 39, no. 3 (April 1986), pp. 361–76.

33. John P. Kohl and David B. Stephens, "Labor Relations, Replacement Workers during

Strikes. Strategic Options for Managers," *Personnel Journal* 65, no. 4 (April 1986), pp. 93–98.

34. Charles J. Morris, ed., *The Developing Labor Law,* 2nd ed. (Washington, D.C.: Bureau of National Affairs, 1983), p. 1017.

35. Ibid., pp. 1020–26.

36. David S. Bradshaw, "Labor Relations, How to Put Teeth into a Labor Injunction," *Personnel Journal* 64, no. 10 (Oct. 1985), pp. 80–85.

37. American Shipbuilders, 380 U.S. 300, 58 LRRM 2672 (1965).

38. *Basic Patterns in Union Contracts,* 1986, pp. 93–97.

39. Ibid, p. 97.

40. John R. Stepp, Robert P. Baker, and Jerome T. Barrett, "Helping Labor and Management See and Solve Problems," *Monthly Labor Review* 105, no. 9 (Sept. 1982), pp. 15–20.

41. Ahmad Karim and Richard Pegnetter, "Mediator Strategies and Qualities and Mediation Effectiveness," *Industrial Relations* 22, no. 1 (Winter 1983), pp. 105–13.

42. Fritz Ihrig, "Labor Contract Negotiations: Behind the Scenes," *Personnel Administrator,* 31, no. 4 (April 1986), pp. 55–60.

Cost of
Labor
Contracts

Wage and Salary Issues

LABOR NEWS

Union Wages Rise Slowly

For four consecutive years, 1982–85, major collective bargaining agreements provided record low or near-record low wage adjustments. Management pressure to restrain labor costs in efforts to remain competitive has dominated negotiations during the early 1980s. In 1985 first year negotiated wage adjustments averaged 2.3 percent, the lowest in seventeen years. Wage adjustments negotiated over the life of multiyear contracts were only slightly higher at 2.7 percent.

When cost-of-living adjustments (COLAs) are added to wage adjustments the total increase averages 4.4 percent annually.

Increased foreign competition and domestic nonunion companies forced union negotiators to agree to major cost-curbing efforts. Common examples include "two-

tiered" compensation systems that pay new employees lower wage rates, "back-loaded" contracts that call for lower specified wage adjustments the first year than in subsequent years, and lump-sum payments in lieu of traditional wage rate increases. At the same time millions of union workers lost their COLAs in newly negotiated contracts. In 1985 alone, 40 percent of the settlements that previously contained COLAs dropped the provision. Those contracts that retained their COLA provisions often included reduced payments or lower caps as cost-cutting measures.

Source: Adapted from Joan Borum and James Conley, "Wage Restraints Continue in 1985 Major Contracts,"Monthly Labor Review 109, no. 4 (April 1986), pp. 22–28.

Wages and other economic benefits for employees are undoubtedly the meat and potatoes of collective bargaining in labor relations. To the employee they represent not only their current income and standard of living but also potential for economic growth and the ability to live comfortably during retirement. Wages are often considered the most important and difficult collective bargaining issue. When negotiated settlements are reported to the public, the first item specified is the percentage wage increase received by employees. In fact, in many cases that may be the only item employees consider critical or an absolute must as they vote to ratify a tentative agreement.

> There is a feeling these days among employees that (the company) is a good place to work and the benefits are good [but] it's just not enough. You can't feed a family on good working conditions. . . . Right or wrong, shortsighted or not—because of inflation money seems to be the prime motivator and driving force.[1]

Most union campaigns in organizations do not necessarily come about because of poor wage and benefit packages offered by nonunion employers. In fact, Gordon Jackson, a labor relations attorney specializing in combating union organizational campaigns, feels that very few campaigns result because of wage and benefit packages offered by employers. To keep economics from becoming a major organizational issue during a union's drive to organize, nonunion employers need only to prove they are paying average rates and providing fairly administered benefits.[2]

According to industrial research, however, pay level is positively related to employee satisfaction.[3] Employees consider their pay to be a primary indicator of the organization's good will. Many in our society consider the salary or income one receives as a measure of one's worth. Employees can get an exact measure of their salary, which can easily be compared to the salaries of fellow employees and those in other organizations and occupations. Therefore, most of us consciously or subconsciously compare our income levels not only to inflation and our cost of living but to incomes of other individuals.

Wages and benefits are also a prime collective bargaining issue to the organization. They represent the largest single cost factor on their income statement. While many management negotiators would like to pay high wages to employees, the reality of competition and the knowledge that competitors may be able to secure less expensive labor make it difficult to survive. Unlike many costs, such as capital and land, wages constantly rise and are not as easy to predict. Wages are the single most important source of tax revenue to federal, state, and local governments and in general are a strong indicator of the economic vitality of a community.

The total economic package of wages and benefits may be negotiated as a complete item rather than treated individually, enabling both sides to accurately estimate the total cost of the contract to the organization in terms of increases over current salary and benefits. In this chapter we will discuss wage issues; employee benefits will be covered in Chapter 7. Wages and benefits are separated to draw a distinction between the two; however, negotiators consider them part of a total economic package.

Labor and management negotiators normally define pay by either time worked or units of output. *Pay for time worked,* or an *hourly wage* or *annual salary,* has

Exhibit 6.1   Job classifications and wage rates

Group		Department
I	Die Repair	Maintenance
II	Maintenance	Maintenance
III	Cage Attendant	Material Handling
	Checker	Shipping
	Head Loader	Shipping
	Guillotine Operator	Window and Prime
	Brake Operator	Millroom and Prime
	Crane Operator	Material Handling
	Automatic Bander	Door and Prime
	Automatic Saw-Punch Machine	Millroom and Prime
IV	K. D. Material Handler	Material Handling
	Utility	Door and Window
	Thermal Break Operator	Prime
	Large Glass Cutter	Specialty
	Large Punch Press Operator	Door and Millroom
	Loading and Receiving	Shipping
	Plant Truck Driver	Shipping
V	Salvage	Material Handling
	Material Handler	Material Handling
	Janitor	Maintenance
	Loader-Unloader	Paint Line and Prime
	Schlegeler	Door, Millroom, Prime and Specialty
VI	(None)	
VII	Glass Cutter	Window, Specialty, Prime and Insulated Glass
	Glass Puller	Door
	Sample Builder	Sample
	Glass Washer and Assembler	Insulated Glass
	Spacer Assembly	Insulated Glass
	Sealant Applicator	Insulated Glass
	Parts Puller (Sash, Screen, Frame)	Window
	Saw Operator	Door, Millroom, Prime, Specialty and Insulated Glass
	Belt Line	Door
	Door Prehanger	Door
VII	Screen Pre-Assembler	Door, Window, Specialty and Prime
	Screener	Door, Window, Specialty and Prime
	Sash Builder	Door, Window, Specialty and Prime
	Frame Builder	Window, Specialty and Prime
VIII	Small Punch Press Operator	Door, Millroom, Specialty and Prime
	Processor	Door, Millroom, Specialty and Prime
	Jamb Wrapper	Door
	Window Wrapper	Shipping
	Miscellaneous Jobs	Material Handling
IX	Packaging	Material Handling
XXIII	Paint Equipment Operator	Paint Line
XXIV	Assistant Paint Equipment Operator	Paint Line

Group	Hire Rate Effective June 1, 1982	Rate After 35 Working Days Effective June 1, 1982
I	$7.80	$8.05
II	$7.62	$7.80
III	$7.28	$7.62
IV	$7.28	$7.54
V	$7.28	$7.48
VI	$6.95	$7.28
VII	$6.95	$7.18
VIII	$6.95	$7.13
IX	$6.95	$7.07
XXIII	$7.62	$7.86
XXIV	$7.62	$7.78

Source: Agreement between Anaconda Aluminum Company and United Steelworkers of America (Sugarcreek, Ohio, 1982), pp. 45–48. Used with permission.

become the predominant means of employee compensation in the United States. Most labor contracts contain specific job titles and associated wage scales agreed upon by labor and management. An example of this is Exhibit 6.1, an agreement between the Anaconda Aluminum Company division of the Atlanta Richmond Company and the United Steelworkers of America AFL-CIO. *Pay for units produced,* usually referred to as *piecework,* is still utilized in many industries as not only a means of wage determination but also a motivational technique. Many piecework systems today provide a guaranteed salary with an additional rate established for units of output above a certain production level.

Union Wage Concerns

Union wage policies affect the distribution of wages in several ways. First, by raising the wages of union workers (compared to nonunion) unionism changes the dispersion of wages in the economy. Unionism has raised the average wages of its organized workers by at least 2–3 points. Second, by negotiating standard rate policies for organized workers, unions have reduced wage differentials among members. The efforts of unions to standardize wage rates across organizations covered by union contracts have reduced wage differentials among jobs and employees within establishments.[4] Thus, unions tend to flatten out wages. Factors such as employee education and work experience have much less effect on wage levels in the union sector than in the nonunion sector.[5] Third, union and management negotiators tend to emphasize cost of living adjustments or increased purchasing power as the justification for pay increases; the union members usually adopt similar views. In nonunion organizations where pay increases are at least partially based on performance, more employees tend to view pay increases as a form of recognition for performance.[6]

"A fair day's pay for a fair day's work" is a commonly used phrase summing up the expectations of many employees. Employees expect and even demand to be treated fairly and honestly by the organization. While most are reasonable in their pay expectations, a few feel they are being underpaid. If employees perceive they are unfairly treated by the organization, particularly in pay matters, they typically will react by leaving the workplace either temporarily through absenteeism and tardiness, or permanently through seeking employment at another organization; by reducing the quantity or quality of their production; or by filing a grievance or enacting a work stoppage through the union. Eventually their pay dissatisfaction will be brought to the bargaining table, leading ultimately to either higher wages or an economic strike. Or they may change their perceptions by simply accepting the inequity although this may become a permanent morale factor.[7]

Obtaining pay equity in the work place is difficult. The slogan "equal pay for equal work" is a guide union and management leaders follow, and employees expect to be maintained. Obviously not all jobs involve work of equal value to an organization. The first-year bookkeeper does not expect the same pay as a tax accountant; the same is true for a punch press operator and a maintenance attendant. Employees understand that the value of the work leads to different pay grades and classifications for different jobs. As shown in Exhibit 6.1, labor agreements commonly provide for different job classifications assigned different pay grades according to level of skill and work demanded. As long as pay grades are fairly structured and evenly applied, employees have no trouble accepting differential pay based upon job classification and internal wage levels.

Some wage systems provide for higher wages to employees with more longevity. Thus, seniority not only helps employees in bidding for open jobs but also in receiving higher pay. Even though less senior employees perform the same work, everyone realizes that longevity pay serves as an incentive to stay with the organization.

Industrial Differentials

Industrial wage differentials also provide a logical basis for differences in pay among employers in the same labor market. Employees recognize that the relationship between labor and total production costs affects their wage levels. Organizations in highly labor-intensive industries are usually less able to provide wage increases than organizations which are in more capital-intensive industries. For example, if a specialized chemical processing plant that has few competitors increases its wage rates by 10 percent, it would need to raise prices by only 0.6 percent to absorb the wage increase because only 6.0 percent of its total production costs are attributable to labor. However, if a southern textile firm raised its wages by 10 percent, it would need to raise prices by 7 percent because its labor costs equal 70 percent of total production costs. A 7 percent price increase could be disastrous to the highly competitive textile organization. Employees accept and understand that not all employers, due to their profitability or current competitive position within the marketplace, can be the highest-paying organization in the industry. If profits decrease so much the organization suffers losses, wage demands usually reflect the reality of the economic times.

Unions affect wages to some extent in many industries. The variation of union power and ability to raise wage levels across industries appears to be related to several factors. Union wage gains are generally greatest where (1) employers' ability to pay is high due to discretionary pricing power and profitability, (2) unions practice centralized bargaining, and (3) unions avoid fragmentation.[8]

Management Wage Concerns

Wage and benefit changes have an impact on the cost of the production of goods and services. Management must consider how a change in wages will affect its pricing policy and ability to compete in the marketplace. It is often mistakenly inferred that management wants to minimize its labor costs for no particular reason, or because employees are not appreciated. The reality is that management needs to maintain competitive labor costs to successfully produce and price products within their industry. Thus, maintaining a competitive position is a primary aim of management in negotiations.

Accurate assessment of competitors' wages and total payroll costs is critical for management in anticipating the future of pricing changes within the industry.

Labor-intensive industries find comparable wages to be even more necessary for long-run success. Thus, when national unions seek to negotiate equal pay increases among employers in the same industry, it is beneficial to management from the standpoint of maintaining a current, competitive position. Union leaders, of course, find it beneficial to offer all members the same wage increases. More competitive and less organized industries, however, cannot provide this type of consistency.

This practice is known as **pattern bargaining**, and can be highly successful for both management and labor. Steel and auto industries as well as meat packing and textile industries have utilized pattern bargaining in the past. Typically, the union leaders choose what they perceive as the weakest company—the one most susceptible to grant wage increases—and begin negotiations. Once negotiations are completed, the union insists that other firms in the industry agree to equal wage and benefit increases.

Pattern bargaining, however, does not prevent firms from negotiating differences according to local labor conditions and the profitability of a particular employer. Instead, when negotiated wage and benefit increases are equal for several employers, they maintain their same relative competitive position with regard to labor costs. However, during the recent economic recession, pattern bargaining has declined in such hard-hit industries as steel, rubber, and automobile. The individual profitability of affected firms becomes more important in many negotiations.

Management is also concerned about the **value added**, labor's theory that wages should equal the contribution of labor to the final product. Out-of-hand labor costs may hamper management's ability to replace and maintain equipment and machinery. It may be tempting in the short run to absorb labor increases by reducing these kinds of expenditures. However, lack of competitive technological improvements and modern machinery can erode productivity. Thus, management wants the value added kept in proportion with the wages paid. The value added by labor to the total product, and the value added by capital and equipment cannot be totally separated because of their interrelationship. One is not useful without the other, and each affects the other's increase or decrease in productivity. Determining labor's share of the value added to the product is a difficult and often debated point in labor negotiations. Sometimes subcontracting bids for specific work can be used to estimate the true value labor has added.

Negotiated Wage Adjustments

Standard Rate, Pay Range Systems

How wage rates are to be defined in the agreement is a critical issue. Most agreements contain a **standard rate** or *flat rate* of pay for each job classification effective during the life of the agreement, as in Exhibit 6.1. Some agreements provide a *pay range* for each job: the person may be paid one of several steps within the range. Usually management will seek flexibility in wage administration by using a range of pay for each grade or category. A common practice in the nonunion sector, this allows management to reward individual differences in employees according to seniority, merit, or quality and quantity of production.

Management usually wishes to hire new, inexperienced employees at the minimum pay rate and allow them to advance during their tenure with the company through merit and/or seniority increases. Management may argue that it makes little sense to pay exactly the same wage rate for a job regardless of the performance level of the employee. The highest-performing employee and the lowest-performing employee in a standard rate system receive the same wage rate, which tends to undermine individual motivation.[9] Union leaders argue that merit increases, which are the primary reason to have pay ranges instead of standard rates, are useful management tools in theory but actually run into severe problems. Union leaders feel that since these systems are normally based upon a supervisor's performance appraisal, they are subject to supervisor bias. The subjectivity and imperfections of performance appraisal systems, which cannot be denied by management, lead most union leaders to argue against a merit pay increase system. Management may then counter with the argument that an imperfect performance appraisal system is better than no system of rewarding individual performance. An example of an arbitrated grievance over an employee's step increase within a pay range is provided in Case 6.1.

An alternative pay system linking pay to performance is a **piece-rate system**. Such a system usually provides employees a standard rate of pay for the average level of production with a bonus rate per piece produced above the agreed-upon level. Union negotiators usually strongly favor this kind of merit system because it is generally more objective. Many negotiators agree that merit wage systems should be used only if performance levels are directly measurable as in a piece-rate system; otherwise automatic across-the-board increases should be combined with a standard rate wage system.[10]

Piece-Rate Systems

Straight piecework is the most common and easily understood individual incentive plan. If an employee is paid $.025 per unit produced and completes 100 units in an hour, then the hour's gross earnings would be $2.50. Variations of straight piecework include falling piece rate and rising piece rate. Exhibit 6.2 is a comparison of the various piece-rate plans.

Plans that use a *falling piece rate* involve a standard time and rate of production. If the employee produces more than the standard, the gain is shared between the employer and the employee. The employee's hourly earnings increase with output above a standard of 100, but the rate per piece falls at various predetermined levels. Thus an employee who has produced 140 units (40 percent above standard) receives only $3.22 (29 percent more) and not $3.50, which would be the case if the $.025 rate were maintained. The employer receives the remainder of the gain, effectively lowering the overhead cost per piece.

Plans that use a *rising piece rate* also involve a standard time and rate of production. But as Exhibit 6.2 illustrates, the worker who increases output by 40 percent has a greater than proportional increase in hourly earnings. After earning $2.50 for the first 100 pieces, the worker earns $2.40 ($4.90 − $2.50) for the next 40 pieces, or 96 percent of the base hourly pay. The increase occurs because the worker earned $0.25 per piece for the first 100 pieces and $.035 per piece for the next 40.

Exhibit 6.2 A comparison of piece-rate plans ($100 per worker overhead cost per hour)

Standard Piece-Rate Plan

Number of Pieces	Piece Rate	Worker's Earnings	Per Piece Overhead Cost	Total Cost
100	$.025	$2.50	$1.000	$1.025
120	.025	3.00	.833	.858
140	.025	3.50	.714	.739
160	.025	4.00	.625	.650
180	.025	4.50	.556	.581
200	.025	5.00	.500	.525

Falling Piece-Rate Plan

Number of Pieces	Piece Rate	Worker's Earnings	Per Piece Overhead Cost	Total Cost
100	$.025	$2.50	$1.000	$1.025
120	.024	2.88	.833	.857
140	.023	3.22	.714	.737
160	.022	3.52	.625	.647
180	.021	3.78	.556	.577
200	.020	4.00	.500	.520

Rising Piece-Rate Plan

Number of Pieces	Piece Rate	Worker's Earnings	Per Piece Overhead Cost	Total Cost
100	$.025	$ 2.50	$1.000	$1.025
120	.030	3.60	.833	.863
140	.035	4.90	.714	.749
160	.040	6.40	.625	.665
180	.045	8.10	.556	.601
200	.050	10.00	.500	.550

Source: Leonard R. Burgess, *Wage and Salary Administration* (Columbus, OH: Merrill, 1984), pp. 241–242.

Management benefits nevertheless: the total cost per piece still declines as more pieces are produced because the fixed overhead cost is spread out over more pieces.[11] Why would management agree to a rising piece-rate system? If the higher hourly earnings are sufficiently motivational, the total cost per piece could be cheaper than under a falling piece-rate plan. For example, if under the falling piece-rate plan of Exhibit 6.2 the employee is only slightly motivated and averages 120 units per hour, then management has an average total piece cost of $.857. But if the rising piece-rate plan is slightly more motivational and the employee averages 140 units per hour, management averages $.749 total per unit cost while the employee averages $4.90 per hour instead of $2.88 (falling rate of 120 pieces).

Piece-rate systems have the advantages of being easily understood, simple to calculate, and motivational. But many jobs do not easily lend themselves to such a pay system because the output of the employee cannot be directly and objectively measured. Also, most employees' output is affected by the output of others, so their productivity is not directly proportional to their input. Finally, union and management negotiators may have a difficult time agreeing on what is a fair production standard. Changes in standards by management can easily lead to union grievances.

Standard hour plans are similar in concept to piece-rate plans except a "standard time" is set to complete a particular job instead of paying the employee a price per piece. For example, an auto mechanic might be given a standard time of two hours to tune up an eight-cylinder car. If the worker's hourly rate is $8.00 per hour and three eight-cylinder tune-ups are finished in six hours, then the employee earns $48.00. If a so-called Halsey 50/50 incentive plan is used, the worker and employer share equally in time saved by the employee. Thus, after completing the three tune-ups in five hours, the employee would be paid $52.00 ($48.00 + $4.00 [1/2 hour saved at $8.00/hour]), and the employer has an additional hour's work time.

Deferred Wage Increases

Many multiyear collective bargaining agreements provide increases in wage rates that are deferred to later years rather than taking effect immediately. Together with the preferred use of COLAs, such **deferred wage rate increases** often make multiyear contracts desirable for both sides. Management can predict labor costs further into the future with a greater degree of accuracy, and union members feel their buying power is protected for a longer period of time and do not have to annually worry about possible strikes.

Deferred wage provisions specify increases in the base pay to take effect on future dates during a multiyear contract. Negotiating multiyear increases often hinges on whether they are *evenly distributed* over the life of the contract, as in the following example of a three-year contract starting July 1, 1988, or whether they are front-end loaded.

Pay Classification	Wage Rate on July 1, 1988	Wage Rate on July 1, 1989	Wage Rate on July 1, 1990
I	$8.80	$9.24	$9.68
II	$8.40	$8.82	$9.24
III	$7.80	$8.19	$8.58

Front-end loading refers to a deferred wage increase with a larger proportion of the total percentage increase in the first year of the agreement. Thus, a three-year total wage increase package might be evenly distributed with an equal percentage provided at the beginning of each year: 5 percent–5 percent–5 percent; or it could be front-end loaded: 10–3–2 . Many contracts provide front-end loading, including providing the total increase in the first year: 15–0–0.

Management generally prefers to spread the increases out over the life of the agreement for cash flow purposes and because the total cost of the agreement is substantially less since higher wages paid only in later years are avoided in early years. For example, the two alternatives for the three-year, 15 percent increase when applied to a $20,000 current wage produce the following wages paid:

Year	Equal Increases 5%–5%–5%	Front-End Loaded 10%–3%–2%	Difference Each Year
0	$20,000	$20,000	—
1	$21,000	$22,000	+ $1,000
2	$22.050	$22,660	+ $ 610
3	$23,153	$23,113	– $ 40
			+ $1,570

Union negotiators often prefer front-end load wage rate increases so their members receive the additional wages ($1,570) and realize a large increase in pay the very first year. However, negotiators acknowledge from past experience that front-end loading may produce long-term problems. Members who were quite happy with a 10 percent increase during the first year of an agreement can easily become dissatisfied with the two subsequent years of small increases, especially during periods of high inflation. Thus, "What have you done for me lately?" becomes a real problem for union and management leaders alike. Also, the annual wage rates at the end of the agreement can easily be lower under a front-end loaded provision than under an equally distributed provision, as in the previously cited example. The union may demand a **wage reopener** provision providing for the reopening of contract talks to discuss only wage rates. Such discussion during the later years of the agreement may become necessary due to unpredictable inflation or company financial success. Management is not obligated to agree to higher wage rates under such a reopener, but realizes this may be necessary to obtain a long-term contract. Also management negotiators realize they will likely be faced with the demands, particularly when they are valid, during the next negotiating session anyway.

Wage reopener clauses are more common in the public sector than the private sector. Private companies prefer the predictability of fixed long-term labor costs while public sector management must deal with short budget periods and longer contracts.

Prior to the 1980s virtually all collective bargaining agreements with multiyear settlements included front-end loaded wage increases. However, foreign and domestic nonunion competition in the 1980s forced management negotiators to seek a variety of cost-curbing measures including **back-loaded contracts.** A back-loaded contract provides a lower wage adjustment in the first year with higher increases in later years of a multiyear contract. For example a 10 percent three-year wage adjustment could be 2–4–4. In many back-loaded contracts workers receive no wage increase in the first year, for example, 0–3–3. Within three years the new cost-curbing strategy spread rapidly and was included in 36 percent of the 1985 settlements.[12]

Cost-of-Living Adjustments

Union negotiators have for years emphasized the need for *cost-of-living adjustments* (**COLAs**) during the life of an agreement. They contend that the *real wage*—the purchasing power negotiated in an agreement as a wage rate—is eroded by inflation during the life of the agreement. Therefore, it is necessary to provide the COLA in an escalator clause so wage rates will keep pace with inflation. General Motors first proposed a COLA clause during negotiations with the UAW in 1948.

Unions and employers were leery of COLAs until the 1950s. Both feared COLAs would include pay cuts, which might have occurred since declines in the Consumer Price Index were at the time quite possible. Union leaders also disliked COLAs because they represented a "substitute for bargaining," meaning they would receive less credit for increases with a COLA. Unions preferred wage reopeners that put them back at the bargaining table. However, by the mid-1950s, both sides worried less about deflation and more about their ability to correctly estimate rising inflation. In addition, in 1950 General Motors and the United Auto Workers signed a historic wage formula, which combined deferred wage adjustments with a COLA—a practice previously avoided by GM but soon followed by many negotiators.[13]

Both labor and management negotiators are careful to specify exact COLA provisions during the agreement. Several critical issues must be carefully spelled out.

1. *Inflation index*   Most provisions use the *Consumer Price Index (CPI)* determined by the Bureau of Labor Statistics as a standard for measuring change in inflation. In 1978 the Bureau of Labor Statistics broke the CPI into two entities: the Urban Family Index or CPI-U for urban families, and the Urban Wage Earner Index or CPI-W for urban wage earners and clerical workers. The CPI-W is the most commonly used index. In addition, an index for a particular standard metropolitan statistical area or the all-cities Consumer Price Index may be utilized.[14]

Increases in the CPI are linked to increases in wages by an adjustment formula. The two most commonly used formulas are a *cents-per-hour* increase for each point increase in the CPI or a *percentage increase* in wage rates equal to some percentage increase in the CPI. The most commonly used formula provides for a 1¢ increase in wages for each 0.3 percent increase in the CPI. An example of this provision is found in Exhibit 6.3, from the agreement between Anaconda Aluminum Company and the Aluminum Workers International Union.

2. *When the increases are to be provided*   The majority of agreements provide for inflation adjustment four times a year following the reported increase in the CPI. This quarterly increase provision is also included in the Anaconda and Aluminum Workers agreement. Other labor agreements provide for adjustments to be made twice a year (semiannually) or once a year (annually).

An alternative for relating changes in wages to cost-of-living changes is through the use of a *corridor COLA plan* enabling wages to automatically rise with CPI increases to a certain point. Then wages will not increase until the next predetermined point, the corridor, is reached. For example, the COLA provision between General Electric and twelve unions called for an increase of 1¢ per hour for each 0.3

percent increase in the CPI. However, the formula is not utilized between 7 and 9 percent (the corridor). If the CPI goes above 9 percent then the COLA again goes into operation. Thus, if during the life of the agreement, prices rose 12 percent, General Electric workers would receive a 9 percent COLA. If they rose 8 percent, workers would receive a 7 percent COLA.[15]

3. *Change in base pay*   If COLAs are treated as additions to the base pay, then other wage adjustments such as shift differential and overtime would increase after a COLA because they are usually a fixed percentage of base pay. Thus the company would find its personnel cost increased by an amount greater than the percentage COLA. The alternative is to treat the COLAs given during the life of the agreement as a benefit and not an addition to the base pay.

4. *COLA maximums*   Some labor agreements provide for a maximum COLA increase made by the company during the life of the agreement. This maximum is usually referred to as a *cap* put on the cost-of-living provision. The cap assures management that wage increases due to CPI increases will not go beyond a certain total.

Critics of COLA provisions state such provisions fuel inflation. However, only a little more than 10 percent of the civilian nonagricultural workforce in the United States is covered by COLA provisions and is therefore able to keep pace with inflation. Most of these are found in the large unions such as the teamsters, steelworkers, and auto workers.[16] Although this excludes over 80 percent of the workforce, critics still

Exhibit 6.3 **COLA contract provision**

ARTICLE XXVIII
Cost of Living

A. For purposes of this Agreement: "Consumer Price Index" refers to the "Consumer Price Index for Urban Wage Earners and Clerical Workers—United States—All Items (1967=100)" published by the Bureau of Labor Statistics, U. S. Department of Labor.

"Consumer Price Index Base" refers to the Consumer Price Index for the month of April 1980 (being that Consumer Price Index which was published by the Bureau in mid-May 1980).

"Adjustment Dates" are September 1, December 1, 1980; March 1, June 1, September 1, December 1, 1981; March 1, June 1, September 1, December 1, 1982; and March 1 and June 1, 1983.

"Change in the Consumer Price Index" is defined as the difference between (i) the Consumer Price Index Base and (ii) the Consumer Price Index for the second calendar month next preceding the month in which the applicable Adjustment Date falls.

"Cost-of-Living Adjustment" is calculated as below and will be payable for the three-month period commencing with the Adjustment Date.

B. Cost-of-Living: Effective on and after August 1, 1980, a Cost-of-Living Adjustment equal to 1¢ will be paid for each full .3 of a point change in Consumer Price Index.

C. Cost-of-Living Roll-In: Effective on each Adjustment Date the quarterly Cost-of-Living Adjustment will be included in the employee's Standard Hourly Wage Scales, commencing on the respective adjustment dates and continuing thereafter. However, such adjustment shall not duplicate the amount, if any, of any prior adjustment which shall have been included in the Standard Hourly Wage Scales.

D. Continuation of the Cost-of-Living Adjustment is dependent upon the availability of the monthly Consumer Price Index in its present form and calculated with the same weighting of individual components and on the same basis as the last index published prior to August 1, 1980. Should the Consumer Price Index be revised from its present form or method of calculation, or discontinued, the parties shall attempt to adjust this Section, or, if agreement is not reached, the parties shall request the Bureau of Labor Statistics to provide an appropriate conversion or adjustment, which shall be applicable as of the appropriate Adjustment Date and thereafter.

E. If the Consumer Price Index falls below the Consumer Price Index Base, there shall be no Cost-of-Living Adjustment.

Source: Agreement between Anaconda Aluminum Co. and Aluminum Workers Local No. 130 and the Aluminum Workers' International Union, AFL-CIO, 1980–83, pp. 36–37. Used with permission.

contend that employers who pay COLAs increase their prices to reflect the increase in labor costs. A circular situation develops, ultimately resulting in increased prices or higher inflation. Inflation causes the CPI to go up which causes COLA provisions in labor agreements to be enacted, causing an increase in wage rates.

Many observers believe that the great increase in COLA clauses during the 1970s made it difficult for the government to reduce inflation and start economic recovery. From 1969 to 1981 the percentage of workers under major private sector agreements of at least 1,000 workers covered by COLAs increased from 25 to 57 percent. More importantly, wage inflation during the 1970s was greater under contracts with *uncapped* COLAs than under all other contracts, including those with capped COLAs and those without COLA clauses.[17]

Labor leaders are quick to point out, however, that since only a small portion of the total labor force is covered by COLA provisions, the effect upon inflation must not be very great. Also, they feel their members should be protected against inflation. Labor leaders point out that government's tying Social Security increases and federal employee retirement increases to the CPI has much more of an impact on inflation than labor agreement COLA adjustments.

A significant problem with COLA adjustments concerning union leaders and management alike is that the increases are taken for granted by employees once given. Members may feel the wage increases they receive due to COLA provisions are not negotiated increases and therefore want further wage increases. Union and management negotiators may feel that they are not given credit for these negotiated increases. Since members come to expect automatic adjustments for inflation, they tend to ask labor negotiators and management, "What have you done for me lately?" Finally, management complains that COLA provisions prevent it from forecasting future labor costs. Management feels it cannot adequately predict the total product cost, and COLA costs hamper the ability to successfully bid on projects or priced items.

As it happens, this highly sought wage enhancement may be on its way out. According to the Bureau of Labor Statistics, only 21 percent of workers were covered by COLAs in major union contracts signed in 1985. Only five years earlier, in 1980, coverage peaked at 61 percent. Although management has always disliked COLAs, to a large degree labor has lost interest because the lower inflation rates of the mid-1980s have decreased their concerns about lost "real" pay. In reality, COLAs themselves may have caused their downfall. Their automatic increases in industries hard hit by low-priced foreign competition may have cost many American workers their jobs, so job security has become a greater concern than COLAs to many union negotiators.[18] While many managers are quick to blame COLAs for high labor costs, they cannot deny they also signed the contracts containing the COLA clauses. If inflation increases, the economy stabilizes, and union negotiators ask for new COLAs, will management again agree to them?

Profit Sharing, Bonus Plans

Compensation systems whereby management agrees to make a lump-sum payment to employees in addition to their regular wages are termed **profit-sharing** or bonus plans. The payments may be based on the profits of the company using an agreed-upon formula (profit-sharing) or an amount specified in the contract based on production or sales levels (bonus). Both are preferred by management over base-wage changes because negotiated increases do not automatically carry over to future years and do not increase the cost of associated benefits such as overtime rates and pension payments, typically based on base-wage earnings.

Profit-sharing plans have increased in popularity and in frequency in labor agreements in the 1980s.[19] Management favors profit sharing to COLAs as a wage supplement for several reasons: (1) payments are made only if the company makes a profit and thus is usually financially strong; (2) unlike COLAs, payments are not tied to inflation, which is not related to the company's financial status and may require increases during difficult times; (3) workers' pay is linked to their productivity and not only the number of hours they work, giving them a direct incentive to see the company become more profitable; (4) workers may feel more a part of the company and develop increased interest in reducing waste and increasing efficiency in all areas as well as their own jobs.

In 1986, for example, the Ford Motor Company distributed $224 million in annual profit-sharing checks to U.S. employees. The average worker received $1,200, a decrease from the 1985 average of $2,100 when Ford reported higher profits. Peter Pestillo, Ford's personnel chief and chief labor negotiator, noted, "We think it's money well spent. They get more, and they get more done. We think we get a payback in the cooperation and enthusiasm of the people." The 1984 Ford–United Auto Workers master agreement was the first to contain a profit-sharing provision pushed by management as a means of avoiding the UAW proposed 3-percent annual raises.[20] The concept of profit sharing within the auto industry is not new, however. Douglas Frasier, former president of the UAW, noted the union first asked for a profit-sharing plan over forty years prior to the 1984 agreement and during several other negotiations, but neither of the U.S. auto giants was interested until they were losing money in the 1980s.[21]

Employee Stock Ownership Plans

Employee stock ownership plans (ESOPs) are generally designed to give employees stock in the company expecting that they will develop ownership interests. Through ESOPs, employees are either given stock bonuses outright or are provided the opportunity to purchase stock, usually at a discount. Management hopes that as employees develop a sense of ownership the company will realize increased production and efficiency.

It has been estimated that by the year 2000, 25 percent of all U.S. workers will have access to an ESOP. The percentage of stock ownership through an ESOP may vary greatly. At W.L. Gore & Associates, a chemical plant in Delaware, the 3,000 employees own about 10 percent of the company's stock, compared to 70-percent ownership at Dan Inc., a textile manufacturer in Virginia. The union and many of the 8,000 employees at Dan River, however, are not at all happy, because they have no voting rights or operational control over the company. The control is held by the 30 percent outside investors and top management. The majority of ESOPs do not allow worker-owners voting rights—a major criticism by unions.[22] One major exception is the Weirton Steel plant where the employees bought the ownership to stop the plant from being shut down by National Steel, a practice which has occurred frequently in recent years. National Steel gave the employees the assets for nothing, avoiding $450 million in shutdown costs (severance pay, continued health insurance, pension benefits, etc.) as provided in the labor contract. The 8,000 employers saved their jobs and gained control and ownership of the company.[23]

Scanlon Group Incentive Plans

A group incentive plan designed to achieve greater production through increased efficiency with accrued savings divided among the workers and the company was developed by Joseph Scanlon. Scanlon at the time was the research director of the United Steelworkers and later joined the faculty at the Massachusetts Institute of Technology.[24] The **Scanlon Plan** became the popular standard in U.S. group incentive plans. It has since become a basis for labor-management cooperation above and beyond its use as a group incentive plan. The plan contains two primary features: (1) departmental committees of union and management representatives meet together at least monthly to consider any cost-savings suggestions; (2) any documented cost savings resulting from implemented committee suggestions are divided 75 percent to employees and 25 percent to the company.[25]

Most other group incentive plans involve programs that set expected levels of productivity, product costs, or sales levels for individual groups and then provide employee bonuses if the targeted goals are exceeded. One widely recognized example is the Nucor Corporation. In 1980 the company reported a staggering growth of 600 percent in sales and 1,500 percent in profits over ten years due to a production incentive program. The company actually developed four separate incentive programs: one each for production employees, department heads, professional employees, and senior officers. Their theory was that "money is the best motivation."[26]

Two-Tier Wage Systems

A wage system that pays newly hired workers less than current employees performing the same or similar jobs is termed "two-tier." Following the historic first **two-tier wage system** in 1977 at General Motors Packard Electric Division in Warren, Ohio, many more union-management negotiations have resulted in similar systems.[27] The basic concept is to provide continued higher wage levels for current employees if the union will accept reduced levels for future employees. Union leaders believe they must accept the two-tier system or face greater layoffs in the future. Management usually claims the system is needed to compete with nonunion and foreign competition. The airline, copper, trucking, auto, food, and aerospace industries have negotiated two-tier systems.[28]

While a two-tier system is contrary to historic union doctrine of "equal pay for equal work" or **pay equity**, when a system is first negotiated the union representatives can claim that they have avoided disaster and saved the jobs and/or wage levels of current members (who must vote on the contract). It is relatively easier to sell such a concept since no workers at that point are accepting the "lower tier." However, five or ten years later when many workers are paid lower wages for the same work as their brother union members it can become a source of conflict and resentment. In some cases the lower-paid workers express their feelings with lower product quality and productivity records than their higher-paid counterparts.[29] In these bargaining units the conflict could present even greater problems to both union and management leaders as the number of lower-tier workers approaches 51 percent of the bargaining unit and they demand equity.

During the early to mid-1980s, labor-management relations focused on union priorities of preserving jobs and aiding displaced workers as well as management cost-saving measures. Three major cost-saving approaches by management negotiators included two-tier pay systems, lump-sum payments in lieu of specified wage increases, and health insurance cost reduction plans. Unions continue to resist two-tier systems because of morale problems that develop as more lower-tier workers are hired. However, when faced with wage cuts or layoffs as the only other means of significantly reducing employer payroll costs, two-tier systems appear more desirable to current members. Lump-sum payments typically appear in three-year contracts, for example, where the first year includes a specified base-wage increase followed by two lump-sum payments in the following years. The employer's cost savings occur due to the avoidance of compounding base wage increases and related benefits such as pensions, which use base wages in payment formulas.[30]

Wage Negotiation Issues

During the negotiation process one or both sides may utilize different wage level theories to stress their economic proposals. One or both sides will bring to light one or more wage theories and issues having an impact upon the negotiation of rates. Which issues might be stressed during negotiations and whether they are even presented depend upon the past history of the company's labor relations and the personalities of the negotiators. In general, either side would utilize an issue it felt was valid or simply useful in providing a significant point for its list of arguments.

Productivity Theory

One of the oldest and broadest negotiation issues concerning wages involves the **productivity theory** that employees should share in increased profits caused by greater productivity. At the heart of the issue is the commonly accepted proposition that the organization's production is a combination of three factors: machinery and equipment, employee labor, and managerial ability. Union and management leaders agree that all three share in the creation of profits since they contribute to the organization's productivity. Whenever figures show that productivity and/or profits have risen, then the question becomes what percentage is attributable to employees' labor as opposed to machinery and equipment, and managerial ability. Labor leaders commonly request that their members get their fair share of the increased profits. Management may request the value-added concept be applied.

Determining labor's fair share then becomes the problem. Management may contend that all they ask is for employees to perform assigned work at stated times and at accepted levels of performance. The union usually counters that employees seek to improve quality and quantity of output, reduce cost, and minimize the waste of resources. However, it is difficult to accurately measure what increases in production can be attributable to employee behavior.[31] If specific production standards are established through negotiation, it is much easier to negotiate accepted wage increases. Yet separating out and measuring profit resulting from individual and group productivity as compared to management and capital equipment are almost impossible.

Ability to Pay

The issue of **ability to pay** is commonly expressed during wage negotiations. During healthy economic times when the company is experiencing high profits, unions will emphasize enhanced financial conditions that should lead to higher wage rates.[32] Similar to the productivity theory, union leaders emphasize that labor is one of the primary inputs into a company's productivity and therefore profitability. Labor negotiators conclude that if the company is experiencing high profits, it can better pay its employees who have contributed to the good financial conditions.

The ability to pay concept, however, has severe limitations according to management negotiators. First and foremost, unions will not press this issue during hard times when profits have decreased or when the company is suffering temporary losses. Unions seldom want to apply the ability to pay doctrine consistently in both good and hard times; instead, they expect wage levels to be maintained during hard times and increased during good times. Second, management will argue that higher profits must be applied back into the company in capital investments. Third, although profit levels fluctuate greatly, negotiated wage rates do not vary accordingly. If higher wage rates were negotiated on the basis of a six-month crest of high profits, the company might find it extremely difficult to maintain the higher wages during a period of sluggish profitability. Unfortunately, wage rates are negotiated for the future, and profit information is only available for the past. Thus, estimating the company's future ability to pay during the life of the new contract is quite difficult.

Job Evaluation

Job evaluation is the process of systematically analyzing jobs to determine their relative worth within the organization. The process is generally part of *job analysis,* the personnel function of systematically reviewing the tasks, duties, and responsibilities of jobs, usually to write job descriptions and minimum qualifications as well as provide information for job evaluation. Generally the result of a job evaluation effort is a pay system with a rate for each job commensurate with its status within the hierarchy of jobs in the organization.[33]

Job evaluation procedures do not include analyzing employee performance; that is referred to as *performance evaluation* or *performance appraisal.* Nor is job evaluation an attempt to review the employees within a position. Rather, the position is reviewed for several carefully selected criteria to determine the relative worth of the job to the organization in comparison to other jobs in the labor market.

Utilizing job evaluation to determine wage rates incurs significant opposition and skepticism from union leaders. Most union leaders feel wage or pay rates should be established at the negotiating table through the process of collective bargaining and not through management discretion.[34] Union leaders generally believe that too much of the job evaluation process is judgmental and therefore subject to human error. However, with participation by union officials in the critical decision-making steps, job evaluation can be effective in unionized organizations.

Union leaders as well as members of management can use job evaluation techniques as guides to negotiate wage agreements and explain paid differentials to employees. An example of how an agreement can provide for the use of job evaluation procedures during the life of a labor contract is shown in the following labor agreement between the Lockheed Company and the International Machinists and Aerospace Workers:

> The job descriptions for each of the factory and for each of the office and technical classifications which are in effect on the date of execution of this agreement, or which are placed into effect pursuant to Paragraph 2 [next paragraph] herewith, shall be a part of this agreement.
>
> In the event that a new job or position is established or there is a substantial change in the duties or requirements of an established job, the company shall develop an appropriate job description and establish within the existing rates structure provided in Section 2 of this article, the basic rates to apply to such job. The company shall furnish the union with the new job description and shall submit for its approval the rate established for such job. In the event that an agreement is not reached within seven calendar days from the date of such submission or within such additional days as may be mutually agreed upon, the company may place the new job description and rate in effect subject to continuing negotiation of rate. Within five working days from the date the job was placed into effect, the union may proceed in accordance with Step 3 of the grievance procedure established in Article 3, Section 1 of this agreement.[35]

Arbitrators usually agree that job evaluation is the only basis for determining how jobs should be classified and assigned to a wage rate. Furthermore, a proper content analysis of jobs within the pay system must be at the heart of the evaluation, and include the employees' regularly assigned duties.[36] Most agreements specify a method of job evaluation and reclassification when duties and responsibilities are changed by management.

Many grievances concerning job content and classification are filed every year. While the negotiated contract may be quite clear, it cannot possibly provide for specific questions of proper content and classification arising as jobs and working conditions change during the life of the agreement. In misclassification disputes, the content of the jobs in question is compared to the duties outlined in the job descriptions, and not the duties performed by the employees, who may not be fulfilling all the requirements. Classification disputes most often deal with the issues of temporary work assignments (see Case 6.4), change in job content, and evaluation of new jobs. Arbitrators have generally ruled that, in the absence of any contract provision to the contrary, whenever an employee is temporarily assigned to perform higher-grade work, she is entitled to the standard rate of that job for the duration of those duties. The employee is not usually entitled to any premium pay received by the previous employee due to merit or seniority.[37]

The most common dispute concerns the reclassification of a job with changed duties that usually carries a change in wage rate. This is illustrated in Case 6.2. In reevaluating changed jobs, the whole job must be re-examined. This is to insure that both decreased and increased duties and responsibilities are considered. Sometimes a new duty or skill counterbalances a skill previously required in the old job, and no wage change is necessary.[38] The evaluation of a new job is often less of a problem since the duties and skills required have usually been evaluated as parts of existing jobs; thus their total evaluation is a sum of the parts. Also new jobs are not filled; thus no one has the vested interest inherent in the classification of an existing job.[39]

Arbitrators usually reject labor's belief that management has only those wage rate and job classification rights expressed in the agreement. Arbitrators feel management has original rights in conducting its operations that are modified only when expressly relinquished by a labor contract. Thus, all rights not altered by the contract are residual rights maintained by management and inherent in operating the business. However, management, even without a specific contract provision, does *not* have the right to revise a job evaluation system, make changes in labor grades, or determine job classifications *without* the consent of the union if the contract establishes wages and working conditions and recognizes the union as the collective bargaining agent. The Wagner Act protects unions' rights to bargain over such wage issues as job evaluation and job classification. A union may exercise its rights in this area in one of three ways: act on an equal basis with management in the initial determination of job classification and wage rates; give prior approval of such management determinations; challenge management unilateral decisions made without union input or approval through the grievance procedure. Unions disagree as to which method is most effective. Many believe job evaluation to be too important to be merely reviewed or challenged after the fact, and insist on equal participation in the decision process.[40]

Unilateral management action regarding wage rates or job classification changes without consent of the union usually constitutes a refusal to bargain collectively, thus violating the National Labor Relations Act. Neither party can refuse to bargain over wage rate or job evaluation issues. If these issues were *not* raised and discussed during negotiations, the union cannot be presumed to have waived its bargaining rights. However, if these matters were brought up during negotiations, even though the agreement is silent regarding these issues, it may be assumed by the NLRB, an arbitrator, or the courts that they were "bargained away for other advantages."[41]

The NLRB has also ruled that if the union has acquiesced to management's unilateral actions over a period of time, the subject need not even be discussed during negotiations to be considered a management right.[42] Such waivers of a union's bargaining rights are applicable only during the life of an existing contract, and do not carry over to negotiations of a new agreement. Thus, during a new contract negotiating session the union can bargain for equal input and review on limitations of management's rights regarding job evaluation or wage issues. The union may even bargain for input into merit ratings, promotion decisions, or in-grade wage increases. However, most agreements permit the employer to make the initial decision on such matters with the union retaining the right to challenge management decisions through grievance and arbitration procedures.[43]

Wage Surveys

Both labor and management conduct their own **wage surveys** to provide information on external labor market conditions. While the job evaluation process is utilized to maintain internal equity for wage rates, it is also important to maintain external equity; that is, both sides want to offer wages competitive with the labor market and industry, so the firm can attract and retain qualified, productive employees. Union leaders want to provide evidence during negotiations to management and their own members that the wage rates they are negotiating are fair and justified by market conditions.

Negotiators seek wage survey information from three general sources. The first source is published labor market information from federal agencies, primarily the U.S. Department of Labor, which provides wage and salary information to all organizations by standard metropolitan statistical area (see Exhibit 6.4). In general the government's employment information is considered complete and accurate. Negotiators in specialized industries may wish to use the second source, industry wage surveys, published by various interested parties within the industry. Or negotiators may choose a third source: their own survey, which is a costly and time-consuming process. One side of the table is less likely to accept the figures produced by the other side unless they have a very strong working relationship or have participated in the survey process.

Conducting their own wage survey can be expensive and difficult for either negotiating team. Job titles alone are no longer acceptable in comparing positions among other organizations. Instead, the surveyor must compare job descriptions and receive detailed information on the duties and responsibilities of various jobs reported in the survey. The wages paid for each job included in the survey must be specifically defined. Information such as initial hiring salary ranges, the value of related benefits, and cost-of-living increases, as well as other wage increases, must be specified so wage rates among different organizations can be compared fairly. Information concerning seniority provisions, paid vacations, sick leave, and other paid time-off work is critical for a valid analysis. Any other paid benefits such as uniform allowance or tuition reimbursement must also be included.[44]

Using wage surveys in negotiations primarily involves two types of problems. First, since survey information is available from many sources, including industry data, the Bureau of Labor Statistics, employer associations, and union groups, it is often difficult to agree which source contains jobs and data applicable to a particular firm. This problem may be compounded if negotiators use survey information from different cities and therefore must agree upon an acceptable cost-of-living difference between the areas as well. One solution is to combine relevant data of two published surveys to determine averages.[45] But even if negotiators agree upon wage survey information, a second problem involves the question of how the negotiating company should compare itself with other firms. Survey information usually provides an average as well as a range of wages paid for different jobs. Negotiating parties must

Exhibit 6.4 Average hourly earnings of selected workers, by sex

Sex, Occupation, and Industry Division	Number of Workers	Average (mean) Hourly Earnings (dollars)
Maintenance, toolroom, and powerplant occupations—men		
Maintenance carpenters	101	11.63
Manufacturing	87	12.06
Maintenance electricians	488	13.01
Manufacturing	459	13.13
Maintenance painters	79	11.38
Nonmanufacturing	61	12.02
Maintenance machinists	358	12.73
Manufacturing	358	12.73
Maintenance mechanics (machinery)	587	13.17
Manufacturing	582	13.21
Maintenance pipefitters	411	12.80
Manufacturing	411	12.80
Millwrights	176	12.53
Manufacturing	176	12.53
Motor vehicle mechanics	523	10.83
Manufacturing	159	11.11
Nonmanufacturing	364	10.71
Transportation and utilities	280	11.33
Maintenance workers (general)	269	6.60
Manufacturing	127	6.85
Nonmanufacturing	142	6.38
Stationary engineers	102	11.48
Manufacturing	98	11.41

Sex, Occupation, and Industry Division	Number of Workers	Average (mean) Hourly Earnings (dollars)
Material movement and custodial occupations—men		
Truckdrivers	1,265	9.93
Manufacturing	432	9.57
Nonmanufacturing	833	10.12
Transportation and utilities	394	11.05
Truckdrivers, light truck	209	7.54
Nonmanufacturing	181	7.10
Truckdrivers, medium truck	350	11.12
Manufacturing	148	10.08
Truckdrivers, heavy truck	294	8.57
Manufacturing	127	9.40
Truckdrivers, tractor-trailer	367	11.46
Manufacturing	94	9.26
Nonmanufacturing	273	12.21
Shippers	111	8.47
Manufacturing	62	8.79
Receivers	296	10.30
Nonmanufacturing	104	8.29
Shippers and receivers	80	8.20
Manufacturing	52	8.07
Nonmanufacturing	28	8.44
Warehousemen	249	8.85
Manufacturing	232	8.66
Order fillers:		
Nonmanufacturing	454	7.54

Sex, Occupation, and Industry Division	Number of Workers	Average (mean) Hourly Earnings (dollars)
Material handling laborers:		
Nonmanufacturing	218	7.07
Forklift operators	1,150	10.05
Manufacturing	1,054	10.14
Power-truck operators (other than forklift)	120	11.26
Guards	1,851	4.94
Manufacturing	381	9.06
Nonmanufacturing	1,470	3.87
Guards I	1,737	4.64
Manufacturing	279	8.71
Nonmanufacturing	1,458	3.86
Janitors, porters, and cleaners	1,278	6.12
Manufacturing	521	9.05
Nonmanufacturing	757	4.10
Material movement and custodial occupations—women		
Forklift operators	45	9.30
Manufacturing	36	9.85
Guards	144	4.32
Nonmanufacturing	128	3.79
Guards I	137	4.04
Nonmanufacturing	128	3.79
Janitors, porters, and cleaners	855	4.80
Manufacturing	170	9.19
Nonmanufacturing	685	3.71

Source: U.S. Department of Labor, *Area Wage Survey: Louisville, Kentucky–Indiana Metropolitan Area*, Bulletin 3020-56 (Washington, D.C.: U.S. Printing Office, Nov. 1983), p. 10.

then agree on whether they want to pay higher, average, or lower wages than the competition.

Thus, wage survey information will not resolve the issue of appropriate wage rates but will at least provide ballpark information to negotiators. Management may argue that what it lacks in wages it makes up in liberal benefits, working conditions, or advancement opportunities. Labor leaders may counter that these advantages are available in higher-paying organizations and/or do not make up for the lack in take-home pay.

Costing Wage Proposals

Many of the changes in contract language may result in indirect or direct long-range cost to the company. However, most changes in wages, benefits, and cost-of-living adjustments are direct and usually substantial cost increases. Other types of changes such as layoff provisions, seniority determination, and subcontracting may result in indirect cost increases to the company. The process of determining the financial impact of a contract provision change is referred to as **costing**.

The costing of labor contracts is obviously a critical aspect in collective bargaining negotiations. Both sides need to accurately estimate the cost of the contract provision so it can be intelligently discussed and bargained for by either side. If it is an item which ultimately is given up by one side so another provision can be gained, then its relative weight is best estimated by knowing its costs.

Although costing is a critical aspect of collective bargaining, it has been neglected in labor relations literature. This neglect may be caused by several important reasons. The proprietors of some successful costing models are unwilling to share their knowledge with the opposition or potential competitors. And, although some models have been developed at substantial costs and are quite valuable, collective bargaining maintains a general atmosphere of secrecy as a part of negotiating strategy.[46]

All economic provisions can be reduced to dollar estimates whereas noneconomic items cannot be as easily valued by either side. The costing process enables both sides to compare the value of different contract provisions and hopefully helps them arrive at a contract agreement. In most cases, accurate costing processes will be accepted by both sides with little disagreement over the methods employed.

The largest single cost incurred by most corporations is labor cost. Even in capital-intensive organizations such as commercial airlines, labor costs account for about 42 percent of total cost, but in labor-intensive organizations, such as the U.S. Postal Service, labor may account for over 80 percent of total cost. For most organizations, labor's impact on profits is critical, and therefore, relatively small changes in labor costs greatly affect the profitability. Therefore, accurate costing of wage proposals in contract negotiations is critical to future cost control for many organizations.[47] Exhibit 6.5 shows how a typical company might cost the wage provision of a contract.

Accountant Michael Granof outlines the four most commonly utilized **methods of costing union wage provisions:**

1. *Annual cost*   This is the total sum expended by the company over a year on a given benefit; usually the sum excludes administrative costs. Most companies make computations similar to those illustrated in Exhibit 6.5 to arrive at the annual cost of a wage agreement or benefit.

Exhibit 6.5 Costing a wage proposal

Data
90 employees at $8.00/hr
60 employees at $6.50/hr
20 employees at $5.75/hr

Proposed wage increase = 6% across the board = 1,900 average number of production hours per year

Annual Cost
Current: 90 × $8.00 = $720
             60 × 6.50 =   390
             20 × 5.75 =   115
                         $1,225/hr

Current annual cost is $1,225 × 1,900 hr = $2,327,500

Proposed: 90 × $8.48 = $763.20
             60 × 6.89 =   413.40
             20 × 6.09 =   121.80
                         $1,298.40/hr

Proposed annual cost is $1,298.40 × 1,900 = $2,466,960
Total cost of proposed increase is $2,466,960 −$2,327,500 = $139,460

Cents-per-hour
$8.48 − 8.00 = $0.48/hr for 90 employees
$6.89 − 6.50 = $0.39/hr for 60 employees
$6.09 − 5.75 = $0.34/hr for 20 employees

Roll-up (Average ÷ Employee)
Cost of benefits per person = $2.00/hr
$1,225 current cost ÷ 170 employees = $7.20 cost of wages/hr
$2.00 benefits cost ÷ $7.20 wages = 27.77% roll-up

Total Cost of Proposed Wage Rates + Roll-up
$139,460.00 + 38,728.04 (27.77% × 139,460.00) = $178,188.04 wages + roll-up

2. *Cost per employee per year*   This is determined by dividing the total costs of the benefit by either the average number of employees for the year or the number of employees covered by a particular program.

3. *Percent of payroll*   This is the total cost of the benefit divided by the total payroll. Companies may include all payments to all employees in the total payroll, but some exclude overtime, shift differential, or premium pay.

4. *Cents-per-hour*   This is derived by dividing the total cost of the benefit or wage provision by the total productive hours worked by all employees during the year.[48]

The two most commonly discussed economic figures are the annual cost figure and the cents-per-hour figure. When the contract is being negotiated, the total value of all additional wages and other economic items is included so the annual cost of the entire package can be accurately estimated. All sides want to know the exact figure of the negotiated wages and benefits. The management negotiator may even offer a lump sum amount, giving the union negotiators the choice of how to divide it among the various proposed economic enhancements. The cents-per-hour figure is perhaps the single most important item to employees in the new contract. Because employees can quickly estimate their additional take-home pay by using the cents-per-hour figure, it becomes vital when they vote on contract ratification. Granof found that most management negotiators agree that the primary goal in bargaining is to minimize the cents-per-hour direct wage increase.[49]

Employers are usually aware that any negotiated economic increases will have to be duplicated for nonunion and management personnel. This **spillover** effect is often quite costly. However, most costing models do not include the spillover costs; unions do not want to consider them part of the contract cost.[50]

Base

The first step in determining compensation costs is to develop the **base** compensation figure. During negotiation, this figure is essential in determining the percentage value of a requested increase in wages. For example, a $500 annual wage increase means a 2.5 percent wage increase on a $20,000 base and a 5 percent increase for an employee with a $10,000 base. The base may be thought of as the employee's annual salary; however, it seldom represents the total payroll costs incurred by the company for that employee. For example, the average salary cost, or *base salary,* for a nurse in a city hospital was $14,073. Under the terms of her contract, a nurse may have also received an average of the following: longevity pay of $505.00, overtime of $486.75, shift differential of $1,033.68, vacation cost of $636.76, holiday pay of $560.72, hospitalization insurance of $515.72, a clothing allowance of $150.00, and pension benefit of $965.89. The total additional paid benefits were $4,854.52 for each nurse, equal to about 34 percent of base pay. When added to the base of $14,073.00, this produced what many think of as the nurse's true gross salary of $18,927.52.[51]

The one absolutely essential figure that every negotiator should have in his mind at all times is *how much a wage increase of 1 percent will cost the company in thousands of dollars per year.* While the overall dollar cost of a contract settlement is important for budget purposes, most negotiators do not consider such costs to be especially pertinent. They find the total cents-per-hour cost of the negotiated wage increase more relevant, and bargain in those terms. Settlements are also evaluated by their superiors in terms of cents-per-hour, but they need to be able to convert cents-per-hour to total dollars for accurate costing.[52]

Roll-up

As hourly wages increase, many benefits also directly increase because they are directly tied to the wage rate or base pay of employees. This direct increase in benefits caused by a negotiated wage increase is referred to as the **roll-up**. Examples of some of these benefits are

1. *Social security and unemployment insurance contributions*   The employer's contribution is computed as a percentage of each employee's wage up to a maximum annual figure. Any negotiated wage increase up to this maximum will cause a direct increase in the employer's contribution.

2. *Life insurance*   Often the amount of life insurance coverage paid by the employer is based upon the employee's annual earnings. Therefore, as annual earnings are increased, the cost of the insurance automatically increases.

3. *Overtime pay and shift premium*   Overtime compensation and shift premium are often computed as a percentage of base wage. Thus, these also increase with the base wage.

4. *Pension benefits*   The pension benefit formula normally includes employees' average annual wages. An increase in wages increases the employer's funding liability for the pension.[53]

Negotiators often determine an agreed-upon percentage attributable to roll-up. The roll-up percentage is computed by dividing the cost of the directly increased benefit by the cost of the wage rate increase. For example, if a $0.50 per hour increase in the base wage directly causes a $0.10 per hour increase in benefits, then the roll-up percentage is $0.10 divided by $0.50 or 20 percent. Therefore, if negotiators agree to increase employees' base wage by $0.50 per hour, from $5.00 per hour to $5.50 per hour, the 10 percent negotiated wage increase would cause a direct cost increase of 12 percent, or $0.60, when the roll-up costs are added.

Computerized Costing

Merlin P. Breaux of the Gulf Oil Corporation in Houston sums up the role of the computer in collective bargaining today:

> Access to computer data banks has significantly shortened our research time prior to negotiations. And, the application of software spread sheets has made contract cost analysis a much easier and more accurate process. In the future of collective bargaining, more development of computer skills is a necessity.

During contract negotiations, the terms of the contract are constantly changing. Negotiators often quickly revise their demands for wages, benefits, and other cost-related items. The time span of a contract is also negotiable. The negotiator needs to estimate the impact of these changes on the total cost of the contract. A labor or management negotiator may ask: What if a time period or other critical contract item is changed? What would the impact be on the bottom line? Thus, a computer is essential in making these quick, accurate, and detailed calculations.[54]

Knowing how *sensitive* a contract is to its individual terms allows the negotiator to manipulate those variables having the least cost to avoid bringing high-cost items to the bargaining table.[55] Company negotiators can use historical records to calculate quickly the cost of the benefits, as, for example, when the union bargains for an additional holiday. The value of this holiday may be the cost of one day's production because of the factory closing or the salary and overtime necessary to pay workers required to work that day.

This cost may be recurring each year once it is added to the contract. Instead of the holiday, therefore, the company might offer a new cafeteria. This one-time capital expense might appear higher than the holiday cost, especially for a small company. But due to its nonrecurring nature and the improvement to the property, the cafeteria would be the item of least cost. The company, knowing the total costs of all terms, will negotiate the least overall cost proposal.

The advent of the "spread sheet" computer modeling systems has given negotiators a tool for accurately and quickly forecasting labor costs during negotiations. Exhibit 6.6 shows an example of a spread sheet, which is set up with the cost categories going from left to right and the individual items going from top to bottom. The system should be designed to compute total outlay of negotiable and nonnegotiable wages and benefits. This can provide a method of illustrating when and how a change in one economic item directly or indirectly affects other items.

Before beginning contract negotiations, base data on the current economic items in the agreement must be formulated. This can be easily accomplished by using

Exhibit 6.6   Impact of hourly increase of labor costs

Effective Date	Wage Increase	Benefit	Overtime	IMPACT ON			
				Regular Benefits	Overtime	Nonscheduled Regular	Overtime Benefits
2-1-83	0.2500		0.0797	0.0135	0.0034	0.0065	0.0011
2-1-83		1 holiday	0.0031	0.0002	0.0001	0.0001	0.0000
2-1-84	0.3000		0.0956	0.0162	0.0042	0.0078	0.0025

Effective Date	Wage Increase	Benefit	Total Impact	Total Net Present Value[a]	Prior Cost	New Cost	Percent Increase
2-1-83	0.2500		0.1042	0.3542	15.4334	15.7876	2.20
2-1-83		1 holiday	0.0035	0.0035	15.7876	15.7911	2.31
2-1-84	0.3000		0.1263	0.1180	15.7911	15.9091	3.08

[a]Net Present Value is a financial technique relating monies received or disbursed in the future to the current period.

information from the company's payroll and general accounting systems, which are often already computerized. Various computer programs create financial reports and other economic models needed to calculate the costs of contract provisions.

For example, assume that cost of labor consists of three elements.

1. Wage-related costs such as hourly wages or roll-up costs
2. Statutory benefits such as unemployment insurance
3. Nonstatutory benefits such as safety shoes or paid holidays

The wage-related costs will vary according to the combination of the number of employees, associated wage rates, and personnel requirements. Statutory benefits can be calculated as percentages of total wages paid. Nonstatutory benefits can be calculated as a lump sum or percent of wage rate. All three types of costs can then be reduced to an hourly cost by dividing the total cost by the appropriate number of hours. This hourly cost estimate serves as a starting point from which economic proposals can be analyzed (see Exhibit 6.7).

To begin contract negotiations, an initial proposal can be developed by the company. The union will also present the company with a list of hoped-for wage and

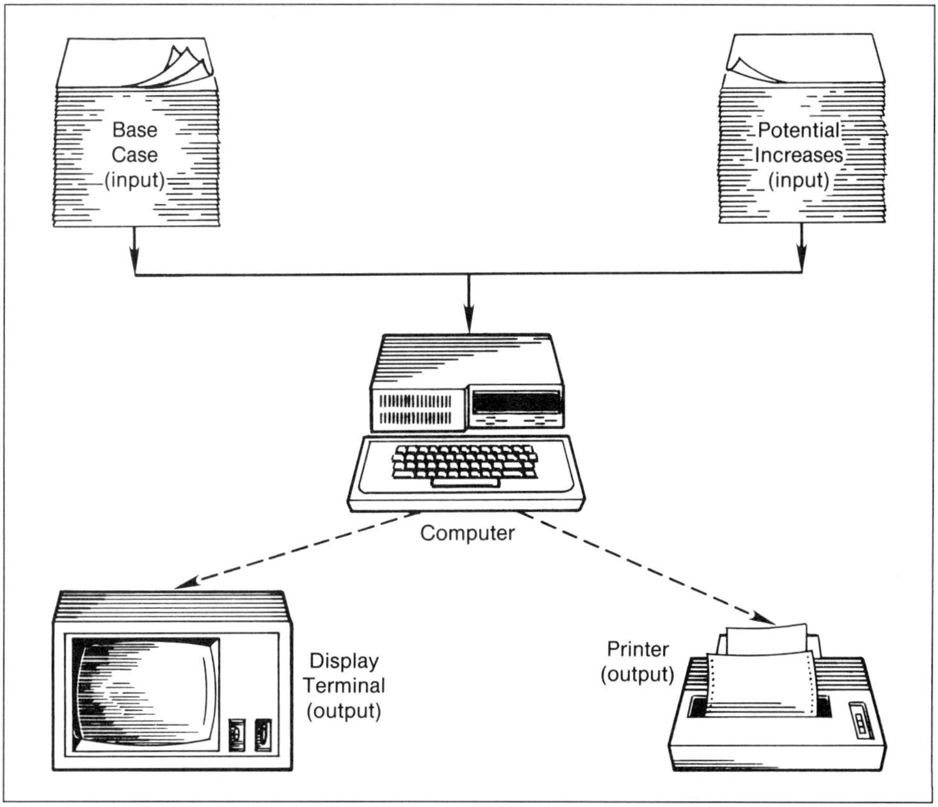

Exhibit 6.7   Basic system flow chart for labor cost negotiations systems

benefit changes. The company, for example, might propose a twenty-five-cent an hour wage increase. The union might propose a fifty-cent an hour increase. The computer will then be programmed to calculate all possible wage increases from twenty-five to fifty cents. Also, the company might propose one additional holiday while the union proposes three. Then the cost of one, two, and three additional holidays will also be programmed into the system.

Thus, before the actual contract negotiations begin, the range of costs will have been calculated. These costs will be the potential increases in labor costs to be added to the base case. To estimate the new cost of the labor contract, the modeling system allows the negotiator to select whatever benefits are being offered the union representatives. The computer will take the selected items, add these to the base case and produce the estimate of new cost. This procedure can be repeated each time there is a change in the negotiated contract items. In fact, the company negotiator can run a cost estimate of several alternative proposals before face-to-face negotiations take place. This will give the negotiator the advantage of knowing in advance the cost of the various changes to the existing contract.

Until a final contract agreement is achieved, the initial model will change as new items are introduced and added to the system. The effect of these items can be shown by relating their behavior to similar items. For example, the cost of one new holiday brought into the discussion through give and take will be the cost of the current dollars for holidays divided by the current number of holidays. Negotiators have instant data on the cost per work hour of the contract proposal.

Labor negotiations are often held at a neutral bargaining site, usually a hotel near the plant. A few years ago this could have presented a problem with using a computer. But due to modern technology, the company representatives can establish a remote data center at the hotel, utilizing a portable terminal, a modem, and the hotel phone to call into the data center at corporate offices. The telephone line links the computer equipment at the hotel and headquarters. It is also possible to use a personal computer that is independent of headquarters.

The model can be used in other projects requiring calculations involving labor cost. If a corporation is planning to expand plant capacity, the system can be used to obtain projections of increased labor costs. The system has calculated all the costs of labor and reduced them to a single hourly cost. Assume a plant expansion will require an average of thirty additional employees, to work twenty-four hours a day, five days a week. It would be simple to multiply the system's hourly cost, which includes all benefits, by thirty employees, twenty-four hours, five days, and fifty-two weeks. This number then would be added to all other costs, such as labor and overhead, to determine the total cost of the plant expansion for a year. More elaborate and difficult proposal changes, such as a change in the pension formulas, can be quickly estimated, possibly eliminating days or even weeks of mathematical calculations. Such time savings can keep negotiations from stalling while leaders wait for information, and even help avoid unnecessary strikes or other labor disruptions.

Further information can be gained by tracking the projection in the modeling system against the actual cost data. This information could provide standards used for cost accounting, as well as prepare the base data for the next contract negotiation sessions. While such computerized costing methods are the exception today, they may become quite common as our society continues to move into the computer age.

Union Wages and Inflation

Unionized wages are often characterized as the spark behind wage-price spirals in the United States. The general public is made aware of large union wage increase settlements, often after any economic strike. However, salary increases received by management and nonunion employees do not receive such publicity. Also, the increased use of COLA provisions in negotiated settlements has received criticism as being a prime cause of inflation.

The causes of inflation are many and complex. The food, energy, and housing sectors make up about 63 percent of the Consumer Price Index. The inflationary period following the Arab oil embargo of 1973 came mostly in these areas and was fueled by increases in capital and energy costs. By 1980, these costs accounted for only nineteen cents of every sales dollar, the lowest percentage in twenty-six years.[56] Between 1970 and 1980 hourly wage rates increased 489 percent in Japan and 464 percent in Germany, compared with 128 percent in the United States.[57]

Many labor critics have claimed that union wage increases have an effect far beyond the organized portion of the labor force. The contention is that nonunion employers, to remain unorganized, follow the lead set by union contracts. However, survey data suggest that such a practice depends on the size of the employer. Large nonunion employers do tend to match the union scale of all levels of unionism in their industry. Medium-size nonunion employers only tend to match the union scale if unionism is a strong presence in their industry. Small nonunion employers tend to maintain wage levels below the union scale regardless of the presence of unionism in the industry.[58] Thus it is difficult to show that union wage increases are followed by a large proportion of employers who may be raising employees' wages for any of several other good reasons.

A comparison between heavily unionized and lightly unionized industries revealed that from 1953 to 1976 earnings rose noticeably faster in the heavily unionized industries, with a long-term widening between union and nonunion earnings. Do, in fact, unions secure higher earnings? Employers might rid themselves of unions if they could avoid strikes and other actions. In the short run nonunion employers might actually pay higher wages than risk union activities.[59]

However, Daniel Mitchell, Director of the UCLA Institute of Labor Relations, suggests that during negotiations employers *offer* less wages than they really intend to pay, or would pay if the company were nonunion, and then they *agree* on higher union-demanded wages. Thus, it appears to the public that the final outcome was a victory for the union, which bargained for more than the employer was willing to give. But the outcome might be similar to the employer's wage determination without a union. Unions may substantially affect only difficult-to-measure, noneconomic items such as work rules, working conditions, and grievance procedures.

Mitchell postulates that higher wages found in unionized industries exist because large organizations have skilled employees who work with little direct supervision and are generally more valued in our society.[60] Many of these highly unionized industries are capital-intensive and thus can more easily afford to pass on higher labor costs in the form of higher prices. They often are also less competitive, and include the auto, steel, rubber, chemical, and transportation industries, and the government.[61]

Summary

Wages and benefits represent the heart of the collective bargaining process. Guarantee of a certain standard of living and a reasonable return for their productive efforts is the major concern for most union members. At the same time management realizes what large percentages of their total costs are wages and benefits. Through job evaluation, wage surveys, and other methods, both sides negotiate either a standard rate or a pay range for each job covered in the agreement. Also, future cost-of-living adjustments are negotiated.

The accurate costing of all negotiated wage changes is critical to successful bargaining and to management's cost containment efforts as well as predictions of future labor cost. Roll-up costs must be included in any estimate when wage increases have been agreed upon. The computer has given both management and labor a negotiating tool to add speed and accuracy to the costing of proposals.

CASE 6.1   *Salary Adjustment*

Adapted from *Bremen Community High School District* 79 LA 778 (1982)

In the contract governing the 1980–81 school year, the parties had agreed that teachers who attended 93 or more calendar days in any school year would be advanced on the salary schedule for the following year. The number of days required for advancement was changed in the contract governing the 1981–82 school year to 130 days. The school board did not advance teachers in the 1981–82 school year who had more than 93 days' but less than 130 days' attendance in the 1980–81 school year. The union grieved the school board's action.

The arbitrator was presented with the following positions. The union claimed that provisions of the 1980–81 collective bargaining contract controlled and had to be honored because the employee who attended the required 93 days had already earned the step increase for the 1981–82 school year. The school board claimed that as the 1981–82 contract was in effect before the school year began, its provisions controlled any salary advancements for that school year and therefore the 130-day rule had to be honored.

Decision

The arbitrator decided in favor of the union. His opinion was based on the fact that the 1981–82 collective bargaining agreement did not specifically provide for retroactivity in the computation of the earned step increase. And while such retroactivity would have been valid if agreed to by the parties, it must be clearly stated in the contract, and cannot be presumed if the contract is silent on the issue.

CASE 6.2   *Piecework to Straight-Time Pay*

Adapted from *Samsonite Corp.* 79 LA 73 (1982)

Under the existing collective bargaining contract, employer paid some employees straight time hourly rates and some employees piecework or incentive rates. In order to change any employee from one rate to the other, the contract required that the employer meet with the union to discuss the change prior to making any change, and justify the change through the application of accepted industrial engineering practices.

As a result of engineering studies conducted in 1980–81, the employer changed the method of pay for three job classifications from piecework to straight time resulting in savings of approximately $275 per month. The union grieved the action.

The union contended that the company could not justify the change based on accepted industrial engineering practices, and that the change was merely a cost-cutting tactic disguised as an improvement in operations. The company defended its action on the basis that the three job classifications involved were deficient in the conditions necessary to apply a professional incentive standard.

Decision

The arbitrator found, first, that the employer complied with the first requirement of the contract, that is, meeting with the union prior to any change. The union participated in the studies undertaken in 1981–82 and in discussions on the performance standards to be improved under the straight line pay rate.

As the second condition, that any change be based on accepted industrial engineering practices, the arbitrator found in the employer's favor.

Third, the arbitrator noted that the employer had from December 1976 through June 1979 spent approximately $1.35 million on equipment used by the employees in the job classifications being grieved. The arbitrator also pointed out that prior to 1976 and after 1979 the same type of variability occurred in the performance of the employees. A previous arbitration award noted that an incentive pay rate can only be awarded if proper performance standards and records are provided, along with uniform equipment conditions and material. A relationship between performance and earnings return must also be shown.

Based on this understanding of the facts, that is, a change in the equipment used by the employees and the continued variable in operations, the arbitrator agreed that a change in standard was justified. That change could also include a change from piecework to straight-time pay.

CASE 6.3 Job Evaluation

Source: Reprinted with permission from Morris Stone, *Labor Grievances and Decisions* (New York: American Arbitration Association, 1970), pp. 35–37

On October 26, Zelda T., an employee in the pattern department of a synthetic rubber products company, was told she would be laid off for lack of work five days later. This notice, required by the collective bargaining agreement, was intended to give an employee facing idleness an opportunity to look around and see whether there was any other job in the shop that her seniority might give her the right to claim.

Zelda and the union steward did just that, and their attention focused on a small parts assembler job in another department. Zelda had once done that work, so there seemed to be no question about her ability, and she had more seniority than the employee who was then on the job.

Management agreed that the small parts operator job was one Zelda might bump into. There was only one trouble: that job was running out too. The result was that Zelda went on layoff on November 2, as scheduled.

On December 7, while still on layoff, Zelda learned that the small parts operator job opened up. But she wasn't recalled for it. Instead, management posted the vacancy and invited only men to bid for the job.

"Because of production needs, we're changing the specifications of that job," the personnel manager explained to the steward. "Whoever does that job will have to handle heavy molds. We've got to have a man on that job."

The steward was not convinced, and he became even more skeptical when he saw that the man who got the job worked only one day on the heavy work, and spent the rest of the time on ordinary work that Zelda, who had more seniority than the man, might have done.

A grievance was filed, and it finally went to arbitration, where the union argued that the assertion that heavy work required a man was only camouflage to deprive Zelda of her seniority rights.

Furthermore, the union argued, management had earlier agreed that Zelda could bump the small parts operator, and it was too late to take a different position now.

Management hotly rejected the accusations. "Everything we did was in good faith," the industrial relations director said. "When we said Zelda was fit to do the work, she was. Later, the heavy work came in and we had to have a man on the job, even if the heavy aspect of the job wasn't a daily occurrence."

Decision

Management was upheld. The arbitrator wrote: "Whether the company breached the seniority provisions of the contract in awarding the job to the junior male employee rather than the grievant, turns more on what the company reasonably thought to be the duties of the job when posted on December 7, 1964, than on what the duties actually turned out to be during the five weeks thereafter. If, on December 7, the company knew or should have known that the job would involve small parts comparable to what it had in mind for the grievant on October 26, then she should have been recalled from the layoff and given the opportunity. On the other hand, if, as the company asserts, the job posting involved different duties, some of which the grievant admittedly could not perform and others

which the company deemed to be too heavy, its earlier agreement with the union would not obtain, and its denial of the opportunity to the grievant would not be violative of the contract."

CASE 6.4   *Wage Rate*

Adapted from *Mobil Oil Corporation,* 79 LA 67 (1982)

An Electrician A position became vacant temporarily due to an employee illness. Electrician B was given the same pay as Electrician A as an incentive for continuing to train an electrician. He performed the work of an Electrician B only. He was not qualified as an Electrician A and his personnel records reflected only the Electrician B classification. He bid on the Electrician A position and was turned down. He grieved the employer's decision. The employer decided that the grievant misunderstood the nature of the pay increase and reduced his pay back to an Electrician B after he filed the grievance. The employee grieved his loss of pay. The loss of pay is the grievance considered here.

The union contended that grievant had been promoted to Electrician A by virtue of the pay increase and that there was no just cause for his demotion. The employer argued that the grievant was never promoted to the Electrician A position because he did not have the qualifications and, indeed, did not perform the duties of an Electrician A. The pay increase was an incentive that the grievant misunderstood. The decision to decrease the pay was to clear up that misunderstanding.

Decision

The arbitrator found that the pay increase was only a reward/incentive pay and not a promotion and that the grievant had been so informed. However, while the employer was free to reduce the pay whenever she wished, she couldn't do so for an improper purpose. The arbitrator found that the employer reduced the pay of grievant as a result of the original grievance for not being given the Electrician A position. As it was the employee's right to grieve the denial of a job bid protected by the contract, the employer could not reduce his pay.

CASE STUDY   *Free Parking*

Adapted from *Social Security Administration* v. *American Federation of Government Employees,* 85 LA 874 (October 22, 1985)

Facts

The dispute involves the interpretation of a national agreement between the par-

ties for numerous employees all over the nation as that agreement affected one office location. The operative sections of the agreement are:

> Any prior benefits and practices and understanding which were in effect on the effective date of this agreement at any level (national, council, regional and local), and which are not specifically covered by this agreement and do not detract from it shall not be changed except in accordance with 5 USC 71.

> The employer agrees to continue to provide secure, adequate, convenient parking.

The Social Security Administration (SSA) was told by the General Services Administration (GSA) (which supervises all government facilities) to move one of its facilities. The old location had approximately thirty-seven parking spaces available to its sixty employees free of charge on a first-come, first-serve basis. The new location had only seven spaces available and these were assigned to car-poolers. The SSA distributed a list of pay parking lots close to the new location for the employees to secure their own parking.

The union grieved the issue claiming that the elimination of free parking for some employees violated the contract.

Lawsuit

The union position is:

1. Advantages enjoyed by employees, whether bargained for or not, become part of their terms of employment and cannot be unilaterally altered by the employer.
2. Free parking at *this* SSA office was a long-established prior benefit, not specifically covered by the agreement (which did not detract from it), and therefore, it cannot be taken away without negotiations.

The SSA position is:

> Parking was specifically addressed in the agreement, and the seven spaces at the new location complied with the provision. No particular number was required.

Questions

1. If you were the arbitrator, what would your decision be, and why?
2. The collective bargaining agreement in this case was a national agreement affecting thousands of employees at different job sites. The parties were aware of individual differences at the various sites when they were negotiating. Can you suggest language changes to the two sections quoted above which could have avoided the problem?

Key Terms and Concepts

Ability to pay	Costing wage proposals
Back-loaded contracts	Deferred wage rate increases
Base	Employee stock ownership plan
COLA	Front-end loading

Job evaluation

Methods of costing wage provisions

Pattern bargaining

Pay equity

Piece-rate systems

Productivity theory

Profit sharing

Roll-up

Scanlon plans

Spillover

Standard rate

Two-tier wage systems

Value added concept

Wage reopener

Wage survey

Review Questions

1. What are the general wage concerns that management and employee representatives bring to the negotiating table?
2. Why have profit-sharing plans replaced COLAs in some recently negotiated agreements?
3. Why does management often prefer profit-sharing increases or bonuses to deferred wage increases?
4. How can wage surveys be effectively used in collective bargaining?
5. Why are labor and management negotiators likely to respond to consideration of the company's ability to pay higher wages?
6. What are some problems with negotiated cost-of-living adjustments?
7. Why must labor and management be able to accurately determine the cost of wage proposals?
8. How should negotiators treat the roll-up costs when negotiating wage changes?
9. Why might union negotiators favor front-end loaded deferred wage increases? Are there potential drawbacks?

Endnotes

1. Mitchell Marks and Philip Mirvis, "Wage Guidelines: Impact on Job Attitudes and Behavior," *Industrial Relations* 20, no. 3 (Fall 1981), p. 296.
2. Gordon E. Jackson, *How To Stay Union Free* (Memphis, Tenn.: Management Press, 1967), pp. 93–94.
3. Chris Berger and Donald Schwab, "Pay Incentives and Pay Satisfaction," Industrial Relations 19, no. 2 (Spring 1980), p. 206.
4. Richard B. Freeman, "Unionism and the Dispersion of Wages," *Industrial and Labor Relations Review* 34, no. 1 (Oct. 1980), pp. 3–24.
5. Jeffrey Pfeffer, "Union-Nonunion Effects on Wage and Status Attainment," *Industrial Relations* 19, no. 2 (Spring 1980), pp. 140–50.
6. Linda A. Krefting, "Differences in Orientations Toward Pay Increases," Industrial Relations 19, no. 1 (Winter 1980), pp. 81–87.
7. Michael R. Carrell, "A Longitudinal Field Assessment of Employee Perceptions of Equitable Treatment," *Organizational Behavior and Human Performance* 21 (1978), pp. 108–18.

8. Lawrence Mishel, "The Structural Determinants of Union Bargaining Power," *Industrial and Labor Relations Review* 40, no. 1 (Oct. 1986), pp. 90–104.

9. Charles Hughes, *Making Unions Unnecessary* (New York: Executive Enterprises, 1976), pp. 105–6.

10. Ibid., p. 106.

11. Leonard R. Burgess, *Wage and Salary Administration* (Columbus, Ohio: Charles E. Merrill, 1984), p. 242.

12. Joan Borum and James Conley, "Wage Restraints Continue in 1985 Major Contracts," *Monthly Labor Review* 109, no. 4 (April 1986), pp. 22–28.

13. Sanford M. Jacoby, "Cost-of-living Escalators Became Prevalent in the 1950's," *Monthly Labor Review* 108, no. 5 (May 1985), pp. 32–33.

14. Richard I. Henderson, *Compensation Management,* (Reston, Va.: Reston, 1979), p. 98.

15. Ibid., p. 100.

16. Victor J. Sheifer, "Cost of Living Adjustment: Keeping up with Inflation?" *Monthly Labor Review* 106, no. 6 (June 1979), pp. 14–17.

17. Wallace E. Hendricks and Lawrence M. Kahn, "Cost of Living Clauses in Union Contracts: Determinants and Effects," *Industrial and Labor Relations Review* 36, no. 3 (April 1983), pp. 447–59.

18. David Paulz, et. al., "The Era of the UNCOLA," *Newsweek,* January 6, 1986, 51–52.

19. *Basic Patterns in Union Contracts* (Washington, D.C.: The Bureau of National Affairs, 1986), pp. 122–123.

20. "Pay Day: Typical Ford Worker Gets $1,200 for Profit-Sharing," *The Courier-Journal,* March 13, 1986, p. B8.

21. Douglas Frasier, speech at the University of Louisville, April 22, 1986.

22. John Hoerr, et al., "ESOPs: Revolution or Ripoff?" *Business Week,* April 15, 1985, 56.

23. William E. Fruhan, Jr., "Management, Labor, and the Golden Goose," *Harvard Business Review* 63 (Sept.–Oct. 1985), pp. 131–141.

24. Harold S. Roberts, *Roberts' Dictionary of Industrial Relations* (Washington, D.C.: The Bureau of National Affairs, 1986), p. 645.

25. Robert J. Schulhof, "Five Years With a Scanlon Plan," *Personnel Administrator,* 24 (June 1979), pp. 55–62.

26. John Savage, "Incentive Programs at Nucor Corporation Boost Productivity," *Personnel Administrator* 22 (Aug. 1981), pp. 33–36.

27. "The Revolutionary Wage Deal at G.M.'s Packard Electric," *Business Week,* August 29, 1983, 54.

28. S.R. Premeaux, R.W. Mondy, A.L. Bethke, "The Two-Tier Wage Systems," *Personnel Administrator* 31, no. 11 (Nov. 1986), pp. 93–100.

29. "The Double Standard That's Setting Worker Against Worker," *Business Week,* April 8, 1983, 70.

30. George Ruben, "Labor and Management Continue to Combat Mutual Problems in 1985," *Monthly Labor Review* 109, no. 1 (Jan. 1986), pp. 3–15.

31. Henderson, *Compensation Management,* pp. 25–26.

32. Sumner Slichter, *Basic Criteria Used in Wage Negotiation* (Chicago: Chicago Association of Commerce and Industry, 1947), p. 25.

33. David W. Belcher, *Wage and Salary Administration* (Englewood Cliffs, N.J.: Prentice-Hall, 1982), pp. 106–13.

34. Harold D. James, "Issues in Job Evaluation: The Union View, 1971–1978," *Personnel Journal* 58 (Feb. 1979), pp. 80–85.

35. *Agreement,* The Lockheed-Georgia Company and the International Association of Machinists and Aerospace Workers, AFL-CIO, 1968–71, pp. 86–87.

36. Clifford M. Baumback, *Structural Wage Issues in Collective Bargaining* (Lexington, Mass.: D.C. Heath, 1971), pp. 4–24.

37. Ibid.

38. Diamond Power Specialty Corp., 46 LA 295.

39. Baumback, *Structural Wage Issues,* pp. 16–19.

40. Ibid., pp. 1–4.

41. C. & C. Plywood Corporation & Veneers, Inc., 163 N.L.R.B. 136 (1967).

42. General Electric Co., 163 N.L.R.B. (1967).

43. Baumback, *Structural Wage Issues,* pp. 26–28.

44. Belcher, *Wage and Salary Administration,* pp. 106–13.

45. Ibid., pp. 236–43.

46. Gordon S. Skinner and E. Edward Herman, "The Importance of Costing Labor Contracts," *Labor Law Journal* 32, no. 8 (Aug. 1981), pp. 497–504.

47. Wayne F. Cascio, *Costing Human Resources: The Financial Impact of Behavior in Organizations* (Boston: Kent Publishing, 1982), p. 99.

48. Michael H. Granof, *How to Cost Your Labor Contract* (Washington, D.C.: Bureau of National Affairs, 1973), pp. 4–5.

49. Ibid., p. 33.

50. Skinner and Herman, "Costing Labor Law Contracts," pp. 500–501.

51. Cascio, *Costing Human Resources,* p. 102.

52. Granof, *Cost Your Labor Contract,* p. 34.

53. Frederick L. Sullivan, *How to Calculate the Manufacturer's Costs in Collective Bargaining* (New York: AMACOM, 1980), pp. 23–26.

54. Michael R. Carrell and Lynn Hampton, "Computer Enhanced Labor Negotiations," *Labor Law Journal* 36, no. 10 (Oct. 1985), pp. 795–800.

55. U.S. Department of Labor, Bureau of Labor Statistics, *Handbook of Labor Statistics* (Washington, D.C.: Government Printing Office, 1980), p. 56.

56. "Labor Cost Decline Seen," *New York Times,* 16 Dec. 1981, p. D-5.

57. Rudolph A. Oswald, "Why Wages Should Not Be Blamed for the Inflation Problem," *Monthly Labor Review* 109, no. 4 (April 1982), p. 45.

58. Michael Podgursky, "Unions, Establishment Size and Intra-Industry Threat Effects," *Industrial and Labor Relation Review* 39, no. 2 (Jan. 1986), pp. 277–294.

59. Daniel J. B. Mitchell, *Unions, Wages, and Inflation* (Washington, D.C.: The Brookings Institution, 1980), pp. 62–64.

60. Ibid., pp. 77–89.

61. Baumback, *Structural Wage Issues,* pp. 76–84.

7

Employee Benefits Issues

Employers may seek to keep employees from leaving too soon by asking them to sign a *"pay-back" agreement* requiring an employee who voluntarily quits before a specified period of time (usually one year) to pay the employer the cost of certain benefits. The most common benefits specified include relocation costs for newly hired employees, training program costs, and tuition assistance. The aim of such agreements is to protect the investment the employer has made in the employee. Companies such as American Airlines (pilot training costs of about $10,000), Electronic Data Systems Corporation (relocation costs), and Lockheed Corporation (tuition assistance) have successfully sued employees who refused to honor their agreements.

Some unions have criticized the agreements; the AFL-CIO has noted their similarity to indentured servitude (a person required to work for another as a servant). However, not all unions dislike the concept. The Sheet Metal Workers Union has required those who complete the union training program to repay the program costs if they work for a nonunion shop within ten years.

Source: Adapted from Judy L. Ward, "Firms Forcing Employees to Repay Some Costs if They Quit Too Soon," The Wall Street Journal, *July 16, 1985, p. 30.*

Today negotiated employee benefits, once referred to as fringe benefits, represent a critical part of the total economic package. Employers may easily find that between 25 and 45 percent of the total economic package now consists of benefits rather than direct compensation. Yet benefits are not usually designed to meet the same employee objectives as the wage portion of the negotiated agreement. From the employee standpoint, the wage portion of the economic package provides income needed for the necessities of life such as food, shelter, and clothing, as well as some luxuries. Management views wages as a means of attracting, retaining, and motivating employees and therefore maximizing their productivity.

Benefits, however, often have different objectives for management as well as the union. For example, many benefits are designed to guarantee employees a stream of income regardless of unforeseen circumstances such as layoff, automation of work, death, or illness. A major effect of a strong benefit package is the reduction of turnover. A substantial cost borne by workers in changing jobs is the loss of associated benefits. A worker leaving behind a pension may forfeit several thousands of dollars of retirement income, along with sizable losses in vacation, insurance, and other benefits.[1]

Retirement income is usually the most expensive negotiated economic benefit. Additional pay for time not worked, such as vacation, holiday, and sick leave, is commonly negotiated as well as premium pay for unusual circumstances such as overtime and call-in pay.

As a percentage of the total compensation provided by management, benefit costs have grown dramatically in recent years. During the period from 1975 to 1985, the cost of benefits provided by employers increased 105 percent, from an average of $77 per week to $157 per week.[2] As Exhibit 7.1 illustrates, the increase in total employee benefits was 13 percent *greater* than the increase in average weekly earnings for the ten-year period. Also, the most expensive areas of employee benefits continue to be pensions, social security, insurance, and paid time-off work. Unions have generally led the way in benefit changes in this country regarding the types of benefits provided by employers and their relative value. Negotiated benefits in collective bargaining agreements generally set the standard for the nonunion sector.

Does collective bargaining affect the benefits received by union members? A comparison of over 10,000 union and nonunion establishments found that unionism had a sizable impact on total benefit expenditures as well as the straight-time wage rate. Exhibit 7.2 illustrates the average dollars spent per hour on voluntary benefits were 140 percent higher ($0.70/hour versus $0.29/hour) in private union firms. The union firm dollar average was also higher for legally required benefits by 55 percent ($0.28/hour versus $0.18/hour).[3]

Givebacks

The 1980s have ushered in a new era in negotiated wage and benefits. High levels of unemployment prompted unions in severely affected industries to seek ways to protect jobs. Through collective bargaining, unions seek to stop further layoffs. Employers are willing to agree to increased employment security only at the high

Exhibit 7.1   Average weekly employee benefits costs

Benefit	1975	1985	Percentage Increase
Insurance (life, hospital, surgical medical, etc.)	$ 11.19	$ 30.02	168%
Old age, survivors, disability, and health insurance	12.23	27.46	125
Paid vacations	11.15	20.17	81
Pensions (nongovernment)	11.92	17.40	46
Paid rest periods, coffee breaks, lunch periods, etc.	7.85	14.46	84
Paid holidays	7.23	11.75	63
Unemployment compensation taxes	2.19	6.62	202
Paid sick leave	2.58	5.50	113
Workers' compensation	2.71	5.02	85
Profit-sharing payments	2.37	4.50	90
Thrift plans	0.60	2.52	320
Other paid nonworking time (guard duty, death in family, personal emergencies, etc.)	0.90	1.90	111
Dental insurance	0.21	1.67	695
Christmas or other special bonuses, suggestion awards, etc.	0.90	1.33	48
Employee education expenditures	0.23	1.21	426
Short-term disability	N.A.	1.17	N.A.
Salary continuation or long-term disability	0.44	0.85	93
Employee meals furnished free	0.40	0.56	40
Discounts on goods and services purchased from company by employees	0.35	0.33	−6
Other employee benefits	1.17	2.60	122
Total employee benefits	**$ 76.62**	**$157.04**	**105%**
Average weekly earnings	**$216.42**	**$416.02**	**92%**

Source: Reprinted by permission from *Nation's Business* (February 1987). Copyright 1987, U.S. Chamber of Commerce.

price of wage and/or benefit freezes. In several cases reductions in benefits, particularly paid time-off work, are required to guarantee employment levels.[4] Thus **givebacks** or *concession bargaining* techniques were born out of necessity.

Concession bargaining first gained national headlines in November 1979 when Chrysler negotiated over $200 million in givebacks. On the brink of bankruptcy, Chrysler used the United Auto Worker concessions to negotiate over $1 billion in long-term, federal government loans. While some concessions were in the area of deferred wage increases, the majority of the savings came in the reduced employee benefits of paid holidays, paid sickness and accident absences, and pension funds.[5] In return Chrysler gave the UAW a seat on its board of directors and a no-layoff guarantee.

The giveback negotiations of the UAW and Chrysler were historical in the labor relations field. The negotiations set a pattern for several other unions and showed that unions preferred reductions in previously negotiated benefits such as paid time-off work to reductions in wage levels. The negotiations also proved that a giant corporation and a major union could work together to keep the company operating.

On Labor Day in 1983, after a single six-hour negotiation session, the new Chrysler Corporation as proclaimed by its president, Lee Iacocca, and the UAW reached another agreement. The new agreement came only a few weeks after Chrysler had reported record quarterly profits and was able to pay off its federal loans several years ahead of schedule. The new contract contained over $1 billion in wage and benefit increases.[6] The UAW had publicly demanded that Chrysler share its wealth with the employees since it had asked them for substantial givebacks during harder times. Management apparently agreed since only one day of negotiating was required.

In many cases concessions are not called "concessions" so that neither side appears to have lost or won in negotiations. Most negotiations involving givebacks

Exhibit 7.2   Dollars spent on compensation

| Compensation per Hour[1] | Manufacturing (n=4074) | | | | All Private Nonfarm (n=10,088) | | | |
| | Union (n=2580) | | Non-union (n=1494) | | Union (n=4973) | | Non-union (n=5115) | |
	Dollars	Share	Dollars	Share	Dollars	Share	Dollars	Share
Total[2]	$3.66	1.000	$2.81	1.000	$4.33	1.000	$2.73	1.000
Straight-time pay	2.75	0.750	2.26	0.804	3.35	0.773	2.25	0.826
All fringes	0.91	0.250	0.55	0.196	0.99	0.227	0.47	0.174
Legally required fringes	0.22	0.059	0.18	0.063	0.28	0.065	0.18	0.067
Voluntary fringes	0.70	0.191	0.37	0.133	0.70	0.162	0.29	0.106
Life, accident, health insurance	0.15	0.041	0.07	0.023	0.16	0.036	0.05	0.017
Vacation	0.15	0.041	0.07	0.026	0.11	0.025	0.06	0.021
Overtime premiums	0.12	0.033	0.09	0.032	0.13	0.031	0.07	0.026
Pensions	0.12	0.033	0.05	0.017	0.15	0.035	0.04	0.013
Holiday	0.09	0.024	0.05	0.018	0.07	0.015	0.04	0.014
Shift premiums	0.03	0.007	0.01	0.004	0.02	0.004	0.01	0.002
Sick leave	0.01	0.003	0.01	0.003	0.01	0.003	0.01	0.004
Bonuses[3]	0.01	0.003	0.02	0.008	0.01	0.003	0.02	0.007
Other[4]	0.03	0.007	0.01	0.002	0.04	0.010	0.01	0.002

[1] All figures are in 1967 labor cost units, obtained by deflating 1968–72 figures by division by the ratio of average hourly earnings in the private sector in each year to average hourly earnings in the private sector in 1967.
[2] Calculated from the Bureau of Labor Statistics, *Expenditures for Employee Compensation Survey*, tapes 1967–68, 1969–70, and 1971–72. Shares are based on dollars carried to additional decimal places. Column sums do not always add to the correct total due to rounding.
[3] Lump-sum payments under profit-sharing plans or seasonal bonuses.
[4] Leave benefits, severance, vacation and holiday funds, supplemental unemployment benefits, savings plans, and other private welfare benefits.

Source: Reprinted, with permission, from Richard B. Freeman, "The Effect of Unionism on Fringe Benefits," *Industrial and Labor Relations Review* 34, no. 4 (July 1981), pp. 489–509. © Cornell University. All rights reserved.

require both labor and management to make some concessions in a true "give-and-take" process.[7] Often, for example, if management demands givebacks in wages and benefits, union negotiators will demand similar reductions in management salaries and benefits. If management requests greater flexibility in work rules and scheduling, labor negotiators might demand greater union participation in management decisions.

Successful concession bargaining hinges on management's ability to convince labor of impending financial crisis that could cause a significant loss of jobs or total shutdown of the operation.[8] However, economic adversity alone may not be enough to bring about concessions. Union negotiators expect management concessions and programs to enhance labor-management relationships. Thus employers as well as unions have made concessions during giveback negotiations, many aimed at increasing quality of work life and worker participation in decision making. Economic concessions have often centered on management's sharing of future "good times" through profit sharing or gain sharing in exchange for immediate union givebacks.[9]

Required Benefits

Some employee benefits are required by law and are therefore not negotiated. However, both labor and management representatives need to be cognizant of these benefits and their impact upon other benefits that can be negotiated. Some negotiated benefit plans are designed to supplement those required by law to guarantee the employee a greater level of benefit. In recent years some union leaders opposed government-imposed benefit programs such as the Occupational Safety and Health Act of 1970, the Pension Reform Act of 1974, and the Health Maintenance Organization Act of 1973, because the benefits provided were previously only for union employees. Union negotiators also felt the government diluted their ability to bargain for even better benefits. Uniformly provided benefits restrict negotiators' ability to bargain for specific programs preferred by their membership.

Unemployment insurance, Social Security, and worker's compensation are three costly and important government-required benefits. **Unemployment insurance** programs have been operating since 1938, helping maintain the economy by stabilizing purchasing power while allowing workers to seek new jobs without significant negative impact.[10] States provide unemployed workers with benefits by imposing payroll taxes on employers. The amount paid normally varies according to the state's unemployment rate. The unemployed person must have worked for a certain period of time and must register with the state bureau of employment to receive benefits.

About 97 percent of all workers are included in the federal-state unemployment insurance system. Employers pay a payroll tax of 6.2 percent on each employee's wages up to $7,000 a year. There are no federal standards for benefits, qualifying requirements, benefit amounts, or duration of benefits; the states each develop their own formulas for workers' benefits. Under all state laws a worker's benefit rights depend on his work experience during a "base period" of time. Most states require a claimant to serve a waiting period before receiving benefits.[11] Workers are usually required to be available for work, able to work, and actively seeking work to receive benefits. Claimants are disqualified for voluntarily leaving without good cause, discharge for misconduct, or refusal to accept suitable work.

In 1935, Congress established the *Social Security* system to provide supplemental income to retired workers. Initially intended to supplement private, often union-negotiated pension plans, Social Security would help retirees live in dignity and comfort. The cost of the system is carried by employers and employees who pay an equal amount of taxes into the system, which then uses the funds to pay benefits to currently retired individuals. Technically, Social Security taxes are Federal Insurance Contributions Act (FICA) taxes. Management often points out that the employees pay only half the cost of the system yet receive all the benefits.

Recently, another phase of the Social Security system was added to provide disability, survivor, and Medicare benefits. To become eligible for retirement benefits, individuals born after 1928 must contribute for forty quarters (ten full years). Required contributions to receive medical benefits vary according to age.

Since the Social Security Revision Act of 1972, the benefits paid to retirement income recipients increase each year by a percentage equal to the increase in the Consumer Price Index, if the CPI increases by 3 percent or more. This automatic and liberal increase has been one of the main causes of the shaky financial condition of the Social Security system.[12] It has also provided management's primary weapon in not increasing employees' private pensions. Employers complain that Social Security taxes have increased each year along with raised salaries since the tax is a percentage of the employees' salary. In addition, Congress raised the employers'/employees' Social Security tax rate from 4.8 percent in 1970 to 6.7 percent in 1982, with a scheduled increase of 7.65 percent in 1990.[13]

Laws requiring **worker's compensation** were enacted by states to protect employees and their families against permanent loss of income and high medical bills due to accidental injury or illness on the job. The primary purpose of most state laws is to keep the question of the cause of the accident out of court. The laws assure employees payment for medical expenses or lost income. Worker's compensation primarily consists of employer contributions into a statewide fund. A state industrial board then reviews cases and determines employee eligibility for compensation due to injury on the job. Employees are often able to recover total medical expenses and up to two-thirds of lost income due to missed work or disability.[14] States may allow employers to purchase worker's compensation insurance from private insurance companies as well as state funds.

Union leaders have played an important role in assuring that worker's compensation laws are updated and employee interests are protected. Their efforts not only protect the interests of the union workers but also the nonunion sector.

"Right-to-Know" Laws

In 1986 the Occupational Safety and Health Administration (OSHA) began requiring employers in all basic industries to meet "right-to-know" rules similar to those in existence in seventeen states.[15] Union leaders had sought federal legislation for years. **Right-to-know laws** require employers to provide workers information about hazardous substances but these laws do not limit sale or use. Workers are given the right to know what they are dealing with on the job. Over 1,000 substances have been listed as hazardous by state and federal agencies, including asbestos, cyanide, and polychlorinated biphenyls (PCB). The information requirements for employers include (1) material safety data sheets (MSDS) that identify the maker, the physical and chemical characteristics of the substance, the known health risks, safety equipment and precautions, and first-aid techniques; (2) warning labels on workplace containers; and (3) employee training programs.[16]

Income Maintenance Plans

Income maintenance provisions have become commonplace in collective bargaining agreements. These plans are negotiable and include supplemental unemployment benefits, severance pay (also called *dismissal* or *termination pay*), and wage employment guarantees. In addition, these plans protect employees from financial disruptions. Private pension plans provide for income during retirement, along with Social Security.

Pension Plans

Private pension plans have become one of the most sought-after and most expensive employee benefits, as illustrated in Exhibit 7.1. In the early stages of the U.S. labor movement, the benefit provided motivation for senior employees to remain with the organization and thus increase their retirement income. However, only in the last twenty-five to thirty years have both labor and management negotiators accepted management's obligation to provide income to employees beyond their productive years. This occurred largely as a result of a 1949 decision by the Supreme Court, *Inland Steel Company* v. *NLRB,* in which the Court declared pension plans to be mandatory collective bargaining subjects. Today pension plans are provided in over 90 percent of the labor contracts in manufacturing industries.[17] In 1980 the Bureau of Labor Statistics estimated that 66 percent of all nonfarm employees were covered by a private pension plan.[18] Likewise, the number of private pension plans throughout the United States has increased dramatically since the *Inland Steel* decision. While fewer than 1,000 private pension plans were in operation in 1940, over 700,000 were in operation in 1982. The number of workers covered by those plans as well as the percentage of the nonfarm work force has also grown to about 35 million workers.[19]

However, today it is estimated that more than 10 million paying American workers will never collect from their pension plans. For example, Christine Clark was a tobacco worker for more than thirty years for several companies with private pension plans. Yet she could not receive a single penny in retirement benefits. The reason: Ms. Clark never became **vested**—had enough years to become eligible for company pension benefits—with any employer. Although she worked for Liggett & Meyers Tobacco Company in Richmond, Virginia, for twenty-three years, only seven years counted toward the pension plan, not enough to qualify her for the minimum of ten years. After several odd jobs, Ms. Clark worked for eight-and-a-half years for American Tobacco Company in Richmond, Virginia, again not long enough to become vested with the pension plan. At the age of fifty-three and having worked for thirty-four years, Ms. Clark has no retirement income other than her Social Security.[20]

Many U.S. workers will not receive private pensions due to their desire to change jobs and leave employers frequently during their productive years. They miss being covered by any one company's pension plan. For other employees, the company either shuts down, lays them off, or dismisses them before they become vested. The lack of pension planning is particularly a problem in the service sector of our economy, which has grown rapidly in recent years.

Unions have been successful in providing private pension plans for their members; this is not commonly found in the nonunion sector. It is estimated that over 91 percent of the union employers in this country have private pension plans compared to only 52 percent of nonunion employers.[21] One major study concluded that unionization has significantly affected retirement systems of private employers, increasing the likelihood that an employer will offer a pension.[22] However, unions apparently are not able to raise actual employer expenditures for pensions once they are established.[23]

Union-negotiated pension plans compared to nonunion plans provide beneficiaries the ability to retire at an earlier age, greater benefits when they retire, and larger increases in their benefits after they retire. Combined with the greater inclusion of union workers in pension plans compared to nonunion, union membership is the dominant factor in determining the private pension dollars received by a retired worker in the United States.[24]

Why the significantly greater pension benefits for union workers? One possibility is because under collective bargaining, the preferences of older workers receive greater weight than those of younger workers. Older workers, who demand more pension benefits, are better able through collective bargaining to affect their level of benefits than nonunion workers. Another possibility is that unions are better able to monitor pension plans and their pension funds. The complexity of benefit formulas, participation, vesting and other pension factors may be simply too difficult for the individual nonunion worker to completely understand and monitor.[25] Finally, union members who directly participate in negotiations are usually older workers with greater knowledge of, and interest in, the pension plan.

Most workers plan to retire at the age when they first become eligible for full private pension benefits.[26] In the past that age, most commonly sixty-five, was also the mandatory retirement age and the age at which full Social Security benefits would first be available. In the future the "typical" retirement age may difficult to estimate. Many workers are living longer and choosing to work longer. The amendment to the Age Discrimination in Employment Act of 1986 made it illegal for employers to require retirement at any age,[27] and the 1983 Social Security Amendment will gradually change the age of full benefits eligibility from sixty-five to sixty-seven. Thus the worker will be faced with a more complex decision when choosing a retirement date.

Private pension systems will play an even more important role in the retirement decision. Undoubtedly, management will consider changing the full benefit eligibility age from sixty-five to sixty-seven to match the change in Social Security benefits and reduce their cost of retirement benefits. In the absence of unexpected events such as sudden wealth or failing health, most workers faced with the choice of working as long as they desire will consider the age at which they first become eligible for full pension benefits to be a critical decision point. Pension plans often use increased benefits to encourage workers not to retire early at reduced benefits, for example, at age sixty-two, but to continue working and each year receive a higher proportion of their total benefits. Labor and management leaders alike are now faced with the reality of no mandatory retirement age and a change in Social Security. Thus they can more easily consider changes in pension benefits, significantly affecting the age at which their workers choose to retire and therefore the cost of the pension system. Just as employee health care plans have seen a great deal of change in recent years, private negotiated pension plans are likely to experience significant change in the future.

Employee Retirement Income Security Act (ERISA)

In 1974 Congress passed the **Employee Retirement Income Security Act (ERISA)**, also known as the Pension Reform Act. The law was passed in response to alleged abuses and incompetence in some private pension plans. ERISA provided a sweeping reform of pension and benefit rules. The lengthy and complicated law primarily affects the following aspects of pension planning.

1. Employers are required to count toward vesting all service from age eighteen and to count toward earned benefits all earnings from age twenty-one. (Prior to the Retirement Equity Act of 1984, accrual toward vesting began at age twenty-two, toward earnings at age twenty-five.)
2. Employers must choose from among three minimum vesting standards (Sec. 203).
3. Each year employers must file reports of their pension plans with the U.S. Secretary of Labor for approval. New plans must be submitted for approval within 120 days of enactment.
4. The Pension Benefit Guarantee Corporation (PBGC) was established within the Department of Labor to encourage voluntary employee pension continuance when changing employment. This is accomplished by providing *portability*—the right of an employee to transfer tax-free pension benefits from one employer to another.
5. Pension plan members are permitted to leave the work force for up to five consecutive years without losing service credit and allowed up to one year maternity or paternity leave without losing service credit.[28]

ERISA substantially reduced the number and scope of pension issues left at the bargaining table. The law has been criticized by employers and labor leaders because it is quite complex and may have encouraged some employers to provide no retirement plan at all.[29]

Issues in Pension Negotiations

Vesting   The conveying of employees' nonforfeitable rights to share in a pension fund is termed **vesting**. As illustrated in the example of Christine Clark, many individuals never receive private pension funds because they leave employers before working enough years to become vested.

Section 203 of ERISA provides that employers choose from among three alternatives of retirement age and service. One alternative is to provide 100 percent vested rights after ten years of service. The other two provide less than 100 percent vested rights with fewer years of service. Union negotiators are very interested in the plan chosen by management. However, no single plan is always preferred by employees.

Qualified plan   A *qualified plan* generally refers to a plan that meets standards set by the Internal Revenue Service (IRS). By qualifying under the IRS provisions, an employer can deduct pension contributions made to the qualified plan as business expenses for tax purposes. This, of course, is a major reason employers seek to qualify their pension plans whenever possible. Employees, however, also benefit since they do not pay taxes on any dollars either they or the employer invest in the plan under current income. Instead, income taxes are paid when the retirement benefits are received. A *nonqualified plan* would not provide the tax advantages of the qualified plan but would be required to meet the strict guidelines set by the IRS.

Funding methods   There are four general methods of funding pension plans. Each method may provide some particular advantage to management.

1. *Trusted or funded plans*   Employers create a separate account or fund and invest dollars annually to provide the future retirement benefits for employees. The fund is usually administered by a bank or separate board that makes decisions as to the investment of the funds and the payment of retirement benefits to individuals. Usually the fund is kept financially sound by an actuarial study of the estimated financial liability of the plan as well as its expected wealth of current assets. If the actuarial study determines that the fund does not have enough money to guarantee benefit payments to both the present and past contributing employees, the employer adds the additional money necessary to keep the fund financially sound. This review of actuarial soundness is normally done annually. In some years if the number of retirement employees decreases and the number of new employees changes, it may not be necessary for the employer to add any additional money to the fund, whereas other years employers may have to add substantial amounts.

2. *Current expenditure plans*   Treating the retirement benefits paid to previous employees as a current expense and therefore paying it out of operating income is known as a *nonfunded* or *pay-as-you-go* funding method. This method is not actuarially sound and guarantees no fund available to current employees to provide later retirement benefits. Yet for many employers the possibility of providing the trusted or funded plan is very small since such plans usually require a large amount of capital to begin operation and create a large fund. The **current expenditure** system can simply provide that the employer will meet an additional expense each year; that is, the retirement benefits due its previous employees, as it meets other expenses. The largest nonfunded plan in the world is the Social Security retirement system.

3. *Insured plans*   Insurance companies often provide pension plans to employers. Normally the insurance company treats the provisions of the pension plan for the employer as it would any other type of collective insurance; the employer pays a premium while the insurance company administers the plan, pays out all benefits due, and assumes future payment liability. Although the employer may pay more to the insurance company than might be necessary under a trusted plan, the expertise and the experience of the insurance company may be well worth the additional fee to the small- or medium-size employer.

4. *Profit-sharing plans*   Some companies provide a pension plan which is funded; however, the funds are provided only through a percentage of company profits. This represents a unique compromise between the current expenditure and the funded methods. Management feels that employees will be more interested in the profitability of the company if their pensions share in the risk of profitability of doing business. Companies with stable profitability and growth have little trouble funding a pension plan through the profit-sharing approach. Sears Roebuck and Company and other firms in this country have successful profit-sharing plans. However, if profits substantially decrease or become nonexistent over several years, the plan may eventually become financially unsound.

Union leaders prefer the trusted and insured methods of funding pension plans that provide greater security for the future retirement benefits of their members. Even if the company had to shut down, most properly funded plans would continue to provide retirement benefits to employee participants.

Contributory plans   All pension plans are either contributory or noncontributory. In a **contributory plan**, the employer pays a portion of the funding and the employee pays the other portion. The percentage paid by employer and employee becomes of keen interest during collective bargaining. Also of interest is the type of benefit plan provided. In a *noncontributory plan,* the employer pays all the administrative and funding costs. Therefore, the question of how much is to be paid by the employer does not arise during collective bargaining; rather, the benefit package provided by the plan becomes the central issue.

About 82 percent of the plans are contributory in manufacturing firms. Management feels that having employees share some of the cost of the pension plan reminds them of the expense of the plan and motivates them to stay with the firm once they have become vested. Union negotiators would prefer that all plans be noncontributory; however, they realize that many employers, particularly small firms, cannot bear the entire cost of a financially sound retirement system.

Age or service requirement   Most pension plans require a minimum age and/or years of service before an employee becomes eligible to receive retirement benefits. The plan may simply require a minimum age such as fifty-five or sixty at which the retired employee begins receiving benefits, or a minimum of twenty-five or thirty years of service. Other plans require a minimum of both, such as twenty-five and sixty, meaning twenty-five years of service and sixty years of age. Under such a plan, the employee who began work with the company at age twenty must work for forty years before becoming eligible to receive retirement benefits, even though she could become eligible at age forty-five under the service requirement. Some systems provide for an option of retirement minimums. For example, an employee may receive 50 percent of the benefits if he retires at age fifty-five, 70 percent at age sixty, 80 percent at age sixty-two, or 100 percent at age sixty-five. Management realizes that the percentages and ages can be changed to motivate employees to retire at an earlier age or to wait until the mandatory retirement age of seventy. A similar type of provision can be created for years of service. The minimum age and/or service requirement is an item of great interest during contract negotiations. If union membership is heavy with senior employees close to retirement, changing the minimum requirement becomes an even greater goal of the union negotiators. Negotiators must try to clearly specify service requirements to avoid disputes as in Case 7.1, where the definition of age was critical.

Benefit formula   Perhaps the most important pension item in collective bargaining is the *benefit formula,* in which benefits due each retiree are calculated. A common benefit formula would appear as follows:

$$\text{Benefit dollars} = \text{Years of service} \times \text{Base pay} \times \underline{\hphantom{XXX}}\%$$

The three variables of importance in the formula, therefore, are years of service, employee's base pay, and a percent to be applied. The percentage is usually a fixed figure that is seldom negotiated to change, 2–3 percent being often used, up to 5 percent or as low as 1 percent. The number of years of service is determined by the individual employee. The determination of the base pay, therefore, becomes critical to many contract negotiations. For many years, base pay was defined to be the average of the employee's annual gross wage received. However, in recent years with high inflation causing rapid salary increases as well as moves through promotion and transfer, base pay often receives other definitions.

Contracts today commonly define *base pay* as the average yearly salary for the last three or five years worked, or the average yearly salary for the highest three of the last five years. The most liberal definition of base pay would be the employee's highest gross salary received in any one year. The more years included in averaging base pay, if one assumes a steadily increasing salary, the lower the average and therefore the lower the benefit. Union negotiators also want to include vacation time and time taken for personal leave as well as time worked in a definition of base pay. Management will naturally resist any redefinition of base pay that would increase its calculated total and the pension benefit in the formula.

Union leaders are keenly aware that private pension plans fail to keep up with inflation. Therefore, their demand priorities for pension benefits usually center on providing fully funded plans with a base defined to be the average of the highest three years of employee service with future benefits tied to increase in the Consumer Price Index. As our work force grows older and union members increasingly get closer to retirement years, their interest in providing cost-of-living adjustments to pension plans will probably increase. However, many plans today still provide for a flat-rate pension benefit as determined by the formula, which never increases during the retirement years. At the same time, however, management negotiators claim that employers cannot afford increases in pension benefits since they are required to pay substantial increases in the Social Security taxes. Since Social Security benefits are also tied to the Consumer Price Index and provide for automatic increases as the index rises, management reasons that private pension plans need not provide similar increases.

Determining the cost of a change in pension plan negotiated through collective bargaining is difficult. Normally such changes cannot be made without an actuarial study to estimate their impact on the total pension plan and possible increase in the company's insurance premium or additional cash contribution. The actual cost of a plan benefit cannot be determined until the employee is actually deceased. Therefore, costs are always estimated and may change. Negotiators may avoid some of the problems in estimating proposed changes in pension plans by assigning cost determination to outside consulting actuaries or trusted employees.[30]

Wage Employment Guarantees

In recent years, union negotiators have fought vigorously for an income maintenance benefit previously provided only to the white collar workers—that of guaranteed income throughout the year regardless of available hours of work or actual work performed. Union negotiators feel their members should also have the security and convenience of regular pay periods. The problems and frustrations of fluctuating income make the guaranteed wage a high priority for many union leaders.

Wage employment guarantees ensure employees a minimum amount of work or compensation during a certain period of time, usually for the life of the contract. Normally all full-time employees who have at least one year's service are eligible. The United Auto Workers contracted a guaranteed wage in its agreement with Ford Motor Company in 1967, a major step for union negotiators in the industry. In 1980, 1.5 million workers received some wage employment guarantee. Of the employees covered by the agreements, most were in the food and primary metals industries, including one-third in manufacturing jobs and the remainder in nonmanufacturing jobs.[31] For example, a wage employment guaranteed provision might read: All regular, full-time employees shall be guaranteed a minimum of forty hours of work per week or compensation in lieu of work being provided.

When negotiating to provide a guaranteed annual wage, management often will insist upon an **escape clause** to suspend the guarantee for production delays beyond the control of management, such as natural or accidental disasters, voluntary absences, employee discharge, or strikes.

Supplemental Unemployment Benefits

In the 1950s, steel and automobile industry union leaders began to negotiate for Supplemental Unemployment Benefits (SUB) plans. These plans provide additional income to supplement state unemployment benefits to employees who are laid off. Union negotiators normally contend that state unemployment benefits do not enable the employee to adequately maintain his style of living. SUB plans are designed to be directly supplemental; employees receive a certain percentage of their gross pay for a maximum number of weeks when unemployed. For example, if each employee subjected to a layoff during the period of the contract receives 75 percent of normal base pay with the company providing the additional funds necessary to the employee's state unemployment benefits, an employee making about $266 a week would receive a total of $200. This 75-percent figure would include $150 per week of state unemployment benefits, with the remaining $50 being provided by the company.

Some negotiated SUB plans will provide only 50 to 75 percent of gross pay; few go beyond 75 percent. Most will provide the additional unemployment benefits for at least a period equal to the state's unemployment, often exceeding that up to one year in length. Employees must have at least one year's service before they are eligible for SUB benefits; they do not receive such benefits if they are on strike or under disciplinary action. Most SUB plan provisions include the escape clauses discussed under wage employment guarantees.

Management usually strongly opposes implementing a SUB plan. Management negotiators emphasize that the company already pays into the state unemployment fund as required by law and that union leaders should lobby their state legislature to increase those funds. Management will also argue that additional unemployment benefits decrease its ability to make technological changes and provide new equipment and processes because of the additional benefits paid to displaced employees.

Although some SUB plans were negotiated as early as 1923 by Procter & Gamble and 1932 by Nunn Shoe Company, the great increase in the number of plans providing coverage for employees came after the 1955 negotiated SUB plan between the Ford Motor Company and the United Auto Workers. Today nearly three million employees are covered by the SUB plans; most are within the garment, rubber, steel, and auto industries.[32]

Most SUB plan provisions require that the company contribute a certain number of cents per hour into a special fund until a required maximum is reached. The maximum is usually expressed in terms of dollars per employee covered. For example, one such agreement provides that the company pays into the fund 7 cents for each paid labor hour until the total market value of the fund reaches $260 per employee. Once that level of funding is reached, the firm contributes 5 cents per labor hour until a maximum funding of $375 per employee is reached. The cost of providing such a benefit, therefore, is usually assumed to be the maximum contribution to the plan per employee, such as $375 in the last example. Employees may draw upon the fund if they have accumulated a sufficient number of *credit units;* that is, the employee may receive one-half credit unit for each work week she receives any compensation other than SUB from the company. The number of credit units accumulated, therefore, is a function of the employee's years of service with the company.[33]

Guaranteed Income Stream

The relatively high unemployment rate and severe layoffs in the 1970s and 1980s caused job security to become a top priority for union negotiation and members.[34] Several innovative provisions in contracts have the intent of improving employment security. One of the most interesting and publicized is the **Guaranteed Income Stream (GIS)** plan in the auto industry.

The GIS plan is an alternative to the traditional supplemental unemployment plan (SUB), although the goal of income maintenance for employees is the same. The typical GIS plan differs from SUB plans in three important areas. First, GIS plans furnish benefits to eligible workers until they retire and thus have been called a "guaranteed lifetime wage," whereas SUB plans end after a short period of time, usually two years. Second, qualification for a GIS plan is based on earnings and not employment, which encourages laid-off workers to seek other employment. Third, the benefits provided by a GIS plan are only partially offset by outside earnings until a "breakeven" point is reached. Under most SUB plans, benefits are completely offset by outside earnings—a deterrent to laid-off workers seeking outside jobs. Thus, GIS plans create incentives for laid-off workers, unlike SUB plans, which tie them to their former employer. Both sides may benefit from GIS plans. If laid-off workers find new jobs, the amount of GIS benefits paid by the former employer may be reduced as they are partially offset by the outside income. However, the employer is encouraged to avoid layoffs by the long-term eligibility aspect of a GIS plan. When layoffs are necessary, the employer has an additional financial incentive to help workers find new employment. The GIS plan may eventually replace SUB plans since both management and labor can realize important advantages.[35]

Severance Pay

Severance pay, sometimes called *dismissal pay,* is income provided to employees who have been permanently terminated from the job through no fault of their own. While similar to SUB in its appearance and formula for provision in determining benefits, severance pay is given under quite different circumstances. SUB pay enables the employee who is temporarily laid off to feel minimum impact from the layoff and anticipate a return to work and full pay. Employees who receive severance pay, however, realize they have no hope for future work with the company. It is not normally provided to employees who are terminated for just cause or who quit.

The purpose of severance pay is to cushion the loss of income due to plant closing, merger, automation, or subcontracting of work. Therefore, union negotiators contend that management should shoulder some of the financial burden while the employee is seeking other permanent work.

The amount of severance pay is usually specified by a formula guaranteeing a percentage of base pay determined by number of years service with the company. The percentage normally increases as the employee's number of years increases to a maximum percentage. To be eligible, employees are normally required to have a minimum number of years service, usually one, except in a case of disability. Management negotiators have been somewhat more sympathetic to severance pay provisions because management controls its cost completely. However, as the economy, technology, and mergers force changes in many of our industries, management negotiators may be likely to resist further increases in severance pay provisions.

If severance pay is included in an agreement, it is considered an employee right. In the case of a merger, plant closing, relocation, or the sale of the company, the liability for severance pay may become a most important issue. Court decisions have upheld the legal right of employees to receive severance pay from the parties involved. In such cases severance pay owed workers is generally regarded as a legal liability of the company.[36] Unions have a legal right to file suit on behalf of employees denied negotiated severance pay under the Labor Management Relations Act, Section 301.[37]

Death and Disability Insurance Plans

Union leaders have also strongly negotiated for death and disability benefits to supplement Social Security. The negotiated benefit may provide for coverage up to a maximum, or it may provide benefits independent of others received by the employee. The need for negotiators to be very specific in providing these benefits is illustrated in Case 7.2, where a disabled employee received far less than expected. However, negotiators are aware of the benefits made available upon death or disability to employees by the Social Security system, and employers remind union officials that they contribute to the Social Security system and therefore provide funding for its death and disability benefits as well as those received through the collective bargaining process. An example of the negotiated benefit is included in an agreement between Anaconda Aluminum Company and Aluminum Workers Local 130 and the Aluminum Workers' International Union, AFL-CIO.

> ARTICLE 19
> *Group Insurance*
> a. The company will provide without cost to the employee the following group insurance and benefits.
> b. Terms and conditions of the coverage called for in paragraph(s) of this article will be contained in the contract between the company and the insurance company with details in a separate booklet which will be furnished to each employee.
> c. Life Insurance—On the fifteenth of the month, following the completion of his probational period, the employee will be covered by $12,000 life insurance. Included in the policy are provisions for coverage after retirement, layoff, and in the event of disability. Retiree benefits do not apply for deferred vested pension.
>
> Source: *Agreement* between Anaconda Aluminum Co. and Aluminum Workers' Local No. 130 and the Aluminum Workers' International Union, AFL-CIO, 1980–83, pp. 26–27. Used with permission.

The company commonly bears the entire premium cost of death and disability insurance. However, often it may be negotiated that employees will be offered additional group insurance through the group plan at reduced rates. Union members, of course, often benefit from such a plan by an amount greater than the premium paid by the company in their behalf. Usually the company can obtain group insurance at a rate cheaper than each individual could purchase on her own. Case 7.3 illustrates how negotiated disability benefits can differ between active employees and pensioners.

Employee life insurance plans are included in over 90 percent of negotiated plans. Most provide a specific benefit, often $10,000.[38] Another common type of benefit provides an amount directly related to the employees' annual earnings. Plans that relate the amount to earnings most often provide a maximum benefit equal to total yearly earnings; some provide twice the earnings.[39] The cost of life insurance coverage is paid entirely by the employer in most agreements.

Group Dental, Legal, and Vision Insurance

Twenty years ago a few labor agreements provided dental, legal, or auto insurance to employees. Such contract provisions are far more common today and are highly sought by unions.

Comprehensive dental care benefits have been developed to provide protection against the cost of basic types of dental protection. Such plans include schedule, comprehensive, and combination.[40] *Schedule plans* have no deductibles and provide specific payments for each procedure covered. *Comprehensive plans* require an initial deductible and then provide a fixed percentage payment of covered expenses. Most *combination plans* provide a fixed fee schedule for routine dental procedures and a deductible on other procedures with a coinsurance clause requiring the covered employee to pay a percentage of the fee.[41]

The provision of full-range legal services through negotiated group plans is relatively new. During the early 1970s, prepaid legal services first became a common subject in labor negotiations due to a U.S. Supreme Court decision upholding such a plan and the 1976 Tax Reform Act declaring legal expenses to be nontaxable.[42]

Two types of prepaid legal plans are commonly negotiated. One, an *open panel,* allows the employee to select any attorney who will perform the service at a stated fee. The other, the *closed panel,* requires employees to use specific attorneys. Most plans require the employee to pay part of the annual fee.[43] Labor negotiators may prefer the open panel so members can utilize familiar attorneys. Closed panels, however, are more easily administered by management.

Routine eye examinations, glasses, and contact lenses are usually included in vision care provisions. Employees may be given the choice of doctors or may be limited to certain ones retained under contract.

Health Care Plan

One of the most common employee benefits negotiated to provide income mainte- nance and insurance to employees is the *health care plan.* This plan assists employees in maintaining their normal standard of living when unusual or unexpected health problems occur by covering medical bills and related costs. In addition to related health care benefits such as Medicare provided by Social Security, worker's compen- sation, and in-house medical services, most contracts provide for hospitalization and major medical insurance.[44] Unions have had a great impact in extending health care insurance. In 1950, relatively few contracts contained health care provisions; today over 95 percent of negotiated contracts have hospitalization or major medical benefits.[45]

Hospitalization plans are either commercial insurance or hospital service plans. *Commercial insurance* involves a contract between an employer and an insurance company providing fixed cash benefits for hospital room, board, and other hospital charges. The employer agrees to pay the premiums to cover the insurance provided by the contract, and the insurance company assumes the liability of qualifying employees. The commercial insurance plan pays directly to the insured company, which reimburses the hospital for costs; this plan can be tailored to the needs of the company as specified by contract.

Under the *hospital service plan,* a nonprofit organization such as Blue Cross-Blue Shield provides coverage for hospital services including room, board, and other costs. The insurance company is directly billed for the covered costs. Blue Cross covers hospital cost; Blue Shield covers physicians' fees. The primary advantage of this is that hospitals offer lower rates to the Blue Cross system; however, these plans are usually less flexible, and the employer and union negotiators must choose from the available options.[46]

Most negotiated health care plans provide for a $100 deductible to be paid by the employee and a maximum percentage, often 80 percent, to be paid by the employer for major medical expenses. The plans also set a maximum figure. Since such benefits usually overlap with benefits provided by other sources such as worker's compensation and other insurance, the contract provision must also specify whether benefit payments are made in lieu of any other benefits received or whether benefits received from other plans are to be deducted from the amount the employee is entitled to under the health insurance plan. An example of the hospitalization, medical, and surgical insurance as well as the major medical insurance negotiated between the Anaconda Aluminum Company and the Aluminum Workers' International Union AFL-CIO follows.

> ARTICLE 19
> *Hospitalization, Medical, and Surgical Insurance*
> d. Hospitalization, Medical, and Surgical Insurance—The plan covers the employee and his dependents, as defined in the booklet, for actual charges for room and board up to the hospital's most common semi-private room rate for up to 730 days; surgical benefits at reasonable and customary charges; out-patient hospital benefits for accidents, illness or surgery; and maternity benefits. Retirees and their spouses will have the same basic coverage (group hospital and surgical coverage) as an active employee. Coverage will cease for the spouse when the retiree dies. Retiree benefits do not apply for deferred vested pension.
> e. The plan of paragraph (d) above also provides for benefits for six months following a layoff for employees with two years seniority; for one year for employees who become disabled because of sickness or injury; and for retiring employee and spouse.
> f. Sickness and accident benefits in accordance with the following schedule for a maximum of 26 weeks for any one illness or injury, subject to a 7-day waiting period in case of non-hospitalized sickness:
>
> Source: *Agreement* between Anaconda Aluminum Co. and Aluminum Workers' Local No. 130 and the Aluminum Workers' International Union, AFL-CIO, 1980–83, pp. 27–30. Used with permission.

Note that the hospitalization provision specifies that actual charges for room and board will be reimbursed, indicating an insurance plan rather than the service benefit. Also the number of days for which an employee can be reimbursed for a semiprivate room rate is specified. The major medical plan covers 80 percent of employee expenses to be paid by the employer, and a cash deductible of $50 paid by the employee with an annual maximum of $100.

Health Maintenance Organizations

In 1973 Congress passed the Health Maintenance Organization Act, which provided for the creation of **Health Maintenance Organizations** (HMOs). An HMO is simply a local medical facility that provides routine checkups, shots, and treatments for injuries or illnesses to employees and their families. In addition, it includes many other benefits, such as maternity benefits, family planning services, vision testing, mental health services, and services for alcohol-drug abuse, not normally found in major medical-hospitalization plans.[47] Many HMOs contract with local hospitals when extensive specialized surgery and other unusual medical treatment are needed.

The act established standards for private individuals to receive federal financing to create HMOs to provide an alternative health care system for employees. Once they become established, the HMOs should become self-sufficient through premiums received from employees and their employers. The act also requires employers with twenty-five or more employees and who currently offer a medical benefit plan to offer the HMO option to employees if a federally approved HMO exists in the local area.

Among the advantages provided by HMOs is comprehensive health care. The plan allows for preventive medicine and includes routine visits to a physician and less expensive periodic health assessments and immunizations. HMOs also provide health care to a family at lower annual total cost than a typical insurance plan. The HMO plan includes many of the additional health care costs families normally incur that are not covered in their group health insurance. Physicians try to prevent unnecessary hospitalization costs by doing many procedures in the office and on an outpatient basis. In one major U.S. industry alone, 5 percent of its employees enrolled in HMOs and saved approximately two million dollars per year in health care costs.[48] In addition, HMOs can be easily administered. Since there is no expensive and time-consuming third-party claim review process, the employer finds it easier to provide HMO insurance to employees. A monthly premium check is paid to the HMO for services to the covered individuals with no other financial transactions or vouchers.

The provision of a wider range of health services is a particularly attractive provision of HMOs. Some HMOs even provide a human relations department offering employee counseling services regarding smoking withdrawal, weight reduction, and abortion, as well as education about diet, diabetes, and hypertension.[49]

However, some union leaders view HMOs as restricting their ability to negotiate benefits, since employees contend that private insurance benefits are needed when extensive specialized surgery and other unusual medical problems arise. Employees may not accept HMOs since their choice of physicians and location of facilities is limited to the HMOs in the area. Many employees simply feel more comfortable with physicians they know and trust and believe that it is unfair for management to put a price tag on the cost of quality health care.

Health Care Cost Containment

General Motors spends more money for employee medical benefits than for steel from its main supplier. Indeed, employers pay almost half the nation's health care bills through insurance programs.[50] Provisions designed to lower the cost of health care are included in over 55 percent of 1986 labor agreements—an indication that management and labor are serious about health care cost containment. Most of the measures are designed to reduce hospitalization costs by requiring surgery on an outpatient basis when possible and requiring second opinions before scheduling surgery.[51]

A Bureau of Labor Research analysis of health insurance trends in the 1980s indicates a continued expansion of cost-control measures. First, employers are raising their employees' share of the total health care bill by eliminating "first-dollar" coverage and requiring increased cost-sharing by employees through higher deductibles and co-insurance provisions. Second, the higher cost of hospital rooms has encouraged more employers to include extended care facilities and home health care as alternatives to hospital care. Third, an increasing number of employers are changing sources of coverage from traditional commercial insurance companies to self-insurance or Health Maintenance Organizations. Finally, entirely new cost-cutting measures include requiring a second opinion before elective surgery, routine physical examinations, and greater testing before hospital admittance. Whereas most benefits have not changed in recent years, two notable exceptions are dental coverage and increased major medical maximums to increase employee protection against catastrophic "out-of-pocket" expenses.[52]

One area of major concern to both labor and management is which, if any, of the various health care cost-containment programs available should be used. Both sides recognize the need to control cost increases. However, some techniques such as self-insurance and expanding coverage to extended care facilities and home health care may be far more palatable to unions than those that directly increase workers' share of medical bills such as higher deductibles or co-insurance provisions.

Wellness Programs

Company-provided **wellness programs** have dramatically risen in number. Most are expanded physical fitness or alcohol and drug rehabilitation programs, but many complete wellness programs include stress management, high blood pressure detection, cancer detection and treatment, and individualized exercise programs. Examples of successful wellness programs include the following:

☐ Mesa Petroleum Company—medical costs for participants in the fitness program averaged $173 per person compared to $434 for nonparticipants[53]

☐ General Motors—an employee assistance program cut medical benefit payments by 60 percent after only one year[54]

☐ Campbell Soup Company—a colon-rectal cancer detection program resulted in a savings of $245,000 in medical payments[55]

☐ Burlington Industries—its "health-back" program decreased absenteeism from 400 days to 19 days annually[56]

Company-sponsored physical fitness programs (PFPs) have become a popular part of wellness programs. Few existed before 1975 but they are common today among large employers. A PFP may only be a basketball hoop in the employee parking lot—or Kimberly Clark Company's $2.5 million physical fitness center.[57]

The shift from traditional hospital service plans to more competitive comprehensive coverage plans has also enabled management to carefully design plans to cut costs and negotiate with several health care providers for the lowest cost. One such strategy is the Preferred Provider Organization (PPO). A PPO is usually a specific contract among the employer, insurance carriers, hospitals and health care providers, dentists, and physicians. The contract allows certain services to be provided at a discount in exchange for a guaranteed number of patients. The employees can be assured of receiving needed health care, and management is given the flexibility to negotiate a low-cost program.

Employee Assistance Programs

Beginning in the early 1970s, the number of **employee assistance programs** (EAPs) significantly increased. By 1980 there were an estimated 4,000 programs in almost every type of service, industrial, and nonprofit organization.[58] The number increased apparently because many labor relations managers believe they can save money by helping employees resolve personal problems that affect job performance. EAPs also provide the union evidence of management's concern for employees' well-being, which should be a strong boost to employee relations. But the primary reason for more company-sponsored EAPs is that they may enhance a company's profitability by reducing absenteeism, turnover, tardiness, accidents, and medical claims.[59]

Many EAPs grew from alcohol-treatment programs. The typical program addresses psychological and physical problems, including stress, chemical dependency (alcohol and drug), depression, marital and family problems, financial problems, health, anxiety, and even job boredom. The procedure in virtually all EAPs is (1) problem identification, (2) intervention, and (3) treatment and recovery. Program operations generally fall into two categories: internal programs that use a full-time specialist who identifies the program, and those that refer the employee to a community agency for treatment.[60]

An example of a successful referral program is the EAP at Bechtel Power Corporation in San Francisco. When a supervisor believes an employee's performance has been adversely affected by personal problems, the supervisor phones the EAP office. (An alternative first step would be an employee self-referral.) Once the supervisor and EAP specialist discuss the particulars of the situation—performance record, absenteeism, and so on—the supervisor is normally advised to suggest that the employee use the EAP. It is carefully explained to the employee that participation is voluntary and does not affect the discipline process, which may be implemented if required by poor work. Strict confidentiality is guaranteed.[61]

Unions have often taken an active role in designing EAPs. Usually both labor and management agree that the troubled employee is a valuable asset, and if rehabilitated, can remain a valuable employee after treatment. However, the EAP is generally not viewed by the union or management as an alternative to the disciplinary process, and at some point an employee may be forced to choose between treatment or termination.

Future Health Care Negotiations

Unions generally have responded positively to cooperative management programs designed to trim health care costs. Since 1958, the Teamsters Union has worked with the city of New York by operating the Teamster Center Services, an advice and referral unit, which provides information on alcoholism, drug abuse, second surgical opinions, insurance, vocational re-education, and legal and financial matters. In 1986, General Motors and the United Auto Workers announced they had reduced health care costs by $200 million in a single year. Their cost reduction program promoted the use of Health Maintenance Organizations, outpatient surgery, and the elimination of unnecessary surgery.[62]

Even though unions are reluctant to abandon their traditional health insurance coverage, there are a number of strategies management negotiators can use that may result in cost-cutting agreements. Among those successfully used are the following:

☐ Proposing to offer coverage equal to the current plan, except under company administration. This strategy may result in lower administrative costs and greater company control.
☐ Eliminating dependent coverage. This tactic may be successful if the work force tends to be married and the spouses have comparable benefits that can cover the family at lower cost.
☐ Freezing company costs, either fully or partially. Such an agreement would require members of the bargaining unit to share in the increases in coverage during the lift of the contract or establish deductibles for emergency room visits to discourage the use of the emergency room "as an out-patient clinic or as a substitute for the family doctor."[63]

Pay for Time Not Worked

What has become one of the most sought-after employee benefits by union members is **payment for time not worked** on the job. Employees today have come to expect to be paid for holidays and vacations, as well as many other absences. These *time-off-with-pay* components of labor agreements are many and varied, and include the following:

Holidays	Maternity leave (infant care)
Vacations	Maternity leave (prenatal care)
Jury duty	Sick leave
Election official	Wellness leave (no sick leave used)
Witness in court	Time off to vote
Civic duty	Blood donation
Military duty	Grievance and contract negotiations

Funeral leave   Lunch, rest, and wash up periods
Illness and family leave   Personal leave
Marriage leave   Sabbatical leave[64]

Paid Holidays

Over 86 percent of labor agreements provide for *paid holidays*. Union negotiators'
demand for increased paid holidays has been great and continues to increase the
average number of paid holidays provided by the agreements. In 1950, the average
number of paid holidays in labor agreements was three; thirty years later the average
was closer to ten. Most contracts provide for between eight and twelve paid holidays,
as illustrated in Exhibit 7.3. Labor agreements in the manufacturing sector contained
paid holiday provisions over 99 percent of the time while only 70 percent of the
nonmanufacturing labor agreements contained similar provisions.[65]

Normally, employees required to work on holidays receive double or even triple
pay in the contract provision. In the chemical, hotel, and restaurant industries that
operate every day, employees may be given double pay for working holidays and
another day off during the following week. If a holiday falls during an employee's paid
vacation, the employee usually receives an extra day of scheduled vacation. Employees
on layoff during a paid holiday usually do not receive pay for that holiday.

Martin Luther King's birthday and **personal days** are two paid holidays that have
grown in popularity over the past decade.[66] The personal day or **"floating holiday"**
started in the rubber industry. Floating holiday provisions allow the selection of the
day on which the holiday is observed to be left to the discretion of the employee or
to be mutually agreed upon between management and the employee. Management
has resisted the concept of a floating holiday on the theory that there is little difference
between a floating holiday and an additional vacation day.

Many labor agreements have observed the *Monday holiday* practice provided by
the federal government. The observance of Monday holidays is, in theory, designed to
give employees more three-day weekends during the year for additional rest and
relaxation. In practice, however, the Monday holiday has increased absenteeism, the
chief administrative problem caused by paid holidays. Employees can easily see that
being absent on Friday or Tuesday would provide them a four-day weekend or almost
a complete week's vacation.

The agreement between the Lockheed-Georgia Company and the Aeronautical
Machinists contains paid holiday provisions that eliminate most problems and abuses.

SECTION 3
Holidays

1. The company recognizes the following ten holidays: New Year's Day; Good Friday;
   Memorial Day; Fourth of July; Labor Day; Thanksgiving Day; the day after Thanksgiving; December 24; Christmas Day, December 25; December 26; and January 2.
2. Full pay (eight hours of straight time including shift bonus and odd work week bonus,
   if any) shall be paid to employees for each of these holidays regardless of the day of
   the week upon which the holiday falls. In addition, two times the regular rate of the
   employee shall be paid for hours worked on holidays.

Exhibit 7.3   Number of paid holidays and pay for time worked

Holiday Provision	Agreements	Workers
Number of paid holidays		
All agreements	1,550	6,593,800
Total with paid holidays[1]	1,301	5,650,050
Fewer than 6 days	22	66,950
6 days	30	101,250
7 days	42	144,600
8 days	76	239,150
9 days	159	655,100
10 days	322	1,587,800
11 days	289	867,700
12 days	146	521,100
13 days	55	165,350
14 days	49	173,400
15 days	17	611,750
16 days	8	51,450
17 days	3	27,900
20 days	5	12,600
Funded holidays	59	348,800
Other[2]	17	69,250
No reference to paid holidays	249	943,750
Pay for time worked on holidays		
All agreements	1,550	6,593,800
Total with work rates on paid holidays	1,278	5,517,150
Straight time	1	1,000
Time and one-half	26	73,150
Double time	152	444,700
Double time and one-half	576	2,778,000
Triple time	387	1,583,500
Equal time off on another day or pay[3]	10	29,950
Funded holidays	60	347,300
Varies with holiday	43	150,150
Varies according to specified criteria	7	48,700
Other[4]	12	46,500
No reference to rates for holidays worked	23	132,900
No reference to paid holidays	249	943,750

[1]For purposes of this table, half-day holidays have been ignored.
[2]Includes agreements that vary the number of holidays by location; that refer holidays to local negotiations; and that refer to paid holidays, but give no further details.
[3]Agreements provide premium pay for time worked and compensatory time off at the option of the employer or the employee.
[4]Includes agreements that pay a flat-sum premium or make arrangements not included above.

Source: U.S. Dept. of Labor, Bureau of Labor Statistics, *Characteristics of Major Collective Bargaining Agreements* (Washington, D.C.: Government Printing Office, 1981), p. 85.

3. In order to be eligible for holiday pay, an employee must have worked or have been on a vacation or a paid leave (other than paid sick leaves) on the last work day before and the first work day after the holiday; except that when the holiday falls on a day before employment, a day after termination, or during an employee's leave, no pay under this section shall be granted.

4. Should a recognized holiday fall upon a Sunday, the Monday immediately following shall be observed as the holiday. Should a recognized holiday fall upon a Saturday, the Friday immediately preceding such Saturday shall be observed as the holiday unless the work schedule of the majority of the employees includes Saturdays, in which event the holiday shall be observed on such Saturday.

5. An additional day's pay (i.e., double pay) shall be granted to an employee on vacation if a holiday for which he would have been paid had he been working falls during his vacation.

Source: *Agreement* between the Lockheed-Georgia Company and the Aeronautical Machinist Local Lodge No. 709, International Association of Machinists and Aerospace Workers, AFL-CIO, 1971, pp. 70–71. Used with permission.

An agreement provision for a paid holiday should specify

1. *Eligibility*   As illustrated in the Lockheed-Georgia Company agreement example, employee eligibility, which requires employees to work the last working day before the holiday and the first scheduled working day after the holiday, helps to minimize the problem of employees stretching holiday periods.

2. *Holiday rate*   If employees are scheduled to work on what was agreed to be a paid holiday, they will receive premium pay.

3. *Which days are paid holidays*   The days determined to be paid holidays should be specified in the agreement as in Section 3–1 of the example.

4. *Holidays falling on nonwork days*   As specified in Section 3–4 of the agreement, provisions for the holiday should be made in case the holiday falls on a nonwork day such as a Sunday.

Paid Vacations

The practice of providing employees with *paid vacations* in labor agreements has become not only commonly accepted but expected by union employees. Over 94 percent of labor contracts provide for paid vacations of 2–6 weeks duration.[67] Unlike paid holidays, however, employers believe that paid vacations are effective in increasing employee productivity. Employees, by taking a physical and mental break from the workplace, are able to return to work refreshed and rejuvenated.

Four different types of vacation plans are commonly negotiated: the graduated plan, the uniform plan, the ratio-to-work plan, and the funded plan. By far the most popular type of plan is the *graduated plan* that provides an increase in the number of weeks vacation according to length of service. The *uniform vacation plan* provides all workers with the same length of vacation. This is most commonly found in manufacturing firms that shut down for specified periods to retool or change product lines, giving employees vacations during the shutdown. The *ratio-to-work plan* commonly found in the printing and transportation industries relates the length of vacation to the number of hours or days the employee works during a given time period, usually the year preceding the allocation of vacation. The *funded plan* requires employers to contribute to a vacation fund from which employees may draw vacation pay during periods when no work is available. This is most often found in the construction and apparel industries where the demand for work varies greatly during the year.[68]

An example of a graduated vacation plan is provided in the agreement between Anaconda Aluminum Company and the Aluminum Workers' International Union, AFL-CIO.

ARTICLE 8
Vacations

a. An employee with one year or more of service with the company and who has worked at least one thousand hours since the employee's anniversary date in the preceding calendar year projecting work hours (if necessary) to the employee's next anniversary date shall receive a paid vacation on the following basis:

Employee's Service	Vacation Pay	Week's Vacation Leave
One year, but less than two	$ 52.00	One
Two years, but less than three	$ 74.00	One
Three years, but less than five	$100.00	Two
Five years, but less than ten	$168.00	Two
Ten years, but less than fifteen	$180.00	Three
Fifteen years, but less than twenty	$200.00	Three
Twenty years, but less than twenty-five	$210.00	Four
Twenty-five years or more	$240.00	Five

b. The amount of vacation pay for each employee shall be computed at his regular bid rate as of January 1 of each year, multiplied at the appropriate number of hours set forth in the table in the paragraph above.

c. An employee entitled to a vacation shall receive his vacation pay on the payday preceding his vacation leave, but no later than the second pay period in December.

d. Vacation shall be taken during the period from January 1 to December 31 each year. Preference of vacation period shall be according to seniority but subject to planned operation schedule. The company shall discuss a vacation schedule with the union regarding preference by seniority. Nothing in this article shall restrict the company from scheduling all or part of a planned shutdown for vacation purposes, should business conditions permit.

Source: *Agreement* between Anaconda Aluminum Co. and Aluminum Workers' Local No. 130 and the Aluminum Workers' International Union, AFL-CIO, 1980–83, pp. 9–11. Used with permission.

This example includes several provisions that should be specified in the labor agreement, including the eligibility for vacation leave and pay, how long the employee has to be with the company to qualify, and any other requirements for vacation leave. Duration of vacation leave must be determined, along with any additional vacation pay such as premium pay or bonuses. Also, the scheduling of vacations, a critical aspect of the contract, must be specified. Normally, scheduling is done on the basis of seniority; however, management often tries to retain some right in the determination of employee scheduling so adequate skills and abilities can be maintained in the workplace. In the agreement between Anaconda Aluminum and the union, the company retains the right to schedule vacations during a planned shutdown that might become necessary for business reasons, an important provision for management to retain.

Determining the annual cost of any negotiated increase in the number of vacation days or holidays is relatively straightforward. One common method is to multiply the number of additional vacation or holiday hours by the base wage rate of employees covered. Another method would be to determine the appropriate percentage of the amount charged to the holiday or vacation pay account from the previous fiscal year. For example, if the company estimates that employees averaged eleven days of paid vacation in the previous year at a total cost of $1,200,000, then the average cost per day was $109,090. Thus, if one additional vacation day is negotiated, the total cost for the next year would be $1,309,090.[69] One problem in determining the cost of additional vacation or holiday benefits is that the cost of continuing production as usual is not provided in the two alternatives. Industries such as the chemical and utility companies that provide around-the-clock service require many employees to work on holidays for premium rates. Thus, it may be necessary to add additional factors to the estimate of negotiated increases in vacation and holiday pay.[70]

Sick Leave

Sick leave is normally accrued by employees at a specific rate such as one day per month from the first day of permanent employment. The subject of many arbitration cases, sick leave is intended to provide for continuation of employment when employees are physically unable to report for work. To minimize grievances and other problems associated with sick leave provisions, the labor agreement should specify the procedure for taking sick leave—the time sick leave must be reported by during the beginning of the work shift, and what verification by a physician or other individuals is required; a definition of *sick;* and the accumulation rights. Some contracts provide that unused sick leave can be accumulated without any maximum to cover employees who require extended sick leave for serious illnesses. A doctor's certification is usually needed only when an employee uses extended sick leave. Many contracts specify a maximum number of days of sick leave that can be accumulated by an employee.

Paid Leaves of Absence

Most agreements provide for *paid leaves of absence* for a variety of purposes including military service, education, and union business, as well as personal reasons. Personal leave may result from a variety of causes such as jury duty, appearing as a witness in a court case, or attending a family funeral. When negotiating a funeral leave benefit, it is important to specify for which family members the leave should apply. Personal leave may also include the awarding of personal days that employees may take without specifying why they missed work or giving advance notice. Military leave is often negotiated for employees in the United States Armed Forces Reserve Units.

There is little consistency across or even within industries as far as what types of leave are negotiated and the number of paid days of work provided for. The most commonly negotiated paid leave is for the conducting of union business, with 60 percent of agreements in 1980 covering one thousand or more workers for this paid benefit. Usually the conducting of union business provision would include contract negotiation as well as handling grievances for arbitration proceedings. Paid leave for military services is included in 59 percent of labor agreements; leave for personal reasons in 53 percent; maternity/paternity leave in 39 percent; and education leave in 9 percent of labor agreements.[71] The provision for paid leave of absence varies greatly by industry but is generally more prevalent in the manufacturing industries.

In general, the labor agreement for paid leave of absence provisions must include employee eligibility requirements; payment received—base wage plus other wages as well as whether additional outside income such as pay for jury duty or reserve pay is to be deducted from the employee's wage; and scheduling considerations.

Premium Pay

Virtually all labor agreements provide a specific work schedule and require **premium pay** for any hours worked beyond the normal schedule. Over 93 percent of labor agreements provide for premium pay for Saturdays or Sundays not part of the normally scheduled work week, and 96 percent provide for specified overtime premium pay rates either on a weekly or daily basis.[72] Overtime premiums are often provided on a daily basis for time over eight hours, as shown in Exhibit 7.4. Such additional pay was termed *penalty pay* in the past because it was intended to discourage employers from requiring employees to work additional hours or weekends. Today employers are anxious to maintain their rights in scheduling additional hours so overtime costs in premium payments can be minimized.

Negotiated increases in overtime in premium pay benefits cannot easily be costed since the actual cost increase per year will be determined by management's scheduling of overtime hours. Therefore, the best estimation of negotiated cost increases is made by multiplying the percentage increase in the benefit by last year's total dollars allocated to that particular benefit. For example, if management spent an additional $550,000 in overtime pay and the overtime rate is increased by 5 percent during the next year, the additional cost of the increase to management would be $27,500 annually.

The **pyramiding of overtime** pay is prohibited in most contracts. Pyramiding is the payment of overtime on overtime, which can occur if the same hours of work qualify for both daily and weekly overtime payment. In contracts where pyramiding is prohibited, provisions specifying how such hours will be paid are usually included.

Exhibit 7.4 Premium pay in contracts (frequency expressed as percentage of provisions)

Overtime Provisions

	Daily	Weekly	6th day	7th day	Saturday	Sunday
All Industries	93	68	24	26	50	58
Manufacturing	96	70	27	32	64	80
Nonmanufacturing	88	65	20	17	29	50

Second-Shift Differentials

	Cents per Hour						Percentage of Hourly Pay					
	1–10¢	11– 20¢	21– 30¢	31– 40¢	41– 50¢	Over 50¢	1– 3%	4– 6%	7– 9%	10– 12%	13– 15%	Over 15%
All Industries	9	37	30	9	9	6	5	35	5	51	2	2
Manufacturing	9	42	31	8	8	2	6	37	4	53	—	—
Nonmanufacturing	10	25	27	11	13	14	—	31	6	44	13	6

Third-Shift Differentials

	Cents per Hour						Percentage of Hourly Pay					
	20¢ and under	21– 30¢	31– 40¢	41– 50¢	51– 60¢	Over 60¢	1– 3%	4– 6%	7– 9%	10– 12%	13– 15%	Over 15%
All Industries	23	35	16	14	7	6	—	15	17	49	17	2
Manufacturing	24	39	15	10	4	7	—	16	16	55	10	3
Nonmanufacturing	17	22	17	24	15	4	—	10	20	30	40	—

Reporting Pay

	Guaranteed Hours							
	1	2	3	4	5	6	7	8
All Industries	2	14	4	65	—	2	1	11
Manufacturing	—	8	5	76	—	2	1	8
Nonmanufacturing	7	33	3	34	—	—	—	23

Call-Back, Call-In Pay

	Guaranteed Hours							
	1	2	3	4	5	6	7	8
All Industries	1	16	13	64	1	2	—	4
Manufacturing	1	13	9	71	1	2	—	2
Nonmanufacturing	2	23	19	48	—	2	—	6

Source: Adapted from *Basic Patterns in Union Contracts,* 11th ed. (Washington, D.C.: The Bureau of National Affairs, 1986), pp. 56, 119, 120, 121.

How overtime work is distributed among employees is also discussed in most labor contracts. The most common provision is a general statement to the effect that overtime will be distributed equally as far as practical. Other provisions assign overtime on the basis of seniority or by rotation. Many agreements limit overtime distribution to employees within a department, shift, job classification, or those specifically qualified.[73]

Premium pay for other undesirable work situations may also be negotiated. *Shift differentials* are negotiated additional hourly rates of pay provided to employees who work the least desirable hours. Usually specified in cents-per-hour in the labor agreement, the cost of the increase in a shift differential would be calculated similarly to that of an overtime premium pay increase. Over 90 percent of all late-shift factory workers receive a shift differential premium over their day-shift counterparts. Usually the differential is provided in the contract clause on a cents-per-hour addition to day-shift rates, averaging about 25 cents per hour or 8 percent of the day-shift rate. Third shift rates often are several cents-per-hour higher than second shift. Employers are willing to pay the higher personnel costs not only because production volumes can be increased but also because they receive maximum use of plant and equipment and may receive lower utility rates for night wage. Continuous process industries such as basic steel and chemical require twenty-four-hour operation to avoid high start-up and shut-down costs. Thus, shift differentials are most common in capital-intensive industries. On the other hand, workers often resist late-shift employment due to biological, psychological, and social problems related to night work.[74]

Still other premium payments often negotiated include reporting pay, call-in pay, and on-call pay. Particularly common in the manufacturing and construction industries, **reporting pay** is the minimum payment guaranteed employees who report for work even if work is not available. If employees have not been given adequate notice of usually twenty-four hours not to report to work, they are eligible to receive either the minimum amount of work or payment usually equal to four hours of scheduled work.

A supplemental payment given to employees called back to work before they were scheduled is usually termed **call-in pay**. Most labor agreements provide a lump sum amount or an amount equal to a minimum hours of pay for employees called in during other than scheduled work hours. Thus, employees who do not take their complete rest between scheduled work days receive a bonus for being called in before their next normal reporting time.

On-call or *standby* **pay** is given to workers available to be called in if needed. This type of pay is commonly negotiated in companies such as the chemical industry or airlines that must provide continuous production or service. Usually a lump sum amount is paid to employees on a daily basis when they must be available to work, whether they are called in or not.

Employee Services

A wide variety of employee services have been negotiated in labor agreements. In general, they are not as commonly found as the previously discussed employee benefits; however, most labor agreements provide for at least a few employee services. Some of the more traditional employee services include sponsoring social and recreational activities such as picnics and athletic events. The cost of these services has been re-examined in recent years since only a relatively small percentage of employees utilize the facilities.

Subsidized food services are a popular employee benefit. Both labor and management feel that providing dining facilities, low-cost meals, or vending machine products minimizes time away from the job spent on breaks or at mealtime in addition to guaranteeing a balanced diet. Credit unions sponsored by the companies are another employee service often sought by union negotiators. While a credit union is normally operated completely independently from the employer, the employer's cooperation in establishing it and providing payroll deductions is critical and must be negotiated.

In recent years, some of the newer employee services negotiated include child care either at the work site or in the form of partial reimbursement. Counseling for employees with medical, financial, or drug and alcohol problems has become highly desirable. Services minimizing work-related costs, such as transportation to and from the job, clothing, and tool allowances are often useful in particular industries. Union negotiators of today stress the fact that these costs represent a liability and should be carried by the company.

Summary

Employee benefit costs have skyrocketed in recent decades. The three most expensive employee benefits for employers continue to be retirement plans, insurance plans, and pay for time not worked. Still, a variety of employee benefits have increased in recent years as employees and union leaders initiate new benefits in labor negotiations. By necessity some benefits are unique to particular industries. For example, the agreement between the Schlitz Brewing Company and the International Union of the United Brewery, Flour, Cereal, Soft Drink, and Distillery Workers of America states that, "Beer shall be given to the employees for consumption on the premises daily free of charge, the amount and the dispensing of which shall be according to regulations fixed by the employer."[75] While no one can predict the future of benefit negotiations between management and labor, the spiraling increases in employee benefits negotiated from the 1950s to the 1970s have slowed down in the 1980s as givebacks have become commonplace.

CASE 7.1 Pensions

Reprinted with permission from Morris Stone, *Labor Grievances and Decisions* (New York: American Arbitration Association, 1970) pp. 148–51

In negotiating a contract with management of a woolen mill, the union insisted upon, and finally got, a retirement-sep-

aration pay plan that gave employees who attained the legal retirement age of 65 for men or 62 for women, and who had fifteen years of service with the company, a lump sum representing one week's pay for each year of service. [The text of the clause read: "It is agreed the company will pay retirement-separation pay to employees who have attained the legal retirement age, which entitles them to Social Security benefits and who voluntarily retire from the employment of the company and have at the time of their retirement completed fifteen (15) years or more years of continuous service with the company with an average employment of one thousand (1000) hours or more for each year of such service. The amount of retirement-separation pay shall be one (1) week's pay for each service year, with a maximum of twenty (20) weeks pay."]

This was obviously not a pension plan as such, for it did not give employees a definite income for the duration of their lives. Nor was it a severance pay plan, for it applied only to employees who quit on reaching retirement age. But the plan clearly had some resemblance to both types of benefits, at least to the extent that it caused employees to expect that if they remained with the company long enough, they would be rewarded with some financial help toward retirement.

But that help was not forthcoming for a number of employees who had worked fifteen or more years for the company but who could not reach retirement age as employees because the company ceased operations in May 1964. There was no question but that the discontinuation was for good-faith reasons; the plant had been losing money steadily and management had no alternative but to go out of business. But a dispute arose as to whether the employees who were otherwise eligible for retirement-separation pay, but who would

never reach retirement age as employees through no fault of their own, lost eligibility for that reason alone.

"It is well settled that fringe benefits are a form of wages," the union attorney pointed out when the issue reached arbitration, "and management cannot escape its obligations to employees with fifteen or more years of service any more than they could avoid paying wages. Moreover, the contractual plan was not simply for retirement, but for separation as well, which is why it was called a *retirement-separation plan* in the contract itself."

"All this talk about fringe benefits being a form of wages is irrelevant," the company attorney answered. "The fact is that not every fringe benefit is given to all employees under any and all circumstances. The contract states the conditions of eligibility, and our contract sets up not only length of service but the legal retirement age as conditions precedent to the lump-sum payment. Employees who have met both conditions are getting the payment, but those who met only one do not."

After hearing these arguments, and after receiving in evidence a copy of the union contract, with the retirement separation pay provision underlined, the arbitrator declared the hearing closed.

Decision

The company won. A straightforward reading of the clause, the arbitrator said, "leaves one with the definite impression that attainment of the legal retirement age is a prerequisite to qualifications of the stated benefit." He acknowledged that there was, as the union had asserted, a trend in favor of considering employee benefits as simply another form of wages, but he agreed with the company that the answer to the question at hand still lay in what this particular contract said. He pointed out that the estate of an employee who dies after working fifteen years for the company, but before reaching retirement age, would not be entitled to the lump sum payment. Yet, if this were simply a form of wages, such a payment would be due. The arbitrator stated that there were other compelling reasons for not upholding the grievance. "When the present clause was drawn up, it was presumably contemplated that the company, as its part of the bargain, would be assured the full benefit of the employees' years of service up to retirement age if the employees had almost thirty more years of potential service on the date of the plant closing. And while it is true that the employees were not responsible for their failure to fulfill their part of the bargain, neither was the company. We are dealing here with a good faith termination of business, brought on by circumstances beyond either party's control. It is difficult, therefore, to see why the company should be thus penalized for having gone out of business."

CASE 7.2   *Cost of Benefits*

Reprinted with permission from Morris Stone, *Labor Grievances and Decisions* (New York: American Arbitration Association, 1970), pp. 157–59

It is possible that when negotiators of a union contract at a paper and pulp mill agreed upon language for supplementary disability pay to employees injured on the job, it did not occur to them that the phrase *normal wages* might be susceptible to more than one interpretation. But conflicting interpretations did come to light during the summer of 1965.

The clause in question stated that when an employee sustains an injury under circumstances entitling him to benefits under the New Hampshire Workmen's Compensation Act, the company would give him additional cash benefits so that his income, for a stated period of time, would be two-thirds of his normal wages. [The text of the clause read: "When an employee sustains a temporary or permanent total disability under circumstances entitling him to benefits under the New Hampshire Workmen's Compensation Act, the company agrees to afford voluntarily additional benefits to such employee equal to the difference between the benefits provided under such law for the period of such disability and an amount equal to 66 2/3 per cent of the normal wages for such employees during such period, subject, however, to a maximum period of three hundred (300) weeks, and further provided that the total of the weekly benefits paid pursuant to said act plus the additional weekly benefits herein provided for shall in no event exceed a maximum of $70 per week. The maximum additional amount to which the employee is entitled is $1,800."]

The conflict came about as a result of an injury to an employee whose normal schedule included Sundays, for which he was regularly paid double-time.

When the time came for the personnel manager to determine the injured employee's normal wages so that the level of supplementary payments might be established, he followed the procedure which, he said, he had followed in every other case of that kind. That is, he took into account the number of hours actually worked, not the number of hours paid for. By that method of computation, the employee's normal wage was of course lower, and the company's supplementary payments were less than they would have been if the normal wage included premium pay.

When a grievance was filed, management made a strong showing that it had followed its usual practice, but the union was not persuaded.

"We don't know how you've been doing things in the past," the shop steward said, "and we have no way of knowing whether circumstances were the same. Even if it happened that an employee who normally put in premium time accepted less than was coming to him, it isn't binding on the grievant in this case. Maybe the other men didn't know their rights. That should not prejudice us now."

Eventually, the case went to arbitration, where two issues were presented: What did the contract's reference to *normal wages* mean, and did it matter that the company's method of computation was applied for over twenty years?

Decision

The union was upheld. The arbitrator wrote: "It seems to the arbitrator that here we have a case wherein past practice is contrary to the most reasonable interpretation of the contract. Absent some qualifying phrase such as average straight time earnings, one would assume that normal wages would equal what the employee normally received. If, as here, his normal work week . . . included Sunday work, then his normal wages included what he was paid for Sunday work, i.e., they included double time." The fact that employees in the past may have overlooked their rights, the arbitrator said, did not affect the union's case here, because there was no evidence that the union had known about the violations at all. He awarded an adjustment in the grievant's favor, but the arbitrator said that there should be no retroactive readjustment for anyone else. He said he was interpreting the contract for the present and the future, not the past.

CASE 7.3   *Medical Benefits*

Reprinted with permission from Morris Stone, *Labor Grievances and Decisions* (New York: American Arbitration Association, 1970), pp. 143–45

About thirty years ago, while he was working for a municipal transportation company, some sparks from a welding machine struck Charles B. in the ear, causing an injury that eventually resulted in some loss of hearing. Despite the limitations of function, Charles continued working for the company until his retirement on pension a few years ago.

Under the pension plan, those who retired continued to have access to medical and surgical services that the company provided for active employees. The language of the current contract read: "The Company shall provide the services of physicians and surgeons as are deemed necessary by the Company's medical advisor, should any full-time or pensioned employee elect to avail himself thereof."

Some time after his retirement, Charles began to feel that his damaged ear was getting worse. He went to see the company doctor, who sent him to an ear specialist. After examining Charles and getting the full history of the case, the specialist reported to the company doctor that he had found a large perforation of the left drum. He said he thought the patient would benefit from corrective ear surgery and closure of the middle ear space with a tympanoplasty. He went on to say, however, that no arrangements were made for the surgery because "this is more or less elective, and I have asked the patient to discuss this with you."

The discussion the specialist referred to did take place, but it did not result in a satisfactory conclusion, as far as Charles was concerned. The company doctor said he did not think the operation was necessary, within the meaning of the union contract clause, and he refused to authorize the surgical service at the company's expense. Instead, he wrote to the partner of the ear specialist who had examined Charles to obtain a clarification of the earlier judgment. He received this reply: "I have reviewed the records on Mr. B. and feel that the ear surgery may or may not correct the hearing problem since statistically this type surgery shows less than a 50 percent result. Specifically, I do not feel the surgery is necessary for the physical well-being of this patient since he has obviously done well with this problem for over thirty years."

On the basis of this judgment, the company doctor confirmed his earlier decision not to authorize payment for Charles's ear operation. A grievance was filed, and the case made its way through grievance procedure to arbitration.

"The company doctor abused his authority in this case," the union's attorney argued at the arbitration hearing. "If Charles had been an employee who was still actively at work, there is no question but that his operation would be paid for. The contract does not give management the right to discriminate against pensioners."

"That's pure speculation," answered the company's attorney. "Nobody knows what the doctor would have advised in the case of a hypothetical employee. The contract says we have to pay for medical services the company doctor deems necessary, and that's all that counts."

Decision

The company won. For one thing, the arbitrator wrote, the company was correct in saying that the decision had to turn on the doctor's decision in this case, not on what he might have decided if Charles had not yet retired. Furthermore, he wrote, "I do not think that every medical service deemed necessary for a pensioner—such factors as age, the nature of the malady, and the probable result of the service might well make it quite proper to provide the service to an active employee and deny it to a pensioner—and, indeed, might well make it quite proper to provide it to a pensioner and deny it to an active employee." Finally, neither of the specialists who wrote letters recommending the surgery had gone so far as to say it was necessary, the arbitrator said.

CASE STUDY   *Vacation Pay*

Adapted from *Vesuvius Crucible Co.* v. *National Labor Relations Board,* 668 F. 2d 162 (CA 3, 1981)

Facts

Company and union had a collective bargaining agreement in effect from November 2, 1973, to October 31, 1976. No agreement for a new contract was reached by the October 31, 1976, expiration date and the employees went on strike. The strike lasted until July 11, 1979—2 years and 8 months.

In June of 1977, the union asked for accrued vacation pay for the ten-month period before the strike (January 1976 through October 1976) for all eligible employees. The company refused, stating that under its interpretation of the contract no vacation pay was yet due. The contract provisions in question are as follows:

> SECTION VII.   VACATIONS
> A. *Eligibility*—To be eligible for a vacation in any calendar year during the term of this Agreement, the employee must have one year or more of continuous service.
> B. *Length of Vacation and Extra Vacation Pay*
>   1. An eligible employee who has attained the years of continuous service indicated in the following table in any calendar year, on the anniversary of his employment with the Company, during the term of this Agreement shall receive a vacation corresponding to such years of continuous service as shown in the following table. . . .
> D. *Vacation Pay*—An employee granted a vacation will receive, for each vacation week, two percent (2%) of his earnings from January 1 to December 31 of the year previous.

> E. *Vacation Allowance in Lieu of Vacation*—While it is recognized that the purpose of the vacation provided by this Section is to grant the employees vacation with pay as annual periods of rest and recreation, the Company may require an employee to work during his vacation, in which event he shall be paid his vacation pay in addition to his regular pay.

Lawsuit

The union charged that the company committed an unfair labor practice by withholding the vacation pay and the NLRB agreed. The company appealed.

Appeal

In defending its position, the NLRB relied on court-tested standards for determining an unfair labor practice when an employer discourages union membership by means of discrimination.

If the conduct complained of could naturally and forseeably have an adverse effect on employee rights, then the conduct is "inherently destructive." In such cases, there is no need to find actual anti-union motivation, and showing a legitimate business purpose will not relieve the employer of the unfair labor charge. IN this instance, the NLRB contended that the company's refusal to pay previously earned vacation benefits to striking workers was "inherently destructive" of important employee rights.

The NLRB further contended that the company's interpretation of the contract was incorrect, and therefore there was no legitimate or substantial business reason for its conduct. Because the conduct was "inherently destructive," however, neither the lack of anti-union sentiment nor a legitimate business purpose was relevant.

The company's position included the following points:

1. Its interpretation of the contract was legitimate and in good faith.
2. The board overstepped its role by disagreeing and substituting its own interpretation of the contract.
3. In the past, vacation rights were not determined by expired contracts but by the contract in effect at the time of payment.
4. Vacation pay was withheld from strikers and nonstrikers alike—no one received the pay.

5. Payment of benefits was contingent upon reaching an agreement on the contract—not on the employees' return to work.

Questions

1. Did the company's action of withholding vacation pay illegally affect the employees' right to collectively bargain? Why or why not?
2. Would you have reached a different decision if nonstriking employees had received vacation benefits? Why or why not?
3. If you were the union, how might you propose changing the eligibility clause to avoid future problems?
4. Should striking employees be paid for accrued vacation time?

Key Terms and Concepts

Call-in pay

Contributory plans

Current expenditure pension plan

Employee Assistance Program

Employee Retirement Income Security Act (ERISA)

Escape clause

Floating holiday

Givebacks

Guaranteed Income Stream

Health Maintenance Organizations

On-call pay

Pay for time not worked

Pay-back agreements

Personal days

Premium pay

Pyramiding of overtime

Reporting pay

Right-to-know laws

Severance pay

Sick leave

Unemployment insurance

Vested

Wage employment guarantees

Wellness program

Worker's compensation

Review Questions

1. How can negotiators reduce health care costs and maintain a good health care benefit?
2. In recent years, management negotiators have increased their resistance to increases in private pension plan funding. Why?
3. Why might workers be ineligible for retirement funds from a private pension plan, even though they have worked all their lives?
4. What is meant by *eligibility* in a holiday clause?
5. Why do workers try to negotiate wage employment guarantees? Supplemental Unemployment Benefits (SUB)?
6. How does a GIS differ from SUB pay?
7. What type of health care plans are normally negotiated? How can a Health Maintenance Organization (HMO) be considered as an alternative to such plans? What are the purposes of HMOs?
8. Why do employees today place a high priority on paid time-off? How has the Monday Holiday caused administrative problems? How can holiday provision problems be minimized?
9. What paid leaves of absence are usually provided by labor agreements?
10. Why does management dislike pyramiding of overtime?

Endnotes

1. Olivia S. Mitchell, "Fringe Benefits and the Cost of Changing Jobs," *Industrial and Labor Relations Review* 37, no. 1 (Oct. 1983), pp. 70–78.
2. James R. Morris, "Those Burgeoning Worker Benefits," *Nation's Business*, Feb. 1987, pp. 53–54.
3. Richard Freeman, "The Effect of Unionism on Fringe Benefits," *Industrial and Labor Relations Review* 34, no. 4 (July 1981), pp. 489–509.
4. Bureau of National Affairs Editorial Staff, "Give-backs Highlight Three Major Bargaining Agreements," *Personnel Administrator* 28, no. 1 (Jan. 1983), pp. 33–35.
5. *Report on Labor Relations in an Economic Recession: Job Losses and Concession Bargaining* (Washington, D.C.: Bureau of National Affairs, 1982), pp. 56–59.
6. "One Billion for the UAW," *Fortune* 108, no. 7 (Oct. 3, 1983), p. 6.
7. Gary N. Chaison and Mark S. Plovnick, "Is There a New Collective Bargaining?" *California Management Review* 28, no. 4 (Summer 1986), pp. 54–61.
8. M. Schuster, "The Impact of Union-Management Cooperation on Productivity and Employment," *Industrial and Labor Relations Review* 36 (1983), pp. 415–430.
9. Mark Plovnick and Gary Chaison, "Relationships Between Concession Bargaining and Labor-Management Cooperation," *Academy of Management Journal* 28, no. 3 (Sept. 1985), pp. 697–704.
10. Evan Claque and Leo Kramer, *Manpower Policies and Programs: A Review 1935-1975* (Kalamazoo, Mich.: W.E. Upjohn, 1976), pp. 82–83.
11. James M. Rosbrow, "Unemployment Insurance System Marks Its 50th Anniversary," *Monthly Labor Review* 108, no. 9 (Sept. 1985), pp. 21–28.
12. Jerry Flint, "The Old Folks," *Forbes* 125, no. 4 (Feb. 18, 1980), pp. 51–56.
13. Dale Detlefs, *1984 Guide to Social Security* (Louisville: Meidinger and Associates, 1984), pp. 6–9.
14. Michael P. Littea and James E. Inman, *The Legal Environment of Business: Text, Cases and Readings* (Columbus, Ohio: Grid, 1980), pp. 464–65.

15. Alaska, California, Connecticut, Illinois, Maine, Maryland, Massachusetts, Michigan, Minnesota, New Hampshire, New Jersey, New York, Oregon, Rhode Island, Washington, West Virginia, Wisconsin.

16. Bruce D. May, "Hazardous Substance: OSHA Mandates the Right to Know," *Personnel Journal* GS, no. 8 (Aug. 1986), pp. 128–130.

17. Michael H. Granof, *How to Cost Your Labor Contract* (Washington, D.C.: Bureau of National Affairs, 1973), pp. 4–5.

18. U.S. Department of Labor, Bureau of Labor Statistics, *Characteristics of Major Collective Bargaining Agreements* (Washington, D.C.: Government Printing Office, 1981), pp. 42–58.

19. Lawrence Meyer, "Many Workers Lose Retirement Benefits Despite Reform Laws," *Washington Post,* Sept. 7, 1982.

20. Ibid.

21. *Characteristics of Major Agreements,* 1981, pp. 42–58.

22. William Alpert, "Unions and Private Wage Supplements," *Journal of Labor Research* 3 (Spring 1982), pp. 179–99.

23. Augustin Fosu, "Impact of Unionism on Pension Fringes," *Industrial Relations* 22, no. 3 (Fall 1983), pp. 419–25.

24. Steven G. Allen and Robert L. Clark, "Unions, Pension Wealth, and Age—Compensation Profits," *Industrial and Labor Relations Review* 39, no. 4 (July 1986), pp. 502–512. Also Steven G. Allen, Robert Clark, and Dan Summer, "Post-Retirement Adjustments of Pension Benefits," *Journal of Human Resources* 21, no. 1 (1986), pp. 118–37.

25. Freeman, "Effect of Unionism," 489–509.

26. K.H. Anderson, R.V. Burkhauser, and J.F. Quinn, "Do Retirement Dreams Come True? The Effect of Unanticipated Events On Retirement Plans," *Industrial and Labor Relations Review* 39, no. 4 (July 1986), pp. 518–526.

27. Vicky Cahan, "Mandatory Retirement Gets Put Out to Pasture," *Business Week* Nov. 3, 1986, p. 31.

28. The Retirement Equity Act of 1984.

29. "When Pension Liabilities Dampen Profits," *Business Week,* June 16, 1983, pp. 80–81.

30. Granof, *How to Cost,* p. 61.

31. *Characteristics of Major Agreements,* 1981, pp. 42–58.

32. Granof, *How to Cost,* p. 64.

33. Ibid., p. 65.

34. D. Quinn Mills, "When Employers Make Concessions," *Harvard Business Review* (May–June 1983), pp. 103–113.

35. Peter Cappelli, "Auto Industry Experiments with the Guaranteed Income Stream," *Monthly Labor Review* 107, no. 7 (July 1984), pp. 37–39.

36. Martin Joy Galvin and Michael Robert Lied, "Severance: A Liability in Waiting?" *Personnel Journal* 65, no. 6 (June 1986), pp. 126–131.

37. UAW vs. Roblin Industries, 114 LRRM 2428 (D.C. Mich., 1984).

38. *Basic Patterns in Union Contracts,* 11th ed. (Washington, D.C.: Bureau of National Affairs, 1986), pp. 13–15.

39. Allan P. Blostin, "Is Employer-Sponsored Life Insurance Declining Relative to Other Benefits?" *Monthly Labor Review* 104, no. 7 (Sept. 1981), pp. 31–33.

40. J. F. Follman Jr., "Dental Insurance," *Pension and Welfare News,* Aug. 9, 1973, pp. 20–24, 72.

41. Richard I. Henderson, *Compensation Management* (Reston, Va.: Reston, 1979), p. 323.

42. Sandy Dement, "A New Bargaining Focus on Legal Services," *American Federationist* 85 (May 7, 1978), pp. 7–9.

43. Henderson, *Compensation Management,* p. 325.

44. Ibid., pp. 321–22.

45. *Characteristics of Major Agreements,* 1981, p. 56.

46. Henderson, *Compensation Management,* p. 321.

47. Michael R. Carrell and Frank E. Kuzmits, *Personnel: The Management of Human Resources,* 2nd ed. (Columbus, Ohio: Merrill, 1986), pp. 405–412.

48. Herbert Notkin and Leland Meader, "Health Care Cost Containment," *The Personnel Administrator* 24, no. 3 (March 1979), pp. 58–59.

49. Robert J. Gunbiner, "Selection of a Health Maintenance Organization," Personnel Journal 57, no. 8 (Aug. 1978), pp. 444–45.

50. Michael R. Carrell, "Employer Provided Health Care—What Are the Alternatives?", *Business Forum,* Summer 1987.

51. *Basic Patterns in Union Contracts,* 11th ed. (Washington, D.C.: The Bureau of National Affairs, 1986), pp. 11–21.

52. Robert N. Frumkin, "Health Insurance Trends in Cost Control and Coverage," *Monthly Labor Review* 109, no. 9 (Sept. 1986), pp. 3–8.

53. "Reduced Costs, Increased Worker Production Are Rationale for Tax-favored Corporate Fitness Plans," *Employee Benefit Plan Review,* Nov. 1983, p. 21.

54. Charles A. Berry, *An Approach to Good Health for Employees and Reduced Health Care Costs for Industry,* Health Insurance Association of America (1981), p. 9.

55. Jane Daniel, "An Offer Your Doctor Can't Refuse," *American Health,* Nov./Dec. 1982, p. 82.

56. Berry, *Approach to Good Health,* p. 15.

57. Jack N. Kondrasuk, "Corporate Physical Fitness Programs: The Role of the Personnel Department," *Personnel Administrators* 29, no. 12 (Dec. 1984), pp. 75–80.

58. Thomas Land, "Global Strategy: Confronting Alcoholism at the Workplace," *Alcoholism* 1, no. 6 (1981), pp. 41–42.

59. Carrell and Kuzmits, *Personnel,* pp. 390–392.

60. Ibid.

61. Roger K. Good, "What Bechtel Learned Creating an Employee Assistance Program," *Personnel Journal* 63, no. 9 (Sept. 1984), pp. 80–86.

62. "Employees Join Efforts to Trim Health Care Costs," *Resource* (Alexandria, Va: American Society for Personnel Administration, January 1986), pp. 1, 6.

63. "Cutting Costs With Unions," *Resource,* (Alexandria, Va: American Society for Personnel Administration, Nov. 1986), p. 6.

64. Henderson, *Compensation Management,* p. 326.

65. *Characteristics of Major Agreements,* 1981, p. 85.

66. *Collective Bargaining Negotiations and Contracts* (Washington, D.C.: The Bureau of National Affairs, 1986), p. 12.

67. U.S. Department of Labor, Bureau of Labor Statistics, Bulletin 2013 (Washington, D.C.: Government Printing Office, 1979), p. 55.

68. *Characteristics of Major Agreements,* 1981, pp. 79–81.

69. Granof, *How to Cost,* pp. 45–51.

70. Ibid, pp. 50–51.

71. *Characteristics of Major Agreements,* 1981, p. 79.

72. Ibid, p. 69.

73. *Basic Patterns in Union Contracts,* 1986, pp. 51–53.

74. Sandra L. King and Harry B. Williams, "Shift Work Pay Differentials and Practices in Manufacturing," *Monthly Labor Review* 108, no. 12 (Dec. 1985), pp. 26–33.

75. *Agreement,* between the Joseph Schlitz Brewing Co. and the International Union of the United Brewery, Flour, Cereal, Soft Drink and Distillery Workers of America, 1965–67, p. 32.

PART

IV

Operational Processes

Job Security and Seniority

LABOR NEWS

Toyota's $32 Million Gamble

During 1986 the U.S. Congress was wrestling with the Internal Revenue Code, which resulted in its most sweeping changes in thirty-two years. Five major automobile construction projects (Toyota, Lexington, Kentucky; General Motors' Saturn plant in Tennessee; Chrysler/Mitsubishi, Normal, Illinois; Mazda, Michigan; and Chrysler, St. Louis) were caught in the transition from the old tax laws to the new ones. Each sought tax breaks under the informal congressional "transition rule" granted to projects begun before new tax rules take effect. Of the five factories, Toyota's was the only one not to receive the tax breaks, at a cost of $32 million to the Japanese auto giant.

Was Toyota too late to be added to the Congress Christmas list? No, Toyota was included in the House version of the tax reform bill while GM's Saturn plant was in neither! The obvious answer was organized labor. Of the five projects only the Toyota plant had not reached a construction agree-

ment with the powerful AFL-CIO Building and Construction Trades Union. Union president Robert Georgine had led an extensive campaign to delete Toyota's name from the final version of the tax bill. Representing fifteen unions and 4.1 million members, Georgine lobbied every member of the House-Senate conference committee.

Toyota's problems with labor stemmed from the decision of the contractor to subcontract work to the lowest bidder instead of negotiating an agreement with the building and trades unions. The result was union and nonunion labor working on the site. Toyota apparently believed labor did not have the political muscle necessary to remove the Lexington site from the transition list; it was a $32 million gamble, and Toyota underestimated the union.

Source: Adapted from Mike Brown, "The Taxing Question Is: Why No Toyota Break?" The Courier-Journal, Sept. 20, 1986.

Over the years workers' interests and demands regarding job security have never waned. Together with wages and benefits, job security is seen by negotiators as a top priority in good and bad economic times. Job security is viewed by many as simply meaning the guarantee of work. However, in reality it means much more, including the rights to remain employed during times of layoffs, to promotion, and to a fair hearing in cases involving discipline; and the need to have work performed by employees within the company rather than subcontracting or increasing the use of automatic equipment. The ultimate job security employment situation occurs in some foreign countries where, after a probationary period, employees are guaranteed a job with good wages and benefits for their entire careers as long as they continue to produce satisfactorily. At the other end of the continuum is the hypothetical lack of job security where management might fire, promote, or lay off employees without rationale or consideration for experience and productivity. Negotiating for better wages or working conditions would be meaningless if management could without reason or with biased intentions terminate employees or remove jobs from the workplace.

The concept of job security has also been termed **industrial jurisprudence** by Sumner Slichter. Slichter's concept contains the primary ingredients of job security in today's collective bargaining: seniority as a determining factor in layoffs, promotions, and transfers; control of entrance to the organization or trade; seniority as a determining factor in job assignments; negotiated management change and work methods, also for the introduction of new machinery; and negotiated wage rates.[1] Industrial jurisprudence generally embodies the principle that the operation of the organization will not be determined by a single individual or group of top management officials. Instead, the employees are given some rights to guarantee input into important decisions regarding their employment.

Guarantees of work and promotion opportunities are less important in some industries such as local government and public utilities that have very little variation in the numbers they employ. However, in most manufacturing industries that are heavily unionized, employment variations are great due to changes in consumer demands; thus job security is a primary concern.

The ultimate labor-management conflict over job security is a basic and important one. Management believes it needs to have a free hand in the operation of the workplace to maximize profits and exercise its abilities. In contrast, labor believes employee experience and skills are critical to productivity. Employees require some protection against unreasonable managers as well as guarantees that important decisions such as promotions and layoffs will be made on a rational basis, and favoritism or union busting will be avoided.

Beginning in the thirties, seniority-based procedures, usually the *last hired, first fired* rule, became common layoff and recall decision criteria. Various theories support this rule, and include the *human capital theory,* where employees increase their productivity with experience and rational employers want to retain the more productive employees; the *implicit contract theory,* where the career strategy of employers encourages employees to commit themselves to steady, productive work, thus laying off senior employees would cause worker distrust in any career planning; and the *internal labor market theory,* in which collective bargaining produces rules and procedures to ease the tension between the parties. Seniority-based layoff procedures are a prime example of such rules in limiting management's actions and increasing employee loyalty.[2]

Permanent layoffs are of particular concern to employees since layoffs result in significant reductions in earnings over the course of employees' work lives. Thus, employees have even stronger expectations that employers will reward loyalty during economic downswings.[3] The last hired, first fired rule has caused lower permanent separation rates among union workers in comparison to nonunion workers, along with more frequent temporary layoffs in the union sector due to senior union members' preference for short layoffs, allowing them to maintain their seniority.[4]

Seniority

A *seniority system* is a set of rules governing the allocation of economic benefits and opportunities on the basis of service with one employer.[5] It is by far the most commonly negotiated means of measuring service and comparing employees for promotion and employment decisions.

Seniority is perhaps the most important measure of job security to employees, and the issue of seniority is popular among unions and viewed as critical to job security. Seniority is highly visible because it is so easy to define and measure. Normally, it is calculated in terms of days beginning with the employee's date of hire, and with a few exceptions, continues over the years during the employee's tenure. Union negotiators will vehemently claim that management, in the absence of a job seniority system, will make promotion, layoff, and other decisions based solely upon possible short-run cost savings or individual biases rather than the objective criteria that seniority easily provides. These criteria include the employee's loyalty to the company and her skills and productivity that increase with time spent on the job.

Management may argue that time worked on the job is only one measure and that the employee's performance record, as well as other criteria, should be considered, especially performance appraisals completed by supervisors. However, performance appraisal systems, even at their best, are heavily dependent upon supervisors' objectivity and ability to honestly and thoroughly evaluate individual performance, something that is often very difficult to do. Therefore, performance appraisals are subjective and do not guarantee employees the objectivity and consistency they expect when promotion or layoff decisions are made.

In nonunionized organizations, it certainly is not unheard-of for employers to terminate or lay off senior employees who have worked into higher pay grades or other junior employees who have unjustifiably suffered a supervisor's contempt. A seniority system provides a means of job security and requires that if a supervisor feels an employee is unproductive or unable to successfully produce, the supervisor must defend and subject his decision to an agreed-upon process. Also, the seniority system utilizes a basic and fair premise that employees who have stayed with the organization longer and provided more service should be given first preference when all other aspects of the employment decision are equal.

To fully define the concepts of seniority, it may be helpful to distinguish between unionized and nonunionized employer/employee relationships. Seniority is not required by federal or local laws, nor is it an inherent right of employees. However, seniority is a mandatory subject in the collective bargaining process. Strict formal seniority systems are commonplace in virtually all unionized organizations, but are rare among nonunion employers. The latter employer typically maintains total decision-making control in all aspects of employment that are partially or totally governed by seniority systems in the unionized organization.[6] A Bureau of National Affairs survey of over 400 labor contracts found that 88 percent of the agreements provided for the seniority system, including 95 percent in the manufacturing industries and 76 percent in the nonmanufacturing industries. In most of the contracts surveyed, seniority played a critical role in the determination of promotion and layoff decisions.

Calculation of Seniority

In general, seniority is considered to be the process of giving preference in employment decisions based upon the length of continuous service with the company. When seniority is involved in promotion considerations, it may be defined as preference in employment based upon the length of continuous service and on the ability and fitness of the employee to perform the job. New employees generally begin acquiring seniority on the date they are first hired. In the case of two or more employees hired on the same date, seniority may be determined by the exact time of hire or the alphabetical listing of their last names. Often, however, seniority is not awarded to employees until after the probationary period, even though they begin accruing seniority from their date of first hire.[7] The contract clause that specifically defines seniority can be quite fairly detailed as in the example of the agreement between General Motors Corporation and the United Auto Workers in Exhibit 8.1. Some clauses may be fairly brief, as the following seniority provision from the agreement between Anaconda Aluminum Company and the Aluminum Workers Trades, AFL-CIO:

> *Section 1:* Plant seniority is defined as an employee's length of continuous service at Anaconda Aluminum Company, division of the Anaconda Company, Columbia Falls reduction plant in Columbia Falls, Montana.
>
> *Section 2:* Departmental seniority is defined as employee's length of continuous service in a department of the plant.
>
> *Section 3:* Granted leaves of absence, vacations and jury duty will not be considered as a break in service. Re-employment rights of employees who enter the armed forces shall be determined by the applicable federal and state laws.[8]

Seniority List

Most agreements have the company prepare and post a **seniority list** so there will be no question about employee, department, or plantwide seniority. There must be total

Exhibit 8.1   Agreement on the terms of seniority

SENIORITY

Acquiring Seniority

(56) Employes shall be regarded as temporary employes until their names have been placed on the seniority list. There shall be no responsibility for the reemployment of temporary employes if they are laid off or discharged during this period. However, any claim by a temporary employe made after 30 days of employment that his layoff or discharge is not for cause may be taken up as a grievance.

(57) Employes may acquire seniority by working ninety days during a period of six continuous months in which event the employe's seniority will date back ninety days from the date seniority is acquired; provided, however, that employes hired pursuant to Appendix A may acquire seniority by working thirty days during a period of six continuous months in which event the employe's seniority will date back thirty days from the date seniority is acquired. (See Appendix D.)

(58) When an employe acquires seniority, his name will be placed on the seniority list for his occupational group in the order of his seniority.

(59) Seniority shall be by non-interchangeable occupational groups within departments, group of departments or plant-wide, as may be negotiated locally in each plant and reduced to writing. It is mutually recognized by the parties that written local seniority agreements are necessary. All local seniority agreements and modifications or supplements thereto shall be reduced to writing and be subject to the approval of the Corporation and the International Union.

When changes in methods, products or policies would otherwise require the permanent laying off of employes, the seniority of the displaced employes shall become plant-wide and they shall be transferred out of the group in line with their seniority to work they are capable of doing, as comparable to the work they have been doing as may be available, at the rate for the job to which they have been transferred.

Seniority Lists

(60) Up-to-date seniority lists shall be made available to all employes for their inspection within the plant either by posting where practical or by a satisfactory equivalent method. The method of displaying seniority lists is a matter for local negotiation.

(60a) The seniority list shall contain each employe's name, occupational group, plant seniority date, and, if different than the employe's plant seniority date, his skilled trades date of entry or his skilled trades seniority date. This will not require a change in any mutually satisfactory local practice now in effect.

(61) Each six (6) months the Chairman of the Shop Committee shall be given two up-to-date copies of the complete seniority list of the plant containing each employe's name, department number, occupational group or classification, plant seniority date, and, if different than the employe's plant seniority date, his skilled trades date of entry or his skilled trades seniority date. This will not require a change in any mutually satisfactory local practice now in effect.

(61a) Following the end of each month the Chairman of the Shop Committee shall be furnished two copies of the list of names, department number and seniority dates of employes who during the preceding month have:

(a) Acquired seniority.

(b) Been granted leaves of absence for military service.

(c) Been granted other types of leave of absence of more than thirty (30) days' duration.

(d) Returned to work from leaves of absence described in (b) and (c) above.

Local Management will designate on the list those employes who ceased to be subject to the check-off and the reason therefor.

(61b) Each week the Chairman of the Shop Committee shall be furnished two copies of the list of names and department numbers of the employes who during the preceding week:

(a) Became new hires into the bargaining unit (designating those hired pursuant to Appendix A and, by classification, those hired as journeymen, including identification of apprentice graduates, and employes-in-training (E.I.T.).

(b) Returned to work from permanent layoff.

(c) Transferred

   (1) into the bargaining unit, or

   (2) out of the bargaining unit (to supervisory or non-supervisory position).

(d) Had their employment terminated while in a temporary employe status, including the date of hire and last day worked of each such employe.

(e) Lost seniority, and the reason therefor (designating those who were hired pursuant to Appendix A).

The list shall contain the seniority dates of employes listed under (b) and (c). It shall also include a notation of the seniority date of the employe with the longest seniority who is laid off or the "leveling off" date.

(61c) Each week the Chairman of the Shop Committee shall be furnished one copy of the names of employes who received S. U. B. checks for regular benefits or alternate benefits and the amount of such benefits.

Source: *Agreement* between General Motors Corporation and the UAW, November 11, 1976, pp. 39–42. Used with permission.

agreement as to the exact calculation and order of employees on seniority lists (see Case 8.1). The method of displaying seniority lists is usually a matter for local negotiation between labor and management. Many contracts provide that seniority lists be updated monthly, and that they contain the employee's name, occupational group or department, any specific skilled trades date of entry, and related seniority. Any disputes over seniority lists are taken through the grievance procedure for resolution.

Depending on the particular labor agreement, seniority rights are vested within a variety of different employee units. The most common unit would be **plantwide seniority** where an individual employee receives credit that becomes applicable whenever that employee competes with any other employee from another unit for the same position. Other common seniority units include departmental, trade, classification, and company-wide. For example, in a **departmental seniority** system, employees accrue seniority according to the amount of time they worked within a particular department, and that seniority credit is valid only within that department.[9] For example, an employee with eleven years seniority in department x could not successfully compete with an employee with seven years in department y for an open position in department y.

Classification seniority, similar to departmental seniority, provides for employee seniority only within the same job classification. *Company-wide seniority* systems combine all employees from various locations and types of facilities. When two employees compete for an open position in a company-wide system, individual experience, length of service, and related departments or job classifications are not considered, but only the seniority with the company. This makes company-wide seniority the most impractical and infrequently used.

Companies often use a seniority system combining plant-wide seniority with departmental seniority. Plantwide seniority may be utilized for determining layoffs, vacations, and other specific benefits. Departmental seniority is often used to determine eligibility for a promotion or a transfer so employees with specific skills and related job experience can be considered for new positions. However, in the case of layoffs, it is often believed that employees' total work experience, and therefore their plantwide seniority, is the most important job security factor.

In situations involving layoffs, seniority systems often use **bumping**; that is, employees with greater seniority whose jobs have been phased out have the right to displace employees with less seniority. Such bumping rights may be limited to departmental or job classification seniority instead of plantwide seniority. In a combined seniority system, plantwide seniority is frequently used to determine bumping rights.[10]

Superseniority

Union officers and committee personnel may be given preferred seniority rights for layoff and recall situations. This is often referred to as **superseniority,** and is granted in the collective bargaining agreement so union stewards and other labor officials will continue to work during periods of layoff so that the union can continue to operate effectively. When agreeing to superseniority for the union, management may ensure that certain labor relations personnel be similarly protected against layoffs. Some superseniority clauses require that protected union officials have the ability to perform available work or that superseniority is provided only within departments or job classifications.

The value of superseniority depends upon the frequency and degree of layoffs typically experienced by the company. In some cases, it is virtually meaningless, because union stewards and officials have high levels of seniority from their many years of experience with the union and company.

The labor agreement should explicitly specify under what conditions an employee might lose seniority. Case 8.2 discusses how some employees lost all their seniority when a new company location replaced an older one. Virtually all contracts provide that employees lose seniority if they voluntarily quit or are discharged. Employees who do not report back to work after a vacation or other leave of absence for an excessive period of time may be also deprived of their seniority. Usually employees on layoff will retain and accumulate seniority for a period of time specified within the agreement. An example of a loss of seniority clause is provided in Chapter 11.

Seniority is normally retained by employees during short-term leaves of absence due to illness as well as during strikes. However, most agreements provide that employees who accept other employment during their leaves of absence forfeit their seniority. The Selective Service Act provides that full seniority is maintained and accumulated during military leaves of absence.[11]

Promotions

Management often disagrees with the use of seniority to determine promotion decisions. The Bureau of National Affairs estimates that seniority is a determining factor in promotional policies as provided by collective bargaining agreements in 67 percent of labor contracts. However, only 9 percent call for promotion decisions based upon seniority as the sole determiner. Another 33 percent provide that the most senior individual will receive promotion if she is qualified for the job.[12] In most promotional policies, seniority is treated as a determining factor along with employee skill and ability.

Some contract clauses that allow promotion according to seniority simply state that promotions to fill vacancies or new job positions on a permanent basis will be based upon length of service within the company and employee skill and ability. Determining which employees have the required skill and ability is difficult and subjective. Management generally contends that promotion should be based on employee's individual performance and required skills rather than length of service.

When labor agreements provide that promotional decisions will be made according to seniority and job skills, it is difficult to determine the weight of each factor and the measurement of individual skills. Although seniority is a factor in promotion decisions in most labor contracts, it is usually not considered to be as important as ability to perform the job. Quite frequently ability becomes more dominant. When management decides to promote a less senior employee on the basis of higher demonstrated ability, employee grievances may result, as in Case 8.3. Management must prove that the more senior employee does not have the ability to perform the job.

Arbitrators usually let the decision of management stand in promotion selections unless it can be substantially shown by the union that the company completely ignored seniority or acted in an arbitrary manner. Arbitrators have generally held that management has the burden of proof to estimate employee ability correctly. However, the selection process must be shown to be free from favoritism or bias.[13] And if there is doubt as to a senior worker's ability to perform the job, arbitrators often have held that a trial period on the new job is the best way to judge the employee's ability.[14] If the contract states that seniority as well as ability will be considered in making promotional decisions, it is expected that seniority will be used as a tiebreaker for two employees with relatively equal ability. If no internal employee bids for a position or is determined by management to be qualified, the company usually is given the right to hire from the outside.[15]

Managers may argue that making important promotional decisions solely on length of service takes away employee incentive. Employees will tend to perform at the status quo knowing that they cannot be promoted before all the senior employees, and when their turn comes, no one can take the promotion away from them. Labor leaders point out that seniority can be objectively and easily measured. Therefore, promotion decisions based upon seniority are far less subject to supervisor bias or inability to assess correctly individual performance and skills.

What weights are given to seniority and ability in actual promotion decisions? Is there a difference between union and nonunion employers? An analysis of over 600 U.S. firms indicated that 60 percent give the person with greater seniority a preference in promotion decisions. In practice both union and nonunion employers reported giving length of service more weight in promotion decisions than required by written policy or union contract. While union employers reported using seniority to a greater extent, the difference in comparison with nonunion employers was not significant.[16]

Nonunion organizations often have promotion policies based primarily upon promoting from within to boost employee morale and assure individuals that they can work hard and get ahead. Like union organizations, they hesitate to promote a less senior employee unless there is concrete evidence to show that a more senior employee is less capable. The effect of such a promotion upon general employee morale, as well as upon the individual involved, also needs to be determined. Therefore, in nonunion organizations, seniority is weighed carefully along with the employee's past record and demonstrated skills.[17]

Job Bidding

It is quite common for the **job bidding** process to be detailed in the labor agreement to minimize misunderstandings and grievances and increase employee morale. An example of a detailed job bidding process follows:

> 1. When a new classification is created or an opening occurs in the existing classification, the opening will be posted on the official bid bulletin boards for a period of four working days, Saturdays, Sundays, and holidays excluded.

2. Bids for such openings will be received from any permanent employee. Temporary employees will not be allowed to bid.

3. Bids will be awarded on an up-bid, down-bid, or lateral-bid. An *up-bid* is a bid from a lower to a higher pay grade or from a pool classification to a specific line classification. A *lateral-bid* is from one classification to another classification in the same pay grade, or from one pool position to another regardless of pay grade. A *down-bid* is from a higher pay grade to a lower pay grade or from a specific line classification to a pool classification.

4. Bids will be based on plant seniority and competency with the following regulations applying:

a. Bids to be classifications and specific lines of progression: an employee awarded a job bid in one specific line cannot bid again for one year from the date qualified in the specific line job except on an up-bid basis within his specific line progression.

b. Bids to classifications in the pool: an employee who down-bids from a specific line of progression to a pool position cannot bid again for a period of six months from the date classified except to a specific line. Or an employee classified in a pool position who down-bids or laterally bids to another pool position cannot bid again for a period of six months from the date classified except through a specific line.

c. Down-bids from classification and pay grades 12 and above will be limited to a maximum of one down-bid per classification in any one sixty day period.

Adapted from *Agreement* between Anaconda Aluminum Co. and Aluminum Workers' Local No. 130 and the Aluminum Workers' International Union, AFL-CIO, 1980–83, pp. 16–17. Used with permission.

Layoff and Recall Actions

Many employers also question the use of seniority as the sole decision criterion in layoff and recall situations. Employers argue that ability should be a greater factor in determining layoff and recall of employees. However, since layoff and recall situations are usually seen as temporary, management's argument against the use of seniority is considerably weaker. Also, in layoff and recall situations, there is less of a question of the employee's ability since he has been performing the job satisfactorily before a layoff occurs. Thus, management has little room to argue that seniority is not more important in layoff and recall than in promotion decisions.

In most labor contracts, probationary employees will be laid off first, with further necessary layoffs being made in accordance with plantwide seniority. Laid-off employees may be given the opportunity to exercise their plantwide seniority and bump employees at the bottom of the seniority list rather than be laid off. When skilled trades or other specialized job classifications are involved, layoffs will commonly occur by seniority within the trades or classifications. Most agreements also provide that the company give reasonable notice and reasons for upcoming layoffs to the unions. If the work force is increased after a layoff, contracts usually provide that laid-off employees will be recalled according to plantwide seniority for appropriate jobs.

Contract layoff procedures may fall into three general categories: layoff based entirely on seniority, layoff based upon seniority among those employees management feels are capable of performing the work, and layoff based upon seniority only if ability and other factors are equal among affected employees. When the last two methods of layoff and recall procedures are utilized, grievances are likely to be filed because of the subjectivity of determining employee ability to perform work, especially when bumping is used and employees are performing new jobs.[18] If a contract provides that seniority and equal ability shall govern in layoff and recall decisions, arbitrators are likely to interpret *equal* as meaning not exactly equal but relatively equal. When contracts provide that ability should be part of the determination in layoff and recall decisions, arbitrators' awards have suggested certain guidelines be considered.[19] Some of the guidelines include the following:

1. When seniority is considered a governing criterion if ability to perform the work is relatively equal, then only the employee's seniority should be considered.[20]
2. A junior employee could be given preference over a senior employee, if the senior requires a much greater amount of supervision in performing the job.[21]
3. Senior employees can be required to demonstrate ability to perform the work by passing a test that would qualify them for jobs held by junior employees.[22]

In cases involving temporary or emergency layoffs, management is often given more flexibility in selecting employees than in indefinite layoffs. If the contract does not specify differences in procedure involving temporary layoffs and indefinite layoffs, arbitrators have generally held that ordinary layoff procedures must be followed even where the lack of work lasted only a few hours or one to two days. However, the more common ruling of arbitrators in such situations has been that cumbersome seniority rules need not be followed to the letter in a brief layoff. Arbitrators have even held that in layoffs caused by emergency breakdowns or natural, unplanned disasters, seniority rules can be disregarded if necessary. However, if the application of seniority rules in the contract does not cause a hardship during the emergency, the employer is advised to follow the contract layoff procedures.[23] A concise layoff and recall contract clause setting forth the procedure and notification requirements and possible emergency exceptions follows:

ARTICLE 10
Reduction of Forces
a. The company agrees that in the event of a reduction in force, plant seniority shall govern and employees covered by the terms of this agreement shall be laid off in the inverse order of seniority, provided that the employee retained has the ability to fill the job. He shall have a reasonable length of time to demonstrate his ability to hold the job.
b. If an emergency such as fire, flood, storm, or major breakdown occurs during a work week, every effort will be made to avoid loss of work and/or to reassign employees on a basis of seniority. However, it is recognized that a layoff out of seniority not exceeding one day may be necessary to avoid a payment of penalty pay.
c. Whenever a reduction in force is necessary, the company will post the names of the employees to be laid off at least three days, excluding Saturday, Sunday, and holidays, prior to such reduction unless cancellation of orders, changes in customer's requirements, breakdowns, or accidents or other emergencies make such notices impossible, in which case a union will be immediately notified.

> When the company again adds to the number of employees, those laid off shall be re-employed in the order of their seniority. A notice of recall or restoration shall be sent by registered mail to the last known address of the employee, and a copy of the notice, before it is mailed, shall be given to the properly designated officer of the union. It shall be the duty of the employee to keep the company informed as to his correct address.

Source: *Agreement* between Anaconda Aluminum Co. and Aluminum Workers' No. 130 and Aluminum Workers' International Union, AFL-CIO, 1983, pp. 14–16. Used with permission.

Typically, the only exceptions to the use of seniority as the total or partial determinant in layoff and recall decisions occur when probationary employees are laid off first without any discussion of ability to perform, or in cases involving superseniority when union officials are laid off last.

A recent development in the issue of seniority rights involves layoffs by companies or governmental agencies subject to court-ordered affirmative action plans. The U.S. Supreme Court, in *Firefighters Local Union No. 1784* v. *Stotts,* upheld a seniority system even though the resulting layoffs adversely affected blacks hired under a consent decree to remedy past discrimination. The Court would not allow the consent decree, which had not dealt with the layoff issue, to be given preference over a collectively bargained seniority system. Advocates of affirmative action plans fear this decision, reaffirming the "last hired, first fired" philosophy, will undermine equal opportunity employment strides made in the last few years. Labor leaders, however, defend the protection afforded by seniority systems as necessary to preserve a basic negotiated job right. They argue that changed hiring practices giving women and blacks more job opportunities will eventually lead to *their* seniority in the various systems. Increased employment and secure job rights will accomplish the desired affirmative action goals without adversely affecting the senior worker.

Shared Work/Short-Time Compensation

Workers who have their worktime (and therefore pay) reduced have become more numerous as management strives to cut personnel costs and remain competitive. This **shared work** concept has affected workers who had their hours cut one day per week (short-time) but at least retained their jobs and 80 percent of their income. Union leaders pressured to accept this proposal can rationalize that it is preferable for 100 percent of the employees to work 80 percent of their regular hours than have 80 percent work 100 percent of their regular hours and have 20 percent laid off. Prior to the 1980s, short-time workers were ineligible for any unemployment insurance benefits since they continued to work a reduced number of hours each week. Thus, a "pro-layoff" bias existed because many would prefer total layoff and therefore receive unemployment benefits.

In response some states[24] adopted short-time compensation programs as part of their unemployment insurance systems, allowing workers to receive partial unemployment benefits after a reduction in work hours. In general, these state programs were designed to reduce the pro-layoff bias and encourage reduced-hours strategies during temporary economic downturns.[25]

Overall, the AFL-CIO has supported the short-time compensation concept as a means of reducing the number of workers who must experience the extreme hardships of total unemployment. However, the AFL-CIO does not endorse long-term use of shared work or view it as an alternative to the creation of permanent full-time jobs. In general, management has been slow to endorse the concept.[26]

Burden of Proof

Arbitrators have generally placed the burden of proof on the employer to show that a bypassed senior employee is not competent for the job during promotions or layoff/recall actions. However, employers are not required to show that junior employees are more competent. When seniority and ability are given practically equal weight in contract clauses, arbitrators expect the employer to prove whether the ability factor was given greater weight than the seniority factor. In general, even though arbitrators may speak in terms of burden of proof when management's decision regarding ability is challenged, both parties are expected to produce any evidence supporting their respective continuances.[27]

While it is generally agreed that management has the right to determine how ability is to be measured in cases involving promotion or layoff and recall decisions, there is no federal law or agreed-upon formula to specify exactly how such decisions should be made. Management generally uses a variety of factors to determine the ability to perform a job. The specific factors may be limited by the contract clause prevailing in a given situation. However, the absence of any such clause gives management the freedom to determine its own factors and measurements. The factors or criteria most commonly used to determine an employee's ability to perform the job and make decisions of promotion or recall are summarized in the following section.

 1. *Tests*   Appropriate written, oral, and aptitude tests have been used to determine the ability of competing employees. Most arbitrators look very favorably upon the use of appropriate tests as fair and objective means of determining employee fitness to perform the job. Arbitrators have generally held that tests, in order to be validly used to determine ability, must be job related, fair and reasonable, administered fairly without discrimination, and evaluated properly and objectively. Management should be prepared to show that the tests are directly related to the skill and ability required in the performance of the job. Also, employers should be able to prove that the tests were administered fairly and without discrimination.

 2. *Experience*   This is the extent to which an employee has performed the particular job or relevant type of work, and is completely separate from seniority. In most situations, experience is an important, related factor considered by management to determine an employee's fitness and ability to perform the job. If other factors are approximately equal and the senior employee had had satisfactory experience performing the job in some capacity, experience may be considered the most important criterion. However, experience on the particular job in question is far more valuable than experience on related jobs.

 3. *Trial period*   Some contract clauses provide that a trial period be given to the senior employee so her ability to perform the job is directly tested. The absence of such a specific provision gives management more flexibility in deciding whether to give the

senior employee a trial period. Some arbitrators consider a fair trial period the best test of an employee's ability. However, management is not required to give the employee training on the job but instead allows a temporary period to determine if the employee has the ability. Thus, arbitrators have generally concluded that if there is a reasonable doubt as to the ability of the senior employee, a trial period should be granted, unless it would cause serious inconvenience to the company. Some labor contracts provide for a specific amount of time for the trial period; others only require a reasonable qualifying period and leave such determination to management.

4. *Opinion of supervisor*   The opinion of the supervisor to determine ability is seriously considered only if supported by factual evidence such as production records, merit ratings, or other specific job-related information. Periodic performance evaluations by supervisors are often an essential part of this documentation. Such merit ratings or rating scales generally include factors such as quality of work, knowledge of the job, cooperation with others, ability to accept orders, and attitude. If supervisory ratings include personal biases, the ratings are given less weight in employment decisions.

5. *Educational background*   Employee training on or off the job can be considered an important criterion. Such training must be job related to the specific job in question. The employee's formal education can also be considered if it is pertinent to the job.

6. *Production records*   Management may rely heavily upon an employee's production record as evidence of fitness and ability to perform the job. Certainly, an employee's past output reflects not only skills and abilities but motivation and effort. If there is a considerable difference among competing employees, arbitrators have held that management can consider production records as the sole factor if the selection is based upon ability.

7. *Attendance records*   If a senior employee has a particularly poor attendance record, she may be bypassed. The promotion of a junior employee over a senior employee on the basis of great differences in their attendance records has been generally upheld by arbitrators. The same is true if the senior employee has a poor disciplinary record.

8. *Physical fitness*   Contracts may specify physical fitness as a job requirement. Arbitrators will generally favor recent medical evidence and discard dated medical records. Unless prohibited by contract, management can require competing employees to take physical examinations, if all employees are required to take such examinations, and the results are job related. A particular physical defect or limitation limiting the employee's ability to perform the job can be considered a pertinent reason to bypass a senior employee. Arbitrators have even upheld management's decision to bypass a senior employee on the grounds of obesity, if it has to some extent affected the employee's past work performance. An employee's temperament or nervousness, as exhibited in his past job performance, may also disqualify a senior employee.

Adapted with permission from *How Arbitration Works,* 3rd ed., by Frank Elkouri and Edna Asper Elkouri (Washington, D.C.: Bureau of National Affairs, 1981), pp. 577–609. Copyright © 1981 by the Bureau of National Affairs, Inc. Washington, D.C.

Company Mergers

When separate companies or different entities merge, how the seniority lists of the two are combined is a critical question. The merger must specify which principle of combining seniority lists will be utilized. The most commonly used methods include the **Surviving Group Principle** where seniority lists are merged by adding the names of the employees of the acquired company to the bottom of the acquiring company. Thus, all the employees of the acquiring company receive greater seniority consideration than any employee of the acquired company. Another method, the **Length of Service Principle**, is used when an employee's length of service is considered, regardless of which company he worked for prior to the merger; therefore, the two seniority lists are combined with no employee losing any previously earned seniority. With the **Follow the Work Principle**, employees are allowed to continue previously earned seniority on separate seniority lists when their work with the merged company can be separately identified. The **Absolute Rank Principle** gives employees rank positions on the merging seniority lists equal to their rank position on the prior seniority lists. Therefore, two employees will be ranked first, followed by two being ranked second, followed by two being ranked third, and so on. The **Ratio-Rank Principle** combines seniority lists by establishing a ratio based upon the total number of employees in the two groups to be merged. If Group A has 150 employees and Group B has 50 employees, the ratio is three to one and, of the first four places on the new seniority lists, the three ranked highest in Group A will be given positions one, two, and three, while highest ranked position in Group B will be given rank four.[28]

A combination of methods is often used to combine seniority lists of merged units or companies, with weight being given to the different principles. For example, in merging two airline pilot seniority lists, one-third weight was given to the Ratio Rank Principle and two-thirds to the Length of Service Principle.[29]

Union Security

As presented in Chapter 2, *union security* refers to the union's ability to perform its exclusive collective bargaining role without interference. A *union security clause* is a provision in the collective bargaining agreement requiring employees to join the union, pay union dues and fees, or in some way support the union as a condition of continued employment. Such a provision ensures that the union, its members, and all of the employees who share the benefits of the collective bargaining agreement pay for the union's support.

Seniority and other job rights of individuals under collective bargaining agreements are subject to negotiation. The survival of a particular union as the agent to preserve previously bargained rights and seniority systems may become important. A union security clause, therefore, helps initiate and strengthen loyalties to a particular union.

Union security clauses may take several forms. The *closed shop provision* provided that the employer hire only union members. Therefore, in order to get a job, a person first had to join the union. Prior to being outlawed by the Taft-Hartley Amendments of 1947, the closed shop provision caused a huge increase in union membership.

The most common type of union security clause is the **union shop**. It provides that, within a specific period of time, usually thirty to ninety days, the employee join the union. Union membership under such a provision must be available on a fair and nondiscriminatory basis. Under relevant Court decisions the extent of an individual's participation in the union under a union shop provision is limited to payment of union dues. A union cannot seek the discharge of a member of a bargaining unit so long as the member's dues to the union are paid.[30]

A **union hiring hall** provision often used in the construction trades requires an employer to hire employees referred by the union if the union can supply a sufficient number of applicants. As long as the union refers union and nonunion members alike and does not require membership before the seventh day of employment, such provisions are legal.

Two milder forms of union security include the *agency shop* provision, requiring employees to contribute a sum equal to membership dues to the union, but not requiring them to join the union; and a *maintenance of membership* provision, requiring union members to remain union members for the duration of the union contract once it is signed. Nonunion members are not required to join. Also, the following are considered union security provisions: a *preferential shop,* which requires the employer to give hiring preference to union members; a **check-off provision** requiring that employers directly deduct union dues from employee paychecks; and **superseniority** that gives union leaders top seniority for layoff purposes and indirectly increases union security by ensuring continuity of its leadership.

In states containing *right-to-work laws,* a collective bargaining agreement cannot contain a union shop clause. The lack of union security in these states has an effect upon the types of seniority and other job rights provisions negotiated by the union. While the negotiated items will affect all the employees, only those who voluntarily join the union truly participate in deciding contract goals. However, in right-to-work states, a large percentage of employees in the bargaining unit often will voluntarily join the union. They realize the importance of their support to the success of the union.

Subcontracting

Although few problems arise when there are specific contract restrictions on management's rights to subcontract, management's insistence upon freedom in this area often leads to grievances. A grievance over management's right to subcontract work during the agreement often results in arbitration. In the past, many arbitrators held that management has the right to subcontract work through independent contractors; however, in recent years, this has been somewhat restricted by arbitrators.

What is subcontracting? It has been termed the "Twilight Zone" of management rights in collective bargaining, and is considered a headache by both labor and management. Basically, **subcontracting** may be defined as arranging to make goods or perform services with another firm that could be accomplished by the bargaining unit employees within the company's current facilities.[31]

Contract provisions against subcontracting may carry over to new employers, as when the Communication Workers of America won a $6 million settlement from

AT&T over subcontracting. The 130 workers who won reinstatement of their jobs claimed AT&T violated the subcontracting clause contained in their agreement with Pennsylvania Bell. The breakup of the Bell system shifted the workers to AT&T where they were laid off and their work, primarily wiring and installation of telephones, was contracted out. The union won reinstatement of their jobs and back-pay for the 130 workers, and in addition, won back-pay for another 900 workers and resolved over 100 pending arbitration cases.[32]

Many union leaders and arbitrators believe that the recognition clause recognizing the union as the exclusive bargaining agent implies an agreement that the employer may not remove work from employees in the unit by subcontracting it to others during the life of an agreement. However, others argue that the National Labor Relations Act requires recognition of the union as a representative of people and not work; the purpose of the recognition clause is to enunciate the legal status of the bargaining unit required by the act. The clause merely describes the unit of the employees for whom the union speaks and thus delineates the agreement in terms of those employees covered. Therefore, it does not deal with and has no bearing upon any specific employment terms or conditions.

An example of a contract clause limiting the ability of management to subcontract is provided in the agreement between Lithonia Lighting Inc. and Local Union no. 613 of the International Brotherhood of Electrical Workers:

SECTION VIII
Subcontracting
The company agrees that wherever possible it will not subcontract work normally performed by members of the bargaining unit while there are employees on layoff capable of performing such work; and in the event work is subcontracted hereunder, such work will not be subcontracted to individuals, firms, or corporations unfair to the IBEW.[33]

This example, however, will allow management to subcontract work. Management could subcontract work currently being performed by employees of the bargaining unit through attrition and additional training. An example of an even more restrictive subcontracting clause is provided in the agreement between the Lockheed-Georgia Company and the International Association of Machinist and Aerospace Workers, AFL-CIO, who perform maintenance work on airplanes:

SECTION 14
Subcontracting
The company agrees that it will not subcontract maintenance work to be performed on company premises when the work operations involved have normally been performed by the employees in the bargaining unit, except for the following instances:

a. Where peculiar skills or specialized equipment are involved which are not available within the company.
b. Where short-term or peak requirements necessitate the need for additional assistance because of an insufficient number of employees that [*sic*] are available possessing of the necessary maintenance skills to perform such work operations within the time of requirement.

c. Where unusual or one-shot jobs are required which are not usually performed by the company.

d. Where the volume of work on any particular job precludes the possibility of its completion within scheduled time limits.

It is not the intent of the company to use on-site contractors for the purpose of reducing or transferring work ordinarily performed by the maintenance employees of the bargaining unit.[34]

Management's right to subcontract is usually judged by arbitrators against the recognition of the bargaining unit, seniority, wages, and other clauses within the agreement. Standards of reasonableness and good faith are applied in determining whether clauses in the contract have been violated by subcontracting. In general, management's right to subcontract is recognized, provided it is exercised in good faith. Arbitrators often recognize that signing a contract does not establish an agreement that all of the jobs will continue to be performed by members of the bargaining unit unless this is specified within the contract. However, the company cannot undermine the unit by subcontracting for the sole purpose of getting rid of work done by union employees in favor of nonunion employees who are paid lower wages. The following standards that arbitrators generally apply to subcontracting cases are summarized:

1. *Past practices*   Whether the company has subcontracted work in the past. (64 LA 101, 63 LA 1143, 61 LA 526)

2. *Justification*   Whether subcontracting is done for reasons such as economy, maintenance of secondary sources for production, plant security, etc. (62 LA 421, 61 LA 530)

3. *Effect on union*   Whether subcontracting is being used as a method of discriminating against the union and substantially prejudicing the status and integrity of the bargaining unit. (64 LA 602)

4. *Effect on unit employees*   Whether members of the union are discriminated against, displaced, laid off, or deprived of jobs previously available to them, or to lose regular or overtime earnings, by reason of the subcontract. (63 LA 798, 62 LA 1000, 62 LA 895, 61 LA 333)

5. *Type of work involved*   Whether it is work that is normally done by unit employees, or work that is frequently the subject of subcontracting in the particular industry, or work that is of a marginal or incidental nature. (62 LA 474)

6. *Availability of properly qualified employees*   Whether the skills possessed by available members of the bargaining unit are sufficient to perform the work. (65 LA 598, 65 LA 431, 63 LA 883)

7. *Availability of equipment and facilities*   Whether necessary equipment and facilities are presently available or can be economically purchased. (64 LA 1244, 63 LA 82, 62 LA 505)

8. *Regularity of subcontracting*   Whether the particular work is frequently or only intermittently subcontracted.

9. *Duration of subcontracted work*   Whether the work is subcontracted for a temporary or limited period, or for a permanent or indefinite period.

10. *Unusual circumstances involved*   Whether an emergency, special job, strike, or other unusual situation exists, necessitating the action.

11. *History of negotiations*   Whether management's right to subcontract has been the subject of contract negotiations. *(How Arbitration Works,* by Frank and Edna Elkouri; published by BNA, 1960)

Source: Reprinted by permission from *Grievance Guide,* 6th ed. (Washington, D.C.: Bureau of National Affairs, 1982), pp. 298–99. Copyright © 1982 by The Bureau of National Affairs, Inc., Washington, D.C.

Technological Change

Union leaders have historically been skeptical of some so-called technological change programs initiated by management. Labor's past resistance is especially deep-rooted in the manufacturing sector, where changes have robbed workers of their special skills. Computer-controlled equipment not only replaced many jobs but also the skills required, undermining labor's traditional position. The unskilled or semiskilled workers following in the wake of these changes do not have the bargaining power of their forerunners, and can be quickly and easily trained on jobs that previously took years to develop experience and a level of competence.[35]

Another deep-rooted resistance to technological change may have resulted from labor's negative experience with past management plans that were sometimes thinly veiled methods of reducing the work force or pay levels rather than implementing true technological changes. Management programs disguised as reorganization attempts, introduction of more efficient equipment, or job enrichment programs, have not always been in good faith and result in the suspicion of union officials.

In recent years, labor leaders have been particularly skeptical of job enrichment programs. Since employees take on additional responsibilities, determining whether a program will result in increased job autonomy or simply increased workloads is difficult at best. William Winpisinger stated what many of his labor colleagues believe to be true:

> . . . Studies tend to prove that workers' dissatisfaction diminishes with age. That's because older workers have accrued more of the kinds of job enrichment that unions have fought for—better wages, shorter hours, vested pensions, a right to have a say in the working conditions, a right to be promoted on the basis of seniority and all the rest. That's the kind of enrichment that unions believe in.[36]

Technological change programs that attempted to reorganize or redesign jobs to reduce the number of union employees or affect pay scales left hard feelings.

Unions have utilized collective bargaining to protect their members against technological changes leading to layoffs, demotions, or the expansion of unskilled versus skilled positions. Many labor agreements contain clauses requiring the retraining of workers displaced by automation, forbidding layoffs due to technological changes, and providing expensive severance pay plans. Such actions tend to reduce cost-effectiveness of proposed technological advances.

However, today many union leaders agree that collective bargaining practices requiring that work be performed by obsolete, low productivity methods are self-destructive. It has taken years for some leaders to develop this attitude, but they realize the company cannot be competitive within the marketplace. Therefore, labor does not always resist technological change, and instead allows management a free hand in the collective bargaining agreement when profits can be shared. For example, in the *Scanlon Plan* productivity and profit sharing are related, and increased earnings are shared. A fair way of dividing up productivity and profits has been agreed upon between labor and management in advance. As the profits grow due to increased productivity, everyone gets a larger total share. With strict agreed-upon means of measuring productivity and profit sharing, the exact wages and benefits due labor are not set forth in the collective bargaining agreement, but rather negotiated with stated productivity and profit-sharing formulas to determine what labor will get at the end of a predetermined period of time. While there is a greater risk to labor and management, there is also the possibility of greater return from such a system.[37] Both labor and management will probably work harder to achieve higher levels of profitability.

Retraining Rights

The need to stay competitive with nonunion and foreign businesses has caused union leaders to accept technology changes as necessary and normal conditions of work. Today, rather than oppose technological change, negotiators anticipate it and bargain for advance notice, retraining rights, and outplacement assistance for affected workers.

A total systematic approach to **technological change and worker retraining** was developed by the Ford Motor Company and the United Auto Workers (UAW) in 1982. The decision to close the San Jose, California plant was announced along with a labor-management initiative to provide assistance to displaced workers. The total program included the following agenda:

☐ *Orientation and benefits*   All workers were included in meetings that provided them information about available services, company benefits, and "personalized" information about specific benefits at the time of shutdown.

☐ *Assessment and testing*   Over 1,600 workers participated in retraining programs after taking a skills test administered by the California Employment Department.

☐ *Basic education and vocational courses*   In-plant courses in basic math, reading, and English enabled 183 workers to pass the general equivalency diploma (GED) examination. In addition, Ford personnel taught courses in computers, welding, statistical quality control, auto mechanics, metal repair, electronics, and so on. More than 2,100 workers participated.

☐ *Seminars and programs*   Additional in-plant seminars were offered in small business, real estate, armed security, and so forth.

☐ *Target vocational retraining*   Local technical training institutions taught over thirty courses in areas such as microwave and machine tool technology, and auto service. The courses were paid for by the 1982 Ford-UAW "Nickel Fund" for training, Job Training Partnership Act (JTPA) of 1982, and the state of California.

☐ *Job search and placement*   Two-day job search workshops were conducted by California Employment Development Department staff workers.

☐ *Ford plant relocation*   Under the 1982 agreement, 117 San Jose hourly workers chose to relocate to other Ford plants in the United States.[38]

As a result of the program, more than 83 percent of those employees who re-entered the labor market secured employment, and 21 percent chose retirement under the agreement's benefit plan. Both labor and management consider the program a model worker-retraining program, a workable approach to the challenge of technological change.

Summary

Job security and seniority are vital to collective bargaining agreements. Both labor and management strongly believe they must maintain certain rights where job security affects the employee's ability to keep her job and successfully compete for higher positions. Seniority, or length of service with the organization, and the employee's ability to perform the job successfully are the two primary factors considered in layoff and promotion situations for both union and nonunion companies. An effective job security system also requires that the labor agreement contain a fair and just discipline and grievance system so management's decisions regarding promotion or layoff and recall can be properly disputed by labor.

Seniority systems have generally been utilized because they are easy to develop and provide an objective, unambiguous means of considering employees when job openings occur. The theory behind using seniority is that if the employees are approximately equal in ability, then the employee who has the greatest length of service should be given the opportunity first. This is commonplace in nonunion as well as union organizations. Unfortunately, there are not always objective measures of ability to perform. The difficulty lies in determining the relative ability of competing employees.

Seniority systems and employee feelings of job security are meaningless unless contract provisions limit management's ability to subcontract work. Without such provisions, management can subcontract work temporarily and force severe hardships on employees, causing them to leave and lose their seniority. Certainly, while union leaders agree that subcontracting is necessary in some situations, it can and has been used to undermine labor unions.

CASE 8.1   *Seniority List*

Adapted from *Clarkston Community Schools,* 79 L.A. 48 (1982)

The union protested the inclusion of administrators on a school district seniority list. The list included the accumulated seniority of former administrators who had returned to teaching, and present administrators who were formerly teachers. The union conceded that teachers promoted to administration retained the seniority accumulated while in the bargaining units, but objected to them accumulating seniority as administrators for the purposes of bumping into the bargaining unit. The school district admitted that administrators are not in the bargaining unit but defended their demands based on the contract and past practices.

Decision

The arbitrator considered the contract language involved and found that when a teacher is promoted to an administrator's position she leaves the bargaining unit for purposes of seniority and does not accumulate seniority for the time spent working as an administrator. In addition, a person who begins employment as an administrator does not accumulate seniority if and when he becomes a teacher. This decision was based on interpretation of the seniority section specifying that system-wide seniority would be computed from the date of employment. While the school district contends that the provision is so broad it allows continuation of seniority accumulation when a teacher is promoted to an administrator's position, the arbitrator found the reference to "teachers with the highest seniority shall be the last to be laid off" reiterated the union's position that the seniority provisions only applied to members of the bargaining unit. In addition, the arbitrator relied upon interpretation of other contracts in the same field that defined *system-wide seniority* as the continuous service with the district. And in interpreting the contract language, the arbitrator found that it did not speak to how seniority would be continued, just from what date it would begin.

CASE 8.2   *Management Decisions*

Reprinted with permission from Morris Stone, *Labor Grievances and Decisions* (New York: American Arbitration Association, 1970), pp. 178–180

For some time, there had been talk at an interstate trucking company about the possibility that the company was going to open a new terminal in a city a few hundred miles away. As is usually the case with rumors, everyone put his own interpretation on the few solid facts that were known. Some said the company was expanding, and new job opportunities would open up. Others, less optimistic, predicted that the company would close its present location and leave all of its employees stranded. The truth lay somewhere in between; management was planning to open a new terminal for improved service to new customers, but what would happen to the old terminal was not yet decided.

Finally, as soon as the picture became a little clearer in management's mind, the company made an official announcement to its employees. Using carefully chosen words, management said that any employees who wished to transfer to the new location would be placed on a preferential hiring list, and they would be given full seniority credit. New drivers would be hired only if there were an insufficient number of voluntary transfers, and the new men would, of course, be outranked by those who did transfer. As to what would happen to the old terminal, management did not say for sure. Those who did not want to transfer could stay behind, but no assurances were given as to how long their jobs would last. They were staying put at their own peril.

Some drivers transferred and others did not. Six months later, the axe fell. Management closed the old terminal, and a number of men were put out of work. They applied for work at the new terminal, hoping that their seniority would still serve, but they soon got the bad news.

"It's too late now to accept the offer we made six months ago," said the president of the freight line. "If we still need anyone there, we will consider you as new job applicants. But if we hire you—and remember, I'm not saying we will—it will be as brand-new drivers."

The prospect of being unemployed or of being junior to men hired only a week earlier was hard to take. A grievance was therefore filed, and it soon reached arbitration.

"You misled us," the business agent of the union said at the hearing. "If you had told us you were going to close down over here, these men would have transferred. But you wanted to get rid of long-seniority men. That was not good faith bargaining."

"Nonsense!" answered the attorney for the trucking company. "Management gave the employees all the facts, exactly as they were known at the time. If business had been good, we would have kept both terminals. As it turned out, we had to close one. The employees who stayed behind knew they were taking a calculated risk. They gambled and lost, that's all."

Finally the arbitrator declared the hearing closed, and retired to write his decision.

Decision

Management won. "I believe the evidence abundantly shows the grieving drivers were well aware of what was going on," the arbitrator wrote. He said it would have been practically impossible for management to give more information than was given in view of "the vicissitudes of competitive business." Even if some management official had given more cause for optimism than was warranted by the facts, the arbitrator added, that would not constitute a binding commitment on the company, because the trucking company would still be bound only by what the collective bargaining agreement required.

CASE 8.3   Promotions

Adapted from *American Sawmill Machine Company,* 79 L.A. 106 (1982)

The company operates a plant in Mississippi. A position came open as a result of the resignation of the incumbent. The open position was posted and four employees bid on the job and were interviewed concerning their interest. Employee Studdard, whose plant seniority

date was November 17, 1980, was selected. Another employee, Welch, whose seniority date was September 9, 1980, filed a grievance. The union's contentions in Mr. Welch's grievance was that management had violated the contract concerning job promotions that stated the job was to be assigned within seven calendar days to the bidder who had the apparent ability to perform the work and the greatest plant seniority. The union contended the company passed over a senior employee without showing that the employee was incapable of performing the job in favor of an employee who was admittedly more qualified. But since the collective bargaining agreement only requires that the bidder with the greatest plant seniority have the apparent ability to perform the work, the company violated the agreement.

The position of the company was that it was not a stringent seniority clause and allowed the company some discretion in selecting the bidder who had the most experience, qualifications, and leadership abilities to perform the job.

Decision

The arbitrator in this case decided for the union. He found that although the seniority clause concerning promotions in this contract was a modified seniority clause, it did give the senior employee preference. While some modified clauses compared the relative ability of a senior and junior employee and promoted the senior only if those abilities were equal, this particular collective bargaining agreement clause required that the senior employee be given preference if he possessed only sufficient ability to perform the job. Therefore, the company was to determine the seniority date of the employees bidding on the job and whether the most senior employee had the apparent ability to perform the work. The interpretation of *apparent* was understood to merely exclude obviously unqualified bidders, and not allow for comparison among those bidding. If the most senior employee apparently had the ability to perform the job, he would have to be appointed.

CASE STUDY   *Union Shop Clause*

Adapted from *United Stanford Employees, Local 680, Service Employees International Union AFL-CIO* v. *NLRB*, 601 F.2d 980 (9th Cir, 1979)

Facts

The 1974–76 collective bargaining agreement between the union and Leland Stanford Junior University contained a standard union shop provision that required employees in the bargaining unit to be union members as a condition of employment. In seeking to enforce this union shop provision, the union did three things:

1. The union notified new bargaining unit members by letter that they were required to join the union on or before the end of their trial period and that joining involved filling out a membership application card and taking an oath. The letter did not say what would happen if they did not join the union.

2. Three employees of the university who were employed prior to the collective bargaining agreement but who joined the bargaining unit after the agreement was signed had not

joined the union (that is, signed application cards and taken oaths). The union filed suit against these three in state court asking the court to require them to perform their contract obligation of becoming union members.

3. The union refused to accept the resignation of two union members.

Lawsuit

The employees complained to the NLRB, which found the union had violated the law and engaged in unfair labor practices by the three aforementioned actions. The union appealed this finding.

Appeal

The union's position on appeal was that while it conceded that "full membership" was not a condition of employment—that is, the employee could not be fired so long as she paid dues—the collective bargaining agreement still required full-fledged membership. Therefore, so long as they did not threaten anyone with loss of employment, they were free to try to enforce the contract any way they could.

The union made three points:

1. The letter sent did not mention discharge.
2. Another provision of the collective bargaining contract made clear that so long as the dues were paid, a member could not be fired.

3. And finally, that the language used in the collective bargaining agreement was the same as in half the agreements in the nation, so how could it have been an unfair labor practice?

In its defense the NLRB noted the following:

1. Although the letter did not threaten discharge for not joining the union, it did not cite for the member the provision of the contract only requiring payment of dues.
2. Even if the employee did not fear loss of his job, the possibility of being sued by the union was enough to be an illegal restraint on the employee's right not to join a union.
3. It was not the language of the agreement that caused the NLRB trouble, but the union's aggressive pursuit of "full-fledged membership."

Questions

1. In this case, should the court uphold the NLRB or rule in the union's favor? Why?
2. If the union must resort to such aggressive action to get members into the union, of what value could those members be to the union?
3. If a majority of the employees desire a union shop, should some employees be allowed not to join?

Key Terms and Concepts

Absolute Rank Principle

Bumping

Check-off provision

Departmental seniority

Follow the Work Principle

Industrial jurisprudence

Job bidding (up, down, lateral)

Length of Service Principle

Plantwide seniority

Ratio-Rank Principle

Seniority list

Shared work

Subcontracting

Superseniority

Surviving Group Principle

Technological change and retraining

Union hiring hall

Union shop

Review Questions

1. Why is seniority considered a critical issue? What are the advantages and disadvantages of using a seniority system?
2. Generally how is seniority calculated?
3. Describe the different methods by which labor agreements might consider seniority in a promotion decision.
4. Why is seniority often used in layoff and recall actions? Specifically how do contract clauses provide for the consideration of seniority in such decisions?
5. Under what circumstances might employers bypass a senior employee and promote a junior employee when the labor agreement contains a seniority clause?
6. Why is a seniority system important to a labor group's union security?
7. Why has management's right to subcontract work been the subject of many grievances?
8. What are some of the reasons behind union mistrust of technological change? How might this be remedied?

Endnotes

1. Sumner H. Slichter, *Union Policies and Industrial Management* (Washington, D.C.: Brooklyn Institute, 1941), pp. 1–5.
2. Daniel Cornfield, "Seniority, Human Capital, and Layoffs: A Case Study," *Industrial Relations* 21, no. 3 (Fall 1982), pp. 352–64.
3. William Cooke, "Permanent Layoffs: What's Implicit in the Contract?" *Industrial Relations* 20, no. 2 (Spring 1981), pp. 186–92.
4. Francine Blau and Lawrence Kahn, "Unionism, Seniority, and Turnover," *Industrial Relations* 22, no. 3 (Fall 1983), pp. 362–73.
5. Maryellen Kelley, "Discrimination In Seniority Systems: A Case Study," *Industrial and Labor Relations Review* 36, no. 1 (Oct. 1982), pp. 40–41.
6. Stephen Cabot, *Labor Management Relations Manual* (Boston: Warren, Gorham, Lamont, 1980), chap. 15, p. 2.
7. Ibid., 1981 Supplement, chap. 15, p. 1.
8. *Agreement* between Anaconda Aluminum Co. and Aluminum Workers' Trades Council of Columbia Falls, AFL-CIO, 1980, p. 6.
9. Cabot, *Labor Management,* chap. 15, p. 4.
10. Ibid., chap. 15, pp. 4–5.
11. 38 U.S.C. sec. 2021 (1976).

12. Bureau of National Affairs Editorial Staff, *Grievance Guide* (Washington, D.C.: Bureau of National Affairs, 1978), p. 2.
13. 44 LA 283 (1965).
14. BNA Editorial Staff, *Grievance Guide,* pp. 173–74.
15. Ibid., p. 165.
16. Katherine G. Abraham and James L. Medaoff, "Length of Service and Promotions in Union and Nonunion Work Groups," *Industrial and Labor Relations Review* 38, no. 3 (April 1985), pp. 408–420. Also D. Quinn Mills, "Seniority Versus Ability in Promotion Decisions," *Industrial and Labor Relations Review* 38, no. 3 (April 1985), pp. 421–425.
17. Michael R. Carrell and Frank E. Kuzmits, *Personnel* (Columbus, Ohio: Charles E. Merrill, 1986), pp. 487–89.
18. BNA Editorial Staff, *Grievance Guide,* pp. 107–9.
19. Ibid.
20. Bethlehem Steel Co., 1924 LA 820 (1955).
21. Copeo Steel & Engineering Co., 12 LA 6 (1979).
22. Metallab, Inc., 65 LA 1191 (1975).
23. BNA Editorial Staff, *Grievance Guide,* pp. 111–12.
24. California passed the first state law in 1978—the Shared Work Unemployment Compensation bill. By 1986, Arizona, Oregon, Washington, Florida, Maryland, and New York passed similar laws.
25. S. Kerachsky, W. Nicholson, E. Cairn, and A. Hershey, "Work-Sharing Programs: An Evaluation of Their Use," *Monthly Labor Review* 109, no. 5 (May 1986), pp. 31–33.
26. John Zalusky, "Short-Time Compensation: The AFL-CIO Perspective," *Monthly Labor Review* 109, no. 5 (May 1986), pp. 33–34.
27. Frank Elkouri and Edna Asper Elkouri, *How Arbitration Works,* 3rd ed. (Washington, D.C.: Bureau of National Affairs, 1981), pp. 4–5.
28. Thomas Kennedy, *Labor Arbitration and Industrial Change* (Washington, D.C.: Bureau of National Affairs, 1963), pp. 1–34.
29. Elkouri, *How Arbitration Works,* pp. 566–67.
30. Hershey Foods Corp., 207 N.L.R.B. 897, 84 LRRM 1004 (1973), enforced, 513 F. 2d 1083, 89 LRRM 2126 (CA 9, 1975).
31. *Winning at Arbitration* (Columbus, Ohio: Crain, 1983), p. 20.
32. "Union Wins $6 Million Settlement With AT&T," *The Courier-Journal,* Jan. 10, 1987, p. B1.
33. *Agreement* between Lithonia Lighting Inc. and The International Brotherhood of Electrical Workers, Local no. 613 of Atlanta, Georgia, 1968, p. 4.
34. *Agreement* between Lockheed-Georgia Company and The International Association of Machinists and Aerospace Workers, AFL-CIO, 1968, pp. 19–20.
35. Robert Schrank, "Are Unions An Anachronism?" *Harvard Business Review* 57, no. 5 (Sept.–Oct. 1979), pp. 56–59.
36. William Winpisinger, "Job Satisfaction," *AFL-CIO American Federationist* 80, no. 2 (1973), pp. 9–10.
37. Robert J. Schulhof, "Five Years With a Scanlon Plan," *Personnel Administrator* 24, no. 6 (June 1979), pp. 55–62.
38. Gary B. Hansen, "Innovative Approach to Plant Closings: The UAW-Ford Experience at San Jose," *Monthly Labor Review* 108, no. 7 (July 1985), pp. 56–59.

Implementing the Collective Bargaining Agreement

LABOR NEWS

Duty to Bargain if Moving Out?

Should a company, privately owned and operated, be forced to negotiate with employees when a decision to move a plant is reached? Should employees have an opportunity to discuss the effects of uprooting their families, creating havoc in the community, and generally causing misery among a segment of society?

These questions have been answered, at least temporarily, by the National Labor Relations Board. In a recent ruling, the board held that the Otis Elevator Company was under no duty to bargain with its employees before moving its operations from one state to another. The move was motivated by a hope of improving the marketability of its products.

The ruling dealt another setback to labor, which has faced increasing difficulty in using existing collective bargaining agreements to thwart relocation moves that cost jobs. Owen Beiber, president of the United Auto Workers, said that the decision "threatens to unleash a new wave of plant closings, joblessness, and community misery as companies are released from any obligation to bargain with their workers before transferring and subcontracting work, or even to supply any information relative to the move."

Adapted from "Ruling Smooths Way for Firms Seeking to Move," Louisville Courier-Journal, 11 April 1984. Reprinted with permission.

Whereas the interest of management and labor is usually focused on the months of negotiations necessary to arrive at a collective bargaining agreement, the negotiated agreement is implemented over a much longer period. It is that period of implementation that tests the success of the collective bargaining process. That success is measured not only by the fact that a contract is signed, but also by the quality of its terms and the willingness of the parties to administer the contract fairly. This chapter will examine implementation and will include an overview of grievance and arbitration issues; economic activity during a contract term; and the rights of labor, management, and individuals under a collective bargaining agreement.

Reducing an Agreement to Writing

Duty

At some point in the labor-management relationship governed by the National Labor Relations Act, agreement is reached on wages, hours, and other terms and conditions of employment. Today the agreement is written, but when the National Labor Relations Act was passed, the act did not expressly require that a collective bargaining agreement be reduced to writing and signed by the parties. Nor did it address whether bargaining was to be a process of continuing negotiations or even what the legal status of a signed agreement might be. These questions were left to the National Labor Relations Board, the courts, and Congress to answer in piecemeal fashion.

As early as 1941, the Supreme Court imposed a **duty** upon the parties in a collective bargaining relationship to reduce to writing and **sign any agreement** reached through the bargaining process. A refusal to sign was declared a refusal to bargain collectively and an unfair labor practice because, the Court found, a signed agreement had long been informally recognized as a final step in the bargaining process. The Court thought it obvious that the employer's refusal to sign an agreement ". . . discredits the [labor] organization, impairs the bargaining process, and tends to frustrate the aim of the statute to secure industrial peace through collective bargaining."[1] In the Taft-Hartley Amendments, Congress recognized the need for a written agreement and defined the bargaining duty as including ". . . the execution of a written contract incorporating any agreement reached if requested by either party. . . ."[2]

Part of the negotiator's role in the collective bargaining process is drafting the final agreement. The negotiator should try to be clear and concise, while accurately reflecting the agreement and understanding of the parties. One author suggests circulating the final agreement to non-negotiating union and management personnel affected for comment prior to signing.

> Once contract provisions are committed to paper, a good test of their meaning is to have a wide variety of different individuals, wholly unfamiliar with what has transpired during negotiations, read and interpret each provision of the contract. Particularly appropriate candidates for this *provisional intent test* are those who enforce/administer, police, or are governed by the terms of the agreement—stewards, foremen, department superintendents, shop chairmen, plant managers, grievance committeemen, rank-and-file members, etc. If provisional meaning is misconstrued, revision is in order.[3]

Nature of the Labor Agreement

The agreement between a union and an employer is not an employment contract. The employment contract is between the employer and the employee. It may be expressed verbally or in writing, or it may simply be a function of the employer's job offer and the employee's acceptance. The union is not a party to this employment contract, but the agreement between the union and the employer does shape the terms of that independent employment contract by establishing company policy in the areas covered by the agreement. The labor agreement also serves to define the union's relationship with management and provides the means to enforce its provisions.

Every labor agreement differs in terms and language but has basic similarities. Most labor contracts contain four main sections: union security and management rights, wage and effort bargain, individual security, and administration.

Union security   The contract needs to identify the parties to the agreement, the parties' authority, and the conditions and duration of that authority. The bargaining unit is described generally in terms of employees in job categories included or excluded from coverage under the agreement. By law the union is the exclusive bargaining agent for the unit described. The contract might go farther than that and provide for certain **union security** provisions. These can include

1. *Union shop*—requires that an employee join a union after employment.
2. *Maintenance of membership*—requires union members to remain members during the contract term.
3. *Agency shop*—requires nonmembers to pay union dues and fees as if they were members.
4. *Hiring halls*—requires an employer to seek employees through a union hiring hall. Nonunion members can and legally must have access to the referrals and can be charged a fee by the union.

A contract must run for a specific term. Most contracts contain renewal provisions, with prior notice of termination or of a time for reopening negotiations. Contracts can have **openers**—clauses that allow for negotiations to proceed during the term of the contract on one or more items, generally wages.

A majority of contracts (about 80 percent) contain three-year terms, as shown in Exhibit 9.1. A movement from one-year to three-year terms was aided by the NLRB in a general ruling that extended the contract bar rule (see next section) to a three-year period.[4] In recent years, the number of contracts with periods extended to four or five years has increased. The desire by both labor and management to provide greater long-term stability in labor relations has greatly motivated negotiators toward longer multiyear agreements.[5]

Wage and effort bargain   With or without a labor agreement, the employer-employee contract contains a wage and effort bargain. If a union exists, collective bargaining can determine the contents of that employment agreement. Areas primarily covered in this section are as follows:

1. *Pay scales*—hourly, weekly, or monthly wage or salary paid for the job, usually determined by job classification and compensation schedules or earnings based on work output such as piecework systems.
2. *The effort bargain*—acceptable standards for the task performance measured in work crew sizes and tasks, quotas, or work rules.
3. *Premium pay*—includes overtime, call-in pay, shift differentials,and weekend work.
4. *Fringe benefit*—such as paid holidays and vacations, bonuses, and coffee breaks.
5. *Contingent benefits*—includes insurance, pensions, sick pay, severance pay, and unemployment benefits.

Exhibit 9.1 Length of contract term
(frequency expressed as percentage of industry contracts)

	Duration in Years			
	1	*2*	*3*	*4 or more*
All Industries	3	13	79	5
Manufacturing	2	12	80	6
Apparel	11	—	78	11
Chemicals	—	13	81	6
Electrical Machinery	—	15	80	5
Fabricated Metals	—	11	74	16
Food	5	19	76	—
Furniture	—	—	100	—
Leather	—	25	50	25
Lumber	—	14	86	—
Machinery	4	8	84	4
Paper	—	14	86	—
Petroleum	—	100	—	—
Primary Metals	—	4	92	4
Printing	13	25	25	38
Rubber	—	—	83	17
Stone, Clay, & Glass	8	—	92	—
Textiles	—	20	80	—
Transportation Equipment	—	3	94	3
Nonmanufacturing	3	14	78	5
Communications	—	—	100	—
Construction	7	10	79	3
Insurance & Finance	—	57	43	—
Maritime	—	—	100	—
Mining	8	8	75	8
Retail	—	4	96	—
Services	4	22	59	15
Transportation	4	12	80	4
Utilities	—	40	60	—

Source: *Basic Patterns in Union Contracts,* 11th ed. (Washington, D.C.: The Bureau of National Affairs, 1986), p. 2. Copyright © 1986 by The Bureau of National Affairs, Inc., Washington, D.C. 20037. Used by Permission.

Management rights   The area of labor relations known as "**management rights**" has evoked more emotion and controversy than any other single issue. At the core of the debate is the concept of management's right to run the operation versus the union's quest for job security and other protections for its numbers.[6] Management rights provisions are found in almost all contracts in a section labeled *management rights*; union rights, however, are usually scattered throughout a contract according to subject matter.[7]

Unquestionably, the question of who controls the workplace is of great interest to both management and labor. Management rights generally include decisions governing the working environment of employees, including supervising the work force, controlling production, setting work rules and procedures, assigning duties, and the use of plant and equipment. Management generally believes that if it is to operate efficiently, it must have control over all decision-making factors of the business. Management also contends that any union involvement in the area is an intrusion on its inherent right to manage. Union advocates respond that where the right to manage involves wages, hours, or working conditions, labor has a legal interest under federal law.[8] Arthur Goldberg, former Secretary of the U.S. Department of Labor and U.S. Supreme Court justice, summarizes the management rights issue:

> . . . Somebody must be boss; somebody has to run the plant. People can't be wandering around at loose ends, each deciding what to do next. Management decides what the employee is to do. However, right to direct or to initiate action does not imply a second-class role for the union. The union has the right to pursue its role of representing the interest of the employee with the same stature accorded it as is accorded management. To assure order, there is a clear procedural line drawn: the company directs and the union grieves when it objects.[9]

A management rights clause often appears at the beginning of a contract following the union recognition and security clauses. An example of a common management rights clause follows:

ARTICLE III
Management
The management of the plant and the direction of its working force are vested exclusively in the Company. These functions are broad in nature and include such things as the right to schedule work and shift starting and stopping time, to hire and to discharge for just cause, to transfer or lay off because of work load distribution or lack of work. In the fulfillment of these functions the Company agrees not to violate the following Articles or the intent and purpose of this Contract, or to discriminate against any member of the Union.

Source: *Agreement* between the Anaconda Company and United Steel Workers of America, AFL-CIO Local Union No. 4612.

Reserved rights.   In addition to explicit management rights specified in the contract (as illustrated in the example), there are also residual, implied, or **reserved rights** not found in the language of the agreement. The "reserved rights theory" generally contends that management retains all rights except those it has expressly agreed to share with or relinquish to the union.[10] Management, under the reserved rights concept, does not review the agreement to determine which rights it has gained but instead reviews the agreement to ascertain which rights it has conceded to labor. All rights remaining reside with management.[11]

Recent NLRB and Court decisions have reflected a shift in one area of management rights, giving the employer the right to relocate work during the contract term without any requirement to negotiate with the union. The Supreme Court in *First National Maintenance Corp.* v. *NLRB* and the NLRB in *Otis Elevator Co.*[12] recognized that plant relocations had an impact on labor, but that not all such decisions were based on "terms and conditions" of employment protected by the act. Management has the right to make decisions based on the economics and profitability of its operation and on a change in scope and direction of the business.

Restricted rights. **Restrictions of management rights** are common in contracts as union negotiators strive to delineate the union's rights in specific areas of decision making. Contracts may contain a general statement restricting management from "taking actions in violation of the terms of the agreement." Specific restrictions of management rights, or conversely the providing of union rights, are most often found in the following contract clauses:

☐ *Subcontracting* of work to outside firms
☐ *Supervisory performance* of bargaining unit work, except for training or in an emergency
☐ *Technological changes* in work methods or equipment (such as robots) without union approval or the retraining of displaced workers
☐ *Plant shutdown or relocation* without advance notice and transfer rights to a new location
☐ *Union rights* of access to bulletin boards, pertinent information, and company premises

Individual security   Without a labor agreement, an employee does not have certain kinds of job rights and security. The interests of the employee in job security and the interests of the employer in having a stable work force coincide under contract provisions that provide for employee seniority and union shops or hiring halls. Job security is also covered in the contract under due process provisions establishing a grievance procedure and/or requiring warnings, notices, and written reprimands prior to disciplinary actions. The basic rule of law is that, ". . . in the absence of some explicit contract provision, every employment is an employment at will and either the employer or employee is free to terminate it at any time without notice."[13]

Administration   Most contracts provide for the machinery necessary to enforce the terms of the agreement. On-the-job representation is given by union shop stewards and officials. External enforcement is provided through arbitration provisions.

Contract Bar

Through its decisions over the years, the National Labor Relations Board established a **contract bar** doctrine stating that a current and valid contract can prevent another union from petitioning for an election and being certified as the exclusive representative. The board developed this doctrine as a balance between two competing interests under the National Labor Relations Act—the right of employees to choose their bargaining representatives, and the need to achieve stability in labor relations through negotiation of collective bargaining agreements.

It is the NLRB's theory that if a union has negotiated and signed an agreement on behalf of its members, another union should not be allowed to seek recognition during the life of that agreement. Certain elements must be present to ensure that the contract acts as a bar to a representational election:

1. The contract must be in writing and signed by the parties. An oral agreement cannot be a bar.
2. The contract must be for a fixed term. An indefinite term expiring upon some happening in the future cannot bar an election, nor will the board honor a contract with an unreasonably long term. Currently, the NLRB views a three-year contract as reasonable. Any contract of longer term will not bar an election to change representation at the end of the three-year period.
3. The contract must provide substantive terms and conditions to ensure a stable employer-employee arrangement. If the contract covers wages alone, it probably would not operate as a bar.
4. The contract must be duly ratified if ratification by the membership is required.
5. The contract must contain only legal provisions. Clauses that discriminate on the basis of race, religion, etc., or that clearly violate union security provisions of the act cannot bar a new election.
6. The contract must not be prematurely extended. The NLRB allows employees the right to change representation during the *open period*—the first 30-day period in the 90 days before termination of the original contract. Once contract negotiations begin, the employee cannot petition for a change in representation. This *insulated period* begins 60 days before the contract is due to expire. Therefore, negotiations must not take place during the open period, so that employees have an opportunity to change representation.

Contract Enforcement

Collective bargaining agreements are enforced by judicial proceedings by either the NLRB or the courts, through adherence to grievance and arbitration procedures by the parties to the contract, and by resort to economic self-help pressure activities.

Judicial Proceedings

National Labor Relations Board   The National Labor Relations Board has the authority to investigate and prevent unfair labor practices as listed in Section 8 of the National Labor Relations Act. Violation of a provision of a collective bargaining agreement is not in and of itself an unfair labor practice. Therefore, enforcement and interpretation of a contract provision might only come within the jurisdiction of the National Labor Relations Board if the matter also involves a violation of the unfair labor practice provision. The board may be involved in contract enforcement if the contract has incorporated a statutory obligation it already has jurisdiction to enforce, or if a contract has incorporated an unlawful provision it is called upon to invalidate.

For example, if an employer is accused of refusing to bargain during the term of the contract by making a unilateral change in the wage structure or other term of employment, by subcontracting work, or by refusing to supply information the union seeks, and if the employer claims the contract justifies his action, the NLRB can *interpret the lawful contract clause*. The board is called upon to investigate and determine the validity of the employer's claim.

The board's interpretive power might also be apparent in a case involving a union security clause or the provisions of a grievance procedure where a contract is used by an employer or a union to defend the discharge or disciplining of an employee, and that employee claims a violation of the National Labor Relations Act.

In representation cases, a party may claim that proper interpretation of a contract places her under its protection and provisions. Thus the NLRB's definition of the parties to a collective bargaining agreement can have great impact.

The NLRB may *invalidate a contract or clause* if it finds that the union acted under an erroneous though good faith claim that it had majority representation; or in a successorship situation where a union has dissolved or merged with another or where a business has changed hands. Contract clauses impinging upon areas prohibited by the act will come before the board for validity tests. Items tested include union security clauses, discriminatory provisions, hot cargo clauses in which union members refuse to handle goods from a nonunion employer, and breach of a union's duty of fair representation. Also, a petition and election for representation not barred by an existing contract may invalidate an existing contract.

The NLRB may also show support of contracts and contract clauses by interpreting the contract as a waiver of statutory rights. Often claims that a statutory right of a party has been violated, based upon specific language in the collective bargaining agreement, result in an NLRB finding that the party waived those rights when entering into the agreement. Numerous cases have come before the board in which a union is found to have waived the right to bargain over such issues as employee qualifications, employer subcontracting, or administration of a merit rating system. These have been so decided because of specific language in the contract reserving those items to the employer.

However, general management rights provisions will usually not be interpreted as waiving statutory rights. The National Labor Relations Board will not uphold an employer when, in defense of an unfair labor practice charge, he claims that his unilateral action is protected by a management rights clause in a collective bargaining agreement unless the clause is specific as to the matter under discussion, is a recognized management function, or is a continuation of long-standing procedures required by the business. The board does not honor the residual rights theory; that is, the employer retains all rights not surrendered under the agreement, nor will it validate unilateral actions taken by the employer if it finds such actions subject to bargaining under the act and not specifically waived by the union in the contract.

The NLRB may even go past the specific language of the contract and explore the bargaining history of the parties to determine if there has been a waiver of a statutory right. The present law on waiver is summarized as follows:

1. There is a continuing statutory duty to bargain, even during the term of a contract.
2. The continuing duty to bargain embraces not only grievances but also all mandatory subjects that are not contained in a contract for a fixed period.
3. A party may waive his right to bargain, either by relinquishing a right to bring up a particular subject or by agreeing that the other party may exercise unilateral control over the subject.
4. Such a waiver must be clear and unmistakable and must indicate an acquiescence, agreement, or conscious yielding to a demand.[14]

However, a statutory right to receive information is not waived by waiving a right to bargain over the issue. In one case, the board found that, while the union gave the employer the prerogative to discharge for lack of work, it did not in the contract forestall a grievance or a claim for information to justify the discharge when the employer took such action.

The enforcement of existing collective bargaining agreements also comes under the NLRB's jurisdiction when it has been claimed that unilateral action by the employer has modified the contract. Or an employer might claim that the union has violated the act by a strike action called to force bargaining on a modification of an existing contract. It is an unfair labor practice to terminate or modify an existing contract during its life except under the conditions outlined in the statute.[15]

Court enforcement   Prior to the Taft-Hartley Amendments, employers and unions could sue in state court for breach of contract if one party believed the other party violated a collective bargaining agreement. Most state courts viewed the collective bargaining agreement as a legally enforceable obligation. Unions could obtain injunctions to restrain employers from violation of wage provisions or to require employers to abide by a union shop agreement. The employer could obtain an injunction against strikes in breach of a valid no-strike clause. Still, contract enforcement for the employer was difficult because many labor unions were not incorporated. In some states such unincorporated organizations could not be sued, thus the employer had to sue each union member individually. Even if the unincorporated union could be sued for specific injunctive relief, monetary damages might not be available.

The Taft-Hartley Amendments were an attempt to lessen the unions' power by allowing access to federal courts on suits for collective bargaining contract violations. The amendments specifically recognized labor unions as entities that could be sued and held liable for monetary damages. The legislative intent of the Taft-Hartley Amendments was interpreted by the Senate as follows:

> If unions can break agreements with relative impunity, then such agreements do not tend to stabilize industrial relations. The execution of an agreement does not by itself promote industrial peace. The chief advantage which an employer can reasonably expect from a collective labor agreement is assurance of uninterrupted operation during the term of the agreement. Without some effective method of assuring freedom from economic warfare

for the term of the agreement, there is little reason why an employer would desire to sign such a contract.

It is apparent that until all jurisdictions, and particularly the federal government, authorize actions against labor unions as legal entities, there will not be the mutual responsibility necessary to vitalize collective-bargaining agreements. The Congress has protected the right of workers to organize. It has passed laws to encourage and promote collective bargaining.

Statutory recognition of the collective agreement as a valid, binding, and enforceable contract is a logical and necessary step. It will promote a higher degree of responsibility upon the parties to such agreements, and will thereby promote industrial peace.

It has been argued that the result of making collective agreements enforceable against unions would be that they would no longer consent to the inclusion of a no-strike clause in a contract.

This argument is not supported by the record in the few states which have enacted their own laws in an effort to secure some measure of union responsibility for breaches of contract. Four states—Minnesota, Colorado, Wisconsin, and California—have thus far enacted such laws and, so far as can be learned, no-strike clauses have been continued about as before.

In any event, it is certainly a point to be bargained over and any union with the status of representative under the NLRA [National Labor Relations Act] which has bargained in good faith with an employer should have no reluctance in including a no-strike clause if it intends to live up to the terms of the contract. The improvement that would result in the stability of industrial relations is, of course, obvious.[16]

Grievance Procedure and Arbitration

Later chapters of this book will deal with the practical aspects of contract enforcement through grievance and arbitration procedures. The development of grievance and arbitration as a means of contract enforcement and the relationship and effectiveness of this type of enforcement as compared to court and NLRB enforcement are discussed here.

Development of arbitration rights
The American common law tradition is that an employee is an employee at will, with the terms and conditions of her employment established by the employer with virtually no restriction. Although this tradition allowed either party to terminate the relationship and therefore was seen as fair and equitable, the employee had little real protection from poverty. It was in the public interest, therefore, that the government enter into the employer-employee relationship. This could be done by enacting laws to regulate terms and conditions of employment, including questions of wages, bonuses, fringe benefits, discharge and employment standards; or by using legislation to regulate the relationship between employer and employee. The National Labor Relations Act reflects the latter choice. Its provisions speak to the requirement for collective bargaining but not to the substantive provisions of the employment contract, and have resulted in the development of *arbitration,* a system of private enforcement of publicly protected rights. The National Labor Relations Act itself did not embody arbitration provisions.

The real development of labor arbitration as we know it today, and indeed the virtual transformation of the usual meaning of the word, came as a result of World War II, the War

Labor Board and the impermissibility of the strike weapon as a method of resolving questions of interpretation and compliance with collective agreements and of providing the interstitial lawmaking which the interpretive process implies.

As a result of this development, we have in this country a system of nongovernmental law which provides not only the rules concerning the rights of employees against employers but also the system of adjudication of controversies concerning the applications of those rules.[17]

The public had become responsible for the enforcement of the right to a specific process but not the right to substantive protections.

The collective bargaining agreements entered into by parties subject to the act after the War Labor Board Policy of World War II gave each side protective rights enforceable through the use of arbitration. In most contracts, a grievance procedure provides a union the right to seek compliance with a contract provision through a system of formal or informal meetings between union and management. Such procedures may cause the employer to comply simply because the grievance is brought to the employer's attention. However, if the grievance involves disagreement over facts, the meaning of the collective bargaining agreement, application or implementation of the agreement, or the reasonableness of an action, it might not be resolved without the intervention of a third party. Thus, *arbitration* can also be the resolution by an outside party of a grievance dispute. If the parties to a collective bargaining agreement agree to a grievance-arbitration procedure in the contract, substantive rights granted under that contract are enforced by the arbitration award.

Court and board enforcement   As discussed earlier, state and federal courts have enforcement powers in collective bargaining agreements. In the **Lincoln Mills** case, the Supreme Court, by accepting such enforcement powers, required specific performance of an employer's promise to arbitrate in a collective bargaining agreement.[18] The Court felt that the agreement to arbitrate grievance disputes was the employer's tradeoff for the union's agreement not to strike.

The role of arbitration and court enforcement of contract agreements was more specifically outlined in three Supreme Court cases known as the *Steelworkers Trilogy*.[19] These cases held that the function of the court is limited to a review of whether or not the issue to be arbitrated is governed by the contract. Any doubt as to the coverage should be resolved in favor of arbitration. And unless the arbitrator's award is ambiguous, it should be enforced by the courts even if the court would not have decided the substantive issue in the same way.

The 1960 *Steelworkers Trilogy* expanded vastly upon the foundation laid in *Lincoln Mills*. Arbitration was acknowledged as the preferred, superior forum for contract interpretation and enforcement. The powers of an arbitrator were held to be bounded by the restrictions of the "four corners of the contract" but arbitral actions were largely immunized from judicial review. As repeatedly stated thereafter, arbitration became the cornerstone of the rapidly arising edifice housing the federal law of the labor agreement.[20]

The Court gave almost complete deference to arbitration as a means of contract enforcement by limiting its own review of an arbitration to whether or not the issue under arbitration is in the agreement.

The National Labor Relations Board also deferred its jurisdiction in certain unfair labor practice cases to an arbitration procedure established under the contract. In the *Collyer* decision, the NLRB agreed to defer jurisdiction if there was a stable collective bargaining relationship between the parties, the party defending the charge was willing to arbitrate the issue, and the dispute centered on the contract and its meaning.[21]

The board also decided to defer to an arbitration award if the arbitration procedure met the following criteria:

1. *Fair and regular proceedings*   That the proceedings are the equivalent of due process, affording parties an opportunity to be heard, cross-examine witnesses, be represented by counsel, and have an unbiased decision maker.

2. *Agreement to be bound*   Both parties must agree to abide by the arbitrator's decision. A hearing over the parties' objections would not be honored.

3. *Award not repugnant to purposes and policies of the act*   Even if due process is followed, the arbitrator's award can be invalidated if it violates the purposes of the National Labor Relations Act. For example, an arbitrator upheld a dismissal of an employee for being disloyal, but his so-called disloyalty was in seeking help from the National Labor Relations Board. The board did not uphold that award.

4. *Unfair labor practice to be considered by arbitrator*   The actual issue surrounding the unfair labor practice must be reviewed and decided by the arbitrator or the NLRB will not defer to the award. Deciding other issues between the parties is immaterial.[22]

Case 9.1 is an example of a decision by the National Labor Relations Board to send the parties to arbitration.

Since the 1971 *Collyer* decision, the NLRB has continued to reaffirm its policy to defer to arbitration in unfair labor cases.[23] A comparison of NLRB awards and arbitration decisions/grievance settlements in a recent study found that when the unfair labor practice involves a complaint from an individual because of discipline of a union member, the arbitration/grievance procedure often results in the same or nearly the same result as an NLRB award. However, cases involving a charge that the employer has refused to bargain in good faith have less frequently been decided by an arbitrator or settled by the parties in the same manner as similar cases that were decided by the NLRB. And in most cases these were to the union's disadvantage.[24]

Arbitration in contract enforcement   As with collective bargaining, the effectiveness of arbitration as a method of contract enforcement is dependent upon the skill of the parties involved. Because arbitrators are not bound by judicial precision, their procedures and decision-making processes determine whether the contract can be effectively enforced.

Arbitration hearings reflect the relationship of the parties. Sometimes they are formal and legalistic—witnesses are sworn, rules of evidence apply, and formal briefs are prepared. Or they may be informal—the parties speak their piece to an arbitrator who separates facts from fiction. An arbitrator can also use different approaches. Contract language may be strictly interpreted and a winner and loser found, or a decision amenable to both parties may be arrived at, regardless of exact contract requirements.

However, certain guidelines in assisting the arbitrator's decision making include

1. *The parole evidence rule*   The arbitrator generally limits the decision to an interpretation of the contract language only. Evidence varying with or contradicting the written labor agreement should not be admitted. If the issue presented includes an ambiguous contract provision, the arbitrator seeks to find clarification within the whole contract.

2. *Intent of the parties*   In some instances, an arbitrator may try to determine what the parties had in mind when they took certain actions. To do this, an arbitrator must look to observable behavioral manifestations of intent and apply a reasonable-person test to it.

3. *Past practice*   Consideration of a specific and identical action, employed over a number of years to the recognition and satisfaction of both parties, is acceptable for an arbitrator when deciding on ambiguous contract language or even resolving problems not covered in the contract.

4. *De minimus*   This refers to an insignificant contract violation. Arbitrators may deny a grievance as trivial and inconsequential under this theory.

5. *Previous arbitration awards*   Previous arbitration awards, although they do not carry the same weight as previous court decisions, can be considered in appropriate cases. However, unless cases are very similar, an arbitrator may find a previous award irrelevant.[25]

Critics believe that arbitration, by nature, is an inconsistent system of adjudication. The parties cannot be assured their case received the same treatment as another party on the same issue. They also feel that the quality of an arbitrator can be reflected in judgments rendered, but the absence of a consistent review mechanism may never uncover incompetence. There is no requirement that an arbitrator know, understand, or apply relevant provisions of the National Labor Relations Act, yet the National Labor Relations Board defers to an arbitrator's award. And, while the NLRB requires adherence to due process principles, often the official record of the arbitration is deficient either because of incompetence or because of the informality of the arbitration hearing.

Further criticisms point out that arbitration is a system of private law administered by management and the union. Union majority interests may submerge or restrict individual or minority rights. And since an arbitrator depends upon the parties for a livelihood, there is speculation that decisions are often rendered with consideration as to future employment rather than on the merits of the grievance.

While advocates of arbitration claim it affords a speedy and cheap resolution of labor disputes, the necessity or desirability of seeking an NLRB determination on the arbitration award may actually result in more time and expense.

Proponents of arbitration point to the obvious advantages of allowing the resolution of contract disputes during the contract term by internal processes without resort to the NLRB, the courts, or economic pressure, such as strikes. Unlike proceedings in court or before the board, the objective of a grievance arbitration proceeding is to reach fair settlements, not win cases. The need for the arbitrator to preserve a relationship between both parties leads to better decisions, furthering the goal of peaceful labor relations. And early recognition of employee dissatisfaction can eliminate disagreements that might otherwise undermine the labor-management relationship. In addition, arbitration is seen as a means to continuing the collective bargaining process after the agreement is signed. If any details of the employment contract are misapplied, the arbitrator, as an objective third party, can more readily address the contract intent.

Economic Activity

The resort to economic pressure as a means to enforce a contract obviously is not the preferred method, as evidenced by the support given arbitration in court decisions. A union slowdown or strike countered by an employer lockout or mass dismissal seems at odds with the National Labor Relations Act's aim of promoting industrial peace. But the resort to economic activity, or at least the ability to resort to economic activity, is a key element in the success of the collective bargaining process.

Earlier chapters detailed the use of economic weapons, strikes, and other concerted activity during recognition campaigns and during negotiations. While use of economic power to enforce an existing contract has become increasingly rare due to mandatory grievance and arbitration procedures and no-strike clauses in labor agreements, such action has not disappeared. Indeed, about one-third of the recorded work stoppages over the last two decades were strikes during a contract term.[26]

The Supreme Court in the **Boys Market, Inc.** case upheld an injunction against a union that struck over an arbitrable grievance despite a no-strike clause and a mandatory grievance procedure.[27] But the Court noted that not all such strikes would be enjoined. It adopted strict standards from an earlier case:

> When a strike is sought to be enjoined because it is over a grievance which both parties are contractually bound to arbitrate, the district court may issue no injunctive order until it holds that the contract does have that effect; and the employer should be ordered to arbitrate, as a condition of his obtaining an injunction against the strike. Beyond this, the district court must, of course, consider whether issuance of an injunction would be warranted under ordinary principles of equity—whether breaches are occurring and will continue, or have been threatened and will be committed; whether they have caused or will cause irreparable injury to the employer; and whether the employer will suffer more from the denial of an injunction than will the union from its issuance.[28]

Thus, a union does have an effective weapon despite a no-strike clause if the grievance does not factually come under the contract arbitration procedure, if the employer is not willing to arbitrate, and if the employer cannot show where he has suffered irreparable injury from the breach of the no-strike obligation.

The Supreme Court later upheld the right of a union to engage in a sympathy strike pending an arbitrator's decision on whether such a strike was forbidden under the particular no-strike clause of the labor agreement.[29] The strike had been called in support of another union properly engaged in an economic strike. While the arbitration procedure could be invoked to decide the scope of the no-strike clause, the Court would not allow the union's strike to be enjoined pending that decision. And while the NLRB in its decision in *Indianapolis Power and Light Company*[30] attempted to create a presumption that broad no-strike clauses were intended to cover sympathy strikes, the U.S. Court of Appeals overruled that presumption in 1986 in *International Brotherhood of Electrical Workers, Local 387* v. *NLRB*.[31] The court said a no-strike clause must be interpreted according to the terms of the particular collective bargaining agreement, the bargaining history, and the past practices of the parties to determine its application to sympathy strikes.

Rights and Prohibited Conduct

Certain rights and duties arise during the term of a contract. These include the rights of the individual under the collective bargaining process, the duty to bargain during a contract term, and the duty to refrain from prohibited economic activities.

Individual Rights

Right to refrain from union activities   Because of the National Labor Relations Act, labor relations has developed into a stylized system of employer-union relations. In an election decided by majority rule, a union is given the authority to represent all the employees of an appropriate unit in negotiation and administration of a contract. Individual employees who may have voted against the union still find their employment contract affected by these negotiations. And while the union has a duty to fairly represent all employees during the negotiation process, absent a showing of actual hostile discrimination, the court will accept a wide range of reasonableness when a question of a breach of that duty arises.

Originally the National Labor Relations Act allowed an employer to make an agreement with a union to require union membership as a prior condition of employment; that is, the closed shop. All forms of union security were permitted, as long as the agreement was made with a bona fide union representing the bargaining unit. Closed shop clauses became common in collective bargaining agreements. Although these clauses protected and promoted the growth of unions, abuses of the system against individuals who were denied job opportunities led to the Taft-Hartley Amendments. These amendments made the closed shop an unfair labor practice, and added the right *not* to organize and engage in union activity. And while union shop clauses still could be negotiated and enforced against existing employees, the employee need only pay dues to abide by that contract clause; no other activity was required. The amendments also allowed state right-to-work laws to outlaw even the union shop requirement.

The union hiring hall is another practice that appears to give equal consideration to union and nonunion personnel. Although a hiring hall operating as a closed shop was technically outlawed by the amendments, a union can still negotiate a contract clause that requires the employer to hire through the union's exclusive referral system. It is then up to the nonunion individual to claim and prove discriminatory referrals. Case 9.2 illustrates the fine line between union discrimination and discrimination in general in union hiring halls.

Union security clauses are not the only prohibited behavior violating the individual employee's right to refrain from union activity. The courts consider union intimidation and reprisals or threats of same against employees as restraint and coercion.

Duty of fair representation   Under its **duty of fair representation**, a union must consider all the employees in the bargaining unit when negotiating an agreement and make an honest effort to serve their interests. This must be a good faith effort, without hostility or arbitrary discrimination. But the end result of such negotiations may still unevenly affect one, several, or a class of employees without the union being considered in breach of its duty.

A far more litigious area concerning fair representation is in contract enforcement. Grievance arbitration has become the most common method of enforcing each party's promise to abide by the contract. That promise to arbitrate is enforceable by either the employer or the union. Fitting the individual into that arbitration system involves balancing conflicting interests.

The National Labor Relations Act adopted the doctrine of majority rule when it granted a union exclusive representation rights if selected by most unit members. The courts confirmed this doctrine by giving the collective agreement precedence over the individual employment contract. To balance the power of the union, the court recognized the union's duty to represent all of its employees.

But there remained a question of whether an individual employee could arbitrate against both or either party. In *Vaca* v. *Sipes, Hines* v. *Anchor Motor Co., Inc.,* and *Bowen* v. *U.S. Postal Service* the Supreme Court indicated that the individual has no absolute right to have a grievance arbitrated, and the union is liable to the employee only if, in processing and settling that grievance, it violates its fair representation duty.[32]

In contract administration issues, the duty of fair representation is breached when a union's conduct is arbitrary, discriminatory, or in bad faith. A union may not arbitrarily ignore a meritorious grievance or process it in a perfunctory manner. Yet proof of the merit of a grievance is not enough under this test; arbitrary or bad faith actions must also be proved.

The subjective nature of the fair representation test has left unions with Hobson's choice. If a union cannot be reasonably certain that its honest and rational decision not to pursue a grievance to arbitration will withstand a *Vaca* challenge, the arbitration process will be so burdened its effectiveness and financial liability will be undermined. But at the same time the *Vaca* rule ensures an individual that, while there is no absolute right to arbitrate a grievance, the union cannot behave in an arbitrary fashion, as demonstrated in Case 9.3.[33]

Due process   The individual employee has a right to due process of law under a collective bargaining agreement. This process includes a right to *substantive due process,* fair treatment by the employer in any action taken against an employee; and a right to *procedural due process,* a fair hearing on that action.

Generally, in substantive due process, the policy or standard invoked must be known by the employee and must be reasonable. In addition, a violation of policies must be proven and the burden is on the employer. The application of rules and policies must be consistent; certain employees cannot be singled out for discipline. Also, actions must be impersonal and based on fact.

In procedural due process, any contractual procedures for employment actions must be followed. Equally important, the arbitration procedure must be fair. The individual must receive fair representation by the union; a hearing must be held so the individual can be heard in an unbiased setting; and the employer's reasons for bringing the action must be made known.

Duty to Bargain During the Contract Term

The standards for good faith collective bargaining contained in the National Labor Relations Act include the duty to bargain during the contract term if a party wishes to terminate or modify that contract. The duty, however, is not absolute. The language of the act provides that a party cannot be required to discuss or agree to terminate or modify the contract during its term. In addition, the contract under which parties operate may limit the duty in the following ways:

1. **Zipper clause**   An abbreviated form of the waiver provision in a collective bargaining agreement, sometimes referred to as a "wrap-up" clause, considered to denote waiver of the right of either party to require the other to bargain on any matter not covered in an agreement during the life of the contract, thus limiting the terms and conditions of employment to those set forth in the contract. A clause of this type would read:[34]

> This contract is complete in itself and sets forth all the terms and conditions of the agreement between the parties hereto.

2. **Opener clause**   A clause that allows negotiations to take place during the contract terms on certain mandatory items, such as wages or insurance coverage.

3. **Separability clause**   A clause in a labor contract that protects the validity of the rest of the contract should any part of it be held invalid.[35]

Union demand to negotiate   A question of bargaining during the contract term may arise when the union seeks to add new items not covered under the contract. This situation highlights the two competing views of collective bargaining. One view is that the collective bargaining agreement does not end the collective bargaining process. It is a continuous process, albeit with rules as to how the process should proceed. Many people believe the grievance-arbitration procedures are a part of that process since those decisions shape the administration of the contract and therefore its terms. The opposite view is that the collective bargaining process must be completed with the signing of the contract to give meaning to the contract terms. Because bargaining should encompass all subjects, the final agreement should settle all subjects either explicitly or implicitly between the parties. Under this view, the grievance-arbitration procedure interprets the contract only, and adds nothing to its terms.

The attitude of the National Labor Relations Board to a union demand for bargaining on a new item during a contract term seems to be that if the item is not contained in the contract, and was not discussed during negotiations, the employer has a duty to bargain on that item.[36]

Employer's unilateral action   Most often the question of the duty to bargain during a contract term arises as a result of unilateral action by the employer. Depending upon the circumstances, such action may be deemed an unfair labor practice as a breach of that duty to bargain. The questions of whether a substantive or procedural provision of a contract was violated arise when an employer takes unilateral action during a contract term and makes a change in some condition of employment.

If the employer's action changes a stated term of the contract, the answer is simple. The employer has committed an unfair labor practice. However, if under a broad management rights clause, the employer takes an action affecting employees in a manner not contemplated by the contract, disagreement as to breach obviously occurs. As a rule, the NLRB considers charges of unfair labor practice by a union in this instance a matter for arbitration and, under the *Collyer* decision, will defer its jurisdiction to the arbitrator.

> As one might expect, the *Collyer* decision has been subject to considerable debate. Unions charge that the National Labor Relations Board has run out on its authority and responsibility to enforce the Taft-Hartley Act, leaving organized labor at a distinct disadvantage in the collective bargaining process. Employers, naturally, are pleased with the decision which they claim allows them the freedom to more efficiently operate their firms. The freedom, in this case, comes from the fact that the National Labor Relations Board will defer to arbitration matters involving changes in existing contracts, hence allowing employers to more easily circumvent the requirement of good-faith bargaining during the administration of the contract.[37]

Even under a management rights clause, a contract may contain a requirement that, while the final decision is the employer's, the union must be consulted prior to any action. An employer who violates this procedural requirement is in breach of the contract and of her duty to bargain during its duration.

Prohibited Economic Activity

The National Labor Relations Act, as amended by Taft-Hartley and Landrum-Griffin, outlawed four specific economic pressure techniques that unions might try to employ during the term of a contract: secondary boycotts, hot cargo agreements, jurisdictional strikes, and featherbedding.

Secondary boycotts   Section 8(b)(4) of the National Labor Relations Act prohibits a union from engaging in, or from inducing others to engage in, a strike or boycott aimed against the goods or services of one employer to force the employer to cease doing business with another employer. This prohibition was a response to the labor movement's use of the **secondary boycott** to affect employer A by exerting economic pressure on those who do business with employer A. Primary economic activity such as a boycott by employees against an employer is not prohibited by this section, nor is a secondary boycott with an objective that is not statutorily forbidden.

The Supreme Court attempted to give guidance on the distinction between a primary and secondary boycott. A *primary boycott* occurs when persons who normally deal directly with the work involved are encouraged to withhold their services. This type of boycott is not prohibited and includes, for example, appeals to replacement workers or delivery men not to cross a picket line, or appeals to employees of subcontractors not to continue work essential to the operation. Even if the picketing takes place at the work site of the secondary employer, it may be protected if the work involved is the object of the dispute.

However, inducement of persons indirectly related to the work in question is a *secondary boycott* and is prohibited. For example, there is a prohibition against attempting to stop a subcontractor from crossing a picket line and entering a plant site if the contractor's work has no relationship to the day-to-day operation. The fine line between a legal boycott and an illegal secondary boycott was illustrated in 1974, when the AFL-CIO supported a boycott of goods from the Farah Mfg. Co., Inc., of El Paso, Texas. Mass picketing demonstrations were organized from New York to Tokyo, in which pickets could legally carry signs saying, "Don't Buy Farah parts at XYZ's" but not those saying "Don't Shop at XYZ's—they carry Farah Parts."[38]

The secondary employer involved must be neutral for the above primary-secondary distinction to be valid. Secondary and primary employers will be considered allied if the secondary employer performs work she would not be doing except for the strike; or if there is common ownership, control, and integration of operation causing the businesses to be treated as a single enterprise.

A union is liable for any actual damages resulting from an unlawful secondary boycott sustained by the secondary or primary employer.

Hot cargo agreement The term **hot cargo agreement** refers to a negotiated contract provision stating that union members of one employer need not handle nonunion or struck goods of other employers. Court decisions after passage of the Taft-Hartley Amendments basically allowed such agreements, stating that the prohibition against secondary boycotts did not prohibit an employer and union from voluntarily including a hot cargo clause in their agreement; but such a provision was not an absolute defense against an unfair labor practice charge. If inducements of employees prohibited by Section 8(b)(4) of the National Labor Relations Act in the absence of a hot cargo provision occurred, the inducements would still violate the act.

The need to analyze such provisions on a case-by-case basis decreased somewhat after the passage of the Landrum-Griffin Amendments outlawing most hot cargo agreements, except for the garment and construction industry. But there still remain numerous similarly negotiated clauses that may or may not violate the act. A picket line clause protecting employees from discharge for refusing to cross a lawful primary picket line at another employer's premises is not a violation of the hot cargo agreement prohibition. However, a struck-work clause stating that an employer will not do business with a nonunion or struck employer is in violation unless the secondary employer is an ally. Clauses completely prohibiting an employer from subcontracting are valid. But a clause forbidding subcontracting with nonunion employers may be a violation if it is aimed at a union's difference with another employer and not designed to protect union standards. A work-preservation clause is lawful if the object of the clause is to protect and preserve work customarily performed by employees in the unit. This is true even if it involves refusing to handle certain cargo, as long as the cargo is refused and not the employer making the cargo. The aim of the clause must be to protect the actual employees of the bargaining unit and not union members as a group.

Jurisdictional disputes   Prior to the 1947 Taft-Hartley Amendments, jurisdictional disputes between labor unions competing for the same work assignments caused numerous work stoppages. The amendments and later court decisions made such activities unfair labor practices and gave the NLRB jurisdiction to decide not only the unfair labor practice charge of participating in a jurisdictional dispute but also the underlying question of which union should get the work assignment. Factors the board uses include

> . . . all relevant factors in determining who is entitled to the work in dispute, e.g., the skills and work involved; certifications by the board; company and industry practice; agreements between unions and between employers and unions; awards of arbitrators, joint boards, and the AFL-CIO in the same or related cases; the assignment made by the employer; and the efficient operation of the employer's business.[39]

Featherbedding   Another prohibited activity is **featherbedding**, "practices on the part of some unions to make work for their members through the limitation of production, the amount of work to be performed, or other make-work arrangements."[40]

Featherbedding was made an unfair labor practice by the Taft-Hartley Amendments only in instances where a union exacts pay from employers in return for services not performed. The Supreme Court upheld a negotiated agreement to provide pay for make-work if the work was actually done regardless of its value to the employer.

Summary

The parties to the collective bargaining process have a duty to bargain in good faith, and, if and when agreement is reached, to commit that agreement to written form. That written agreement becomes the basis for the labor/management relationship during the contract term.

The contract is enforced at various times and for various purposes by the courts and the National Labor Relations Board through arbitration and grievance procedures and through employee job actions.

The National Labor Relations Board through its power to prevent unfair labor practices, can interpret, invalidate, and enforce collective bargaining agreements in appropriate cases. The courts also have jurisdiction to enforce the labor agreement as binding on both the employer and the labor organization. But as a rule, both the board and the courts defer to a grievance-arbitration process for contract administration whenever possible. The arbitration process allows the parties to resolve their differences during the life of the contract as a continuation of collective bargaining. Resort to economic activity to enforce contracts cannot always be avoided, and the strike is one aspect of contract enforcement.

Contract administration includes recognition of rights under collective bargaining agreements. Individual workers have the right to refrain from union activity, to be fairly represented by the union, and to receive due process in their dealings with the union and the employer.

The union and the employer operate under a good faith duty to bargain during the contract term in appropriate circumstances. Neither party has the right to resort to secondary economic activities that violate the collective bargaining agreement or the law.

CASE 9.1   *Deferring to Arbitration*

Adapted from *Electronic Reproduction Service Corp.*, 213 N.L.R.B. 110, 87 LRRM 1211 (1974)

The union and the company were unable to reach agreement on a contract and a strike ensued. A strike settlement agreement provided that all unresolved contractual issues after thirty more days of negotiations would be submitted to final and binding arbitration. This was done and an arbitration award resolving major contractual provisions was made. The company refused to sign the contract and instead announced that it would close down its plant. In preparation for such closing, it began to lay off employees. The union grieved and alleged that the company was discriminating in its layoffs against union members who had participated in the strike. The arbitrator began hearing the cases but only examined the layoffs from the standpoint of discharge for "just cause" and did not address the discrimination issue. The company requested that the union be directed to submit whatever proof it had on discrimination; the union did not comply. After the individual employees who were laid off were given arbitration awards, the union charged the company with an unfair labor practice based on discrimination and sought relief from the National Labor Relations Board.

Decision

The National Labor Relations Board reiterated its decisions in the *Spielberg* and the *Collyer* cases: to discourage dual litigation and forum shopping, the board would encourage parties to settle their contractual disputes through arbitration. In this case, the issue of discrimination could clearly have been presented to and decided by the arbitrator. The union chose not to do so, believing it could decide the issues of unjust dismissal with the arbitrator and then go to the National Labor Relations Board for a decision on the discrimination charge.

Therefore, the board refused to review the discrimination charge because the union failed to present it at the arbitration level.

CASE 9.2   Union Hiring Hall

Adapted from *Local 357, Teamsters* v. *N.L.R.B.* 47 LRRM 2906 (1961)

The union and the companies signed a three-year collective bargaining agreement that included a provision relating to the hiring of casual or temporary employees as follows:

> Casual employees shall, wherever the union maintains a dispatching service, be employed only on a seniority basis in the industry wherever such seniority employees are available. . . . Seniority rating of such employees shall begin with a minimum of three months service in the industry, irrespective of whether such employee is or is not a member of the union.

The union did indeed maintain such a hiring hall and would refer casual laborers to the employers upon request. One union member who had customarily used the hiring hall was employed without going through the hiring hall. When the union complained to the employer, the union member was fired. The union member filed charges against both the union and the employer to the NLRB, and the NLRB found that the hiring hall provision in the contract was unlawful per se and that the discharge of the union member at the union's request was a violation of both the employer's and the union's duty not to discriminate against union members. The board further ordered that the company and the union cease using the hiring hall provision. The union appealed the board's ruling to the federal courts.

Decision

The district court reversed the NLRB decision and found in favor of the union. The court pointed out that Congress had not outlawed the hiring hall, although it had outlawed the closed shop and the use of hiring halls as a de facto closed shop. As the language of the hiring hall provision itself provided that nonunion members would not be discriminated against, the board could not find that the hiring hall arrangement was discriminatory per se. Although the court did find discrimination in the actual facts of the case, it was personal and not the encouraging/discouraging union membership discrimination that is outlawed by the Taft-Hartley Amendments.

CASE 9.3   Duty of Fair Representation

Adapted from *Ruzicka* v. *General Motors Corp.* 523 F.2d 6th Cir. (1975)

The plaintiff had been discharged by the company for intoxication and abusive language. He filed a timely grievance protesting his discharge. The grievance proceeded to the third step, which required the union to file a statement of unadjusted grievance to invoke arbitration. The local union never filed such a statement although it sought and received two extensions to do so. After missing the two extensions, the company disclaimed any further obligation under the agreement to arbitrate. The plaintiff instituted intra-union procedures charging unfair representation by the union and, having lost, filed in federal court. The plaintiff alleged that a union official's hostility toward him had caused that official not to file the statement of unadjusted grievance. The lower court concluded that there was no unfair representation because the union official had merely neglected to file the required statement and that, even if the official was hostile toward the plaintiff, the plaintiff had to show that the hostility caused the official's neglect. Therefore, the lower court concluded that the union had not unfairly represented the plaintiff because it had merely neglected to file the grievance and had not acted in bad faith.

Decision

The Supreme Court reversed the lower court's decision and found that the union had violated its duty of fair representation by violating at least one of the three tests in the *Vaca* decision—arbitrary, discriminatory, or in bad faith. It pointed out that a union must adhere to three separate standards: first, it must treat all factions and segments of its membership without hostility or discrimination; second, in asserting the rights of its individual members, the union must exercise its discretion in complete good faith and honesty; and, third, it must avoid arbitrary conduct. Any one of these standards may be violated and cause the union to be charged with unfair representation. In this case, the appropriate official's neglect in filing the third stage of the grievance procedure without deciding the plaintiff's claim was without merit, was clearly arbitrary, and was a perfunctory handling of agreements. As such, it was unfair representation.

CASE STUDY   *Duty to Bargain*

Adapted from *Tocco Division of Park-Ohio Industries, Inc.* v. *NLRB*, 702 F. 2d 624 (CA6, 1983)

Facts

The company, prior to 1976, manufactured all its products at a unionized plant in Cleveland. In 1976 it built a nonunion plant in Alabama, originally intending to duplicate the Cleveland operation. Unfavorable economic condition, however, caused the company to transfer certain operations from Cleveland to Alabama, resulting in the layoff of seven union employees. The union filed unfair labor practice charges, which were settled when the company promised not to transfer work from the Cleveland plant without bargaining with the union. The settlement was reached during the same time the company and union were negotiating a new collective bargaining agreement.

During negotiations, the company, despite the aforementioned settlement, repeatedly submitted to the union a written statement asserting its right to decide what product ". . . is made where by whom . . ." and asked the union to submit any proposal it had to limit the company's right to transfer work. The union made no such proposal. It did, however, submit a severance pay proposal, which became part of the contract. That provision provided for severance pay for layoffs as a result of plant closure or operational transfers.

A month after the agreement was signed, and again within a year, the company informed the union of certain operational transfers to the Alabama plant. The actions did not cause layoffs and the union did not object to either move. However, the next operational move did result in four layoffs, and the union objected and asserted that the company should have bargained before moving. The company disagreed. After twenty-three more employees were laid off, the union filed unfair labor charges against the company.

Lawsuit

The company's position was that the union waived its right to bargain over the work transfers (a) in the language of the collective bargaining agreement; (b) during negotiations of the agreement; and (c) by acquiescing in the previous work transfers.

Language of Agreement

COMPANY POSITION: The severance pay provision in the contract showed the union accepted compensation in lieu of bargaining over work relocation. They pointed to the wording of the section, "In the event the company *determines* to . . . transfer . . . severance allowances will be payable . . ." to show that discretion to relocate was given solely to the company in return for the pay.

UNION POSITION: The severance pay provision was in the supplemental unemployment benefits section, not the man-

agement rights section where a union waiver would normally be located. In addition, the law requires a waiver to be "clear and unmistakable." The company's interpretation of the severance pay section gave too much weight to one word, *determines*. That word was taken out of context as to a clear union waiver of rights.

During Negotiations

COMPANY POSITION: During negotiations, the company asserted it had no restraints on its right to relocate work and asked that if the union wished to restrict the company's right, it should propose constraints. Instead, the union proposed the severance pay provision, definitely a quid pro quo, which constituted a waiver.

UNION POSITION: Because work transfers are a mandatory subject of bargaining, the union did not have to bargain on the subject to avoid waiving it. It was the company's duty to show an unequivocal waiver. In addition, the severance pay proposal during negotiations occurred *before* the union and company settled the original unfair labor practice charge in which the company agreed to bargain before relocating work. Obviously the union was still interested in bargaining on the issue and did not waive it by the severance pay proposal.

Failure to Object

COMPANY POSITION: The union's failure to object to the two initial work transfers constituted a waiver by acquiescence.

UNION POSITION: The union did not object because no member of the unit was affected by the first two transfers. The union did object when the work relocation resulted in layoffs.

Questions

1. Did the union waive its right to negotiate transfers? Why or why not?
2. Do you think the company would have allowed the collective bargaining agreement to remain silent on transfers if it believed it would have to negotiate each transfer?
3. Should a collective bargaining agreement end the bargaining process, or should the administration of the agreement be part of the process? Why or why not?

Key Terms and Concepts

Boys Market case

Collyer case

Contract bar

Duty of fair representation

Duty to sign a contract

Featherbedding

Hot cargo agreements

Lincoln Mills case

Management rights

Opener clause

Reserved rights

Restricted rights

Secondary boycotts

Separability clause

Union security

Zipper clause

Review Questions

1. How can labor negotiators ensure that the agreement reached will be easily understood by others?
2. What are some common management rights that might be found in labor agreements?
3. Describe elements of an agreement ensuring that other unions are barred from representing a union's employees.
4. By what methods can collective bargaining agreements be enforced?
5. What is meant by the phrase "employee at will with the terms and conditions of his employment?" How does it apply in labor relations?
6. How did the *Steelworkers Trilogy* help clarify the role of arbitration and court enforcement of contracts?
7. What individual rights do employees have within the collective bargaining process?
8. What kind of economic pressures are illegal?

Endnotes

1. H. J. Heinz Co. v. N.L.R.B., 311 U.S. 514, 51 S.Ct. 320, 85 L.Ed. 309 (1941).
2. 29 U.S.C. §158(b) (1982).
3. David A. Dilts and Clarence Deitsch, *Labor Relations* (New York: Macmillan, 1983), p. 152.

4. *Basic Patterns in Union Contracts*, 11th ed. (Washington, D.C.: The Bureau of National Affairs, 1986), pp. 1–3.

5. Harold S. Roberts, *Roberts' Dictionary of Industrial Relations*, 3rd ed. (Washington, D.C.: The Bureau of National Affairs, 1986), p. 396.

6. Marvin Hill, Jr. and Anthony V. Sinicrope, *Management Rights* (Washington, D.C.: The Bureau of National Affairs, 1986), p. 3.

7. *Basic Patterns in Union Contracts*, 1986, p. 11.

8. *Management Rights*, 1986, pp. 4–5.

9. Arthur J. Goldberg, "Management's Reserved Rights: A Labor View," *Proceedings of the 9th Annual Meeting of The National Arbitration Association*, 118 (1956), pp. 120–121.

10. *Management Rights*, 1986, pp. 6–7.

11. Paul Prasow and Edward Peters, *Arbitration and Collective Bargaining: Conflict Resolution in Labor Relations*, 2nd ed. (New York: McGraw-Hill, 1983), pp. 33–34.

12. 452 U.S. 666, 107 LRRM 2705 (1981); 269 N.L.R.B. 891, 115 LRRM 1281 (1984).

13. Benjamin Aaron et al., *The Future of Labor Arbitration in America* (New York: American Arbitration Association, 1976), p. 168.

14. Charles J. Morris, ed., *The Developing Labor Law* (Washington, D.C.: Bureau of National Affairs, 1971), p. 469.

15. 29 U.S.C. 158(d) (1982).

16. U.S. Senate, Committee on Labor and Public Welfare, *Committee Report,* S. Rep. 105, 80th Cong., 1st sess., 1947, pp. 16–18.

17. Aaron, *Future of Labor,* p. 87.

18. Textile Workers Union v. Lincoln Mills, 353 U.S. 448, 40 LRRM 2113 (1957).

19. United Steelworkers v. American Mfg. Co., 363 U.S. 564, 46 LRRM 2414 (1960); United Steelworkers v. Warrior & Gulf Navigation Co., 363 U.S. 574, 46 LRRM 2416 (1960); United Steelworkers v. Enterprise Wheel & Car Corp., 363 U.S. 593, 46 LRRM 2423 (1960).

20. Aaron, *Future of Labor,* p. 56.

21. Collyer Insulated Wire, 192 N.L.R.B. 837, 77 LRRM 1931 (1971).

22. Spielberg Manufacturing Company, 112 N.L.R.B. 1080, 36 LRRM 1152 (1955).

23. Olin Corp. 268 N.L.R.B. 573 (1984), Combustions Engineering, Inc. 272 N.L.R.B. No. 32 (1984); Badger Meter, Inc. 272 N.L.R.B. No. 123 (1984).

24. Benjamin W. Wolkinson, "The Impact of the *Collyer*. Policy of Deferral: An Empirical Study," *Industrial and Labor Relations Review* 38, no. 3 (April 1985), pp. 377–391.

25. William H. Holley, Jr., and Kenneth M. Jennings, *The Labor Relations Process* (Hinsdale, Ill.: Dryden, 1980), pp. 286–90.

26. Sean Flaherty, "Contract Status and the Economic Determinants of Strike Activity," *Industrial Relations* 22, no. 1 (Winter 1983), pp. 20–33.

27. Boys Market, Inc. v. Retail Clerks Union Local 770, 398 U.S. 235, 90 S.Ct. 1583, 26 L.Ed. 2d 199 (1970).

28. Sinclair Refining Company v. Atchison, 370 U.S. 195, 82 S.Ct. 1328, 8 L.Ed. 440 (1962).

29. Buffalo Forge Company v. United Steelworkers of America, 428 U.S. 397, 96 S.Ct. 3141, 49 L.Ed. 2d 1022 (1976).

30. 276 N.L.R.B. No. 211 (1985).

31. No. 85-7129 (9th Cir., May 6, 1986).

32. Vaca v. Sipes, 386 U.S. 171, 64 LRRM 2369 (1967); Hines v. Anchor Motor Co., Inc., 424 U.S. 554, 91 LRRM 2481 (1976), and Bowen v. U.S. Postal Service, 112 LRRM 2281 (1983).

33. See George W. Bohlander, "Fair Representation: Not Just a Union Problem," *The Personnel Administrator* 25, no. 3 (March 1980), pp. 36–40, 82.

34. Roberts, *Dictionary of Industrial Relations*, p. 285.

35. Roberts, *Dictionary of Industrial Relations*, p. 659.

36. Jacobs Manufacturing Company, 94 N.L.R.B. 1214 (1951).
37. Dilts, *Labor Relations,* p. 122.
38. Daniel D. Cook, "Boycott! Labor's Last Resort," *Industry Week* 189 (June 18, 1976), pp. 23–32.
39. Morris, *Developing Labor Law,* p. 684.
40. Ibid., p. 688.

10

Grievance and Disciplinary Procedures

LABOR NEWS

Alan Moseley: Union "Griever"

The job of shop steward, or union "griever," is on the front line in the growing battle over jobs in America's steel industry. Alan Moseley works in a steel mill in East Chicago, Indiana. His employer, Inland Steel Industries Inc., is struggling to meet foreign competition and a shrinking domestic market by eliminating jobs wherever possible. Alan Moseley is also a shop steward for the United Steelworkers Local 1010 and handles members' grievances against his employer. Today he describes most grievances as a "daily battle over jobs."

The job of union griever is considered critical by management and labor leaders. "We can't do a thing without the support of the grievers," says William Boehler, the head of labor relations at Inland Steel. While labor relations at Inland are better than at most other steel producers, new machines, computers, work rules, and labor-saving devices continue to eliminate blue-collar jobs.

Technological change has complicated the grievance process. In one case, for example, four jobs were at stake and manage-

ment wanted only management personnel to operate a computer that controlled a heat-treatment machine that had replaced union workers. The company hired outside lawyers to argue the case against Moseley and the union, who believed union workers should be given an opportunity to learn to operate the equipment. The union won the battle in arbitration after 2½ years.

The union griever is caught in a fight for survival. In 1986 workers cut the brake lines of a griever's car and another was punched out at a union meeting. The job was much more fun in the 1960s when Moseley became a steelworker at age 18 and was elected assistant griever. Back then, most grievances concerned the company's efforts to discipline a young work force, and job security seemed almost guaranteed.

Source: Adapted from Alex Kotlowitz, "Grievous Work: Job of Shop Steward Has New Frustrations in Era of Payroll Cuts," The Wall Street Journal, April 1, 1987, pp. 1, 20. Used by permission.

In the day-to-day administration of a collective bargaining agreement, the majority of time is spent on grievance handling.[1] A detailed study of the time devoted to the formal meetings required to process a typical grievance found that, on the average, over nine direct working hours were required. This time did not include the hours of investigations and preparation spent by each side.[2] The extreme importance of a good grievance procedure has been described as the "life blood of a collective bargaining relationship."[3]

Regardless of the completeness and clarity of the labor agreement, disagreements will arise during the life of the contract. Thus a *grievance procedure,* a previously agreed-upon procedure to resolve such disputes, must be provided in the agreement. The grievance handling process must settle disputes arising during the term of the agreement—if not, strikes, lockouts, or other work disruptions may result.

A **grievance** is often defined as any perceived violation of a contract provision. This definition could be broadened to include any gripe by an employee against an employer, or vice versa. One arbitrator has said that "if a man thinks he has a grievance, he has a grievance."[4] However, a more precise definition might include any formal complaint lodged by persons who believe they have been wronged.[5]

Fortunately, most collective bargaining agreements are similar to Exhibit 10.1 and delineate a grievance procedure that consists of a specified series of four or five procedural steps that an aggrieved employee, union, and management representatives must follow when a complaint arises. Typically, the grievant is provided with a systematic set of appeals through successively higher levels of union and management representatives. The fact that most contracts provide for specific grievance procedures clearly indicates that while both sides try to develop a clear and precise document during the contract negotiation process, some areas will be subject to misunderstanding during the life of the contract. Indeed, as shown in Case 10.1, the grievance procedure itself is sometimes the subject of a grievance.

The signing of a contract spells out a new relationship between labor and management, and the agreement specifies a new set of rules legally binding labor and management during the life of the contract. The administration of the contract is substantially provided by a formal grievance process agreed upon in the contract. While the number and contents of the procedural steps in a formal grievance process vary from contract to contract, most involve four or five steps.

Sources of Employee Grievances

Whatever the subject matter of a particular grievance may be, exactly *why* the grievance was filed may provide far greater understanding of the union's and/or employee's motives. One or more of the following situations might be a **source of employee grievance.**

Clarifying Contract Provisions under Changing Conditions

After contracts are agreed upon and signed by both parties, unforeseen circumstances change some operating conditions. Even with the best of intentions, both manage-

Exhibit 10.1   Grievance procedure

ARTICLE IX
Adjustment of Grievances

A grievance shall consist of a dispute between an employee, the Union, and the Company as to the meaning or application of any provisions of this Agreement.

When it becomes necessary for a Union officer, steward or employee to process a grievance during working hours, he shall notify the foreman involved in advance and ring out his card and receive no pay for the time spent processing the grievances. It is the Union's desire that a minimum of time be spent processing the grievances during regular shift hours of the employees and the Union officers concerned.

The President of the Union, or his duly appointed representatives chosen from the Grievance Committee, shall have access to departments other than his own for the purpose of transacting the legitimate business of the grievance procedure, after reasonable notice has been given to the head of the department to be visited and permission from his own department has been obtained.

An employee ordered to report to the office for disciplinary purposes shall have the right to be represented by a Union official (steward, committeeman, or officer). The representative will be treated as though processing a grievance. The employee shall be advised of the purpose of the meeting in advance and advised of the provisions of this paragraph.

The Union Committee or Union officers shall conduct no Union activities, other than processing of grievances, on Company premises without the consent of the Company.

Step 1. Within three (3) working days after the first occurrence of the situation, condition, or actions of the Company giving rise to the grievance, the employee affected shall personally discuss his grievance with his foreman. He shall ring out his card (unless it can be discussed on an off-shift hour) and his steward shall be present.

Within twenty-four (24) hours after the grievance is discussed, the foreman shall give his verbal decision to the aggrieved employee and/or his steward.

Step 2. In the event that a satisfactory settlement has not been reached at the verbal level, the aggrieved employee, or his steward, may within 48 hours present the grievance in writing, and within 48 hours shall receive a written answer from his foreman.

Step 3. Within three (3) working days after the written decision has been given, the Local Union may present the grievance in writing to a representative designated by the Company.

All third step grievances (except discharge cases which may, if requested by the Union, be discussed at special meetings to meet deadlines) shall be considered at the next scheduled grievance meeting attended by an International Representative, unless he waives the right to be present; but upon demand by the Company, such representative shall attend at least one meeting a month to consider pending grievances.

Within four (4) working days after the grievance meeting, the Company shall give to the Local Union its written decision. The time limits in this step may be extended by mutual agreement.

The aggrieved, or in case of a group grievance, a representative of the aggrieved group, may be present at the meetings at all steps of this grievance procedure if he so requests to be present.

The Union shall certify in writing to the Company, over the signature of the Local Union Recording Secretary, a list of the officers, committeemen and stewards who are to be recognized by the Company.

The Union Grievance Committee shall consist of not less than three (3) members.

The Union Grievance Committee shall have the right to file a grievance in behalf of an employee and/or employees if there is a contract violation, and if filed within three (3) working days of the occurrence.

Source: *Agreement* between The Anaconda Company Aluminum Division and United Steelworkers of America, AFL-CIO, 1900–79, pp. 19–23. Used with permission.

ment and labor may find that they honestly disagree on the contract provision relevant to the new operations. For example, workers at the Diamond Shamrock Corporation normally worked the evening shift from 3:00–11:00 P.M. and received a shift differential under the existing contract. Management changed the hours of the shift to 11:00 A.M.–7:00 P.M., resulting in a grievance requesting shift differential pay for the four new hours of work overlapping with the old hours for which they received shift differential pay. Management declined, claiming that shift differential was only required by contract when the entire shift was from 3:00–7:00 P.M. The arbitrator agreed with management that the contract did not provide shift differential on a per-hour basis, but on a per-shift basis.[6]

Support for Future Negotiations

Unions often encourage their members to file grievances in certain areas to provide a file of supporting evidence during future negotiations. The negotiators may then point to the grievances as evidence of their members' concern over a particular management practice or lack of an employee benefit or service. The union does not intend to prevail in many of these cases, but wants to alert management to the issue. Thus, the administration of one contract becomes a basis of negotiation for a future contract.

Rectifying a Contract Violation

Contract negotiators have one primary goal—to sign a contract. While many contracts are quite lengthy and involved, they will specify how each debatable issue should be resolved. In fact, both sides expect that disagreements will occur during the life of the contract, which is why grievance arbitration is included.

One of the most common sources of grievances is the union's honest belief that management has violated a provision of the existing contract. For example, an arbitrator ruled that the contract clause stating that the parties may negotiate necessary schedule changes from the standard work week did not require the union's consent before changes could be made if negotiations were provided. The union believed the contract phrase did in fact require management to gain its consent before changes were made.[7]

Show of Power

Sometimes employees and union officials file grievances to demonstrate their authority and influence. Union officials may feel a need to remind employees that they are on their side and work hard to represent their interests. After all, union leaders are elected by their members, and members expect something in return. While the union leadership may realize that a particular employee grievance is without substantial merit, the issue will be pursued if it is of great concern to the membership. Individual employees may also, for a variety of reasons, file grievances. Some may simply be letting off steam while others may use the grievance process as a means of settling a score with management. No contract language can eliminate grievances when these kinds of motives are involved. Some management and labor relations personnel claim such meritless grievances waste time and resources. However, critics should consider that the grievance process is partially designed to provide a safety valve to employees who might otherwise express their normal anxiety and frustration in more harmful ways, such as absenteeism, sabotage, or even alcoholism.

Increased Pay

One of labor's primary motives in bargaining is to provide assurances of pay that might otherwise be at the discretion of management. Labor negotiations have initiated many types of pay incentives and premiums not found in the nonunion sector. Many grievances result from employees believing they are entitled to additional pay that management believes is not required.

The union, in one instance, claimed that the contract providing that employees working on Sunday receive double the straight-time hourly rate required double-time pay for all Sunday hours. Management contended that since it began opening on Sunday as a regular business day after a state blue law was repealed, the double-time pay was not required since Sunday became a normal work day. The arbitrator agreed with management.[8]

Steps in a Grievance Procedure

Step 1: Employee, Steward, Supervisor

The initial **step in a grievance procedure** usually instructs the employee to discuss the grievance with the shop steward and/or go directly to the supervisor. The employee has the legal right to do the latter; the supervisor must resolve the grievance consistent with the contract. The supervisor must also notify the union of the grievance. The shop steward is, however, usually the first person contacted. Therefore, the steward must be experienced in handling grievance matters and familiar with the terms of the contract and its provisions. The steward must also be able to recognize grievances containing some merit as well as those that are trivial and should be dropped. A steward will encourage and help the employee to pursue a legitimate grievance, and in some cases must convince the employee that a grievance contains no merit.

The extent to which grievances are resolved at the lowest possible level is an important indicator of effective grievance handling. One means of attaining resolution at the lowest possible level is the use of feedback from previous grievance cases. The outcome of previous similar cases provides cues to both parties that tend to focus their discussion and provide a faster resolution of the grievance. Generally the purpose of feedback is not to "set precedent" but instead to provide both parties with an array of possible likely solutions.[9] In practice, if both sides introduce the results of previous similar grievances at the first level of grievance discussions, a compromise may well be reached more quickly than if they wait until the issue goes to arbitration.

Step 2: Written Grievance

If steward and employee agree that the grievance has some merit and should be pursued, then the grievance is reduced to writing. At this point, the grievance is said to have moved from the informal to the formal stage. A grievance form is completed by the steward and employee within forty-eight hours of the occurrence, or within the time limit specified in the contract. The process of writing out the complaint forces the grievant to set forth the facts, contract provisions, and contingencies early on in the process.

Most company and union representatives feel it is important to formalize the grievance in written format at this stage.[10] Once the grievance has been reduced to writing, the steward and the employee meet with the supervisor to discuss the grievance in an honest effort to quickly settle the matter. Both sides can assess the strengths and weaknesses of the claim. Usually, most grievances containing little merit will be dropped quickly.

Research indicates that most grievances are settled in this step of the grievance process. If the grievance cannot be resolved at this stage, the employee may choose to appeal.

Step 3: Shop Steward, Department Head

When the shop steward and supervisor cannot resolve the grievance, then it may be appealed to the next higher level of management and union representative, usually within seven calendar days. At this point, the union representative continues to be the shop steward or business agent. However, the management representative usually represents a higher level and may be a plant superintendent or department head. At this stage, the two sides review the written grievance and try to reach a resolution.

Step 4: Union Grievance Committee, Director of Personnel and Industrial Relations

At this point, the employee's grievance is reviewed by a plantwide union grievance committee that may further appeal the answer to Step 5, usually within thirty calendar days. The plant manager or department head may be assisted by the director of personnel and industrial relations in reviewing the grievance from a management perspective. As with the second step, they review the written grievance and discuss the case with the employee's representatives. Both sides continue to honestly try to resolve the grievance rather than go to the final stage of the process, final and binding arbitration. This final step is more expensive, represents a failure to reach an agreement in the matter, and brings greater tension to the grievance. Both sides realize that they may completely lose the case before an independent arbitrator.

Step 5: Arbitration

Approximately 95 percent of all collective bargaining agreements provide for a binding arbitration as the final step in the handling of grievances.[11] The contract provisions usually include that either management or labor request arbitration as a final step in resolving the grievance. This request must be made within sixty calendar days of the receipt of the answer of Step 4. The outside independent arbitrator will study the evidence and listen to the arguments of both sides before rendering a decision. The arbitrator's decision, as agreed upon in the collective bargaining contract, is final and binding on both parties and can be appealed to the courts only on the grounds of collusion, if the arbitrator's award exceeded his authority, or if the arbitrator's decision was not based on the essence of the labor agreement.[12]

Functions of Grievance Procedures

Formal grievance procedures have been found to be the most common tool to resolve conflicts arising between labor and management during the life of the agreement. In general, the functions provided by a grievance procedure are as follows:

1. *Conflict management resolution*   Before grievance procedures and arbitration became popular, strikes and slowdowns were often used by employees and unions to resolve complaints over the interpretation of labor agreements. Without grievance procedures, questions would probably be resolved by a test of economic strength, harmful to both management and the union. Case 10.2, however, illustrates that having a grievance procedure does not always prevent job actions.

2. *Agreement clarification*   All agreements contain a certain amount of unintentional ambiguity that develops questions requiring contract interpretation. The dynamics of employer and employee relationships cannot be fully anticipated by the parties at the bargaining table; thus, negotiating language often must be applied to unforeseen situations.

3. *Communication*   Grievance procedures provide a vehicle for individual employees to express their problems and perceptions. They offer employees a formal process to air perceived inequities in the workplace.

4. *Due process*   The most widely heralded function of grievance procedures is that of a third party intervention. Most grievance procedures provide a fair and equitable due process containing binding arbitration as a final step. Without this process, management would likely have an upper hand in most grievance situations. However, employee and union strikes would be heightened, with economic measures used to balance management's authority.

5. *Strength enhancement*   The grievance mechanism helps unions to develop employee loyalty and trust. Grievance processing emphasizes union presence and strength during the term of the collective bargaining agreement and reminds employees of the union efforts to protect their interests. The formal grievance also strengthens management's and labor's communication skills, since first-level stewards and supervisors are almost always involved in the initial step of the grievance procedure. Both sides come to better understand each other's perspectives and develop a closer working relationship.[13]

Grievance Categories

Grievances may be categorized according to issues that arise most frequently:

Suspension	An employee has been ordered not to work for a period of time usually ranging from one day to two weeks. Almost all of these suspensions are the result of absenteeism, avoidable accidents, insubordination, or job performance.
Seniority	An employee is grieving because of seniority bypass. Almost all such grievances are filed because an employee has been overlooked for overtime, transfers, promotions, training, or scheduling.
Transfer	Most grievances in this category are filed because an employee has been refused a transfer for which he or she has applied. This may be

because of low supervisory ratings, excessive absenteeism, medical transfers receiving priority, and so forth.

Termination	Simply, the employee has been fired. Almost all actions in this category are because of excessive absenteeism, a history of avoidable accidents, insubordination, or job performance.
Disciplinary Memoranda	This is essentially a warning to an employee which presumably will be followed by more serious consequences should the employee continue or repeat the incident. Ordinarily, these are a reaction to absenteeism, accidents, insubordination, tardiness, and job performance.
Vacation	This occurs because employees do not receive the vacation dates they prefer. This may be because junior employees have been given the dates of preference, or because the organization has limited the number of employees who may be on vacation at any given time.
Grievance Process	The union ordinarily charges that the company has not met in good faith on a grievance. Also, a case is occasionally found when the company is alleged not to have met the conditions of a grievance settlement.
Management Performing Productive Work	This is self-explanatory. The union alleges that management employees are doing work which is (or should be) restricted to union personnel.
Safety	The union alleges that a procedure or a condition involving employees is unsafe. The union, in this case, is usually asking that this procedure or condition be modified.
Discrimination	This may be a forum for Title VII disagreements. However, this is not ordinarily the case. Grievances in this category are catchalls. Discrimination here means that an employee charges that he or she is not being treated the same as other employees. These grievances do not necessarily, indeed, rarely have race, sex, or national origin overtones.
Performance Evaluations	An employee charges that his or her annual performance evaluation is not a fair representation of his or her job performance over that period.
Union Representation	The union files a grievance in this case because an employee, facing a disciplinary hearing, has requested union representation and has had this request denied.
Sick Benefits Denial	An employee has not come to work for some period. This employee claims to have been ill and requests sick pay compensation. For whatever reasons, the company has refused to pay this sick leave.
Pay (differentials, travel, etc.)	These grievances usually occur over the nonpayment of special pay provisions (not ordinarily hourly wages). Meal allowances, night shift differentials, travel reimbursements are most common.

Excused or Complimentary Time	An employee has requested time off without pay. The company has denied the request.
Work out of Classification	An employee is asked to do a job which is allegedly not in his or her job description. It is argued that this particular job should be done by someone in a different job classification.
Training	An employee has requested training for some aspect of his or her job. The company has denied the request.

Source: Dan R. Dalton and William D. Tudor, "Grievance Arbitration May Be Expensive, but What of the Alternative?" *Personnel Administrator* 26, no. 3 (March 1981), pp. 25–27. Reprinted from the March 1981 issue of *Personnel Administrator,* copyright 1981, The American Society for Personnel Administration, 606 North Washington St., Alexandria, VA 22314, $30 per year.

Disciplinary Procedures

A primary objective of a grievance process is to provide employees with a fair review and, if necessary, an appeal of disciplinary actions taken by management. Regardless of size or industry, every company at some time must administer corrective discipline. Certain employees may need such attention only once or twice in their careers and quickly respond to fair procedures; others may never correct their behavior and will exhaust any progressive disciplinary process. Case 10.3 involves a rare situation in which an employee could not benefit from disciplinary procedures. However, it is important that *other* employees believe the disciplined employee was given a fair chance and equitable punishment. In order to maintain good labor relations, both labor and management should strive for fair and effective disciplinary policies.

Employers need a comprehensive and effective discipline system to maintain control over the work force. Otherwise, satisfactory employee attendance, conduct, and productivity could not be achieved. A well-structured and uniformly enforced discipline program also may reduce employee discontent, along with any manager's tendency to treat employees in an arbitrary or biased manner. Employees are more satisfied when they know what consequences to expect from rule violations, and see discipline procedures consistently administered.[14]

Labor and management officials want to minimize the use of disciplinary actions, but both realize such actions will be needed in some situations. Therefore, virtually all collective bargaining agreements outline a **disciplinary procedure.**

Other than the economic benefits of a labor agreement, the disciplinary process may be the most vital aspect of a labor-management relationship. Management views the right and ability to discipline its employees effectively as the heart of maintaining a productive work force. If work rules can be accidentally or willfully violated by one employee, the total result could be very costly. For example, if one employee continues to neglect wearing protective goggles because they are uncomfortable or inconvenient, others may follow because they think the rule has been relaxed. The eventual penalty is OSHA citations and fines or possibly an individual's loss of eyesight in an accident due to one minor infraction.

Any degree of discipline—even if it is only an oral warning—is both stressful and embarrassing to the employee because of the economic and psychological penalties of a layoff or termination. If such discipline was not warranted by the facts of the situation, if the employee was ignorant of any wrongdoing, or if the penalty was unusually harsh, other employees will react very negatively. Protection from biased or thoughtless supervisors in disciplinary matters has been a prime motive behind many union organizing campaigns.

A variety of disciplinary policies may be provided in the labor contract. A study by the Bureau of National Affairs suggests these policies be encouraged by management and labor officials and utilized:

    1. *Explain company rules*   Orientation courses, employee handbooks, bulletin board notices, and other devices must be used to bring work rules to the attention of employees.

    2. *Get the facts*   Interview witnesses and investigate testimony to ensure both sides of a story are presented. Circumstantial evidence, personality factors, and unproven assumptions cannot be easily defended before arbitrators.

    3. *Give adequate warning*   Most grievance warning steps are given to the employee in writing; however, all warnings, even oral warnings, should be noted in the employee's personnel record. Copies of warning notices should go to the union.

    4. *Ascertain motive*   People usually have a reason for what they do. Seldom will employees intentionally and maliciously violate rules. The penalty should be adjusted to the degree the employee's action was intentional.

    5. *Consider employee's past record*   Before disciplinary action is taken, the employee's past record should be taken into account. A good work record and seniority are considered, especially in cases of minor offenses.

    6. *Discipline without discharge*   Wherever possible, avoid the use of discharge. Only when any hope of future improvement is past, or the offense is so severe, should discharge be used.[15]

A critical aspect of the disciplinary procedure is the face-to-face counseling provided by the supervisor. Such encounters often can become explosive and lead to subjective and emotional behavior. Employees may feel they need a union to provide them protection against what they perceive are unfair supervisory actions. Any corrective supervisory counseling should provide the employee feedback stating the problem, the preferred action, and future expectations as well as the disciplinary action to be taken. Exhibit 10.2 illustrates a disciplinary system designed to provide maximum employee control, minimum discontent, and reduced exposure to legal problems.

The Labor-Management Relations Act, in addition to civil and anti-discrimination laws, provides restrictions on employee discipline. The act prohibits disciplinary action against employees for union-related activity. Most related charges of such employer actions arise out of union organizational campaigns. The second most common source of unfair discipline charges arises from conflict between the union steward and management. The steward must file the grievances of union members and advocate their point of view. In this situation, the NLRB may view disciplinary actions against the steward as an unfair labor practice. Thus, employers should have

Exhibit 10.2 Discipline rules to protect us all

Whenever people gather together, some rules and regulations are needed to help everyone work together harmoniously. This is especially true in a company such as ours which needs to have efficient operations. It is our aim to be patient and firm in running the company. Our sincere desire is to help each employee in every possible way to perform his or her job well. However, responsibilities are shared by everyone. You have the responsibility to us and to your fellow workers to conduct yourself according to certain rules of behavior and conduct. The purpose of these rules is not to restrict the rights of anyone but, rather, to define them. By keeping you informed of your rights, you will be more satisfied and the company can maintain an orderly and efficient operation. We ask for the wholehearted cooperation of all members of our team of employees in the observance of these rules which are necessary to protect the best interests of all.

The following rules are listed with their attending penalties for your information.

GROUP I

1. Failure to attend scheduled meetings.
2. Stopping work before time specified for such purposes.
3. Loitering and loafing during working hours.
4. Leaving your department or assigned working areas during working hours without permission of a supervisor, except for the use of the restrooms. (No smoking in restrooms.)
5. Failure to keep your own time card accurately or completing another employee's time card.
6. Repeated failure to be at the work station to work at starting time.
7. Creating or contributing to unsanitary conditions.
8. Posting or removal of notices, signs or writing in any form on any bulletin board on company property without permission of management.
9. Neglect or mishandling of equipment or any other supplies.
10. Unsatisfactory work and/or attitude.
11. Waste or personal use of company supplies.
12. Untidy attire, extreme makeup, and hairstyles; torn uniforms and other failure to maintain a clean, neat appearance.
13. Failure to follow any other company rule, regulation, or job requirement not specifically mentioned herein.

PENALTIES FOR GROUP I VIOLATIONS

First offense—Oral warning.
Second offense—Written warning.
Third offense—One (1) day's suspension without pay.
Fourth offense—Termination of employment.

GROUP II

1. Leaving the premises during working hours without permission of a supervisor.
2. Fighting of any type on company premises at any time.
3. Attempting bodily injury to another.
4. Two (2) days' unexcused absence during any thirty (30) calendar days.
5. Violation of the no solicitation/nor distribution rule.
6. Failure to report off from work in accordance with current regulations.

Exhibit 10.2 (continued)

PENALTIES FOR GROUP II VIOLATIONS

First offense—Written warning.
Second offense—Two (2) days' suspension without pay.
Third offense—Termination of employment.

GROUP III

1. Deliberately making or using falsified records, material requisition, passes, time cards, etc.
2. Use of intoxicating liquids or narcotics of any kind on company premises.
3. Insubordination.
4. Sabotage.
5. Theft of any property.
6. Concerted or deliberate restriction of output (slowdown, delaying other employees' work, etc.).
7. Reporting for work under the influence of any alcoholic beverage or illegal narcotic.
8. Improperly discussing or disclosing confidential information.
9. Using the eating, drinking, and smoking facilities to excess.
10. Excessive absenteeism.
11. Discourtesy to the public.
12. Refusal to accept any reasonable work assignment.
13. Gambling.
14. Immoral conduct.
15. Incompetence.
16. Gross negligence of duty.
17. Willful or consistently careless destruction of company property.
18. Violation of safety rules.
19. Sleeping on duty.
20. Profanity.
21. Possession of firearms or other illegal weapon on company premises.

PENALTIES FOR GROUP III VIOLATIONS

First offense—Termination of employment.

Source: Stephen Cabot, *Labor-Management Relations Manual* (Boston: Warren, Gorham, Lamont, 1979), chap. 16, pp. 7–9, by permission of Warren, Gorham, Lamont, Inc.

a uniformly applied and well-documented disciplinary program they can defend against possible claims of unfair labor practice discrimination.[16]

Grounds for Discharge

Employees may be terminated or discharged for "cause" or "just cause" for specific offenses. Most contracts specify the offenses that are sufficient grounds for immediate

Exhibit 10.3 Grounds for immediate discharge

	Percent of Contracts	
Cause	*Manufacturing*	*Nonmanufacturing*
Violation of leave provision	43	26
Unauthorized strike participation	41	25
Unauthorized absence	36	16
Dishonesty or theft	19	29
Violation of company rules	25	15
Insubordination	17	22
Intoxication	16	32
Incompetence	20	15
Failure to obey safety rules	13	15
Misconduct	11	11
Tardiness	12	5

discharge, but also provide for an appeal procedure in that event. The contract may require that the union be notified in advance of a discharge or that a predischarge hearing be held with the employee and union present. The most common grounds for discharge specified in contracts include those listed in Exhibit 10.3.[17]

Absenteeism

Unexpected employee absences cause major problems for management. Supervisors who receive an employee's call notifying them of their absence that day must quickly transfer personnel and possibly call in additional employees. The absent employee causes several problems:

1. *Lost productivity*   Replacement employees usually cannot be as efficient on a job as those who perform it daily. If they are shifted from another area two or more jobs may be affected by one absence.

2. *Additional costs*   Often the use of a replacement employee causes the employer to pay overtime. Thus, even if the absent employee is not paid for hours missed (which is usually not the case), personnel costs increase significantly.

3. *Benefits*   Most contracts provide that the absent employee continues to receive almost all benefits. If a replacement employee also receives some additional benefits, the hourly cost can approach $5.00.

4. *Administrative time*   Several people may be needed to provide replacement help. The immediate supervisor may need not only to contact additional help, but also to provide them with more instruction during the day. Personnel department people, department heads, and others may also be required to use part of their day in arranging for replacement help.

Management considers absenteeism a controllable problem and usually seeks to minimize the number of absences through the use of control or disciplinary techniques. While hesitant to implement new or additional control techniques that may be abused by management, unions recognize the seriousness of the problems caused by unexpected absences and have agreed to a variety of control measures in contracts, including those listed in Exhibit 10.4.[18]

One example of union-management ability to control absenteeism is the H.J. Scheirich Company, a cabinet manufacturer with over 400 employees. Several years ago the firm's management concluded that absenteeism was causing major production problems and had inflated labor costs. Together Scheirich and the union negotiated an innovative **"no-fault" absenteeism** policy. The new policy centered on the policy statement, "Action may be taken when cumulative time lost from work for any reason substantially reduces the employee's services to the company."

In practice, excessive absenteeism was considered to be three percentage points above the plant average; however, no exact figure was used. Instead, abuses were examined on a case-by-case basis. In the first six years of the new program, eleven employees were terminated for "unavailability for work." Eight of the eleven grieved their terminations through the union; five went to arbitration. The arbitrators upheld the termination in four of the five cases, and in the fifth case the award was given to the employee only because management failed to notify her with sufficient warnings. In general, the arbitrators issued opinions stating that management has a right to terminate employees for excessive absences even when due to illness or other factors. They found the case-by-case method of comparing the employee's percentage of absenteeism to the company average to be reasonable.[19]

Exhibit 10.4   Control of absenteeism

Method of Control	Percent Use
Employee call-in to give notice of absence	99
Termination based on excessive absenteeism	97
Progressive discipline for excessive absenteeism	97
Identification and discipline of employees abusing attendance policies	92
Inclusion of absenteeism rate on employee job performance appraisal	47
Consistency in applying attendance policy	83
Clearly written attendance policy	77
Requirement of doctor's written excuse for illness/accidents	89
Component on attendance in a formal employee-orientation program for new hire	73
Daily attendance records maintained by supervisors	66
Screening of recruit's past attendance records before making a selection decision	66
Analysis of daily attendance information at least monthly	68

Source: Steve Markham and Dow Smith, "Controlling Absenteeism: Union and Nonunion Differences," *Personnel Administrator* 30, no. 2 (Feb. 1985), pp. 87–102. Reprinted from the Feb. 1985 issue of *Personnel Administrator,* copyright 1985, The American Society for Personnel Administration, 606 North Washington St., Alexandria, VA 22314.

Managers may believe that unions present barriers to effective absenteeism programs and policies. In fact, campaigns to remain union-free often include information implying that significant differences in absence rates and programs exist between union and nonunion employers. However, a survey report of 959 employers in 1985 suggested that the presence of a union is not associated with employee-absence levels any higher or lower than those of nonunion employers. Also, the most common absenteeism control mechanism, employee call-in to given notice of absence, was reported by 99 percent of both types of employers. The only method reported to significantly decrease absenteeism, a monthly analysis of attendance data, was used more often by union organizations than nonunion. Nonunion employers in general had fewer control techniques than union employers.[20]

Nonunion Grievance Procedures

The use of formal grievance procedures where employees may advance their complaints and problems is often recognized by many organizational managers as critical in remaining nonunion. Formal grievance procedures are far less common and more varied in nonunion organizations.[21] A 1977 survey of 1,958 *Harvard Business Review* readers resulted in only 14 percent nonunion workers reporting that their companies had a management grievance committee.[22]

Formal grievance procedures in nonunion organizations are normally patterned after procedures in unionized organizations. An example of the grievance procedure for a nonunion organization is presented in the following:

> In order to protect the individual rights of the employee, the hospitals have established and maintain a grievance procedure, whereby an employee may present what he/she considers to be a personal injustice regarding his/her employment relationship. Such a grievance must be filed by the employee within five days from the time the situation occurred that may have caused the grievance. Also the following steps should be taken in pursuing the grievance:
>
> 1. The aggrieved employee should first let his/her supervisor know of the complaint. If the employee does not receive a satisfactory reply within two working days, he/she should proceed to Step 2.
> 2. At this step, the department head is notified of the complaint in writing by the employee. If the employee wishes assistance in writing the grievance, he/she may request assistance from the personnel department. If a satisfactory reply to the grievance is not received in three working days, then the employee should proceed to Step 3.
> 3. At this stage, the director of personnel services or his/her designate is informed of the grievance by the employee. After a review of the facts, the personnel director or his/her designate and the employee may reach a satisfactory solution to the grievance. However, if this does not occur, then the fourth step should be taken.
> 4. A peer review committee composed of three impartial employees will be established to review the grievance and establish the facts of the complaint. The members of this committee are subject to the approval of the aggrieved employee. The director of personnel services or his/her designate will serve as a resource person for the committee. However, the peer review committee, alone, makes the recommendation of how the

complaint is to be resolved. Within five working days of the hearing, the employee will receive the committee's written recommendation.

5.   Finally, if the employee and/or the department head is not satisfied with the committee's recommendations, then the last step in the appeal process is administration where the final determination is made.

In no way, either directly or indirectly, is the employee to consider his/her job in jeopardy as a result of participating in this procedure.

Source: *Norton-Children's Hospitals Employee Handbook* (Louisville, Kentucky: Norton-Children's Hospitals, undated), pp. 17–18, by permission of Norton-Children's Hospitals, Inc.

The example illustrates the absence of binding arbitration as a final step, the major difference between union and nonunion procedures. Also, nonunion firms are more likely to use suggestion boxes or open-door grievance procedures. The theory behind nonunion firms having a grievance procedure where employees, without reprisal, can seek relief against unfair practices or procedures has considerable merit. However, making it a reality presents many problems.

Most nonunion employees are relatively unsophisticated about grievance procedures and what the procedures can accomplish. Nonunion employees may believe that their company carries a smaller percentage of grievances through to the final step than unionized organizations. This is usually not the case. The unionized organization usually has a similar percentage of grievances that reach the final level because the steward effectively communicates that a grievance is without substantial merit to the employee. The employee in the unionized firm realizes the steward usually has the employee's best interest in mind and accepts this advice more readily than the nonunion employee, who generally does not have as much trust in management.

Formal nonunion grievance procedures raise the employees' expectations of relief and intensify their feelings about problems because they know some of the problems will be addressed. If the grievance procedure takes a long time to resolve, employees may begin to feel that management is delaying the process. In some cases, the entire plant may become empathetically involved, and small problems may be magnified into large ones.

Nonunion employees may be more hesitant to use the formal grievance procedure since they do not have the support and understanding of union representatives. Unless both top management and the first-level supervisors enthusiastically support the grievance procedure, the employees quickly discount it as truly objective for airing complaints. In the unionized organization, the employees feel safer knowing that the union structure is supporting them. Therefore, grievances must be quickly aired and objectively heard in nonunion organizations. Management must understand that there is no union hierarchy to protect the employees' interests and views.[23]

Demand for Grievance Arbitration

There are no prescribed rules for grievance arbitration as in the judicial process. Arbitration procedures should be based upon the wishes and needs of the parties involved to the extent possible within the judgment of the arbitrator. The arbitration process is more private and is therefore unique to the parties, as compared with the public judicial process. Also, the grievance arbitration procedure involves more sophisticated and knowledgeable parties than those in most judicial proceedings, and the arbitrator is more knowledgeable than the judge in most cases.

The law has played a relatively limited role in labor and management arbitration in the United States. Grievance arbitration fundamentally is the product of a private contract between labor and management and is the final step of a grievance resolution process. Parties involved have honored their agreement to arbitrate the final and binding process in grievance cases and carry out the award of the arbitrator with little or no thought to the legal stance of arbitration. Only a very small percentage of cases have resulted in court action in connection with any aspect of arbitration.[24] The courts have required arbitration in situations when the termination date of an agreement was not specifically stated or when the wording of a contract implied arbitral settlements of disputes, although the word *arbitration* was not specifically used in the agreement.

There are two common kinds of arbitration. **Interest arbitration** refers to situations where the parties have chosen to submit their arbitration for the determination of the provisions of a new contract. **Rights** or *contract interpretation* **arbitration** involves interpretation of existing contract terms.[25] Exhibit 10.5 is an example of a typical contract interpretation demand.

While many labor disputes are clearly suitable for arbitration, judgment must be exercised in deciding whether to arbitrate a particular dispute. Factors to be considered are the merits of the case, the importance of the issue, the effect of winning or losing the dispute, the possibilities of settlement, and psychological and face-saving aspects. The most popular use of labor arbitration is interpreting applications of the collective bargaining agreements. However, labor arbitration is not always the solution. Management will hesitate to arbitrate issues regarding normal prerogatives such as determining methods of production and operating policies and finances. Labor likewise considers the settlement of an internal union conflict as a topic in which management should not participate.[26]

Legal State of Arbitration

Section 301 of the Taft-Hartley Amendments provided that suits for a violation of a contract between an employer and the labor organization may be brought to a United States District Court having jurisdiction over the parties. This clarified the enforceability of arbitrators' decisions through the court process. In 1957, the Supreme Court in the case of *Textile Workers Union of America* v. *Lincoln Mills of Alabama* further delineated the meaning of Section 301. In the **Lincoln Mills** **case**, the labor contracts included a grievance procedure with final arbitration as the terminal step in the process. The union had requested arbitration of several grievances, but the employer had refused. Therefore, the union brought suit under Section 301 of Taft-Hartley, compelling management to go to arbitration. The Court ruled that the intent of Section 301 was to ensure that management mainly bargained in good faith in a responsible manner as set forth in the amendments. Management was ordered to arbitrate, as provided in the contract. The Court also determined that the agreement

Exhibit 10.5 Demand for arbitration

To: _ABC Company_   Date: _10/8/88_
  (Name)
  (of part upon whom the Demand is made)
  (Address) _10 East Street_
  (City and state) _Pittsburgh, Pa_

The undersigned, a Party to an Arbitration Agreement contained in a written contract, dated _5/6/88_, which agreement provides as follows

(Quote arbitration clause)

Any dispute, claim or grievance arising out of or relating to the interpretation or application of this agreement shall be submitted to arbitration under the Voluntary Labor Arbitration Rules of the American Arbitration Association. The parties further agree that there shall be no suspension of work when such dispute arises and while it is in process of adjustment, or arbitration.

NATURE OF DISPUTE:

The union claims that _John Smith_ was unjustly discharged.

REMEDY SOUGHT:

Reinstatement with full back pay and all seniority rights to the date of discharge.

You are hereby notified that copies of our Arbitration Agreement and of this Demand are being filed with the American Arbitration Association at its _Pittsburgh_ Regional Office, with the request that it commence the administration of arbitration.

Signed _George Green_
  (Title) _XYZ Union, Local 777 International Representative_
  (Address) _122 West Street_
  (City and state) _Pittsburgh, Pa._
  (Telephone) _412-555-1890_

Source: Theodore Kheel, *Labor Law* (New York: Matthew Bender, 1983), p. 21, by permission of Matthew Bender.

to arbitrate grievance disputes is an agreement by the union not to interrupt production by use of a strike.

This decision established that federal courts should enforce collective bargaining agreements providing for binding arbitration on behalf of or against labor organizations and that industrial peace can be obtained by providing grievance arbitration. Therefore, in the landmark *Lincoln Mills* case, the United States Supreme Court held that the Taft-Hartley Amendments provide a forceful support for the use of binding arbitration.[27]

In 1960, the United States Supreme Court further clarified the legal status of the arbitrator's role with three decisions commonly referred to as the ***Steelworkers Trilogy* cases**. The significant aspects of these cases may be summarized as follows:

1.   The question of interpretation of the agreement is for the arbitrator, and the courts "have no business overruling him because their interpretation of the contract is different from his."[28]

2.   The function of the court is very limited when parties have agreed to submit all questions of contract interpretation to the arbitrator. The courts, therefore, have no business weighing the merits of the grievance, considering whether there is equity in a particular claim, or determining whether there is particular language in the written instrument supporting the claim.[29]

3.   The labor arbitrator's source of law is not confined to the expressed provisions of a contract. The industrial common law—the practices of the industry and the shop—is equally a part of the collective bargaining agreement, although not expressed in it. The labor arbitrator is usually chosen because of the parties' confidence in her knowledge of the common law of the shop and their trust in her personal judgment in considerations not expressed in the contract.[30]

Grievance Resolution and Title VII

The grievance resolution process in collective bargaining agreements is no longer free from legal challenges. The employer's authority to make decisions and take actions involving employee discipline and grievances was substantially altered by **Title VII** of the 1964 Civil Rights Act and the 1967 Age Discrimination Act. These laws gave employees the right to appeal to the Equal Employment Opportunity Commission and the courts in discriminatory cases involving disciplinary treatment. Title VII of the Civil Rights Act prohibits the use of race, color, religion, sex, or national origin as the basis of any employment decision. The Age Discrimination Act prohibits such actions involving persons age 40–70. A disciplinary penalty, even if provided for by a contract grievance clause, is governed by both of these laws.[31]

A landmark case, ***Alexander v. Gardner—Denver, Co.*** provided a Supreme Court decision on the possible conflict between the courts and grievance arbitration. The Court ruled that an arbitrator's decision would not keep an employee from utilizing the courts in matters involving possible discrimination, even though this avenue is closed in most grievance issues. However, the Court did provide that great weight should be given to the arbitrator's decision and that Title VII should supplement rather than replace the contractual grievance arbitration process.[32] In such cases the employer must prove that any disciplinary penalty was applied for legitimate reasons and in a nondiscriminatory manner.[33]

Grievance Mediation

While the use of mediation to resolve employee grievances is not new in labor relations, it is less visible than arbitration. **Grievance mediation** can be defined as "the intervention of an outside mediator into a potential or actual impasse over the interpretation or application of contract terms."[34] The process should be viewed as a means of reducing the need for arbitration since it is usually utilized as the last step *before* arbitration.

The former Director of the Federal Mediation and Conciliation Service, William Simkin, has suggested that mediation is a most useful means of avoiding the need for binding arbitration as a means of resolving grievances.[35] Reducing the use of expensive, time-consuming arbitration is one of the primary advantages of mediation. Small unions and employers might be particularly interested in using mediation as an alternative.[36] Also, mediation is *not* a decision process in which one side must lose. If a compromise is reached, it is far less likely that either side will bear the image of a loser as is often the case in arbitration. Mediation is not a final step, yet it allows the voluntary use of a neutral third party to help resolve the conflict without going to arbitration.

The bituminous coal industry illustrates one of the most successful uses of grievance mediation. The unionized sector of the industry has historically been plagued by wildcat strikes, expensive arbitration, and a great deal of labor unrest.[37] In the fall of 1980, several coal districts began experimenting with the use of mediation as the final step in a grievance resolution process before binding arbitration. After two six-month trial periods in four districts of the United Mine Workers of America, 89 percent of the 153 grievances taken to mediation were resolved before arbitration. Total savings were almost $100,000 and the average grievance was resolved three months earlier than it was under arbitration.[38]

The use of grievance mediation in the coal industry has been considered a success for several reasons. Most grievances were resolved regardless of the mechanism by which the grievance was brought to mediation (by request of one party or by mutual consent), and regardless of the nature of the issue. Mediation saved, on the average, $700 and three months per case in comparison to arbitration. Also, labor and management leaders greatly preferred the informality of mediation and their ability to control the outcome through negotiation. The key to the use of mediation was the willingness of both parties to *negotiate* a solution with the mediator and other party.[39]

The NLRB and other agencies should accept the intervention of grievance mediation if the following guidelines by mediator and arbitrator Mollie Bowers are followed:

1. Include the grievant in any and all meetings.
2. Hold meetings in reasonable times and locations.
3. Guard against any charge that the neutral party conspired to obtain a result that conflicts with case law, the contract, or statutory law.
4. The mediators should have a good working knowledge of laws, the contract language, and prevailing practices.
5. The parties *must* agree on the settlement.[40]

Summary

Grievance procedures and the arbitration of disputes provide an important tool to collective bargaining. Without such procedures, labor and management, as well as the community, would suffer greatly from economic recriminations, such as strikes and walkouts. Instead, issues such as a supervisor's disciplining an employee, as well as instances of "letting off steam," can be logically decided. The Supreme Court and the NLRB have given sufficient authority to agreed-upon grievance procedures and arbitration as a final step, making the practices commonplace and effective. However, specific steps to be utilized in employee grievances should be detailed in the labor agreement. Grievance mediation provides a useful alternative to arbitration as a final step and should be considered when possible.

CASE 10.1   *Union Official*

Reprinted with permission from Morris Stone, *Labor Grievances and Decisions* (New York: American Arbitration Association, 1970), pp. 64–67

For several days, trouble had been brewing in a household appliance manufacturing company over temporary transfers of employees, which the union thought were not being carried out in accordance with contractual requirements, and over the frequent scheduling of overtime. The collective bargaining agreement contained grievance procedures for resolving such disputes, but when a flare-up of anger occurred over still another temporary transfer, Fred R., an employee who was then acting president of the local, decided to call a union meeting at 4:00 P.M. that very day to see what action the members wanted him to take.

Four o'clock seemed to be the proper time because that was when the regular shift ended. It happened, however, that the company had scheduled two hours of overtime for most of the departments, and the union meeting was going to be a serious interference with production plans.

At first, management did not object to the calling of a union meeting during scheduled work time as such. An officer of the company only suggested that the meeting be postponed to another day, on which overtime had also been scheduled. When Fred refused to change his plans, he was told that employees who left work to attend the meeting might get warning slips. No other threat of discipline was made.

Fred remained adamant. The upshot was that about ninety-five employees—25 percent of the work force—clocked out at the end of the shift and performed none of the overtime for which they had been scheduled. For this, the company discharged Fred, citing a contractual provision which stated: "The union agrees that it will not, while the contract is in force, authorize or condone any strike, work stoppage, or slowdown of any kind over grievance and complaints."

"Fred knew he was violating the contract when he called a meeting during working hours," the plant manager said, when the discharge grievance reached arbitration. "The overtime had been properly scheduled in advance, and the contract is clear that stoppages of any kind are forbidden." He went on to explain to the arbitrator that the negotiators of the collective bargaining agreement had taken special pains to avoid irresponsible conduct by union officers. He cited a clause which stated that, in case of a strike over a matter which is subject to grievance procedure, a notice would be sent to the general president of the union, who would have to order the employees back to work. Those who failed to do so could be discharged.

The union's attorney answered that the meeting was not a work stoppage within the meaning of the contract, and

that it had been necessary to call it that very day if an illegal walkout was to be forestalled.

In the course of the arbitration hearing, it was also brought out that Fred, although an employee with long seniority, was inexperienced as a union president, that the regular union president had approved the stand Fred had taken, [and] that neither the regular president nor any employees other than Fred had been disciplined when new contract negotiations were under way.

After hearing all the evidence and arguments, the arbitrator declared the hearing closed and retired to write his decision.

Decision

The arbitrator agreed that the company had the right to discipline Fred under the circumstances, but he said that discharge was too severe. He reinstated Fred, but without back pay. The arbitrator held it against the company that its officer had acted indecisively by first urging that the meeting be rescheduled to another time, when it would also have interfered with production, and that the only words of caution were that employees would be subject to warning slips if they did not perform overtime. He wrote: "The grievant acted improperly and in violation of the agreement, but it must be found that while discipline was justified, discharge was not . . . . Considering the grievant's fine work record, and the type of penalty extended to others who participated in the meeting, it is found that discharge was an excessive penalty."

CASE 10.2   *Grievance Procedures*

Reprinted with permission from Morris Stone, *Labor Grievances and Decisions* (New York: American Arbitration Association, 1970), p. 192

For eighteen years, it had been the practice at an industrial instrument manufacturing plant for management and the union's grievance committee to meet one morning a week to discuss and decide all grievances on hand. As a rule, these meetings lasted from about 9:00 A.M. to noon, and the employees occupied in these discussions were paid by the company for those hours.

As time went on, the feeling grew on the part of the personnel manager that the meetings were dragging on unnecessarily and that if the company was not paying for the time, there would be a more businesslike atmosphere. Early in February 1964, therefore, management sent the union a letter informing it that henceforward grievance meetings would take place every other week during the last hour of the day. If meetings lasted longer than that, they would run into the employees' own time. The letter also indicated that if the "privilege" of one hour on company time should be abused, the company would reconsider the matter and perhaps abolish even that paid-for hour.

The personnel manager was wise enough in the ways of labor relations and arbitration to know that a long-standing practice is not easily abolished. But he was confident that past practice, by itself, would not stand in the way of what he was trying to accomplish, because the contract specifically said:

> No other agreements, understandings or practice contemporaneous or preexisting, except to the extent that they are

expressly included in this Agreement, shall be binding on either party. Similarly, no subsequent agreements, understandings, or practices shall be valid unless reduced to writing and signed by authorized representatives of both parties.

The grievance the personnel manager expected was quick in coming. It was, of course, based upon past practice, but not on that alone. The union pointed out that the grievance procedure set time limits for each step—one day for the first, two days for the second, and three days for the third step, unless the time is extended by mutual agreement.

"We've been extending the time limit freely, when necessary, because for eighteen years we had a reasonable procedure for grievance meetings," the business agent pointed out. "But if your new plan goes into effect, we will have to process every grievance immediately as it arises in accordance with time limits and we will not permit exceptions. That will be jungle warfare, not grievance settling."

Management refused to yield, and the matter finally went to arbitration.

Decision

Neither party won in full. Although there was no contractual obligation on the part of the company to schedule three-hour meetings on any particular day, the arbitrator explained, any changes that were put into effect would have to be consistent with the time limits of the grievance procedure clause which, as the union pointed out, allowed only six days for the first three steps. Furthermore, he wrote, the grievance procedure clause does not contemplate unilateral changes of meeting dates and times. "I believe that a reasonable implementation of (the grievance procedure clause) is that grievance meetings should be held during working hours as they have been so held in the past here and as is common industrial practice. The number of meetings obviously depends on the number and nature of the grievances to be heard. On the basis of the record and

the time limits of (the contract), I believe that the parties should schedule grievance meetings to be held within a maximum of three working hours but not necessarily in the morning." Although he upheld the grievance in general, the arbitrator rejected the union's view that this conclusion had to be reached because of past practice. The practice alone could not be binding, precisely for the reason the employer had asserted— the presence in the contract of the clause barring understandings which were not reduced to writing.

CASE 10.3 *Absenteeism*

Reprinted with permission from Morris Stone, *Employee Discipline and Arbitration* (New York: American Arbitration Association, 1977), pp. 34–36

From the very beginning of her employment at an automobile parts manufacturing plant, Mrs. H. was an absenteeism problem. The only difference between her case and that of others, however, was that her absences were always caused by genuine illnesses, accidents, and, during one year, a pregnancy.

According to the personnel department's records, in no year was Mrs. H. absent less than 2.5 percent of her working time. In some years, the absences were 20 percent and more. Her worst record of all was during the past year, when she was away from her job 46.4 percent of the time due to illness.

Management had talked to her from time to time about her attendance, but nothing had been said or done that would amount to an official warning that she would be discharged if her record did not improve.

Finally, the company notified Mrs. H. that she was discharged. The facts about Mrs. H.'s absences could not be

disputed, and the union made no attempt to do so. Mrs. H. found a basis for a grievance in the company's published rules.

"Your own rules state that employees will be warned for absenteeism before they are discharged," she said. "I was never warned officially, so you can't discharge me all of a sudden."

"That rule has nothing to do with your kind of absence," replied the personnel manager. "You were not AWOL, and we are not accusing you of irresponsible conduct. What would be the sense of warning you about something you couldn't help? It's just a question of the point having been reached where we can no longer stand for so much absence, even when caused by the best of reasons."

The union supported Mrs. H. and carried the case to arbitration. "Our contract provides for sick leaves of up to twenty-four months," the international representative pointed out. "That shows us that negotiators did not expect employees to be fired for getting sick."

"The sick leave provision was put into the contract for the benefit of an employee who might have a medical problem once in a while and then come back to work fully cured," was the reply of the company's attorney. He handed the arbitrator medical records showing that Mrs. H.'s illnesses were of a kind that could be expected to bother her now and then for the rest of her life.

After all the evidence was in, the arbitrator closed the hearing and wrote his award.

Decision

The company was upheld. It was irrelevant, the arbitrator stated, that a company rule provided for warnings prior to discharge. That rule was, as the com-

pany said, directed at absences which could be regarded as misbehavior or misconduct. In short, warning Mrs. H. could not result in any improvement because her absences were for causes beyond her control. This case, he said, did not present a problem of discipline. Rather, it was just a question of the time having come when the employer may discharge an employee who is unable to keep up a regular work schedule. He thought it worth noting that there was no reason to believe Mrs. H.'s attendance would be better in the future than it had been in the past. In answer to the union's argument about the sick leave clause, the arbitrator said that leaves were intended "for the now-and-then unfortunate employee" who gets sick. It does not "create a haven for the chronically ill."

CASE STUDY   *Work Schedules*

Adapted from *Thrifty Corp.* v. *United Food and Commercial Workers,* 85 LA 780 (Sept. 2, 1985)

Facts

The issue presented for arbitration is whether the company violated the contract by requiring the grievant to work weekends. The applicable sections of the contract are as follows:

> [t]he Employer *shall endeavor* to rotate *all* full-time employees on night and Sunday work, *except* when such rotation adversely affects the Employer's operation.

> *All* full-time clerks upon completion of one (1) year's service *shall be provided* with two (2) consecutive days off at least once each calendar month on either a Friday-Saturday, Saturday-Sunday or Sunday-Monday . . .

> It is further agreed that *no employee shall suffer any reduction* in rates or *general working conditions* by reason of the signing of this Agreement . . .

Section J of this same Article addresses "effective dates" and states:

> All economic terms and conditions of this Agreement shall be effective July 1, 1983 except as specified herein. *All operational terms and conditions which change previously existing practices shall be effective not later than the date of execution of this Agreement.*

Grievant was a full-time sales clerk who, when she was rehired by the company, had an oral agreement with the manager that she did not have to work weekends. She had been sought out for reemployment and worked from September 1972 until June of 1984 without working weekends. In June of 1984, the company began to rotate her schedule and required work on some weekend days. The grievant complained and she was told the new collective bargaining agreement required the rotation.

Lawsuit

The grievant filed her grievance. The company's position was as follows:

1. The previous contract had provided that the rotation was subject to the employee's agreement, but the new contract had been changed. In order to accommodate the union-requested mandatory guarantee of two days off together each month, the rotation schedule could not be subject to the agreement of individual employees.
2. The specific change in the contract cut off any past practice argument.
3. The contract provision (Article XXI, J) that changes in existing practices would be taking effect on a certain date confirmed that previous practices would be changed by the agreement.

The union position was as follows:

1. It was a mutually recognized and long-standing practice that the grievant did not work weekends.
2. Article VI, Section D of the agreement protected employees from any reduction of rates or general working conditions by the signing of the agreement. In this case, grievant's work schedule was a general working condition.
3. Continuing her present work schedule would not harm the company nor the other employees.

Questions

1. If you were the arbitrator, what would you decide, and why?
2. The union had bargained away an individual employee's right to agree to work weekends, and yet the union supported the grievant in this case. What reasons could the union give for this seemingly contradictory position?
3. The grievant in this case was seeking special treatment. What justification could there be for treating one member of the bargaining unit in a different manner? What problems could such treatment cause?

Key Terms and Concepts

Absenteeism (no-fault)

Alexander v. *Gardner—Denver, Co.*

Disciplinary procedures

Formal grievance

Grievance

Grievance mediation

Interest arbitration

Lincoln Mills case

Rights arbitration

Sources of employee grievances

Steelworkers Trilogy cases

Steps of a grievance procedure

Review Questions

1. What are the advantages of using a grievance process to settle disputes instead of other labor relations processes? How does a community benefit?
2. Why do grievance procedures contain several steps? What are the general functions of a grievance procedure?
3. How do nonunion grievance procedures compare with those commonly found in the unionized sector?
4. What are the factors that should be considered before a grievance is taken to arbitration?
5. According to U.S. Supreme Court decisions, what is the legal status of arbitration as a means of resolving grievances?
6. Describe a system of fair and effective disciplinary policies.
7. Compared with arbitration, what are the advantages and disadvantages of grievance mediation? What are some guidelines for the effective use of grievance mediation?

Endnotes

1. David Levin and Richard B. Peterson, "A Model for Measuring Effectiveness of the Grievance Process," *Monthly Labor Review* 106, no 4 (April 1983), pp. 47–49.
2. Dan R. Dalton and William D. Tudor, "Grievance Arbitration May Be Expensive, But What of the Alternative?" *Personnel Administrator* 26, no. 3 (March 1981), pp. 25–29.
3. Frank Elkouri and Edna A. Elkouri, *How Arbitration Works,* 3rd ed. (Washington, D.C.: Bureau of National Affairs, 1981), pp. 106–7.
4. Cudahy Packing Co., 7 LA G45, G46 (1947).
5. Elkouri and Elkouri, *How Arbitration Works,* pp. 109–10; and E.I. DuPont DeNemours and Co., 29 LA 646, 650 (1957).
6. Diamond Shamrock Corp., 55 LA 827 (1946).
7. BNA Editorial Staff, *Grievance Guide,* 6th ed. (Washington, D.C.: Bureau of National Affairs, 1978), p. 306.
8. Alexander's Personnel Providers, Inc., 68 LA 249 (1947).
9. Thomas B. Knight, "Feedback and Grievance Resolution," *Industrial and Labor Relations Review* 39, no. 4 (July 1986), pp. 585–598.
10. Harold Davey, Mario Bognanno, and David Estenson, *Contemporary Collective Bargaining,* 4th ed. (Englewood Cliffs, N.J.: Prentice-Hall, 1982), p. 169.
11. W. J. Usery, Jr., "Some Attempts to Reduce Arbitration Costs and Delays," *Monthly Labor Review* 105, no. 11 (Nov. 1972), p. 3.
12. See the Steelworkers Trilogy Cases: United Steelworkers of America v. Enterprise Wheel & Car Corp., 80 S.Ct. 1358, 34 LA 569 (1960); United Steelworkers of America v. American Mfg. Co., 363 U.S. 566–67 (1960); and United Steelworkers of America v. Warrior and Gulf Navigation Company, 363 U.S. 582 (1960).
13. Steven Briggs, "The Grievance Procedure," *Personnel Journal* 60, no. 6 (June 1981), pp. 471–74.
14. Stephen Cabot, *Labor Management Relations Manual* (Boston: Warren, Gorham, Lamont, 1979) chap. 16, pp. 1–2.
15. BNA Editorial Staff, *Grievance Guide,* pp. 4–5.
16. Cabot, *Labor Management,* chap. 16, pp. 3–5.

17. *Basic Patterns in Union Contracts,* 11th ed. (Washington, D.C.: The Bureau of National Affairs, 1986), pp. 2–12.

18. Steve Markham and Dow Scott, "Controlling Absenteeism: Union and Nonunion Differences," *Personnel Administrator* 30, no. 2 (Feb. 1985), pp. 87–102.

19. Ibid.

20. Frank E. Kuzmits, "What To Do About Long-Term Absenteeism," *Personnel Administrator* (Oct. 1986), pp. 93–100. See also Elkouri and Elkouri, *How Arbitration Works,* p. 545.

21. Maurice S. Trotta, *Arbitration of Labor-Management Disputes* (New York: American Management Association, 1974), p. 218.

22. David W. Ewing, "What Business Thinks About Employee Rights," Harvard Business Review 55, no. 5 (Sept.–Oct. 1977), pp. 81–94.

23. James P. Swann, "Formal Grievance Procedures In Non-union Plants," *Personnel Administrator* 26, no. 8 (Aug. 1981), pp. 66–70.

24. Elkouri and Elkouri, *How Arbitration Works,* p. 26.

25. Theodore Kheel, *Labor Law* (New York: Matthew Bender, 1983), chap. 24, p. 1.

26. Elkouri and Elkouri, *How Arbitration Works,* p. 44.

27. Textile Workers Union of America v. Lincoln Mills of Alabama, 353 U.S. 456(1957).

28. United Steelworkers of America v. Enterprise Wheel & Car Corp., 80 S.Ct. 1358, 34 LA 569 (1960).

29. United Steelworkers of America v. American Mfg. Co., 363 U.S. 566–67 (1960).

30. United Steelworkers of America v. Warrior and Gulf Navigation Company, 363 U.S. 582 (1960).

31. Edward L. Harrison, "Legal Restrictions on the Employer's Authority to Discipline," *Personnel Journal* 61, no. 2 (Feb. 1982), pp. 136–37.

32. 415 U.S. 36 (1978).

33. Harrison, "Legal Restrictions," p. 137.

34. Mollie H. Bowers, "Grievance Mediation: Another Route to Resolution," *Personnel Journal* 61, no. 2 (Feb. 1982), pp. 132–33.

35. William E. Simkin, *Mediation and the Dynamics of Collective Bargaining* (Washington, D.C.: Bureau of National Affairs, 1971), p. 300.

36. Bowers, "Grievance Mediation," p. 131.

37. Jeanne M. Brett and Steven B. Goldberg, "Wildcat Strikes in Bituminous Coal Mining," *Industrial and Labor Relations Review* 32, no. 4 (July 1979), pp. 467–83.

38. Jeanne M. Brett and Steven B. Goldberg, "Grievance Mediation in the Coal Industry: A Field Experiment," *Industrial and Labor Relations Review* 37, no. 1 (Oct. 1983), pp. 49–68.

39. Ibid., pp. 67–68.

40. Bowers, "Grievance Mediation," pp. 134–36.

The Arbitration Process

LABOR NEWS

Arbitration after a Contract Expires?

In 1986 the U.S. Court of Appeals, Eighth Circuit, ruled that a grievance was not arbitratable because it involved an employee's discharge more than a year after the union agreement had expired. The union, Teamsters Local 238, and management, CRST Inc., had not negotiated a new agreement, and the old one expired on June 30, 1982. In December 1982, the employer posted a schedule of wages, hours, and working conditions. The schedule included grievance arbitration on the matter of employee seniority.

Jeffrey Ottaway, a truck driver for CRST, was fired in July 1983 for reckless driving, and the Teamsters filed a grievance. After CRST refused to arbitrate the case, the Teamsters filed suit in federal court. The district court held that since there was no collective bargaining agreement in force in July 1983 the grievance was not arbitratable. The eighth circuit court noted, however, that the employer's posted schedule did not spe-

cifically abandon the contract's grievance arbitration procedure.

The eighth circuit's decision may appear to be contrary to the 1977 Nolde Brothers, Inc. *v.* Local 358, Bakery & Confectionary Worker's Union. *In the* Nolde *case the Supreme Court ruled that "there is a presumption that an arbitration clause survives the expiration of a union contract absent a clear indication to the contrary." The eighth circuit in its 1986 CRST decision noted this presumption of arbitrability. However, since the grievance occurred more than a year after the contract expired and the employer had, in the posted schedule, agreed only to arbitrate seniority rights cases, Ottaway's firing was not arbitratable.*

Source: "Contract Expires; Arbitration Denied," Resource *pamphlet (Alexandria, Va: American Society for Personnel Administration, Oct. 1986), p. 16, by permission of American Society for Personnel Administration.*

Arbitration is a negotiated procedure whereby labor and management agree to submit disputes arising under the terms of the contract to an impartial third party. The two parties accept as final and binding the decision of the independent arbitrator. Labor and management must also arbitrate any grievance if so requested by the other party.

Almost all collective bargaining agreements today provide for the arbitration of grievances that cannot be settled otherwise by labor and management. It is the dominant third party method of settling labor disputes and the key to the successful administration of day-to-day contracts. About 27,000 grievance arbitrations are conducted annually through the American Arbitration Association and the Federal Mediation and Conciliation Service.[1]

The concepts of collective bargaining, mediation, fact finding, and arbitration constitute stages in the relationship between labor and management. Collective bargaining is the first stage as labor and management agree upon a contract for a stipulated period of time. Conciliation, mediation, and fact finding can be considered intermediate stages. Grievance mediation helps resolve employee grievances.

Conciliation and mediation may be used to resolve conflicts between labor and management. The two are practically interchangeable, although mediation applies the intervention of an outside third party to help reach a compromise and conciliation is carried on without a third party. Mediators and conciliators do not make a decision but instead aid in the negotiation process and assist parties in coming to voluntary agreements.

Fact finding is also an intermediate process. It allows outside individuals to investigate and assemble all facts surrounding a dispute and issue a report of the evidence. The hope is that the process prevents labor and management from using retaliatory techniques such as strikes and walkouts until a report has been issued.

Arbitration is often the last stage of the relationship between labor and management. In the arbitration process the parties are compelled by their own agreement to accept the decision of an outside third party as *final* and *binding* in settling disputes. Arbitration can also be used as a conflict resolution technique after such techniques as conciliation and mediation have failed to produce an agreement.

Proponents of arbitration have claimed among its many advantages the saving of time, expense, and the reduction of labor strikes. The prolonged and technical procedures of the courts are not as well adapted to the particular needs of labor and management relations as arbitration. In general, the arbitration process is more informal than court proceedings. As a result, it can concentrate on key issues and usually resolve disputes faster than litigation.

The U.S. Supreme Court has acknowledged the superiority of arbitration in resolving labor/management disputes under collective bargaining agreements:

> The labor arbitrator performs functions which are not normal to the courts; the considerations which help him fashion judgments may indeed be foreign to the confines of courts. The parties expect that his judgments of a particular grievance will not only reflect what the contract says but, insofar as the collective bargaining agreement permits, such factors as the effect upon productivity of a particular result, its consequence to the morale of the shop, his judgment whether detentions will be heightened or diminished.

For the parties' objective in using the arbitration process is primarily to further their common goal of uninterrupted production under the agreement, to make the agreement meet their specialized needs. The ablest judge cannot be expected to bring the same experience and confidence to bear upon the determination of a grievance, because he cannot be similarly informed.[2]

The courts have further stressed that arbitrators' decisions, as long as they are based on interpretation of the contract, should be final and binding and not questioned by the courts. For example, in 1986 the seventh circuit upheld an arbitrator's decision and overturned a district court's reversal of that decision. In this case, an employee of E.I. DuPont de Nemours & Company, during a nervous breakdown, attacked fellow employees and damaged company property. The arbitrator had concluded the incident was a result of a mental breakdown (not drug use as the company contended) and would most likely not recur. The arbitrator's decisions, vacated by the district court, was upheld by the seventh circuit court. The court stated, "So long as the arbitrator interpreted the contract in making his award, his award must be affirmed even if he clearly misinterpreted the contract."[3]

Another advantage of arbitration over litigation is the final and binding provision contained in most agreements to arbitrate grievances. This provides a final step for settling labor disputes in comparison to the court process requiring a series of lengthy appeals and many steps before a final decision. In addition, the technical rules of evidence found in the courtroom need not be applied to the proceedings. Arbitration hearings are less formal than litigation and the advocates need not have legal training.

Courts of general jurisdiction are not usually well-versed in problems unique to labor-management grievances. Arbitrators are presumed to be familiar with the needs and techniques of the industry, and therefore, both parties feel more confident that they will be able to adapt to the awards of the arbitrator.[4]

In our society, the use of voluntary arbitration to settle labor-management disputes provides an important role in minimizing disruptions of the productions of goods and services. It serves as a safety valve for our capitalistic system. Society as a whole benefits greatly when disputes are arbitrated quickly without the use of strikes or walkouts.

Selecting the Arbitrator

Both labor and management pay the arbitration fees and have a hand in the choice of arbitrator; he is not an outside party imposed upon them to resolve disputes. The arbitrator's jurisdiction evolves from the contract negotiated by the two parties. Therefore, the arbitrator's performance must generally be satisfactory; the parties can dispense with an incompetent arbitrator. The arbitrator is well aware that he provides a service for a fee and is expected to meet certain professional standards.

Because of the very real need to keep both parties satisfied with arbitration decisions, arbitrator decisions and awards are far from uniform on almost any issue.[5] However, no two grievance situations are the same.

The arbitrator may be a permanent umpire chosen beforehand by labor and management to decide disputes arising during the life of the collective bargaining agreement. However, most arbitrations take place on an ad hoc basis, with arbitrators selected to hear disputes case by case.

Collective bargaining agreements with arbitration normally also provide for the selection process of arbitrators. If a permanent arbitrator is not designated in the contract, then an impartial agency is often agreed upon as a source of arbitrators. The American Arbitration Association and Federal Mediation and Conciliation Service are two agencies that are the most frequent sources of arbitrators.

The American Arbitration Association has developed this process for selecting an arbitrator:

1.   On receiving the demand for arbitration or submission agreement, the tribunal administrator (a staff member of the association) acknowledges receipt thereof and sends each party a copy of a specially prepared list of proposed arbitrators. In drawing up this list, he is guided by the statement of the nature of the dispute. Basic information about each arbitrator is appended to the list.

2.   Parties are allowed seven days to study the list, cross off any names objected to, and number the remaining names in the order of preference. If parties want more information about a proposed arbitrator, such information is gladly given upon request.

3.   Where parties are unable to find a mutual choice on the list, the association will submit additional lists, at the request of both parties.

4.   If, despite all efforts to arrive at a mutual choice, parties cannot agree upon an arbitrator, the association will make an administrative appointment. But in no case will an arbitrator whose name was crossed out by either party be so appointed.[6]

The arbitrator would be required to follow the contract language regardless of any personal opinion as to the reasonableness of the agreement language if the intent of the provision is clear. However, the language is often ambiguous, and the arbitrator must interpret the provision in question.

In interpreting contract language, two **role models for arbitrators** have been developed. One role model sees the arbitrator as a judge or umpire. Under this model the arbitrator, as a judge, reviews the arguments and proofs presented by the parties and makes a decision according to the rules imposed by the contract.[7] The second role model is much broader. The arbitrator's role is that of a mediator or impartial chairman, and is primarily to help resolve the dispute rather than decide which party was right or wrong under the contract. The fact that the future relationship of both parties would be stronger if they resolve their own disputes is emphasized. The arbitrator issues a binding decision only as a last resort.[8] Today the latter role is more often viewed as proper for a grievance mediator, as discussed in Chapter 10. Arbitrators are more likely to serve as judges. Was the arbitrator in Case 11.1 more of a judge than a mediator in resolving the disputed contract language?

Qualifications of Arbitrators

Arbitrators are not required to have any specific educational or technical training unless specified by the collective bargaining agreement. However, if rigid qualifications are required, it may become very difficult to find an available arbitrator.

Various characteristics including experience, education, occupation, and visibility have been identified as affecting arbitrator selection. Both labor and management prefer arbitrators with specific attributes. Research has shown that age and experience are the most significant *demographic* factors affecting arbitration decisions. Surprisingly, though, labor lawyers have not been able to distinguish between the decisions of experienced and inexperienced arbitrators.[9]

In addition to these demographic variables, other variables affecting arbitrator selection include *visibility,* such as public speaking and professional association membership, and *past arbitration decisions.* All three appear to determine which arbitrator might be selected for a case. Empirical data indicate that visibility in the community may be the single most important variable.[10]

Arbitrators are secured from a wide variety of backgrounds and include attorneys, judges, and university professors. Elkouri and Elkouri outline some general **qualifications of an arbitrator**:

1. *Impartiality*   While no one can be absolutely free from bias or prejudice, the arbitrator is expected to divest himself from personal inclinations during negotiations, even though he decides cases according to his own judgment. The element of honesty and impartiality is the most critical, and the arbitrator must always be able to be up front with both parties. Otherwise, he might not be selected again.

2. *Integrity*   Arbitrators are expected to be of the highest integrity. Both parties can review backgrounds and affiliations of prospective arbitrators; personal, financial, or business interests in the affairs of either party are primary considerations. The Code of Ethics for Arbitrators requires the arbitrator to disclose any association or relation that might reasonably bring any doubt to her objectivity. Records of past decisions and if the arbitrator has expressed strong opinions in favor of either labor or management are also reviewed. Arbitrators are expected to exercise fairness and good judgment in issuing awards, and not just please both sides by splitting awards.

3. *Ability and expertise*   A labor-management arbitrator should have a broad background, experience, and education. Maturity of judgment and a quick, analytical mind are also necessary. The arbitrator is not expected to be a subject matter specialist; such an expert may be difficult or impossible to find. Both parties may prefer someone with general business or financial expertise.

4. *Legal training*   Labor-management arbitrators often are lawyers. Legal training may help an arbitrator to be objective and to analyze and evaluate facts without personal bias or extraneous evidence. However, all lawyers do not make good arbitrators, nor are all good arbitrators lawyers.[11]

Tripartite Arbitration Board

The labor agreement may provide for multiple arbitrators. A **tripartite arbitration board** usually has one or more members selected by management, an equal number of members selected by labor, and a neutral member who serves as chairperson. The labor and management members act as partisans or advocates for their respective sides and, in essence, the neutral chairperson becomes a single arbitrator.

Tripartite boards sometimes do not reach decisions unanimously. Collective bargaining agreements often provide that a majority award of the board is final and binding. Some agreements may even give the neutral member the sole right and responsibility for making the final decision. The advantage of using a tripartite board rather than a single arbitrator is to provide the neutral member with valuable advice and assistance from the partisan members. Each party may be able to give a more realistic and informed picture of the issues involved to the neutral arbitrator than to formally present these issues itself. The disadvantage of such a board, of course, is the additional time and expense incurred.[12]

The following is an example of a panel selection procedure:

ARTICLE 27
Section 2
If the issue cannot be resolved by the Joint Conference Committee, a panel of seven (7) impartial arbitrators will be promptly secured from the Federal Mediation and Conciliation Service. The employer and the union shall each have the right to reject one panel of impartial arbitrators, but they must select an arbitrator from the third panel of arbitrators if they cannot agree to select from the first or second panels. The arbitrator will be selected by each party striking an equal number of arbitrators from the panel. The remaining individual shall be the arbitrator and his decision shall be final and binding on the employer, the union, and the employees. Expenses incurred in any arbitration under the provision of this article will be borne equally by the employer and the union.[13]

Determining Arbitrability

If both parties in a dispute submit the dispute to arbitration, there is no question of **arbitrability** since a submission by both parties identifies their agreement to go to arbitration. However, if only one party invokes the arbitration clause in a collective bargaining agreement by notice of intent to arbitrate a dispute, the other party may resist the intent to arbitrate on the grounds that the dispute is not arbitrable. Such a challenge to arbitrability is presented either to the arbitrator or to the courts. While most questions of arbitrability are left in the hands of the arbitrator, they may be taken to the courts. The courts may be involved with arbitrability in one of several ways as outlined by Elkouri.

1. The party challenging arbitrability may seek a temporary injunction or stay of arbitration, pending determination of arbitrability.
2. The party demanding arbitration may seek a court order compelling the other party to arbitrate where the applicable law upholds agreements to arbitrate future disputes; the latter party then raises the issue of arbitrability.
3. The issue of arbitrability may be considered when an award is taken to court for review or enforcement, unless the parties have clearly vested the arbitrator with exclusive and final right of determining arbitrability, or unless the right to

challenge arbitrability is held by the court to have been otherwise waived under the circumstances of the case.[14]

The Supreme Court in the *Warrior and Gulf* case declared that congressional policy in favor of settlement of disputes through arbitration restricts the judicial process and strictly confines it to questions of whether the reluctant party agreed to arbitrate the grievance in the collective bargaining contract. A labor-management agreement to arbitrate therefore should not be denied unless a court is absolutely positive that the arbitration clause in the collective bargaining contract is not susceptible to interpretation covering the dispute. Any doubt in questions of arbitrability should be *resolved in favor of the grievance being arbitrated.*[15] The case study at the end of this chapter, however, illustrates a necessary exception to this rule.

Questions of arbitrability are most often left up to the arbitrator, who tries to avoid or delay the expense of court proceedings. Usually the collective bargaining agreement itself specifies that the arbitrator is to rule on questions of arbitrability as well as on the merits of the dispute. It is usually felt that a preliminary decision relating to arbitrability by the arbitrator is an inherent part of his duty. Procedurally, however, the arbitrator determines whether he rules on arbitrability before the presentation of the merits of the case or reserves his ruling after the full case has been presented. Therefore, the arbitrator's authority is derived from the collective bargaining agreement. Even if the courts are utilized to decide whether the contract obligates both parties to arbitrate a grievance, once that determination is made, the arbitrator decides if a particular grievance should be resolved within the framework of the contract. In other words, the court generally decides whether the union and employer have agreed to arbitration. But the arbitrator determines whether a particular grievance under a contract is arbitrable. The arbitrator also decides all procedural issues pertaining to the grievance.[16]

Hearing Procedures

The arbitrator fixes the date of the hearing after consulting with both sides and makes the necessary arrangements. The hearing procedure for the arbitration of a grievance normally follows a certain series of steps:

1. An opening statement by the initiating party (except that the company goes first in discharge or discipline cases)
2. An opening statement by the other side
3. The presentation of evidence, witnesses, and arguments by the initiating party
4. A cross-examination by the other side
5. The presentation of evidence, witnesses, and arguments by the defense
6. A cross-examination by the initiating party
7. A summation by the initiating party (optional)
8. A summation by the other side (optional)
9. Filing of briefs (optional)
10. The arbitrator's award[17]

The Opening Statement

The opening statement lays the groundwork for the testimony of witnesses and helps the arbitrator understand the relevance of oral and written evidence. The statement should clearly identify the issue, indicate what is to be proved, and specify the relief sought. Sometimes parties will present the opening statement in writing to the arbitrator with a copy given to the other side. Usually, however, the opening statement is also made orally so that appropriate points can be highlighted and given emphasis if to the advantage of the presenting side.[18]

Rules of Evidence

Strict legal **rules of evidence** are not usually observed unless expressly required by the parties. The arbitrator determines how the hearing is run and how evidence is presented.

> In arbitration, the parties have submitted the matter to persons whose judgment they trust, and it is for the arbitrators to determine the weight or credibility of evidence presented to them without restrictions as to rules of admissibility which would apply in a court of law.[19]

In Case 11.2, the arbitration involved rules of evidence traditionally used in criminal actions.

Generally, any pertinent information or testimony is acceptable as evidence if it helps the arbitrator understand and decide the issue. Arbitrators are usually extremely receptive to evidence, giving both parties a free hand in presenting any type they choose to strengthen and clarify their case.[20] The arbitrator decides how much weight to give evidence in making her decision.

Presenting Documents

Most arbitration cases provide for the presentation of essential documents. Most important, of course, are those sections of the collective bargaining agreement that have some bearing on the grievance. Other documentation would include records of settled grievances, jointly signed memoranda, official minutes of contract negotiation meetings, personnel records, office reports, and organizational information. Documentary evidence is usually presented to the arbitrator with a copy made available to the other party but is also explained orally to emphasize its importance.[21]

Examination of Witnesses

Each party depends upon the direct examination of its own witnesses during an arbitration hearing. The witness is identified and qualified as an authority on the facts to which he will testify and is generally permitted to tell his story without interruptions and without the extensive use of leading questions as in legal cases. The witness in an arbitration proceeding would rarely be cut off, and some arbitrators even ask the witness if he would want to add anything to the testimony as relevant to the case. Arbitrators generally uphold the right of cross-examination of witnesses, but not as strongly as courts.

The arbitrator also does not usually limit the rights of parties to call witnesses from the other side for cross-examination. However, opinion is split concerning the right of the company to call the grievant as a witness. One side believes that the application of the privilege against self-incrimination should apply in arbitration proceedings, even though there is no applicable constitutional privilege. The opposing view is that the privilege against self-incrimination in the field of criminal law is not present in grievance cases.[22]

The Summation

Before the hearing is closed by the arbitrator, both sides are given equal time for closing statements. This is the last chance for each side to convince the arbitrator and to refute all the other side's arguments. Each side can summarize the situation and emphasize relevant facts and issues.[23]

The Arbitrator's Award and Opinion

The **award** is the arbitrator's decision in the grievance case. Awards are usually short, are presented in written format, and are signed by the arbitrator. Even if an oral award is rendered, the arbitrator usually produces a written award later. Awards of arbitration boards must be signed by all members if a unanimous decision is required; otherwise, it must be signed by a majority.

The arbitrator will also often present a written **opinion** stating the reasons for her decision. This opinion is separate from the award and clearly indicates where the opinion ends and the award begins. It is generally felt that a well-reasoned opinion can contribute greatly to the acceptance of the award. The U.S. Supreme Court has emphasized the need of arbitrator opinions and encouraged their use.[24]

Case Preparation

When a grievance has reached the point of arbitration, both parties have probably gone through several steps of discussion in negotiation to resolve the issue. The issues disputed by the parties usually have been fairly well defined by the time the case reaches arbitration. To prepare the case for arbitration, the American Arbitration Association recommends the following steps in hearing preparation:

1. Study the original statement of the grievance and review its history through every step of the grievance machinery.

2. Carefully examine the initiating grievance paper (submission or demand) to help determine the arbitrator's role. It might be found, for instance, that while the original grievance contains many elements, the arbitrator, under the contract, is restricted to resolving only certain aspects.

3. Review the collective bargaining agreement from beginning to end. Often clauses which at first glance seem to be unrelated to the grievance will be found to have some bearing.

4. Assemble all necessary documents and papers at the hearing. Where feasible, make postdated copies for the arbitrator and the other party. If some of the documents are in the possession of the other party, ask in advance that they be brought to the arbitration. Under some arbitration laws, the arbitrator has authority to subpoena documents and witnesses if they cannot be made available in any other way.

5. If you think the arbitrator should visit the plant or job site for on-the-spot investigation, make plans in advance. The arbitrator should be accompanied by representatives of both parties.

6. Interview all witnesses. They should certainly understand the whole case and particularly the importance of their own testimony.

7. Make a written summary of each proposed witness's testimony. This will be useful as a checklist at the hearing to make sure nothing is overlooked.

8. Study the other side of the case. Be prepared to answer the opposing evidence and arguments.

9. Discuss your outline of the case with others in your organization. Another's viewpoint will often disclose weak spots or previously overlooked details.

10. Read as many articles and published awards as you can on the general subject matter and dispute. While awards by other arbitrators or other parties have no binding present value, they may help clarify the thinking of parties and arbitrators alike.[25]

On the basis of its extensive experience in administering arbitration proceedings, the American Arbitration Association has concluded that a party may harm its case by the following practices:

1. Using arbitration and arbitration costs as a harassing technique.
2. Overemphasis of the grievance by the union or exaggeration of an employee's fault by management.
3. Reliance on a minimum of facts and a maximum of arguments.
4. Concealing essential facts; distorting the truth.
5. Holding back books, records, and other supporting documents.
6. Tying up proceedings with legal technicalities.
7. Introducing witnesses who have not been properly instructed on demeanor and on the place of their testimony in the entire case.
8. Withholding full cooperation from the arbitrator.
9. Disregarding the ordinary rules of courtesy and decorum.
10. Becoming involved in arguments with the other side. The time to try to convince the other party is before arbitration, during grievance processing. At the arbitration hearing, all efforts should be concentrated on convincing the arbitrator.

Source: Reprinted with permission from *How Arbitration Works,* 3rd ed., by Frank Elkouri and Edna Asper Elkouri (Washington, D.C.: Bureau of National Affairs, 1981), p. 249. Copyright © 1981 by the Bureau of National Affairs, Inc., Washington, D.C.

Contractual Issues

While both labor and management strive to produce a contract that results in as few disagreements as possible, contractual disputes will arise. Some of these, of course, end up in arbitration after other avenues for resolution have been explored. Historically, certain **contractual issues** seem to develop an agreed-upon solution mechanism that eventually enables both parties to resolve their dispute before arbitration is needed. However, many issues simply cannot be easily resolved with *any* contractual language and therefore end up going to arbitration for final resolution. Some of the most commonly arbitrated issues are discussed in the following paragraphs.

Just Cause

Most collective bargaining agreements provide that management has the right to discipline or discharge employees for **just cause**. While most labor and management negotiators can agree upon general concept, specifying exactly what constitutes just cause appears impossible. Some contracts will specify specific grounds that constitute just cause and usually also include other less specific provisions that are open to dispute. The inability to specify exactly what employee offenses constitute just cause is a major reason why employee discipline and discharge procedures continue to be one of the most frequently arbitrated contractual issues. The overwhelming majority of discipline cases also involve disagreement over the concept of just cause.[26] Case 11.3 presents an unusual set of circumstances leading to an employee discharge later found to be unjust. An example of the just cause provisions appears in the *Agreement* between the National Conference of Brewery and Soft Drink Workers and Teamsters Local No. 745 and the Schlitz Brewing Company.

> ARTICLE V
> *Section 1*
> The right of the company to discharge, suspend, or otherwise discipline in a fair and impartial manner for just and sufficient cause is hereby acknowledged. Whenever employees are discharged, suspended, or otherwise disciplined, the union and the employees shall promptly be notified in writing of such discharge, suspension, or other disciplinary action and the reason therefore. No discipline, written notice of which has not been given to the union and the employee, nor any discipline which has been given more than twelve months prior to the current act, shall be considered by the company in any subsequent discharge, suspension, or other disciplinary action.
> *Section 2*
> If the union is dissatisfied with the discharge, suspension, or other disciplinary action, the questions as to whether the employee was properly discharged, suspended, or otherwise disciplined shall, upon request of the union, be reviewed in accordance with the grievance procedure set forth . . . . [27]

The criteria used by arbitrators for just cause will obviously vary from case to case and from arbitrator to arbitrator. However, the Bureau of National Affairs has provided tests for determining whether a company has just cause for disciplining an employee.

1. *Adequate warning*   Is the employee given adequate, oral or printed, warning as to the consequences of his conduct? Employees should be warned by the employer as to punishments either in the contract, handbook, or other means in disciplinary cases. Certain conducts such as insubordination, drunkenness, or stealing are considered so serious the employee is expected to know they will be punishable.

2. *Prior investigation*   Did management investigate the case before administering the discipline? Thorough investigation should have normally been made before the decision to discipline. When immediate action is required, the employee should be suspended pending investigation with the understanding that he will be returned to his job and paid for time lost if found not guilty.

3. *Evidence*   Did the investigation produce substantial evidence or proof of guilt? It is not required that evidence be conclusive or beyond reasonable doubt, except when the misconduct is of such a criminal nature it seriously impairs the accused's chances for future employment.

4. *Equal treatment*   Were all employees judged by the same standards, with rules applied equally? The same penalty, however, may not be always given since it may be a second offense, or other factors may logically suggest a different punishment.

5. *Reasonable penalty*   Was the penalty reasonably related to the seriousness of the offense and the past record of the employee? The level of the offense should be related to the level of the penalty, and the employee's past record should be taken under consideration.

6. *Rule of reason*   Is the disciplinary action fairly administered? Even in the absence of specific provisions, a collective bargaining agreement protects employees against unjust discipline. Employees may reasonably challenge any company procedure that threatens to deprive employees of their negotiated rights.

7. *Internal consistency*   Was management enforcement of the rule or procedure consistent? The company should not electively enforce codes of conduct against certain employees. Enforcement should be consistent, whether the company disciplines on a case-by-case basis or uses a handbook. The *past practice* of management in similar cases will be carefully reviewed by an arbitrator.[28]

The more common remedies used by arbitrators in overturning management actions in discipline and discharge cases include reinstatement with back pay, without back pay, or with partial back pay, with other rights and privileges remaining unimpaired; commuting the discharge to suspension for a specified period of time, or further reducing the penalty to only a reprimand or a warning; reversing management's assessment of suspension because the arbitrator believes the penalty is too severe. Back pay will usually be ordered consistent with the elimination of suspension.[29] Most arbitrators apply accepted common law with contracts not specifying just cause. This usually means that management action is subjected to tests of prior standards and procedural requirements. If the action meets both criteria, it will generally be found to be a valid prerogative of management.[30]

Seniority Recognition

The most severe limitation of managerial discretion is perhaps the negotiated requirement of seniority recognition. It significantly reduces the employer's control over the work force and the filling of positions. **Seniority** is commonly understood to mean the length of service with the employer either on a company-wide basis or within the particular unit of the organization. People retain their jobs according to their length of service with the employer or within the particular unit and will be promoted to better jobs on the same basis.

The purpose of seniority is to provide maximum security to workers with the longest continuous service.[31] Arbitrators often hear cases involving loss of seniority or management's failure to promote the most senior person. Collective bargaining agreements often provide sections describing the loss of seniority similar to this agreement between General Motors Corporation and the United Auto Workers.

> *Section 64*
> Seniority shall be broken for the following reasons: (a) if the employee quits, (b) if the employee is discharged, (c) if the employee is absent for three working days without properly notifying the management, unless a satisfactory reason is given, (d) if the employee fails to return to work within three working days after being notified to report for work, and does not give a satisfactory reason, [and] (e) if the employee is laid off for a continuous period equal to the seniority he had acquired at a time of such layoff.[32]

The agreement commonly requires management to prepare seniority lists to be made available to all employees. The seniority list usually contains each employee's name, occupational group, plant seniority date, and new seniority date where applicable. If the contract does not require the posting of a seniority list, the employer may be held to be under an implied obligation to make proper and reasonable disclosure of seniority. An arbitrator has ruled the following:

> An employee—and the union as his representative—clearly has a right to be informed of a seniority date and length of continuous service credited to him on the company's records. By the same token, since most seniority issues involve a comparison of the relative rights of two or more employees, the employee—and the union as his representative—has a right to know the seniority dates and length of continuous service credited to the other employees in the seniority unit applicable to him at any given time. The only accurate source of such information is obviously the company. It has the records. It is initiating the various transfers, promotions, demotions, thumps, layoffs, recalls, etc. . . . which are daily causing changes in those records.[33]

Incompetence

Arbitrators in general recognize management's right to set reasonable production standards and to enforce such standards through discipline. However, incompetence generally should not be treated the same as a disciplinary problem since proper remedies usually include additional training, transfer, or demotion instead of warnings, suspension, or discharge. In incompetence cases arising over the reasonableness of management's action, arbitrators will consider the adequacy of the employee's training, supervision, and ability to perform the job. The arbitrator must decide if the contract has been followed. While both labor and management have the responsibility for producing evidence supporting their case, the burden of proof is usually on management to verify the employee's incompetence.[34]

The discharge or severe discipline of an employee for incompetence will not likely be upheld by an arbitrator under the following conditions:

1. The charge of incompetence is not properly investigated or substantiated.

2. The employee is not given adequate warning and opportunity to improve his or her performance.
3. Other employees with equally poor performance records are not treated in the same manner.
4. The employee shows substantial improvement after being warned.
5. Poor work is due to inability, and there is other work available that the employee can perform.[35]

Holiday Pay Eligibility

In recent years, most contracts have come to provide for **paid holidays eligibility**. Certain contract eligibility requirements must be fulfilled to receive pay for the holiday. Since the creation of Monday holidays by the federal government has increased labor's demand for three-day weekends, employers have become even more concerned with attendance problems due to employees trying to stretch three-day weekends into four days, substantially disrupting production. An example of a common eligibility requirement is provided in the labor agreement between the National Conference of Brewery and Soft Drink Workers and the Schlitz Brewing Company.

> ARTICLE XII
> *Holidays*
> . . . to be eligible for holiday pay, an employee must work his full shift on the day before the holiday and his full shift on the day after the holiday. Approved absence on either of these days shall not disqualify the employee for holiday pay. Holiday pay shall be at the straight time rate, excluding shift differentials.[36]

Because paid holidays represent one of the most costly benefits given to the employees, management often will pursue disagreements to arbitration. The most common dispute concerning paid holidays involves the eligibility of employees. Other disputes concern avoidance of *holiday stretching;* that is, requiring work on the day before or after the holiday. Holiday pay is generally given to workers who fail to meet work requirements through no fault of their own. For example, an employee of the John Deere Tractor Co. was awarded holiday pay by an arbitrator even though he had left work a half hour early the day before the holiday so he could catch a train. The arbitrator felt the employee was simply making the holiday available.[37] Also, if a contract provides holiday pay without restriction, laid-off workers continue to be employees of the company and are entitled to the holiday pay. Still another disputed topic is holidays falling on nonwork days. These must be paid for if the contract designates certain days as paid holidays and does not limit pay to holidays falling on scheduled work days.[38]

Arbitrators generally agree that the common attendance requirement for employees to work the days before and after the holiday are not limited to the days immediately preceding and following the holiday. For example, a contract stated that holiday pay would be provided if the employee worked the work day previous to and following the holiday. The holiday fell on a Thursday and the plant was closed for the rest of the week. The employee was denied pay for the holiday because he was absent the following Monday, the next scheduled work day. The arbitration board upheld the company's position that the days preceding and following the holiday do not have to fall on the same work week.[39] In general, the prior and following work days are considered to be the last and first scheduled work days surrounding the holiday.

Management Rights

A common issue in arbitration cases is **management rights** in the areas not expressly discussed in the contract. Often it is believed that in the absence of restrictive or specific provisions, managerial rights are retained by management. However, arbitrators do not always take the view that management retains *all* unstated rights.

The following contract provides a general statement of management rights covering items such as the size of the work force and operational methods.

> ARTICLE V
> *Management Rights*
> (a) It is the intent of parties to this agreement that the employee will furnish a full fair day's work for a full fair day's pay. (b) Management shall be the sole determiner of the size and composition of the work force. Management shall have the prerogative of controlling its operations, inducing new or improved methods or facilities, subject to the limitations set forth in this agreement. (c) Management shall retain all rights and privileges which are not specifically abridged by the terms of this agreement.[40]

Arbitrators usually impose a standard of reasonableness and good faith on managerial actions that adversely affect employees, whether or not the contract provides management's discretion in the area. Arbitrators generally agree that the union cannot block technological improvement, even if the work force is reduced, unless there is a specific contract restriction. Likewise, arbitrators generally give management broad authority in assigning work to employees and in controlling plant operations and procedures, unless specifically restricted by the contract.[41]

The following summarizes points to consider in management rights cases:

1. If a company brought up a subject in negotiations but failed to get its demands written into the contract, it may have lost its right to take unilateral action in that area.
2. Management generally is conceded to have the right to make technological improvements, even if some workers are adversely affected, unless its contract says otherwise.
3. Similarly, a company normally has the right to eliminate a job it no longer considers necessary. The union will be watchful, though, to make sure the duties of the job aren't in fact transferred to other workers.
4. Even in the absence of a contract clause forbidding supervisors to do bargaining unit work, arbitrators sometimes have held that they could not do such work if people in the bargaining unit would be adversely affected.[42]

Summary

The arbitration process has been developed and refined over many years. The selection of an arbitrator or board of arbitrators is generally specified in the labor agreement. The hearing procedure, however, which is not bound by legal precedent, is quite flexible and is subject to the arbitrator's discretion. The courts have generally left the questions of arbitrability and case decisions to arbitrators.

A great variety of important and complex issues end up in arbitration. The issue of just cause for employee discipline or discharge is difficult to define within the contract and in most cases involves emotional situations. Seniority is another deceptively simple yet important contractual issue. Disagreements over incompetence, holiday pay, and management rights are also common arbitration subjects. The increased use of arbitration in recent years has greatly reduced the occurrence of strikes and similar actions to settle labor disputes.

CASE 11.1 Contract Language

Reprinted with permission from Morris Stone, *Labor Grievances and Decisions* (New York: American Arbitration Association, 1970), p. 17

It is customary, in American industrial relations, for employers to guarantee their employees a minimum of four hours' work or wages on any day they report as scheduled and find no work available. The purpose is twofold: to compensate employees for the trouble of appearing for work, and to penalize the company for managerial thoughtlessness or carelessness. By the same token, the typical reporting pay clause also includes certain exceptions, intended to relieve management of reporting pay obligations when the reason for the cancellation of work orders was beyond the control of the company.

At a mine owned by a steel company, the company's obligations to provide work or wages was expressed in this language:

Whenever an employee reports for work on any regularly scheduled working day, he shall be guaranteed by the company, except in cases of breakdowns or other conditions beyond the control of the company, at least four hours of work that day or its equivalent in pay at his regular rate unless said employee has been notified before his scheduled starting time not to report for work.

This clause seemed very clear, and no doubt the negotiators were quite certain its meaning could not be in dispute. But a dispute did arise one day, as a result of a fairly typical combination of circumstances.

At about eleven o'clock one night, a hoist broke down because of an electrical failure. The company's maintenance men set to work immediately, hoping to effect the repairs before the day shift was due to arrive at 8 A.M. By three o'clock, they decided to call the service department of the electric utility company.

It was not until ten o'clock in the morning that the servicemen located the burned-out resistor coil that had caused all the trouble. By that time, the day shift had come and gone, without doing any work.

Management did not think the men were entitled to any reporting pay because the circumstance making work impossible seemed clearly "beyond the control of the company." The union took a different view. It insisted that only timely notification of the shift cancellation could relieve management of its obligation to give reporting pay.

"Why do you suppose we put language into the contract about conditions beyond the control of the company if it was not to cover exactly such situations?" the company's attorney demanded to know, when the matter was argued before the hearing. Moreover, he pointed out, cancellation of the shift was not feasible, because the company hoped all along to repair the equipment before the morning.

"And why do you suppose we put language into the contract about notification before the start of the shift?" replied the union's attorney. "The fact is that you let the men come in even though you must have known by five or six o'clock that you would have to send them right home again."

"That's your interpretation of events, not ours," management retorted. "In any case, the machine breakdown is an absolute defense against reporting-pay claims, and notification has nothing to do with it."

Finally, the arbitrator declared the hearing closed and retired to write his decision.

Decision

The union won. The arbitrator said that the contract could not be construed, as the company would have liked, on the basis of the syntax of the reporting pay clause alone. This clause must be understood in the broader context of the parties' total agreement, evaluated by customary relevant standards in collective bargaining. He said that employees who were already at work when the machine broke down would not have to be given the four-hour guarantee (assuming they had not yet worked that many hours when the breakdown occurred), but those who surely could have been notified in sufficient time not to report for the next scheduled shift were in a different position. To uphold the company, he concluded, would be to say that the company could permit employees to come in for days on end even though a major breakdown made work impossible. He concluded: "So long as the company voluntarily chooses not to 'unschedule' or otherwise to lift the requirement upon employees who are under a duty to report for work, it owes them the correlative duty to provide the four hours of some work or of equivalent pay when they faithfully comply by being on hand."

CASE 11.2   *Rules of Evidence*

Reprinted with permission from Morris Stone, *Employee Discipline and Arbitration* (New York: American Arbitration Association, 1977), p. 9

On arriving for work one morning, the supervisor of the shipping department saw a deep, ugly gouged-out area on the main door to the storage space and on the cinder blocks adjoining the door. He called the plant manager, and the two of them began an investigation to determine how it happened.

Actually, one didn't need to be a detective to find the cause. When one lined up the company's fork lift trucks against the damaged door, it became perfectly clear that the scratch was the result of careless operation of a truck. It seemed clear that either Ben T. or Arthur G., the night-shift fork lift operators, had done the damage.

Both men were questioned about it, and both absolutely denied responsibility. Management then asked the union to help determine who was guilty. Some time passed, and the union reported that it was unable to solve the mystery. "It's just one of those things," the business agent said. "Why don't you forget about it?"

But the plant manager refused to forget. "We're going to suspend both of you two fork lift operators until the guilty party comes forward and admits it," he told the two men. This occurred on October 7, and the union promptly filed grievances. On October 18, the men were called back to work, although neither had broken his silence.

A few months later, the matter was in arbitration. "If the man who did the damage had come forward, we would have disciplined him lightly, and the other would not have been involved," the personnel manager said, "It's obvious that one of the men did the damage, and both had to know who it was. The suspension they got was deserved."

"We're not admitting that one of the men was careless," the union representative replied. "But even if that were admitted for the sake of argument, it still remains for the company to prove which one was at fault. You can't punish an innocent man, and you can't even punish a guilty man unless you can prove your case."

Decision

The union won this case. The company has the right to discipline for cause, the arbitrator wrote, but the company must be able to show by a preponderance of evidence that the punished employee was guilty. True, inferences could be drawn from physical facts, but inferences are not substitutes for evidence in a case of this kind. He concluded: "A fundamental rule of law and justice is the presumed innocence of accused persons until proven guilty." In a kind of aside, the arbitrator said he was aware of the company's fear that a union victory in this case might undermine managerial authority in general. To this he replied: "This decision is obviously not to be interpreted as a license to ignore company rules or instructions."

CASE 11.3   *For Cause Discharge*

Reprinted with permission from Morris Stone, *Employee Discipline and Arbitration* (New York: American Arbitration Association, 1977), pp. 51–54

In many years as a foreman in an Ohio asphalt roofing materials company, Al K. had never encountered a situation like this. Joseph T., one of the men in his department, had been absent one Monday in August, without having notified the company in advance and without having called in. When the man showed up on Tuesday, Al naturally asked him where he had been. Since this was Joseph's first absence in more than six months, Al expected a conventional reply, and, depending upon the reason given, he would decide whether to invoke a schedule of penalties the company and the union had agreed upon. The agreed-upon schedule read: "The company and the union have agreed to a procedure relative to absenteeism, as follows: warning notice; warning notice with three day layoff; and dismissal. All notices shall be effective for a period of six months."

What Al did not expect was this reply: "I was absent for personal reasons and I don't want to tell you what they were."

Al insisted on a better answer and Joseph refused. Meanwhile the argument became more intense and less polite. Finally, Al reported this to the personnel manager, who gave Joseph a direct order to answer. Joseph still insisted his reason was personal and did not have to be disclosed.

"Well, now it's not just a question of an unauthorized absence," the personnel manager said. "It's insubordination. And the penalty for insubordination is discharge."

At this, Joseph's manner became really defiant, and he expressed himself in language that was clearly insubordinate and disrespectful.

Unlike many discharge and discipline cases reaching arbitration, this one was singularly free of dispute as to facts. It all turned on the company's view that an employee is under an obligation to disclose the reasons for his absence, on pain of discharge for insubordination. The union asked not only for reinstate-

ment and back pay, but for interest on the money he lost by the discharge.

Decision

The union won this case. An employee does have an obligation to justify his absence if he can, the arbitrator conceded, but if he does not try to do so, the employer can only assume that the reason was not an acceptable one. The employee then becomes subject for the discipline for absenteeism that the parties had agreed would be appropriate in view of the employee's previous record. In Joseph's case, that would be a warning. The arbitrator wrote: "An employee with a poor excuse for absence, no excuse at all, or a refusal to give an excuse has not proved that he had reasonable and just cause for his absence. He, in other words, was absent without just cause, and assumes the responsibility for whatever penalty the parties understand will be applied to unexcused absences. But the employer-employee relationship does not impose an obligation on an employee to inform the employer of his activities while engaged in matters not affecting the employer-employee status."

Nor did the intemperate language Joseph used after the argument was under way justify the discharge. "A threat of discharge under these circumstances could well provoke a response in kind," the arbitrator said. As a remedy for the wrongful discharge, the arbitrator granted back wages, including what Joseph would have received in overtime, holiday, and vacation pay. But he did not grant interest. The granting of such a remedy, he said, is possible in the courts, but it is not clearly within the arbitrator's authority. "I believe it reasonable to assume that these parties at the time the contract was negotiated contemplated the usual back pay award in the event that a discharge was found not for just cause," he explained. The award also added: "Unemployment insurance payments, if any, shall not be deducted from the back pay award. This is a matter between the grievant and state authorities under existing Ohio law on the subject."

CASE STUDY   *Arbitrability*

Adapted from *Communication Workers of America* v. *Western Electric* 751 F. 2d 203 (CA 7, 1984)

Facts

In September 1981, the union grieved the company's announced intention to lay off seventy-nine employees from its Chicago location. The union contended there was no lack of work at that site and that under the contract the company can only lay off from the site where there is a lack of work. Despite the grievance, the company laid off the employees and transferred approximately eighty employees from other locations to the Chicago location.

The union demanded that the dispute be arbitrated and the company refused. The company claimed that the "management functions" clause of the contract gives it the prerogative to determine "lack of work," and so long as it lays off in the order prescribed by the contract, there is nothing to arbitrate. The union contended that certain provisions of the contract modified the "management functions" clause and requested the court to order arbitration.

The lower court found that there were arguable issues to arbitrate and ordered the parties to arbitrate the arbitrability issue—in order words, an arbitrator would decide if she had jurisdiction under the contract of the issue in dispute.

Before this could happen, the company appealed the lower court's ruling.

Appeal

The company argued that the lower court erred in not simply deciding whether the dispute was subject to arbitration. It contended that under the *Steelworkers Trilogy* cases the *courts* must decide if the issue is subject to arbitration, not the arbitrator. The company proposed the following points:

1. Arbitration is a matter of contract, and parties cannot be forced to submit issues to arbitration they have not agreed to submit.
2. Unless the contract clearly provides otherwise, arbitrability is a judicial determination.
3. In deciding arbitrability, the court is not to decide on the merits of the claim.
4. Where the contract has an arbitration clause, the presumption is for arbitrability.

The lower court pointed out, however, that the exception to the rule is found when deciding the arbitrability of the case would also involve the court in interpreting the substantive provisions of the labor agreement.

The union's position was that the layoffs were subject to arbitration, and they pointed to sections of the labor agreement to prove this. The "management functions" clause, the "adjustment to the working force" clause, and the "arbitration" clause must be read together and interpreted. The court could not decide arbitrability in this case without interpreting these sections and therefore deciding the substantive issue. It is for an arbitrator to decide the substantive issues.

Questions

1. Should the court decide whether there is an issue to arbitrate or should an arbitrator? Why?
2. Give the reasons you think arbitration is a superior resolution process to court action in contract disputes.
3. Give the reasons you think a court action is a superior resolution process to arbitration in contract disputes.

Key Terms and Concepts

Arbitrability

Arbitrator role models

Arbitrator's award

Arbitrator's opinion

Contractual issues

Holiday pay eligibility

Just cause

Management rights

Qualifications of an arbitrator

Rules of evidence

Seniority

Tripartite arbitration board

Review Questions

1. What is the process normally utilized in the selection of an arbitrator? How does the selected arbitrator interpret ambiguous contract provisions?
2. How is binding arbitration superior to the courts in settling labor disputes? How does it differ from mediation and conciliation?
3. What information can be presented as evidence during arbitration proceedings? What are the usual hearing procedures?
4. Can a party harm its own case during arbitration proceedings? If so, how?
5. How does an arbitrator determine that a company had just cause for taking a disciplinary action? What remedy might an arbitrator choose if a company did not have just cause?
6. How do labor contracts prevent holiday stretching?

Endnotes

1. Robert Coulson, *Labor Arbitration—What You Need to Know,* booklet (New York: American Arbitration Association, 1978), pp. 19–22; and Steven Briggs and John Anderson,

"An Empirical Investigation of Arbitrator Acceptability," *Industrial Relations* 19, no. 2 (Spring 1980), pp. 163–64.

2. United Steelworkers v. Warrior & Gulf Navigation Co., 80 S.Ct. 1347, 1352–1353 (1960).

3. E.I. DuPont de Nemours & Co. v. Grasselli Employees Independent Association of East Chicago, Inc. No. 85–1577 (7th Cir. May 9, 1986).

4. Frank Elkouri and Edna Asper Elkouri, *How Arbitration Works,* 3rd ed. (Washington, D.C.: Bureau of National Affairs, 1981), pp. 8–9.

5. Ibid., p. 26.

6. *Labor Arbitration Procedures and Techniques* (New York: American Arbitration Association, 1978), pp. 12–13.

7. Stephen Cabot, *Labor Management Relations Manual* (Boston: Warren, Gorham, Lamont, 1979), chap. 18, pp. 4–6.

8. Steven B. Goldberg, "The Mediation of Grievances Under a Collective Bargaining Contract: An Alternative to Arbitration," *Northwestern University Law Review* 77, no. 3 (Oct. 1982), pp. 270–73.

9. Nels Nelson and Earl Curry, "Arbitrator Characteristics and Arbitral Decisions," *Industrial Relations* 20, no. 3 (Fall 1981), pp. 312–17.

10. Briggs and Anderson, "An Empirical Investigation," pp. 163–73.

11. Elkouri and Elkouri, *How Arbitration Works,* pp. 169–70.

12. Ibid., pp. 81–84.

13. *Agreement* between the Mechanical Contractors Association and Plumbers and Gas Fitters Local Union No. 107, 1979–82, p. 21.

14. Elkouri and Elkouri, *How Arbitration Works,* pp. 169–71.

15. United Steelworkers v. Warrior & Gulf Navigation Co., 80 S.Ct. 1347, 1352–1353 (1960).

16. Theodore Kheel, *Labor Law* (New York: Matthew Bender, 1982), chap. 24, p. 5.

17. *Labor Arbitration Procedures,* pp. 17–20.

18. Ibid.

19. Instrument Workers v. Minneapolis Honeywell Co., 54 L.R.R.M. 2660, 2661 (1963).

20. Cabot, *Labor Management Relations,* chap. 18, p. 6.

21. Kheel, *Labor Law,* chap. 24, pp. 35–42.

22. Cabot, *Labor Management Relations,* chap. 18, pp. 7–8.

23. Kheel, *Labor Law,* chap. 24, p. 26.

24. Elkouri and Elkouri, *How Arbitration Works,* pp. 236–39.

25. Kheel, *Labor Law,* chap. 24, p. 42.

26. Wallace B. Nelson, "The Role of Common Law in Just Cause Disputes," *Personnel Journal* 58, no. 8 (Aug. 1979), pp. 541–43.

27. *Agreement,* National Conference of Brewery and Soft Drink Workers and Teamsters Local No. 745 and Jos. Schlitz Brewing Co., Longview, Texas, 1979, pp. 13–15.

28. BNA Editorial Staff, *Grievance Guide* (Washington, D.C.: Bureau of National Affairs, 1978), pp. 1–3.

29. Elkouri and Elkouri, *How Arbitration Works,* p. 648.

30. Nelson, "The Role of Common Law," pp. 541–43.

31. Ibid., p. 551.

32. *Agreement,* General Motors Corporations and the United Auto Workers, 1970, p. 43.

33. Bethlehem Steel Co., 24 LA 699, 702 (1955).

34. BNA Editorial Staff, *Grievance Guide,* p. 87.

35. Gail Schur White, "Past and Current Trends in Negligence and Incompetence Arbitration," *Personnel Journal* 58, no. 11.

36. *Agreement,* Schlitz Co., p. 24.

37. LA 21 (1948).

38. BNA Editorial Staff, *Grievance Guide,* p. 204.
39. 11 LA 33 (1949).
40. *Agreement,* Mechanical Contractors Association of Kentucky, Inc. and Plumbers and Gas Fitters Local Union No. 107, 1979–82, p. 6.
41. BNA Editorial Staff, *Grievance Guide,* pp. 226–27.
42. Ibid., p. 225.

Related
Issues

12

Labor Relations in the Public Sector

Should Public Union Strikes Be Legal?

At a time when new state collective bargaining laws in Ohio and Illinois have been opening the door to more public unions, a crucial question has been raised. The California Supreme Court on May 13, 1985 addressed this key issue of public sector collective bargaining—the no-strike rule.

Critics of public sector collective bargaining have long contended that government must exercise its duties without interference of any outside party, including unions. The rights of the people that government serves could not be protected in the case of a public union strike. This was why President Ronald Reagan could not recognize or tolerate the air traffic controllers' (PATCO) strike in 1981.

Advocates of public sector collective bargaining have countered that the critics were correct in that the public's rights do need protection, and thus public employees should be denied the right to strike. However, public employees should be allowed collective bargaining to negotiate wages, benefits,

grievance resolution, and so on, without the right to strike.

Therefore the California decision may have upset the delicate balance of public sector collective bargaining rights. The dispute arose from a strike by Los Angeles County sanitation workers. The California state law required employers to "meet and confer" with employee representatives, but did not grant or deny the right to strike. The Los Angeles Sanitation District won a lower court decision awarding over $300,000 for damages caused by the stike. The supreme court recognized the traditional position against public sector strikes at all levels of government. However, the court rejected the notion that government cannot provide essential public services in a strike, citing the 1981 PATCO strike. The court also noted the legislature had not specifically banned public strikes by law, a provision common in other state laws. The court did, however, state that public strikes that create a "substantial and immi-

nent threat to the health and safety of the public" are unlawful.

The historic decision is likely to have significant effects on public sector labor relations. Unions will likely lobby to change other state laws to allow nonthreatening strikes; in fact, ten states now may allow strikes either directly or by not banning them.[1] Public unions in California may re-

evaluate their ability to successfully strike an employer, and public unions in other states may press for a similar state supreme court ruling.

Source: Adapted from County Sanitation District No. 2 of Los Angeles County v. Los Angeles County Employees Association, Local 660, *38 CH. 3d, 85* Daily Journal D.A.R. 1625 (1985).

The National Labor Relations Act, passed in 1935, established a national labor policy to be enforced by federal action. This policy recognized the need for collective bargaining as a way to eliminate and mitigate industrial strife. The act established equality of bargaining power between employers and employees and gave employees substantive rights to organize themselves into labor unions, presenting themselves to the employer for recognition. Employers were required to meet with their employees at the bargaining table to discuss the terms and conditions of the job. The right to strike was given government protection and served as an economic equalizer for the employee.

Public employees, however, were not guaranteed rights under the National Labor Relations Act. This chapter will examine the development of labor relations in the public sector, how the parties and the interests differ from those in the private sector, and how disputes are resolved.

Evolution of Public Sector Labor Relations

Congress excluded federal, state, and local government employees from the provisions of the National Labor Relations Act until the Postal Reorganization Act of 1970 allowed postal workers to come under the National Labor Relations Act's provisions.[2] In the traditional sense, Congress did not view government as an employer, but as a representative of the people, supplying certain necessary services. Therefore, people employed by the government were not employees but public servants, and they were protected from the arbitrary actions of private employers by already existing systems. Such systems addressed basic employee concerns—wages, benefits, job security— even as the sovereignty of the government was maintained.

Such was not always the case. In the early 1800s, citizens were scandalized by the use of party patronage in federal, state, and local governments. This *spoils system* caused a turnover of government workers based on their political affiliation, not ability or dedication. Government workers were expected to support political candidates with time and money or fear losing their jobs. The government lost continuity and efficiency because of the repeated replacement of trained employees.

In 1871, the first Civil Service Commission was established to propose reforms in the national government. Congress, however, failed to make an appropriation for the commission and it disbanded. In 1883, an outgoing Republican Congress passed the

Pendleton Act, which provided for a bipartisan three-member Civil Service Commission to draw up and administer competitive examinations to determine the fitness of appointees to federal office. The act protected federal employees from being fired for failure to make political contributions and actually forbade political campaign contributions by certain employees. The Pendleton Act affected only about 10 percent of the federal employees at the time, but enabled the president to broaden the merit system and was the foundation of the present federal civil service system.

Many states followed the federal government's lead and instituted civil service merit systems for their employees. Thus, the **civil service system** provided job security for government workers. Rules governing hiring, firing, and discipline protected the worker from arbitrary actions. Due process hearings gave workers a forum to protest an employer's actions.

The Pendleton Act also gave Congress the right to regulate wages, hours, and working conditions of public employees. These employees began to lobby Congress for wage increases and improved benefits. In the early 1900s, Presidents Theodore Roosevelt and William Howard Taft issued restrictive executive orders aimed at preventing such lobbying. But in 1912 Congress enacted the Lloyd-LaFollette Act allowing unaffiliated organizations to present their grievances to Congress without fear of retaliation.[3]

In the public sector, therefore, organizations of government employees, such as the National Federation of Employees formed in 1917 and the American Federation of Government Employees formed in 1932, concentrated on lobbying to obtain legislation favorable to their members. For most government workers, such lobbying proved to be successful. While income was modest, fringe benefits such as vacations, paid holidays, paid sick leave, and pensions offered the public employee rewards not found in the private sector. Before the National Labor Relations Act was passed, public employees, represented by employee associations and organizations, could boast of an indirect participation in decisions affecting their employment. Unlike their counterparts in the private sector, their employer also could be reached in the legislatures and at the ballot box. However, the growth of public employment at every level soon began to erode that accessibility.

The Rise of Public Sector Unions

During the 1930s and 1940s, private sector unionization flourished under the protection of the National Labor Relations Act. These unions sought job security, higher wages, improved benefits, grievance procedures, and arbitration rights and, more important, recognition as participants in the decision-making process. Since many public employees already had these conditions, unionization held no attraction for them. The successes of private unions, however, began to surpass the public employees' ability to lobby, and changes in their job classifications and numbers gave an impetus to public sector unionization.

In the private sector, wages and benefits improved year after year, and job security was increased through the establishment of grievance and arbitration procedures in collective bargaining agreements. The organized worker also became cognizant of the respect a union could demand from an employer. Since strikes were protected under the act, the employer did not hold all of the bargaining strength.

Public employees discovered that lobbying efforts alone could not supply them with the controls and benefits of collective bargaining. Their swelling ranks made this process increasingly cumbersome and contributed to the rise of public sector unionism.[4] From 1956 to 1976, state and local government employment increased 140 percent, while federal employment increased by 23 percent.

The organizational size and complexity of government contributed to mismanagement and job dissatisfaction. It became increasingly difficult for employees to influence legislative action because the numerous layers of bureaucracy freed politicians from responsibility. In addition, the civil service systems developed to protect public employees were perceived as employer-recruited, employer-directed personnel mechanisms. As one expert observed, "It is the labor-management inadequacy of the civil service system that has been a prime cause of the remarkable thrust of union organization among public employees in recent years."[5]

Organized labor recognized an opportunity to add public employees to its forces. Through labor's efforts, changes were made in federal, state, and local laws that led to public sector collective bargaining rights. However, these laws were not changed easily, and collective bargaining in the public sector is still accepted with reservations.

The Sovereignty Doctrine

As discussed in earlier chapters, the key to employers' resistance to collective bargaining in the private sector was the desire to protect their private property rights. The National Labor Relations Act tried to balance the employer's private property rights against the employee's right to organize and to bargain collectively. And although the purpose of the act was to place employees in an equal bargaining position, employers still held all rights not taken from them at the bargaining table.

In the public sector, governments were able to resist collective bargaining because of the **sovereignty doctrine**. *Sovereignty* is defined as ". . . the supreme, absolute, and uncontrollable power by which an independent state is governed."[6] In a democracy, the source of that supreme power is the people who have vested their government with rights and responsibilities as caretakers of that power. The sovereignty doctrine requires that the government exercise its power unfettered by any force other than the people—all of the people. Collective bargaining was seen as a threat to that sovereignty doctrine if government were to share decision-making authority with employees. Obviously, decisions made at the collective bargaining table would affect the way government provides services and the amount those services would cost the taxpayer.

But the sovereignty doctrine had numerous weak points. Government contracts extensively with members of the private sector, and negotiation of those contracts takes place bilaterally. This disputes the claim that government must make its decisions unilaterally. Government's voluntary recognition of the employee's right to bargain collectively with it has also weakened the sovereignty doctrine. And the sovereignty doctrine can no longer be used to support the theory that government— the ruler—can do no wrong when numerous court decisions have ruled against the sovereign. The Supreme Court has allowed citizens to claim civil rights, torts, and contract violations against state and local governments, subjecting such institutions to monetary damages and remedial actions. In some states, federal judges have taken over the responsibility for administering the prison system until court-mandated improvements are made.

Laws

Executive orders In January 1962, the President's Task Force on Employee-Management Relations reported that one-third of the federal employees belonged to labor organizations. It recommended that the government officially acknowledge this and respond affirmatively to employees' desire for collective bargaining. President John F. Kennedy signed **Executive Order (E.O.) 10988**, which recognized the rights of federal employees to join or to refrain from joining labor organizations, granted recognition to those labor organizations, and detailed bargaining subjects. While this executive order can be cited as having established the framework for labor-management relations in the federal government, comparison to its private sector counterpart, the National Labor Relations Act, showed glaring deficiencies.

As in the National Labor Relations Act, the right to organize was granted to federal civilian employees under E.O. 10988. However, the head of an agency could determine that a bureau or office was primarily performing intelligence, investigative, or security functions, and the employees of that bureau or office could be excluded from the E.O. for national security reasons.

Under the National Labor Relations Act, a labor organization receiving a majority vote of the members of the bargaining unit gains exclusive recognition. Under Executive Order 10988, exclusive recognition could be gained in the same manner, but two other types of recognition were also proffered. The first type granted formal recognition if there was no exclusive representative for the bargaining unit and the organization had at least 10 percent of the employees in the unit. Such an organization would represent only its members. A second type consisted of informal recognition of an employee organization that did not meet the majority vote or 10 percent membership qualifications. This system generated much confusion since an agency might have to deal with two unions representing the same class of employees. For example, 10 percent of the service personnel could gain formal recognition while a different 8 percent could claim informal. The agency would be negotiating with two unions consisting of 18 percent of one class of employee.

In the private sector, bargaining subjects protected by the act included wages, hours, and conditions of employment. Under E.O. 10988, bargaining subjects were limited. The employees could not mandate negotiations on economic issues. A management rights clause reserved the government's power to direct and discipline employees. And the grievance procedure could not result in binding arbitration.

Another deficiency in the E.O. was the lack of a central authority to determine bargaining unit recognition and to resolve disputes. Instead, many decisions were left to agency heads who were the immediate employers of the labor organization's members.

The most significant difference between the National Labor Relations Act and Executive Order 10988 was the right to engage in work stoppages. Strikes were specifically denied the public labor organizations.

From 1970 to 1975, Executive Order 10988 was amended three times, primarily by E.O. 11491. Improvements included the granting of exclusive recognition rights for the union having majority support and eliminating formal and informal recognition. Amendments provided for creation of the National Labor Relations Council to interpret the executive orders and resolve major policy disputes, and the Federal Service Impasse Panel to assist in resolving impasses in negotiations. Finally, the amendments expanded the mandatory bargaining subjects covered by E.O. 10988 to include agency regulations and changes in agency personnel policies.

The Civil Service Reform Act of 1978   Currently, federal employee labor relations are governed by the provisions of Title VII of the **Civil Service Reform Act of 1978** and Reorganization Plan No. 2 of 1978.

Title VII, Federal Service Labor-Management Relations, is modeled after the National Labor Relations Act. Central authority was placed in a three-member panel, the Federal Labor Relations Authority. This panel oversees labor-management relations within the federal government, its three members being appointed by the president of the United States. The president also appoints a general counsel empowered to investigate alleged unfair labor practices and file and prosecute complaints.

The Federal Labor Relations Authority oversees creation of bargaining units, conducts elections and decides representation cases, determines unfair labor practices, and seeks enforcement of its decisions in the federal courts. The Federal Service Impasse Panel was continued by the act and provides assistance in resolving negotiation impasses.

The unfair labor practice provision of Title VII generally mirrors the unfair labor practice provision in legislation for private employers and employees. The government is prohibited from the following practices:

1. Restraint and coercion of employees in the exercise of their organizational rights
2. Encouragement or discouragement of union membership
3. Sponsorship of labor organizations
4. Refusal to bargain in good faith with a recognized organization
5. Refusal to cooperate in impasse procedures
6. Disciplining a union member who files a complaint
7. Enforcement of a new regulation that conflicts with an existent collective bargaining agreement[7]

A labor organization is prohibited from these actions:

1. Interference with an employee's right to organize or to refrain from organizing
2. Discrimination against or causing the employer to discriminate against employees because of union activity
3. Refusal to cooperate in impasse procedures
4. Refusal to bargain in good faith or to call for or engage in a work stoppage or slowdown[8]

Unlike private sector labor laws, Title VII mandates inclusion of a grievance procedure with binding arbitration as a final step in all federal collective bargaining agreements:

(B) Any negotiated grievance procedure referred to in subsection (A) of this section shall
1. Be fair and simple
2. Provide for expeditious processing
3. Include procedures that
   a) Assure an exclusive representative the right, in its own behalf or on behalf of any employee in the unit represented by the exclusive representative, to present and process grievances
   b) Assure such an employee the right to present a grievance on the employee's own behalf, and assure the exclusive representative the right to be present during the grievance proceeding
   c) Provide that any grievance not satisfactorily settled under the negotiated grievance procedure shall be subject to binding arbitration which may be invoked by either the exclusive representative or the agency.[9]

Title VII codifies presidential policies toward federal labor-management relations and improves the opportunities for the growth of collective bargaining in the public sector.

State and local government laws Title VII does not cover state and local employees, who must look to state and local laws for their collective bargaining rights. Over two-thirds of the states have enacted legislation granting public sector collective bargaining rights to some groups, such as teachers, police, and firefighters. Local, county, and municipal governments may also adopt collective bargaining laws or, by practice, recognize and bargain with employee organizations.

While state and local laws may differ as to particulars, some patterns emerge. Legislation is more favorable to collective bargaining in the northern, northeastern, midwestern, and far western part of the United States. The sunbelt states located along the lower Atlantic Ocean, the southeast, southwest, and southwest Rocky Mountains generally do not have comprehensive public sector labor laws.

State legislation usually includes bargaining over wages, hours, terms of employment, and working conditions. Unfair labor practices and limits on or prohibitions of the right to strike also are legislated. The bargaining obligation is enforced by an administrative agency, and procedures are established should there be an impasse.[10]

A developing campaign to include state and municipal employees under federal legislation was substantially undermined by the Supreme Court decision in *National League of Cities* v. *Usery*.[11] That case reconfirmed the specific state's sovereignty over its own employees and denied that the commerce power of the federal government could be invoked to regulate that relationship. A recent study of the growth of teacher bargaining concluded that, while teacher bargaining in large cities typically starts before collective bargaining laws are passed, the passage of the laws spurs subsequent union growth.[12]

Bargaining Parties in the Public Sector

Public Employment

Unlike employees in the private sector, public employees provide education, police, fire, and sanitation services, and maintenance of public improvements. In recent years, legislation has increased government jobs for social workers, clerical and office employees, and computer technicians. Citizens depend upon the services of these employees. The nature of the services provided—social security checks, food stamps, recordkeeping—are such that private industry is unable or unwilling to offer them; thus, a government monopoly is created.

The lack of competition by the private sector can cause collective bargaining problems. Without consumer control, quality can suffer, subjecting the public employee to adverse public sentiment. The lack of another provider makes the continuation of the public service critical; it prevents the employees from using economic pressure to reach a collective bargaining agreement. The absence of marketplace control on costs might also encourage intemperate collective bargaining settlements by public employers. The public employer, often an elected official, might give more than the tax dollars warrant to a certain project, then let a succeeding administration solve the deficit.

Public sector collective bargaining also differs because of its extensive unionization of professional employees. Measures of productivity are more difficult to devise for professional employees than for production and maintenance employees. In addition, the use of a service in the public sector cannot be related to the need for such service when participating in collective bargaining. Since providing public transportation is necessary, a bus driver should not be expected to have his pay affected by the number of people who choose to use that service.

The Public Employer

The public employer represents and provides services to the public. That employer is either an elected official serving for a limited term or someone placed in a position by that official. While the legislative and executive branches of governments are almost always separate, the government as an employer is a combination of the two. Their roles may be clearly distinguished or may merge as the employee seeks the decision maker for collective bargaining rights. The source of funds available to the public employer may be limited by totally external factors—Proposition 13 type taxing limitations; or grants of funds from a higher government level with constraints on their use, for example, the Job Training Partnership Act of 1982.[13]

By using the sovereignty doctrine, the public employer may seek to control the collective bargaining process by limiting the issues to be bargained. Also, the public employer can be influenced by a lack of competition in the necessary services.[14]

Bargaining Unit Determination

Under Title VII of the Civil Service Reform Act, the Federal Labor Relations Authority must determine an appropriate bargaining unit. Borrowing from court decisions under the National Labor Relations Act, the federal law applies a **community of interest** test to identify an appropriate unit on an agency, plant, installation, functional, or other basis. The criteria used to determine a clear and identifiable community of interest include common skills, similar working conditions, common supervision, common work site, and identical duties. An appropriate unit must promote effective dealings with the agency; the extent of unionization by a bargaining unit is not a factor in its recognition. At the federal level, confidential employees, managers and supervisory personnel, and personnel employees are excluded from the bargaining unit. Professional employees are excluded from nonprofessional units unless the professional employees vote in favor of their own inclusion.

A community of interest test is also used in state and local government to determine an appropriate unit. Guidelines for such determination may or may not be outlined in the legislation. The following criteria have been developed by the Advisory Committee on Intergovernmental Relations (ACIR) to define community of interest:

1. Similar wages, hours, working rules, and conditions of employment
2. Maintaining a negotiating pattern based on common history
3. Maintaining the craft or professional line status
4. Representation rights, which involve the inclusion or exclusion of supervisors or nonprofessionals (this refers to organizations such as police or fire departments).[15]

On the state and local level, the inclusion of supervisory personnel within the bargaining unit has presented a difficult question. Those in favor of such inclusion point to the need to consolidate employees and to limit the number of unions involved. It has been suggested that supervisors moderate demands and create less militant organizations. In some instances, supervisory titles in the public sector do not reflect actual supervisory authority because of the way decisions are made in the public sector, as illustrated in Case 12.1. In addition, all supervisory and nonsupervisory career employees share common interests, especially in money issues. Those who oppose the inclusion of supervisory personnel point out that supervisors face a potential conflict of interest when they themselves are affected by a contract they must enforce. Also, in pursuing grievance procedures, the distinction between management and employee needs to be clear. And supervisors may need to continue an operation during a work stoppage by the bargaining unit.

The size of a public employee unit can give a strategic advantage to either side. The public employer may encourage a larger unit, hoping the diverse interests and backgrounds of a larger unit will prevent the union from gaining majority status. Larger units prevent or reduce the possibility that multiunion negotiation will be used against the employer. The time and cost of bargaining is greatly reduced with larger units. Still, employers realize the political power of public employee unions may be increased if the unit is very large. Because unions seek to represent the unit most likely to give it majority status, size is not the only determining factor in their organization efforts.

In addition, because of the mix of service and clerical employees being organized on a local or state level, the employees often have to choose between two labor organizations—a trade union and an employee association. Their choice will have significant impact upon the labor-management relationship.[16]

Bargaining Interests in the Public Sector

The Scope of Negotiations

Management rights   More management rights are reserved for the employer in the public sector than in the private sector. Under the sovereignty theory, government avoids many issues at the bargaining table. For example, in Title VII, an agency is given the right to make a unilateral decision to determine the mission, budget, organization, number of employees, and internal security practices. Questions of hiring, employee assignment, promotions, firings, suspensions, and other disciplinary actions are all at the agency's discretion. A union may be able to negotiate procedures for actions taken by the employer and appropriate arrangements for adversely affected employees, but, as stated earlier, the basic content of a grievance procedure is also legislated. Most state and local governments use similar language to ensure that policy and quality of service remain the prerogative of management.

Union security   *Union security* refers to the ability of the union to grow and to perform its collective bargaining role without interference from management or other unions. As the exclusive representative of certain employees, a union enjoys a high degree of security. But unions seek more. In the private sector, union security provisions include automatic dues deductions, a union or agency shop, and maintenance of membership provisions. These ensure a dependable source of revenue.

Automatic dues deduction is the most commonly allowed **public sector union security** provision. Each employee is asked to sign an authorization card; union dues are withheld from the employee's checks and transmitted to the union.

An agency shop provision requires financial support of the union, whether the employee joins or not. This is a popular provision in public employee contracts because it assists the union financially, but does not require compulsory unionization. A union shop requires that the employee join the union after being hired, and a maintenance of membership clause keeps the employee in the union during the life of the contract. Both of these provisions can run afoul of employee rights under civil service or merit systems where an employee can be discharged only for a job-related reason. The agency shop provision has come under some question in a Supreme Court decision, *Abood* v. *Detroit Board of Education*, limiting the amount of dues to be paid by nonunion members to the amount actually spent on collective bargaining, contract administration, and grievance adjustment.[17]

In recent years, state and local governments have been subjected to numerous civil rights actions in which allegations have been made that the power of the government was used to deprive a citizen of a constitutional right.[18] Such actions have led many public officials to believe that union security and maintenance of membership clauses could subject the governmental entity to a civil rights charge of depriving the employees of their property right in employment.

Claims that such union security clauses can violate merit principles and possibly the employee's civil rights reinforce the public employer's aversion to such clauses.[19] The employer also recognizes that the bargaining power of the employee increases with the security of the union.

Wages and fringes   In most cases the negotiation of wages and fringe benefits is a union's principal function. Public employee unions, however, often find this subject out of their reach. Under Title VII, the federal statute governing employee rights, the right to collectively bargain is limited to issues concerning conditions of employment and excludes wages and fringe benefits. For most state and municipal employees, union contract negotiations take place during or after the respective legislative body has determined a budget. Unions may be limited to a negotiation on how the available dollars are to be divided among classes of employees or distributed as base wages, fringe benefits, bonuses, and incentive pay. Despite these limitations, collective bargaining does have an impact on public sector wage levels. One recent analysis shows that the gap is narrowing between union impact on wage increases in the private and public sectors.[20]

Hours   The nature of the job performed often determines the amount of flexibility available in the negotiation of hours. Police, fire, and other emergency services must operate around the clock. Transportation and public utilities cannot be subject to variation. Determination of total hours of employment, therefore, is jealously guarded by the public employer as a basic policy decision.

Working conditions   Unlike in the private sector, negotiation of working conditions in the public sector does not center on promotions, discipline, and production standards. Working conditions directly affect the provision of service to the public. Therefore, the number of police in a patrol car or firefighters on a fire alarm run are issues that may be decided at a negotiating table. Classroom size, the number of bus routes, or the frequency of trash pickup are determined by the public employer, often through negotiations. The public employee is often better able to determine the quality of service than the manager.

Grievance procedure   Under the federal statute, a grievance procedure must be included in federal contracts. That procedure includes binding arbitration if necessary. State and local government contracts, while containing grievance procedures, frequently stop at advisory arbitration.

   Public employers believe that the sovereignty doctrine prohibits the delegation of decision-making authority to a nonelected body. That legal theory weakens, however, when the binding arbitration concerns only adjudication of contract provisions already negotiated and agreed to by the public employers.

> Although not entirely dead, the sovereignty and extraloyalty theory are moribund; and it is clear that the federal policy in favor of grievance arbitration in the public sector, as well as recent state legislation, has had a considerable influence on state court decisions involving public sector arbitration. The trend is strongly in the direction of upholding the legality of voluntary agreements to submit grievance to final and binding arbitration and of enforcing such agreements.[21]

Negotiating the Public Employee Contract

As collective bargaining gains acceptance in the public sector, the contract has become increasingly important to the public "helping" professions, such as the police.

In many of today's law enforcement agencies, collective bargaining and labor relations have been and can continue to be a catalyst for changing old methods and old attitudes. Police agencies are reflections of society and the career professional police officer demands to be heard and considered. Police departments and public sector administrators have an obligation through collective bargaining, to change with the changing times, or risk the possibility of stagnation, unrest, and dissatisfaction, both in the ranks and in the eyes of the public.

Police officers are no longer the ultraconservative public employees who will grudgingly accept whatever they are given without regard for personal needs and wants. Police officers have been conditioned through the sixties and seventies of seeing others accomplish missions by united action. With public demands of law enforcement at its highest level, collective bargaining has and must be the avenue to demonstrate the ability to discuss with administrators and bargain in good faith, to improve upon economic conditions, hours, and improvement of the hazardous working conditions.

When there is a reluctance of police officers to use collective bargaining, normally, it is the uncertainty of what it is, and what it can do, due to the many historical myths surrounding the process. The public sector process goes beyond actual bargaining. It should be an ongoing, daily process designed to administer contractual provisions, resolve personnel grievances, and most importantly—promote an atmosphere of harmonious relationships, which ultimately will provide an efficient and productive police agency.

Source: Charles R. Orms, "Police Officers' Need for Collective Bargaining," unpublished. Used with permission of Charles R. Orms, President, Kentucky State Lodge, Fraternal Order of Police.

The bargaining process Fundamental ideas regarding bargaining theories and the bargaining process in the private sector hold true for the public sector with a few variations. As outlined in Chapter 5, union negotiators derive their authority to negotiate from their membership. That authority is generally limited in that the contract must be taken back to the membership for a vote. On the other hand, management negotiators have the authority to commit to a negotiated agreement at the bargaining table. This is often referred to as *bilateral bargaining*. In the public sector, where *management's* authority to negotiate flows from the people, the decision cannot be made by one official and is referred to as *multilateral bargaining*.

Multilateral bargaining The governmental entities involved in collective bargaining fall into two categories: a council form and an executive-legislative form. For example, an elected or appointed *council* of a school district acts as a board of directors for a corporation that appoints its own chief executive officer. The public negotiator for management may find her role similar to that of the negotiator for labor, i.e., she is charged with returning a negotiated agreement for approval to the final authority. Such approval is usually given because of the close relationship between the negotiator and the council.

In an *executive/legislative* form, the executive authority resides with a president, governor, or mayor who is the *manager* of the governmental entity. The legislative authority resides with a congress, a legislature, or a council that is the *law maker* of the governmental entity. Together, the two parties make up *management*; both are employers to the public employees. This joint management authority is seldom a problem because the executive manages personnel policies on a day-to-day basis under directives put in place by the legislators. During labor negotiations, however, when the decisions affecting employees are subject to collective bargaining, conflicts can arise. The negotiator is employed by the executive branch, and may be understood to be negotiating on behalf of the executive branch. Settlement may be reached by the negotiator and endorsed by the executive (mayor, governor, etc.), but it must be approved by the legislative body. The legislative body may not approve the negotiated agreement, thereby undermining the collective bargaining process.

Obviously, the disadvantage of multilateral negotiations to the employer is the union's ability to appeal to the legislative body for a more favorable settlement before, during, or after the negotiations, thus undermining the work of the executive. On the other hand, the executive and legislative branches may not agree on a settlement, leaving the union up in the air while each side blames the other for indecision.[22]

The legislative body may seek to play the role of a mediator between the executive branch and the union when an impasse develops.[23] The legislative body is a part of management and, as such, has no legitimate role as mediator. Because the legislature has the authority to determine the budget, involvement at an impasse stage of negotiations represents a new level of negotiation rather than mediation. That level may involve a restatement of the executive's position or a new offer by the legislative branch. Such a practice undermines the public employer's negotiating posture. Intervention after the fact by a third party may destroy the fairness of a negotiated agreement and the commitment to compromise so important to collective bargaining.

Open negotiations Public employee collective bargaining makes news. Press coverage of public employee collective bargaining can harm the bargaining process in several ways. If an impasse is reached, the parties may try to explain their side to the media, hoping to influence public opinion and in turn the negotiating process. Rushing for media coverage may cause a party to present proposals publicly before they have presented them to the other party at the negotiating table. By emphasizing the differences between the parties instead of the points of agreement, reporters can actually prolong the posturing stage. In the normal course of events, agreement of public employees and employers at the collective bargaining table is not newsworthy; therefore, media coverage often will be confined to reporting on the items separating the parties and not the items of agreement. Publicity might also encourage the negative tactic of turning to the legislative body for impasse resolution. Coverage reinforces the bad feelings too often present in negotiations in a way the private sector rarely experiences.

Sunshine laws (see Case 12.2) require that collective bargaining sessions be open to the public, often thwarting the parties' ability to compromise.[24] Some initial posturing is necessary on both sides so the negotiator's constituency is assured he is acting on their behalf. Negotiators may find it difficult to stop posturing if they are under constant scrutiny. At any particular juncture during the negotiation process, it may seem as if one side or the other is winning or losing. A fear of "loss of face" by either side may endanger the fair compromise so necessary to successful negotiations.

However, press coverage of public sector collective bargaining is necessary because the ultimate decision does rest with the public. Without contribution by the public at some point during the process, the parties will not be able to gauge its reaction. By making the progress of negotiations public, elected officials and union members are able to get a response and so can modify their positions. For example, if a union representing teachers learns through news coverage of their negotiations that the public would support tax increases to improve the teacher-student ratio but not to raise salaries, its posture during the negotiations might change.

The right to strike   In the private sector, an impasse in collective bargaining negotiations can result in a strike. The National Labor Relations Act reserves that right to the employee as an economic weapon. In the public sector, the right to strike is usually denied to the public employee either by the collective bargaining statute or by court actions.

The right-to-strike issue is to the public sector what the right-to-work issue was to the private. Those who believe the public employee should have the right to strike cite the following reasons:

1.   Despite legislation to the contrary, public employees do go on strike.[25] Attention is then focused upon the strike issue and not upon the reason for the disagreement, thereby thwarting resolution of the impasse.

2.   Strikes, or at least credible strike threats, facilitate agreement at the bargaining table. Good faith bargaining alone cannot equalize the parties' bargaining power.[26]

3.   Strikes test the union's strength as a bargaining representative; this strength can be used as a bargaining strategy.

4.   Nonessential public employees should have the same rights as their counterparts in the private sector to strike.[27]

Those who believe that public employees should not have the right to strike cite the following reasons:

1.   The primary reason for prohibiting public employee strikes is that the services provided by employees are essential to the general welfare. A distinction between police and fire services and motor pool operations may or may not be made. Case 12.3 points out the public's interest in curtailing the right to strike.

2.   Under the sovereignty theory, giving unions the right to strike places too much power in the hands of the employees rather than in the elected representatives of the people.

3.   Since there are no market controls on government services, the strike threat could cause public employers to make unwise agreements at the expense of the taxpayer.[28]

Despite the traditional bias against public employees' right to strike, ten states allow workers to strike either directly or by not prohibiting it.[29]

The Professional Air Traffic Controllers (PATCO)   In 1968 a group of New York controllers formed the Professional Air Traffic Controllers (PATCO). Increased frustration with the Federal Aviation Association's (FAA) poor management of the air traffic control system led to a slowdown beginning in New York and spreading to other cities. In 1969, PATCO counsel F. Lee Bailey discussed the controller's frustrations with overcrowding in the skies on the *Tonight Show* and said, "I'd start walking, if I were you."[30] The next day several hundred controllers conducted a work stoppage and the FAA suspended eighty. In 1970 almost 3,000 controllers informally went on strike; 52 were fired and 1,000 suspended.[31]

Several other instances gave PATCO the reputation of being an independent and feisty union. Certainly some of their members' feelings of independence were rooted in the belief they were highly skilled professionals who could not easily be replaced. Then in 1981, PATCO leaders called the first declared national strike against the federal government.

However, at least twenty-two strikes *unauthorized* by law against the federal government occurred before the 1981 PATCO strike:

1962—Tennessee Valley Authority craft workers' strike. Eighty were fired, none rehired.
1969—Sick-in by 500 PATCO members over F. Lee Bailey's remarks. No disciplinary action taken.
1969—Postal workers in Massachusetts strike over wages. No disciplinary action taken.
1970—Over 2,300 PATCO members engaged in a two week sick-in during contract negotiations. Sixty were fired, 59 rehired.
1970—Over 152,000 postal workers strike for nine days for higher wages. The issue was negotiated. No disciplinary action taken.
1970—One-day strike by 1,400 Printing Office workers over wages. Issue was negotiated. No disciplinary action taken.
1971—Library of Congress employees' strike. Thirteen were fired and none rehired.
1973—Tennessee Valley Authority craft workers' strike. One hundred ninety-two were fired, but all were rehired.
1974—New Jersey postal workers (475) walkout. Federal judge orders arbitration of issue. No disciplinary action taken.
1978—California and New Jersey postal workers (4,750) engage in wildcat strike. Two hundred twenty-six were fired, 104 rehired.[32]

Therefore, when over 13,000 air traffic controllers followed PATCO's call for the first nationwide declared strike a critical moment in U.S. history had arrived. Never before had so many federal workers directly violated the no-strike clause of their contracts and endangered the lives of Americans.

President Reagan quickly warned that such direct disobedience of the law would not be tolerated. He stated, "There is no strike, what they did was to terminate their own employment by quitting."[33] Reagan gave workers a deadline that most ignored, then he fired all but the few who returned to work. Not one controller was given amnesty or rehired.

The success of the Reagan Administration in replacing such highly skilled workers, together with widespread public support, left little doubt in the minds of government workers as to what might happen if they went on strike. PATCO miscalculated its ability to gain concessions by striking. It sacrificed a substantial pay increase, a generous benefits package, and its very existence in its attempt to legitimize strikes in the public sector.[34]

Impasse Settlement Procedures

Legislation that allows public sector collective bargaining but prohibits strikes often details the procedures available to resolve an impasse.

Mediation is provided in almost all states with collective bargaining in the public sector. As with the private sector, the mediator has no independent authority but uses acquired skills to bring the parties back together. It has been suggested that the mediator represent the public's interest at the bargaining table. Such a role does not seem to facilitate resolution of a dispute.

Fact finding and *advisory arbitration* can be far more successful in the public sector than the private because of political pressures. Under fact finding and advisory arbitration, an unbiased third party examines the collective bargaining impasse and issues findings and recommendations. The findings may move the process by simply eliminating the distrust one party feels for the other party's facts or figures. Reasonable recommendations may also pressure a party to accept an offer that otherwise would not have been considered.

Interest arbitration allows a panel to make a final and binding decision on a negotiation dispute and has been used in the public sector to resolve impasses. However, the legality of allowing a third party to set the terms of the contract has been questioned.[35]

The use of such a compulsory mechanism seems incompatible with collective bargaining. A fundamental tenet of American industrial relations is that the bargaining outcome be determined by the parties to the greatest extent possible. Interest arbitration violates that tenet by substituting a third party's decision for that of the negotiating parties. Interest arbitration can become a substitute for the arduous demands of bargaining and can discourage the concessions so necessary to negotiations. The award merely becomes a compromise between the parties' final positions.[36]

Proponents of interest arbitration, however, believe that the threat of arbitration, like the threat of a strike, provides an incentive to negotiate when the parties understand and appreciate the final offer procedure.[37]

The 1984 interest arbitration involving the U.S. Postal Service (USPS) and its two largest unions, the American Postal Workers Union and the National Association of Letter Carriers, was historic. The five-member arbitration panel's award covered more than 500,000 employees, a record number for a single arbitration in the United States.

The postal negotiations were the first postal labor talks since the landmark air traffic controllers' (PATCO) strike in 1981. The tone of the talks was set when the USPS Board of Governors proposed a two-tier wage structure with a new scale 33 percent below the current scale. The unions believed the wage concession was unwarranted by the financial condition of USPS. Negotiations quickly went to impasse and led to binding arbitration as provided for in the 1970 Postal Reorganization Act.[38]

The central issue was the interpretation of a section of the 1970 act that gives USPS the ability to maintain compensation and benefits "on a standard of comparability" to the private sector. The arbitration award provided for a three-year agreement with 2.7 percent annual increases for incumbent employees. New employees in a two-tier system would start at wage levels below those of current employees.

The Public Employee Contract

Reducing the Contract to Writing

Title VII of the Civil Service Reform Act requires that any agreement must be incorporated into a written document if either party requests it.[39] The subjects covered in a public sector collective bargaining agreement may differ from those in the private sector. An analysis of the differences can be made using four contract groups: union security and management rights, wage and effort bargaining, job security, and contract administration. Union security will generally be included in the collective bargaining agreement as an automatic check-off provision. The federal statute mirrors the National Labor Relations Board in regard to a valid contract as a bar to an election for recognition by a different union. State and local statutes are usually not that comprehensive. The management rights issue is indirectly addressed by detailing procedures to be followed by the employer.[40]

Although wages and benefits are not subject to negotiation, such items as merit raise systems and premium pay may be covered. Local government and state contracts may include wage provisions and often include procedures for testing standards of performance.

Job security, seniority, and due process often are covered under merit and civil service systems already in place. If the contract touches upon these areas at all, the rights and procedures would be in addition to the civil service system.

In the area of contract administration, federal law requires that a grievance procedure with binding arbitration be part of each contract. Such procedures usually stop at advisory arbitration at the state and local level.

Contract Enforcement

The Federal Labor Relations Authority performs the same role in federal labor contract enforcement as the private sector National Labor Relations Board. If a contract interpretation or violation issue is also an unfair labor practice, the authority has jurisdiction. However, unlike the NLRB, the authority has jurisdiction in all the arbitration awards appealed to it, regardless of the issue involved. The authority performs a quasi-judicial role when it determines if the arbitrator's award is contrary to any law, rule, or regulation or if it is deficient ". . . on other grounds similar to those applied by federal courts in private sector labor-management relations."[41]

Grievance Arbitration

Grievance arbitration in the private sector has proven to be a more effective means of contract enforcement than strikes, in addition to continuing the collective bargaining process through the life of the contract. At the federal, state, and local level, the grievance arbitration procedure has borrowed heavily from the private sector.[42]

In the area of discipline and dismissal, however, public sector labor law has developed along completely different lines because of the constitutional protection afforded government employees. When government acts at any level to discipline or dismiss an employee, a form of state action has occurred. The power of the state over an individual is curtailed by the Bill of Rights, and if any constitutionally protected right is infringed upon by the discipline or dismissal of an employee, that employee has a valid claim against the governmental entity regardless of contractual rights. Examples of constitutionally protected rights follow.

1. Privilege against self-incrimination
2. Freedom of association
3. Right to participate in partisan politics
4. Freedom of expression

These constitutionally protected rights, as well as specific statutes allowing government employees to appeal to various courts, have assured public employees of multiple forms of relief not available to private sector employees. While this tends to weaken the grievance-arbitration system, it guarantees the rights of the individual over those of the unions.[43]

Summary

Widespread unionization in the public sector developed later than in the private sector. Presently, unionization is still limited because of the sovereignty doctrine curtailing the scope of collective bargaining in the public sector.

Under Executive Order 10988, as updated under the Civil Service Reform Act of 1978, federal employees are granted limited collective bargaining rights.

The nature of public employment affects the bargaining units, along with the scope and conduct of negotiations. The restriction on the ability to strike in the public sector further limits the effectiveness of the collective bargaining process, even though that restriction is not always followed.

Alternative remedies available to the public employee prevent the grievance-arbitration procedure from becoming the predominant means of contract enforcement as in the private sector.

CASE 12.1   *Bargaining Unit Determination*

Adapted from *Seattle* v. *Amalgamated Transit Union Local 587*, 1977–78, P.B.C. para. 36,046

The union in this case was recognized as the exclusive bargaining representative of a group of public employees who worked in mass transit. The city appealed this finding because the bargaining unit contained certain employees who the city claimed were supervisory and should not be included. While the State Department of Labor had reviewed this contention by the city and found that those employees were properly a part of the unit, a lower court reversed that finding and the union appealed.

Decision

The Court overruled the lower court and reinstated the Department of Labor's finding. It pointed out that the lower court had based its reversal of the Department of Labor's decision on the fact that the department had not followed its own

procedures in determining which employees were supervisory. The Court stated that the lower court was wrong in requiring that those procedures be followed because, unlike the National Labor Relations Act, which excludes supervisory employees from bargaining units, the state law excludes only employees designated as deputy, administrative assistant, or secretary who have a confidential relationship to the executive head of the actual bargaining unit. Therefore, even though the Department of Labor may have applied some type of past procedure in determining the supervisory nature of the public employee, the state law merely excludes the employees in those three classifications who maintain a confidential relationship with the director.

CASE 12.2   *Negotiating in Open Session*

Adapted from *City of Springfield, Missouri* v. *John C. Crow, Judge*, 1979-80, P.B.C. para. 36,815

The members of the City of Springfield Public Utilities Board were negotiating with several labor unions. During the course of those negotiations, the board held numerous meetings with its principal negotiator to discuss issues remaining in dispute. These meetings were not announced to the general public, and it was voted they go into closed session. A newspaper reporter filed suit charging that the board could not meet in closed session to discuss the contract negotiations because of the state's Open Meetings Act.

Decision

The court found that while the state's Open Meetings Act was applicable to the utility board and that it held no specific exemption for collective bargaining sessions, such sessions were not subject to the act. The court based this decision on an interpretation of the rights granted public employees to bargain collectively under another state law. It was the court's opinion that the public employees' right to meaningful collective bargaining would be destroyed if full publicity were accorded at each step of the negotiations. However, the final agreement negotiated by the parties would be subject to an open session.

CASE 12.3 *The Right to Strike*

Adapted from *Burke and Thomas, Inc.* v. *International Organization of Masters, Mates, and Pilots*, 1979-80, P.B.C. para. 36,785

On the eve of Labor Day weekend, the union called a strike of its members, preventing public employees who normally ran ferry services to a tourist island from providing such services over the holiday weekend. The strike was called to protest the change in the wording of a contract under negotiation after the union believed agreement had been reached on the language. The strike was held to be in breach of an existing collective bargaining agreement and was voluntarily ended after the weekend. Members of the public who resided or owned businesses on the islands and were left without a ferry system filed suit against the union, claiming inconvenience and economic harm as a result of the strike. The plaintiffs claimed damages from the union in excess of $1 million.

The plaintiffs based their case on the union's action as being a tortious interference with their business relationships. The plaintiffs also held that they were third-party beneficiaries of the public employee contract, and that the union had breached its duty to them.

The union protested that the plaintiffs were seeking to create a new law to hold public employee unions strictly accountable to the public if anyone was injured by their strikes.

Decision

The court held that the plaintiffs, as members of the public, were not third-party beneficiaries of the collective bargaining agreement between the union and the public employer. To create third-party beneficiary rights, the contract between the first and second party must convey such rights to the third party. In this instance, the purpose of the collective bargaining agreement between the union and the employer was to improve the relationship between the employer and its employees. As to the plaintiffs' contention that the strike was a tortious interference in the business relationships, the court found no such intent. The court held that, although the strike does affect members of the public, the purpose is to use economic force to gain bargaining leverage during contract negotiations. The court also declined to create a tort doctrine to permit public collection of damages from strikes. It felt that decisions affecting resolution of public employee labor relations issues should be left to the legislature. Although a tort doctrine would not hold up in court in this instance, citizens could still require that employees either resume their work or be held in contempt of court.

CASE STUDY   *Bargaining Unit*

Adapted from *School Committee of Wellesley v. Labor Relations Commission*, 1977–78 PBC, 36, 404(1978)

Facts

A bargaining unit consisting of principals, assistant principals, coordinators, and department heads had been represented by the Wellesley Teachers Association for a number of years and had been recognized by the school board. After the effective date of a state statute granting collective bargaining rights to certain public employees, the school board stopped bargaining with the union on the grounds that the employees in the unit were "managerial employees" and excluded from coverage of the state act.

Lawsuit

The state statute in question defines *managerial employees* as those who (a) participate to a substantial degree in formulating or determining policy; (b) assist to a substantial degree in the preparation for or the conduct of collective bargaining for the public employer; and (c) have substantial authority to act independently in an appeal under a collective bargaining agreement.

The parties to this suit analyzed the facts as to the powers, duties, and responsibilities of the unit members quite differently compared to the statutory requirements.

A. *Policy Formation*

FACT: Members of the unit attended and participated in periodic discussions with higher administrators. The meetings were characterized as "input" meetings, and some members were consulted before policy was implemented. Two committees made up of unit members met regularly with the superintendent to discuss policy. Suggestions formulated at these meetings could be forwarded to the school board for action.

UNION POSITION: Unit members participated only in an advisory and consulting role, *not* with authority to make a final decision. Therefore, their participation was not to a "substantial degree."

SCHOOL BOARD POSITION: Statute includes "participation . . . in formulating" policy as well as determining policy. These meetings were for that purpose and put the employees in the "managerial" group.

B. *Collective Bargaining*

FACT: One principal, a member of the unit, attended one negotiating session between the board and the secretary's union. Members of the unit are asked for their opinions on administering the teachers' and secretaries' contracts. The superintendent would like members of the unit to participate with the board in negotiating teachers' and secretaries' contracts.

UNION POSITION: Members did not participate in collective bargaining for the public agency.

SCHOOL BOARD POSITION: The positions of the members of the unit as principals and department heads made them uniquely qualified to assist the board in contract negotiations with other groups, and their status as "non-managerial" obviously presented a conflict of interest to these duties.

C. *Administering Collective Bargaining Agreement*

FACT: Members of the unit are part of the grievance procedure in the collective bargaining agreements of teachers and secretaries. In the two grievances filed under those agreements, the principal was not actually allowed to settle the grievances but served as a conduit to pass them on to the superintendent.

UNION POSITION: The members of the unit do not possess "substantial responsibility," as the actual authority exercised is perfunctory, clerical, routine, or automatic.

SCHOOL BOARD POSITION: Regardless of the actual authority previously exercised, the collective bargaining agreements state the potential authority of the principals to settle grievances. That potential is enough to satisfy the statute.

Questions

1. If you were the judge would you decide the employees are "managerial employees" and therefore not eligible for collective bargaining, or not? Why?
2. Would the fact that these are public employees influence your decision?
3. Do you think the employees in this case would have sought bargaining rights if their participation in management had been as substantial as the school board argued it was?

Key Terms and Concepts

Civil Service Reform Act of 1978

Civil Service System

Community of interest

Executive Order 10988

Fact-finding

Interest arbitration

Pendleton Act

Public sector union security

Sovereignty doctrine

Sunshine laws

Review Questions

1. How are public employees provided the right of collective bargaining? Do state and local government employees have the same rights as federal employees?
2. Why did the government resist collective bargaining?
3. How do public employees' rights and interests differ from those of private sector employees? How do management rights differ between the public and private sectors?
4. Can the news media affect the bargaining process in the public sector? Should their news coverage be curtailed?
5. Give some valid reasons for and against giving public employees the right to strike.

Endnotes

1. Bernard F. Ashe, "Current Trends in Public Employment," *The Labor Lawyer* 2, no. 2 (Spring 1986), pp. 277–298.
2. Pub. L. 91-375, 84 Stat. 737, 39 U.S.C. sec. 1209 (1970).
3. Benjamin Aaron et al., *Public-Sector Bargaining* (Washington, D.C.: Bureau of National Affairs, 1979), p. 46.
4. David Lewin and Shirley B. Goldenberg, "Public Sector Unionism in the U.S. and Canada," *Industrial Relations* 19, no. 3 (Fall 1980), pp. 239–56.
5. Jerry Wurf, "Establishing the Legal Right of Public Employees to Bargain," *Monthly Labor Review* 92, no. 7 (July 1969), p. 66.
6. Henry Campbell Black, *Black's Law Dictionary,* 4th ed. (St. Paul, Minn.: West Publishing, 1968), p. 1568.
7. 5 U.S.C. sec. 7116 (a) (1982).
8. 5 U.S.C. sec. 7116 (b) (1982).
9. 5 U.S.C. sec. 7121 (b) (1982).
10. For an overview of state and local legislation see Aaron, *Public-Sector Bargaining*, pp. 191–223; and Nels E. Nelson, "Public Policy and Union Security in the Public Sector," *Journal of Collective Negotiations in the Public Sector* 7, no. 2 (1978), pp. 87–117.
11. 426 U.S. 833 (1976).
12. Gregory M. Saltzman, "Bargaining Laws as a Cause and Consequence of the Growth of Teacher Unionism," *Industrial and Labor Relations Review* 38, no. 3 (April 1985), pp. 335–351.
13. Lewin, "Public Sector Unionism," p. 245.
14. Aaron, *Public-Sector Bargaining*, pp. 80–117.
15. E. Edward Herman and Alfred Kuhn, *Collective Bargaining and Labor Relations* (Englewood Cliffs, N.J.: Prentice-Hall, 1981), p. 101.
16. James E. Martin, "Employee Characteristics and Representation Election Outcomes," *Industrial and Labor Relations Review* 38, no. 3 (April 1985) pp. 365–376.
17. Ellis v. Brotherhood of Railway, Airline and Steamship Clerks, 446 U.S. 435, 104 S. Ct. 1883, 80 L.Ed. 2d 428 (1984). See also Abood v. Detroit Board of Education, 230 N.W.2d 322, 90 LRRM 2152 (1975). Charles M. Rehmus and Benjamin A. Kerner, "The Agency Shop After *ABOOD:* No Free Ride, but What's the Fare?" *Industrial and Labor Relations Review* 34, no. 1 (Oct. 1980), pp. 90–100.
18. Elrod v. Burns, 427 U.S. 347 (1976).
19. "Compulsory Unionism in Government Employment," Public Service Research Council, reprinted in *Should the Federal Government Significantly Curtail the Powers of Labor Unions in the United States?* (Washington, D.C.: Government Printing Office, 1981), pp. 473–82.
20. William J. Moore and John Raisian, "Public-Sector Union Wage Effects: A Time Series Analysis," *Monthly Labor Review* 105, no. 8 (Aug. 1982): pp. 49–53.
21. Benjamin Aaron et al., *The Future of Labor Arbitration in America* (New York: American Arbitration Association, 1976), p. 18.
22. Lewin, "Public Sector Unionism," p. 249.
23. Peter Feuille and John C. Anderson, "Public Sector Bargaining: Policy and Practice," *Industrial Relations* 19, no. 3 (Fall 1980), pp. 309–24.
24. Roger L. Bowlby and William R. Schriver, "The Behavioral Interpretation of Bluffing: A Public Sector Case," *Labor Law Journal* 32, no. 8 (Aug. 1981), pp. 469–73.

25. Eugene H. Becker, "Analysis of Work Stoppages in the Federal Sector, 1962–81," *Monthly Labor Review* 105, no. 8 (Aug. 1982), pp. 49–53.

26. Theodore W. Kheel, "Resolving Deadlocks Without Banning Strikes," *Monthly Labor Review* 92, no. 7 (July 1969), p. 62.

27. John M. Capozzola, "Public Employee Strikes: Myths and Realities," *National Civic Review* 68, no. 4 (April 1979), pp. 178–88.

28. Aaron, *Public-Sector Bargaining*, p. 151.

29. Bernard F. Ashe, "Current Trends in Public Employment," *The Labor Lawyer* 2, no. 2 (Spring 1986), pp. 277–298.

30. Randy Steele, "The Rise of PATCO," *Flying* 109 (March 1982), p. 35.

31. Ibid.

32. Michael Doan, "When Workers Took On Uncle Sam," *U.S. News and World Report* (Aug. 1981), pp. 17–20.

33. Steele, "The Rise of PATCO," p. 35.

34. Herbert R. Northrup, "The Rise and Demise of PATCO," *Industrial and Labor Relations Review* 37, no. 2 (Jan. 1984), pp. 167–84.

35. Kenneth P. Swan, "Public Bargaining in Canada and the U.S.: A Legal View," *Industrial Relations* 19, no. 3 (Fall 1980), pp. 272–91.

36. David E. Bloom, "Is Arbitration Really Compatible with Bargaining?" *Industrial Relations* 20, no. 3 (Fall 1981), pp. 233–44. See also Patricia Compton-Forbes, "Interest Arbitration Hasn't Worked Well in the Public Sector," *Personnel Administrator* 29, no. 2 (Feb. 1984), pp. 99–104.

37. Angelo S. DeNisi and James B. Dworkin, "Final-Offer Arbitration and the Naive Negotiator," *Industrial and Labor Relations Review* 35, no. 1 (Oct. 1981), pp. 78–87, and John C. Anderson, "The Impact of Arbitration: A Methodological Assessment," *Industrial Relations* 20, no. 2 (Spring 1981), pp. 129–48.

38. J. Joseph Loewenberg, "The 1984 Postal Arbitration: Issues Surrounding the Award," *Monthly Labor Review* 109, no. 6 (June 1986), pp. 31–32.

39. 5 U.S.C. sec. 7103(a)(12) (1982).

40. 5 U.S.C. sec. 7106 (1982).

41. 5 U.S.C. sec. 7122 (1982).

42. Henry Graham and Virginia Wallace, "Trends in Public Sector Arbitration," *Personnel Administrator* 27 (April 1982), pp. 73–77.

43. David L. Dilts and Clarence K. Deitsch, "Arbitration Lost: The Public Sector Assault on Arbitration," *Labor Law Journal* 35, no. 3 (March 1984), pp. 182–88.

Equal Employment Opportunity

LABOR NEWS

Affirmative Action Reaffirmed by U.S. Supreme Court

In 1986 and 1987, the United States Supreme Court upheld and extended the general principles of affirmative action as they have evolved since the 1960s. In three related decisions in 1986, the court ruled that minority-preference hiring and promotion plans are not limited to actual victims of job discrimination, and employment goals by employers may be used. In 1987, the Court ruled employers may favor women and minorities over better qualified men and whites. The landmark cases include Wygant v. Jackson Board of Education, *U.S. Supreme Court, 1986, 40 FEB Cases 1321;* Local 28, Sheet Metal Workers v. EEOC, *U.S. Supreme Court, 1986, 41 FEP Cases 107;* Local 93, Firefighters v. City of Cleveland, *U.S. Supreme Court, 1986, 41 FEP Cases 139;* Johnson v. Transportation Agency, *U.S. Supreme Court, 1987.*

In Wygant *the Court held that affirmative action plans need not be victim specific and*

may benefit individuals who did not suffer actual discrimination. Also the Court endorsed the concept that underuse of minorities or women can justify establishing an affirmative action plan. Actual discrimination need not be found. Affirmative action goals in hiring are allowed because no one has a right to a job, and such affirmative action would diffuse the impact of preferences. Affirmative action goals in promotion are allowed if strictly tailored to specific jobs, but affirmative action in layoffs is only allowed under the most stringent set of circumstances. The Court generally upheld the use of a seniority system in layoff situations.

In Sheet Metal Workers, *the Court said a court may order a union to use quotas to overcome a history of discrimination. Also, black and hispanic applicants can benefit even if they personally were not victims of past union bias. The Court also pointed out the benefits of a flexible affirmative action plan rather than the rigid application of a color-blind policy.*

And in Firefighters *the Court upheld a consent decree even though the promotional goals caused the seniority of white firefighters to be ignored. It upheld a voluntary agreement between a union and a public employer to promote minorities on a one-to-one basis.*

In Johnson *the Court ruled that employers may voluntarily correct a "manifest imbalance" in the work force through an affirmative action plan. In this case Diane Joyce, a road maintenance worker in Santa Clara County, California, received a promotion over Paul Johnson, another road worker who had scored higher on an interview. The transportation agency decided to promote Joyce due to a shortage of women in its work force. A federal district court had declared illegal the* affirmative action plan used by the agency when Johnson sued the county. The Supreme Court, however, ruled the county could hire a woman over a better qualified man as part of an affirmative action program. This was the Court's first decision upholding hiring goals based on sex rather than race.

In summary, the Court upheld court-ordered or voluntary affirmative action plans, including numerical standards, to address underuse even if such a plan benefits nonvictims of discrimination. Within their affirmative action plan, private and public employers may hire or promote women and minorities over more qualified white men. Union-negotiated seniority systems, however, may be followed in layoff/recall situations even though they do not follow affirmative action goals.

Since the creation of equal employment opportunity and related laws and court decisions, few aspects of employment have been as controversial, overlapping, and conflicting. Compounded by their relationship to labor unions and collective bargaining, employers find it difficult to comply with equal employment opportunity laws as interpreted by the courts. In some areas, employment discrimination principles and collective bargaining coexist with little problem; however, often their practice and principles seem to clash. The intent of laws and subsequent Supreme Court decisions was to provide equal employment opportunity and affirmative action, along with collective bargaining, to determine issues such as wages, seniority, and promotions. Yet many unions provided for minority training and nondiscrimination within their membership prior to this legislation.

Four major federal laws regulate fair and equal rights in employment. The oldest is the Fair Labor Standards Act of 1938. The 1938 act has as its broad objectives minimum wage provision to provide a rudimentary standard of living, the establishment of the standard forty-hour work week, and the discouragement of child labor.[1] The other major federal laws include the Civil Rights Act of 1964, as amended by the Equal Employment Opportunities Act of 1972; the Equal Pay Act of 1963, as amended in 1974; and the Age Discrimination Employment Act of 1967, as amended in 1978. Each of these acts forbids union and employer discrimination against certain categories of individuals. They apply not only to the hiring process but also to pay, promotion, and other employment opportunities.

Prior to the landmark Supreme Court decision in *Griggs* v. *Duke Power Co.*, discrimination in employment was usually in the context of an individual worker rather than a group of employees.[2] The *Griggs* decision shifted the focus of employment discrimination from individuals to groups subjected to adverse impact by employers. This adverse impact theory opened up a new area of industrial relations to include the equal employment, compensation, and mobility of minorities and females.[3]

Unions and Minority Employment

The AFL-CIO and other union organizations have often supported the concept of equal employment opportunity. The AFL-CIO supported the Civil Rights Act of 1964 and supports the ratification of the Equal Rights Amendment to the U.S. Constitution "to provide equality of the sexes under the law that can be used in efforts to eliminate employment discrimination against women."[4]

In March 1974 women within the U.S. labor movement organized the founding conference of the Coalition of Labor Union Women (CLUW). Recognizing that less than 12 percent of the women in the labor force are unionized and that most working women are suffering economically, the CLUW was formed to promote unionism. Following is the statement of purpose adopted at the CLUW founding conference:

> It is imperative that within the framework of the union movement the Coalition of Labor Union Women take aggressive steps to more effectively address the critical needs of millions of unorganized sisters and make our unions more responsive to the needs of all women, especially the needs of minority women who have traditionally been singled out for particularly blatant oppression.
>
> Union women work in almost every industry, in almost every part of the country. Despite their geographical, industrial and occupational separations, union women share common concerns and goals.
>
> Full equality of opportunities and rights in the labor force require the full attention of the labor movement . . . and especially, the full attention of women who are part of the labor movement.
>
> The primary purpose of this National Coalition is to unify all union women in a viable organization to determine our common problems and concerns and to develop action programs within the framework of our unions to deal effectively with our objectives. This struggle goes beyond the borders of this Nation and we urge our working sisters throughout the world to join us in accomplishing these objectives through their labor organizations.[5]

Today the CLUW is a nonpartisan organization within the union movement and has seventy-five chapters across the nation. The stated goals of the CLUW include the following:

☐ To promote affirmative action in the workplace
☐ To strengthen the role of women within their unions
☐ To organize unorganized women
☐ To increase the involvement of women in the political and legislative process[6]

The effect of unionism on the employment of minorities and women is not clear. Black employment appears to be greater in the union sectors of the economy than in the nonunion sectors. Blacks in general have a greater preference for union membership than whites.[7] Women and Hispanics do not exhibit the same preference for union membership, nor has their employment been greater in the union sector.[8]

Civil Rights Legislation

The Civil Rights Act of 1964

In the early 1960s Congress and the nation witnessed hundreds of demonstrations throughout the country when minorities, particularly blacks, demanded their civil rights as provided by the Constitution. The primary federal law in the field of fair employment practice is the **Civil Rights Act of 1964**, passed only months after the assassination of President John F. Kennedy, its major supporter and author. The act requires employment and compensation of employees without discrimination based on race, color, religion, sex, or national origin:

> *Title VII, Section 703:* It is unlawful for an employer to discriminate against an individual with respect to his compensation, terms, conditions, or privileges of employment because of such individual's race, color, religion, sex, or national origin; or to limit, segregate, or classify his employees in any way which would deprive or tend to deprive any individual of employment opportunities or otherwise adversely affect his status as an employee, because of such individual's race, color, religion, sex, or national origin.[9]

Both employer and union are responsible for fair treatment under **Title VII** of the Civil Rights Act. Case 13.1 describes how a union's handling of a grievance can be challenged under the Civil Rights Act. The employer may not blame failure to comply with the act on barriers in the union contract or threat of a suit if such action is taken. Courts have held this is not a justifiable necessity.[10]

The union and the employer must assure the labor contract provides for equal employment opportunity. Legally the union is obligated to revise any provisions having a discriminatory effect, regardless of the wishes of its membership. The employer is required to unilaterally comply with Title VII, and if such compliance conflicts with the collective bargaining agreement, it is not a violation of the good faith bargaining provision of the National Labor Relations Act. In fact there are several indications that bargaining is the foundation of the EEO process. For example, Title VII requires the Equal Opportunity Employment Commission (EEOC) to settle disputes by informal methods of conciliation.[11]

Title VII requires the removal of artificial, arbitrary, and unnecessary barriers to employment when the barriers discriminate on the basis of racial or other nonpermissible classifications.[12] Such barriers identified by the Supreme Court and other federal courts include practices and policies of recruitment, selection, placement, testing, transfer, promotion, and seniority as well as other basic terms and conditions of employment.[13]

Equal Employment Opportunity Commission
The 1964 act established the federal **Equal Employment Opportunity Commission (EEOC)**. The EEOC was given

the authority to investigate employee complaints of discrimination arising under the provisions of the act. The EEOC can bring suit in federal court against employers and unions if it finds such action justified. When investigating an employee complaint, the EEOC will determine if there is **probable cause**—a reasonable possibility—of discrimination. If probable cause exists, the EEOC may arrange a conciliation meeting with the employer to discuss the complaint and, if necessary, take the complaint to federal court. A court procedure in a discrimination case generally follows that specified by the Supreme Court in the *McDonnell-Douglas Corporation* v. *Green* case.[14] In that case it was outlined that the aggrieved employee must generally prove that he or she is a minority or female, was qualified for the position and available, and was not hired for the position. The employee must also prove that the employer continues to seek others for the job.

As a defense, the employer may choose to claim that the employee did not have the required bona fide occupational qualifications (BFOQ). Title VII provides that an employer may in certain instances hire employees of a particular religion, sex, or national origin if such is a bona fide occupational qualification to perform the job. An example of a maximum hiring age BFOQ upheld by a court is presented in Case 13.2. Or, the employer may prove it was a business necessity not to hire the complainant. This defense requires proof that the individual could not have successfully performed the job due to inability to work required hours or relate to specific clientele. Or, the person hired is, in fact, better qualified for the job than the complainant. The last is the most common defense of employers with professional personnel systems.

In 1972, Congress amended the 1964 Civil Rights Act to include under Title VII all private employers and labor unions with fifteen or more employees or members; state and local governments; and public and private educational institutions. The amendment also strengthened the 1964 act by giving the EEOC the power to bring suits directly to federal courts when employer conciliation efforts have failed. Following the 1972 amendment, labor unions and employers were required to provide survey information to the EEOC, as in Exhibit 13.1. This information is used to compile workforce analysis and labor market information.

Court-ordered remedies   When the courts have found discrimination under Title VII, a variety of remedies may be applied including the reinstatement or hiring of employees, the awarding of back pay and seniority rights, and the payment of the cost of litigation. The courts have ruled that remedies must not only open the doors to equal employment for all, but also must make whole and restore the rightful economic status of those affected. In practice this has resulted in extremely expensive assessment for back-pay and legal costs. The lengthy process of investigation by the EEOC and eventual legal action add substantially to the cost of the remedy.[15] The 1972 amendment to the Civil Rights Act limits back-pay court orders to a period of two years prior to the filing of the charge.[16] The Supreme Court in ***Albemarle Paper Company*** **v.** ***Moody*** in 1975 held that back-pay should be denied only in very limited situations. In that landmark case the Court noted

> If employers faced only the prospect of an injunctive order, they would have little incentive to shun practices of dubious legality. It is a reasonably certain prospect of a back pay award that is the spur or catalyst which causes employers and unions to self-examine

Exhibit 13.1 Union information report

OMB NO 124-R0016

EQUAL EMPLOYMENT OPPORTUNITY
LOCAL UNION REPORT (EEO-3)

SAMPLE

Mail Completed Report to:
Union Reporting Program (EEO-3)
Benjamin Franklin Station
P.O. Box 14267
Washington, D.C. 20044

Part A. LOCAL UNIONS REQUIRED TO FILE

1. Approximately how many members does the local union have?

_____ members

If the local union has at all times since last December 31, had less than 100 members, fill in Parts A, B, and F, and return the form to Union Reporting Program at the above address, so that you will not receive additional correspondence with respect to this form.

If the local union has had 100 members or more at any time since last December 31, complete the form as instructed.

NOTE—A labor organization is deemed to be a local union if it performs, in a specific jurisdiction, the functions ordinarily performed by a local union, whether or not it is so designated.

Part B. LOCAL UNION IDENTIFICATION

1. Full name of local union for which this report is filed. (Include local number, if any.)

b. Union office, if different from 2a.

Number and street

City

County

State   ZIP Code

2. Mailing address

a. Where official mail should be sent to the union

Number and street

City

County

State

ZIP Code

3. Indicate type of local union report by a check in applicable box

☐ Report filed by local union in its own behalf

☐ Other (explain)

4a. Are you affiliated with or chartered by a national or international union or national federation?   Yes ☐   No ☐

b. If "Yes" to item 4a, give name and address of such national or international organization.

5. Are you affiliated with the AFL—CIO?   Yes ☐   No ☐

Part C. LOCAL UNION PRACTICES

1. To the best of your knowledge, does your membership include any

	Yes	No
a. Blacks (Non-Hispanic)?	☐	☐
b. Hispanics?	☐	☐
c. Women?	☐	☐

3. To the best of your knowledge, has your international union chartered a separate local within the same work and/or area jurisdiction which consists only of

	Yes	No
a. Persons of the same race/ethnic identity	☐	☐
b. Persons of the same sex?	☐	☐

2. If "No" to any items 1a, 1b, or 1c, is this because the group or groups not represented

(CHECK ALL APPLICABLE BOXES)

	BLACK NON-HISPANIC 1 (a)	HISPANIC 1 (b)	WOMEN 1 (c)
a. Are not in the local community?			
b. Are not in the bargaining unit?			
c. Are excluded by provision in constitution or bylaws?			
d. Have not applied for membership?			
e. Have applied, but did not have a sponsor?			
f. Have applied, but did not meet qualifications other than sponsorship?			

g. Other reason(s) (Explain) _____

Part D. REQUIREMENTS FOR FILING SCHEDULE I

1. Does the local union, or any unit, division, or agent of the local union, or any labor organization which performs, within a specific jurisdiction, the functions ordinarily performed by a local union, whether or not it is so designated:

	Yes	No
a. Operate a hiring hall or hiring office?	☐	☐
b. Have an arrangement under which one or more employers are required to consider or hire persons referred by the local union or an agent of the local union?	☐	☐
c. Have 10 percent or more of its members employed by employers which customarily and regularly look to the union, or any agent of the union, for employees to be hired on a casual or temporary basis, for a specified period of time, or for the duration of a specified job?	☐	☐

2. You are required to file Schedule I:

If the answer is "Yes" to any of the three questions in item 1.

(See item 12 of instructions explaining who must file Schedule I.)

If the answer is "No" to all three questions, then the local union is considered to be a "Non-Referral Union". Check this box, ☐ and complete only Parts A through F.

(See definition of "Referral Union" in Section 4 of the general instructions.)

EEOC FORM 274   SEPT 79   PREVIOUS EDITIONS ARE OBSOLETE

EEOC ORIGINAL

PAGE 1

Part E. REMARKS

Part F. IDENTIFICATION AND SIGNATURE

To the best of my knowledge and belief, the information contained in this report is true and complete. It is further certified that to the extent any data in Schedule I, Items 2 or 3, are based on self-identification by individuals, this information was gathered only after they were advised of its confidential nature and purposes.

1. Type or print name, title, work address, and telephone number of designated representative

Name _____

Title _____

Work address _____

Telephone number (including area code) _____

2. Signature of designated representative _____

3. Date _____

"Whoever, in any matter within the jurisdiction of any department or agency of the United States knowingly and willfully falsifies, conceals, or covers up by any trick, scheme, or device a material fact, or makes any false, fictitious or fraudulent statements or representations, or makes or uses any false writing or document knowing the same to contain any false, fictitious or fraudulent statement or entry, shall be fined not more than $10,000 or imprisoned not more than 5 years, or both." Title 18, Section 1001, United States Code.

Exhibit 13.1   (continued)

SCHEDULE I—REFERRAL UNION INFORMATION LOCAL UNION REPORT (EEO—3)

TO BE ANSWERED BY "REFERRAL UNIONS" ONLY

This schedule must be filled out by all local unions which answer "Yes" to any one of the three questions in Part D, Item 1 of Report EEO—3.

1. Name, local number, and address of union as shown in Part B, Items 1 and 2 of Report EEO—3.

Control (LM) Number

2. Method of Identification

Check applicable box(es)

How was information as to race/ethnic identification and sex in item 3 below obtained?

This information may be obtained by visual survey, from records made after employment, from personal knowledge or by self-identification. The self-identification method may be used subject to the conditions set forth in the instructions. No State law prohibiting the self-identification method applies, since the Equal Employment Opportunity Commission's regulations supersede such laws.

a. Existing Record	
b. Visual Survey	
c. Tally from Personal Knowledge	
d. Self-Identification	
e. Other (specify)	

3. Statistics

Membership in Referral Bargaining Units Only

a. Membership

	(1) All Members	(2) MEMBERS BY RACE/ETHNIC CATEGORY	MALE	FEMALE
TOTAL		WHITE (NON-HISPANIC)		
		BLACK (NON-HISPANIC)		
Male		HISPANIC		
		ASIAN AMERICAN or PACIFIC ISLANDER		
Female		AMERICAN INDIAN or ALASKAN NATIVE		

b. Referrals

Referrals During 2-Month Period

	(1) All Referrals	(2) REFERRALS BY RACE/ETHNIC CATEGORY	MALE	FEMALE
TOTAL		WHITE (NON-HISPANIC)		
		BLACK (NON-HISPANIC)		
Male		HISPANIC		
		ASIAN AMERICAN or PACIFIC ISLANDER		
Female		AMERICAN INDIAN or ALASKAN NATIVE		

(3) Period used for Referral Date (you should obtain the figures on referrals during any 2-month period between August 1 and November 30)

(Dates)_____

c. Applicants

To the best of your knowledge, enter the number of applicants for membership and for referral.

(1) APPLICANTS FOR UNION MEMBERSHIP DURING THE PAST YEAR		(2) APPLICANTS FOR JOB REFERRAL DURING 2-MONTH PERIOD	
ALL APPLICANTS		ALL APPLICANTS	
MINORITIES		MINORITIES	
BLACK (NON-HISPANIC)		BLACK (NON-HISPANIC)	
HISPANIC		HISPANIC	
ASIAN AMERICAN or PACIFIC ISLANDER		ASIAN AMERICAN or PACIFIC ISLANDER	
AMERICAN INDIAN or ALASKAN NATIVE		AMERICAN INDIAN or ALASKAN NATIVE	

EEOC FORM 274
SEPT. 79   PREVIOUS EDITIONS ARE OBSOLETE

EEOC ORIGINAL

PAGE 2

and self-evaluate their employment practices and endeavor to eliminate, so far as possible, the last bastions of unfortunate and ignominious pages in this country's history.

It is also the purpose of Title VII to make whole for injuries suffered on account of unlawful employment discrimination. This is shown by the very fact that Congress took care to arm the courts with full equitable powers. The "make whole" purpose of Title VII is made evident by the legislative history. The back pay provision was expressly modeled on the back pay provision of the National Labor Relations Act. Under that act "making the workers whole for losses suffered on account of unfair labor practice is part of the vindication of the public policy which the board enforces." We may assume that Congress is aware that the board, since its inception, has awarded back pay as a matter of course, not randomly or in the exercise of a standard list discretion, and not merely where employer violations were peculiarly deliberate, aggrievous, or inexcusable. Furthermore, in passing the Equal Employment Opportunity Act of 1972 Congress considered several bills to limit the judicial power to award back pay. These limiting efforts were rejected, and the back pay provision was reenacted substantially in its original form.[17]

The **make whole concept** refers to a concept of providing back-pay, position, and lost seniority as a remedy to persons who have suffered discrimination. The phrase refers to the practice of providing remedies that totally place the person in the position she would have been in had she not been discriminated against originally.

The awarding of remedies can lead to conflict among employees within a collective bargaining unit. If a group of employees is awarded back-pay and/or additional seniority from a court case, resentment from other employees can lead to internal conflict within the union as well as with the employer. Some unions, with total support of their membership, are admirably able to represent minority employees who suffered past discrimination. Many unions won court-ordered remedies for minority members; however, such cases often result in animosity between the few minority members and the majority of the members of their bargaining unit.

Sexual harassment   Based on the Civil Rights Act, the EEOC developed guidelines that declared **sexual harassment** a form of illegal sex discrimination. Sexual harassment constitutes a form of behavior directed towards an employee specifically because of his or her sex. (Most incidences of sexual harassment are directed towards women, but research shows that male employees are also sexually harassed on the job, though such incidences are few compared to the problems reported by women.) The EEOC also issued guidelines that set forth a working definition of sexual harassment:

> Unwelcome sexual advances, requests for sexual favors, and other verbal or physical conduct of a sexual nature constitute sexual harassment when (1) submission to such conduct is made either explicitly or implicitly a term or condition of an individual's employment, (2) submission to or rejection of such conduct by an individual is used as a basis for employment decisions affecting such individual, or (3) such conduct has the purpose or effect of unreasonably interfering with an individual's work performance or creating an intimidating, hostile, or offensive working environment.[18]

Sexual harassment may include verbal abuse; sexist remarks; patting, pinching, or brushing against the body; leering or ogling; demand for sexual favors in return for a job or promotion; and physical assault.[19]

The U.S. Supreme Court in 1986 issued its first ruling on sexual harassment. The historic decision, *Meritor Savings Bank* v. *Vinson*, clarified the duty of employers and unions in instances involving possible sexual harassment. The Court stated that business may be held liable for sexual harassment by their employees even if they are unaware of the illegal actions. Furthermore, the Court decided that "without question, when a supervisor sexually harasses a subordinate because of the subordinate's sex, that supervisor discriminates on the basis of sex."[20]

In the *Meritor* case the Supreme Court focused on whether the sexual conduct was unwelcome and concluded that a person may be the victim of illegal sexual harassment even though she voluntarily participated in sexual acts.[21] The harassment may occur at a later date when the employee no longer wishes to be participating in sexual activities or finds such participation a requirement for favorable employment decisions. The Court also criticized the employer's harassment policy, which required employees to report incidents to their immediate supervisor, who may be the harasser. The court suggested a procedure whereby employees can state their complaints to an objective, supportive party. Obviously, unions have realized their standard grievance and arbitration procedures would provide such a mechanism to hear complaints and represent a victim's interests.

Reverse discrimination In a 1979 case, *United Steelworkers* v. *Weber,* the Supreme Court ruled on what is considered as the landmark decision on **reverse discrimination**.[22] In the suit, Weber alleged that the Kaiser Aluminum Voluntary Affirmative Action Program, in reserving 50 percent of the craft training openings for blacks, had discriminated against white employees with more seniority by giving preference to blacks with less time on the job. Weber contended that Congress intended in Title VII to make discrimination illegal in the broadest of interpretations of the Civil Rights Act. Thus, reserving 50 percent of the openings for members of a particular race was reverse discrimination against nonblack employees. The Court noted that while the argument made by Weber had some merit, it did not consider the spirit of the 1964 Civil Rights Act. The act was primarily concerned with the plight of blacks in our economy. Congress intended to open employment opportunities for them in previously closed occupations; the court contended that Congress did not want to prohibit the private sector from accomplishing the goal of the act.

The *Weber* decision established that the Civil Rights Act cannot be literally interpreted but must be considered in terms of Congressional intention and in view of historical discrimination against minorities, especially blacks, in this country. The *Weber* decision also permits employers to voluntarily establish affirmative action plans that can include quotas or require that a certain number or percentage of positions can be reserved for minorities or women. Thus, while the concept of reverse discrimination may exist in the minds of some people, it is not prohibited under the Civil Rights Act as interpreted by the Supreme Court. The Court noted, however, that the Kaiser plan did not unnecessarily trammel the interest of white males; no white males were terminated and the plan was temporary.[23]

Another Supreme Court decision, *Bakke* v. *University of California,* came shortly before the *Weber* case.[24] In the *Bakke* case, a white male claimed reverse discrimination when denied admission to the University of California medical school, even though he had scored higher on entrance exams than some minority students. The school had reserved a certain number of positions for minority candidates. The Supreme Court, in a 5–4 decision, ruled that Bakke should be admitted even though race could be considered in a school's admission plan. To clarify the Court's position on reverse discrimination in employment, many felt it decided to rule on the *Weber* case to establish a precedent reverse discrimination case. The Court did not consider *Bakke* to be a landmark reverse discrimination case, but in the wake of the national publicity concerning it, the Court clarified the issue of reverse discrimination in the *Weber* case.[25]

Affirmative Action Programs

Affirmative action programs require employers or unions to increase the employment and promotion of certain persons or groups of individuals. This goes a step beyond the equal employment opportunity laws that merely require that organizations obey them and not discriminate against minorities and women. However, affirmative action programs require that the employer or union take specific steps to be nondiscriminatory in their employment opportunities and to improve their record of minority employment.

With Executive Order (E.O.) 11246, President Lyndon B. Johnson created the most important source of affirmative action requirements. While an E.O. does not have the impact of federal law, it directly affects governmental agencies and organizations with contracts or subcontracts with federal government programs. In addition, many employers and unions voluntarily developed affirmative action programs similar to the requirements stated by this and succeeding executive orders.

The development and administration of an affirmative action program for either an employer or union generally have these requirements:

1. *Written policy*   Provide a copy of the affirmative action policy specifying a commitment to equal employment opportunity to all employees and to all applicants. The company must reaffirm this commitment in public notices and recruitment ads.

2. *Director*   Appoint a top-ranking official as the individual responsible for monitoring the affirmative action program. This individual must have the authority to receive the assistance and cooperation of all employees of the organization in developing and carrying out the program. The affirmative action director must also have the authority to intervene in any organizational actions contrary to the affirmative action plan.

3. *Work force analysis*   Complete a current work force analysis for the organization consisting of a head count of the employees, classifying them by job category and minority or nonminority states (see Exhibit 13.2). Then determine whether the organization has underutilized minorities or females in any job classification. This is done by comparing the percentage of minorities or females within the job classification to the relevant percentages within the local labor market as estimated by the U.S. Department of Labor. If underutilization exists, then the organization must take the proper steps to increase the employment of minorities or women in that particular job category.

4. *Goals and timetables*   Where underutilization exists, specify goals and timetables to estimate future openings within those job categories so the organization will increase utilization equal to that of the local labor market.

5. *Recruitment plans*   Recruitment methods the organization used in the past must be changed, because obviously they have not allowed for successful recruitment of minorities or females as compared to other employers within the labor market. A specific plan to attract these groups into deficient job categories must be developed.

The heart of affirmative action is the commitment of the union and the employer to not discriminate and, in job categories with a lower percentage of minorities or females than other firms in the local labor market, to take positive steps to increase the recruitment and employment of minorities and females in those job categories. Thus, a minority or female candidate will not only have an equal opportunity of being hired

Exhibit 13.2 Work force analysis

COMPLIANCE SURVEY

AFFIRMATIVE ACTION YEAR FROM: _____ , 19 ____ TO _____ , 19 ____

COMPANY NAME: _____

ADDRESS: _____ Phone: (Area Code ____)

FACILITY COVERED BY PLAN: _____

ADDRESS: _____ Phone: (Area Code ____)

JOB CATEGORIES	TOTAL	PRESENT WORKFORCE															JOB VACANCIES DURING PAST YEAR HOW FILLED					% AVAIL-ABILITY				UNDER UTILI-ZATION (Yes/No)		PROJECTED OPENINGS	GOALS								
		MALE							FEMALE																					CURRENT YEAR						ULTIMATE	
																														Hires		Promotes				%/Year	
		White	Black	Hispanic	Asian/ P.I.	Am. Ind. Ak. Nat.	White	Black	Hispanic	Asian/ P.I.	Am. Ind. Ak. Nat.					Total	Male	Fem.	Min.	Fem.	Min.	Fem.	Min.		Fem.	Min.		Fem.	Min.	Fem.	Min.	Fem.	Min.
OFFICIALS AND MANAGERS																																	
PROFESSIONALS																																	
TECHNICIANS																																	
SALES WORKERS																																	
OFFICE AND CLERICAL																																	
CRAFTSWORKERS (Skilled)																																	
OPERATIVES (Semi-Skilled)																																	
LABORERS (Unskilled)																																	
SERVICE WORKERS																																	
TOTALS																																	

EQUAL EMPLOYMENT OFFICER NAME _____

SIGNATURE _____ DATE _____

Form No. 3-80

or offered union apprentice training in deficient job categories, but if they are substantially equal in their qualifications, they will be given preference.

The labor agreement may implement the affirmative action plan in three basic steps. First, it will focus on the recruitment and selection of minority employees rather than attempting to change employees' attitudes toward minorities and females. Experience shows that many managers and union members still do not recognize the importance of or agree with the principles of affirmative action. It is difficult, if not impossible, to change attitudes that have built up over time. Instead, the affirmative action program must concentrate on the recruitment and selection of qualified minorities and females who will become productive employees. Second, the agreement should encourage participation in the design and implementation of the program from all levels within the union and the organization. Over time, people will realize the importance and the positive nature of the program. Third, the agreement should relate the organization's overall affirmative action goals to each department's specific goals and timetables. Each department will realize it must meet its individual goals if the entire organization is to have a successful affirmative action program.[26]

The Office of Federal Contract Compliance Executive Order 11246 also created the **Office of Federal Contract Compliance (OFCC)** for its administration. The OFCC thus has the responsibility of implementing equal employment opportunity in the federal procurement process and specifies the regulations and processes applying to federal organizations and all contractors and subcontractors. The OFCC conducts compliance reviews for federal agencies such as the Department of Defense and Housing and Urban Development, as well as other agencies and governmental contractors. The OFCC can also cancel or suspend contracts if the contractor fails to comply with equal employment opportunity or affirmative action provisions. The director of the OFCC may initiate proceedings to correct the situation. Thus, both management and labor realize it is in their best interest to develop OFCC-approved affirmative action plans.

The Age Discrimination in Employment Act

The **Age Discrimination in Employment Act (ADEA)** was passed by Congress in 1967 and amended in 1978 and 1986. The act makes it illegal for employers with twenty or more employees, state and local governments, as well as labor unions with twenty-five or more employees to discriminate against individuals over age forty. Employers cannot refuse to hire or discriminate in terms of compensation, promotion, or other conditions based solely on an individual's age. Employers are also prohibited from using age as a preference in their recruiting practices. However, the Supreme Court developed a *determining factor test* in *Laugesen* v. *Anaconda Company*:

> We believe that it was essential for the jury to understand from the instructions that there could be more than one factor to discharge him, and that he was nevertheless entitled to recover [damages] if one such factor was his age and if, in fact, it made a difference whether he was retained or discharged . . . thus, even though age may only be one factor in determining an employment decision, it cannot be used as a basis for discrimination against individuals.[27]

The 1986 amendment prohibits any mandatory retirement age for workers (previously set at age seventy [1978 amendment] and originally at age sixty-five [1967 act]). Public safety employees of state and local governments are exempt until 1994, a measure intended to allow the EEOC adequate time to determine the validity of mental and fitness tests in such areas as police, fire, and emergency medical services. The 1986 amendment also mandates employers to continue the same group health insurance for employees over age seventy that is offered to younger employees. The elimination of mandatory retirement age has received ardent support from senior citizens, labor leaders, and civil rights groups.[28]

Section 4 (f) of the ADEA allows employers and labor unions to discipline or terminate an employee for a job-related reason such as incompetence, theft, or some other just cause that is "not age related." The courts have upheld employers' age policies where health and safety are of concern. In a landmark case, *Hodgson* v. *Greyhound Lines, Inc.* a court of appeals upheld Greyhound's policy of barring applicants under the age of thirty-five for the job of bus driver.[29]

The Vocational Rehabilitation Act of 1973

The **Vocational Rehabilitation Act of 1973** requires employers with government contracts of $2,500 or more to develop approved affirmative action programs for the handicapped. These affirmative action programs include special recruitment efforts for the handicapped as well as procedures to promote and develop handicapped employees within the organization. Under the act, a *handicapped person* is defined as an individual with a physical or mental disability resulting in a substantial handicap to employment. Such an individual would benefit from vocational rehabilitation services.[30]

The courts have generally not broadened the definition of handicapped. In *Forrisi* v. *Bowen,* the U.S. Court of Appeals for the Fourth Circuit ruled that acrophobia (abnormal fear of heights) is not a handicap protected under the 1973 act. While the court did not dispute the worker's claim of having a fear of heights, it concluded that the Rehabilitation Act was only designed to protect individuals who are "truly disabled."[31]

The Rehabilitation Act does not require the establishment of specific goals and timetables for the handicapped. Instead employers are required to make reasonable accommodations, such as adding ramps to their businesses. However, *reasonable* is not specifically defined, and accommodations must be made whether or not they are provided for in the collective bargaining contract. Even if the act conflicts with provisions of the collective bargaining contract, the employer is still required to develop an affirmative action plan for the handicapped. Such a conflict might occur with respect to job assignment or other related circumstances, such as not providing accessible restrooms or office space.

Critics of the 1973 act point out that the seriously handicapped are still primarily limited to small, nonunion employers in the service industry. The factors contributing to this concentration include high wages and institutional rules in the large union employers that lead to low turnover and few promotion opportunities.

Acquired Immune Deficiency Syndrome   There has been intense debate as to whether **Acquired Immune Deficiency Syndrome (AIDS)** is a handicap under the Rehabilitation Act. In 1986 the Justice Department ruled that under the act employers could not discriminate against an employee solely because he had the fatal disease. However, an employer could legally terminate an employee with the disease if it was feared that the condition would spread to other employees.[32]

American Airlines, in a possible precedent case, was sued for $12 million by a woman who claimed she was bitten by a ticket agent who later tested positive for exposure to AIDS. On February 10, 1986, the claimant arrived late at the airport and attempted to board an American Airlines flight without a boarding pass. An altercation resulted when the boarding agent refused to let her board and closed the jetway. She asked the employee his name and he refused to tell her and tried to walk past her. She grabbed his arm and he kicked her in the shins and bit her. The claimant, acting through her attorney, requested that an AIDS antibody test be performed, and she was informed that the result was positive.[33] The woman sued American Airlines for negligently hiring an employee who had been exposed to AIDS and was a violent person. The results of this case could have a major impact on employers' hiring standards.

The Vietnam Era Veterans' Readjustment Act of 1974

In 1974, Congress passed the **Vietnam Era Veterans' Readjustment Act** for veterans who had difficulty in securing employment. The act requires all organizations with government contracts of $10,000 or more to hire and promote veterans of the Vietnam era. Administered by the Veterans' Employment Service of the U.S. Department of Labor, employers holding government contracts are required to list their job openings with local and state employment offices. These offices then contact unemployed veterans as well as other individuals. Employers are not required to set specific goals and timetables in this affirmative action process.[34]

The Office of Federal Contract Compliance Programs has the authority to ensure compliance of both the handicapped and veterans' affirmative action requirements. Individual charges of discrimination are investigated by state agencies and the U.S. Department of Labor.

Seniority and Title VII

In the late 1970s, a number of Supreme Court cases attempted to resolve the critical conflict between Title VII and the collective bargaining process in the area of employee seniority. In collective bargaining, a seniority system usually provides an individual with certain rights related to her date of employment. In general, seniority is used to determine employment decisions based on the first hired receiving first preference; for example, when two qualified employees bid for a job opening and the one with the greater seniority receives the promotion. Another common example occurs when the last employee hired is the first to be laid off.

Section 703 of the 1964 Civil Rights Act provides that differences in employment conditions resulting from a bona fide seniority system are permitted as long as the system was not developed with discriminatory intentions. Congress provided that employees with longer service can be given greater rewards by the employer solely on the basis of seniority, and, even if an employer had discriminated, those employees should not be held responsible.

With the passage of the Civil Rights Act, a common scenario occurs: An employer for many years has not hired minorities or females, then due to an active equal employment opportunity program or court order, he begins to include a larger percentage of these groups in the work force. Due to past hiring practices, white males have far greater seniority than minorities or females. In terms of promotion or necessary layoffs, white males as a group fare better due to their greater seniority. This can represent a no-win situation for all parties concerned and can result in litigation.

Interpreting Section 703 of Title VII has provided the Supreme Court with difficult and interesting cases. In two 1977 landmark decisions, the Court issued its interpretation of Section 703 of the Civil Rights Act. In the first landmark decision, **Franks** v. **Bowman Transportation Company**, the Court ruled that the routine operation of a seniority system is not an unlawful employment practice under Title VII, even if the seniority system has some discriminatory consequences. Only if the seniority system was designed with an intention to discriminate, a rare occurrence, could it be considered a violation of the act.[35] However, the Court held that if a seniority system perpetuates discrimination and is a violation of Title VII due to its intention, the victims of discrimination are entitled to retroactive seniority. Also, the Supreme Court has ruled in cases such as *United Paper Makers and Paper Workers* v. *The United States* that Title VII was not intended to make incumbent white employees suffer for the past discriminatory acts of the employer.[36]

Therefore, Title VII does not usually permit retroactive seniority or bumping privileges to minority or female employees. However, in *Meadows* v. *Ford Motor Company*, an appeals court ruled that women had been discriminated against by the hiring process at a new truck plant, and therefore, the new seniority system had a discriminatory design.[37] The court held that retroactive seniority and back-pay be awarded under Title VII.

In the second landmark case, *International Brotherhood of Teamsters* v. *United States*, the Supreme Court held that employees who had been discriminated against since Title VII became law were entitled to be made whole for discrimination by the company and were granted back seniority.[38] However, the Court interpreted Section 703 as covering seniority-related discrimination only after July 2, 1965.

Thus, the relationship between discrimination under Title VII and seniority systems is complicated. In the *Franks* decision, the Court issued an interpretation of Section 703 generally providing that a seniority system per se is not an unlawful violation of Title VII, even if it provides for more frequent promotion of white male employees or a greater percentage of layoffs of minority and female employees. Only if the system was, in fact, designed with *intentional discrimination*—difficult to prove in a court of law—can it be questioned under Title VII. However, courts have found in some cases that back-seniority and back-pay are remedies that can compensate individuals who have suffered discrimination. The concept and practice of a seniority system was further upheld under a precedent 1984 Supreme Court decision, *Firefighters Local 1784* v. *Stotts*.[39]

In *Firefighters* v. *Stotts*, the Court decided that the affirmative action goals of a consent decree requiring the hiring and promotion of black employees cannot be given greater protection than the seniority system in the event of unanticipated layoffs. The Court said an award of competitive seniority can be made only to actual victims of discrimination.

A city agreed to a consent decree to settle charges of race discrimination in the fire department. When the city later responded to a budget crunch by preparing to lay off firefighters based on their seniority, the district court enjoined any layoffs that would decrease the percentage of blacks in the department.

On appeal, the Supreme Court differed with the district court's ruling. The injunction's interference with a collectively bargained seniority system cannot be justified as an effort to enforce the decree, the Court said, because the decree, to which the union was not a party, mentioned neither layoffs nor an intent to depart from the lawful seniority system. Nor could the district court grant competitive seniority to black employees as a "modification" of its decree, the Court explained, because there was no finding that any of the blacks protected from layoff had been victims of discrimination.[40]

Nondiscrimination Clauses

The EEOC today recommends that every collective bargaining agreement include a nondiscrimination clause to avoid both civil rights violations and pay inequities.[41] The EEOC stipulates that unions and employers emphasize the following key areas:

1. Open membership to all employees regardless of race, national origin, or sex
2. Job referrals by a union to management without discrimination
3. Design or redesign of departmental or plantwide seniority systems so past discriminatory effects are eliminated
4. Grievance arbitration procedures in the collective bargaining agreement to provide for discrimination along with other types of union member grievances

If a nondiscrimination clause is violated by the employer, the union has grounds to file a grievance. The following is an example of a nondiscrimination clause:

> It is the continuing policy and recognized obligation of the company and the union that the provisions of this agreement shall be applied fairly and in accordance with those federal and state employment laws relating to race, color, sex, religious creed, age, national origin, handicap, disabled veterans and Veterans of the Vietnam Era.[42]

Equal Pay for Equal Work

In 1963, Congress amended the 1938 Fair Labor Standards Act with what is often termed the Equal Pay Act. This act contains the principle of **equal pay for equal work**, regardless of sex. Under the Equal Pay Act, employers are prohibited from discriminating against employees covered by the minimum wage provision of the Fair Labor Standards Act.[43] The Equal Pay Act has wider application than any other employment legislation because it does not define a statutory minimum number of employees for compliance, and it applies to organizations of all sizes.[44]

The definition of the word *sex* received little discussion during the 1960s when the Equal Pay Act and Civil Rights Act were debated in Congress. However, from the gay rights movement, an interesting and difficult question—the legal sex of a transsexual—is discussed in Case 13.3. Even more difficult questions concerning the transsexual's and other employees' rights in using locker and restroom facilities, and employer's affirmative action rights need to be answered by the courts.

Equal pay for equal work does *not,* in fact, require that jobs be identical to receive equal wages, nor does it require that jobs that are not exactly identical be placed in separate wage categories. Instead the act as prescribed by Congress requires that organizations pay men and women approximately the same wages for substantially equal work. The concept of **substantially equal** refers to jobs containing similar skill, effort, responsibility, and working conditions.[45] Thus, employers and labor unions must be able to defend their negotiated wage scales by analyzing the content of the jobs. They must also provide evidence that jobs requiring substantially equal work in the areas of skill, effort, responsibility, and working conditions are paid similar wages usually within the same pay grade. In the case of *Corning Glass Works* v. *Brennan* the Supreme Court established this important relationship between an analysis of the content of jobs and the Equal Pay Act.[46]

The Equal Pay Act does provide for legal variances in wages paid to individuals performing identical jobs. Employees may receive different wage rates while performing the same work if such differences are based on seniority, merit, quantity or quality of production, or factors other than sex.[47] These important exceptions provide the basis on which organizations and unions can defend the fact that men performing the same work as women receive, on the average, higher levels of pay. This common occurrence in commerce and industry is due to the fact that men often have greater seniority. Another very important phrase found in the act and in many court cases requires that employers "shall not, in order to comply with the provisions of this subsection, reduce the wage rate of any employee." In essence, this means that employers who are striving to change their pay system to comply with the act may not lower the wages of any individual, but instead must raise wages of those individuals who have suffered discrimination.[48]

Many employers and labor unions have developed new wage and salary systems based upon formal job analysis and job evaluation programs to comply with the Equal Pay Act. Such programs ensure that employees are paid according to the content of their jobs and not according to other factors such as sex, supervisory bias, or job titles.

The vagueness of the substantially equal concept creates areas for disagreement between litigants in cases involving equal pay for equal work.[49] Even the most skilled job analysts would not completely agree upon the level of skill, effort, responsibility, and working conditions required in an organization. Modern job evaluation systems are simply not that accurate. Instead, by allowing jobs of substantially equal content to be put in the same pay grade, the principle of equal pay for equal work can be achieved.

The Pregnancy Discrimination Act

The question of whether shorter maternity leave benefits compared to normal disability benefits provided by employers or in collective bargaining agreements constituted sex discrimination was an issue that had not been thoroughly discussed or addressed by existing legislation. Several lower courts interpreted shorter pregnancy disability durations as constituting sex discrimination. However, in 1976 the Supreme Court reversed these lower court decisions.[50] The issue was finally clarified with the passage of the Pregnancy Discrimination Act of 1977 as an amendment to Title VII of the Civil Rights Act.[51] With the act, employers did not have to offer new benefits they did not already have as of October 31, 1978. Employers, however, were given a grace period to equalize pregnancy benefits with other disability benefits or compensation provided any employee from the date the act was effective until one year, or until an applicable collective bargaining agreement had been determined.[52]

Today, employers and unions must treat pregnancy disability the same as any other disability. They may choose to reduce all disability benefits to six weeks maximum, or increase pregnancy disability benefits to match other disability benefits if provided for a longer period of time. Or, all disability benefits could be completely eliminated in the negotiation process.

Comparable Worth

According to Winn Newman of the General Council of the Coalition of Labor Union Women, the leading women's labor economic issue of the 1980s is pay equity or **comparable worth**.[53] The Equal Pay Act does not enable women always to obtain relief from discrimination; it only guarantees women equal pay on jobs with the same job classification. And, twenty years after the passage of the Equal Pay Act, the average full-time female worker still earns less than 60 percent of the average male's wage.

At the heart of the issue is the concept of comparable worth, which the U.S. Supreme Court acknowledged as a valid legal doctrine in a 1981 decision.[54] The *comparable worth doctrine* requires that pay be equal not just for men and women performing the same job, but for all jobs requiring comparable skills, effort, responsibility, and working conditions. According to supporters, the doctrine represents the spirit and the letter of the Equal Pay Act. Opponents of the comparable worth doctrine argue that the large percentage of women in lower-paying jobs such as secretary, nurse, and elementary school teacher is a result of a woman's attraction to those jobs. The pay levels are a result of the external marketplace, as verified by wage surveys. Furthermore, opponents argue that comparable worth is not a demand for equal opportunity but a demand to be protected against one's career choice.[55]

The debate on the comparable worth issue remains heated, with billions of dollars in employee wages at stake. It is not an easy issue to decide—what is the comparable worth of a secretary in comparison with a security guard? Even women's groups do not agree. For example, a bill introduced by Senator Alan Cranston

(D-Calif.) requiring comparable worth in federal jobs was not supported by the National Organization for Women (NOW).

Public employers are the primary targets of comparable worth advocates because they are more vulnerable legally and because they show the greatest pay inequities.[56] Yet most labor and management representatives agree that the comparable worth issue should be pursued primarily by labor unions and not the government. So labor unions active in the public sector, such as the American Federation of State, County and Municipal Employees (AFSCME), have been taking the initiative. Such unions have the financial and legal resources to assist their members.

According to a 1986 report by the National Academy of Sciences, from 1972 to 1981 women's occupational options expanded greatly. Their participation has increased in several previously male-dominated occupations, including lawyers, bank managers, insurance adjusters, postal clerks, bus drivers, and janitors. Women also experienced a rapid increase in their representation in law enforcement, coal mining, and engineering. Although women continue to dominate several clerical and service occupations, in some cases a shortage of skilled workers has been felt in those fields, as women begin to choose other occupations.[57]

Legal battles over comparable worth are not over yet. Four years after the Supreme Court acknowledged the doctrine, the EEOC formally rejected the concept as a means of determining job discrimination. The commission, in a five-to-zero decision, stated that the theory of comparable worth is not recognized under Title VII of the Civil Rights Act. The case involved alleged sexual discrimination by a Rockford, Illinois, housing authority. The administrative staff was 85 percent female and was paid considerably less than the maintenance staff, which was 88 percent male. The EEOC claimed there was no evidence that any barriers existed that prevented females from moving into maintenance jobs—only their own personal career choices. The Service Employees International Union claimed the EEOC's decision left unions no choice but to resort to court actions in cases involving comparable worth.

In 1986 a record settlement between the AFSCME and the State of Washington provided $97.2 million to 34,000 state employees, the largest settlement to date in a comparable worth case. Both sides of the landmark case claimed the settlement supported their interest. Supporters of comparable worth noted that the settlement provided their goal of pay equity across jobs of equal worth according to a 1981 state-commissioned study. Opponents claimed victory because the September 1985 ruling of the U.S. Ninth Circuit Court of Appeals will stand uncontested. This circuit court decision had posited that federal laws do not require employers to alter market-place job inequities. Instead, the court contended, federal discrimination laws require employers to allow equal access to jobs by both men and women.[58]

Summary

Since the 1960s, the federal and state governments have influenced and have at times created conflict in the collective bargaining process. The most common conflict revolves around seniority. How do plantwide and departmental seniority systems differ in their discriminatory practices? Some view departmental seniority systems as discriminatory. In practice they may tend to keep minorities and females in certain departments and in certain types of jobs. Other job opportunities may be less available to them. However, the courts have generally supported seniority systems as prescribed in collective bargaining agreements unless they are obviously designed to create a discriminatory situation, as shown in the case study for this chapter.

The courts have tried to provide for seniority systems that reward loyal and productive employees. Seniority systems per se are not discriminatory, yet problems arise with employers who have only recently begun to hire minorities and females, who naturally have less seniority than white males. The courts have tried not to penalize those white male employees while providing greater employment opportunities for females and minorities.

The courts have used the remedies of awarding back-pay, seniority, cost of litigation, and reinstatement of position in discrimination cases since the 1960s. These court-ordered remedies are similar to those used in labor relations cases involving unfair labor practices.

The comparable worth or wage equity issue represents an area where collective bargaining principles and equal employment principles are quite similar. While unions historically have demanded equal pay for jobs comparable in the areas of skills, effort, responsibility, and working conditions, they have also recognized in practice the use of wage surveys to determine wage rates. If, however, unions can become the champion of the comparable worth issue, they may be able to successfully organize some largely nonunion professions such as clerical and nursing.

CASE 13.1   *Race Discrimination*

Adapted from *Fort v. Roadway Express, Inc.*, 29 EPD para. 32,904 (1982)

The plaintiff was a black male driver for the company. He and three other black drivers filed charges with the Equal Employment Opportunity Commission against the company and the union alleging racial discrimination in employment conditions. The plaintiff was also dismissed for allegedly tampering with the governor on a truck tractor to increase speed; this was unrelated to the charges of discrimination. This type of offense under the collective bargaining agreement subjected the employee to immediate discharge. The union processed the plaintiff's grievance but the discharge was sustained. The plaintiff filed suit against the company and the union charging discrimination against him because of his race and in retaliation for having filed charges with the EEOC. The plaintiff claimed the union did not fairly represent him in the grievance procedure because of his race.

Decision

The court found that the union fairly processed the grievance of the plaintiffs through the steps provided by the collective bargaining agreement and that similar grievances by white truck drivers were handled in the same manner. In fact, a recently discharged white driver was reinstated upon acceptance of a suspension without pay and the union had proposed a similar resolution for the plaintiff, which he refused. The court concluded that the reasons given by the company for discharging the plaintiff were not pretextral. There had been no showing of fraudulent, deceitful, dishonest, or bad faith conduct by the union.

CASE 13.2   *Age Discrimination*

Adapted from *EEOC* v. *Missouri State Highway Patrol*, 30 EPD para. 33,293 (1982)

The EEOC on behalf of three classes of employees sued the Missouri State Highway Patrol for age discrimination under the Age Discrimination in Employment Act (ADEA). The ADEA prohibits age discrimination against persons age forty to seventy unless age is a bona fide occupational qualification or is reasonably necessary for the normal operation of a particular business. The classes of employees involved are patrolmen who must retire at the age of sixty, and persons over the age of thirty-two who are not hired as troopers or radio operators.

The defendants claimed that in regard to the mandatory retirement rule, adequate aerobic capacity (the ability to use oxygen) is needed by members of the highway patrol and decreases with age. And that, according to its physiologist, an average sedentary forty-five-year-old adult male does not have sufficient aerobic capacity to perform his duties. According to its expert cardiologist, the risk of coronary artery disease increases with age, with the risk peaking in one's fifties. Further, the defendants claimed that keeping the mandatory retirement age is necessary to protect the retirement benefits; that it promotes morale and ensures opportunities for advancement; and that requiring a regular physical fitness program would hurt morale.

The plaintiffs pointed out that the findings of the defendant as to aerobic capacity and coronary artery disease would not support mandatory retirement at sixty but a much earlier age, and that regular physical exams could determine physical changes associated with aging and those associated with disease. And that while the physical abilities needed for law enforcement duties are easy to test, the highway patrol refuses to do so.

As to the maximum hiring age of radio operators, the defendant claimed that persons over the age of forty are unable to safely and efficiently perform the duties of a radio operator because such duties include repairing and installing equipment, hearing and transmitting information, typing, and, in some instances, climbing radio towers. The defendant suggested that hearing and vision generally decline with age but offered no medical evidence.

The plaintiff countered with the fact that the patrol presently employs persons over the age of forty to perform those duties; that the traits necessary for a radio operator can be tested; and that indeed it periodically tested the ability of radio operators to hear, see, and master technical skills. Therefore, the highway patrol could determine the ability of a candidate by the tests and not based on the person's age.

The defendants claimed that, regarding troopers being hired over the age of thirty-two, troopers spend almost all of their time doing road work and must be able to perform all the attendant strenuous physical activities. They presented evidence that the most effective patrolman has had several years of experience and that it takes approximately eleven years for a trooper to gain sufficient experience.

Decision

The court found that the policies not to hire persons over the age of thirty-two to be troopers or radio operators and to mandatorily retire patrolmen over the age of sixty were per se violations of the ADEA and that the defendants must demonstrate that the arbitrary age restrictions are bona fide occupational qualifications reasonably necessary to the normal operation of the patrol.

The court felt that, as to the mandatory retirement rule, the patrol did not prove that persons over the age of sixty were unable to perform the duties of the patrolmen and that individuals could be tested as to whether they are unfit due to advanced age. Also, the court did not accept the defendant's reasons for not

hiring radio operators over age thirty-two and that tests were also available to ascertain an individual's qualifications for the job.

The court, however, found that the defendants proved that their maximum hiring age of thirty-two for troopers was a bona fide occupational qualification. It stated,

> The troopers spent almost all of their time doing road work. Though the patrol requires all of its members to be able to perform all the strenuous physical activities which a trooper encounters daily, the evidence clearly demonstrated that the highest-ranking members of the patrol spent almost all of their time doing administrative work. The safest patrolman is one who had acquired several years of experience. An experienced patrolman is best able to protect the public and serve as an administrator. It takes approximately eleven years for a trooper to gain sufficient experience to serve the patrol in that administrative capacity. Thus, the maximum hiring age requirement of thirty-two for troopers is a bona fide occupational qualification.

CASE 13.3 *Sex Discrimination*

Adapted from *Audrey Summers a/k/a Timothy Kevin Cornish* v. *Budget Marketing, Inc.*, 27 Employment Practices Decisions, para. 32,318 (1982)

The plaintiff Audrey Summers also known as Timothy Cornish applied to and was hired by the company to perform clerical duties as a woman when in fact she/he was an anatomical male. The company dismissed the plaintiff because she/he misrepresented "herself" as an anatomical female when she/he applied for the job. Such misrepresentation led to a disruption of the work rou-

tine; a number of female employees indicated they would quit if the plaintiff was permitted to use the female restroom facilities.

The plaintiff sued the company alleging that "she" had been discharged on the basis of sex in violation of Title VII of the Civil Rights Act of 1964. Plaintiff claimed "she" was discriminated against because of her status as a female (that is, a female with the anatomical body of a male) and that Title VII should cover persons like "herself." The company moved to dismiss the employee's complaint based on the fact that Title VII does not cover persons discriminated against because of their transsexuality. The lower court accepted the company's argument and granted summary judgment.

Decision

The plaintiff appealed the decision and the circuit court upheld the lower court's summary judgment on the basis that for purposes of Title VII, the literal meaning of the term *sex* must be ascribed to unless there is congressional intent to

do otherwise. The legislative history of the Civil Rights Act shows that the act was amended on the day prior to its passage by adding the word *sex* with little debate, and it is recognized that the purpose of that addition was toward providing equal opportunities for women. Subsequent proposals to amend the Civil Rights Act to prohibit discrimination on the basis of sexual preference were defeated. The plaintiff's claim did not deal with discrimination on the basis of sexual preference, nor had Congress shown any intent to protect transsexuals. Therefore, the court did not find that discrimination based on one's transsexualism was within the protection of the act.

CASE STUDY   *Sex Discrimination*

Adapted from *Maguire v. Marquette Univ.* 40 FEP Cases 167 (Feb. 12, 1986)

Facts

The plaintiff, Maguire, is a white Roman Catholic woman who applied for a position as an associate professor of theology at Marquette University. Marquette University was begun and sustained under the auspices of the Jesuits, an organization of Roman Catholic priests. Maguire was denied the job and she brought suit claiming sex discrimination under Title VII.

Marquette's theology department is run by the Jesuits, and about half the members are Jesuits, and by definition male. In fact, the affirmative action plan for the university gives it the right to give preferences to Jesuits in hiring and the right to reserve half the teaching positions in the theology department for Jesuits. Of the other half of the department, all but one are male.

Maguire claimed that Marquette violated Title VII by discriminating against her because of her sex. In general, female candidates are asked different questions when being interviewed for a job, and sexist comments have been recorded. In particular, although she is Roman Catholic, she believed she was not hired because of the perception by the Jesuits that her religious beliefs differed from theirs on the abortion issue.

The defendant, Marquette University, defended its actions by claiming the court has no jurisdiction because of the First Amendment's separation of church and state. Also, there is an exception in Title VII for educational institutions controlled by religious groups. "It shall not be unlawful . . . for a school . . . to hire and employ employees of a particular religion if such school . . . is controlled . . . by a particular religion."

Maguire claimed this exception is not available to Marquette because she is a Catholic and the school is Catholic. Therefore, the court must look past the religion issue and examine the sex discrimination issue.

Marquette claimed, however, that Maguire was neither Catholic nor Jesuit. The issue at trial would then be for the court to determine what it is to be a Catholic—obviously an impermissible decision for a court under the First Amendment.

Questions

1. Would you rule for Maguire or Marquette? Why?
2. Marquette claimed the issue was Maguire's religion, and therefore not subject to a court ruling. If that issue was not part of this case, do you think Maguire could have proven sex discrimination? Why or why not?
3. If church-associated schools are exempt from Title VII, should church-associated apartment buildings, day-care centers, and so on also be exempt?

Key Terms and Concepts

Acquired Immune Deficiency Syndrome (AIDS)

Affirmative action programs

Age Discrimination in Employment Act of 1967 (ADEA)

Albemarle Paper Co. v. *Moody*

Civil Rights Act of 1964

Comparable worth

Equal Employment Opportunity Commission (EEOC)

Equal pay for equal work

Firefighters v. *Stotts*

Franks v. *Bowman Transportation Co.*

Make whole concept

Office of Federal Contract Compliance (OFCC)

Probable cause

Reverse discrimination

Sexual harassment

Substantially equal

Title VII

United Steelworkers v. *Weber*

Vietnam Era Veterans' Readjustment Act of 1974

Vocational Rehabilitation Act of 1973

Review Questions

1. Why does the collective bargaining process fall under Title VII? Does Title VII affect negotiated contracts?
2. Discuss the question of Title VII and its relationship to seniority systems.
3. What does the *make whole* concept in discrimination cases refer to? What remedies do courts normally use to compensate individuals?

4. Why is the 1979 *Weber* case considered to have great importance in discrimination and labor relations?

5. How do affirmative action programs differ from federal employment laws? What specifics are usually included in such programs?

6. What does the principle of *equal pay for equal work* entail?

7. Explain the *comparable worth* concept. Why is it critical to women's issues?

8. What items should appear in a nondiscrimination contract clause? In what other areas can unions and employers help promote nondiscrimination?

Endnotes

1. Michael P. Litka and James E. Inman, *The Legal Environment of Business: Text, Readings, and Cases* (Columbus, Ohio: Grid Publishing, 1980), pp. 452–53.
2. Griggs v. Duke Power Co., 401 U.S. 424 (1971).
3. Marc Rosenblum, "Evolving EEO Decision Law and Applied Research," *Industrial Relations* 21, no. 3 (Fall 1982), pp. 340–51.
4. *AFL-CIO Manual for Shop Stewards* (Washington, D.C.: AFL-CIO, 1980): pp. 52–53.
5. *Forging Change for a New Generation of Families, Workers, and Unions* (New York, NY: The Coalition of Labor Union Women).
6. Ibid.
7. Henry Farber, "The Determination of the Union Status of Workers," *Econometrica* S1, no. 5 (Sept. 1983), pp. 1417–38.
8. Jonathan S. Leonard, "The Effect of Unions on the Employment of Blacks, Hispanics, and Women," *Industrial and Labor Relations Review* 39, no. 1 (Oct. 1985), pp. 115–32.
9. Civil Rights Act of 1964, Title VII 42 U.S.C. Sec. 2000e.
10. U.S. Equal Employment Opportunity Commission, *Affirmative Action and Equal Employment: A Guidebook for Employers* (Washington, D.C.: Government Printing Office, 1974), pp. 57–58.
11. Peter Feuille and David Lewin, "Equal Employment Opportunity Bargaining," *Industrial Relations* 20, no. 3 (Fall 1981), p. 322.
12. Griggs v. Duke Power Co., 401 U.S. 424 (1971).
13. Ibid.
14. McDonnell-Douglas Corp. v. Green, 441 U.S. 792 (1972).
15. U.S. Equal Employment Opportunity Commission, *Guidebook for Employers*, pp. 7–8.
16. 42 U.S.C. Sec. 706(g).
17. Albermarle Paper Co. v. Moody, 422 U.S. 405 (1975).
18. Equal Employment Opportunity Commission, *1980 Guidelines*.
19. Michael R. Carrell and Frank K. Kuzmits, *Personnel* 2d ed. (Columbus, Ohio: Merrill, 1986), pp. 555–59. For further reading see T. L. Leap and E. R. Gray, "Corporate Responsibility in Cases of Sexual Harassment," *Business Horizons* (Oct. 1980), p. 58.
20. Meritor Savings Bank v. Vinson, U.S. Supreme Court 1986, 40 FEP Cases 1822.
21. David S. Bradshaw, "Sexual Harassment: Confronting the Troublesome Issues," *Personnel Administrator* 32, no. 1 (Jan. 1987), pp. 51–53.
22. United Steelworkers v. Weber, 443 U.S. 193 (1979).
23. Ronald Johnson, "Voluntary Affirmative Action in the Post-Weber Era: Issues and Answers," *Labor Law Journal* 32, no. 9 (Sept. 1981), pp. 409–11.
24. Bakke v. University of California 443 U.S. 187 (1978).

25. David Brookmirl, "Designing and Implementing Your Company's Affirmative Action Program," *Personnel Journal* 58, no. 4 (April 1979), pp. 232–37.
26. 41 C.F.R. 60-741.2.
27. Laugesen v. Anaconda Co., 510 F.2d 307, 6th Circuit (1975).
28. Michael R. Carrell and Frank E. Kuzmits, "Amended ADEA's Effects on HR Strategies Remain Dubious" *Personnel Journal* 66, no. 5 (May 1987), pp. 111–120.
29. Hodgson v. Greyhound Lines, Inc., 499 F. 2d 859, 7th Circuit (1974).
30. James H. Craft, Thomas J. Benecki, and Yitzchak M. Shkop, "Who Hires the Seriously Handicapped?" *Industrial Relations* 19, no. 1 (Winter 1980), pp. 94–99.
31. Forrisi v. Bowen, 41 Fair Employment Practices Cases, 190 (4th Circuit 1986).
32. "A Narrow View on AIDS Bias," *Resource*, pamphlet (Alexandria, Va: American Society for Personnel Administration, July 1986), p. 2.
33. *Labor Relations Reporter* (BNA: Washington, D.C.) 123 LRR 61 (15 Sept. 1986), p. 1.
34. Carrell, *Personnel*, pp. 142–46.
35. Franks v. Bowman Transportation Co., 424 U.S. 747 (1976).
36. Local 189, United Papermakers and Paperworkers v. United States, 416 F.2d 980, 5th Cir. (1969).
37. Meadows v. Ford Motor Co., 510 F.2d 939, 6th Cir. (1975).
38. International Brotherhood of Teamsters v. United States, 431 U.S. 324 (1977).
39. Firefighters Local 1784 v. Stotts no. 82–206 U.S. (1984).
40. "Blacks Hired Under Consent Decree Subject to Seniority-Based Layoffs," *U.S. Law Week* 52, no. 49 (June 19, 1984), p. 1193.
41. U.S. Equal Employment Opportunity Commission, *Guidebook for Employers*, pp. 57–58.
42. Ibid.
43. 29 U.S.C. Sec. 206 (d)(1) (1977).
44. George Wendt, "Should Courts Write Your Job Descriptions?" *Personnel Journal* 55, no. 9 (Sept. 1976), pp. 424–44.
45. Schultz v. Wheaton Glass Co., 421 F.2d 259, 3rd Cir. (1970).
46. Corning Glass Works v. Brennan, 415 U.S. 972 (1974).
47. 29 U.S.C. Sec. 206 (d)(1) (1977).
48. Wendt, "Should Courts," p. 423.
49. Ibid.
50. Paul S. Greenlaw and Diana Foderaro, "Some Practical Implications of the Pregnancy Discrimination Act," *Personnel Journal* 58, no. 10 (Oct. 1979), pp.677–81.
51. Pregnancy Discrimination Act of 1977, P.L. 95-955, 92 Stat. 2076–77.
52. Greenlaw, "Some Practical Implications," pp. 78–79.
53. Winn Newman, "Pay Equity Emerges as a Top Labor Issue in the 1980s," *Monthly Labor Review* 105, no. 4 (April 1982), pp. 49–50.
54. Editorial Staff, American Society for Personnel Administration, *Resource,* pamphlet (Alexandria, Va.: American Society for Personnel Administration, Oct. 1983) pp. 1, 8.
55. Robert D. Hershey, "The Wage Gap Between Men and Women Faces a New Assault," *The Courier-Journal*, Nov. 6 1983, pp. 1, 4.
56. Newman, "Pay Equity," p. 50.
57. "Labor Month in Review," *Monthly Labor Review* 109, no. 2 (Feb. 1986), p. 2. See also The National Academy of Sciences Report, *Women's Work, Men's Work: Sex Segregation on the Job* (Washington, D.C.: National Academy Press, 1986).
58. *American Federation of State, County and Municipal Employees* v. *State of Washington*, 770 F. 2d 1401 (Ninth Circuit, 1985).

14

The Future of Collective Bargaining

LABOR NEWS

Employer Drug Screening: Legal or Privacy Invasion?

Mandatory drug screening is the most significant privacy issue in a decade. Employers claim that employee use of illegal drugs is a problem growing out of control, forcing them to use blood and urine tests to screen employees.

Labor unions have mounted the most significant legal challenges, hoping eventually to win in the Supreme Court. They claim the tests are unreliable and may be biased against black and Hispanic workers. Their greatest criticism is the perceived invasion of personal privacy.

The use of illegal drugs by rock stars, professional athletes, and movie stars no longer raises eyebrows, but use in hospitals, courtrooms, nuclear plants, and on construction sites is causing new concerns. "Perfectly respectable professionals" in virtually all lines of work have dramatically increased their use of illegal drugs. It is such a widespread problem that the superintendent of

the Boston Police Department notes that today undercover agents wear three-piece suits instead of hippie-type clothes. The total cost to the U.S. economy is estimated to be $26 billion. Employees who use drugs on the job are estimated to be one-third less productive than their counterparts. The indirect costs such as theft by employees to cover their habits and reprisal by angry customers cannot even be estimated. National Car Rental's personnel director calls it the greatest employee problem in industry today—nothing else is even in second place.

The problem is more difficult today because alcohol, still the most abused drug, can be detected by supervisors much more easily than most other drugs such as Percodan, Diladid, and Quaaludes.

Businesses are beginning to respond with employee assistance programs (EAPs) and supervisor training. Some are even using counteroffensives, like the Boston Blue

Cross-Blue Shield office that requested an undercover police investigation. The Mobay Chemical Corporation of Baytown, Texas, uses drug-sniffing dogs to search work areas. In Ontario, California, the Sunkist Products Company requires all new and "strange-acting employees" to take urine tests.

President Reagan's Commission on Organized Crime recommended routine testing of all workers as a means of reducing illegal

drug traffic. One program, at the Lockheed–California Company in Burbank, found drug usage in 21 percent of job applicants.

Source: Adapted from Robert Lindsey, New York Times News Service. "Employers' Drug-Screening Programs Spark Legal Dispute," The Courier-Journal May 6, 1986, p. 1; and adapted from John Brecher et al., "Taking Drugs on the Job," Newsweek, Aug. 22, 1983, pp. 54–60.

The collective bargaining process has changed notably in recent years. In the past two decades, binding arbitration has become a totally acceptable means of resolving grievances during the life of a contract, reducing the number of lost work days. Labor and management have worked together to make equal employment opportunity and affirmative action a real part of their employment programs. The general view of our society toward unions and the collective bargaining process has also changed greatly. Robert Schrank, scholar, Ford Foundation author, and former union official, sees a different motivation behind union activities and collective bargaining today.

> In the 1930s and the 1940s, I spent some of the best years of my life in the labor movement, as an organizer and union official. They were years of crusading against what we in the unions thought were the worst kinds of industrial exploitation. The crusaders marched to "Solidarity Forever" . . . the labor movement slowly but surely has lost its crusading spirit. Today the major inspiration running through labor's blood may be new ways to invest the pension funds. I do not mean to criticize, merely to mark the end of an era. The crusade has accomplished its mission, the movement phase is over. It is no mean achievement that the major objectives of those organizing years have been met and some of the worst evils of the industrial workplace eradicated. It was an honor to participate in that good work, and I feel great about it.[1]

Sixteen-hour work days, unsafe machinery, child labor, and unsanitary working conditions are mostly gone, thanks to collective bargaining sessions of the past. However, some modern collective bargaining topics have remained unchanged since the 1930s: increased government regulation, job security, and a reasonable wage. New topics include termination-at-will, robotics, technological change, health care, compressed work weeks, employee retraining, affirmative action, and codetermination.

Termination-at-will

Employers in the United States terminate about 3 million employees per year for "cause," a frequency much greater than in other industrialized countries. The possible reasons for this variance include the higher U.S. unemployment rate (which makes it easier to replace workers), the strong U.S. belief in owners' property rights, and a lack of legal protection for individual employees.

Historically, U.S. employers have enjoyed the right to terminate employees for almost any reason, sometimes referred to as "**termination-at-will**" or "employment-at-will."[2] Unless they violate a discrimination law, employers traditionally could fire employees for "good reason, bad reason, or no reason at all." In recent years, state courts have narrowed this doctrine to a limited extent.[3] In general, the courts have found a wrongful discharge when public policy has been violated (firing an employee for refusal to give false testimony, serving on a jury, or reporting illegal conduct of an employer), an implied contract exists (personnel policy or oral statements promising job tenure), or there has been a good faith violation (employment is not at-will).[4] These examples exemplify state court decisions on the termination-at-will doctrine:

☐ International Business Machines (IBM) was ordered to pay $300,000 to a sales manager who was dismissed for dating a former IBM salesman who had gone to work for a competing firm.

☐ Courts in Indiana and Kentucky have determined it is against public policy to fire an employee for filing a worker's compensation claim.

☐ A California court decided that an employer's discharge of a Teamsters' Union business agent for refusing to commit perjury before a state legislative committee was wrongful and contrary to public policy.

☐ Courts in several jurisdictions have ruled in favor of employees who were discharged for "whistle blowing," or disclosing an employer's violations of state or federal laws. In these cases, public policy was said to have been violated by the employers.

☐ The Michigan Supreme Court, in a case involving an employee of Blue Cross–Blue Shield of Michigan, held that the employer's personnel-manual clause stating that employees would be discharged only for "cause" created an *implied contractual agreement* between the employer and employee.[5]

Some employers are responding to the state court decisions by requesting new employees sign an "at-will" statement that decreases possible court litigation over an employment-at-will issue. Employers are also scrutinizing their personnel practices to eliminate any that might be interpreted as an implied contract.

The principle of termination-at-will has inspired widespread discussion and criticism. Defenders of the doctrine argue that employers have property and management rights. Critics of the doctrine have begun to call for federal legislation to protect employees' rights to fair treatment, but opponents counter that legislation already gives employees the mechanism to deal with the problem—collective bargaining. The best protection against unjust discharge is afforded by a collective bargaining agreement. In fact, about 99 percent of all agreements contain a grievance and arbitration procedure covering discharge situations.[6] Representation against perceived unfair employment decisions has historically been a major issue in union organizing campaigns. Union leaders may be able to mobilize greater membership if they present unionization as a solution to growing worker unrest over termination-at-will.

Robotics

Some experts believe the technological revolution sweeping industry today rivals the Industrial Revolution of the nineteenth century.[7] Undoubtedly more jobs will be replaced and greater increases in efficiency will result.

One of the most dramatic areas of development has been in the science of **robotics**, using robots to perform tasks. Industrial robots are often divided into two classes: **anthropomorphic robots** approximate the appearance and functions of humans; and *nonanthropomorphic* robots are very machine-like and have limited functions.[8]

During the 1950s and 1960s, robots could not compete with human dexterity and ability to make instant or complicated decisions. And although computerized automation was desirable, automated machinery could not be easily adapted to various production functions.

The development of the *microprocessor,* which automates production functions, and the *silicon chip,* a miniaturized system of integrated circuits about the size of the quarter, in the 1970s gave robots greater capabilities than previously envisioned. The silicon chip can perform millions of multiplications per second. It has been estimated that a calculation costing 80% with 1950s computer technology now costs less than 1% today after adjusting for inflation.[9] As a result, the use of robots in manufacturing quadrupled between 1979 and 1981.

The first generation of robots of the 1950s performed simple jobs and had limited capabilities. The second generation of robots have the senses of vision and touch, making them more anthropomorphic in their complex capabilities and more adaptable to production needs. Carl Remick, a General Motors official, believes that second-generation robots also have decision-making capabilities, enabling them to react to their environment much like humans.[10]

Second-generation robots are particularly desirable for hazardous and dangerous jobs. And, a study conducted at Carnegie-Mellon University estimates that it will become technically feasible to replace *all* manufacturing operations in the automotive, electrical equipment, machinery, and fabricated metals industries with robots.[11]

The economics of robotics is quite simple. Robots, as compared with human labor, can provide lower cost, higher reliability, and fewer errors. For example, the average labor cost in the United States has increased to about $15 per hour, while the average cost of a utilized robot is less than $5 per hour. Even more dramatic is the fact that inflation will *increase* human labor costs, but additional technological advances will most likely *reduce* the costs of robotics.[12] General Motors, for example, recognizes it can use robots at an average cost of $6 per hour for many functions previously performed by skilled workers at $20 per hour.[13]

The increased use of robotics is supported by both labor and management because of their growing concern for quality control and competitiveness in international markets. Union leaders, anticipating the robotics revolution, have recently bargained for advance notice of the implementation of robots and for retraining rights so members have new skills for long-term employment. William Winpisinger, president of the International Association of Machinists, argued that the replacement of human skills with robots will occur slowly and that unions should be concerned with a shortage of skilled workers to build and maintain the robots of the future.[14] In general, unions have not been opposed to robots *if* the affected workers are provided with the training necessary for the new jobs created by technological change. Although unions realize robotics will cut into their membership, it is preferable to losing all jobs due to foreign competition.[15]

A Japanese auto manufacturer first introduced a robot in an assembly plant in 1971; by 1981 the company had 730 robots and output had increased 186 percent. Over 90 percent of the robots perform welding, painting, and loading functions, hazardous jobs previously performed by humans. The company has found that the average robot pays for itself in two years. Since each robot replaced 0.7 worker, theoretically 1,022 workers have been replaced. However, the company's success led to expansion, no workers were laid off, and in many cases employees were trained for more highly skilled jobs. The plant's trade unions were consulted prior to the introduction of robots and have provided input to maintain good labor relations.[16]

Robotics and Composites

The robotics industry within the automobile industry steadily grew during the 1980s. Outside the auto industry, however, use of robots has experienced little growth. General Electric shut down its robot business and GMF (General Motors and Fanuc Ltd. of Japan), the industry leader, had laid off a third of its work force by 1987. In fact, from 1982 to 1987 over 25 percent of all American machine tools companies failed and over one-third of their jobs had vanished. Why the decline when robots and other advanced machines demonstrate the cost advantages just discussed? According to James Geier, Chairman of Cincinnati Milacron, a leader in the industry, the answer is composites.[17]

Composites are products consisting of graphite fibers and epoxies, which can be stronger than steel and cost considerably less. The very material machines work with is changing from steel, glass, and paper to plastics, synthetics, and "things we haven't even thought of yet." Fifty percent of the composites Milacron sold in 1985 did not exist in 1980. The effect on the machine tool work force—a traditional union industry—could be dramatic. For example, Milacron's employment dropped by more than 4,000 in five years as "well-educated computer programmers and laser engineers increasingly replaced a larger cadre of blue-collar assemblers and machine operators."[18]

Electronic Supervisors

In the age of high technology and robots it was bound to happen: "big brother" is watching millions of U.S. workers every second of the day. Fiction? Not at all. Major corporations, including United Airlines, Equitable Life, AT&T, and Ford Motor Company, have installed monitoring systems on employee computer terminals. An estimated 13 million American workers in 1986 were being scrutinized as they worked, a number that may grow to as many as 40 million by 1990.

Software installed on a central computer can easily monitor how many inputs are made by an employee, how much time each customer contact requires, how many items a grocery clerk can ring up per hour, and how much idle time each employee has taken for such things as bathroom and coffee breaks. Some companies have piece-rate or pay-for-performance programs. Labor groups contend that such programs may result in 19th century sweatshops, but managers contend they can make better decisions based on facts, not biases.[19]

Quality of Working Life (QWL)

In the 1970s many different programs, often referred to as **Quality of Working Life** (**QWL**), were designed and implemented to increase employee satisfaction with their work environment along with productivity. "Quality of working life" is a catch-all phrase characterizing the process by which management, union, and employees determine together what action, changes, and improvements can improve the quality of life at work for all members of the organization and the effectiveness of both the company and the union.[20] QWL programs attempt to establish practical relationships outside the traditional union-management means of negotiations, grievance handling, and joint committees.

QWL programs, some believe, hold the potential for significantly altering the conduct of labor relations. The national press and media have given a great deal of exposure to the so-called new industrial relations.[21] Unlike past efforts, QWL programs try to establish direct channels of communication between workers and their supervisors and give workers a greater voice in decision making.

One of the most widely heralded QWL programs was introduced by General Motors and the United Automobile Workers in the mid-1970s. This program was adopted by eighteen similar GM plants and was subjected to careful empirical review. It was designed to enrich jobs by removing the most boring, repetitive tasks and by increasing employee autonomy. Results of plant-level data from the years 1970–79 showed that more intensive QWL programs were associated with product quality and lower grievance and absentee rates. It was then concluded that QWL efforts represent one possible strategy for breaking the traditional union-management cycle of high conflict and low trust. Such change might be evident in a displacement of resources and energies from dealing with conflicts to concentrating on work problems; increased worker motivation due to greater participation in job-related decision making; and greater flexibility in human resource management resulting from less reliance on strict work rules and assignments. While the GM experience with QWL programs has been quite positive, such efforts will not likely produce an end to all labor-management differences, as is sometimes predicted.[22]

Quality Circles

One employee participation technique that quickly became popular is **Quality Circles** (**QC**). William Ouchi, author of *Theory Z*, predicts that quality circles' success may cause them to become the "management fad of the 80s." He further states that QC success will be longer lived than management by objectives (MBO) or zero-based budgeting.[23]

The QC concept is generally one of people building rather than people using. Usually five to ten employees with common work interests meet voluntarily in groups once a week. The purpose of their meeting is to identify, analyze, and develop solutions to work problems. Solutions are presented to management for final approval. There is no reward for the circle members other than the recognition and satisfaction they receive from helping to increase the efficiency of the organization. QC programs generally start with only two to three circles and add circles as more employees become interested. Circles are independent—they are not part of the organization chart, members volunteer to participate, and they choose what problems to address and how to analyze them.

Quality circles began in Japan in the early 1960s as a major effort to overcome its image of a producer of cheap, inferior goods. By the 1980s there was no question that Sony, Panasonic, Datsun, Toyota, and others had built a reputation for excellence. It has been estimated that 80 percent of Japanese production workers belong to quality circles.

The most obvious advantage to quality circles is that they produce solutions to work-related problems and thus increase quality and efficiency. However, managers and employees have been amazed at the intrinsic rewards—personal satisfaction and peer recognition—that also result.

Thus far unions in the United States have adopted a neutral attitude toward the QC concept. They probably recognize that circles do increase efficiency, helping the job security of their members. However, they also are aware that employees do not directly share in the reduced costs. As the QC concept grows, union leaders may wish to take a closer look at their operation and resulting savings.

Alternate Work Schedules

Increasing numbers of workers in the United States are desiring more diversity in their work schedules. The 1985 Current Population Survey (CPS) indicated a substantial erosion of the standard workweek in the prior twelve years. The increased desire for leisure time resulted in over 34 percent of all work schedules to include compressed workweeks, part-time work, or long-hour schemes (common in twenty-four-hour organizations such as hospitals and chemical processing plants). Among alternate schedules, the compressed workweek is the most common, increasing in use about 4.5 times as fast as the rate of total employment between 1973 and 1985.[24]

About 12 percent of all workers in 1985 worked flexible schedules, and it is fairly certain that more workers will desire alternate work schedules.[25] Most important, it is one area where both labor and management can realize real advantages to a negotiated change and can look to several successful examples when developing a new proposal.

The term *alternate work schedules* refers to programs allowing employees to change the standard five-day, eight-hour-per-day workweek established following the

Fair Labor Standards Act of 1938. This act provided mandatory overtime pay for more than forty hours worked per week. Unlike many QWL programs, alternate work schedule programs change neither the nature nor the type of work performed but only the scheduling to provide motivation and other benefits to employees. Common forms of alternate work schedules have included the four-day workweek, flextime, and part-time work. Successful alternate work schedule techniques generally fall into one of three categories:

Compressed Workweek

4/40

4/48 + 3/36

4½/40 or 4½/36

Discretionary Workweek

Flextime

Staggered Start

Variable Hours

Telecommuting

Part-time

Job Sharing

Job Splitting

Permanent Part-time

Work Sharing

Compressed Workweek

One of the first forms of alternate work schedules was the **compressed workweek**, usually implemented as the four-day week. Successfully utilized by manufacturing organizations, the four-day week provides employees with three-day weekends as well as a weekday to take care of personal business. Management generally reports substantial savings by reducing startup time and decreasing energy consumption, as well as the savings typically gained from increased employee morale and productivity.[26] The usual four-day workweek is four ten-hour days. Sixty percent of all compressed work weeks fall within this 4/40 category.

Another compressed workweek schedule, 4/48 and 3/36, was negotiated by the union and management of Monsanto Company. The program allows three- and four-day work week schedules that rotate a four-day shift with a three-day shift. In this technique, employees who work four twelve-hour days are off three days and then follow with three twelve-hour days and a four-day layoff. For example, one crew of employees may work from 9:00 P.M. to 9:00 A.M. while a second crew works from 9:00 A.M. to 9:00 P.M. In total, then, four shifts of employees are used. The Monsanto example produced considerable savings due to fewer shift changes and a substantial increase in employee morale, as well as a substantial decrease in turnover and absenteeism. Fatigue, often a factor in compressed workweeks, was surprisingly absent with the twelve-hour work days.[27]

Still another form of the compressed workweek is to provide for a half-day on Friday, giving employees time to go to the grocery or the bank or to perform other personal business, yet still providing the organization with a five-day production schedule and allowing the business to be open for the convenience of customers.

Discretionary Workweek

Discretionary workweek examples of alternate work schedules provide the employee with greater freedom in regulating her own work schedule within certain guidelines. **Flextime**, the most liberal of discretionary workweek schedules, allows employees to determine their beginning and ending times each day as long as they work a specified core of hours and a certain total number of hours per day or week. Flextime, developed in Europe in the 1960s, is often mistakenly used to define other types of alternate work scheduling techniques.

The flextime discretionary workweek is often utilized by both union (see Case 14.1) and nonunion organizations. At the heart of its popularity is the employees' actual control of their working hours and greater sense of independence and self-worth.

The importance of the feeling of control has been directly linked to critical motivation and behavior of employees. Employees become motivated to achieve higher levels of productivity due to their perception of an increased autonomy and personal control over their work environment. This is compared to employees who perceive they have no control over their work environment and are therefore more likely to "go through the motions," with less commitment and involvement in the organization.[28] The substantial increase in personal satisfaction with the work schedule and environment that employees typically report from flextime programs may also carry over to their family and friends, since employees report increased satisfaction with their personal lives. Increased quality of customer service is another advantage in flextime implementations.[29]

Flextime was initially resented by union leaders who contended that it increased employees' productivity but did not affect their weekly wage. Employees working flexible hours often decide to stay to finish a job and involuntarily offset these hours by taking time off during a slack period of the day. Thus the company's overtime costs are significantly reduced because the total hours worked per week do not exceed forty. In recent years, however, union resistance has somewhat diminished due to employees' increased demand for flextime. Union leaders will likely be more interested in negotiating guarantees for flextime, as well as increased wages where merited by increased productivity.

The **staggered start** system of discretionary workweek allows employees to choose one of several alternative starting times and work an eight-hour day. Management determines how many employees will be needed at different hours and defines the different options. This gives management greater control over the workplace but substantially reduces the employees' control over their work environment. Similarly, the **variable hours** system allows employees to contract with their supervisors to work for a specified time each day or week, with the possibility of varying schedules on a daily basis whenever agreeable to both parties. Again, employees have less latitude in setting their time schedules, while management maintains greater control.

In Europe, some German companies negotiated *flexiyear schedules.* In one such experiment, a trade company of 850 employees negotiated a working year contract system, allowing an employee to choose how many hours he would work within a month, within parameters. Through the careful use of core time, management was able to guarantee it would have adequate labor to meet production demand, while giving employees a maximum of flexibility with a monthly system.[30]

New technological opportunities such as electronic mail and bulk-data transmission have created a new alternative in work scheduling called **telecommuting**. Telecommuting allows employees to complete some or all of their work at home. For example, computerized clerical work and computer programming can be accomplished at home because the job does not require constant supervision or contact with customers or co-workers. In 1984 about 30,000 employees were working at home.[31] Estimates of the number of Americans who will use home offices by the year 2000 range as high as 22 percent of all jobs; the most common use by the 1980s was with computer data-entry tasks. In 1984, IBM had over 2,000 employees with terminals at home.[32]

A company allows employees to work outside of direct supervision because of cost savings. For example, less expensive office space is required. Employees enjoy flexibility in their work schedules, cost savings because of lunch at home and no commuting, and the opportunity to stay with their families. But there are disadvantages to telecommuting. Employees miss the social contacts at work that are important for personal and professional needs. Also, they are not privy to the office grapevine or "old boy network."

Federal and state laws do not apply to telecommuters in many areas, such as safe working conditions, equipment, and employment status (full or part time).[33] In fact, the 1938 Fair Labor Standards Act contains a "no homeworking" provision, which was upheld by a U.S. Appeals Court in 1984. The case involved the International Ladies Garment Workers' Union, who objected to retired women and housewives knitting at home because the union could not prevent "sweatshop" conditions.[34] Unions in general are likely to be concerned about an increase in telecommuters, who are difficult to organize.

Telecommuting projects have produced an unexpected benefit in some cases— substantial productivity increases. Control Data conducted a program which resulted in productivity increases for individual employees of between 20 and 35 percent. New York Telephone reported increases of between 15 and 85 percent. The J. C. Penney telecommuting catalog-order program experienced not one paid sick day in its first two years.[35]

Part-time Work

The Bureau of Labor Statistics defines *part-time workers* as those who work less than thirty-five hours a week and divides them into three groups: (1) those who voluntarily work part-time (students, retirees, second-income households), (2) those working part-time for economic reasons (their hours have been reduced by employers), and (3) those who usually work full-time (but worked less than 35 hours in a week due to vacation, illness, etc.). Younger (ages 16 to 24) and older (65 and over) workers account for a much higher proportion of the part-time workforce than of the full-time employed.[36]

Part-time work has become an alternate scheduling system that has recently increased in usage. Part-time techniques include *permanent part-time* work as traditionally used by organizations; **job splitting**, when a single job is divided into two or more part-time positions; and **job sharing**, involving two individuals dividing one full-time position. With job splitting, the two people perform the same work but at different set schedules. They often have no direct contact. In job sharing, the two people decide who does what, when, and how for the single full-time position.

There is little doubt that part-time jobs will be increased in the future. Union negotiators, due to hard economic times, have sometimes favored increased part-time work to provide their members with at least some income as opposed to total unemployment. As the number of two-income families increases, union members will also demand more part-time jobs due to child-rearing or other pursuits. Benefits will continue to be provided by the full-time member. Some unions, however, have opposed part-time work because it has sometimes been forced on members who desire full-time employment.

Strong economic growth and low unemployment in the post–World War II era generally resulted in few layoffs for employees. But severe recessions in the 1970s and 1980s brought long-term, and in many cases permanent, layoffs of many thousands of U.S. workers. Economic recessions have become a way of life for many industries in the United States.

Work sharing reduces the number of employees who are laid off by asking all employees to work fewer hours. For example, Motorola, Inc., used work sharing in 1983 by offering to keep employees scheduled for layoff if employees would work four days a week instead of five. Employees included in the plan would only receive 80 percent of their normal wages. Motorola had helped pass a 1981 Arizona state law that allowed workers to collect unemployment compensation for the time not worked during work sharing. One employee, for example, received $12 in state unemployment due to a $40 cut in wages as a result of the work-sharing program. Only a few states, however, have enacted similar laws.[37] Many employees avoided economic hardship with the system. In addition, work sharing improved labor-management relations because everyone was pulling together during hard times. Although Motorola continued to pay benefits to employees who would otherwise have been laid off, management believed higher productivity from thankful employees made up for the increased cost. Unions favor work sharing because they do not lose members during recessions. Perhaps the greatest advantage of work sharing is that employees and their families are not subjected to the destructive psychological and financial stresses of a layoff, which sometimes leave life-long scars.

Trends in Occupational Employment

The overall downward trend in union membership is a major concern to labor leaders. Although the number of organized workers increased from 14.2 million in 1950 to 20 million in 1980, the percentage of union membership has continued to gradually decline from its peak of over twenty-five years ago. Even though there have been significant membership increases in the public and professional sectors, the overall figures are still greatly disappointing to labor leaders. Public sentiment, once strongly behind unions and the collective bargaining process, has waned in recent years. For example, AT&T and PATCO strikers found that the public support so necessary to the success of their walkouts never materialized. The lack of strength in numbers and general public support will have a long-term impact on the collective bargaining process. Public sympathy for strikes, boycotts, and other union activities is often in the minds of labor and management as they consider the tools available in their arsenals.

The U.S. Bureau of Labor Statistics (BLS) has estimated that the total employment picture in the United States through 1990 will see a continued expansion of service occupations. Service personnel, not including private household workers, will increase faster than any other occupation group throughout the 1980s. Projected increases range from 35 to 45 percent, with particularly rapid expansion in food and health service jobs. Blue collar occupations are also expected to increase slightly faster than average, with construction trade workers and mechanics being the two largest categories in this group. The demand for housing starts and other new construction will greatly influence not only the construction industry but related blue collar industries as well. Growth among white collar groups is still expected to continue at a higher-than-average rate, but will slow from the rapid increase experienced in the 1970s and early 1980s. These jobs increased twice as fast as all occupations from 1966 to 1980. White collar jobs include professions requiring postsecondary education, teachers, medical professionals, health technologists, engineers, and scientists.[38] The twenty most rapidly growing occupations with estimates of percentage growth are provided in Exhibit 14.1.

Labor leaders are concerned with employment patterns because the greatest degree of labor market penetration occurs in areas where employment growth has been slower than the national average. In 1985, seven out of every ten U.S. workers were employed in the service-producing sector, while only two of ten worked in factories. From 1970 to 1985 the fastest-growing U.S. industries were business services, health services, and banking. The greatest declines were in the steel, apparel, and textiles industries.[39] One might conclude that since employment in the most heavily unionized industries is not increasing as rapidly as employment in less unionized industries, the percentage of unionized workers would be expected to decrease by 1990 and continue the trend of the past two decades. However, one might also conclude that the industries with the greatest expected growth also have the fewest union members currently and therefore provide for enormous expansion potential. The key, then, is to organize in those industries where unions traditionally have not been successful. Industries such as health care, fast food, and retail have experienced the greatest employment growth and have the greatest potential for unions.

Union leaders are concerned about the future of the labor movement. In a Bureau of Labor Statistics survey of union presidents and other leaders, over 62 percent believed their members do not know what their union does for them, and 51 percent believed there is a crisis in the American labor movement. The primary causes

Exhibit 14.1   The twenty most rapidly growing occupations

Occupation	Percent growth in employment, 1978–90
Data processing machine mechanics	147.6
Paralegal personnel	132.4
Computer systems analysts	107.8
Computer operators	87.9
Office machine and cash register servicers	80.8
Computer programmers	73.6
Aero-astronautic engineers	70.4
Food preparation and service workers, fast food restaurants	68.8
Employment interviewers	66.6
Tax preparers	64.5
Correction officials and jailers	60.3
Architects	60.2
Dental hygienists	57.9
Physical therapists	57.6
Dental assistants	57.5
Peripheral EDP equipment operators	57.3
Child-care attendants	56.3
Veterinarians	56.1
Travel agents and accommodations appraisers	55.6
Nurses' aides and orderlies	54.6

Source: Max L. Carey: "Occupational Employment Growth Through 1990," *Monthly Labor Review* 104 (Aug. 1981), p. 48, by permission of the *Monthly Labor Review.*

of the crisis are felt to be union policies and structure, "antilabor" government policies, and labor's public image. While the leaders surveyed did not express panic, one union leader did respond that organized labor "has not been able to persuade the majority of workers of the worth of unions." Another expressed the exasperation of many officials: "The unions are blamed for productivity problems—why doesn't anyone . . . chide the corporations for failing to modernize instead of paying stock dividends?" An identical survey of the BLS twenty years prior produced some interesting differences. In the 1963 survey only a few listed union leadership and public image as a major concern; instead automation and unemployment were cited as the major problems of the day.[40]

In a long-term effort to attract a new generation of union supporters, the AFL-CIO at its 1985 convention broke historic ground. Lead by Lane Kirkland, president, the union federation voted to offer associated membership to former union members and nonunion workers. Jack Sheinkman of the Clothing and Textile Workers Union said, for example, associate memberships would be offered to the 3,500 workers who voted for the union in its unsuccessful attempt to organize at Cannon Mills in North Carolina.[41] The large volume of people the union hopes to include (starting with their 13.5 million members) will enable the AFL-CIO to offer low-cost group life, auto, and health insurance, dental insurance, prescription drugs, legal services, retirement accounts, and even low-interest credit cards. Union strategists hope the associate members will develop strong ties to the union movement and someday demand union representation through collective bargaining.

Working Women

One way that unions might become successful is to increase their attractiveness to working women. From 1960 to 1980, the BLS estimated that the percentage of men in the labor force decreased from over 82 percent in 1960 to 77 percent in 1980. During the same period, the number of working women in the labor force rose from 37 percent to over 50 percent—an increase of about 20 million.[42] Blacks and immigrants were the pioneers, followed by young single women and mothers re-entering the labor force after their children had grown. The latest influx has included young mothers.

Past social and cultural factors that created a stigma associated with working women have disappeared. Although some women want to break from the traditional household role, others work out of necessity. Twenty-five percent of the female labor force is single, and an additional 20 percent is divorced, separated, or widowed. The remaining 55 percent needs the second income to keep pace with inflation or perhaps the sporadic employment of their husbands.[43]

In the past, occupations with a large percentage of women were harder for unions to organize, perhaps because women disliked the concept of organizing a union instead of dealing with management one-on-one, or considered union membership unnecessary because they were earning "pin money." However, today's women view the collective bargaining process as a way to guarantee the right of equal pay for equal work and job advancement, opening new doors for union organizers. Case 14.3 exemplifies how unions can aid women on the job.

Illegal Aliens

The immigration of illegal aliens has become a prominent issue during the last portion of this century. Most of the estimated 2 to 5 million illegal aliens come from Mexico, Cuba, Central America, and the Caribbean to escape civil wars, overpopulation, and poverty. Their numbers are likely to increase, and they will be competing directly with U.S. citizens for jobs.[44] While some people suggest that recent immigrants fill only low-wage jobs left vacant by domestic workers, labor economists believe that illegal aliens depress the wages even further and cause higher unemployment rates for lower-skilled U.S. workers. Employers and investors may actually benefit from the flow of immigrants who provide lower labor costs and thus higher returns.[45]

Immigrants are an untapped resource for labor leaders. Once aliens get their papers and become legal, they may be willing to unionize. Their children might also be sympathetic to unions when they become part of the work force.

Concession Bargaining

On the brink of bankruptcy, the Chrysler Corporation negotiated over $1 billion in federally secured loans to stay afloat in 1979–80. The United Auto Workers (UAW), in a critical part of the total plan to keep Chrysler financially stable, agreed to defer scheduled wage increases and give up paid personal holidays secured in past negotiations. UAW President Douglas Fraser termed these concessions "the worst we've ever made, and the only thing that is worse is the alternative, no jobs for Chrysler workers."[46] This radical departure from the typical collective bargaining process began a period of U.S. collective bargaining sometimes referred to as *concession, giveback,* or *nontraditional bargaining.* This new bargaining process is caused by economic hardship in many industries.

The early 1980s were characterized by the highest rate of unemployment in this country since before World War II, the greatest number of business failures since the Great Depression, and the lowest percentage of factory utilization in a thirty-five-year period. In 1982, the smallest average wage increase was negotiated by major collective bargaining settlements covering 1,000 workers or more since the Bureau of Labor Statistics began compiling its data.[47]

Collective bargaining in the United States has been marked by much conflict and hostility. American labor relations traditionally have been characterized by confrontation and a "get the boss" attitude by labor, as well as a "keep the union in its place" attitude by management.[48] However, the general pattern of collective bargaining has been one of concession by employers to unions in building upon past agreements. Each new agreement provided for additional wages, benefits, and other employee advantages. With most economists predicting the continuation of recession and slow growth and the increase in foreign competition, the collective bargaining environment may experience an expansion of concession bargaining.[49]

In 1982, Ford Motor Company and the UAW negotiated a break-through in greater job security for union members. At that time, 55,000 Ford workers were on indefinite layoff while the remaining 105,000 feared for their future employment. The UAW agreed to defer cost-of-living increases for eighteen months and eliminate nine previously negotiated personal paid holidays each year. In exchange, Ford Motor Company agreed to a two-year moratorium on plant closings, which would have resulted in subcontracting the manufacturing of parts to non-UAW suppliers.

Of particular significance in the Ford agreement was the new *guaranteed income stream* program in which laid-off employees with fifteen years or more of service would be guaranteed 50 percent of their hourly rate of pay until age sixty-two or retirement. In addition, Ford agreed to undertake an experimental *lifetime job security* program at two plants so jobs would not be eliminated due to technological change or the economy.

Concession bargaining between General Motors and the UAW provided an estimated additional $3 billion in savings to this country's largest auto maker. General Motors agreed to rescind a decision to close four additional plants employing 11,000 employees.[50]

In the meat packing industry, giveback bargaining began in 1981 when the United Food and Commercial Workers Union and Armour and Company agreed on a wage and benefit package. Armour had lost almost $6 million in 1980 and had closed twenty-four plants in the past ten years. The workers gave up specified wage increases and agreed to suspend semiannual cost-of-living pay adjustments. The Food and Commercial Workers Union negotiated similar terms under what was referred to as the "Armour pattern" with several other employers, including Wilson Foods Corporation, George A. Hormel and Company, and Rath Packing Company. Similarly, in 1981, the Teamsters, with nearly half of its members indefinitely laid off, negotiated a thirty-seven-month national master freight agreement calling for a freeze on general wages. The agreement provided for a reopening of negotiations in 1984 only if the parties agreed that the financial status of the industry had substantially changed. The tire, steel, and airline industries, as well as others, also began similar concession bargaining agreements.[51]

An analysis of successfully concluded concession negotiations showed that in more than half, the union agreed to wage and benefit reductions. In the remaining contracts, unions consented to a wage and benefit freeze. The most common concession, found in 40 percent of the contracts, was an agreement to give up paid holidays. The second most common concession involved a work rule or production change. In exchange, employers generally agreed to future wage and benefit improvements and greater job security.[52]

Union concessions generally involve wage, benefit, or work rule changes, with reduced benefits generally more acceptable to employees than wage concessions, although future wage increases may be renegotiated. Often work rule changes are easier to sell to employees and have a more lasting effect. Employers, however, must expect to pay the price of these concessions through one or more of five areas of negotiation:

1. *Increased job security*   The union will most likely try to extract a promise not to close plants or not to subcontract with nonunion producers. The Ford Motor Company example of a guaranteed income stream will be pursued by many unions. Such restrictions can be very expensive and limiting to employers.

2. *Increased financial disclosure*   The employer will have to make a claim of inability to pay or financial hardship. While the company's financial information normally need not be disclosed in collective bargaining, when the employer puts profitability or financial condition in contention, the financial data must be provided to substantiate the position.

3. *Profit-sharing plans*   Union members generally feel that sharing in austerity now should mean sharing profits in the future. For example, in 1983, Chrysler Corporation's employees demanded a share of the record profits, only three years after the UAW made major concessions to guarantee the federal loan to Chrysler. In 1984, over 158,000 union and nonunion employees of the Ford Motor Company received an average of $440 as their part of the new Ford-UAW profit-sharing plan.[53]

4. *Equality of sacrifice*   Employers must demand the same sacrifices from management and nonunion employees as union employees. For instance, General Motors tried to increase its executive bonus program just after the UAW made major concessions in 1982. The UAW and its members demanded, and got, the increases rescinded.

5. *Participation in decision making*   Unions may seek greater participation in various management decisions, including plant closings and the use of new technological methods. If properly utilized, this concession can help develop greater understanding and improve employee relations.[54]

The essence of successful and continued concession bargaining is the development of mutual trust and respect by both parties. The union must be willing to give up some gains made through the years, especially in terms of nonproductive paid time off and other expensive benefits. The employer, in somewhat of a role reversal, must convince the union of the need to negotiate concessions to guarantee survival of the business. The obvious and ultimate proof is that the company is losing money, which usually must be verified by an objective third party such as an outside auditor.

Generally, the reduction of pay for time not worked is more acceptable to employees than outright wage reductions. Reduction of pay for time not worked also enables employers to increase productivity. Contract provisions that are particularly vulnerable to concession bargaining include the following:

1. *Vacation pay*   Lengthening service or work time requirements and shortening length of time off are usually acceptable.
2. *Holiday pay*   Elimination of paid personal holidays or lowering the number of general days granted generates savings and more production time with fewer employees.
3. *Break periods*   Eliminate or shorten rest periods and wash-up time to produce relief but not in direct ratio to minutes saved. Productive output is more often merely spread over the extra time. Breaks are very necessary in some operations, so approach proposals in this area cautiously.
4. *Nonproductive downtime and classification inflexibility*   Propose work be done for all time paid so a productive effort is given even when the standard job is not operating because of irregularities. This can eliminate indirect labor costs in custodial or quality control areas.
5. *Pension benefits*   This is a complex area. There are real cash flow benefits to be realized from changing assumptions and delaying or postponing contributions. Changing from a defined benefit plan to defined contributions or, even better, a profit-sharing plan, will shift the costs to more profitable times and not hold corporate assets hostage.
6. *Insurance program*   Benefit amount, timing, and deductibles can be changed to save considerable costs in this area. Pay particular attention to health, medical, sickness, and accident coverages, which are most costly. Pay for extended coverage on layoff, leave of absence, and retirement can be eliminated or paid by employees. Preserve flexibility to change carriers to obtain premium reductions.
7. *Seniority provisions*   Streamline bidding and bumping procedures to eliminate excessive turmoil and retraining. Ensure assignment of qualified, experienced personnel to jobs to maintain peak efficiency.
8. *Overtime assignment*   Provide for only qualified people to work and eliminate unnecessary make-work assignments.
9. *Bonus payments*   Eliminate or reduce extra payments.
10. *Wages*   Consider eliminating or suspending future increases and cost-of-living allowances. If this doesn't achieve your economic objective, propose a wage reduction. Reductions of over $1 per hour have been approved in many companies.

Source: John W. Falahee, "Concession Bargaining: The Time Is Now!" *Personnel Administrator* 28, no. 1 (Jan. 1983), pp. 27–28. Reprinted from the Jan. 1983 issue of *Personnel Administrator,* copyright 1983, The American Society for Personnel Administration, 606 North Washington St., Alexandria, VA 22314, $30 per year.

Some labor leaders caution that unions should beware of employers who ask for concessions they truly do not need. It is also important to realize that what the media term as "concessions" by unions are in fact not one-sided. For example, the increased job security gained by the UAW in its agreements was a goal the union had pursued since the 1940s.[55]

Codetermination

After Chrysler Corporation agreed to appoint UAW President Douglas Fraser to its board of directors, it was speculated that union leaders would be given a greater voice in managerial decision making.[56] However, the European practice of **codetermination**—allowing union members significant representation on policy-making corporate boards—has attracted very little interest in the United States. Some UAW leaders even questioned Chrysler's motives, stating that labor can best serve its membership through the "traditional adversary relationship between labor and management and that it [labor] has no business mixing in boardroom affairs."[57] While some believe that codetermination provides labor with a voice in managerial decision making and therefore improves communications between labor and management, others question whether labor leaders can sit with management at both board meetings and the bargaining table with the union's best interests in mind.

New Cooperation in the Future?

As the United States struggles to meet greater international competition and domestic needs, the process of collective bargaining will need to undergo substantial changes. From the early 1800s management fought labor as combinations in restraint of trade and used other techniques to combat its very existence. The passage of the National Labor Relations Act in the 1930s and the subsequent Taft-Hartley Amendments legitimized the rules of collective bargaining. But the general adversarial relationship has remained the same.[58]

A Harris poll reported that a majority of the general public believed that unions contribute significantly less than they once did to the growth and efficiency of business.[59] While a majority of union leaders surveyed disagreed with this judgment, the Harris poll reflects a change of attitude toward unions. Many people do not feel that unions aid in the process of making organizations more efficient and productive.

Can labor and management change from an adversarial relationship to a problem-solving one? Such a change should, of course, benefit both management and employees. At least one successful example occurred in a large, modern manufacturing plant that was plagued by union-management conflict. Both union and management were dependent upon each other for their very existence and had a long history of bitter hostility. The plant had suffered two major strikes within a few years, and a third strike due to upcoming negotiations seemed inevitable. The employee relations manager, realizing that both sides had more to lose than to gain in an increasingly competitive marketplace, proposed a development seminar to improve relations. Both sides reluctantly agreed to participate rather than to suffer through a third strike. External labor consultants, using *behavioral science intervention* techniques, set four primary goals for the seminar: establish a basis for a problem-solving relationship; develop concrete plans for moving away from an adversarial relationship toward one of mutual trust; create task forces to solve identified problems; and plan follow-up and re-evaluation programs.

After a considerable amount of antagonism and disagreement, each side conceded major changes in policy that indicated its willingness to cooperate. Both groups saw the real need to pursue a superordinate goal of keeping the plant productive and competitive if there were to be a prosperous future for the company. Once both groups adopted a positive attitude, they were able to develop specific means of improving labor-management relations.

Toward the end of the seminar, the plant manager admitted that management had painted itself into a corner by its labor relations policy. Management then issued a summary statement to the union describing its thoughts and feelings:

1. We recognize we have a deep win-lose orientation toward the union.
2. We want to change!
3. Barriers to overcome: convince the union we want to change; convince ourselves we have the patience, skill and convictions to change.
4. We're responsible to bring the rest [of the management team] on board.
5. We recognize the risk, but want to resist the temptation to revert to win-lose when it gets tough.[60]

Before the use of behavioral intervention, the plant ranked last in economic performance among eleven similar companies; five years later, it was number one. While this experience may not be the solution for all companies and unions, it might be one to consider when faced with the economic consequences of a shutdown.

In 1986 the U.S. Department of Labor (DOL) began a comprehensive review of the nation's labor laws and practices.[61] The purpose of this first-ever study is to determine how the federal government could support increased labor-management cooperation and a "mutual respect for collective bargaining." The review will include an analysis of many of the more experimental cooperative efforts such as worker participation plans (AT&T and CWA), worker retraining programs (Ford and UAW), and the Fremont, California joint venture (GM-Toyota and UAW). According to DOL Secretary William E. Brock, the framework of our existing labor laws and culture often hinders cooperative efforts such as QWL programs and worker participation. Too often our present values foster confrontation rather than goals that encourage cooperation. When the review is completed, the DOL hopes to work with labor and management leaders in the formulation of legislative strategy to modify existing laws to encourage cooperation and innovation.[62]

Union Avoidance versus Cooperation

Today many corporate executives and political leaders are calling for an expansion of cooperative efforts at the workplace, such as quality circles, QWL programs, and continued moderation in wage demands. At the same time, however, the dominant trend among management is to shift investments and jobs to nonunion employment settings.[63] This trend is furthered by Supreme Court decisions allowing plant relocations, liquidations, and partial closings without union input by declaring such practices to be permissive items and not mandatory.[64] It is difficult to see how unions can act cooperatively when management practices undermine their basic existence. If the trend of the early 1980s continues, unions may face life and death struggle, forcing them into confrontation rather than cooperation. American unions will strive to avoid further membership losses by promoting innovation in the workplace to maintain organizational competitiveness, increasing their influence on strategic business and governmental decisions that affect membership, and pursuing new organizing strategies.[65]

Business Schools

U.S. Labor Secretary William E. Brock has strongly suggested that the nation's business schools take the lead in training individuals in labor-management cooperation. Business schools, he noted, can teach the skills necessary for workers and managers to realize their mutual goals. In the past, inadequate preparation in labor-management relations may have aided in developing adversarial positions. Brock asked the business schools in our universities to modify their curricula and train future labor and management leaders about the totality of the work relationship, with particular emphasis on labor-management relations and cooperation.[66]

Summary

The commonplace use of binding arbitration to settle grievances and a new spirit of cooperation to meet outside competition have changed the face of labor relations. Unions recognize that they can no longer count on public sympathy to make strikes and other economic actions successful.

As jobs change due to robotics, technology, and a surging service sector, employees demand more satisfying and challenging jobs. Workers want greater participation in the workplace through QWL, quality circles, and other techniques. They also want more leisure time and alternative work schedules to fit their lifestyles. Collective bargaining can help them realize these goals.

How well unions can bargain for these demands and organize a younger, minority-based, and female-populated labor force may determine their future.

CASE 14.1   *Flextime*

Adapted from *U.S. Department of Health & Human Services* v. *American Federation of Government Employees Local 112*, 83 LA 883 (1984)

Facts

In 1977, the company (Food and Drug Administration, a federal agency) instituted a flextime plan after negotiations between the company and the union. The plan allowed employees, within certain boundaries, to choose their own starting and quitting times. One provision allowed either party to cancel the plan at any time. The plan could be modified by the company after negotiations with the union.

In 1980, the company and the union entered into a new contract. The new contract referenced the flextime plan in the following section:

Article 20   *Hours of Work and Tour of Duty*

1. The District agrees to consult with the Union regarding any changes in the Flextime Plan currently in force in the Chicago District. The District agrees to negotiate with the Union on the impact and implementation of any changes in the Plan.

And it included the following definitions.

Consultations: Verbal or written discussion between representatives of the District and representatives of the Union for the purpose of obtaining or exchanging viewpoints on any aspect of working conditions, and on new or changed policies or programs that affect the morale and general working conditions of employees in the bargaining unit. It is not mandatory that the end result of consultation be agreement between the parties.

Negotiation: Joint discussions by representatives of the District and the Union on subjects appropriate for negotiations as set forth in the Civil Service Reform Act of 1978 to include policies affecting personnel and practices, and matters affecting working conditions which are under control of the District Director. Negotiation should result in execution of a written agreement, including amendments or supplements thereto, or a memorandum of understanding.

In 1983 the company sent the union major modifications to the flextime plan and notified the union that it would meet to negotiate the "impact and implementation" of those changes as required by the contract. The union protested that the company was required to negotiate the substance of the modifications to the plan as well as the impact and implementation, and a grievance was filed.

Grievance

The Union's position was that "hours of work" is a mandatory bargaining subject, and any change during the term of the contract must be negotiated.

The company agreed with this basic premise but pointed out that the union waived its right to bargain under Article 20 of the contract. In the company's opinion the language of Article 20 clearly delineates the responsibilities vis-a-vis the flextime plan. The company must "consult" on changes and "negotiate" on impact and implementation. Article I includes definitions for "consultation" and "negotiation," which clearly provide that consulting is an exchange of ideas with no agreement necessary and negotiating is discussions that result in an agreement.

The union pointed out that a waiver must be clear and unequivocable and disagreed with the company's interpretation of these sections. It stated that Article 20 is vague as to what the difference between "changes" and "impact and implementation" might be, and therefore, the vagueness precludes and waiver of rights by the union.

The company acknowledged that "changes" and "impact and implementation" are not defined in this collective bargaining agreement but are clearly defined in the federal statute that created the bargaining obligation on federal agencies.

> (1) Nothing in the Section shall preclude any agency and any labor organization from negotiating—
>
> (2) procedures which management officials of the agency will observe in exercising any authority under this Section; or
>
> (3) appropriate arrangements for employees adversely affected by the exercise of any authority under this Section by such management officials.

Even if the contract looks like a waiver, using bargaining history and past practice the union believed it could show it did not intend to waive its rights. Article 20 was added to the 1980 contract to counteract the provision of the flexitime plan that allows either party to cancel it any time. Obviously, the union wanted its rights preserved. Also it pointed out that changes made in the plan from 1980 to 1983 were submitted to the union for negotiation prior to approval.

The company pointed out first that unless the contract is ambiguous, the parties cannot rely on bargaining history or past practice to interpret it. But in the event the arbitrator does review those facts, the history of bargaining on the flexitime plan is too vague to establish any proof that the language as written is not the agreement of the parties. As to past practice, the parties' argued changes to the flextime plan before 1983 were minor, and the parties may have only negotiated the impact of those changes.

Decision

The arbitrator agreed with the company that the language of the contract was clearly and unequivocably a waiver.

CASE 14.2   *Subcontracting*

Adapted from *Pennsylvania Power Co.* v. *International Brotherhood of Electrical Workers Local 272* 85 LA 797 (1985)

Facts

The company allowed a non-bargaining unit employee to repair an electrical relay on the plant's security system, and the union filed a grievance.

Grievance

The union contended that the contract was violated because it prohibits supervisors from performing the work normally performed by members of the bargaining unit except in emergencies, for training purposes, or to check equipment.

The company's position was that maintenance of the plant's security system is not work normally performed by the union members, but that it is contracted out to an outside contractor. Therefore, the repair is not within the scope of the contract.

The union acknowledged that the normal maintenance is done by an outside contractor but that those contracts were entered into pursuant to provisions of the collective bargaining agreement that stated prior to outside contracting, the company and union would agree on the scope of the contract. The scope of this contract did not allow supervisors to perform the work. It was the union's position that they agreed to have an outside contractor maintain the security system but not to allow supervisors to make repairs on the system. The union believed they have some control on the scope of outside contracts but none on work assigned to supervisors.

Decision

The arbitrator decided this grievance on the past practice of the parties. The security system had never been maintained by union members. Because it had not, it was not work normally done by the unit members, and therefore the section prohibiting supervisors from performing the work did not apply. The union's point on agreeing to the scope of an outside contract only was simply dismissed as irrelevant to this case.

CASE 14.3   *Maternity Leave*

Adapted from *Ambridge Borough* v. *American Federation of State, County, and Municipal Employees, Local 1051-A* 81 LA 915 (1983)

Facts

A member of the bargaining unit represented by the union adopted a baby girl. She delayed the adoption for 3 weeks to avoid missing work because it was a busy time for her employer. When she finally adopted the baby, she took a two week vacation then applied for a six month unpaid maternity leave pursuant to the contract, which read in part:

ARTICLE X
Leaves of Absence

SECTION 4
UNPAID LEAVES

Reasonable Purpose
1.   Leaves of absence for a limited period without pay—not to exceed ninety (90) days, shall be granted for any reasonable purpose. Extension to be granted with approval of Borough Council.
2.   Reasonable purpose in each case shall be agreed upon by the Union and the Borough.

Maternity
1.   Maternity Leaves—not to exceed six months—shall be granted at the request of an employee. Maternity leaves shall, upon the request of the employee, be extended or renewed for a period not to exceed six (6) months."

The employer denied her maternity leave request but offered her a first and second ninety-day leave for "reasonable purpose." The employee filed a grievance.

Grievance

The employer contended the employee is not entitled to maternity leave because she did not conceive and bear the child. The term "maternity" modifies "leaves" and as such is an adjective defined by *Webster's Dictionary* to refer to "women during pregnancy and confinement." Other collective bargaining agreements correctly refer to the leave as "childbirth leave" and this is obviously the purpose. The employer offered the grievant a "reasonable purpose leave" she refused to take, which would have been the same six months off.

The grievant contended that the term "maternity leaves" in the contract is a noun defined by *Webster's Dictionary* to refer to "the quality or state of being a mother." Maternity leaves are to provide both for the physical health and recovery of the mother and for the child-rearing after birth. The length of time, an initial six months, and the ability to request another six months would not have been provided if it were for the purpose of physical recovery *alone*. Obviously, the maternal relationship during the first months of life is important to an infant's development, whether the infant is adopted or natural.

Decision

The arbitrator found no basis for the employer's contention that the leave was limited to childbirth leave. Other contracts which mean childbirth leave use that term. This contract said "maternity leaves" and the arbitrator agreed that maternity included acting as mother after the child is born. The six-month leave was granted.

CASE STUDY   Dual-employee

Adapted from *National Labor Relations Board* v. *Georgia Florida Alabama Transportation Co.,* 566 F. 2d 520 (CA 5, 1978)

Facts

The bargaining unit of the company consisted of all full-time and regular part-time drivers and dock workers employed at the Alabama terminal of the company. The duties of these employees were loading and unloading trucks and pickup and delivery of local freight. Excluded from the unit were over-the-road drivers and office personnel. One employee, Henderson, was a dual-function employee who spent 80 percent of his time as an over-the-road driver and only 20 percent of his time as a dock worker and local freight driver. His over-the-road duties were paid by the trip, but he was paid for his dock work the same as everyone else. He had been regular part-time on the dock for two years and was expected to continue. When the bargaining unit voted on union representation, Henderson was not permitted to vote because of a determination by the NLRB that he was not part of the bargaining unit. The union won the election on a six-to-five vote, but the company refused to bargain contending that there was doubt as to its majority status because Henderson was not allowed to vote as part of the unit.

Appeal

The union and the NLRB contended Henderson was not part of the unit because to include dual employees there must be a "community of interest" with the bargaining unit. The main focus of their contention that Henderson lacked a community of interest was the amount of time spent as a dock worker (20 percent). Although other regular part-time employees were in the unit, the remainder of their workweek was not devoted to over-the-road driving for the same company. Henderson should be considered part of the over-the-road unit for "community of interest" purposes.

The company disagreed. The previous case law on the community of interest does not rely on the *time* spent by the employee but on such factors as schedules, rates of pay, benefits, day-to-day contacts, and consistency. Time is only one factor. When Henderson was on the dock he was treated exactly the same as the other employees. He had to be considered part of the unit.

Questions

1. Was Henderson a part of the unit or not? Why or why not?
2. The union presumably would not know how Henderson would vote, so what reasons could the union have for excluding employees such as Henderson from the unit?
3. What reason could the employer have for including employees such as Henderson in the unit?

Key Terms and Concepts

Anthropomorphic robots

Codetermination

Composites

Compressed workweek

Discretionary workweek

Flextime

Job sharing

Job splitting

Quality Circles (QC)

Quality of Working Life (QWL)

Robotics

Staggered start

Telecommuting

Termination-at-will

Variable hours

Work sharing

Review Questions

1. How have the central issues of collective bargaining changed since the 1930s? Which issues are still critical today?
2. Why has the silicon chip been important in the development of robotics? Will the field of robotics expand in the future? Why?

3. How do Quality of Working Life (QWL) programs differ from past union-management communications?

4. Which alternate work schedule techniques are likely to be used? What new alternatives might develop?

5. What employment trends should labor leaders study in expanding their membership? What new opportunities for membership would you suggest?

6. What is the cause of recent nontraditional bargaining? Why do many believe that it must continue in the future?

Endnotes

1. Robert Schrank, "Are Unions an Anachronism?" *Harvard Business Review* 57, no. 5 (Sept./Oct. 1979), pp. 107–15.

2. Jack Stieber, "Most U.S. Workers Still May Be Fixed under the Employment-at-will Doctrine," *Monthly Labor Review* 107, no. 5 (May 1984), pp. 34–37.

3. K. B. Stickler, "Limitations on an Employer's Right to Discipline and Discharge Employees," *Employer Relations Law Journal* (Summer 1983), pp. 70–80.

4. As of January, 1987, twenty states have recognized the public policy exception, fourteen states have recognized the implied contract exception, and three states the good faith exception.

5. Michael R. Carrell and Frank E. Kuzmits, *Personnel,* 2d ed. (Columbus, Ohio: Merrill, 1986), pp. 520–21.

6. Stieber, "Employment-at-will Doctrine," p. 36.

7. Sar A. Levitan and Clifford M. Johnson, "The Future of Work: Does It Belong to Us or to the Robots?" *Monthly Labor Review* 105, no. 9 (Sept. 1982), p. 10.

8. George L. Whaley, "The Impact of Robotics Technology upon Human Resource Management," *Personnel Administrator* 27, no. 9 (Sept. 1982), p. 61.

9. Levitan and Johnson, "The Future of Work," p. 10.

10. Carl Remick, "Robots: New Faces on the Production Line," *Management Review* 68 (May 1979), p. 26.

11. Levitan and Johnson, "The Future of Work," pp. 11–12.

12. Whaley, "The Impact of Robotics," p. 61.

13. Levitan and Johnson, "The Future of Work," p. 12.

14. Ibid., p. 13.

15. "Some Lessons Learned for the Decade Ahead," *U.S. News and World Report* 87, no. 27 (Dec. 31, 1979), pp. 73–74.

16. Kazvtoshi Koshiro, "Robots Are a Big Success at Auto Plant in Japan," *Monthly Labor Review* 107, no. 8 (Aug. 1984), pp. 35–36.

17. Jonathan P. Hicks, "Machine-Tooling Firm Eyes Future," *The Courier-Journal* (Feb. 15, 1987), pp. E1, E4.

18. Ibid.

19. Stephen Koepp, et al., "The Boss That Never Blinks," *Time,* July 28, 1986, pp. 46–47.

20. Lee M. Oyley and Judith S. Ball, "Quality of Work Life: Initiating Success in Labor-Management Organizations," *Personnel Administrator* 27, no. 5 (May 1982), pp. 27–29.

21. "The New Industrial Relations," *Business Week* 2687 (May 11, 1981), pp. 85–98.

22. Harry C. Katz, Thomas A. Kochan, and Kenneth R. Gobeille, "Industrial Relations Performance and QWL Programs: An Interplant Analysis," *Industrial and Labor Relations Review* 37, no. 1 (Oct. 1983), pp. 3–17.

23. William G. Ouchi, *Theory Z* (Reading, Mass.: Addison-Wesley, 1981), chap. 11, pp. 1–7.

24. Shirley J. Smith, "The Growing Diversity of Work Schedules," *Monthly Labor Review* 109, no. 11 (Nov. 1986), p. 743.

25. Earl F. Mellor, "Shift Work and Flextime: How Prevalent Are They?" *Monthly Labor Review* 109, no. 11 (Nov. 1986), pp. 14–21.

26. Michael R. Carrell and Frank E. Kuzmits, *Personnel: Management of Human Resources,* 2nd ed. (Columbus, Ohio: Merrill, 1986), pp. 70–81.

27. "Flexible Work Schedules," *Small Business Report,* Oct. 1978, pp. 24–25.

28. John R. Turney, "Alternative Work Schedules Increase Employee Satisfaction," *Personnel Journal* 62, no. 3 (March 1983), pp. 202–7.

29. Randall B. Dunham and John L. Pierce, "The Design and Evaluation of Alternative Work Schedules," *Personnel Administrator* 28 (April 1983), pp. 67–75.

30. Bernhard Teriet, "Flexiyear Schedules in Germany," *Personnel Journal* 61 (June 1982), pp. 428–29.

31. Richard Upton, "The 'Home Office' and the New Homeworkers," *Personnel Management* 21 (Sept. 1984), pp. 39–43.

32. Toby Kahn, "Vermont Home Knitters," *People Weekly* 21 (March 19, 1984), p. 64.

33. Marcia M. Kelley, "Exploring the Potentials of Decentralized Work Settings," *Personnel Administrator* 29, no. 2 (Feb. 1984), pp. 48–49.

34. Grett S. Meier, *Job Sharing* (Kalamazoo, Mich.: Upjohn Institute, 1978), pp. 1–3.

35. Michael Frease and Robert A. Zawacki, "Job-Sharing: An Answer to Productivity Problems?" *The Personnel Administrator* 24, no. 10 (Oct. 1979), pp. 35–37.

36. Thomas J. Nardone, "Part-Time Workers: Who Are They?" *Monthly Labor Review* 109, no. 2 (Feb. 1986), pp. 13–19.

37. Heywood Klein, "Interest Grows in Worksharing, Which Lets Concerns Cut Workweeks to Avoid Layoffs," *Wall Street Journal,* April 7, 1983, p. 27.

38. Max L. Carey, "Occupational Employment Growth Through 1990," *Monthly Labor Review* 104 (Aug. 1981), pp. 42–55.

39. "Labor Month in Review," *Monthly Labor Review* 108, no. 10 (Oct. 1985), p. 2.

40. Brian Heshizer and Harvey Graham, "Are Unions Facing a Crisis? Labor Officials are Divided," *Monthly Labor Review* 107, no. 8 (Aug. 1984), pp. 23–25.

41. "Now It's Unions Offering Fringe Benefits to Workers, *U.S. News & World Report,* Nov. 11, 1985, p. 86.

42. U.S. Bureau of Labor Statistics, *Special Labor Force Reports* (Washington, D.C.: Government Printing Office, 1980), pp. 18–26.

43. Sar A. Levitan, Garth L. Mangum, and Ray Marshall, *Human Resources and Labor Markets: Employment and Training in the American Economy,* 3rd ed. (New York: Harper and Row, 1981), pp. 275–77.

44. George E. Johnson, "The Labor Market Effects of Immigration," *Industrial and Labor Relations Review* 33, no. 3 (April 1980), pp. 331–40.

45. Michael L. Wachter, "The Labor Market and Illegal Immigration: The Outlook for the 1980s," *Industrial and Labor Relations Review* 33, no. 3 (April 1980), pp. 342–54.

46. Bureau of National Affairs, *Report on Labor Relations in an Economic Recession: Job Losses and Concession Bargaining* (Washington, D.C.: Bureau of National Affairs, 1982), p. 16.

47. George Ruben, "Collective Bargaining in 1982: Results Dictated by Economy," *Monthly Labor Review* 106 (Jan. 1983), pp. 28–33.

48. Scott A. Kruse, "Giveback Bargaining: One Answer to Current Labor Problems?" *Personnel Journal* 62 (April 1983), pp. 286–89.

49. Ibid.

50. Bureau of National Affairs, *Report on Labor Relations,* p. 3.

51. Ruben, "Collective Bargaining," pp. 30–33.

52. Bureau of National Affairs, *Collective Bargaining and Labor Relations Database* (Washington, D.C.: Bureau of National Affairs, 1984), p. 21.

53. "Ford Employees Average $440 as Part of Profit-Sharing Plan," *Resource,* pamphlet (Alexandria, Va.: American Society for Personnel Administration, April 1984), p. 12.

54. Krus, "Giveback Bargaining," pp. 289–91.

55. Bureau of National Affairs, *Report on Labor Relations,* p. 5.

56. D. Quinn Mills, "Reforming the U.S. System of Collective Bargaining," *Monthly Labor Review* 106, no. 3 (March 1983), pp. 18–22.

57. Ibid.

58. Robert R. Blake and Jane S. Mouton, "Developing a Positive Union-Management Relationship," *Personnel Administrator* 28, no. 6 (June 1983), pp. 23–31.

59. Louis Harris, *Daily Labor Report* (Washington, D.C.: Bureau of National Affairs, June 3, 1981), pp. A14–A16.

60. Mills, "Reforming the U.S. System," pp. 21–22.

61. Stephen J. Schlossberg and Steven M. Fetter, Department of Labor, Office of Labor-Management Relations and Cooperative Programs Press Release, June 16, 1986, U.S. Department of Labor, Washington, D.C. 20210.

62. "Labor Month in Review," *Monthly Labor Review* 109, no. 7 (July 1986), p. 2.

63. T.A. Kochan, R.B. McKersie, and H.C. Katz, "U.S. Industrial Relations in Transition," *Monthly Labor Review* 108, no. 5 (May 1985), pp. 28–29.

64. First National Maintenance Corp. v. NLRB, 452 U.S. 666 (1981); Otis Elevator Company, 269 NLRB 891 (1984).

65. Kochan, "U.S. Industrial Relations," pp. 28–29.

66. William E. Brock, speech at the 40th Anniversary of the New York School of Industrial and Labor Relations, Cornell University, May 2, 1986.

Text of the National Labor Relations Act

TEXT OF NATIONAL LABOR RELATIONS ACT

49 Stat. 449–57 (1935), as amended by 61 Stat. 136–52 (1947), 65 Stat. 601 (1951), 72 Stat. 945 (1958), 73 Stat. 525–42 (1959), 84 Stat. 930 (1970), 88 Stat. 395–97 (1974), 88 Stat. 1972 (1975), 94 Stat. 347 (1980), 94 Stat. 3452 (1980); 29 U.S.C. §169 (Supp. 1981)

FINDINGS AND POLICIES

Section 1. The denial by some employers of the right of employees to organize and the refusal by some employers to accept the procedure of collective bargaining lead to strikes and other forms of industrial strife or unrest, which have the intent or the necessary effect of burdening or obstructing commerce by (a) impairing the efficiency, safety, or operation of the instrumentalities of commerce; (b) occurring in the current of commerce; (c) materially affecting, restraining, or controlling the flow of raw materials or manufactured or processed goods from or into the channels of commerce, or the prices of such materials or goods in commerce; or (d) causing diminution of employment and wages in such volume as substantially to impair or disrupt the market for goods flowing from or into the channels of commerce.

The inequality of bargaining power between employees who do not possess full freedom of association or actual liberty of contract, and employers who are organized in the corporate or other forms of ownership association substantially burdens and affects the flow of commerce, and tends to aggravate recurrent business depressions by depressing wage rates and the purchasing power of wage earners in industry and by preventing the stabilization of competitive wage rates and working conditions within and between industries.

Experience has proved that protection by law of the right of employees to organize and bargain collectively safeguards commerce from injury, impairment, or interruption, and promotes the flow of commerce by removing certain recognized sources of industrial strife and unrest, by encouraging practices fundamental to the friendly adjustment of industrial disputes arising out of differences as to wages, hours, or other working conditions, and by restoring equality of bargaining power between employers and employees.

Experience has further demonstrated that certain practices by some labor organizations, their officers, and members have the intent or the necessary effect of burdening or obstructing commerce by preventing the free flow of goods in such commerce through strikes and other forms of industrial unrest or through concerted activities which impair the interest of the public in the free flow of such commerce. The elimination of such practices is a necessary condition to the assurance of the rights herein guaranteed.

It is hereby declared to be the policy of the United States to eliminate the causes of certain substantial obstructions to the free flow of commerce and to mitigate and eliminate these obstructions when they have occurred by encouraging the practice and procedure of collective bargaining and by protecting the exercise by workers of full freedom of association, self-organization, and designation of representatives of their own choosing, for the purpose of negotiating the terms and conditions of their employment or other mutual aid or protection.

DEFINITIONS

Sec. 2. When used in this Act—

(1) The term "person" includes one or more individuals, labor organizations, partnerships, associations, corporations, legal representatives, trustees, trustees in cases under Title II of the United States Code or receivers.*

(2) The term "employer" includes any person acting as an agent of an employer, directly or indirectly, but shall not include the United States or any wholly owned Government corporation, or any Federal Reserve Bank, or any State or political

---

*Amended by Public Law 95-598, effective Oct. 1, 1979.

subdivision thereof, or any person subject to the Railway Labor Act, as amended from time to time, or any labor organization (other than when acting as an employer), or anyone acting in the capacity of officer or agent of such labor organization.

(3) The term "employee" shall include any employee, and shall not be limited to the employees of a particular employer, unless the Act explicitly states otherwise, and shall include any individual whose work has ceased as a consequence of, or in connection with, any current labor dispute or because of any unfair labor practice, and who has not obtained any other regular and substantially equivalent employment, but shall not include any individual employed as an agricultural laborer, or in the domestic service of any family or person at his home, or any individual employed by his parent or spouse, or any individual having the status of an independent contractor, or any individual employed as a supervisor, or any individual employed by an employer subject to the Railway Labor Act, as amended from time to time, or by any other person who is not an employer as herein defined.

(4) The term "representatives" includes any individual or labor organization.

(5) The term "labor organization" means any organization of any kind, or any agency or employee representation committee or plan, in which employees participate and which exists for the purpose, in whole or in part, of dealing with employers concerning grievances, labor disputes, wages, rates of pay, hours of employment, or conditions of work.

(6) The term "commerce" means trade, traffic, commerce, transportation, or communication among the several States, or between the District of Columbia or any Territory of the United States and any State or other Territory, or between any foreign country and any State, Territory, or the District of Columbia, or within the District of Columbia or any Territory, or between points in the same State but through any other State or any Territory or the District of Columbia or any foreign country.

(7) The term "affecting commerce" means in commerce, or burdening or obstructing commerce or the free flow of commerce, or having led or tending to lead to a labor dispute burdening or obstructing commerce or the free flow of commerce.

(8) The term "unfair labor practice" means any unfair labor practice listed in section 8.

(9) The term "labor dispute" includes any controversy concerning terms, tenure or conditions of employment, or concerning the association or representation of persons in negotiating, fixing, maintaining, changing, or seeking to arrange terms or conditions of employment, regardless of whether the disputants stand in the proximate relation of employer and employee.

(10) The term "National Labor Relations Board" means the National Labor Relations Board provided for in section 3 of this Act.

(11) The term "supervisor" means any individual having authority, in the interest of the employer, to hire, transfer, suspend, lay off, recall, promote, discharge, assign, reward, or discipline other employees, or responsibly to direct them, or to adjust their grievances, or effectively to recommend such action, if in connection with the foregoing the exercise of such authority is not of a merely routine or clerical nature, but requires the use of independent judgment.

(12) The term "professional employee" means—

(a) any employee engaged in work (i) predominantly intellectual and varied in character as opposed to routine mental, manual, mechanical, or physical work; (ii) involving the consistent exercise of discretion and judgment in its performance; (iii) of such a character that the output produced or the result accomplished cannot be standardized in relation to a given period of time; (iv) requiring knowledge of an advanced type in a field of science or learning customarily acquired by a prolonged course of specialized intellectual instruction and study in an institution of higher learning or a hospital, as distinguished from a general academic education or from an apprenticeship or from training in the performance of routine mental, manual, or physical processes; or

(b) any employee, who (i) has completed the courses of specialized intellectual instruction and study described in clause (iv) of paragraph (a), and (ii) is performing related work under the supervision of a professional person to qualify himself to become a professional employee as defined in paragraph (a).

(13) In determining whether any person is acting as an "agent" of another person so as to make such other person responsible for his acts, the question of whether the specific acts performed were actually authorized or subsequently ratified shall not be controlling.

(14) The term "health care institution" shall include any hospital, convalescent hospital, health maintenance organization, health clinic, nursing home, extended care facility, or other institution devoted to the care of sick, infirm, or aged person.

NATIONAL LABOR RELATIONS BOARD

Sec. 3. (a) The National Labor Relations Board (hereinafter called the "Board") created by this Act prior to its amendment by the Labor Management Relations Act, 1947, is hereby continued as an agency of the United States, except that the Board shall consist of five instead of three members, appointed by the President by and with the advice and consent of the Senate. Of the two additional members so provided for, one shall be appointed for a term of five years and the other for a term of two years. Their successors, and the successors of the other members, shall be appointed for terms of five years each, excepting that any individual chosen to fill a vacancy shall be appointed only for the unexpired term of the member whom he shall succeed. The President shall designate one member to serve as Chairman of the Board. Any member of the Board may be removed by the President, upon notice and hearing, for neglect of duty or malfeasance in office, but for no other cause.

(b) The Board is authorized to delegate to any group of three or more members any or all the powers which it may itself exercise. The Board is also authorized to delegate to its regional directors its powers under section 9 to determine the unit appropriate for the purpose of collective bargaining, to investigate and provide for hearings, and determine whether a question of representation exists, and to direct an election or take a secret ballot under subsection (c) or (e) of section 9 and certify the results thereof, except that upon the filing of a request therefor with the Board by any interested person, the Board may review any action of a regional director delegated to him under this paragraph, but such a review shall not, unless specifically ordered by the Board, operate as a stay of any action taken by the regional director. A vacancy in the Board shall not impair the right of the remaining members to exercise all of the powers of the Board, and three members of the Board shall, at all times, constitute a quorum of the Board, except that two members shall constitute a quorum of any group designated pursuant to the first sentence hereof. The Board shall have an official seal which shall be judicially noted.

(c) The Board shall at the close of each fiscal year make a report in writing to Congress and to the President stating in detail the cases it has heard, the decisions it has rendered, and an account of all moneys it has disbursed.

(d) There shall be a General Counsel of the Board who shall be appointed by the President, by and with the advice and consent of the Senate, for a term of four years. The General Counsel of the Board shall exercise general supervision over all attorneys employed by the Board (other than trial examiners and legal assistants to Board members) and over the officers and employees in the regional offices. He shall have final authority, on behalf of the Board, in respect of the investigation of charges and issuance of complaints under section 10, and in respect of the prosecution of such complaints before the Board, and shall have such other duties as the Board may prescribe or as may be provided by law. In case of a vacancy in the office of the General Counsel the President is authorized to designate the officer or employee who shall act as General Counsel during such vacancy, but no person or persons so designated shall so act (1) for more than forty days when the Congress is in session unless a nomination to fill such vacancy shall have been submitted to the Senate, or (2) after the adjournment *sine die* of the session of the Senate in which such nomination was submitted.

Sec. 4. (a) Each member of the Board and the General Counsel of the Board shall receive a salary of $12,000* a year, shall be eligible for reappointment, and shall not engage in any other business, vocation, or employment. The Board shall appoint an executive secretary, and such attorneys, examiners, and regional directors, and such other employees as it may from time to time find necessary for the proper performance of its duties. The Board may not employ any attorneys for the purpose of reviewing transcripts of hearings or preparing drafts of opinions except that any attorney employed for assignment as a legal assistant to any Board member may for such Board member review such transcripts and prepare such drafts. No trial examiner's report shall be reviewed, either before or after its publication, by any person other than a member of the Board or his legal assistant,

---

*Pursuant to Public Law 96-369, approved Oct. 1, 1980, the salary of the Chairman of the Board shall be $55,387 per year and the salaries of the General Counsel and each Board member shall be $52,750 per year.

and no trial examiner shall advise or consult with the Board with respect to exceptions taken to his findings, rulings, or recommendations. The Board may establish or utilize such regional, local, or other agencies, and utilize such voluntary and uncompensated services, as may from time to time be needed. Attorneys appointed under this section may, at the direction of the Board, appear for and represent the Board in any case in court. Nothing in this Act shall be construed to authorize the Board to appoint individuals for the purpose of conciliation or mediation, or for economic analysis.

(b) All of the expenses of the Board, including all necessary traveling and subsistence expenses outside the District of Columbia incurred by the members or employees of the Board under its orders, shall be allowed and paid on the presentation of itemized vouchers therefor approved by the Board or by any individual it designates for that purpose.

Sec. 5. The principal office of the Board shall be in the District of Columbia, but it may meet and exercise any or all of its powers at any other place. The Board may, by one or more of its members or by such agents or agencies as it may designate, prosecute any inquiry necessary to its functions in any part of the United States. A member who participates in such an inquiry shall not be disqualified from subsequently participating in a decision of the Board in the same case.

Sec. 6. The Board shall have authority from time to time to make, amend, and rescind, in the manner prescribed by the Administrative Procedure Act, such rules and regulations as may be necessary to carry out the provisions of this Act.

Rights of Employees

Sec. 7. Employees shall have the right to self-organization, to form, join, or assist labor organizations, to bargain collectively through representatives of their own choosing, and to engage in other concerted activities for the purpose of collective bargaining or other mutual aid or protection, and shall also have the right to refrain from any or all such activities except to the extent that such right may be affected by an agreement requiring membership in a labor organization as a condition of employment as authorized in section 8(a)(3).

Unfair Labor Practices

Sec. 8. (a) It shall be an unfair labor practice for an employer—

(1) to interfere with, restrain, or coerce employees in the exercise of the rights guaranteed in section 7;

(2) to dominate or interfere with the formation or administration of any labor organization or contribute financial or other support to it: *Provided*, That subject to rules and regulations made and published by the Board pursuant to section 6, an employer shall not be prohibited from permitting employees to confer with him during working hours without loss of time or pay;

(3) by discrimination in regard to hire or tenure of employment or any term or condition of employment to encourage or discourage membership in any labor organization: *Provided*, That nothing in this Act, or in any other statute of the United States, shall preclude an employer from making an agreement with a labor organization (not established, maintained, or assisted by any action defined in section 8(a) of this Act as an unfair labor practice) to require as a condition of employment membership therein on or after the thirtieth day following the beginning of such employment or the effective date of such agreement, whichever is the later, (i) if such labor organization is the representative of the employees as provided in section 9(a), in the appropriate collective-bargaining unit covered by such agreement when made, and (ii) unless following an election held as provided in section 9(e) within one year preceding the effective date of such agreement, the Board shall have certified that at least a majority of the employees eligible to vote in such election have voted to rescind the authority of such labor organization to make such an agreement: *Provided further*, That no employer shall justify any discrimination against an employee for non-membership in a labor organization (A) if he has reasonable grounds for believing that such membership was not available to the employee on the same terms and conditions generally applicable to other members, or (B) if he has reasonable grounds for believing that membership was denied or terminated for reasons other than the failure of the employee to tender the periodic dues and the initiation fees uniformly required as a condition of acquiring or retaining membership;

(4) to discharge or otherwise discriminate against an employee because he has filed charges or given testimony under this Act;

(5) to refuse to bargain collectively with the representatives of his employees, subject to the provisions of section 9(a).

(b) It shall be an unfair labor practice for a labor organization or its agents—

(1) to restrain or coerce (A) employees in the exercise of the rights guaranteed in section 7: *Provided,* That this paragraph shall not impair the right of a labor organization to prescribe its own rules with respect to the acquisition or retention of membership therein; or (B) an employer in the selection of his representatives for the purpose of collective bargaining or the adjustment of grievances;

(2) to cause or attempt to cause an employer to discriminate against an employee in violation of subsection (a)(3) or to discriminate against an employee with respect to whom membership in such organization has been denied or terminated on some ground other than his failure to tender the periodic dues and the initiation fees uniformly required as a condition of acquiring or retaining membership;

(3) to refuse to bargain collectively with an employer, provided it is the representative of his employees subject to the provisions of section 9(a);

(4) (i) to engage in, or to induce or encourage any individual employed by any person engaged in commerce or in an industry affecting commerce to engage in, a strike or a refusal in the course of his employment to use, manufacture, process, transport, or otherwise handle or work on any goods, articles, materials, or commodities or to perform any services; or (ii) to threaten, coerce, or restrain any person engaged in commerce or in an industry affecting commerce, where in either case an object thereof is:

(A) forcing or requiring any employer or self-employed person to join any labor or employer organization or to enter into any agreement which is prohibited by section 8(e);

(B) forcing or requiring any person to cease using, selling, handling, transporting, or otherwise dealing in the products of any other producer, processor, or manufacturer, or to cease doing business with any other person, or forcing or requiring any other employer to recognize or bargain with a labor organization as the representative of his employees unless such labor organization has been certified as the representative of such employees under the provisions of section 9: *Provided,* That nothing contained in this clause (B) shall be construed to make unlawful, where not otherwise unlawful, any primary strike or primary picketing;

(C) forcing or requiring any employer to recognize or bargain with a particular labor organization as the representative of his employees if another labor organization has been certified as the representative of such employees under the provisions of section 9;

(D) forcing or requiring any employer to assign particular work to employees in a particular labor organization or in a particular trade, craft, or class rather than to employees in another labor organization or in another trade, craft, or class, unless such employer is failing to conform to an order or certification of the Board determining the bargaining representative for employees performing such work:

Provided, That nothing contained in this subsection (b) shall be construed to make unlawful a refusal by any person to enter upon the premises of any employer (other than his own employer), if the employees of such employer are engaged in a strike ratified or approved by a representative of such employees whom such employer is required to recognize under this Act: *Provided further,* That for the purposes of this paragraph (4) only, nothing contained in such paragraph shall be construed to prohibit publicity, other than picketing, for the purpose of truthfully advising the public, including consumers and members of a labor organization, that a product or products are produced by an employer with whom the labor organization has a primary dispute and are distributed by another employer, as long as such publicity does not have an effect of inducing any individual employed by any person other than the primary employer in the course of his employment to refuse to pick up, deliver, or transport any goods, or not to perform any services, at the establishment of the employer engaged in such distribution;

(5) to require of employees covered by an agreement authorized under subsection (a)(3) the payment, as a condition precedent to becoming a member of such organization, of a fee in an amount which the Board finds excessive or discriminatory under all the circumstances. In making such a finding, the Board shall consider, among other relevant factors, the practices and customs of labor organizations in the particular industry, and the wages currently paid to the employees affected;

(6) to cause or attempt to cause an employer to pay or deliver or agree to pay or deliver any money or other thing of value, in

the nature of an exaction for services which are not performed or not to be performed; and

(7) to picket or cause to be picketed, or threaten to picket or cause to be picketed, any employer where an object thereof is forcing or requiring an employer to recognize or bargain with a labor organization as the representative of his employees, or forcing or requiring the employees of an employer to accept or select such labor organization as their collective bargaining representative, unless such labor organization is currently certified as the representative of such employees:

(A) where the employer has lawfully recognized in accordance with this Act any other labor organization and a question concerning representation may not appropriately be raised under section 9(c) of this Act,

(B) where within the preceding twelve months a valid election under section 9(c) of this Act has been conducted, or

(C) where such picketing has been conducted without a petition under section 9(c) being filed within a reasonable period of time not to exceed thirty days from the commencement of such picketing: *Provided,* That when such a petition has been filed the Board shall forthwith, without regard to the provisions of section 9(c)(1) or the absence of a showing of a substantial interest on the part of the labor organization, direct an election in such unit as the Board finds to be appropriate and shall certify the results thereof: *Provided further,* That nothing in this subparagraph (C) shall be construed to prohibit any picketing or other publicity for the purpose of truthfully advising the public (including consumers) that an employer does not employ members of, or have a contract with, a labor organization, unless an effect of such picketing is to induce any individual employed by any other person in the course of his employment, not to pick up, deliver or transport any goods or not to perform any services.

Nothing in this paragraph (7) shall be construed to permit any act which would otherwise be an unfair labor practice under this section 8(b).

(c) The expressing of any views, argument, or opinion, or the dissemination thereof, whether in written, printed, graphic, or visual form, shall not constitute or be evidence of an unfair labor practice under any of the provisions of this Act, if such expression contains no threat of reprisal or force or promise of benefit.

(d) For the purposes of this section, to bargain collectively is the performance of the mutual obligation of the employer and the representative of the employees to meet at reasonable times and confer in good faith with respect to wages, hours, and other terms and conditions of employment, or the negotiation of an agreement or any question arising thereunder, and the execution of a written contract incorporating any agreement reached if requested by either party, but such obligation does not compel either party to agree to a proposal or require the making of a concession: *Provided,* That where there is in effect a collective-bargaining contract covering employees in an industry affecting commerce, the duty to bargain collectively shall also mean that no party to such contract shall terminate or modify such contract, unless the party desiring such termination or modification—

(1) serves a written notice upon the party to the contract of the proposed termination or modification sixty days prior to the expiration date thereof, or in the event such contract contains no expiration date, sixty days prior to the time it is proposed to make such termination or modification;

(2) offers to meet and confer with the other party for the purpose of negotiating a new contract or a contract containing the proposed modifications;

(3) notifies the Federal Mediation and Conciliation Service within thirty days after such notice of the existence of a dispute, and simultaneously therewith notifies any State or Territorial agency established to mediate and conciliate disputes within the State or Territory where the dispute occurred, provided no agreement has been reached by that time; and

(4) continues in full force and effect, without resorting to strike or lockout, all the terms and conditions of the existing contract for a period of sixty days after such notice is given or until the expiration date of such contract, whichever occurs later.

The duties imposed upon employers, employees, and labor organizations by paragraphs (2), (3), and (4) shall become inapplicable upon an intervening certification of the Board, under which the labor organization or individual, which is a party to the contract, has been superseded as or ceased to be the representative of the employees subject to the provisions of section 9(a), and the duties so imposed shall not be construed as requiring either party to discuss or agree to any modification of the terms and conditions contained in a contract for a fixed period, if such modification is to become effective before such terms and conditions can be reopened under the provisions of the contract. Any employee who engages in a strike within any notice period specified in this subsection, or who engages in any strike with the appropriate period specified in subsection (g) of this section, shall lose his status as an employee of the employer engaged in the particular labor dispute, for the purposes of sections 8, 9, and 10 of this Act, as amended, but such loss of status for such employee shall terminate if and when he is reemployed by such employer. Whenever the collective bargaining involves employees of a health care institution, the provisions of this section 8(d) shall be modified as follows:

(A) The notice of section 8(d)(1) shall be ninety days; the notice of section 8(d)(3) shall be sixty days; and the contract period of section 8(d)(4) shall be ninety days.

(B) Where the bargaining is for an initial agreement following certification or recognition, at least thirty days' notice of the existence of a dispute shall be given by the labor organization to the agencies set forth in section 8(d)(3).

(C) After notice is given to the Federal Mediation and Conciliation Service under either clause (A) or (B) of this sentence, the Service shall promptly communicate with the parties and use its best efforts, by mediation and conciliation, to bring them to agreement. The parties shall participate fully and promptly in such meetings as may be undertaken by the Service for the purpose of aiding in a settlement of the dispute.

(e) It shall be an unfair labor practice for any labor organization and any employer to enter into any contract or agreement, express or implied, whereby such employer ceases or refrains or agrees to cease or refrain from handling, using, selling, transporting or otherwise dealing in any of the products of any other employer, or to cease doing business with any other person, and any contract or agreement entered into heretofore or hereafter containing such an agreement shall be to such extent unenforceable and void: *Provided,* That nothing in this subsection (e) shall apply to an agreement between a labor organization and an employer in the construction industry relating to the contracting or subcontracting of work to be done at the site of the construction, alteration, painting, or repair of a building, structure, or other work: *Provided further,* That for the purposes of this subsection (e) and section 8(b)(4)(B) the terms "any employer," "any person engaged in commerce or in industry affecting commerce," and "any person" when used in relation to the terms "any other producer, processor, or manufacturer," "any other employer," or "any other person" shall not include persons in the relation of a jobber, manufacturer, contractor, or subcontractor working on the goods or premises of the jobber or manufacturer or performing parts of an integrated process of production in the apparel and clothing industry: *Provided further,* That nothing in this Act shall prohibit the enforcement of any agreement which is within the foregoing exception.

(f) It shall not be an unfair labor practice under subsections (a) and (b) of this section for an employer engaged primarily in the building and construction industry to make an agreement covering employees engaged (or who, upon their employment, will be engaged) in the building and construction industry with a labor organization of which building and construction employees are members (not established, maintained, or assisted by any action defined in section 8(a) of this Act as an unfair labor practice) because (1) the majority status of such labor organization has not been established under the provisions of section 9 of this Act prior to the making of such agreement, or (2) such agreement requires as a condition of employment, membership in such labor organization after the seventh day following the beginning of such employment or the effective date of the agreement, whichever is later, or (3) such agreement requires the employer to notify such labor organization of opportunities for employment with such employer, or gives such labor organization an opportunity to refer qualified applicants for such employment, or (4) such agreement specifies minimum training or experience qualifications for employment or provides for priority in opportunities for employment based upon length of service with such employer, in the industry or in the particular geographical area: *Provided,* That nothing in this subsection shall set aside the final proviso to section 8(a)(3) of this Act: *Provided further,* That any agreement which would be invalid, but for clause (1) of this subsection, shall not be a bar to a petition filed pursuant to section 9(c) or 9(e).*

---

*Sec. 8(f) is inserted in the Act by subsec. (a) of Sec. 705 of Public Law 86-257 (1959). Sec. 705(b) provides:

Nothing contained in the amendment made by subsection (a) shall be construed as authorizing the execution or application of agreements requiring membership in a labor organization as a condition of employment in any State or Territory in which such execution or application is prohibited by State or Territorial law.

(g) A labor organization before engaging in any strike, picketing, or other concerted refusal to work at any health care institution shall, not less than ten days prior to such action, notify the institution in writing and the Federal Mediation and Conciliation Service of that intention, except that in the case of bargaining for an initial agreement following certification or recognition the notice required by this subsection shall not be given the expiration of the period specified in clause (B) of the last sentence of section 8(d) of this Act. The notice shall state the date and time that such action will commerce. The notice, once given, may be extended by the written agreement of both parties.

REPRESENTATIVES AND ELECTIONS

Sec. 9. (a) Representatives designated or selected for the purposes of collective bargaining by the majority of the employees in a unit appropriate for such purposes, shall be the exclusive representatives of all the employees in such unit for the purposes of collective bargaining in respect to rates of pay, wages, hours of employment, or other conditions of employment: *Provided,* That any individual employee or a group of employees shall have the right at any time to present grievances to their employer and to have such grievances adjusted, without the intervention of the bargaining representative, as long as the adjustment is not inconsistent with the terms of a collective-bargaining contract or agreement then in effect: *Provided further,* That the bargaining representative has been given opportunity to be present at such adjustment.

(b) The Board shall decide in each case whether, in order to assure to employees the fullest freedom in exercising the rights guaranteed by this Act, the unit appropriate for the purposes of collective bargaining shall be the employer unit, craft unit, plant unit, or subdivision thereof: *Provided,* That the Board shall not (1) decide that any unit is appropriate for such purposes if such unit includes both professional employees and employees who are not professional employees unless a majority of such professional employees vote for inclusion in such unit; or (2) decide that any craft unit is inappropriate for such purposes on the ground that a different unit has been established by a prior Board determination, unless a majority of the employees in the proposed craft unit votes against separate representation or; (3)

decide that any unit is appropriate for such purposes if it includes, together with other employees, any individual employed as a guard to enforce against employees and other persons rules to protect property of the employer or to protect the safety of persons on the employer's premises; but no labor organization shall be certified as the representative of employees in a bargaining unit of guards if such organization admits to membership, or is affiliated directly or indirectly with an organization which admits to membership, employees other than guards.

(c)(1) Wherever a petition shall have been filed, in accordance with such regulations as may be prescribed by the Board—

(A) by an employee or group of employees or any individual or labor organization acting in their behalf alleging that a substantial number of employees (i) wish to be represented for collective bargaining and that their employer declines to recognize their representative as the representative defined in section 9(a), or (ii) assert that the individual or labor organization, which has been certified or is being recognized by their employer as the bargaining representative, is no longer a representative as defined in section 9(a); or

(B) by an employer, alleging that one or more individuals or labor organizations have presented to him a claim to be recognized as the representative defined in section 9(a):
the Board shall investigate such petition and if it has reasonable cause to believe that a question of representation affecting commerce exists shall provide for an appropriate hearing upon due notice. Such hearing may be conducted by an officer or employee of the regional office, who shall not make any recommendations with respect thereto. If the Board finds upon the record of such hearing that such a question of representation exists, it shall direct an election by secret ballot and shall certify the results thereof.

(2) In determining whether or not a question of representation affecting commerce exists, the same regulations and rules of decision shall apply irrespective of the identity of the person filing the petition or the kind of relief sought and in no case shall the Board deny a labor organization a place on the ballot by reason of an order with respect to such labor organization or its predecessor not issued in conformity with section 10(c).

(3) No election shall be directed in any bargaining unit or any subdivision within which, in the preceding twelve-month period, a valid election shall have been held. Employees engaged in an

economic strike who are not entitled to reinstatement shall be eligible to vote under such regulations as the Board shall find are consistent with the purposes and provisions of this Act in any election conducted within twelve months after the commencement of the strike. In any election where none of the choices on the ballot receives a majority, a run-off shall be conducted, the ballot providing for a selection between the two choices receiving the largest and second largest number of valid votes cast in the election.

(4) Nothing in this section shall be construed to prohibit the waiving of hearings by stipulation for the purpose of a consent election in conformity with regulations and rules of decision of the Board.

(5) In determining whether a unit is appropriate for the purposes specified in subsection (b) the extent to which the employees have organized shall not be controlling.

(d) Whenever an order of the Board made pursuant to section 10(c) is based in whole or in part upon facts certified following an investigation pursuant to subsection (c) of this section and there is a petition for the enforcement or review of such order, such certification and the record of such investigation shall be included in the transcript of the entire record required to be filed under section 10(e) or 10(f), and thereupon the decree of the court enforcing, modifying, or setting aside in whole or in part the order of the Board shall be made and entered upon the pleadings, testimony, and proceedings set forth in such transcript.

(e)(1) Upon the filing with the Board, by 30 per centum or more of the employees in a bargaining unit covered by an agreement between their employer and a labor organization made pursuant to section 8(a)(3), of a petition alleging they desire that such authority be rescinded, the Board shall take a secret ballot of the employees in such unit and certify the results thereof to such labor organization and to the employer.

(2) No election shall be conducted pursuant to this subsection in any bargaining unit or any subdivision within which, in the preceding twelve-month period, a valid election shall have been held.

PREVENTION OF UNFAIR LABOR PRACTICES

Sec. 10. (a) The Board is empowered, as hereinafter provided, to prevent any person from engaging in any unfair labor practice (listed in section 8) affecting commerce. This power shall not be affected by any other means of adjustment or prevention that has been or may be established by agreement, law, or otherwise: *Provided,* That the Board is empowered by agreement with any agency of any State or Territory to cede to such agency jurisdiction over any cases in any industry (other than mining, manufacturing, communications, and transportation except where predominantly local in character) even though such cases may involve labor disputes affecting commerce, unless the provision of the State or Territorial statute applicable to the determination of such cases by such agency is inconsistent with the corresponding provision of this Act or has received a construction inconsistent therewith.

(b) Whenever it is charged that any person has engaged in or is engaging in any such unfair labor practice, the Board, or any agent or agency designated by the Board for such purposes, shall have power to issue and cause to be served upon such person a complaint stating the charges in that respect, and containing a notice of hearing before the Board or a member thereof, or before a designated agent or agency, at a place therein fixed, not less than five days after the serving of said complaint: *Provided,* That no complaint shall issue based upon any unfair labor practice occurring more than six months prior to the filing of the charge with the Board and the service of a copy thereof upon the person against whom such charge is made, unless the person aggrieved thereby was prevented from filing such charge by reason of service in the armed forces, in which event the six-month period shall be computed from the day of his discharge. Any such complaint may be amended by the member, agent, or agency conducting the hearing or the Board in its discretion at any time prior to the issuance of an order based thereon. The person so complained of shall have the right to file an answer to the original or amended complaint and to appear in person or otherwise and give testimony at the place and time fixed in the complaint. In the discretion of the member, agent, or agency conducting the hearing or the Board, any other person may be allowed to intervene in the said proceeding and to present testimony. Any such proceeding shall, so far as practicable, be conducted in accordance with the rules of evidence applicable in the district courts of the United States under the rules of civil procedure for the district courts of the

United States, adopted by the Supreme Court of the United States pursuant to the Act of June 19, 1934 (U.S.C., title 28, secs. 723-B, 723-C).

(c) The testimony taken by such member, agent, or agency or the Board shall be reduced to writing and filed with the Board. Thereafter, in its discretion, the Board upon notice may take further testimony or hear argument. If upon the preponderance of the testimony taken the Board shall be of the opinion that any person named in the complaint has engaged in or is engaging in any such unfair labor practice, then the Board shall state its findings of fact and shall issue and cause to be served on such person an order requiring such person to cease and desist from such unfair labor practice, and to take such affirmative action including reinstatement of employees with or without back pay, as will effectuate the policies of this Act: *Provided,* That where an order directs reinstatement of an employee, back pay may be required of the employer or labor organization, as the case may be, responsible for the discrimination suffered by him: *And provided further,* That in determining whether a complaint shall issue alleging a violation of section 8(a)(1) or section 8(a)(2), and in deciding such cases, the same regulations and rules of decision shall apply irrespective of whether or not the labor organization affected is affiliated with a labor organization national or international in scope. Such order may further require such person to make reports from time to time showing the extent to which it has complied with the order. If upon the preponderance of the testimony taken the Board shall not be of the opinion that the person named in the complaint has engaged in or is engaging in any such unfair labor practice, then the Board shall state its findings of fact and shall issue an order dismissing the said complaint. No order of the Board shall require the reinstatement of any individual as an employee who has been suspended or discharged, or the payment to him of any back pay, if such individual was suspended or discharged for cause. In case the evidence is presented before a member of the Board, or before an examiner or examiners thereof, such member, or such examiner or examiners, as the case may be, shall issue and cause to be served on the parties to the proceeding a proposed report, together with a recommended order, which shall be filed with the Board, and if no exceptions are filed within twenty days after service thereof upon such parties, or within such further period as the Board may authorize, such recommended order shall become the order of the Board and become effective as therein prescribed.

(d) Until the record in the case shall have been filed in a court, as hereinafter provided, the Board may at any time, upon reasonable notice and in such manner as it shall deem proper, modify or set aside, in whole or in part, any finding or order made or issued by it.

(e) The Board shall have power to petition any court of appeals of the United States, or if all the courts of appeals to which application may be made are in vacation, any district court of the United States, within any circuit or district, respectively, wherein the unfair labor practice in question occurred or wherein such person resides or transacts business, for the enforcement of such order and for appropriate temporary relief or restraining order, and shall file in the court the record in the proceedings, as provided in section 2112 of title 28, United States Code. Upon the filing of such petition, the court shall cause notice thereof to be served upon such person, and thereupon shall have jurisdiction of the proceeding and of the question determined therein, and shall have power to grant such temporary relief or restraining order as it deems just and proper, and to make and enter a decree enforcing, modifying, and enforcing as so modified, or setting aside in whole or in part the order of the Board. No objection that has not been urged before the Board, its member, agent, or agency, shall be considered by the court, unless the failure or neglect to urge such objection shall be excused because of extraordinary circumstances. The findings of the Board with respect to questions of fact if supported by substantial evidence on the record considered as a whole shall be conclusive. If either party shall apply to the court for leave to adduce additional evidence and shall show to the satisfaction of the court that such additional evidence is material and that there were reasonable grounds for the failure to adduce such evidence in the hearing before the Board, its member, agent, or agency, the court may order such additional evidence to be taken before the Board, its member, agent, or agency, and to be made a part of the record. The Board may modify its findings as to the facts, or make new findings, by reason of additional evidence so taken and filed, and it shall file such modified or new findings, which findings with respect to question of fact if supported by substantial evidence on the record considered as a whole shall be conclusive, and shall file its recommendations, if any, for the modification or setting aside of its original order. Upon the filing of the record with it the jurisdiction of the court shall be exclusive and its judgment and decree shall be final, except that the court shall be subject to review by the appropriate United States court of appeals if application was made to the district court as hereinabove provided, and by the Supreme Court of the United States upon writ of certiorari or certification as provided in section 1254 of title 28.

(f) Any person aggrieved by a final order of the Board granting or denying in whole or in part the relief sought may obtain a review of such order in any circuit court of appeals of the United States in the circuit wherein the unfair labor practice in question was alleged to have been engaged in or wherein such person resides or transacts business, or in the United States Court of Appeals for the District of Columbia, by filing in such court a written petition praying that the order of the Board be modified or set aside. A copy of such petition shall be forthwith transmitted by the clerk of the court to the Board, and thereupon the aggrieved party shall file in the court the record in the proceeding, certified by the Board, as provided in section 2112 of title 28, United States Code. Upon the filing of such petition, the court shall proceed in the same manner as in the case of an application by the Board under subsection (e) of this section, and shall have the same jurisdiction to grant to the Board such temporary relief or restraining order as it deems just and proper, and in like manner to make and enter a decree enforcing, modifying, and enforcing as so modified, or setting aside in whole or in part the order of the Board; the findings of the Board with respect to questions of fact if supported by substantial evidence on the record considered as a whole shall in like manner be conclusive.

(g) The commencement of proceedings under subsection (e) or (f) of this section shall not, unless specifically ordered by the court, operate as a stay of the Board's order.

(h) When granting appropriate temporary relief or a restraining order, or making and entering a decree enforcing, modifying, and enforcing as so modified, or setting aside in whole or in part an order of the Board, as provided in this section, the jurisdiction of courts sitting in equity shall not be limited by the Act entitled "An Act to amend the Judicial Code and to define and limit the jurisdiction of courts sitting in equity, and for other purposes," approved March 23, 1932 (U.S.C., Supp. VII, title 29, secs. 101–115).

(i) Petitions filed under this Act shall be heard expeditiously, and if possible within ten days after they have been docketed.

(j) The Board shall have power, upon issuance of a complaint as provided in subsection (b) charging that any person has engaged in or is engaging in an unfair labor practice, to petition any district court of the United States (including the District Court of the United States for the District of Columbia), within any district wherein the unfair labor practice in question is alleged to have occurred or wherein such person resides or transacts business, for appropriate temporary relief or restraining order. Upon the filing of any such petition the court shall cause notice thereof to be served upon such person, and thereupon shall have jurisdiction to grant to the Board such temporary relief or restraining order as it deems just and proper.

(k) Whenever it is charged that any person has engaged in an unfair labor practice within the meaning of paragraph (4)(D) of section 8(b), the Board is empowered and directed to hear and determine the dispute out of which such unfair labor practice shall have arisen, unless, within ten days after notice that such charge has been filed, the parties to such dispute submit to the Board satisfactory evidence that they have adjusted, or agreed upon methods for the voluntary adjustment of, the dispute. Upon compliance by the parties to the dispute with the decision of the Board or upon such voluntary adjustment of the dispute, such charge shall be dismissed.

(1) Whenever it is charged that any person has engaged in an unfair labor practice within the meaning of paragraph (4) (A), (B), or (C) of section 8(b), or section 8(e) or section 8(b)(7), the preliminary investigation of such charge shall be made forthwith and given priority over all other cases except cases of like character in the office where it is filed or to which it is referred. If, after such investigation, the officer or regional attorney to whom the matter may be referred has reasonable cause to believe such charge is true and that a complaint should issue, he shall, on behalf of the Board, petition any district court of the United States (including the District Court of the United States for the District of Columbia) within any district where the unfair labor practice in question has occurred, is alleged to have occurred, or wherein such person resides or transacts business, for appropriate injunctive relief pending the final adjudication of the

Board with respect to such matter. Upon the filing of any such petition the district court shall have jurisdiction to grant such injunctive relief or temporary restraining order as it deems just and proper, not withstanding any other provision of law: *Provided further,* That no temporary restraining order shall be issued without notice unless a petition alleges that substantial and irreparable injury to the charging party will be unavoidable and such temporary restraining order shall be effective no longer than five days and will become void at the expiration of such period: *Provided further,* That such officer or regional attorney shall not apply for any restraining order under section 8(b)(7) if a charge against the employer under section 8(a)(2) has been filed and after the preliminary investigation, he has reasonable cause to believe that such charge is true and that a complaint should issue. Upon filing of any such petition the courts shall cause notice thereof to be served upon any person involved in the charge and such person, including the charging party, shall be given an opportunity to appear by counsel and present any relevant testimony: *Provided further,* That for the purposes of this subsection district courts shall be deemed to have jurisdiction of a labor organization (1) in the district in which such organization maintains its principal office, or (2) in any district in which its duly authorized officers or agents are engaged in promoting or protecting the interests of employee members. The service of legal process upon such officer or agent shall constitute service upon the labor organization and make such organizations a party to the suit. In situations where such relief is appropriate the procedure specified herein shall apply to charges with respect to section 8(b)(4)(D).

(m) Whenever it is charged that any person has engaged in an unfair labor practice within the meaning of subsection (a)(3) or (b)(2) of section 8, such charge shall be given priority over all other cases except cases of like character in the office where it is filed or to which it is referred and cases given priority under subsection (1).

INVESTIGATORY POWERS

Sec. 11. For the purpose of all hearings and investigations, which, in the opinion of the Board, are necessary and proper for the exercise of the powers vested in it by section 9 and section 10—

(1) The Board, or its duly authorized agents or agencies, shall at all reasonable times have access to, for the purpose of examination, and the right to copy any evidence of any person being investigated or proceeded against that relates to any matter under investigation or in question. The Board, or any member thereof, shall upon application of any party to such proceedings, forthwith issue to such party subpenas requiring the attendance and testimony of witnesses or the production of any evidence in such proceeding or investigation requested in such application. Within five days after the service of a subpena on any person requiring the production of any evidence in his possession or under his control, such person may petition the Board to revoke, and the Board shall revoke, such subpena if in its opinion the evidence whose production is required does not relate to any matter under investigation, or any matter in question in such proceedings, or if in its opinion such subpena does not describe with sufficient particularity the evidence whose production is required. Any member of the Board, or any agent or agency designated by the Board for such purposes, may administer oaths and affirmations, examine witnesses, and receive evidence. Such attendance of witnesses and the production of such evidence may be required from any place in the United States or any Territory or possession thereof, at any designated place of hearing.

(2) In case of contumacy or refusal to obey a subpena issued to any person, any district court of the United States or the United States courts of any Territory or possession, or the District Court of the United States for the District of Columbia, within the jurisdiction of which the inquiry is carried on or within the jurisdiction of which said person guilty of contumacy or refusal to obey is found or resides or transacts business, upon application by the Board shall have jurisdiction to issue to such person an order requiring such person to appear before the Board, its member, agent, or agency, there to produce evidence if so ordered, or there to give testimony touching the matter under investigation or in question; and any failure to obey such order of the court may be punished by said court as a contempt thereof.

(3)*

(4) Complaints, orders, and other process and papers of the Board, its member, agent, or agency, may be served either personally or by registered or certified mail or by telegraph or by leaving a copy thereof at the principal office or place of business of the person required to be served. The verified return by the individual so serving the same setting forth the manner of such service shall be proof of the same, and the return post office receipt or telegraph receipt therefor when registered or certified and mailed or telegraphed as aforesaid shall be proof of service of the same. Witnesses summoned before the Board, its member, agent, or agency, shall be paid the same fees and mileage that are paid witnesses in the courts of the United States, and witnesses whose depositions are taken and the persons taking the same shall severally be entitled to the same fees as are paid for like services in the courts of the United States.

(5) All process of any court to which application may be made under this Act may be served in the judicial district where the defendant or other person required to be served resides or may be found.

(6) The several departments and agencies of the Government, when directed by the President, shall furnish the Board, upon its request, all records, papers, and information in their possession relating to any matter before the Board.

Sec. 12. Any person who shall willfully resist, prevent, impede, or interfere with any member of the Board or any of its agents or agencies in the performance of duties pursuant to this Act shall be punished by a fine of not more than $5,000 or by imprisonment for not more than one year, or both.

LIMITATIONS

Sec. 13. Nothing in this Act, except as specifically provided for herein, shall be construed so as either to interfere with or impede or diminish in any way the right to strike, or to affect the limitations or qualifications on that right.

Sec. 14. (a) Nothing herein shall prohibit any individual employed as a supervisor from becoming or remaining a member of a labor organization, but no employer subject to this Act

---

*Sec. 11(3) is repealed by Sec. 234, Public Law 91-452, 91st Cong., S. 30, 84 Stat. 926, Oct. 15, 1970. See Title 18, U.S.C. § 6001, *et seq.*

shall be compelled to deem individuals defined herein as supervisors as employees for the purpose of any law, either national or local, relating to collective bargaining.

(b) Nothing in this Act shall be construed as authorizing the execution or application of agreements requiring membership in a labor organization as a condition of employment in any State or Territory in which such execution or application is prohibited by State or Territorial law.

(c)(1) The Board, in its discretion, may, by rule of decision or by published rules adopted pursuant to the Administrative Procedure Act, decline to assert jurisdiction over any labor dispute involving any class or category of employers, where, in the opinion of the Board, the effect of such labor dispute on commerce is not sufficiently substantial to warrant the exercise of its jurisdiction: *Provided,* That the Board shall not decline to assert jurisdiction over any labor dispute over which it would assert jurisdiction under the standards prevailing upon August 1, 1959.

(2) Nothing in this Act shall be deemed to prevent or bar any agency or the courts of any State or Territory (including the Commonwealth of Puerto Rico, Guam, and the Virgin Islands), from assuming and asserting jurisdiction over labor disputes over which the Board declines, pursuant to paragraph (1) of this subsection, to assert jurisdiction.

Sec. 15. Wherever the application of the provisions of section 272 of chapter 10 of the Act entitled "An Act to establish a uniform system of bankruptcy throughout the United States," approved July 1, 1898, and Acts amendatory thereof and supplementary thereto (U.S.C., title 11, sec. 672), conflicts with the application of the provisions of this Act, this Act shall prevail: *Provided,* That in any situation where the provisions of this Act cannot be validly enforced, the provisions of such other Acts shall remain in full force and effect.

Sec. 16. If any provision of this Act, or the application of such provision to any person or circumstances, shall be held invalid, the remainder of this Act, or the application of such provision to persons or circumstances other than those as to which it is held invalid, shall not be affected thereby.

Sec. 17. This Act may be cited as the "National Labor Relations Act."

Sec. 18. No petition entertained, no investigation made, no election held, and no certification issued by the National Labor

Relations Board, under any of the provisions of section 9 of the National Labor Relations Act, as amended, shall be invalid by reason of the failure of the Congress of Industrial Organizations to have complied with the requirements of section 9(f), (g), or (h) of the aforesaid Act prior to December 22, 1949, or by reason of the failure of the American Federation of Labor to have complied with the provisions of section 9(f), (g), or (h) of the aforesaid Act prior to November 7, 1947: *Provided,* That no liability shall be imposed under any provision of this Act upon any person for failure to honor any election or certificate referred to above, prior to the effective date of this amendment: *Provided, however,* That this proviso shall not have the effect of setting aside or in any way affecting judgments or decrees heretofore entered under section 10(e) or (f) and which have become final.

INDIVIDUALS WITH RELIGIOUS CONVICTIONS

Sec. 19. Any employee who is a member of and adheres to established and traditional tenets or teachings of a bona fide religion, body, or sect which has historically held conscientious objections to joining or financially supporting labor organizations shall not be required to join or financially support any labor organization as a condition of employment; except that such employee may be required in a contract between such employees' employer and a labor organization in lieu of periodic dues and initiation fees, to pay sums equal to such dues and initiation fees to a nonreligious nonlabor organization charitable fund exempt from taxation under section 501(c)(3) of title 26 of the Internal Revenue Code, chosen by such employee from a list of at least three such funds, designated in such contract or if the contract fails to designate such funds, then to any such fund chosen by the employee. If such employee who holds conscientious objections pursuant to this section requests the labor organization to use the grievance-arbitration procedure on the employee's behalf, the labor organization is authorized to charge the employee for the reasonable cost of using such procedure.

Text of the Labor-Management Relations Act

TEXT OF LABOR MANAGEMENT RELATIONS ACT

61 Stat. 136–52 (1947), as amended by 73 Stat. 519ff (1959), 83 Stat. 133 (1969), 87 Stat. 314 (1973), 88 Stat. 396–97 (1974); 29 U.S.C. §§141–97 (Supp. 1981)

AN ACT

To amend the National Labor Relations Act, to provide additional facilities for the mediation of labor disputes affecting commerce, to equalize legal responsibilities of labor organizations and employers, and for other purposes.

Be it enacted by the Senate and House of Representatives of the United States of America in Congress assembled,

SHORT TITLE AND DECLARATION OF POLICY

Section 1. (a) This Act may be cited as the "Labor Management Relations Act, 1947."

(b) Industrial strife which interferes with the normal flow of commerce and with the full production of articles and commodities for commerce, can be avoided or substantially minimized if employers, employees, and labor organizations each recognize under law one another's legitimate rights in their relations with each other, and above all recognize under law that neither party has any right in its relations with any other to engage in acts or practices which jeopardize the public health, safety, or interest.

It is the purpose and policy of this Act, in order to promote the full flow of commerce, to prescribe the legitimate rights of both employees and employers in their relations affecting commerce, to provide orderly and peaceful procedures for preventing the interference by either with the legitimate rights of the other, to protect the rights of individual employees in their relations with labor organizations whose activities affect commerce, to define and proscribe practices on the part of labor and management which affect commerce and are inimical to the general welfare, and to protect the rights of the public in connection with labor disputes affecting commerce.

TITLE I

AMENDMENTS OF NATIONAL LABOR RELATIONS ACT

Sec. 101. The National Labor Relations Act is hereby amended to read as follows:

(The text of the National Labor Relations Act as amended appears in Appendix A, *supra.*)

EFFECTIVE DATE OF CERTAIN CHANGES

Sec. 102. [Omitted.]
Sec. 103. [Omitted.]
Sec. 104. [Omitted.]

TITLE II

CONCILIATION OF LABOR DISPUTES IN INDUSTRIES AFFECTING COMMERCE; NATIONAL EMERGENCIES

Sec. 201. That it is the policy of the United States that—

(a) sound and stable industrial peace and the advancement of the general welfare, health, and safety of the Nation and of the best interest of employers and employees can most satisfactorily be secured by the settlement of issues between employers and employees through the processes of conference and collective bargaining between employers and the representatives of their employees;

(b) the settlement of issues between employers and employees through collective bargaining may be advanced by making available full and adequate governmental facilities for conciliation, mediation, and voluntary arbitration to aid and encourage employers and the representatives of their employees to reach and maintain agreements concerning rates of pay, hours, and working conditions, and to make all reasonable efforts to settle their differences by mutual agreement reached through conferences and collective bargaining or by such methods as may be provided for in any applicable agreement for the settlement of disputes; and

(c) certain controversies which arise between parties to collective-bargaining agreements may be avoided or minimized by making available full and adequate governmental facilities for furnishing assistance to employers and the representatives of their employees in formulating for inclusion within such agreements provision for adequate notice of any proposed changes in the terms of such agreements, for the final adjustment of grievances or questions regarding the application or interpretation of such agreements, and other provisions designed to prevent the subsequent arising of such controversies.

Sec. 202. (a) There is hereby created an independent agency to be known as the Federal Mediation and Conciliation Service (herein referred to as the "Service," except that for sixty days after the date of the enactment of this Act such term shall refer to the Conciliation Service of the Department of Labor). The Service shall be under the direction of a Federal Mediation and Conciliation Director (hereinafter referred to as the "Director"), who shall be appointed by the President by and with the advice and consent of the Senate. The Director shall receive compensation at the rate of $12,000* per annum. The Director shall not engage in any other business, vocation, or employment.

(b) The Director is authorized, subject to the civil-service laws, to appoint such clerical and other personnel as may be necessary for the execution of the functions of the Service, and shall fix their compensations in accordance with the Classification Act of 1923, as amended, and may, without regard to the provisions of the civil-service laws and the Classification Act of 1923, as amended, appoint and fix the compensation of such conciliators and mediators as may be necessary to carry out the functions of the Service. The Director is authorized to make such expenditures for supplies, facilities, and services as he deems necessary. Such expenditures shall be allowed and paid upon presentation of itemized vouchers therefor approved by the Director or by any employee designated by him for that purpose.

---

*Pursuant to Public Law 90-206, 90th Cong., 81 Stat. 644, approved Dec. 16, 1967, and in accordance with Sec. 225(f) (ii) thereof, effective in 1977, the salary of the Director shall be $52,500 per year.

(c) The principal office of the Service shall be in the District of Columbia, but the Director may establish regional offices convenient to localities in which labor controversies are likely to arise. The Director may by order, subject to revocation at any time, delegate any authority and discretion conferred upon him by this Act to any regional director, or other officer or employee of the Service. The Director may establish suitable procedures for cooperation with State and local mediation agencies. The Director shall make an annual report in writing to Congress at the end of the fiscal year.

(d) All mediation and conciliation functions of the Secretary of Labor or the United States Conciliation Service under section 8 of the Act entitled "An Act to create a Department of Labor," approved March 4, 1913 (U.S.C., title 29, sec. 51), and all functions of the United States Conciliation Service under any other law are hereby transferred to the Federal Mediation and Conciliation Service, together with the personnel and records of the United States Conciliation Service. Such transfer shall take effect upon the sixtieth day after the date of enactment of this Act. Such transfer shall not affect any proceedings pending before the United States Conciliation Service or any certification, order, rule, or regulation theretofore made by it or by the Secretary of Labor. The Director and the Service shall not be subject in any way to the jurisdiction or authority of the Secretary of Labor or any official or division of the Department of Labor.

FUNCTIONS OF THE SERVICE

Sec. 203. (a) It shall be the duty of the Service, in order to prevent or minimize interruptions of the free flow of commerce growing out of labor disputes, to assist parties to labor disputes in industries affecting commerce to settle such disputes, through conciliation and mediation.

(b) The Service may proffer it services in any labor dispute in any industry affecting commerce, either upon its own motion or upon the request of one or more of the parties to the dispute, whenever in its judgment such dispute threatens to cause a substantial interruption of commerce. The Director and the Service are directed to avoid attempting to mediate disputes which would have only a minor effect on interstate commerce if State or other conciliation services are available to the parties. Whenever the Service does proffer its services in any dispute, it shall be the duty of the Service promptly to put itself in communication with the parties and to use its best efforts, by mediation and conciliation, to bring them to agreement.

(c) If the Director is not able to bring the parties to agreement by conciliation within a reasonable time, he shall seek to induce the parties voluntarily to seek other means of settling the dispute without resort to strike, lock-out, or other coercion, including submission to the employees in the bargaining unit of the employer's last offer of settlement for approval or rejection in a secret ballot. The failure or refusal of either party to agree to any procedure suggested by the Director shall not be deemed a violation of any duty or obligation imposed by this Act.

(d) Final adjustment by a method agreed upon by the parties is hereby declared to be the desirable method for settlement of grievance disputes arising over the application or interpretation of an existing collective-bargaining agreement. The Service is directed to make its conciliation and mediation services available in the settlement of such grievance disputes only as a last resort and in exceptional cases.

(e) The Service is authorized and directed to encourage and support the establishment and operation of joint labor management activities conducted by plant, area, and industrywide committees designed to improve labor management relationships, job security and organizational effectiveness, in accordance with the provisions of section 205A.*

Sec. 204. (a) In order to prevent or minimize interruptions of the free flow of commerce growing out of labor disputes, employers and employees and their representatives, in any industry affecting commerce, shall—

(1) exert every reasonable effort to make and maintain agreements concerning rates of pay, hours, and working conditions, including provision for adequate notice of any proposed change in the terms of such agreements;

(2) whenever a dispute arises over the terms or application of a collective-bargaining agreement and a conference is requested by a party or prospective party thereto, arrange promptly for such a conference to be held and endeavor in such conference to settle such dispute expeditiously; and

(3) in case such dispute is not settled by conference, participate fully and promptly in such meetings as may be undertaken by

---

*Sec. 203(e) was added by Public Law 95-524, enacted Oct. 27, 1978.

the Service under this Act for the purpose of aiding a settlement of the dispute.

Sec. 205. (a) There is hereby created a National Labor-Management Panel which shall be composed of twelve members appointed by the President, six of whom shall be selected from among persons outstanding in the field of management and six of whom shall be selected from among persons outstanding in the field of labor. Each member shall hold office for a term of three years, except that any member appointed to fill a vacancy occurring prior to the expiration of the term for which his predecessor was appointed shall be appointed for the remainder of such term, and the terms of office of the members first taking office shall expire, as designated by the President at the time of appointment, four at the end of the first year, four at the end of the second year, and four at the end of the third year after the date of appointment. Members of the panel, when serving on business of the panel, shall be paid compensation at the rate of $25 per day, and shall also be entitled to receive an allowance for actual and necessary travel and subsistence expenses while so serving away from their places of residence.

(b) It shall be the duty of the panel, at the request of the Director, to advise in the avoidance of industrial controversies and the manner in which mediation and voluntary adjustment shall be administered, particularly with reference to controversies affecting the general welfare of the country.

Sec. 205A. (a)(1) The Service is authorized and directed to provide assistance in the establishment and operation of plant, area and industrywide labor management committees which—

(A) have been organized jointly by employers and labor organizations representing employees in that plant, area, or industry; and

(B) are established for the purpose of improving labor management relationships, job security, organizational effectiveness, enhancing economic development or involving workers in decisions affecting their jobs including improving communication with respect to subjects of mutual interest and concern.

(2) The Service is authorized and directed to enter into contracts and to make grants, where necessary or appropriate, to fulfill its responsibilities under this section.

(b)(1) No grant may be made, no contract may be entered into and no other assistance may be provided under the provisions of this section to a plant labor management committee unless the employees in that plant are represented by a labor organization and there is in effect at that plant a collective bargaining agreement.

(2) No grant may be made, no contract may be entered into and no other assistance may be provided under the provisions of this section to an area or industrywide labor management committee unless its participants include any labor organizations certified or recognized as the representative of the employees of an employer participating in such committee. Nothing in this clause shall prohibit participation in an area or industrywide committee by an employer whose employees are not represented by a labor organization.

(3) No grant may be made under the provisions of this section to any labor management committee which the Service finds to have as one of its purposes the discouragement of the exercise of rights contained in section 7 of the National Labor Relations Act (29 U.S.C. 157), or the interference with collective bargaining in any plant, or industry.

(c) The Service shall carry out the provisions of this section through an office established for that purpose.

(d) There are authorized to be appropriated to carry out the provisions of this section $10,000,000 for the fiscal year 1979, and such sums as may be necessary thereafter.

(e) Nothing in this section or the amendments made by this section shall affect the terms and conditions of any collective bargaining agreement whether in effect prior to or entered into after the date of enactment of this section.*

National Emergencies

Sec. 206. Whenever in the opinion of the President of the United States, a threatened or actual strike or lock-out affecting

---

*Sec. 205A was added by Public Law 95-524, enacted Oct. 27, 1978.

an entire industry or a substantial part thereof engaged in trade, commerce, transportation, transmission, or communication among the several States or with foreign nations, or engaged in the production of goods for commerce, will, if permitted to occur or to continue, imperil the national health or safety, he may appoint a board of inquiry to inquire into the issues involved in the dispute and to make a written report to him within such time as he shall prescribe. Such report shall include a statement of the facts with respect to the dispute, including each party's statement of its position but shall not contain any recommendations. The President shall file a copy of such report with the Service and shall make its contents available to the public.

Sec. 207. (a) A board of inquiry shall be composed of a chairman and such other members as the President shall determine, and shall have power to sit and act in any place within the United States and to conduct such hearings either in public or in private, as it may deem necessary or proper, to ascertain the facts with respect to the causes and circumstances of the dispute.

(b) Members of a board of inquiry shall receive compensation at the rate of $50 for each day actually spent by them in the work of the board, together with necessary travel and subsistence expenses.

(c) For the purpose of any hearing or inquiry conducted by any board appointed under this title, the provisions of section 9 and 10 (relating to the attendance of witnesses and the production of books, papers, and documents) of the Federal Trade Commission Act of September 16, 1914, as amended (U.S.C. 19, title 15, secs. 49 and 50, as amended), are hereby made applicable to the powers and duties of such board.

Sec. 208. (a) Upon receiving a report from a board of inquiry the President may direct the Attorney General to petition any district court of the United States having jurisdiction of the parties to enjoin such strike or lock-out or the continuing thereof, and if the court finds that such threatened or actual strike or lock-out—

(i) affects an entire industry or a substantial part thereof engaged in trade, commerce, transportation, transmission, or communication among the several States or with foreign nations, or engaged in the production of goods for commerce; and

(ii) if permitted to occur or to continue, will imperil the national health or safety, it shall have jurisdiction to enjoin any such strike or lock-out, or the continuing thereof, and to make such other orders as may be appropriate.

(b) In any case, the provisions of the Act of March 23, 1932, entitled "An Act to amend the Judicial Code and to define and limit the jurisdiction of courts sitting in equity, and for other purposes," shall not be applicable.

(c) The order or orders of the court shall be subject to review by the appropriate circuit court of appeals and by the Supreme Court upon writ of certiorari or certification as provided in sections 239 and 240 of the Judicial Code, as amended (U.S.C., title 29, secs. 346 and 347).

Sec. 209. (a) Whenever a district court has issued an order under section 208 enjoining acts or practices which imperil or threaten to imperil the national health or safety, it shall be the duty of the parties to the labor dispute giving rise to such order to make every effort to adjust and settle their differences, with the assistance of the Service created by this Act. Neither party shall be under any duty to accept, in whole or in part, any proposal of settlement made by the Service.

(b) Upon the issuance of such order, the President shall reconvene the board of inquiry which has previously reported with respect to the dispute. At the end of a sixty-day period (unless the dispute has been settled by that time), the board of inquiry shall report to the President the current position of the parties and the effort which has been made for settlement, and shall include a statement by each party of its position and a statement of the employer's last offer of settlement. The President shall make such report available to the public. The National Labor Relations Board, within the succeeding fifteen days, shall take a secret ballot of the employees of each employer involved in the dispute on the question of whether they wish to accept the final offer of settlement made by their employer as stated by him and shall certify the results thereof to the Attorney General within five days thereafter.

Sec. 210. Upon the certification of the results of such ballot or upon a settlement being reached, whichever happens sooner, the Attorney General shall move the court to discharge the injunction, which motion shall then be granted and the injunction discharged. When such motion is granted, the President shall submit to the Congress a full and comprehensive report of the proceedings, including the findings of the board of inquiry and the ballot taken by the National Labor Relations Board, together with such recommendations as he may see fit to make for consideration and appropriate action.

COMPILATION OF COLLECTIVE-BARGAINING AGREEMENTS, ETC.

Sec. 211. (a) For the guidance and information of interested representatives of employers, employees, and the general public, the Bureau of Labor Statistics of the Department of Labor shall maintain a file of copies of all available collective-bargaining agreements and other available agreements and actions thereunder settling or adjusting labor disputes. Such file shall be open to inspection under appropriate conditions prescribed by the Secretary of Labor, except that no specific information submitted in confidence shall be disclosed.

(b) The Bureau of Labor Statistics in the Department of Labor is authorized to furnish upon request of the Service, or employers, employees, or their representatives, all available data and factual information which may aid in the settlement of any labor dispute, except that no specific information submitted in confidence shall be disclosed.

EXEMPTION OF RAILWAY LABOR ACT

Sec. 212. The provisions of this title shall not be applicable with respect to any matter which is subject to the provisions of the Railway Labor Act, as amended from time to time.

CONCILIATION OF LABOR DISPUTES IN THE HEALTH CARE INDUSTRY

Sec. 213. (a) If, in the opinion of the Director of the Federal Mediation and Conciliation Service a threatened or actual strike or lockout affecting a health care institution will, if permitted to occur or to continue, substantially interrupt the delivery of health care in the locality concerned, the Director may further assist in the resolution of the impasse by establishing within 30 days after the notice to the Federal Mediation and Conciliation Service under clause (A) of the last sentence of section 8(d) (which is required by clause (3) of such section 8(d)), or within 10 days after the notice under clause (B), an impartial Board of Inquiry to investigate the issues involved in the dispute and to make a written report thereon to the parties within fifteen (15) days after the establishment of such a Board. The written report shall contain the finding of fact together with the Board's recommendations for settling the dispute, with the objective of achieving a prompt, peaceful and just settlement of the dispute. Each such Board shall be composed of such number of individuals as the Director may deem desirable. No member appointed under this section shall have any interest or involvement in the health care institutions or the employee organizations involved in the dispute.

(b)(1) Members of any board established under this section who are otherwise employed by the Federal Government shall serve without compensation but shall be reimbursed for travel, subsistence, and other necessary expenses incurred by them in carrying out its duties under this section.

(2) Members of any board established under this section who are not subject to paragraph (1) shall receive compensation at a rate prescribed by the Director but not to exceed the daily rate prescribed for GS-18 of the General Schedule under section 5332 of title 5, United States Code, including travel for each day they are engaged in the performance of their duties under this section and shall be entitled to reimbursement for travel, subsistence, and other necessary expenses incurred by them in carrying out their duties under this section.

(c) After the establishment of a board under subsection (a) of this section and for 15 days after any such board has issued its report, no change in the status quo in effect prior to the expiration of the contract in the case of negotiations for a contract renewal, or in effect prior to the time of the impasse in the case of an initial bargaining negotiation, except by agreement, shall be made by the parties to the controversy.

(d) There are authorized to be appropriated such sums as may be necessary to carry out the provisions of this section.

TITLE III
SUITS BY AND AGAINST LABOR ORGANIZATIONS

Sec. 301. (a) Suits for violation of contracts between an employer and a labor organization representing employees in an industry affecting commerce as defined in this Act, or between any such labor organization, may be brought in any district court of the United States having jurisdiction of the parties, without respect to the amount in controversy or without regard to the citizenship of the parties.

(b) Any labor organization which represents employees in an industry affecting commerce as defined in this Act and any employer whose activities affect commerce as defined in this Act shall be bound by the acts of its agents. Any such labor organization may sue or be sued as an entity and in behalf of the employees whom it represents in the courts of the United States. Any money judgment against a labor organization in a district court of the United States shall be enforceable only against the organization as an entity and against its assets, and shall not be enforceable against any individual member or his assets.

(c) For the purposes of actions and proceedings by or against labor organizations in the district courts of the United States, district courts shall be deemed to have jurisdiction of a labor organization (1) in the district in which such organization maintains its principal offices, or (2) in any district in which its duly authorized officers or agents are engaged in representing or acting for employee members.

(d) The service of summons, subpena, or other legal process of any court of the United States upon an officer or agent of a labor organization, in his capacity as such, shall constitute service upon the labor organization.

(e) For the purpose of this section, in determining whether any person is acting as an "agent" of another person so as to make such other person responsible for his acts, the question of whether the specific acts performed were actually authorized or subsequently ratified shall not be controlling.

Restrictions on Payments to Employee Representatives

Sec. 302. (a) It shall be unlawful for any employer or association of employers or any person who acts as a labor relations expert, adviser, or consultant to an employer or who acts in the interest of an employer to pay, lend, or deliver, or agree to pay, lend, or deliver, any money or other thing of value—

(1) to any representative of any of his employees who are employed in an industry affecting commerce; or

(2) to any labor organization, or any officer or employee thereof, which represents, seeks to represent, or would admit

to membership, any of the employees of such employer who are employed in an industry affecting commerce;

(3) to any employee or group or committee of employees of such employer employed in an industry affecting commerce in excess of their normal compensation for the purpose of causing such employee or group or committee directly or indirectly to influence any other employees in the exercise of the right to organize and bargain collectively through representation of their own choosing; or

(4) to any officer or employee of a labor organization engaged in an industry affecting commerce with intent to influence him in respect to any of his actions, decisions, or duties as a representative of employees or as such officer or employee of such labor organization.

(b)(1) It shall be unlawful for any person to request, demand, receive, or accept, or agree to receive or accept, any payment, loan, or delivery of any money or other thing of value prohibited by subsection (a).

(2) It shall be unlawful for any labor organization, or for any person acting as an officer, agent, representative, or employee of such labor organization, to demand or accept from the operator of any motor vehicle (as defined in part II of the Interstate Commerce Act) employed in the transportation of property in commerce, or the employer of any such operator, any money or other thing of value payable to such organization or to an officer, agent, representative or employee thereof as a fee or charge for the unloading, or the connection with the unloading, of the cargo of such vehicle: *Provided,* That nothing in this paragraph shall be construed to make unlawful any payment by an employer to any of his employees as compensation for their services as employees.

(c) The provisions of this section shall not be applicable (1) in respect to any money or other thing of value payable by an employer to any of his employees whose established duties include acting openly for such employer in matters of labor relations or personnel administration or to any representative of his employees, or to any officer or employee of a labor organization, who is also an employee or former employee of such employer, as compensation for, or by reason of, his service as an employee of such employer; (2) with respect to the payment or delivery of any money or other thing of value in satisfaction of a judgment of any court or a decision or award of an arbitrator or impartial chairman or in compromise, adjustment, settlement, or release of any claim, complaint, grievance or dispute in the absence of fraud or duress; (3) with respect to the sale or purchase of an article or commodity at the prevailing market price in the regular course of business; (4) with respect to money deducted from the wages of employees in payment of membership dues in a labor organization: *Provided,* That the employer has received from each employee, on whose account such deductions are made, a written assignment which shall not be irrevocable for a period of more than one year, or beyond the termination date of the applicable collective agreement, whichever occurs sooner; (5) with respect to money or other thing of value paid to a trust fund established by such representative, for the sole and exclusive benefit of the employees of such employer, and their families and dependents (or of such employees, families, and dependents jointly with the employees of other employers making similar payments, and their families and dependents): *Provided,* That (A) such payments are held in trust for the purpose of paying, either from principal or income or both, for the benefit of employees, their families and dependents, for medical or hospital care, pensions on retirement or death of employees, compensation for injuries or illness resulting from occupational activity or insurance to provide any of the foregoing, or unemployment benefits or life insurance, disability and sickness insurance, or accident insurance; (B) the detailed basis on which such payments are to be made is specified in a written agreement with the employer, and employees and employers are equally represented in the administration of such fund, together with such neutral persons as the representatives of the employers and the representatives of employees may agree upon and in the event the employer and employee groups deadlock on the administration of such fund and there are no neutral persons empowered to break such deadlock, such agreement provides that the two groups shall agree on an impartial umpire to decide such dispute, or in event of their failure to agree within a reasonable length of time, an impartial umpire to decide such dispute shall, on petition of either group, be appointed by the district court of the United States for the district where the trust fund has its principal office, and shall also contain provisions for an annual audit of the trust fund, a statement of the results of which shall be available for inspection by interested persons at the principal office of the trust fund and at such other places as may be designated in such written agreement; and (C) such payments as are intended to be used for the purpose of providing pensions or annuities for employees are made to a separate trust which provides that the funds held therein cannot be used for any purpose other than paying such pensions or annuities; (6) with respect to money or other thing of value paid by any employer to a trust fund established by such representative for the purpose of pooled vacation, holiday, severance or similar benefits, or defraying costs of apprenticeship or other training program: *Provided,* That the requirements of clause (B) of the proviso to clause (5) of this subsection shall apply to such trust funds; (7) with respect to money or other thing of value paid by any employer to a pooled or individual trust fund established by such representative for the purpose of (A) scholarships for the benefit of employees, their families, and dependents for study at educational institutions, or (B) child care centers for preschool and school age dependents of employees: *Provided,* That no labor organization or employer shall be required to bargain on the establishment of any such trust fund, and refusal to do so shall not constitute an unfair labor practice: *Provided further,* That the requirements of clause (B) of the proviso to clause (5) of this subsection shall apply to such trust funds; (8) with respect to money or any other thing of value paid by any employer to a trust fund established by such representative for the purpose of defraying the costs of legal services for employees, their families, and dependents for counsel or plan of their choice: *Provided,* That the requirements of clause (B) of the proviso to clause (5) of this subsection shall apply to such trust funds: *Provided further,* That no such legal services shall be furnished: (A) to initiate any proceeding directed (i) against any such employer or its officers or agents except in workman's compensation cases, or (ii) against such labor organization, or its parent or subordinate bodies, or their officers or agents, or (iii) against any other employer or labor organization, or their officers or agents, in any matter arising under the National Labor Relations Act, as amended, or this Act; and (B) in any proceeding where a labor organization would be prohibited from defraying the costs of legal services by the provisions of the Labor-Management Reporting and Disclosure Act of 1959; or (9) with respect to money or other things of value paid by an employer to a plant, area or industrywide labor management committee established for one or more of the purposes set forth in section 5(b) of the Labor Management Cooperation Act of 1978.*

(d) Any person who willfully violates any of the provisions of this section shall, upon conviction thereof, be guilty of a misdemeanor and be subject to a fine of not more than $10,000 or to imprisonment for not more than one year, or both.

(e) The district courts of the United States and the United States courts of the Territories and possessions shall have jurisdiction, for cause shown, and subject to the provisions of section 17 (relating to notice to opposite party) of the Act entitled "An Act to supplement existing laws against unlawful restraints and monopolies, and for other purposes," approved October 15, 1914, as amended (U.S.C., title 28, sec. 381), to restrain violations of this section, without regard to the provisions of sections 6 and 20 of such Act of October 15, 1914, as amended (U.S.C., title 15, sec. 17 and title 29, sec. 52), and the provisions of the Act entitled "An Act to amend the Judicial Code to define and limit the jurisdiction of courts sitting in equity, and for other purposes," approved March 23, 1932 (U.S.C., title 29, secs. 101–115).

(f) This section shall not apply to any contract in force on the date of enactment of this Act, until the expiration of such contract, or until July 1, 1948, whichever first occurs.

(g) Compliance with the restrictions contained in subsection (c)(5)(B) upon contributions to trust funds, otherwise lawful, shall not be applicable to contributions to such trust funds established by collective agreement prior to January 1, 1946, nor shall subsection (c)(5)(A) be construed as prohibiting contributions to such trust funds if prior to January 1, 1947, such funds contained provisions for pooled vacation benefits.

BOYCOTTS AND OTHER UNLAWFUL COMBINATIONS

Sec. 303. (a) It shall be unlawful, for the purpose of this section only, in an industry or activity affecting commerce, for any labor organization to engage in any activity or conduct defined as an unfair labor practice in section 8(b)(4) of the National Labor Relations Act, as amended.

---

*As amended Aug. 15, 1973, Public Law 93-95, 87 Stat. 314; Oct. 27, 1978, Public Law 95-524, sec. 6(d), 92 Stat. 2021.

(b) Whoever shall be injured in his business or property by reason of any violation of subsection (a) may sue therefore in any district court of the United States subject to the limitations and provisions of section 301 hereof without respect to the amount in controversy, or in any other court having jurisdiction of the parties, and shall recover the damages by him sustained and the cost of the suit.

Restriction on Political Contributions

Sec. 304. Section 313 of the Federal Corrupt Practices Act, 1925 (U.S.C., 1940 edition, title 2, sec. 251; Supp. V, title 50, App., sec. 1509), as amended, is amended to read as follows:

Sec. 313. It is unlawful for any national bank, or any corporation organized by authority of any law of Congress to make a contribution or expenditure in connection with any election to any political office, or in connection with any primary election or political convention or caucus held to select candidates for any political office, or for any corporation whatever, or any labor organization to make a contribution or expenditure in connection with any election at which Presidential and Vice Presidential electors or a Senator or Representative in, or a Delegate or Resident Commissioner to Congress are to be voted for, or in connection with any primary election or political convention or caucus held to select candidates for any of the foregoing offices, or for any candidate, political committee, or other person to accept or receive any contribution prohibited by this section. Every corporation or labor organization which makes any contribution or expenditure in violation of this section shall be fined not more that $5,000; and every officer or director of any corporation, or officer of any labor organization, who consents to any contribution or expenditure by the corporation or labor organization, as the case may be, in violation of this section shall be fined not more than $1,000 or imprisoned for not more than one year, or both. For the purposes of this section, "labor organization" means any organization of any kind, or any agency or employee representation committee or plan, in which employees participate and which exists for the purpose, in whole or in part, of dealing with employers concerning grievances, labor disputes, wages, rates of pay, hours of employment, or conditions of work.

STRIKES BY GOVERNMENT EMPLOYEES

Sec. 305. [Repealed by Ch. 690, 69 Stat. 624, effective August 9, 1955. Sec. 305 made it unlawful for government employees to strike and made strikers subject to immediate discharge, forfeiture of civil-service status, and three-year blacklisting for federal employment.]

TITLE IV

CREATION OF JOINT COMMITTEE TO STUDY AND REPORT ON BASIC PROBLEMS AFFECTING FRIENDLY LABOR RELATIONS AND PRODUCTIVITY

Sec. 401. There is hereby established a joint congressional committee to be known as the Joint Committee on Labor-Management Relations (hereafter referred to as the committee), and to be composed of seven Members of the Senate Committee on Labor and Public Welfare, to be appointed by the President pro tempore of the Senate, and seven Members of the House of Representatives Committee on Education and Labor, to be appointed by the Speaker of the House of Representatives. A vacancy in membership of the committee, shall not affect the powers of the remaining members to execute the functions of the committee, and shall be filled in the same manner as the original selection. The committee shall select a chairman and a vice chairman from among its members.

Sec. 402. The committee, acting as a whole or by subcommittee shall conduct a thorough study and investigation of the entire field of labor-management relations, including but not limited to—

(1) the means by which permanent friendly cooperation between employers and employees and stability of labor relations may be secured throughout the United States;

(2) the means by which the individual employee may achieve a greater productivity and higher wages, including plans for guaranteed annual wages, incentive profit-sharing and bonus systems;

(3) the internal organization and administration of labor unions, with special attention to the impact on individuals of collective agreements requiring membership in unions as a condition of employment;

(4) the labor relations policies and practices of employers and associations of employers;

(5) the desirability of welfare funds for the benefit of employees and their relation to the social-security system;

(6) the methods and procedures for best carrying out the collective-bargaining processes, with special attention to the effects of industrywide or regional bargaining upon the national economy;

(7) the administration and operation of existing Federal laws relating to labor relations; and

(8) such other problems and subjects in the field of labor-management relations as the committee deems appropriate.

Sec. 403. The committee shall report to the Senate and the House of Representatives not later than March 15, 1948, the results of its study and investigation, together with such recommendations as to necessary legislation and such other recommendations as it may deem advisable, and shall make its final report not later than January 2, 1949.

Sec. 404. The committee shall have the power, without regard to the civil-service laws and the Classification Act of 1923, as amended, to employ and fix the compensation of such officers, experts, and employees as it deems necessary for the performance of its duties, including consultants who shall receive compensation at a rate not to exceed $35 for each day actually spent by them in the work of the committee, together with their necessary travel and subsistence expenses. The committee is further authorized with the consent of the head of the department or agency concerned, to utilize the services, information, facilities, and personnel of all agencies in the executive branch of the Government and may request the governments of the several States, representatives of business, industry, finance, and labor, and such other persons, agencies, organizations, and instrumentalities as it deems appropriate to attend its hearings and to give and present information, advice, and recommendations.

Sec. 405. The committee, or any subcommittee thereof, is authorized to hold such hearings; to sit and act at such times and places during the sessions, recesses, and adjourned periods of the Eightieth Congress; to require by subpena or otherwise the attendance of such witnesses and the production of such books, papers, and documents; to administer oaths; to take such testimony; to have such printing and binding done; and to make such expenditures within the amount appropriated therefor; as it deems advisable. The cost of stenographic services in reporting such hearings shall not be in excess of 25 cents per one hundred words. Subpenas shall be issued under the signature of the chairman or vice chairman of the committee and shall be served by any person designated by them.

Sec. 406. The members of the committee shall be reimbursed for travel, subsistence, and other necessary expenses incurred by them in the performance of the duties vested in the committee, other than expenses in connection with meetings of the committee held in the District of Columbia during such times as the Congress is in session.

Sec. 407. There is hereby authorized to be appropriated the sum of $150,000, or so much thereof as may be necessary, to carry out the provisions of this title, to be disbursed by the Secretary of the Senate on vouchers signed by the chairman.

TITLE V

DEFINITIONS

Sec. 501. When used in this Act—

(1) The term "industry affecting commerce" means any industry or activity in commerce or in which a labor dispute would burden or obstruct commerce or tend to burden or obstruct commerce or the free flow of commerce.

(2) The term "strike" includes any strike or other concerted stoppage of work by employees (including a stoppage by reason of the expiration of a collective-bargaining agreement) and any concerted slow-down or other concerted interruption of operations by employees.

(3) The terms "commerce," "labor disputes," "employer," "employee," "labor organization," "representative," "person," and "supervisor" shall have the same meaning as when used in the National Labor Relations Act as amended by this Act.

SAVING PROVISION

Sec. 502. Nothing in this Act shall be construed to require an individual employee to render labor or service without his consent, nor shall anything in this Act be construed to make the quitting of his labor by an individual employee an illegal act; nor shall any court issue any process to compel the performance by an individual of such labor or service, without his consent; nor shall the quitting of labor by an employee or employees in good faith because of abnormally dangerous conditions for work at the place of employment of such employee or employees be deemed a strike under this Act.

SEPARABILITY

Sec. 503. If any provision of this Act, or the application of such provision to any person or circumstance, shall be invalid, the remainder of this Act, or the application of such provision to persons or circumstances other than those as to which it is held invalid, shall not be affected thereby.

Index